America's Two Constitutions

America's Two Constitutions

A Study of the Treatment of Dissenters in Time of War

Thomas J. Reed

FAIRLEIGH DICKINSON UNIVERSITY PRESS
Madison • Teaneck

Published by Fairleigh Dickinson University Press
Copublished by The Rowman & Littlefield Publishing Group, Inc.
4501 Forbes Boulevard, Suite 200, Lanham, Maryland 20706
www.rowman.com

Unit A, Whitacre Mews, 26-34 Stannary Street, London SE11 4AB

British Library Cataloguing in Publication Information Available

Library of Congress Cataloging-in-Publication Data

Names: Reed, Thomas J. (Thomas James), 1940– author.
Title: America's two constitutions : a study of the treatment of dissenters in time of war / Thomas J. Reed.
Description: Madison, New Jersey : Fairleigh Dickinson University Press ; Lanham, Maryland : The Rowman & Littlefield Publishing Group, Inc., 2017. | Includes bibliographical references and index.
Identifiers: LCCN 2017029703 (print) | LCCN 2017035184 (ebook) | ISBN 9781683931133 (electronic) | ISBN 9781683931126 (hardcover : alk. paper)
Subjects: LCSH: War and emergency legislation—United States—History. | Subversive activities—Law and legislation—United States—History. | Sedition—Law and legislation—United States—History. | Freedom of expression—United States—History. | Peace movements—United States—History. | Pacifists—Legal status, laws, etc.—United States—History.
Classification: LCC KF5900 (ebook) | LCC KF5900 .R44 2017 (print) | DDC 342.73/062—dc23

LC record available at https://lccn.loc.gov/2017029703

™ The paper used in this publication meets the minimum requirements of American National Standard for Information Sciences Permanence of Paper for Printed Library Materials, ANSI/NISO Z39.48-1992.

Printed in the United States of America

Contents

Illustrations

Acknowledgments

This study of the government treatment of anti-war dissenters is a project that started in 1999. I could not have written this book without the assistance of many individuals and institutions. Associate Dean Michael Slinger and Associate Dean and Prof. Erin Daly contributed important comments and suggestions that made this book a better product. During the past fifteen years, I enjoyed the support of Widener University of Delaware Law School that made it possible to take time to research the many subtopics in this book. My thanks to law librarians Enza Klotsbucher, Janet Lindemuth, and Mary Jane Mallonee for the time they spent securing books and articles via interlibrary loan. Thanks also to the staff of the New Jersey State Library who assisted me in locating documents relating to the treatment of Tories during the Revolution and to the staff of the Delaware Historical Society. The Morris Library of the University of Delaware supplied me with many volumes relating to my topic.

Portions of this book relating to the Civil War were taken from my lecture "Abraham Lincoln and the Simple-Minded Soldier Boy" originally given to the Lincoln Club of Delaware in 2007. I am grateful to the Lincoln Club and its then-president David Swayze for allowing me to set out the thesis for the suspension of civil liberties during the Civil War. I owe a special debt of gratitude to the late Prof. Robert Lipkin, who encouraged me to continue with this project because he was convinced that this story needed to be told to judges, lawyers, and law students. Last but not least, my editorial supervisors at Fairleigh Dickinson University Press, Dr. Harry Keyishian and Dr. Kalman Goldstein, gave my manuscript a careful reading and suggested many constructive changes. Lynn Weber, my copy editor, made numerous helpful suggestions and corrections to this manuscript. My wife Emily Reed, Ph.D., helped me deal with a very critical computer software problem and contributed her valuable time to adjusting and correcting the manuscript for this book to ready the text for publication.

Introduction

The living United States Constitution is an inherently flexible compromise between special interest groups that has been given meaning and consistency by the decisions of the U.S. Supreme Court interpreting the paper Constitution's often vague and contradictory provisions. Like the Bible, the paper Constitution is open to many shades of interpretation. The relationship between the presidential power to make war and the basic civil rights of U.S. citizens and resident aliens spelled out in the Bill of Rights is tenuous, uncertain, and capable of contradictory interpretations. One school, exemplified by Chief Justice William H. Rehnquist's *All the Laws But One*,[1] argues that civil liberties are subordinate to national survival and that war is the kind of "exigent circumstance" that justifies suspension of civil liberties due to the armed services' need to defend the nation from external or internal aggression. Another school, exemplified by James G. Randall, tends to deplore some of the excesses of military rule, especially during the Civil War, but accepts the limitation of civil liberties as an inevitable consequence of armed combat.[2] A third school of thought considers the war power subordinate to or limited by the Bill of Rights. An unpopular view during most wars, it was the rhetoric of the peace-at-any-price Democrats during the Civil War and also the gospel of the draft resisters of the 1960s.

This book is an examination of the interaction of the war power and the First, Fourth, Fifth, and Sixth Amendments to the Constitution. President George W. Bush's executive order instituting military commissions for the purpose of trying aliens on criminal charges arising from participation in terrorist acts against the United States makes this something more than an academic debate. The U.S. Supreme Court has been the arbiter of the interaction between the war power and the rest of the Constitution for more than 160 years. The Court has provided no coherent constitutional perspective on this issue, although it has been called upon to decide a series of high-profile cases involving the alleged ability of the war power to trump other parts of the Constitution.

The moral choices made by government politicians from the beginning of the Revolution until the present time also reflect a general inarticulate opinion that the end justifies the means.

This doctrine is the heart of consequentialism, a moral philosophy that looks to the achievement of the political end as the ultimate arbiter of the means used by the government to attain that end. If the end is attained then the means used to achieve the end are morally correct. If the end is not achieved, then the means used were morally wrong. Although there are two other modern schools of thought that reject consequentialist morality, these schools have little impact on the operation of the government or on the opinion of the people of the United States. The story of treatment of dissenters in time of war generally supports a consequentialist moral behavior model for politicians and the people of the United States as the chapters in this book will show.

Chapter 1 introduces the subject and examines the American Revolution and the suppression of civil liberties from 1775 through the Alien and Sedition Acts of 1798. The American Revolution was a true civil war. Large numbers of colonists sided with the mother country, joined its armed forces, and fought unsuccessfully to suppress the rebellion. There was no national prosecutorial system, and each colony had to deal with dissent in its own way. Since most of the thirteen colonies had adopted a bill of rights declaring freedom of assembly, freedom of speech, and basic rights to public trial by jury, each colony in turn had to deal with the Tory problem without destroying the alleged reason for resisting British rule: tyranny and abuse of power.

The end of hostilities did not immediately stop the suppression of the rights of Tories. Confiscation acts deprived them of property without any pretense of due process and culminated in a case that reached the U.S. Supreme Court once the judicial apparatus of the U.S. government had been set up in 1789, *Martin v. Hunter's Lessee*. At the same time that the seizure cases were wending their way through the judicial system of the new United States, Congress, expecting a war with revolutionary France, passed the Alien Act and the Sedition Act limiting anti-war dissent. Prosecutions under these statutes were more than a comic opera: none reached the U.S. Supreme Court before the Jefferson administration put a stop to prosecutions under both acts.

The relationship between the war power and the rest of the Constitution was not a significant issue again until the Civil War, when President Lincoln suspended civil liberties in a number of instances and ordered civilians to be tried before military commissions rather than civilian courts. Chapter 2 is a detailed examination of the history of suspension of civil liberties by the Lincoln administration and the legal fallout from that suspension. In 1861, President Lincoln used the State Department to put down civil dissent in the non-seceding states. Secretary of State William H. Seward ordered the arrest of hundreds of civilians for anti-administration speech or protest activities and locked these unfortunates up without formal indictment in U.S. military installations. President Lincoln invoked the war power to suspend the writ of habeas corpus in the vital transportation corridor from Washington, D.C., to Philadelphia, thence northward to Maine. Although Chief Justice Roger B. Taney held that arrest without notice of the charges laid against the defendant and without right of counsel was illegal and issued a writ of habeas corpus as supervising circuit justice in *Ex parte Merryman*, the Lincoln administration refused to obey the court and kept its prisoner incommunicado.

In 1862, the civil dissent program was turned over to Secretary of War Edwin M. Stanton, who vigorously enforced the proscription against dissent, aided by additional proclamations of the president suspending the writ of habeas corpus along major railroad routes, then in all the border states, and finally throughout the United States. In 1862, Congress ratified suspension of the writ of habeas corpus and authorized a national draft to commence in July 1863. The law authorizing the draft also set up military provost marshal's offices for all the states to aid in enforcing the draft. The secretary of war also authorized trial of civilians before military commissions for sabotage and resisting the draft. Thousands of U.S. nationals were arrested and imprisoned under this new regime for suspected anti-war dissent. Hundreds were tried by military commission and convicted of vague charges of disloyalty and resistance to the draft, resulting in a number of death sentences.

There were two very high-profile cases during the war that tested the legality of the provost martial system of justice. In *Ex parte Vallandigham*, the court upheld the expulsion of a sitting U.S. member of Congress from Ohio to the Confederacy for a virulent anti-war speech. In the prize cases, the Supreme Court granted quasi-belligerent status to the Confederate States of America and permitted confiscation and sale of captured Confederate shipping under a very broad definition of the war power.

The assassination of Abraham Lincoln on April 14, 1865, provoked another wave of arrests without probable cause or charges as hundreds of alleged Confederate sympathizers were jailed throughout the United States as a precaution against further assassination attempts. Eight of those jailed hundreds turned out to be directly implicated in the assassination conspiracy. They were tried before a military commission presided over by Maj. Gen. David M. Hunter, and four were sentenced to death in May 1865. A last-minute attempt to seek a writ of habeas corpus to free the conspirators failed, and the four sentenced to die were executed in the Washington Arsenal Penitentiary yard in July 1865.

After the Civil War ended, the U.S. Supreme Court tried to reverse the course of history in *Ex parte Milligan* without, as later events would prove, making any real change in the relationship between the war power and the Bill of Rights. Lamden Milligan, an Indiana lawyer and devout anti-war Democrat, had been implicated in a conspiracy to free thousands of Confederate prisoners of war held at Camp Douglas in Chicago. Another admitted conspirator named him as a "general" in the secret order known as the Sons of Liberty who would command a column of anti-war Democrats that would seize the prison and free the Confederates. Tried by military commission in Indianapolis just before the end of the war, Milligan and four other alleged conspirators were sentenced to die. Milligan sought a writ of habeas corpus in the U.S. Circuit Court for Indiana. The circuit judges split on the issue of suspension of habeas corpus, generating an appeal by right to the Supreme Court. The Supreme Court ordered Milligan to be freed, holding that trial by military commission was neither authorized by Congress nor constitutional when the civilian courts were open for business and there was no threat of invasion by a hostile power.

Chapter 3 examines President Wilson's well-engineered program of suppression of civil liberties during World War I. Congress added the Espionage Act of 1917 and the Sedition Act of 1918 to the legal implements that the Department of Justice could employ to suppress those who opposed the war and the draft. The principal targets of the program were Socialists and members of the Industrial Workers of the World. The United States also prosecuted individuals who were of German descent for alleged seditious statements against the war, in some cases statements made before the United States declared war in April 1917 when the United States was officially neutral. Wilson's attorneys general also countenanced the formation of a civilian vigilante group to ferret out anti-war protesters and draft dodgers, granting it quasi-official status as an arm of the Justice Department. Vigilantes who murdered IWW union organizers were not prosecuted by local authorities. The Wilson administration used its official public information apparatus headed by George Creel to suppress anti-war sentiments by inflated claims of battlefield success and by cutting off access to press bulletins and stories among major anti-war newspapers and magazines.

Chapter 4 follows the suppression of civil liberties by the Franklin D. Roosevelt administration during World War II, highly publicized at the time and widely criticized since that time by scholars. Martial law was declared in Hawaii and kept in force for more than two years after Pearl Harbor. German saboteurs were tried by military commission and sentenced to death. U.S. citizens of Japanese ancestry were interned in concentration camps for the duration of the war as a security precaution. At war's end, high-ranking Japanese officers were tried by a military commission for war crimes and sentenced to death. The Roosevelt administration avoided out-and-out suppression of political dissenters but used other means to ensure that anti-war protesters were excluded from the public forum from 1941 to 1945.

Chapter 5 examines the Cold War. During the 1940s and 1950s, the United States directed its efforts against the tiny U.S. Communist Party, rooting out known Communists and fellow travelers in federal jobs under a loyalty oath program established by President Truman and continued by President Eisenhower. State and local governments adopted the loyalty oath program and engaged in their own purges of job holders who were felt to be pro-Communist.

Vigilante action during the Cold War period consisted of local self-appointed censors forcing public libraries to remove allegedly pro-Communist books from bookshelves. Self-appointed censors also had a well-organized "clearance" program for stage, screen, television, and radio performers that forced Hollywood studios and media networks to buy the screening service in order to prevent the screeners from accusing the recalcitrant media outlet of being "soft on Communism."

Congress also took a hand in the hue and cry after Communists. The House Un-American Activities Committee held a series of hearings intended to expose Communists in government, leading to the perjury prosecution of Alger Hiss. Hiss told the committee that he was not a Communist and had never been a Communist. Whittaker Chambers, a confessed former Communist, identified Hiss as the man who funneled secret documents to Chambers for transmission to the Soviet Union's spy apparatus in the United States. Public opinion supported Chambers and the Committee against Hiss's denials. Wisconsin's junior senator Joseph R. McCarthy launched a blacklisting program in Wheeling, West Virginia, in 1950, accusing the State Department of harboring known Communists. McCarthy's Senate Committee attacked minor government employees for pro-Communist sympathy, eventually challenging the Department of the Army for pro-Communist leanings among its employees at Fort Dix, New Jersey. The public generally supported Sen. McCarthy until he was censured by the Senate for multiple violations of Senate rules of decorum.

Chapter 6 examines the extent of governmental suppression of civil liberties during the Vietnam War. The Johnson and Nixon administrations carefully avoided direct suppression of the anti-war movement. Both administrations pursued criminal prosecutions against men who refused to report for induction claiming that they were morally opposed to all wars or to the Vietnam war alone. In *United States v. Seeger,*[3] decided in 1965, the Supreme Court recognized that a man who was opposed to all wars on moral grounds and who did accept the existence of a higher power but not the religious Supreme Being was entitled to conscientious objector status. The draft prosecutions included the conviction of boxer Muhammad Ali for failing to report for induction. Ali, a member of the Nation of Islam, claimed exemption as a minister. Eventually Ali would be exonerated by the U.S. Supreme Court. Other men who made similar claims were not as successful.

State authorities did pursue repressive measures, the most notorious being the 1970 shooting of students on the Kent State University campus by Ohio National Guard soldiers during the suppression of a student anti-war protest riot that featured firebombing of the campus ROTC building the day before the shooting.

The United States invaded personal privacy during the Vietnam war on the pretext of ferreting out Communists and pro-Communists. The

FBI conducted an unauthorized surveillance program called COINTEL that started before U.S. ground troops were committed to Vietnam and continued until exposed after a clandestine raid on the Media, Pennsylvania, FBI field office in 1971. COINTEL was justified as a necessary measure to identify pro-Communist sympathizers who would hinder the war effort. The Central Intelligence Agency surreptitiously opened incoming and outgoing U.S. mail from alleged pro-Communists, read and copied the documents in the mail, and resealed the mail. This invasion of privacy was known as Operation Chaos. The Justice Department was convinced that the Black Panther Party was a threat to the war effort. The FBI and local law enforcement officers in Chicago raided the Black Panther Party's Chicago headquarters. Party member Fred Hampton was shot and killed during the raid.[4]

Chapter 7 examines the issue raised by the Bush administration's actions after September 11, 2001. The PATRIOT Act extended governmental surveillance activities, but the most egregious invasion of privacy was surreptitious telephone monitoring by the NSA, CIA, and FBI, programs that were largely judicially unsupervised.

Military operations in Afghanistan and Iraq produced hundreds of supposed Taliban and Al Qaida members who were thought to possess valuable military intelligence that could be extracted by interrogators using techniques that many knowledgeable experts considered to be torture. The CIA established secret prisons in states that had not signed the Geneva Convention against torture of captives and in some instances turned over suspects to states with no qualms about using torture to extract information, called "extraordinary rendition."

Most of the captives were interned at Guantanamo Bay, Cuba, thought to be beyond U.S. jurisdiction. The Bush administration was unable to ward off habeas corpus petitions filed on behalf of some Guantanamo captives on the ground of lack of jurisdiction. Congress responded by suspending habeas corpus for the first time since President Lincoln's days, barring use of the writ to test the confinement of Guantanamo captives.

President Bush resurrected military commissions as a vehicle to try non-U.S. citizens captured in Afghanistan and Iraq for violating the international law of war. Bush's first attempt to establish trial by military commission without congressional authorization foundered before the Supreme Court. Congress then enacted enabling legislation permitting trial of captives by military commission that has withstood judicial review.

Chapter 8 is a reexamination of the data and a series of conclusions that are not particularly comforting. The United States is unlikely to adopt a written series of amendments to the Constitution defining emergency power. Rather, in typically American fashion, the United States will muddle through times of national emergency, following the lead of the executive branch in most instances during the life of the emergency, the legislative and judicial branches condoning suspension of civil liberties guaranteed by the Bill of Rights. When the emergency ends, Congress and the courts will retreat from enabling the executive branch to restrict civil liberties and will try to undo, usually without success, the worst effects from the suspension of civil liberties.

NOTES

1. William H. Rehnquist, *All the Laws But One* (New York: Knopf, 1998).
2. James G. Randall, *Constitutional Problems under Lincoln* (New York: D. Appleton, 1926; Urbana: University of Illinois Press, 1956).
3. 380 U.S. 163 (1965).
4. Jeffrey Haas, "The Assassination of Fred Hampton: How the FBI and the Chicago Police Murdered a Black Panther," DemocracyNow!, 2009, last accessed March 14, 2017,http://www.democracynow.org/2009/12/4/the_assassination_of_fred_hampton_how.

ONE

The Whigs and the Tories

Dissent during the Revolution

> "It is an error to represent the Tories of our Revolution as composed of Americans lacking in love for their native country, or in zeal for its liberty, or in willingness to labor, or fight, or even to die, for what they conceived to be its interests."
>
> —Moses Coit Tyler, *The Party of the Loyalists in the American Revolution*

The American Revolution was a civil war.[1] From 1764 to April 1775, the elite leadership of the thirteen Royal and proprietary colonies[2] along the Atlantic seaboard was involved in a continuing factional argument about the best way to deal with Royal imposition of control over colonial government via a series of taxes imposed by Parliament on the colonists that were not the product of the colonial popularly elected legislatures, who by charter were empowered to tax property in each colony.[3] Parliament imposed a series of direct taxes on trade goods to pay for the cost of the French and Indian War and continued costs of keeping up garrisons of Royal soldiers stationed to protect colonists from Native American raids. Parliament also passed an act imposing on individual colonists the duty to quarter soldiers in their homes if barracks space proved insufficient to house troops. Finally, Parliament imposed the vice admiralty courts on its colonists, a court that tried persons accused of smuggling without benefit of a jury.[4]

THE BEGINNING OF RESISTANCE TO THE MOTHER COUNTRY

The colonial elite, permitted to manage their colonies for decades without parliamentary interference, fought to keep their autonomy. One branch of the elite eventually came to the idea that the colonies could never regain their autonomous status as British dependencies. The only solution to autonomy, according to this minority, was to become independent states. The leadership of the Whig faction came from this minority. A second group, probably the majority, believed that colonial grievances could be reconciled and local autonomy restored permitting the colonies to remain part of the British Empire. The leadership of the Loyalist or Tory faction was drawn from this second group.[5]

The Stamp Tax of 1764

In 1764, Parliament imposed a direct document tax on legal documents and other paper products used in the colonies. All legal papers required a tax stamp costing anywhere from 3d to 10s. Playing cards required a 1s stamp. Newspapers required a 1d stamp for every copy in circulation. Anyone who wished to practice law had to buy a 10s stamp. In several colonies, citizens organized boycotts of the paper products requiring a stamp. Attorneys were admitted to practice without a stamp and court documents were filed without stamps.[6] Vigilante groups threatened the Royal tax commissioners with bodily harm, and at least one Stamp Act commissioner was tarred and feathered.[7] James Otis, a Boston attorney and a member of the Massachusetts General Assembly Committee to seek ways and means to deal with the Stamp Tax, sent invitations to the legislatures of the thirteen colonies, asking each to send delegates to a Congress in New York to discuss what to do about the Stamp Tax.[8] The Congress adopted a major declaration of policy called the Declaration of Rights and Grievances, drafted by Pennsylvania delegate John Dickinson.[9] The declaration asserted that Parliament lacked authority to levy a direct tax on the colonies. It claimed that the people of each colony had the right by nature and as Englishmen to imposition of any tax levy only after the levy had been approved by popular vote or by vote of their elected representatives. The petition implored the king and Parliament to repeal the Stamp Tax in recognition of that fundamental right. The Declaration of Rights and Grievances was sent to Parliament to the leaders of the Whig party. It carried some weight with the Whigs who were advocating repeal of the Stamp Tax.[10]

Following the adjournment of the Stamp Act Congress, more than two hundred New York City merchants signed a non-importation agreement. The New York merchants' declaration was followed by similar non-importation agreements from Philadelphia and Boston mercantile groups. This precursor of the boycott was highly effective because English merchants who shipped paper products, legal documents, and other goods subject to the Stamp Tax were losing business. The colonies were their best customers. Under pressure from English merchants doing business with the colonies, Parliament repealed the Stamp Tax in March 1766.[11] At the same time, Parliament passed the Declaratory Act asserting its right to direct taxation of the property of the citizens of the twelve colonies.[12]

The Townshend Duties

Repeal of the Stamp Tax didn't end the tension: Parliament replaced the Stamp Tax with a series of import duties collectively known as the Townshend Acts.[13] The twelve colonies reacted to this latest attempt to impose a direct tax predictably: meetings of indignant citizens, petitions to Parliament to repeal the Townshend Acts, and speeches condemning Parliament for violating the rights of free Englishmen. Most of the colonial legislatures passed a non-importation act forbidding importation of any goods from England listed in the Townshend Acts' schedule of duties. The Townshend duties were never put into effect: Parliament repealed the Townshend duties before one shilling was collected. Parliament left open the imposition of a duty on tea, which would later be the source of great tribulation.

In March 1770, a Boston anti-Parliamentary mob pelted a detail of Royal soldiers from the 29th Regiment of Foot in support of a sentry stationed before the Boston State House with snowballs and rocks. The detail was commanded by Capt. Thomas Preston of the 29th Foot. Someone hit a soldier with a rock and that soldier fired his musket. The rest of the detail fired into the crowd, killing three mob members and mortally wounding two others. Captain Preston, the eight soldiers, and four civilians were charged with homicide by the Massachusetts attorney general, leading to a state trial. Whig lawyers John Adams, assisted by Josiah Quincy III and Tory Robert Auchmuty, skillfully defended Capt. Preston who was acquitted. Adams and his fellow attorneys presented the defense for the eight soldiers. Six were acquitted and two convicted of manslaughter. The four civilians were acquitted.[14]

The Duty on Tea

In 1772, Parliament reenacted a duty on tea shipped from the mother country. Shiploads of tea arriving in the colonies did not land their cargoes. In Boston in early 1773, a mob of men dressed like Native Americans dumped three shiploads of tea into Boston Harbor. Other retaliatory vigilante acts occurred in other colonies, including demonstrations against landing cargoes of tea, throwing tea cargoes overboard, and at least one act of vandalism, burning a ship loaded with tea. South Carolina Whigs also reacted to the duty on tea after the first cargo of tea under the duty to arrive at Charleston was seized by the Crown and impounded before it could be destroyed. The second cargo was dumped into the Cooper River by Whigs. Whigs at Annapolis, Maryland, burned a cargo of tea after it was off-loaded from a British East India cargo ship.

New York governor Tryon refused to allow East Indiamen to unload tea at the port of New York after an angry crowd demonstrated against off-loading tea cargos. The Whigs also campaigned for a boycott of all tea in the colonies.[15]

Prior to 1773, there was no serious talk about overthrowing the government of any of the colonies. That year, a vigilante group called the "Regulators" took up arms and drove off Royal judges and officials in the recently settled western North and South Carolina. The Regulators complained that the Royal judges enforced unjust property tax indebtedness on the provinces. The North Carolina Regulars were dispersed by Royal militia at the crossing of the Alamance in 1771 after a brief firefight.[16] The South Carolina Regulators conducted a guerrilla war against Royal authority for more than a year before the South Carolina government granted the Regulators' demand for local courts and Royal offices for acceptance of deeds and wills in western South Carolina.[17]

The Intolerable Acts

A semi-secret organization called the Sons of Liberty was organized in the 1760s in Boston to oppose Parliament's attempts to lay a direct tax on Massachusetts Colony. The Sons of Liberty eventually spread to other New England towns and to other colonies (e.g., New York and Pennsylvania). The group conducted demonstrations against the Stamp Act and were instrumental in forcing Stamp Tax collectors to resign their offices before the tax took effect.[18] Sons of Liberty opposition to Royal authority turned ugly in Massachusetts. The Sons of Liberty who threw tea cargoes into Boston Harbor in 1773 dressed as Native Americans were doing the bidding of a small group of upper-class members, merchants such as John Hancock, who was under Royal surveillance for smuggling activities; lawyers Samuel Adams, John Adams, and James Otis; and highly respected craftsmen such as Paul Revere. Parliament retaliated against the tea-dumping incident by closing the port of Boston in 1774, essentially destroying the livelihood of thousands of people and also cutting off food shipments.[19] Parliament also passed a revised version of the Quartering Act, authorizing the Royal Army to quarter troops in private homes,[20] and the Quebec Act that declared that the conquered province of Quebec included all the land west of the Alleghenies and north of the Ohio River, which were off limits to English colonists. The same act also recognized the Roman Catholic religion as the state religion of Quebec and extended Catholicism to regions of the future states of Illinois, Indiana, and Ohio that the colonies of Connecticut and Virginia claimed to be land within their charters and jurisdiction.[21] The last straw was the Massachusetts government act that restructured the government of Massachusetts Colony imposing a Royal governor whose salary was paid out of taxes collected by Parliament, assisted by a counsel of men handpicked to be supporters of the king by the colonial secretary, and disbanding the general assembly and forbidding town meetings without the governor's approval.[22]

Prime Minister Lord North sent orders to Gen. Thomas Gage, commanding general of all Royal forces in the colonies, to occupy Boston with four regiments of foot and grenadiers to keep the contumacious citizens of Boston in hand. Gage's troops arrived in 1774 and were forcibly quartered in Boston private homes because there were no local barracks to accommodate Gage's four regiments. Gage was also appointed acting Royal governor of the colony.[23] Massachusetts Colony was a province under military rule without any popularly elected assembly sitting to appoint officers and levy taxes on the colonists.

THE FIRST CONTINENTAL CONGRESS

The closing of the port of Boston brought out a common desire among the upper class of the other colonies to aid Massachusetts by shipping food and other supplies overland to Boston to be brought in via Boston Neck to keep the city alive. It also provoked the convening of a Continental Congress made up of delegates from the thirteen colonies appointed by the colonial legislatures to represent each colony. The first Continental Congress met in Philadelphia in September 1774.[24] Delegates passed resolutions condemning the closing of the port of Boston and calling for removal of Royal troops from Boston.

The Continental Congress first discussed the response to be made to Parliament concerning the Intolerable Acts on September 6, 1774.[25] On September 7, Congress appointed two delegates from each of the thirteen colonies to a great committee to prepare the responses. The detail work of drafting the document was assigned to John Adams of Massachusetts and John Rutledge of South Carolina.[26] Their draft was reported to the Great Committee on September 14. The Continental Congress approved the Continental Association, a document that called for each colony and all of its citizens to commit itself to stopping all importation of any British-made goods, tea, molasses, syrups, paneles, coffee, or pimento as of December 1, 1774.[27] The Association stated that slaves should not be imported as of December 1. The Association also called for stopping exportation of colonial crops and livestock (except rice) as of September 1, 1775. The final draft was passed by Congress on October 20, 1774.[28] The Association required a complete boycott of British goods and a corresponding embargo on shipment of foodstuffs and raw materials to Britain.

The Continental Association also established the Continental Congress as a de facto central quasi-governmental authority that presumed to speak for all colonists. The members of Congress, who were de jure representatives of their colonial assemblies, all of whom signed the Association, committed their colonies and their citizens to non-importation and non-exportation as a unified protest against the Intolerable Acts. The Association resolution instructed the colonies that they were responsible for "establishing such farther regulations as they may think proper for carrying into execution the Association."[29] The document required each colony to ensure compliance with the document by setting up committees of observation in counties, cities, and towns to ensure that every citizen of the colony lived up to the Association.[30] The Association required signers to publish the names of those who refused to sign the Association, then to "break off all dealings" with the Non-Associator thereafter.[31] The immediate impact of the Association varied from colony to colony. Since the Association was extra-governmental, the colonial committees of safety and correspondence were initially responsible for setting up machinery to obtain the signatures of Associators. In South Carolina, for example, in January 1775, a non-governmental body known as the Provincial Congress set up local parish committees of observation to oversee obtaining signatures and to identify the non-signers, publish their names, and make sure that they were ostracized.[32]

Lexington and Concord

On the morning of April 19, 1775, Massachusetts townsmen fired upon a Royal battalion of infantry sent to take John Hancock into custody and to seize illegally held gunpowder and weapons from storage spaces in Lexington and Concord, Massachusetts. The skirmish at Lexington was a disaster for the local militia, known as the "minutemen." The fight at Concord an hour or so later that morning was an inconclusive draw, and the Royal Army began its trudge back to Boston without Hancock or any of the illegal gunpowder. About a thousand local militiamen scurried after the Royal Army taking potshots from behind stone walls and trees at the retreating soldiers, killing and wounding dozens of men.[33] The colony of Massachusetts was now in armed rebellion against its Royal governor and the Royal Army.

Only a fraction of the settlers in Massachusetts actually engaged in armed opposition to Royal authority. The Massachusetts Whig or Patriot faction operated through a shadow government of committees of correspondence throughout the colony. The Massachusetts Whigs were in communication with similar non-governmental committees of correspondence in the twelve other colonies. The thirteen British North American colonies responded to the crisis provoked by the affair at Lexington and Concord through the Continental Congress, which was originally empowered by resolutions from the thirteen colonial legislatures to meet and consider common problems associated with British rule. Members of

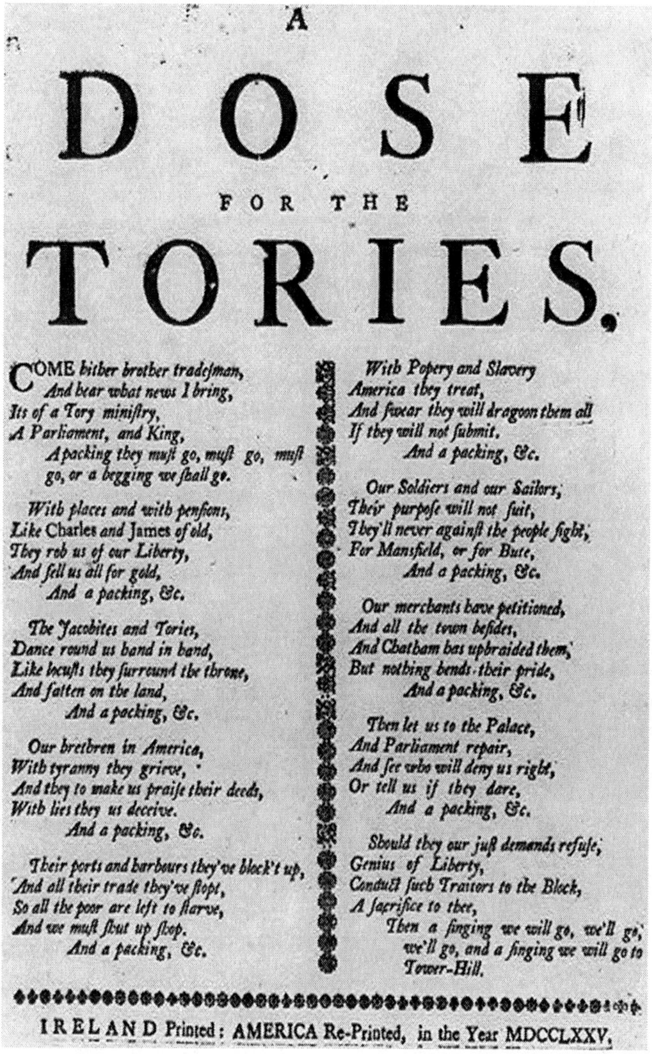

A
DOSE
FOR THE
TORIES.

COME *hither brother tradesman,*
And hear what news I bring,
Its of a Tory ministry,
A Parliament, and King,
A packing they must go, must go, must go, or a begging we shall go.

With places and with pensions,
Like Charles *and* James *of old,*
They rob us of our Liberty,
And sell us all for gold,
And a packing, &c.

The Jacobites and Tories,
Dance round us hand in hand,
Like locusts they surround the throne,
And fatten on the land,
And a packing, &c.

Our brethren in America,
With tyranny they grieve,
And they to make us praise their deeds,
With lies they us deceive.
And a packing, &c.

Their ports and harbours they've block't up,
And all their trade they've stopt,
So all the poor are left to starve,
And we must shut up shop.
And a packing, &c.

With Popery and Slavery
America they treat,
And swear they will dragoon them all
If they will not submit.
And a packing, &c.

Our Soldiers and our Sailors,
Their purpose will not suit,
They'll never against the people fight,
For Mansfield, or for Bute,
And a packing, &c.

Our merchants have petitioned,
And all the town besides,
And Chatham has upbraided them,
But nothing bends their pride,
And a packing, &c.

Then let us to the Palace,
And Parliament repair,
And see who will deny us right,
Or tell us if they dare,
And a packing, &c.

Should they our just demands refuse,
Genius of Liberty,
Conduct such Traitors to the Block,
A sacrifice to thee,
Then a singing we will go, we'll go, we'll go, and a singing we will go to Tower-Hill.

IRELAND Printed: AMERICA Re-Printed, in the Year MDCCLXXV.

Figure 1.1. A Dose of Tories (Library of Congress).

the colonial legislatures were often members of the colony's committee of correspondence.[34]

The committees of correspondence bypassed the legislatures and dealt directly with raising troops, provisioning them and sending them to surround Boston. The twelve colonies were still governed by the British Crown. All but Connecticut, Maryland, Pennsylvania, and Rhode Island were headed by Royal governors appointed by Parliament. The governors of Connecticut and Rhode Island were popularly elected by the citizens. Both had unicameral elected legislative assemblies.[35] Pennsylvania and Maryland were proprietary colonies managed by private citizens.[36] All the colonies had popularly elected legislatures that had the power to enact direct taxes on the citizens. The Whig non-governmental organizations somehow managed to capture the machinery of government in all the colonies by the end of 1775. The Whig governments promptly dealt with the rights of those citizens who were loyal to the Crown by passing acts suggested by the Continental Congress requiring that any person holding public office take an oath of allegiance to the new states of the United States.[37]

The Continental Congress acted as the de facto governing body of the thirteen united colonies. It was based on delegations chosen by the legislative assemblies of the thirteen colonies. Each colony had one vote.[38] It appointed George Washington of Virginia as lieutenant general commanding the Continental army at Cambridge, Massachusetts.[39] Other army officers were also appointed by Congress. Congress had no power to tax the citizens of the colonies. It could only ask the individual colonies to contribute to the support of the insurrection.

The Whig party controlled the Continental Congress and the colonial assemblies that were reconvened after May 1775. By mid-1775, the Royal governors of the ten colonies had fled their capitals, and the governor's councils had ceased to meet. The Tory party had been expelled from power by the Whigs in every colony, and the Massachusetts insurrection had expanded into a full-dress civil war following the Battle of Bunker Hill. Gage's Royal Army was bottled up in Boston. The Continentals occupied the hills overlooking Boston and Boston Harbor. The stalemate continued into 1776, when the Continentals finally positioned siege artillery captured at Fort Ticonderoga to bombard the city. Gage decided to evacuate Boston, taking with him hundreds of citizens loyal to the Crown. The stage was set for the Whigs to carry out reprisals against the Tories. Beginning in 1775, the Continental Congress obligingly passed resolutions prescribing a program of repression that every one of the thirteen new states was strongly urged to adopt. The result was a concerted program to disenfranchise the Tories, to appropriate their land and personal property, and to drive them out of the thirteen newly independent states. The program was not entirely successful, but it led to the exile of thousands of Tories to England, Canada, and the Bahamas, many of whom did not return after the Treaty of Paris ended the war.

THE WHIG AND TORY PARTIES IN THE COLONIES

Colonial society, like that of the mother country, was based on a class structure requiring deference to be shown by members of the lower classes to those who were of the higher class. The upper class, the colonial gentry, was made up of men of wealth and substance, ministers of the established Anglican church, and most professional men and their families. Beneath the upper class, a solid middle class, consisting of yeoman farmers, tradesmen, and some professionals (e.g., physicians and ministers of the Presbyterian and Baptist churches), along with many younger men involved in mercantile adventures, generally deferred to the upper class on most political matters. Most had hopes of rising into the upper class by acquiring wealth. Below the middle class, white tenant farmers, laborers, and other poor white people formed the lower class, and free and slave African Americans composed the bottom of the social order.

The Tory Faction

As the quarrel with Parliament continued, the upper class divided into two groups: neither group supported Parliament's imposition of taxes. One group, nominally labeled "Tories," represented the more conservative element of the elite, willing to work out accommodations with the mother country on the question of taxation, quartering of troops, and the jurisdiction of the vice admiralty courts. Royal officeholders, members of the clergy of the Church of England, Quakers, a majority of wealthy New England and Mid-Atlantic merchants, and a minority of southern planters made up the leadership of the Tories. The Tory faction generally refused to sign the Continental Association in 1774 because the Tories believed that the Association was an act of open rebellion against the Crown. The other wing, labeled the "Whigs," responsible for most of the direct action against the Stamp Act, the Townshend duties, and the tea duty, were willing to oppose imposition of Parliamentary control, even if it meant armed insurrection. Whigs generally signed the 1774 Association and considered those who did not sign it to be disloyal to their colony.[40] Whig leadership consisted of a minority of New England and Mid-Atlantic merchants, Congregational and Presbyterian clergymen, some minor officeholders, the majority of the colonial legislatures in Massachusetts, Rhode Island, Connecticut, Maryland, and Virginia, and a substantial number of southern planters, the groups most affected by imposition of direct taxes and duties.

In April 1775, at the outbreak of hostilities, the Tory faction may have been in the majority among New York citizens, but the extra-legal provincial convention was under Whig control.[41] New Jersey and Delaware had significant Tory populations who opposed breaking with the mother country.[42] In Pennsylvania, loyalists and anti-war Quakers, Dunkards, and Mennonites probably outnumbered Pennsylvania Whigs, who came principally from the Irish immigrant population.[43] The Tories also controlled Savannah and southern Georgia[44] and maintained a strong presence in South Carolina.[45] A substantial plurality of the Irish Presbyterian immigrants who settled in the South Carolina backcountry after 1765, the backbone of the Regulation movement, were Tory adherents.[46] Maryland Tories were principally confined to Maryland's Eastern Shore counties.[47] North Carolina Tories were a curious amalgamation of Royal officeholders, Anglican clergymen, some planters, backcountry Scottish highlanders resettled in or near Buies Creek, and Irish immigrants who were the moving force in the Regulation movement put down by Governor Tryon.[48] New England Tories were a small minority and had limited control over the actions of the local Sons of Liberty. Hundreds of New England Tories, including most of the elite Tory leadership, fled to Boston after Lexington and Concord and then went into voluntary exile when Gen. Howe evacuated Boston in 1776.[49] The middle class was divided along the same lines. Most lawyers were Tories, but in Massachusetts the Whig leadership consisted of lawyers such as James Otis, John Adams, and Samuel Adams.[50] Samuel Adams was the founder of the Sons of Liberty, a semi-secret club that took direct action (e.g., the Boston Tea Party) against taxes imposed by Parliament.

The Whig faction had an opposition in each of the colonies. Large numbers of colonists sided with the mother country, joined its armed forces, and fought unsuccessfully to suppress the rebellion. Simulating the political division in the mother country, the anti-Whig faction was labeled the Tory party. Again, there is no scientific way to project the actual percentage of the adult male population in every one of the thirteen colonies that made up the Tory faction. The estimate made by John Adams of Massachusetts during the Revolution that one-third of the population were Whigs, one-third were Tories, and the remainder were committed to the winning side has the appeal of firsthand observation but cannot be verified from the data. The Tory faction was characterized by refusal to break with the Crown. There was no national prosecutorial system, and each colony had to deal with dissent in its own way. Since several of the thirteen colonies had adopted a bill of rights declaring freedom of assembly, freedom of speech, and basic rights to public trial by jury, each colony in turn had to deal with the Tory problem without destroying the alleged reason for resisting British rule: tyranny and abuse of power.[51]

The Tory faction was further divided into active and passive participants in the war of 1775–1783. Thousands of Tories enlisted in the British army and navy or in Loyalist units formed by Provincial officers or by British regular officers. Most Tories served in units that were not part of the regular British establishment. Tory units consisted of "regular" Provincial commands, the Loyalist militia, the Volunteer Local Corps, and Refugees and Associators. A conservative count of the various Tory units numbered 183 different Tory units ranging in size from small companies to brigades. More than 1,500 Tories were granted commissions by the Crown for service in Tory units during the war.[52] No accurate count of enlisted men is known to exist. Scholars such as Prof. Calhoon estimate that fifty thousand Tories served in all branches of the army and navy.[53] About nineteen thousand Tories served in Provincial commands. Provincial regiments were raised under the authority of the commander in chief in America, Canada, or Jamaica. The commander in chief signed all the commissions for Provincial officers. A Provincial regiment could be drafted or disbanded at the commander in chief's whim. Provincial soldiers enlisted for the duration of the war, unlike Continental soldiers who served for one year. Provincials were paid, clothed, armed, and fed, the same as a British soldier; they were liable to the same military discipline; and they could serve anywhere in North America. Almost all Provincial commands served in the thirteen former Atlantic seaboard colonies between Nova Scotia and West Florida.[54]

Provincial units were mustered by the muster master general, Massachusetts' Tory Edward Winslow. Their uniforms were distributed by the inspector general of Provincial forces, Col. Alexander Innes. Clothing and pay for the Provincials came through the Treasury Office as an extraordinary expense—that is, an expense over and above the normal costs of the Royal Army.[55] Provincial companies and regiments fought in most of the major battles of the Revolution after 1775. Five Provincial regiments were included in the American establishment by war's end. Officers of the five establishment regiments were entitled to half-pay retirement when the war ended. All Provincial regiments were eligible to obtain a higher status of sorts by going on the American establishment. This status was to be conferred on those Provincial units that had achieved their quota of men and had performed valuable services during the war. The five regiments of the establishment were the Queen's American Rangers, the Volunteers of Ireland, the New York Volunteers, the King's American Regiment, and the British Legion. The five were renumbered the 1st through 5th American Regiments respectively and could order their clothing directly from England instead of taking what they could get from the Provincial stores. Their buttons were generally marked with the number of their regiment. Their officers were automatically entitled to half pay and permanent rank in America upon the reduction of their corps. This establishment did not alter their pay, jurisdiction, or form of muster.[56]

About ten thousand Loyalists served in Tory militias or as Associators. Militia units were formed from local Tory farmers and mechanics in Georgia, New Jersey, New York, North Carolina, and South Carolina. Militia units were supposed to serve in their home colony, although some militia units crossed borders to fight. Militias were formed in Quebec, Nova Scotia, East Florida, and West Florida as well as in six colonies out of the thirteen in rebellion. Militiamen usually served without pay and provided their own weapons. North Carolina and South Carolina provided for payment for their militias, leaving the only extant militia muster records because militias in other colonies were never formally mustered. Thomas Allen estimates that the New York Loyalist militia numbered more than seven thousand soldiers. The governor of the province controlled the formation and commissioning of militia officers. The Loyalist militias were compulsory in those portions of the colonies that came under British control during the war. The Loyalists exempted Quakers and other peace church members from militia musters and service, as well as public officials.[57] The number of Tory militiamen in New York, New Jersey, and other reconquered provinces cannot be ascertained due to lack of muster records. Volunteer Local Corps, units halfway between the militia and the Provincial regiments, were also organized in several provinces. The members of the Local Corps served for a fixed period of time and wore uniforms. Volunteer Local Corps units served only in their provinces of origin. The ranks of Volunteer Local Corps included the Queen's Own Loyal Virginia Regiment, the East Florida Rangers, the Bucks County Volunteers, and two troops of cavalry raised in Georgia by Governor Wright in 1781.[58]

The final classes of Tory fighting units were the Refugees and Associators. The units were auxiliary troops used in pioneering work or sent out to raid the enemy to return with supplies for the Royal Army. Tories serving in these units were not paid and did not have uniforms. The British high command expected that Refugees and Associators would provide food, clothing, and arms for themselves by raiding the enemy or selling firewood to local Tory families. Refugee and Associator units were raised by order of the British commander in chief or by a Royal governor or garrison commander. Refugees and Associators units were popular after 1777 in the northern provinces. The first such organization, the Loyal American Association, was recruited in Boston in 1775. The soldiers in Refugee and Associator units served without pay or uniforms. They were considered auxiliary troops that were able to support themselves in the field by woodcutting, procuring supplies for the British from the Rebels, or by plundering. These auxiliary troops were outside regular army discipline and proved difficult to control. Examples are the Loyal Refugee Volunteers, the Hazard's Corps, the Loyal Associated Refugees, the King's Militia Volunteers, and the Associated Loyalists.[59]

None of the thirteen states of the United States were immune from Loyalist military activity. Tory military units constituted a clear and present danger to the continued, precarious existence of the United States during the Revolution. Tory military units operated with the main British army from 1775 to 1782. Tory commands also campaigned independently during the Revolution. The New York frontier was a battleground between Tory ranger commands led by Walter Butler and John Johnson and local Whig militia and Continental troops of the line from 1777 through 1782.[60] New Jersey's infamous "Neutral Ground" was dominated by Tory units raised by Royal governor William Franklin and the forces commanded by New York's Royal governor, William Tryon.[61] Tory units conducted operations in South Carolina against Whig irregular units such as Francis Marion's guerrillas and engaged in pitched battles with Whig militiamen at Kings Mountain[62] and the Cowpens,[63] and they fought the Continental army under Maj. Gen. Horatio Gates at Camden in 1780[64] and at Guilford Courthouse in 1781.[65] Tory irregulars spearheaded a Loyalist uprising in Worcester County, Maryland, and neighboring Sussex County, Delaware.[66]

Notable Tory military leaders included Brigadier General Donald MacDonald, leader of the Tory forces consisting mainly of recent Highland Scot immigrants at the Battle of Moore's Creek Bridge in North Carolina;[67] Brigadier General Oliver Delancy, a scion of one of the wealthiest and most distinguished families in New York, who commanded a brigade at the Battle of Long Island;[68] Maj. Robert Rogers, a hero of the French and Indian War who commanded a second Rogers' Rangers unit for the Royal Army in 1776–1777;[69] John Butler, organizer of Butler's Rangers, which included Native Americans recruited by Iroquois chief Joseph Brant;[70] Walter Butler, his son, who took over command from his father; Sir John Johnson, son of Sir William Johnson, the British Indian agent for the northern colonies and frontier;[71] and Guy Johnson, Sir William Johnson's nephew.[72] Tory units were also recruited by regular British officers. Lieutenant Colonel Banastre Tarleton recruited Loyalists for his American Legion, a command originally put together by another British officer, John Graves Simcoe, who blended the Pennsylvania Light Dragoons, the Bucks County Light Dragoons, and the Caledonia Volunteers into the British Legion. Tarleton took over the command and fought a two-year irregular war against Whig guerillas in South Carolina and North Carolina.[73] Captain Patrick Ferguson, the inventor of the practical breech-loading rifle, recruited the American Volunteers, which he led in several engagements, including the disastrous engagement at Kings Mountain where Ferguson was killed in battle and his command was slaughtered.[74]

Civilian Tory activists organized military units, provided weapons and ammunition to British and Tory military units, or formed shadow governments to deal out punishment to Whigs in the same way that Whig committees of correspondence and committees of observation had done to Tories. William Franklin was the most notable civilian activist. He was the illegitimate son of Benjamin Franklin who became Royal governor of New Jersey in 1762 in his early thirties. William Franklin was educated for the law in London under his father's indulgent supervision. He disagreed with his father's Whiggish stand on provincial rights of self-government, and when hostilities broke out, he remained loyal to the king. In June 1776, the New Jersey Provincial Congress passed a resolution for his arrest as "an enemy to the liberties of this country."[75] Franklin was arrested and put in custody of Whig Connecticut governor John Trumbull. After signing a parole, Franklin was allowed to walk about town and immediately began corresponding with Tory leadership in

Connecticut and New Jersey. Trumbull judged that this violated his parole and imprisoned him in the Litchfield, Connecticut, town jail until he was exchanged in October 1778 for Delaware president John McKinley.[76] Franklin was released in New York City and formed a "Refugee Club" for Tories who had escaped Whig harassment in New Jersey and other provinces. Franklin proposed a plan to enlist Associators from New Jersey and elsewhere for the purpose of carrying out a guerilla war in the Neutral Ground. The plan was approved by New York Royal governor Maj. Gen. William Tryon. The Associators were managed by the Board of Associated Loyalists, a body headed by Franklin and including former North Carolina Royal governor Josiah Martin. Sir Henry Clinton issued commissions for the Associators' officers and furnished weapons and ammunition for the Associators. Franklin's Associators mustered more than four hundred soldiers at the height of this recruiting campaign. The Associators carried out raids in New Jersey from 1778 through the end of the war, the largest and best organized being the March 1780 descent upon Hackensack.[77]

Joseph Galloway of Pennsylvania had been a member of the First Continental Congress in 1774. He put together a plan for an American parliament representing the thirteen provinces and an executive president general for America appointed by the Crown. He believed that this body could redress the grievances that related to taxation issues and manage unrest in the provinces. Unfortunately, Galloway's plan had no other supporters. He then disassociated himself from the Whig party and the Continental Congress. In 1776 he fled to New York to escape Whig retribution. When General Howe captured Philadelphia in September 1777, Galloway became the head of the town watch, a Tory paramilitary police force that arrested Whigs and punished them for resisting Royal authority.[78] When Howe abandoned Philadelphia in 1778, Galloway returned to New York and eventually made his way to England.[79]

William Allen, the chief justice of Pennsylvania, also sided with Royal authority. He left Pennsylvania in 1774, frustrated by the first Continental Congress's decision to boycott British goods. His sons James and William Allen worked with Joseph Galloway during the British occupation of Philadelphia in support of return to Royal rule.[80] Reverend Jonathan Boucher, the pastor of an Anglican church in Maryland and tutor to George Washington's stepson, continued to pray for the king at services despite threats from Whigs that he would he shot. Boucher had opposed the Stamp Tax and the Quebec Act but was unwilling to accept nonimportation and the disassociation of Maryland from the Crown. In May 1775, Boucher, the pastor of St. Barnabas Church, Upper Marlboro, Maryland, took a brace of pistols with him to the pulpit for a farewell sermon. At the conclusion of services, he seized Osborn Sprigg, a notorious Whig, and escorted him out of church to their waiting horses. Boucher fled Maryland to the mother country after this incident.[81]

The great majority of Tories were passive bystanders who wished for success of British arms but neither fought for their sovereign nor supplied British units with weapons or ammunition and avoided head-on conflict, if possible, with their Whig neighbors. For example, Matthew Lymberger, a farmer in Penobscot, Massachusetts, was a confirmed Loyalist who in public was neutral. The majority of eighty thousand Tory exiles in Nova Scotia and Canada were farmers. Around five thousand backcountry farmers from Georgia and South Carolina fled to British East Florida.[82] The Loyalist claims filed after the Revolution included over eight hundred men who listed their pre-war occupation as "farmer." Many of these claimants were not soldiers or suppliers.[83] A few case histories of passive Tories are enlightening. Philip Barton Key of Maryland was a "bystander" Loyalist who had been studying law in Annapolis in 1775. Key's brother accepted a commission in the Continental army. He never enlisted or sought a commission in the Royal Army or Navy and did not supply the British forces with weapons, ammunition, or provisions. He refused to take the test oath in 1777. He was forbidden to go within seven miles of any navigable water. Key fled to Philadelphia after the city had been occupied by Sir William Howe. When Howe evacuated Philadelphia, Key followed the army to New York and eventually left the United States. Key was repatriated without incident after the end of hostilities in 1783.[84]

The thousands of claims submitted by Loyalists who fled the United States to avoid arrest and persecution contain the stories of many humble farmers who were loyal to the Crown. The case of John Woodcock of New York is typical of so many similar claims. According to his declaration before the Loyalist Claims Commission, he lived in Whig territory on the Susquehanna River during the war. In 1781, he was living at Warren's Bush on a four-hundred-acre farm. Woodcock swore he assisted other Loyalists to escape from Whig control. His son and his brother's son-in-law served in the Royal Army. Woodcock was sentenced to be deported as an enemy of the state in 1781. Woodcock produced a departure order signed by a New York official named G. Putnam. Woodcock produced three witnesses who swore that Woodcock was a Loyalist who furnished livestock to the king's forces. One witness, Garret Dingman, corroborated Woodcock's claim that he was deported by order of the State of New York.[85]

Alexander White, the last Royalist sheriff of Tryon County, New York, asserted in support of his claim that he published Gov. Tryon's proclamation banning committees of correspondence and Safety and followed the proclamation by opposing the meeting of the county committees of safety and inquiry, arresting the individuals who formed both committees. Sheriff White was then attacked by a Whig mob and besieged in his house until Sr. John Johnson managed to free him from the Whigs. White then fled to Canada and returned in 1775, only to be taken prisoner at

Lake Champlain and transported to Albany Goal and put in irons. Sheriff White was eventually sent to New England for about a year and a half, escaping in time to join Gen. Burgoyne's expedition. White was captured a second time after Burgoyne had surrendered and held for about twelve months before being exchanged in October 1778. Sheriff White went to New York City and worked as a barracks master for the Royal Army until New York City was evacuated. He produced a certificate from former governor Tryon attesting to his loyalty to the Crown, along with attestations from Tryon, James Delancy, Sir John Johnson and Col. Johnson, stating that White was a loyal subject of the Crown, corroborating his imprisonment for the cause. Sheriff White was a tenant farmer holding a lease from Sir William Johnson on a farm on the Mohawk River where he lived and a claim to a portion of a thousand-acre patent near Fort Edward. He lost his home, livestock, and all possessions.[86] These claims affidavits give the reader some idea of the great mass of Tories who fled the United States between 1775 and 1783 to escape persecution by the Whigs.

The Traditional Religious Pacifists

The thirteen states also dealt harshly with members of the traditional pacifist sects, members of the Society of Friends and the Anabaptist denominations, Mennonite, Dunkard, and Amish people, citizens whose religious beliefs included a literal interpretation of Christ's message requiring them to abstain from all forms of warfare. Members of the Society of Friends generally remained neutral throughout the war. In Rhode Island, Friends were subject to the militia act and could escape military service, but their town had to hire substitutes. The Friends had a portion of their real and personal property confiscated to pay substitutes. Massachusetts later adopted the same policy regarding the exemption of Friends from militia muster and conscription.[87] Prior to Sir William Howe's occupation of Philadelphia, forty prominent Friends such as James Pemberton, Henry Drinker, and Thomas Wharton were placed under arrest by Pennsylvania authorities according to a request issued by the Continental Congress as "persons inimical" to the new government. Their homes and shops were searched, but the searchers failed to find any pro-British documents or evidence that these men cooperated with the British in any way. Nonetheless, the forty Friends were ordered to be deported to Virginia. The group eventually was exiled to Winchester, Virginia, until returned and released in 1778.[88] Pennsylvania also imposed fines and taxes on its Amish, Dunkard, Mennonite, Moravian, and Schwenkfelder citizens to support the war effort.[89]

The Whig Faction

The Whig faction was also a cross-section of the colonial population. Some of the great landowners of the southern colonies (e.g., Charles Carroll of Carrollton of Maryland, Arthur Middleton and Robert Barnwell of South Carolina, George Washington and Richard Henry Lee of Virginia)[90] were Whigs, as were numerous of yeoman farmers, mechanics, and laborers. The Whig faction had more than its fair share of the tiny professional class in the colonies, particularly the lawyers. Religiously, the Whig faction in most of the colonies included members of the Established Church and many Dissenters (i.e., Presbyterians).

There is no scientific way of determining the size of the Whig faction at the outbreak of armed conflict in the spring of 1775. Lists of Associators and non-Associators from some of the colonies prepared in the late 1770s provide some rough way of estimating the strength of the Whig faction later in the Revolution. Shortly after the end of hostilities, John Adams estimated that one-third of the population of the thirteen colonies were Loyalists. Some scholars have made projections based on these lists which indicate that the Whigs numbered more than one out of every three male citizens in the colonies.[91] Although other scholars challenge this estimate, no one has projected that a substantially higher proportion of the adult male population actually supported the Whig cause. In a later era, the Whig faction might have been described as a vanguard of the revolutionary party.

THE PROGRAM TO SUPPRESS THE TORIES

The Whig party started persecuting Tories by mob action and vigilante action several years before the Declaration of Independence. In Massachusetts, vigilante Sons of Liberty bands roamed the streets of Boston during the Stamp Act crisis. The Sons of Liberty were responsible for dumping tea into Boston Harbor, and after the Coercive Acts were passed by Parliament, the Sons of Liberty used mob action against Royal lieutenant governor and Governor's Council member Thomas Oliver. In August 1774, a delegation of "landowners" went to Oliver's home in Cambridge to protest the Coercive Acts. Oliver met with the delegates on his doorstep and accompanied the delegation to Cambridge's town square where a larger audience was assembled. A rumor spread that Gen. Gage was sending troops to Cambridge, and the crowd demanded that Oliver send a message to Gage instructing him not to send troops to Cambridge. Oliver did as requested. The crowd then asked him to resign from the council. He refused and returned home. Several hours later, a crowd estimated at around four thousand, some bearing muskets and other weapons, surrounded his house. The delegation went to his door with a pre-written letter of resignation from the council. They told Oliver that the crowd was unhappy that he had not resigned. Oliver signed the resignation under duress and later repudiated it.[92]

The vigilantes also favored tarring and feathering Royal officers and notable Tories.[93] The victim would be forcibly taken out of his home or shop, stripped naked, and then covered with pine tar followed by a roll in a blanket full of chicken or goose feathers.[94] "Smoking the Tory" was another favorite vigilante tactic: the suspected disloyal person was locked in a cabin, the windows and doors were shut, a fire was started in the fireplace, and then the chimney top was closed off, causing smoke to back up into the cabin, nearly suffocating the disloyal person, who was then encouraged to sign a loyalty oath.[95]

The Association and Non-Associators

The Continental Congress could not pass legislation commanding the colonies to do anything. It could pass resolutions directed to the legislatures of the colonies recommending action. Congress developed a coordinated plan to deal with the Tories that appeared in a series of resolutions from 1775 to 1780. The Association was the first step in the process of muzzling Tory dissent. Those who signed the Association were considered good Whigs; those who did not sign were identified as Tories.[96] Many Non-Associators were members of the traditional "peace denominations" (e.g., Society of Friends, Mennonites, or Dunkers). These individuals were lumped together with people who refused to betray their loyalty to King George. The thirteen colonies had no legal requirement for signatures on the Association. Non-Associators were persecuted intermittently by vigilantes using tar and feathers and other coercive techniques to punish Non-Associators.[97]

Post-Independence Treatment of Tories

Loyalty Oaths

The situation regarding Loyalists deteriorated rapidly after the signing of the Declaration of Independence. In March 1776, the Continental Congress had passed a resolution calling on the colonies to disarm Non-Associators and use the arms to provide weapons to the Continental Line and the colonial militia.[98] Some colonies were already requiring test oaths for all citizens. Massachusetts passed a statute in 1775 requiring all officeholders to take a loyalty oath to the colony.[99] Connecticut followed suit later in May 1776 with a test oath requiring all citizens to take an oath of fidelity to the colony to preserve their civil rights.[100] By 1778, all thirteen states passed test oath statutes requiring all male citizens to execute a loyalty oath to the state and a renunciation of any claim to sovereignty by Great Britain.[101] Two states required youths over eighteen[102] and five required youths sixteen or older to take the loyalty oath.[103] The remainder did not specify any age requirement for taking the oath. Those who refused to sign were to be brought before a local magistrate. If the person who refused to sign persisted in refusing to sign, he would be deprived of all firearms, of the right to hold any political office, and of the right to vote and to serve on juries. If the non-juror was a lawyer, he would be barred from practicing law. Pennsylvania barred non-jurors from practicing medicine or acting as an apothecary.[104] A non-juror could not commence a civil lawsuit. Most states assessed a treble property tax on non-jurors to help finance the war.[105] A few states allowed a non-juror a second chance to sign the oath.[106] Quakers, Mennonites, and Dunkards were usually exempted from the oath requirement.[107]

The enforcement of the loyalty oath was uneven; a number of states reenacted their original loyalty oath act twice or three times.[108] The preambles to the reenacted loyalty oath statutes usually recited that the people who had failed to comply with the original statute's deadline were entitled to a second chance due to matters beyond their control. Tories who refused to take the oath, and even those who had joined British military units, were often given a chance to repent their allegiance by taking a loyalty oath and agreeing to serve in a Continental or state naval warship for the duration of the war.[109]

Treason

The Continental Congress passed a resolution that all the provincial assemblies should pass an act stating that anyone who served in the Royal Army or Navy or aided and abetted the Royal military with supplies or by acting as a guide or a pilot was guilty of treason. The thirteen states followed suit by passing treason acts based on English precedents.[110] The statutes were remarkably similar in scope. Maryland's treason act is typical. According to Acts 1777 passed February 5, 1777, any subject or inhabitant of Maryland who would levy war against the united colonies, or afford aid and comfort to Great Britain's armed forces, or give intelligence to Great Britain, would be guilty of treason, punishable by death without benefit of clergy if convicted. Conviction required the testimony of two witnesses to the treasonable act. Second, the statute made any Maryland subject or inhabitant who concealed the treason of another person guilty of misprision of treason, also punishable by death without benefit of clergy. Persons who were convicted of treason or misprision of treason would also be punished by forfeiture of all real and personal property belonging to the offender. Third, any Maryland subject who affirms that the king or Parliament has authority over Maryland was subject to a fine of up to £10,000 and imprisoned for up to five years. Fourth, any Maryland subject who excited or persuaded any inhabitant to obstruct the execution of any law of Maryland would be fined £2,000 and imprisoned up to two years if convicted.[111]

A number of states also added statutes defining trading with the enemy as a separate crime punishable by fine and imprisonment. These statutes permitted private parties to enforce the law by apprehending anyone on his way to trade with the enemy without a passport. The trader's goods would be confiscated and sold. Half the proceeds of sale were earmarked for the private party who apprehended the trader. Typically, a person who was caught trading with the enemy without a passport or licenses would be fined and have a portion of his real and personal property seized as a fine.[112]

Some states passed deportation statutes requiring that citizens who were deemed inimical to the Whig order who refused to take the test oath be deported to another jurisdiction.[113] Georgia adopted a statute deporting non-resident persons who came to Georgia and sought citizenship without producing a certificate of loyalty issued by a judicial officer in another U.S. jurisdiction.[114]

Confiscation of Tory Property

In November 1777, a resolution of the Continental Congress called for the states to set up a system for confiscation of the land and personal property of Loyalists.[115] All thirteen states adopted confiscation acts that permitted the seizure of real and personal property owned by resident Tories and by Tories who were absent from the jurisdiction. Typically, these statutes called for condemnation of all real and personal property owned by a Tory convicted of treason or misprision of treason. Estates of absentees were to be confiscated, saving an allowance for the spouse of an absentee Tory. Any suspected disloyal person was also likely to have condemnation proceedings brought against him.[116] The property condemned would then be managed to produce income for the state to be used to support the war effort.[117] The duty to find and ferret out real and personal property belonging to convicted people and absentees was variously assigned to the town selectmen in some New England states[118] or an administrative commissioner in some states.[119] Private parties who caught a person trading with the British were permitted to confiscate the offender's trade goods and recover half the value in compensation.[120] The early confiscation acts required the person who discovered the estate of an alleged disloyal person to appear before a justice of the peace or a special commissioner with an inventory of real and personal property.[121] The judicial officer would then schedule a hearing on condemnation of the disloyal person's estate, with notice to the disloyal person and to all his creditors.[122] Some states provided for jury trials in condemnation.[123] Most states provided for jury trials for persons accused of treason. Forfeitures resulting from attainder for treason were the product of the jury trial on the merits for treason.[124] If the defendant was adjudged to be disloyal, his property would be confiscated and turned over to the commissioner or to a trustee to manage. If he was not found to be disloyal, the case would be dismissed and the alleged disloyal person would recover possession of his property. Delaware, Georgia, and Maryland permitted non-judicially supervised seizure of Tory real and personal property. In these states commissioners appointed by the state legislature seized the real and personal estate of men convicted of treason or misprision of treason. The treason statutes did not provide for judicial review of these seizures apart from the criminal trial brought against the alleged offender.[125]

No one knows how many condemnation proceedings were filed between 1775 and 1783 and how many resulted in confiscation. No one knows how many people were convicted of treason or misprision of treason, forfeiting their real and personal property to the state without further judicial review. Some of the states passed pardon acts toward the end of the war, granting Loyalists who recanted their allegiance to King George a pardon once the former Loyalist took a loyalty oath. If the former Loyalist's estate had not been sold, it would be returned to him. If all or part had been sold, the state would compensate the former Loyalist with a partial cash payment for the loss.[126]

Confiscation acts were generally amended around 1780 to permit the trustee or commissioner holding real and personal property to sell the confiscated estates to the highest bidder at public sale.[127] Some states authorized sale of confiscated property earlier than 1780,[128] and the practice of sale at auction was generally available by 1782 in most jurisdictions.

Some states also passed special acts naming Tories whose real and personal property would be seized on account of disloyalty, directing commissioners or trustees to take possession of the named individuals' real and personal property.[129] Most of the thirteen states also had condemnation proceedings on the books for property confiscated from persons wrongfully trading with the enemy.[130]

THE TREATY OF PARIS AND CHALLENGES TO TREASON ACTS AND CONFISCATIONS

By the end of the war, between sixty thousand and eighty thousand Loyalists had fled the United States to East and West Florida, New Brunswick, Quebec, the Bahamas, Jamaica, and Great Britain.[131] Most of these people lost their real and personal property through confiscation by the government of the thirteen states. The number and value of estates confiscated between 1775 and 1783 is unknown. More than three thousand refugees filed claims with the British Loyalist Claims Commission. The commission adjudicated 3,225 claims for lost or confiscated estates between 1783 and 1789. The commission granted partial compensation to 2,291 claimants.[132] The Treaty of Paris of 1783 ending hostilities contained Article V urging the Continental Congress to influence the thirteen states to restore the confiscated estates of Loyalists to their pre-war owners.[133] The clause could not be enforced, and the governments of the thirteen states continued to sell confiscated estates into the late 1780s.

Raymond Lambert, who researched the wartime confiscations in Georgia, reported that the Georgia Confiscation Commissioners sold £410,218 worth of real and personal property between 1782 and 1786. Buyers were unable to complete payment for £281,716 worth of confiscated estates, which were returned to the state for resale.[134] The state conducted eight major sales of confiscated estates between June and October 1782 after the British evacuated Augusta and Savannah.[135] Lambert noted that some of the estates sold were already occupied by prominent Whigs, lending credence to the accusations made that confiscation of estates simply benefitted well-off Whigs at the expense of Tories who had fled the jurisdiction to save their lives.[136]

Maryland's commissioners sold more than £450,000 worth of confiscated real estate.[137] In 1776, the Massachusetts Great and General Court had considered confiscating the lands of Royal officials. The legislature ordered the estates of former officials to be seized without notice or hearing and authorized the commissioners who took possession of these estates to farm them out on one-year leases. The Massachusetts confiscation program was opposed by prominent Whigs who feared that confiscation of Tory estates was an unwarranted interference with private property.[138] Massachusetts' confiscation program had started as a small-scale seizure of the estates of Royal officials, but a second Confiscation Act threatened to subject more than two thousand Massachusetts citizens to loss of their estates.[139] Article I of the 1780 Massachusetts Declaration of Rights stated that:

> All men are born free and equal, and have certain natural, essential, and unalienable rights; among which may be reckoned the right of enjoying and defending their lives and liberties; that of acquiring, possessing, and protecting property; in fine, that of seeking and obtaining their safety and happiness.[140]

The confiscation of the estates of men who were not convicted of treason flaunted this provision of the constitution. The 1779 general confiscation act did include trial by jury in Superior Court after the presenters that submitted their case to a justice of the peace. The earlier act attainted former Royal officials without notice or hearing. The government seized their estates without judicial review. The second act also provided for an allowance to the spouse or widow of the "conspirator" whose property was to be seized.[141]

Some years after the end of hostilities, a "blacklist" was published listing more than 250 New York citizens who were deemed to be Loyalist conspirators who had forfeited their estates.[142] In 1939, Harry Yoshpe published a scholarly study of confiscations in the lower counties of New York.[143] He reported that the commissioners of forfeiture filed a report stating that they had sold forfeited estates located in the southern district of New York valued at £502,709 10s as of 1787.[144] Some but not all of the owners of these forfeited estates had been included in the "blacklist." Pennsylvania's Council of Safety confiscated the estates of nearly five hundred Loyalists who were attainted for treason between 1778 and 1781.[145] Virginia confiscated the seignory of Lord Fairfax in the Northern Neck of Virginia and sold off large tracts from the enormous Fairfax grants to local landowners.[146]

Forfeited estates often ended up in the hands of wealthy Whigs. Yoshpe reported that the commissioners of forfeiture sold the East Farm estate of Loyalist merchant James Delancy, comprising most of today's lower east side of New York City, to twenty-five prominent Whigs, including members of the rival mercantile family of Philip Livingston.[147] This same pattern appeared time and again in other colonies.

Testing the Constitutionality of Confiscation

The end of hostilities in 1783 did not stop the suppression of the rights of Tories. The Treaty of Paris did not bind the thirteen states to return Tory property. They were free to continue to sell confiscated estates. The treason acts that permitted ex parte bills of attainder and the confiscation acts that permitted ex parte seizure of property deprived persons identified as Tories of life, liberty, and property without any pretense of due process of law. In North Carolina and New Jersey, aggrieved Tories pursued a remedy for their confiscated estates in the courts with some success.

Bayard v. Singleton

While not all states had a bill of rights in their constitutions, North Carolina did. The constitutionality of North Carolina's confiscation act was tested in *Bayard v. Singleton*.[148] Samuel Cornell, a New Bern merchant who was also a Loyalist and a member of Royal governor Martin's council fled North Carolina in 1775, leaving land and personal property behind. In December 1777, Cornell attempted to return to New Bern. He was turned away because he would not take a loyalty oath. Cornell took ship for New York, but not before he conveyed his land and personal property to his wife and daughter. The State of North Carolina confiscated Cornell's estate and sold it to another New Bern Whig merchant, Spyers Singleton. In 1787, Cornell's daughter, Elizabeth Cornell Bayard, filed suit against Singleton to recover the land and personal property conveyed to her by her late father. She was represented by future North Carolina governor Samuel Johnston and William R. Davie. Singleton hired former governor Abner Nash and Alfred Moore, the only North Carolinian ever appointed to the U.S. Supreme Court, as his counsel.[149] While this lawsuit was pending, the North Carolina General Assembly passed a statute quieting title in any person who purchased confiscated land at public sale from the commissioners of forfeited estates. Singleton's counsel moved to dismiss Bayard's suit on the ground that the quiet title act barred any right she may have derived from her late father's conveyance.[150] Bayard's counsel argued that the quiet title act was contrary to Articles XII, XIII, and XIV because Bayard would be deprived of her estate without a hearing and trial by jury.[151]

Twenty-seven other litigants had pending cases for recovery of confiscated estates in the North Carolina court system at the time *Bayard* was decided.[152] The Court of Conferences (predecessor of the North Carolina Supreme Court) denied the motion to dismiss on the ground that the 1785 act deprived the plaintiff of due course of law and ordered the case to be tried. The court said:

> That by the constitution every citizen had undoubtedly a right to a decision of his property by a trial by jury. For that if the Legislature could take away this right, and require him to stand condemned in his property without a trial, it might with as much authority require his life to be taken away without a trial by jury, and that he should stand condemned to die, without the formality of any trial at all: that if the members of the General Assembly could do this, they might with equal authority, not only render themselves the Legislators of the State for life, without any further election of the people, from thence transmit the dignity and authority of legislation down to their heirs male forever.
>
> But that it was clear, that no act they could pass, could by any means repeal or alter the constitution, because if they could do this, they would at the same instant of time, destroy their own existence as a Legislature, and dissolve the government thereby established. Consequently the constitution (which the judicial power was bound to take notice of as much as of any other law whatever,) standing in full force as the fundamental law of the land, notwithstanding the act on which the present motion was grounded, the same act must of course, in that instance, stand as abrogated and without any effect.[153]

The court held that at the time Cornell conveyed his estate to his wife and daughter, he was an alien, having chosen to live under the Crown's protection. The court then stated that Cornell had forfeited the right to convey his property.[154] The Court rejected an argument based on Vattel's international law treatise "of the majority of the inhabitants of any country deliberately dissolving their old government."[155] This reference is obscure and does not appear to relate to anything in Vattel's volume 1. The case was set for trial. The jury gave a verdict for the defendant, and Bayard's case and the twenty-seven other cases were dismissed by means of a voluntary nonsuit.[156] The case did determine that the judicial branch could find that an act of the general assembly was unconstitutional and unenforceable. *Bayard* preceded *Marbury v. Madison* by almost twenty years.

Holmes v. Walton

John Holmes and Solomon Ketchum were apprehended by Elisha Walton allegedly heading for British lines to trade goods with the British army. They were charged with violating New Jersey's Trading with the Enemy Act.[157] According to the statute, they were to be tried before a jury of six citizens of the vicinage.[158] Holmes and Ketchum were convicted by the six-person jury, and their trading goods were seized and ordered sold.[159] Holmes and Ketchum listed eight points of error meriting reversal of their conviction. Item 7 read as follows: "Because the Jury sworn and who tryed the above cause, and on whose Verdict Judgment was entered, consisted of six men only, when by the Laws of the Land, it should have consisted of twelve men."[160] The defendants did not challenge the constitutionality of the 1778 Trading with the Enemy Act.

Meanwhile, on Christmas Day 1779 the New Jersey legislature passed a statute authorizing trial by a jury of twelve in forfeiture cases.[161] On September 7, 1780, the New Jersey Supreme Court entered judgment reversing the conviction of Holmes and Ketcham and remanded their case for a new trial.[162] The court did not state the grounds for the reversal. Modern commentators have asserted that the court reversed the case because the New Jersey Constitution of 1776 contained a clause stating that the common law of England and trial by jury would remain in force until altered by a future legislature. The 1776 constitution did not say that trial by a jury of twelve was required.[163] Despite this analytical faux pas, modern commentators claim that the New Jersey Supreme Court "measured the statute against the state constitution, found that the former violated the latter, and refused to apply it to the case at hand."[164] The basis for this assertion is highly speculative, since the defendants listed seven other grounds for reversing their convictions in their certiorari petition.

Rutgers v. Waddington

In 1783, the New York General Assembly passed an act permitting displaced Whigs who lost their estates by flight to avoid the British occupation to bring trespass acts to recover damages for loss or destruction of their real and personal property against the current owner or possessor of the estate.[165] Pre-war Elizabeth Rutgers owned a brewery in Manhattan. In August 1778, Waddington occupied her brewery and remained in possession under British rule up to March 17, 1783. Waddington cited and pled Article 5 of the Treaty of Paris in support of his right to remain in possession and to be free of Rutgers's claim for damages.[166]

Alexander Hamilton argued that the New York Constitution incorporated the law of nations when it adopted the common law. Article XXXV of the New York Constitution provided:

> And this convention doth further, in the name and by the authority of the good people of this State, ordain, determine, and declare that such parts of the common law of England, and of the statute law of England and Great Britain, and of the acts of the legislature of the colony of New York, as together did form the law of the said colony on the 19th day of April, in the year of our Lord one thousand seven hundred and seventy-five, shall be and continue the law of this State, subject to such alterations and provisions as the legislature of this State shall, from time to time, make concerning the same. That such of the said acts, as are temporary, shall expire at the times limited for their duration, respectively. That all such parts of the said common law, and all such of the said statutes and acts aforesaid, or parts thereof, as may be construed to establish or maintain any particular denomination of Christians or their ministers, or concern the allegiance heretofore yielded to, and the supremacy, sovereignty, government, or prerogatives claimed or exercised by, the King of Great Britain and his predecessors, over the colony of New York and its inhabitants, or are repugnant to this constitution, be, and they hereby are, abrogated and rejected. And this convention doth further ordain, that the resolves or resolutions of the congresses of the colony of New York, and of the convention of the State of New York, now in force, and not repugnant to the government established by this constitution, shall be considered as making part of the laws of this State; subject, nevertheless, to such alterations and provisions as the legislature of this State may, from time to time, make concerning the same.[167]

He asserted that the New York General Assembly could not violate the law of nations and had not intended to violate the law of nations when it passed the Trespass Act.[168] Hamilton claimed that under the law of nations, a civilian occupying land pursuant to military order could not be ousted. Therefore, Waddington, who had occupied the brewery under military order in 1778 was not required to respond in damages to Rutgers's complaint. Hamilton argued that the court should follow the law of nations because the Articles of Confederation established the right of Congress to conduct foreign relations for the states, making the law of nations applicable to each state. The Treaty of Paris adopted the law of nations implicitly, said Hamilton, because it conferred amnesty for all trespasses carried out under military orders, and the treaty was the supreme law of the land, binding on New York.[169]

Rutgers's attorney demurred to Hamilton's plea and argument, asserting that the Trespass Act did not allow a plea based on the law of nations as a bar to an action brought under the statute. Hamilton responded with his demurrer asserting that the claim was barred by force of the Treaty of Paris and the law of nations.[170] Upon joining of the issues, Mayor Duane issued a unanimous decision in favor of Mrs. Rutgers. The court held that the Trespass Act of 1783 did not contemplate any exception to the act grounded in the law of nations. Nor did the Treaty of Paris include a provision that barred Mrs. Rutgers from recovering damages, the court said.[171] The plaintiff's demurrer was sustained, and the parties later settled out of court.

The Mayor's Court did not hold that the Treaty of Paris barred the Trespass Act, although it specifically provided for amnesty between the warring parties. The opinion left the subject of the effect of treaties on domestic statutes hanging in the air without any analysis of the Articles of Confederation.[172] Article 9, § 1, authorized Congress to make treaties, but that article did not state what force and effect a treaty would have after ratification.[173]

As far as the law of nations was concerned, assuming that the British and the Continentals were engaged in a just war over issues of sovereignty, Hamilton was correct in asserting that property seized by military authority was immune from process while under military control, but he conveniently ignored the international law principle that required the return of property seized by the enemy when the sovereign retook territory occupied by the enemy. By that standard, Mrs. Rutgers would have prevailed.[174] Vattel describes an unjust war as: "The immediate consequence of the premises is, that if a nation takes up arms when she has received no injury, nor is threatened with any, she undertakes an unjust war. Those alone, to whom an injury is done or intended, have a right to make war."[175] Vattel argued that a sovereign should not start a war unless the sovereign had a just cause for war.[176] Vattel elaborated on the right to seize enemy property asserting that in war, enemy property may be seized in order to diminish the enemy's capability to wage war.[177] However, when war ends, the people injured by seizure of their property have a right to restitution of the confiscated property if their sovereign recovers the territory lost to the enemy.[178] That is precisely the position of Mrs. Rutgers upon the Continental army's repossession of New York City in 1783 after the British evacuation. Vattel stated in *The Law of Nations*, vol. 3, ch. 18, § 294, that the general rules of the law of war apply to a civil war. This makes Hamilton's argument plausible, but the doctrine of postliminium undercuts his major premise.

Testing Bills of Attainder against Tories

In 1778, Virginia operated under its 1776 Declaration of Rights that contained a specific guaranty of procedural due process to the accused in Article VIII. The accused was entitled to notice of the charges put against him, to be confronted by the witnesses against him, to have a trial by jury, and to call witnesses on his behalf.[179] The Declaration of Rights did not mention bills of attainder, although the provisions of Article VIII would be in conflict with the process of legislative attaint for treason.

Attaint for treason was part of the judicial punishment imposed on a traitor by a court after conviction. The malefactor who was attained for treason would lose all civil rights, including the right to title to real and personal property. One who was attainted for treason could not convey or will his estate to his family, and his property would be confiscated by the state.[180] Attaint for treason prior to the adoption of the U.S. Constitution in 1789 could also be accomplished by bill of attainder, an ex parte legislative condemnation of an individual.[181]

Josiah Philips, a Tory who lived in southern Princess Anne County, Virginia, was the leader of a gang of Tory outlaws that raided Whig supporters, seizing livestock and valuables and occasionally killing a Whig or two. In 1778, the Virginia General Assembly passed a statute attainting Philips for treason.[182] The statute was drafted by Thomas Jefferson.[183] Josiah Philips and several of his gang were captured before Jefferson's bill of attainder became law. Virginia attorney general Edmund Randolph decided to try Philips and several gang members on robbery charges rather than to proceed to execute Philips according to the terms of the bill of attainder. Philips was convicted and sentenced to death. The Philips case is often cited as an early example of judicial review of state legislation regarding constitutionality. Actually, the attorney general made the decision to indict Philips for robbery rather than order his execution according to the bill of attainder.

Commonworth v. Caton[184]

In 1782, the Virginia Supreme Court sustained the 1776 Treason Act on a challenge that the act violated the 1776 Declaration of Rights. The issue was whether a pardon voted on by the House of Delegates but not ratified by the Virginia Senate was effective. The 1776 act required both houses to concur in granting a legislative pardon.[185] James Lamb, Joshua Hopkins, and John Caton were convicted of treason by the General Court of Virginia. A resolution to pardon the three offenders was passed by the House of Delegates, but the senate refused to consider the pardon resolution.[186] The attorney general then moved to execute the death sentence for the three men. The defendants opposed the motion, invoking the pardon and citing the Virginia Declaration of Rights as authority, arguing that the Treason Act of 1776 was unconstitutional.[187]

The Virginia Constitution provided that the governor had the power to pardon defendants except where the law directed otherwise.[188] Caton's lawyers, led by St. George Tucker, argued that the court should set aside any statute of Virginia that contradicted the 1776 Virginia Constitution.[189]

The court's opinion, crafted by George Wythe, declared that the legislative pardon issued by the House of Delegates was inconsistent with the general power to pardon under the Virginia Constitution. Since the house had not prosecuted Caton and the others, it did not have exclusive power to pardon the offenders.[190]

Wythe asserted that "If the whole legislature . . . should attempt to overleap the bounds, prescribed to them by the people, I, in administering the public justice of the country, will meet the united powers, at my seat in this tribunal; and, pointing to the constitution, will say, to them, here is the limit of your authority; and, hither, shall you go, but no further."[191]

The court did not hold that the pardon was unconstitutional. Judge Wythe's opinion stated in dicta that the court had the right to hold a statute or resolution unconstitutional but chose instead to set aside the pardon resolution because it had not been approved by the council as required by the 1776 constitution. President Justice Pendelton's separate opinion did not contradict that of Judge Wythe. Both opinions cited the pardoning power clause of the 1776 Virginia Constitution and proceeded to construe the pardon resolution as inconsistent with the constitution. By implication, Judge Wythe's dicta is correct: the court could hold that a statute or resolution was invalid because it contradicted the express language of the constitution.

Martin v. Hunter's Lessee

The real challenge to confiscation of Tory estates arose after the adoption of the U.S. Constitution. In 1813 during the midst of the War of 1812 with Great Britain, the U.S. Supreme Court was called to decide the rightful ownership of the thousands of acres originally granted to Thomas Lord Fairfax in 1736.[192] The original Fairfax grant consisted of five million acres, originally granted by King Charles II to seven peers loyal to the Stuart dynasty. By 1719, the tract had been inherited by Thomas, the Sixth Lord Fairfax. Settlers on this immense Royal grant were Virginia colonists who paid annual quitrents to Lord Fairfax's agent for the privilege of owning land in the grant. The original grant description was:

> All that entire tract, territory or parcel of land, situate, &c. and bounded by, and within the heads of the rivers Tappahannock, &c. together with the rivers themselves, and all the islands, &c. and all woods, underwoods, timber, &c. mines of gold and silver, lead, tin, &c. and quarries of stone and coal, &c. to have, hold, and enjoy the said tract of land, &c. to the said [patentees] their heirs and assigns forever, to their only use and behoof, and to no other use, intent or purpose whatsoever.[193]

Lord Fairfax, a confirmed bachelor, took up permanent residence at Greenway Court in modern-day Clarke County, Virginia, in 1742. He hired George Washington in 1748 to act as one of the surveyors who were to establish the boundary line between the Fairfax grant and lands belonging to Virginia Colony. Washington, only sixteen, became one of Lord Fairfax's closest associates, a relationship he maintained until Lord Fairfax, a dedicated Tory, died in 1781. The Fairfax estates were inherited by Robert Fairfax, Lord Thomas's nephew, who died in 1793 in England. Lord Robert Fairfax willed his Northern Neck grant to Rev. Denny Martin, who was the son of Lord Thomas Fairfax's sister. Martin was required to change his surname to "Fairfax" in order to take title to the estate. In 1786, Denny Martin Fairfax went to Virginia to challenge the confiscation of the Northern Neck. He succeeded in recovering an interest in the grant.

In 1777, the Virginia General Assembly passed a sequestration act appointing commissioners for all Virginia counties to take possession of the estates of British subjects, to manage them, and to collect income from the sequestered estates, pay all expenses associated with the upkeep of the estates, and deposit the balance, if any, in the Virginia loan office evidenced by a certificate showing the balance payable to the British subject.[194] The act did not define "British subject," allowing the commissioners to follow their own notion of who was and was not a British subject. Lord Fairfax's Virginia holdings were sequestered by the Commonwealth. In 1779, the Virginia General Assembly passed an act providing for appointments of escheators for all Virginia counties save the Northern Neck. The county escheator was directed to hold an inquest on estates that were sequestered by the act of 1777, with notice to the titular British subject owner, and after the inquest hold the property for twelve months before selling it, allowing anyone with claims against the British subject to file those claims with the office of the general court.[195] After the expiration of twelve months' time, the escheator was free to sell the estate.[196] The liquidation of the estates of British subjects confiscated the remaining Fairfax grant lands.[197] Article 5 of the Treaty of Paris contained a clause recommending to all the states "that the Estates, Rights, and Properties of such last mentioned Persons shall be restored to them."[198] Virginia's general assembly stopped all future confiscation of Tory estates in October 1784.[199] In 1785, the general assembly amended the 1779 escheat act to add "the counties of the Northern Neck" to the list of counties where escheators were to be appointed, making the remaining portion of the sequestered Fairfax grant subject to sale.[200] Lord Fairfax and his agents kept the records of leases, deeds, and quitrents at Greenway Court. A 1785 statute, companion to the escheat act amendment, provided that Lord Fairfax's records be removed to a central office. The same act made all unappropriated lands in the Fairfax grant subject to the general land laws of the Commonwealth, allowing the Commonwealth to grant title to or to lease any land to any willing purchaser. The 1785 act also exonerated Fairfax grant copy holders from all quitrents and compositions.[201]

David Hunter, the lessee of the "waste lands" under the escheat act of 1779, brought an ejectment against Denny Martin Fairfax in district court in Winchester, Virginia. The district court in Winchester gave judgment for the defendant in 1796, and Hunter appealed. His cause was argued in 1796 and reargued in 1810.[202] Denny Martin Fairfax died on April 3, 1800, in England. Denny Martin Fairfax devised his Virginia holdings to Philip Martin, who was a Virginia citizen.[203] Martin was substituted as party defendant. At stake was title to the remaining thousands of ungranted acres and the annual quitrent payments from settled lands. The Virginia Court of Appeals reversed the district court, holding that Denny Martin Fairfax was an alien when title to the Northern Neck allegedly passed to him from Lord Robert Fairfax. He was ineligible to own real estate in Virginia, and Philip Martin was in no better position than his devisor.[204]

Philip Martin brought a writ of error in the U.S. Supreme Court. The Court handed down its opinion in 1813, during the second war with Great Britain. The majority opinion of the court delivered by Justice Joseph Story concluded that Lord Fairfax held fee simple title to the Northern Neck lands prior to his death in 1781.[205] The Court then dealt with the issue of the kind of title, if any, transferred to Denny Martin Fairfax by Lord Fairfax's will. The Court concluded that Lord Fairfax could transfer fee simple title to Denny Martin Fairfax, an alien, by the terms of his will, but not by inheritance.[206] Unless Denny Martin Fairfax somehow lost his right to title of the remaining Northern Neck lands by some other means, he was the owner in fee simple of the Northern Neck lands when the ejectment was first brought.[207] The Court said that Fairfax

"had a complete, though defeasible title, by virtue of the devise, and as the possession was either vacant or not adverse, of course the law united a seizin to his title in the lands in controversy; and this title could only be divested by an inquest of office, perfected by an entry and seizure where the possession was not vacant." As an aside the Court mentioned that there was no distinction to be drawn between an enemy alien and a friendly alien once peace had been restored, although any enemy alien's property could be confiscated during time of war.[208]

Phillip Martin, by implication, had taken title by will, that is, by purchase, from Denny Martin Fairfax. The Court noted that Lord Fairfax's lands were not seized during the war nor was any inquest held relating to Lord Fairfax's or Denny Martin Fairfax's title to the Northern Neck from 1775 to 1783.[209] Since Hunter's grant dated from 1789, six years after the end of hostilities, he would lose. Hunter had contended that the Virginia wartime and post-war statutes that subjected the Northern Neck to escheat overrode the common law and vested title in him. The Court considered this claim and rejected it. The 1777 confiscation act applied to lands held by British subjects. Lord Fairfax was a Virginia citizen, and the act did not apply to him. The 1782 act, noting that Lord Fairfax had died and had willed the Northern Neck to an enemy alien, ordered the Northern Neck quitrents to be sequestered.[210] The act did not reach Denny Martin Fairfax's title to the remaining lands that were unsold.[211] The second 1782 act confirmed Northern Neck entries and surveys made after Lord Fairfax's death "until some mode shall be taken up and adopted by the General Assembly concerning the Northern Neck."[212] Hunter asserted that the 1785 act that confirmed the right of the Commonwealth of Virginia to issue land patents to unappropriated Northern Neck lands was a legislative appropriation of the remaining portions of the Fairfax grant to the Commonwealth of Virginia. The Court rejected this contention:

> In acts of sovereignty so highly penal, it is against the ordinary rule to enlarge, by implication and inference, the extent of the language employed. It would be to declare purposes which the legislature have not chosen to avow, and to create vested estates, when the common law would pronounce a contrary sentence, and the guardians of the public interests have not expressed an intention to abrogate that law. If the legislature have proceeded upon the supposition that the lands were already vested in the commonwealth, we do not perceive how it helps the case. If the legislature, upon a mistake of facts, proceed to grant defective titles, we know of no rule of law which requires a Court to declare, in penal cases, that to be actually done which ought previously to have been done. The patent of the original Plaintiff manifestly issued under the succeeding section—and upon a construction, which we give to this section, it issued improvidently and passed no title whatever.[213]

The Court reversed the Virginia Court of Appeals and remanded the case to that court.[214] The Court did not expressly state that the Treaty of Paris overrode any later Virginia statute that attempted to deprive Denny Martin Fairfax or Philip Martin of title to the Northern Neck lands. It disposed of Hunter's claim to title by construing the effect of the Virginia statutes on the title of Denny Martin Fairfax. Justice Johnson's dissenting opinion states that the Treaty of Paris had no impact on the issue of title to Northern Neck lands.[215] Justice Johnson asserted, "Whether an alien devisee is to be considered as a purchaser according to the meaning of that term as applied to an alien, or whether his estate is to be considered as one of those which are cast on him by operation of law, is an alternative, either branch of which may be laid hold of with some confidence."[216] Justice Johnson believed the better rule was that a devise to an alien was void, which would have destroyed Denny Martin Fairfax's title to the Northern Neck.[217]

On remand, the Virginia Court of Appeals declined to follow the Supreme Court's decision and again affirmed its 1810 ruling that Denny Martin Fairfax had no title to the remaining Northern Neck lands.[218] The

Virginia Court of Appeals held that federal and state sovereignty were separate, distinct, and mutually exclusive. That court denied that Article VI of the U.S. Constitution required it to follow and accept a decision of the U.S. Supreme Court.[219]

Philip Martin applied for another writ of error to the U.S. Supreme Court after the court of appeals had ruled against him. The case was argued in 1815, and the Supreme Court issued its decision in 1816. *Martin v. Hunter's Lessee* established several crucial points of constitutional law. First, the Constitution was not an act of the sovereign states; it was an act of the people of the United States.[220] Second, the judicial power of the United States is a declaration of the whole American people, not a concession by the individual states.[221] Third, Article III, § 1, of the Constitution vests the judicial power of the United States in the Supreme Court and any inferior court established by Congress. That power extends to all cases arising under the Constitution or the laws of the United States or under any treaties to which the United States is signatory.[222] The Constitution was not an offshoot of the Articles of Confederation; it was a wholly independent compact among the people of the United States.[223] Fourth, the appellate jurisdiction of the Supreme Court via writ of error reaches cases arising in state courts, and state courts are bound by decisions of the Supreme Court with respect to those cases.[224]

The Court sustained its original 1813 decision, holding that the second writ of error was based on the Virginia Court of Appeals' failure to follow the mandate of the Court.[225] Despite this holding, the Court revisited the basis for its jurisdiction over the Fairfax Grant controversy.

The Court said, "It is apparent, from this summary explanation, that the title thus set up by the plaintiff might be open to other objections; but the title of the defendant was perfect and complete, if it was protected by the treaty of 1783."[226] The Court stated that when a suit questions the construction of a treaty and a state court issues a decision against the construction of the treaty, the Supreme Court, on writ of error, reviews the entire decision.[227] The Court then reversed the Virginia Court of Appeals and affirmed the original 1796 judgment of the District Court of Winchester.[228]

Martin v. Hunter's Lessee did not squarely hold that the Treaty of Paris compelled the security of Philip Martin's title to unsold lands in the Northern Neck. It recognized that Article 6 of the Treaty of Paris applied to the case but did not construe that article.

THE QUASI-WAR WITH FRANCE AND THE ALIEN AND SEDITION ACT

At the same time that *Martin v. Hunter's Lessee* was wending its way through the judicial system of the new United States, U.S. vessels were fired on by vessels of the French Republic. French privateers captured and seized U.S. merchantmen from 1796 onward. The French Republic asserted that the John Jay Treaty of 1794 was a violation of the 1778 treaty of alliance between the United States and France, making the United States a foreign belligerent and ally of Great Britain. Congress rescinded the 1778 treaty on July 7, 1798, and the U.S. Navy commenced retaliatory operations against the French Republic. By 1800, the diminutive U.S. Navy had captured hundreds of French merchant ships and in two frigate-to-/frigate duels had defeated and captured the French frigate *L'Insurgente* and defeated the badly damaged *La Vengeance*, which escaped capture by a very narrow margin.[229]

Congress, expecting a full-scale war with revolutionary France, passed the Alien Acts and the Sedition Act in 1798.[230] The Sedition Act defined two new federal crimes: (1) conspiring to oppose any measure of the U.S. government, to intimidate a U.S. officer from performing his dues, or to procure an insurrection or riot and (2) writing, publishing, or uttering or knowingly assisting someone else to write, publish, or utter a statement that was false or malicious that attacked the U.S. Constitution or one that proposed to resist a statute of the United States or to aid a foreign nation's hostile designs on the United States.[231] Thomas Jefferson's Democratic-Republican Party members viewed the Sedition Act as a Federalist measure directed at Jefferson's opposition. The Democratic-Republican legislatures of Virginia and Kentucky passed resolutions that declared the Alien and Sedition Acts unconstitutional statutes violating the First Amendment to the Constitution. Both states attempted to nullify the act.[232] The act expired in 1800 before any judicial review of the constitutionality of the acts or of nullification.

Twenty-five men were arrested for violating the Sedition Act between 1798 and 1800 during the two-year life of the act.[233] Eleven were prosecuted and ten were convicted. The violators included James T. Callender, who was arrested for writing *The Prospect before Us*, a pamphlet that referred to the Adams administration as "a continual tempest of malignant passions." Vermont Democratic-Republican congressman Matthew Lyon wrote an essay criticizing the Adams administration as characterized by "ridiculous pomp, foolish adulation, and selfish avarice." He was reelected while serving his sentence. Benjamin Franklin Bache, Benjamin Franklin's grandson and editor of the Philadelphia *Aurora*, wrote an editorial criticizing Lt. Gen. George Washington as incompetent and describing President Adams as "the blind, bald, crippled, toothless querulous Adams." Bache died of yellow fever while awaiting trial.[234] None of these federal prosecutions were subjects of writs of error to the U.S. Supreme Court before the acts expired. President Jefferson pardoned all the individuals who were convicted under these acts.[235]

CONCLUSION

The Continental Congress, a Whig semi-governmental body, had no direct authority over the thirteen states that sent delegates to it. Congress set a pattern by passing the Associators resolution in 1774, calling for citizens of the thirteen colonies to sign a pledge not to import British goods and to stop shipments of colonial raw materials to England and its other colonies. Non-Associators, those who believed the Association was an act of rebellion, were subjected to vigilante coercion and reprisal before the first shot was fired at Lexington in April 1775. By the late summer of 1776, the Continental Congress had passed a resolution requiring all male citizens to swear to their loyalty to the new United States. All thirteen states adopted a loyalty oath. Those who failed to take the oath were marked men. Congress then passed a resolution calling on the member states to adopt statutes defining treason, broad enough to snare Tories who had joined the Royal Army or Navy, Tories who supplied goods to the Royal Army or Navy, and anyone who was aware that a Tory had become a traitor and did not denounce that Tory. Tories attainted for treason would suffer the death penalty, and their estates would be attainted and the states could seize these estates and sell them.

Congress recommended that the states pass laws to confiscate the estates of disloyal people, including those who were not guilty of overt treason. Each state followed suit—some states calling for judicially supervised confiscation proceedings before a judge, others setting up commissioners to deal with confiscations administratively, and in at least one instance confiscating an alleged traitor's land by legislative fiat. Some states passed deportation acts, ejecting Tories from the state forever. By war's end, more than eighty thousand Tories had either fled or been exiled for siding with the king. Although some Tories did not leave the United States and some of the eighty thousand fugitives returned, the vast majority of Tories never returned and lost their estates to escheators and state forfeiture commissioners.

All this occurred years before the adoption of the U.S. Constitution. Only a handful of the thirteen states had one form or another of a bill of rights in their constitutions, and the Articles of Confederation were silent on the issue of deprivation of property rights. One can draw the conclusion that the 1787 Constitution that failed to include any bill of rights left to the states the authority to brand people as traitors, seize their estates, and liquidate those estates. The adoption of the 1791 Bill of Rights imported language in the Fifth Amendment taken from Virginia's and Massachusetts' state bills or declarations of rights. Prior to ratification of the Constitution in 1787–1788, there were no federal checks on state action to arraign Tories for treason, seize their estates, and eject them from the state. The Fifth Amendment limited federal power over the property of alleged offenders; it did not limit state power to seize Tory estates. More than twenty years after 1789, the U.S. Supreme Court concluded that treaties entered into by the United States were part of the law of the land.

The power to limit Tory dissent during the Revolution was jointly held by the legislatures of the thirteen states and by the presidents or governors of those states. That power was tested in court only once in North Carolina, the only state to hold that ex parte confiscations of Tory estates was a denial of due process of law guaranteed by the state's bill of rights. The effect of clauses 5 and 6 of the Treaty of Paris on confiscations was never really reviewed by the courts. Post-1789, *Martin v. Hunter's Lessee* invalidated the sequestration, confiscation, and sale of Lord Fairfax's grant in Virginia's Northern Neck. The original 1813 decision of the U.S. Supreme Court was based on a construction of the rights of aliens to transfer property by will; the 1816 decision declared that the decisions of the U.S. Supreme Court respecting the law of the case were mandatory directions to inferior state courts to act in accordance with the Court's Article III, § 1, grant of judicial power. No court really addressed the systematic suppression of the Tory party during the Revolution.

The U.S. Constitution was adopted without specific reference to the Articles of Confederation. Article I of the U.S. Constitution appropriated the right to wage war, formerly granted to the Continental Congress by the Articles of Confederation. Part of this power remained legislative and was capable of exercise by vote of Congress.[236] The states could no longer brand anyone a traitor nor punish anyone for treason or trading with the enemy. Part of this power was delegated to the president under Article II, § 2, where the president was made commander in chief of the armed forces of the United States.[237]

The 1787 Constitution did not define or explain how the president and Congress were to deal with dissenters in time of war. The example of the treatment of Tories during the Revolution would support an implied joint congressional/executive power to take measures to suppress dissent in time of war without regard to the limitations of the First Amendment on government action to suppress free speech and free assembly; the Fourth Amendment prohibition of unreasonable searches and seizures; the Fifth Amendment guaranty that citizens were free from loss of life, liberty, or property except by due process of law; and the Sixth Amendment list of rights available to the accused in criminal proceedings. Judicial review of any of the convictions under the Sedition Act of 1798 could have been the litmus for the implied power to suppress dissent. In the absence of judicial review, the extraordinary implied power to suppress dissent would haunt the halls of Congress and the White House in later decades.

NOTES

1. This is the viewpoint taken by Broaddus Mitchell in *The Price of Independence* (London: Oxford University Press, 1974) and by Thomas B. Allen in *Tories: Fighting for the King in America's First Civil War* (New York: HarperCollins, 2010). See also Emerich de Vattel, *The Law of Nations or Principles of Natural Law in Four Books*, vol. 3, trans. Joseph Chitty (London: 1833; orig. publ. 1758), 414.

2. Delaware did not become an independent entity until 1775; although Kent, New Castle, and Sussex counties, the three counties comprising modern Delaware, had their own legislature, the three lower counties were part of Pennsylvania Province and were governed by the Penn proprietors.

3. The series of acts of Parliament that asserted Parliament's right to impose direct or indirect taxes on the twelve colonies without the consent of the colonial legislators were the Stamp Tax Act of 1765, 5 Geo. III ch. 12; the Quartering Act of 1765, 5 Geo. II ch. 33 (commonly known as the Mutiny Act); the American Colonies Act of 1766, 6 Geo. III ch. 12 (commonly known as the Declaratory Act); the Townshend Acts; the Revenue Act of 1767, 7 Geo. III ch. 46; the Indemnity Act of 1767, 7 Geo. III ch. 56; the Commissioner of Customs Act of 1767, 7 Geo. III ch. 41; the Vice Admiralty Court Act of 1767, 7 Geo. III ch. 22; and the Act of 1774, 14 Geo. III ch. 19. Closing the port of Boston should be added to this list because it triggered the calling of the Continental Congress of 1774 and ultimately led to the engagements at Lexington and Concord, Massachusetts, in April 1775.

4. See Quartering Act of 1765. For a description of the resistance to the Quartering Act in New York and other colonies, see John C. Miller, *Origins of the American Revolution* (Palo Alto, CA: Stanford University Press, 1943; rev. ed., 1959), 237–241.

5. See Jackson Turner Main, *The Sovereign States, 1775–1783* (New York: New Viewpoints, 1975), 269–273 (composition of Loyalist faction); Mitchell, *The Price of Independence*, 18–21.

6. Miller, *Origins of the American Revolution*, 240.

7. Miller, *Origins of the American Revolution*, 109–164.

8. John Clark Ridpath, *James Otis the Pre-Revolutionist* (Chicago: Literary Association, 1898), last accessed Feb. 1, 2017, Project Gutenberg, http://www.gutenberg.org/cache/epub/722/pg722-images.html.

9. John Dickinson, *Declaration of Rights and Grievances*, 1765, last accessed Feb. 1, 2017, http://www.constitution.org/bcp/dor_sac.htm. See also *Journal of the First Congress of the American Colonies, in Opposition to the Tyrannical Acts of the British Parliament. Held at New York, October 7, 1765* (New York, 1845), 27–29.

10. Miller, *Origins of the American Revolution*, 138–140. New Hampshire, North Carolina, Nova Scotia, and Virginia did not send delegates to the Stamp Act Congress. The Connecticut, New York, and South Carolina delegates lacked the authority to sign any documents on behalf of their colonies. The Stamp Act Congress approved (with dissenting votes) a petition to Parliament asserting that by charter and the Royal prerogative, the colonies could not be taxed by Parliament where no colony was represented.

11. Miller, *Origins of the American Revolution*, 156–159.

12. American Colonies Act of 1766.

13. Miller, *Origins of the American Revolution*, 235–252. The Townshend Act placed an internal customs duty on paper, paint, glass, lead, and tea imported by colonial merchants from the mother country. The Navigation Acts passed in the late seventeenth century forbade colonists from importing these products from any country other than Great Britain and her overseas colonies.

14. For the Royal account, see *Fair Account of the Unhappy Disturbance at Boston in New England Extracted from the Depositions That Have Been Made by All Parties with an Appendix Containing Some Affidavits and Other Evidences Not Mentioned in the Narrative of It That Has Been Published in Boston* (London: B. White Fleet St., 1770). For the account by the Sons of Liberty, see *Short Narrative of the Horrid Massacre in Boston Perpetrated in the Evening of the Fifth Day of March by Soldiers of the XXIXth Regiment with Which the*

XIVth Regiment Was Quartered There: With Some Observations on the State of Things Prior to the Catastrophe, to Which Is Added an Appendix, Containing the Several Depositions Referred to in the Preceding Narrative; And Also Other Depositions Relative to the Subject of It (Boston: Edes & Gill, 1770).

15. Miller, *Origins of the American Revolution*, 338–348.

16. John Spencer Bassett, *The Regulators of North Carolina* (Washington, DC: Government Printing Office, 1895), 164–205, last accessed Feb. 1, 2017, http://docsouth.unc.edu/nc/bassett95/bassett95.html. See also http://www.nchistoricsites.org/alamance/alamanc.htm.

17. Rachel N. Klein, "Ordering the Back Country: The South Carolina Regulation," *William & Mary Quarterly (Third Series)* 38 (1981): 661–680.

18. Herbert M. Morais, "Artisan Democracy and the American Revolution," *Science & Society* 6, no. 3 (1942): 227–241; Thomas W. Ramsby, "The Sons of Liberty: The Early Inter-Colonial Organization," *International Review of Modern Sociology* 17 (1987): 313–334.

19. Boston Port Act, USHistory.org, last accessed Feb. 1, 2017, http://www.ushistory.org/declaration/related/bpb.htm.

20. Quartering Act, U-S-History.com, last accessed Feb. 1, 2017, http://www.u-s-history.com/pages/h1242.html.

21. The Quebec Act of 1774, 14 Geo. III ch. 83, last accessed Feb. 1, 2017, http://www.usconstitution.net/quebecact.html.

22. Massachusetts Government Act, U-S-History.com, last accessed Feb. 1, 2017, http://www.u-s-history.com/pages/h1244.html.

23. "Thomas Gage," *Encyclopaedia Britannica Online*, last modified Jan. 30, 2015, last accessed Feb. 1, 2017, http://www.britannica.com/EBchecked/topic/223455/Thomas-Gage.

24. Miller, *Origins of the American Revolution*, 379–382; "First Continental Congress," USHistory.org, last accessed Jan. 30, 2017, http://www.ushistory.org/declaration/related/congress.html.

25. Worthington Chauncy Ford, ed., *Journal of the Continental Congress 1774–1789 Edited from the Original Records in the Library of Congress by Worthington Chauncy Ford Chief, Division of Manuscripts*, vol. 1 (Washington, DC: Government Printing Office, 1904), 25–26.

26. Ford, *Journal of the Continental Congress*, vol. 1, 28n1, 41. Congress accepted the final report on Sept. 23, 1774.

27. Library of Congress, *Continental Association*, Oct. 20, 1774 (unpaginated), last accessed Jan. 30, 2017, http://www.loc.gov/teachers/classroommaterials/presentationsandactivities/presentations/timeline/amrev/rebelln/assoc.html(hereafter "*Continental Association*").

28. *Continental Association*.

29. *Continental Association*.

30. *Continental Association*.

31. Allen, *Tories: Fighting for the King*, 24–25, describing the refusal of tradespeople in Massachusetts to deal with Non-Associators; *Continental Association*.

32. Christopher Gould, "The South Carolina and Continental Associations: Prelude to Revolution," *South Carolina Historical Magazine* 87 (1986): 36.

33. "Lexington and Concord," USHistory.org, last accessed Jan. 30, 2017, http://www.ushistory.org/us/11c.asp.

34. Virginia is a good example of the interlocking membership of the colonial legislature and the colony's committee of correspondence. See I. Miller, "The Second Virginia Committee of Correspondence," *William & Mary Quarterly (Second Series)* 22 (1913): 99.

35. "Historical Sketch of Battles of Lexington and Concord," last accessed June 12, 2014, http://www.yale.edu/ynhti/curriculum/units/1980/cthistory/80.ch.02.x.html. See also "Lexington and Concord," USHistory.org, last accessed July 3, 2017, www.ushistory.org/us/11c.asp.

36. For the governmental structure of the thirteen colonies, see "New Hampshire," *Son of the South,* last accessed Jan. 30, 2017, http://www.sonofthesouth.net/revolutionary-war/colonies/new-hampshire.htm. See also Henry Cabot Lodge, *Short History of the English Colonies in America* (New York: Harper, 1881), chs. 1–2 (Virginia), chs. 3–4 (Maryland), chs. 5–6 (North Carolina), chs. 9–10 (Georgia), ch. 11 (Delaware), ch. 15 (Massachusetts), ch. 19 (Connecticut), ch. 21 (New Hampshire), ch. 22 (Rhode Island). See also John Doyle, *English Colonies in America: The Middle Colonies,* vols. 2 and 3 (New York: Henry Holt, 1907), vol. 2, chs. 1–6 (New York); vol. 2, chs. 7–8 (New Jersey); vol. 2., ch. 9 (Virginia); vol. 2, chs. 7–9 (Pennsylvania); vol. 2, chs. 12–13; vol. 2, ch. 22; vol. 3, chs. 10–11 (Maryland); vol. 3, chs. 12–13 (North Carolina).

37. See, e.g., Maryland: Convention Proceedings, July 26, 1776 ("Resolution: Resolved unanimously that the following association be signed by the members of the Convention and by all other the freemen of this province") (Maryland State Archives, SC M 3145, 53); Massachusetts: Acts 1775, ch. 5, An Act Prescribing the Form of an Oath to Be Taken by All Commission Officers Both Civil and Military, Who Have Been Commissionated for This Colony, since the Nineteenth Day of July Last, or May Be Hereafter Commissionated, until the Further Order of the Great and General Court; New Hampshire: Acts 1777, Nov. 8, 1777, An Act to Oblige the Members of the COUNCIL and House of Representatives, All Officers, Civil and Military, Barristers and Attorneys at Law to Take and Subscribe an Oath of Fidelity to the State; New Jersey: Acts 1776, ch. 2, Sept. 19, 1776, An Act for the Security of the Government of New Jersey; South Carolina: Acts 1776, Apr. 6, 1776, An Ordinance for Establishing an Oath of Office to Be Taken in Manner Therein Mentioned; Virginia: Acts 1776, ch. 3, An Ordinance Prescribing the Oath of Office to Be Taken by the Governor and Privy Counsel, and Other Officers of the Commonwealth of Virginia.

38. "Continental Congress," *Encyclopaedia Britannica Online,* last accessed Jan. 30, 2017, http://www.britannica.com/topic/Continental-Congress.

39. Ford, *Journal of the Continental Congress,* vol. 2 (June 15, 1775), 91.

40. See "Articles of Association in Pennsylvania," *Mother Bedford,* last accessed Jan. 30, 2017, http://www.motherbedford.com/Articles3.htm. Non-Associators (including Quakers, Mennonites, and Dunkards) were heavily taxed by the Pennsylvania General Assembly in 1775 after the proprietary government abdicated its authority over the colony ("Resolutions Directing the Mode of Levying Taxes on Non-Associators," *Mother Bedford,* http://www.motherbedford.com/Articles4.htm). See Christopher Gould, "South Carolina and Continental Associations: Prelude to Revolution," *South Carolina Historical Magazine* 87 (1986): 30–48.

41. Main, *The Sovereign States,* 272–273, 285–287, 431 (loyalist farmers in New York).

42. Main, *The Sovereign States,* 431. See Harold B. Hancock, *The Loyalists of Revolutionary Delaware* (Newark: University of Delaware Press, 1977), 1–11.

43. Robert McC. Calhoon, *The Loyalists in Revolutionary America, 1760–1781* (New York: Harcourt Brace Jovanovich, 1973), 382–393 (Pennsylvania); Main, *The Sovereign States,* 431.

44. Main, *The Sovereign States,* 308–310.

45. Robert S. Lambert, *South Carolina Loyalists in the American Revolution* (Columbia: University of South Carolina Press, 1987), 33–41, 47–48.

46. Lambert, *South Carolina Loyalists in the American Revolution,* 199–212 (describing the "civil war" in the Up Country); Main, *The Sovereign States,* 306–308.

47. Maryland was a proprietary colony, a personal fiefdom of the Calvert family. Main, *The Sovereign States,* 295–296.

48. Calhoon, *The Loyalists in Revolutionary America,* 442–447; Main, *The Sovereign States,* 272–273; Lloyd Johnson, "Highland Scots," North Carolina History Project, last accessed June 22, 2017, http://northcarolinahistory.org/commentary/110/entry.

49. "The Loyalists," U-S-History.com, last accessed Aug. 8, 2012, http://www.u-s-history.com/pages/h568.html.

50. See Claude H. Van Tyne, *The Loyalists in the American Revolution* (New York: Macmillan, 1902; repr., 1959), 28, 30, 111.

51. Virginia's 1775 declaration of rights and Massachusetts declaration of rights are the best-known antecedents of the federal Bill of Rights. A majority of the thirteen states did not adopt any version of a bill of rights and had no "due process" clauses in their constitutions. Rhode Island, for example, continued under its colonial charter until Dorr's Rebellion in 1842.

52. Thomas B. Allen, "Tories: Fighting for the King," last accessed Jan. 30, 2017, http://www.toriesfightingfortheking.com/ToryArmy.htm. This page was prepared by Thomas Allen, author of the book by the same title, and by Roger McBride Allen. According to the On-Line Institute for Advanced Loyalist Studies (last accessed Jan. 30, 2017, http://www.royalprovincial.com/military/milit.htm, hereafter "Advanced Loyalist Studies"), more than fifty thousand Loyalist men served in the British army or navy during the Revolutionary War.

53. See Advanced Loyalist Studies; see also Calhoon, *The Loyalists in Revolutionary America*, 502.

54. Advanced Loyalist Studies.

55. Advanced Loyalist Studies.

56. Advanced Loyalist Studies.

57. Advanced Loyalist Studies.

58. Advanced Loyalist Studies.

59. Advanced Loyalist Studies.

60. For an account of the Wyoming Valley massacre and other engagements in New York and Pennsylvania, see Allen, *Tories: Fighting for the King*, 209–229, 252–275.

61. Allen, *Tories: Fighting for the King*, 184–208. In addition to Provincial regiments and Associators, the "Neutral Ground" was patrolled by "cow-boys," irregular Loyalist guerilla bands who preyed on Whig farmers and merchants and assassinated Continental soldiers on foraging expeditions.

62. Maj. Patrick Ferguson's riflemen was a Tory unit. It was the only British unit at Kings Mountain. See "Battle of King's Mountain," *TheAmericanRevolution.org*, last accessed Mar. 14, 2017, http://www.theamericanrevolution.org/battledetail.aspx?battle=25. See also "Battle of King's Mountain," BritishBattles.com, last accessed Mar. 14, 2017, http://www.britishbattles.com/war-of-the-revolution-1775-to-1783/battle-of-kings-mountain.

63. The principal component of the British army at Cowpens was Lt. Col. Banastre Tarleton's British Legion, a Loyalist force of cavalry and infantry. See "The Battles of Lexington and Concord," TheAmericanRevolution.org, last accessed Jan. 30, 2017, http://www.theamericanrevolution.org/battledetail.aspx?battle'26; "Battle of Cowpens," BritishBattles.com, last accessed Mar. 14, 2017, http://www.britishbattles.com/war-of-the-revolution-1775-to-1783/battle-of-cowpens.

64. Tarleton's Legion and Lord Rawdon's Irish Volunteers fought alongside regular establishment units such as the 23rd Foot (Royal Welch Fusiliers) and the 33rd Foot ("Battle of Camden," BritishBattles.com, last accessed Jan. 30, 2017, http://www.britishbattles.com/war-of-the-revolution-1775-to-1783/battle-of-camden).

65. Tarleton's Legion and Tarleton's Light Dragoons represented the Loyalist units on the field at Guilford Court House. "Battle of Guilford Courthouse," BritishBattles.com, last accessed Jan. 30, 2017, http://www.britishbattles.com/war-of-the-revolution-1775-to-1783/battle-of-guilford-courthouse.

66. Hancock, *The Loyalists of Revolutionary Delaware*, 77–80. See also *Journals of the Continental Congress*.

67. "The Battle of Moores Creek Bridge," National Park Service, last accessed Mar. 14, 2017, https://www.nps.gov/parkhistory/online_books/mocr/adhi_1.htm.

68. Allen, *Tories: Fighting for the King*, 166–167.

69. Allen, *Tories: Fighting for the King*, 175–178; Sir John Simcoe relieved Rogers in 1777 and changed the name of the United to the Queen's American Rangers. Simcoe's rangers saw action during the Saratoga campaign of 1777 and along the New York–Canadian border until war's end. Allen, *Tories: Fighting for the King*, 182.

70. Allen, *Tories: Fighting for the King*, 182.

71. Allen, *Tories: Fighting for the King*, 182.

72. Allen, *Tories: Fighting for the King*, 214–216. Tory units were also recruited by regular British officers. Lt. Col. Banastre Tarleton recruited Loyalists for his American Legion, a command originally put together by another British officer, John Graves Simcoe, who blended the Pennsylvania Light Dragoons, the Bucks County Light Dragoons, and the Caledonia Volunteers into the British Legion. Tarleton took over the command and fought a two-year irregular war against Whig guerillas in South Carolina and North Carolina. Allen, *Tories: Fighting for the King*, 285–287. Captain Patrick Ferguson, the inventor of the practical breech-loading rifle, recruited the American Volunteers, which he led in several engagements, including the disastrous engagement at Kings Mountain, where Ferguson was killed in battle and his command was slaughtered. Allen, *Tories: Fighting for the King*, 282–283, 288–289.

73. Allen, *Tories: Fighting for the King*, 285–287.

74. Allen, *Tories: Fighting for the King*, 282–283, 288–289.

75. *Minutes of the Provincial Congress and the Council of Safety of the State of New Jersey* (Trenton, NJ: Naar, Day & Narr, 1879), 454–456. The text of the resolution reads as follows: "3. Resolved, That, in the opinion of this Congress, the said William Franklin, Esquire, has discovered himself to be an enemy to the liberties of this country; and that measures ought to be immediately taken for securing the person of the said William Franklin, Esquire." *Minutes of the Provincial Congress*, 456; Allen, *Tories: Fighting for the King*, 298–302.

76. Allen, *Tories: Fighting for the King*, 300–301.

77. Allen, *Tories: Fighting for the King*, 307–309.

78. Calhoon, *The Loyalists in Revolutionary America*, 392–394.

79. John E, Ferling, *The Loyalist Mind: Joseph Galloway and the American Revolution* (State College: Pennsylvania State University Press, 1977).

80. George R. Fisher, "Philadelphia Reflections: Philadelphia's Revolutionary Loyalists," last accessed Jan. 30, 2017, http://www.philadelphia-reflections.com/topic/68.htm.

81. Jonathan Boucher, ed., *Reminiscences of an American Loyalist 1738–1789, Being the Autobiography of the Rev'd Jonathan Boucher, Rector of Annapolis in Maryland and afterwards Vicar of Epson, Surrey, England* (New York: Houghton Mifflin; Cambridge and New York: Riverside Press, 1925).

82. Wallace Brown, "The American Farmer during the Revolution," *Agricultural History* 42 (1968): 327, 331.

83. Brown, "The American Farmer during the Revolution," 334–335.

84. M. Christopher New, *Maryland Loyalists in the American Revolution* (Centreville, MD: Tidewater, 1996), 47–49.

85. Claim No. 949 before the Loyalist Claims Commission Taken American Loyalist Claims 1776–1835, AO 12–13, National Archives United Kingdom, Kew Surry, England (hereafter "Loyalist Claims Commission").

86. Loyalist Claims Commission, Claim No. 967.

87. Calhoon, *The Loyalists in Revolutionary America*, 336–337.

88. Calhoon, *The Loyalists in Revolutionary America*, 387–389.

89. See "U.S. Anabaptists during the Revolutionary War," Anabaptists.org, last accessed Mar. 14, 2017, http://www.anabaptists.org/history/anabaptists-during-revolutionary-war.html.

90. Most of the great southern landowners were members of the second Continental Congress. See "Second Continental Congress," John Adams Historical Society, last accessed Mar. 14, 2017, http://www.john-adams-heritage.com/second-continental-congress, and "First Continental Congress," John Adams Historical Society, last accessed Mar. 14, 2017, http://www.john-adams-heritage.com/first-continental-congress.

91. See, e.g., names of authors and various estimates of Whigs.

92. Calhoon, *The Loyalists in Revolutionary America*, 272–274.

93. Calhoon describes the tarring and feathering of Abner Beebe, a Connecticut Tory who complained that the local vigilantes had mistreated his uncle, the parish

clerk of the Established Church in East Haddam. See Calhoon, *The Loyalists in Revolutionary America*, 283. Calhoon also reports on the tarring and feathering of Rev. Samuel Peters, a Connecticut Church of England minister. Calhoon, *The Loyalists in Revolutionary America*, 282.

94. See Benjamin H. Irvin, "Tar and Feathers in Revolutionary America," *American Revolution Essays*, last accessed Mar. 14, 2017, http://revolution.h-net.msu.edu/essays/irvin.feathers.html. See also Stuart Jeffries, "Tarring and Feathering: A Brief History of Brutal Revenge," *The Guardian*, Aug. 29, 2007, last accessed Jan. 30, 2017, http://www.theguardian.com/uk/2007/aug/30/northernireland.humanrights.

95. Allen, *Tories: Fighting for the King*, 27–28, describes the "smoking" of elderly Israel Williams, one of Gage's appointed counselors, until he signed a document renouncing his appointment as counselor.

96. Calhoon, *The Loyalists in Revolutionary America*, 275–276. The Continental Association dated back to 1774 and at first was a simple non-importation agreement relating to British goods.

97. For instances of vigilante action against Non-Associators in New England, see Calhoon, *The Loyalists in Revolutionary America*, 271–280. Main, *The Sovereign States*, 274–276, also describes vigilante retaliation against Non-Associators.

98. The Continental Congress passed a resolution on March 14, 1776, calling upon all the United Colonies to take action against Non-Associators. *Journals of the Continental Congress*, vol. 4, p. 204, Mar. 14, 1776.

99. Acts 1775, ch. 5, provided that any civil or military officer appointed since April 19, 1775, take an oath of office. The office did not specifically state that the oath taker renounced allegiance to King George.

100. Acts 1776, 432, May 1776.

101. Connecticut: Acts 1776, 421, May 1776, An Act in Alteration of an Act Intitled an Act for Prescribing and Establishing Forms of Oath for This Colony; superseded by Acts 1776, 432, An Act for Prescribing an Oath of Fidelity to This State; repealed by Acts 1776, 451, An Act for Repealing an Act for Prescribing an Oath of Fidelity to This State; replaced by Acts 1777, 457, An Act for Prescribing an Oath of Fidelity to This State; amended by Acts 1777, 475.Delaware: Acts 1778, 1, An Act for the Further Security of the Government.

Georgia: Acts 1781, Aug. 20, 1781, Pardon Act [permits former Loyalists to take a loyalty oath to escape conviction for treason].

Maryland: Convention Proceedings, Jul. 26, 1775, "Resolution: Resolved unanimously that the following association be signed by the members of the Convention and by all other the freemen of this province." Maryland State Archives, SC M 3145, 53; Convention Proceedings, Jan. 16, 1776: "Resolution to print 240 copies of the Association. All free men who have not signed the Association by Apr. 11 1776 must surrender all weapons within 5 days after Apr. 11. Any non-associator who wishes to leave province may take personal property. Any estate (real or personal) left behind by a non-associator who leaves the province will be burdened with a lien to support the war effort." Maryland State Archives, SC M 3145, 120–121.

Massachusetts: Acts 1776, ch. 7, An Act for the Execution in the Colony of the Massachusetts Bay, in New England, on Resolve of the American Congress Dated March 14, 1776 [test oath for all male citizens above age sixteen].

New Hampshire: Acts 1778, Mar. 14, 1778, An Act in Addition to an Act Intitled An Act to Oblige the Members of the COUNCIL and House of Representatives, All Officers, Civil and Military, Barristers and Attorneys at Law to Take and Subscribe an Oath of Fidelity to the State Act Passed in the Late General Assembly of this State; the 8th day of November, d. 1777 [applying test oath to all male citizens].

New Jersey: Acts 1776, ch. 2, Sept. 19, 1776, An Act for the Security of the Government of New Jersey [all current and future civil and military officers to take loyalty oath to New Jersey]; Acts 1777, ch. 30, Sept. 24, 1777, An Act for Regulating the Election of the Members of the Legislative Council and Assembly, Sheriffs and Coroners of the State of New Jersey [any voter in election must take loyalty oath in order to vote].

Acts 1777, ch. 50, An Act to Oblige Certain Persons Therein Described to Take the Oaths of Adjuration and Allegiance [lawyers, persons called to serve as grand or petit jurors must take loyalty oath prior to filing writs and processes or engaging in jury service. Every school teacher must take loyalty oath by Dec. 24, 1777].

New York: Acts 1778, ch. 16, Mar. 27, 1778, An Act to Regulate Elections within This State [any resident who is otherwise eligible to vote who has gone over to the enemy, who acknowledges allegiance to Great Britain, who has joined or aided and abetted the armed forces of Great Britain is disqualified from voting]; Acts 1778, ch. 47, June 30, 1778, An Act More Effectually to Prevent the Mischiefs Arising from the Example and Influence of Persons of Equivocal and Suspected Characters in This State.

North Carolina: Acts 1777, ch. 6, An Act to Amend an Act for Declaring What Crimes and Practices against the State Shall Be Treason, and What Shall be Misprison of Treason and Proving Punishment Adequate to Crimes of Both Classes, and for Preventing the Danger Which May Arise from Persons Disaffected to the State [all free males above sixteen must take loyalty oath].

Pennsylvania: Acts 1777, ch. 12, June 13, 1777, An Act, Obliging the Male White Inhabitants of This State to Give Assurances of Allegiance to the Same, and for Other Purposes Therein Mentioned [all white males above age eighteen must take loyalty oath].

Acts 1778, ch. 61, Apr. 7, 1778, An Act for the Further Security of the Government [all white males over eighteen who have not taken the loyalty oath by Jun. 1, 1778, shall be liable to all the disabilities mentioned in the act].

Rhode Island: Acts 1776, June 1776, An Act Empowering the Members of the Upper and Lower Houses of Assembly to Tender to Such of the Inhabitants as Are herein Mentioned, a Declaration or Test for Subscription [all white males over sixteen must subscribe to an oath of allegiance to Rhode Island].

South Carolina: Acts 1776, Apr. 6, 1776, An Ordinance for Establishing an Oath of Office to Be Taken in Manner Therein Mentioned [any person elected or appointed to an office of public trust shall take a Loyalty Oath to South Carolina before assuming office]; Acts 1778, Mar. 28, 1778, An Act to Oblige Every Free Male Inhabitant of This State above a Certain Age, to Give Assurance of Fidelity and Allegiance to the Same; and for Other Purposes Therein Mentioned [any person within this state above the age of sixteen shall take a test oath].

Virginia: Acts 1776, ch. 3, An Ordinance Prescribing the Oath of Office to Be Taken by the Governor and Privy Counsel, and Other Officers of the Commonwealth of Virginia [prescribes loyalty oath for governor and privy council members to take before assuming office]; Hening's Stats., vol. 9, 381, May 28, 1777, An Act to Oblige the Free Male Inhabitants of This State above a Certain Age to Give Assurance of Allegiance to the Same and for Other Purposes [all free white males over sixteen are to appear before justice of peace and take test oath].

102. Those states are Maryland: Acts 1777, ch. 10, Oct. 31, 1777, An Act for the Better Security of the Government; Pennsylvania: Acts 1777, ch. 12, June 13, 1777, An Act, Obliging the Male White Inhabitants of This State to Give Assurances of Allegiance to the Same, and for Other Purposes Therein Mentioned; and Acts 1778, ch. 61, Apr. 7, 1778, An Act for the Further Security of the Government.

103. Those states are Massachusetts: Acts 1776, ch. 7; North Carolina: Acts 1777, ch. 6; Rhode Island: Acts 1776, June 1776; South Carolina: Acts 1778, Mar. 28, 1778; Virginia: Hening's Stats., vol. 9, 381, May 28, 1777.

104. Acts 1777, ch. 12, June 13, 1777.

105. See, e.g., Maryland: Acts 1777, ch. 20, Oct. 31, 1777, An Act for the Better Security of the Government [any free male person above eighteen who refuses to take the oath of fidelity before March 1, 1778, will lose the right to vote and to serve as jurors, and will pay a treble tax].Massachusetts: Acts 1776, ch. 7, An Act for the Execution in the Colony of the Massachusetts Bay, in New England, One Resolve of the American

Congress dated March 14, 1776, Recommending the Disarming Such Persons as Are Notoriously Disaffected to the Cause of America, or Who Refuse to Associate to Defend by Arms the United American Colonies against the Hostile Attempts of the British Fleets and Armies, and for the Restraining and Punishing Persons Who Are Inimical to the Rights and Liberties of the Said United Colonies and for Directing Proceedings Therein [any person over sixteen who fails to take the oath will be disqualified from holding any public office, will surrender his arms and be disqualified as a voter].

New Hampshire: Acts 1781, Nov. 28, 1781, An Act for Preventing the Subjects of His Britannic Majesty and All Other Persons Inimical to the United States of North-America, from prosecuting actions, serving as jurors or acting as town officers within this state [non-jurors are barred from holding public office and may not file a civil suit or serve as a juror].

New Jersey: Acts 1777, ch. 50, An Act to Oblige Certain Persons Therein Described to Take the Oaths of Adjuration and Allegiance [lawyers, persons called to serve as grand or petit jurors must take loyalty oath; failure to take oath bars any person from practice of law or jury service].

New York: Acts 1778, ch. 47, June 30, 1778, An Act More Effectually to Prevent the Mischiefs Arising from the Example and Influence of Persons of Equivocal and Suspected Characters in This State [non-jurors to pay treble tax]; Acts 1778, ch. 16, May 27, 1778, An Act to Regulate Elections within This State [non-jurors lose right to vote if deemed "gone over to the enemy"]; Acts 1779, ch. 12, Oct. 1779, An Act Making It Necessary for the Attornies, Solicitors and Counselors at Law Who Have Been Licensed to Plead or Practice in Any of the Courts of Law or Equity within the Late Colony of New York, to produce certificates of their attachment to the liberties and independence of America [all lawyers admitted before Apr. 21, 1776, have licenses suspended. Lawyers must apply to supreme court of judicature for reinstatement attaching a petition supported by signatures of eight to sixteen persons attesting that the attorney has been a zealous friend of the American cause, who shall respond to a writ of inquiry concerning the attorney's loyalty. Members of general assembly and Congress exempted from this requirement].

North Carolina: Acts 1777, ch. 6, An Act to Amend an Act for Declaring What Crimes and Practices against the State Shall Be Treason, and What Shall Be Misprision of Treason and Proving Punishment Adequate to Crimes of Both Classes, and for preventing the danger which may arise from persons disaffected to the state [every person who fails to take the oath is disabled from voting or holding any office of public trust. Non-jurors also disabled from conveying any land for the next ten years. Non-jurors must turn in all arms to the county court. Any person who fails to take the oath will be banished].

Pennsylvania: Acts 1777, ch. 12, June 13, 1777, An Act, Obliging the Male White Inhabitants of This State to Give Assurances of Allegiance to the Same, and for Other Purposes Therein Mentioned [any person who refuses to take the oath shall be unable to hold any office of public trust or to vote and shall surrender his arms to the county lieutenant or sub-lieutenant]; Acts 1778, ch. 61, Apr. 7, 1778, An Act for the Further Security of the Government [all white males over eighteen who have not taken the loyalty oath by June 1, 1778, shall be liable to all the disabilities mentioned in the Act of June 13, 1777. In addition, no person may practice law, or physic, act as a druggist, or serve as proctor or notary who has not taken the oath].

South Carolina: Acts 1778, Mar. 28, 1778, An Act to Oblige Every Free Male Inhabitant of This State above a Certain Age, to give assurance of fidelity and allegiance to the same; and for other purposes therein mentioned.

Virginia: Hening's Stats., vol. 9, 28, May 28, 1777, An Act to Oblige the Free Male Inhabitants of This State above a Certain Age to Give Assurance of Allegiance to the Same and for Other Purposes.

106. See, e.g., New York: Acts 1780, ch. 59, An Act for Relieving Certain Persons in the County of West Chester against the Penalty Contained in the Resolution of Con-

vention Passed the Twenty-Seventh of December Eighteen [*sic*] Hundred and Seventy Six, requiring the inhabitants of the said county to take the oath of allegiance.

107. See, e.g., Maryland: Acts 1781, ch. 17, An Act Concerning Non-jurors [act imposing disability to sue, practice physick, or carry on trade, repealed. No quaker, dunkard or mennonite will be fined for preaching the gospel].North Carolina: Acts 1779, ch. 10, An Act to Prescribe the Affirmation of Allegiance and Fidelity to This State to Be Taken by the Unitus Fratrem, or Moravians, Quakers, Mennonites and Dunkards, and granting them certain indulgences herein mentioned and other purposes; Acts 1780, ch. 13, An Act for the Relief of the People Called Moravians, Quakers Mennonites and Dunkards within This State.

Virginia: Hening's Stats., vol. 11, 252, ch. 14, An Act to Repeal So Much of Any Act or Acts of the Assembly as Subject the People Called Quakers and Menonists to Penalties or Disabilities for Non-juring.

108. See, e.g., Connecticut: Acts 1776, 421, May 1776, An Act in Alteration of an Act Intitled An Act for Prescribing and Establishing Forms of Oath for This Colony; superseded by Acts 1776, 432, An Act for Prescribing an Oath of Fidelity to This State; repealed by Acts 1776, 451, An Act for Repealing an Act for Prescribing an Oath of Fidelity to This State; replaced by Acts 1777, 457, An Act for Prescribing an Oath of Fidelity to This State Amended by Acts 1777, 475, Acts 1776, ch. 2, Sept. 19, 1776.New Jersey: An Act for the Security of the Government of New Jersey [all current and future civil and military officers to take loyalty oath to New Jersey]; Acts 1777, ch. 30, Sept. 24, 1777, An Act for Regulating the Election of the Members of the Legislative Council and Assembly, Sheriffs and Coroners of the State of New Jersey [any voter in election must take loyalty oath in order to vote]; Acts 1777, ch. 50, An Act to Oblige Certain Persons Therein Described to Take the Oaths of "Adjuration and Allegiance" [lawyers, persons called to serve as grand or petit jurors must take loyalty oath prior to filing writs and processes or engaging in jury service. Every school teacher must take loyalty oath by Dec. 24, 1777].

109. See, e.g., Delaware: Acts 1778, 1, An Act of Free Pardon and Oblivion, and for other purposes therein mentioned [any person who took up arms against the state aided and abetted the enemy may purge treason by taking oath before justice of peace]; New Jersey: Acts 1777, ch. 34, June 5, 1777, An Act of Free and General Pardon, and for other purposes [any disaffected person who has joined the British army or otherwise aided and abetted the enemy may appear before a Supreme Court justice, common pleas court judge, or justice of peace by Aug. 1, 1777, and take the oath of allegiance, purging himself from treason or similar crimes].

110. Connecticut: Acts 1777, 432, An Act for the Punishment of High Treason and Other Atrocious Crimes against the State.Delaware: Acts 1776, ch. 88, An Act to Punish Treason and Dissaffected Persons and for the Security of the Government. Reenacted Acts 1777, ch. 98, An Act to Punish Treason and Disaffected Persons and for Security of the Government.

Georgia: Acts 1778, Mar. 1, 1778, An Act for Attaining Such Persons as Therein Mentioned of High Treason; and for confiscating their estates, both real and personal to the use of this state; for establishing boards of commissioners for the sale of such estates, and for other purposes therein mentioned.

Maryland: Acts 1777, ch. 20, Feb. 5, 1777, An Act to Punish Certain Crimes and Misdemeanors, and to Prevent Toryism.

Massachusetts: Acts 1777, ch. 32, An Act against Treason and Misprision of Treason and for Regulating Trials in Such Cases and for Directing the Mode of Executing Judgments against Persons Attainted of Felony.

New Hampshire: Acts 1777, Jan. 17, 1777, An Act against Treason and Misprision of Treason, and for misprision of treason and regulating trials in such cases, and for directing the mode of treason executing judgments against persons convicted of those crimes.

New Jersey: Acts 1777, ch. 31, June 5, 1777, An Act for Rendering More Effectual Two Certain Acts Therein Mentioned.

North Carolina: Acts 1777, ch. 6, An Act to Amend an Act for Declaring What Crimes and Practices against the State Shall Be Treason, and what shall be misprision of treason and proving punishment adequate to crimes of both classes, and for preventing the danger which may arise from persons disaffected to the state.

Pennsylvania: Acts 1777, ch. 5, Feb. 17, 1777, An Act Declaring What Shall Be Treason, and what other crimes and practices against the state shall be misprision of treason.

Rhode Island: Acts 1775, Oct. 1775, An Act for the Punishment of Persons Who Shall Be Found Guilty of Holding a Traitorous Correspondence with the Ministry of Great Britain or Any of Their Officers or Agents or of Supplying the Ministerial Army or Navy, that now is or may be employed in America against the United Colonies, with provisions, cannon, arms, ammunition, warlike or naval stores or of acting as pilots on board their ships and vessels.

South Carolina: Acts 1776, Apr. 11, 1776, An Act for Preventing Sedition, and Punish Insurgents and Disturbers of the Public Peace.

Virginia: Hening's Stats., vol. 9, Dec. 10, 1775, An Ordinance for Establishing a Mode of Punishment for the Enemies to America in This Colony, supplemented by Hening's Stats., vol. 9, Oct. 18, 1776, An Act Declaring What Shall Be Treason [any man who levy war against the commonwealth, or be adherent to the enemies].

111. Acts 1777, ch. 20, Feb. 5, 1777. Other states confined their treason acts to describing treason and misprision of treason, passing separate acts to punish affirmations that Great Britain still had authority over the states and seditious speech. See, e.g., Massachusetts: Acts 1777, ch. 29, An Act for Preventing or Punishing Crimes That May Be Committed against the Public Safety below the Degree of Treason and Misprision of Treason; New Hampshire: Acts 1777, Jan. 17, 1777, An Act for Preventing and Punishing Such Offenses against the State, as do not amount to treason or misprision of treason; New York: Acts 1781, ch. 48, An Act More Effectually to Punish Adherence to the King of Great Britain within This State; Rhode Island: Acts 1776, July 1776, An Act to Punish Persons Who Shall Acknowledge the King of Great-Britain to Be Their Sovereign; Virginia: 9 Hening's Stats., 170, An Act for the Punishment of Certain Offenses.

112. See, e.g., Connecticut: Acts 1777, 458, An Act to Prevent Traitorous Conspiracies against This and the United States of America [travel pass required for trading goods within enemy lines], modified by Acts 1780, 553, An Act in Further Addition to, and in Alteration of the Act, Entitled An Act More Effectually to Prevent Illicit Trade [shifts burden of proof of lawful importation to the party whose goods have been seized; penalty for violation prison from three months to three years].Delaware: Acts 1778, 151, An Act to Prevent the Inhabitants of this State from Dealing and Furnishing the Enemies Thereof with Supplies, and for other purposes therein mentioned [horses, teams, and goods used in trading with enemy forfeit].

Massachusetts: Acts 1781, ch. 7, An Act in Addition to an Act Intitled An Act for Preventing All Commerce and Illegal Correspondence with the Enemies of the United States of America.

113. See, e.g., Massachusetts: Acts 1777, ch. 48, An Act for Securing This and the Other United States against the Danger to Which They Are Exposed by the Internal Enemies Thereof; Acts 1778, ch. 13, An Act to Prevent the Return to This State of Certain Persons Therein Named, and Others, who have left this state, or either of the United States, and joined the enemies thereof [list of three hundred men who have left Massachusetts and allegedly joined the enemy. If any have returned to Massachusetts, the sheriff, a constable, or other officials are empowered to arrest the returnees and take the returnee before a justice of the peace to be deported from Massachusetts], modified by Acts 1783, ch. 6.New Hampshire: Acts 1778, Nov. 19, 1778, An Act to Prevent the Return to this State, of Certain Persons Therein Named, and of others who have left or shall leave this state, or either of the United States of America, or shall join the enemies thereof.

South Carolina: Acts 1783, Mar. 16, 1783, An Act to Alter and Amend an Act Entitled An Act for Disposing of Certain Estates and Banishing Certain Persons Therein "mentioned."

114. Acts 1782, Aug. 5. 1782, *Colonial Records of Georgia*, vol. 19, 162, An Act for Preventing Improper or Disaffected Persons Emigrating from Other Places, and Becoming Citizens of This State, and for Other Purses Therein Mentioned.

115. Main, *The Sovereign States*, 280.

116. See, e.g., Connecticut: Acts 1778, 495, An Act for Confiscating the Estates of Persons Inimical to the Independence and Liberties of the United States, within This State, and for Payment of Their Debts, and Directing Proceedings Therein.

Delaware: Acts 1778, 1, An Act of Free Pardon and Oblivion, and for Other Purposes Therein Mentioned.

Georgia: Act of Mar. 1, 1778, High Treason; and for Confiscating Their Estates, both real and personal to the use of this state; for establishing boards of commissioners for the sale of such estates, and for other purposes therein mentioned [*Revolutionary Records of Georgia*, vol. 1, 326], modified by Acts 1778, Nov. 25, 1778, An Act to Compel Non-residents to Return within a Certain Time or in Default Thereof, that their estates be confiscated and for confiscating the estate of William Knox, formerly provost marshal of the then province now state of Georgia, *Colonial Records of Georgia*, vol. 19, 126 [non-residents living in Great Britain must return to Georgia within one year of date or lands will be confiscated]; Acts 1782, May 4, 1782, An Act for Inflicting Penalties on, and Confiscating the Estate of Such Persons as Are Therein Declared Guilty of Treason, and for Other Purposes Therein Mentioned [more than two hundred men listed by name are banished from Georgia due to collaborating with the British Crown. Must leave within sixty days or be imprisoned without bail. Real and personal property to be confiscated. Act also applies to persons not named discovered to be collaborators]. Acts 1778, Oct. 30, 1778, An Act to Alter and Amend a Clause or Clauses of an Act Entitled An Act for Attaining Such Persons as Therein Mentioned of High Treason; and for confiscating their estates, both real and personal to the use of this state; for establishing boards of commissioners for the sale of such estates, and for other purposes therein mentioned, and for the better and more effectual carrying the other purposes of the said act into execution [*Colonial Records of Georgia*, vol. 19, 100—changes requirement for purchasers to 25 percent of purchase price down payment at sale].

Maryland: Maryland initiated confiscation of Tory lands before it became a state. See Convention Proceedings, Dec. 8, 1775, Confiscation of Estate of William Bartlett Townsend for Carrying Persons to Lord Dunmore; *Convention Proceedings*, Dec. 17, 1775, Report from Samuel Sharp Custodian of the Estate of Isaac Atkinson, Who Has Fled from the State. Resolved that William Hayward take custody of Atkinson's estate, take an inventory and await further proceedings of this state. (Maryland State Archives, SC M 3145, 276.) Maryland's general confiscation act dated from 1780. Acts 1780, ch. 45, An Act to Seize, Confiscate and Appropriate, All British Property within This State [all property except debts belonging to British subjects within the state will be seized, including those of Maryland residents who fled the state after Apr. 30, 1775. Former Gov. Sharp is excepted from this act].

Massachusetts: Acts 1777, ch. 38, An Act to Prevent the Waste, Destruction and Embezzlement of the Goods or Estates of Such Persons Who Have Left the Same and Fled to Our Enemies for Protection; and also for the payment of their just debts out of their estates; Acts 1778, ch. 11, An Act in Addition to an Act Entitled An Act to Prevent the Waste, Destruction and Embezzlement of the Goods or Estates of Such Persons Who Have Left the Same and Fled to Our Enemies for Protection; and also for payment of their just debts out of their estates [supplements Acts 1777, ch. 37, Agents to manage confiscated estates to be appointed for every county. Probate judge to appoint three commissioners to review claims of creditors]; Acts 1779, ch. 10, An Act for Confiscating the Estates of Certain Persons Commonly Called Absentees [real and personal property of any Massachusetts resident who has left the state after April 19,

1775, who has levied war against the state or given aid and comfort to the enemy held to have renounced allegiance to the United States. All real and personal property within Massachusetts is to be confiscated. Property to be administered by probate court judge]. Acts 1779, ch. 12, An Act in Further Addition to an Act Entitled An Act to Prevent the Waste, Destruction and Embezzlement of the Goods or Estates of Such Persons Who Have Left the Same and Fled to Our Enemies for Protection; and also for payment of their just debts out of their estates [if administrator of estate of anyone who has fled the state flees the state, probate judge is to order estate administered as if administrator was dead].

New Hampshire: Acts 1777, Nov. 29, 1777, An Act to Prevent the Transfer or Conveyance of the Estates and Property of All Such Persons Who Have Been or Shall Be Apprehended upon Suspicion of Being Guilty of Treason, Misprision of Treason or Other Inimical Practices Respecting This State, the United States, Any or Either of Them, and Also for Securing All Lands within This State, as well of such persons as have traitorously deserted, or may hereafter desert the common cause of America, and have gone over to or in any way or manner joined our enemies, as of those who belong to, or reside in Great Britain [attempted transfer of land or personal property by any person taken into custody on suspicion of treason, or misprision of treason or who have joined the enemy are declared void. The land and personal property of any person who made the transfer set aside will be confiscated. An inventory of real and personal property to be made within two months after seizure. Select men to seize the lands of persons who are in custody for the use of the state].

New Jersey: Acts 1778, ch. 27, Apr. 18, 1778, An Act for Taking Charge of and Leasing the Real Estate, and for forfeiting the personal estates of certain fugitives and offenders, and for enlarging and continuing the powers of commissioners appointed to seize and dispose of such personal estates, and for ascertaining and discharging the lawful debts and claims thereon; Acts 1778, ch. 14, Dec. 10, 1778, An Act for Forfeiting and Selling, in the State of New Jersey, the Real Estates of Certain Fugitives and Offenders and for Directing the Mode of Determining and Satisfying the Lawful Debts and Demands Which May Be Due from, or Made against, Such Fugitives and Offenders, and for other purposes therein mentioned [act also applies to land owned by persons who are not New Jersey citizens or residents lying in New Jersey who commit the same offenses].

New York: No statute.

North Carolina: Acts 1777, ch. 17, An Act for Confiscating the Property of All Such Persons as Are Inimical to the United States, and of such persons as shall not, within a certain time therein mentioned, appear and submit to the State whether they shall be received as citizens thereof, and of such persons as fail to appear and shall not be admitted as citizens, and for other purposes therein mentioned; Acts 1779, ch. 2, An Act to Carry into Effect an Act Passed at Newbern in November in the Year One Thousand Seven Hundred and Seventy Seven Intitled An Act for Confiscating the Property of All Such Persons as Are Inimical to the United States, and of such persons as shall not, within a certain time therein mentioned, appear and submit to the state whether they shall be received as citizens thereof, and of such persons as fail to appear and shall not be admitted as citizens, and for other purposes therein mentioned.

Pennsylvania: Acts 1777, ch. 5, Feb. 17, 1777, An Act Declaring What Shall Be Treason, and what other crimes and practices against the state shall be misprision of treason; Acts 1778, ch. 49, An Act for the Attainder of Diverse Traitors, if they render not themselves by a certain day and for vesting their estates in this common-wealth; and for more effectually discovering the same; and for ascertaining and satisfying the lawful debts and claims thereupon; Acts 1778, ch. 97, Mar. 29, 1779, Supplement to an Act Intitled An Act for the Attainder of Diverse Traitors, if they render not themselves by a certain day and for vesting their estates in this common-wealth; and for more effectually discovering the same; and for ascertaining and satisfying the lawful debts and claims thereupon.

Rhode Island: Acts 1775, Oct. 1775, An Act for the Punishment of Persons Who Shall Be Found Guilty of Holding a Traitorous Correspondence with the Ministry of Great Britain or Any of Their Officers or Agents or of Supplying the Ministerial Army or Navy, that now is or may be employed in America against the United Colonies, with provisions, cannon, arms, ammunition, warlike or naval stores or of acting as pilots on board their ships and vessels; Acts 1779, Oct. 1779, An Act for the Confiscation of the Estates of Certain Persons Therein Described.

South Carolina: Acts 1776, Apr. 11, 1776, An Act for Preventing Sedition, and Punish Insurgents and Disturbers of the Public Peace; Acts 1782, ch. 13, Feb. 26, 1782, An Act for Disposing of Certain Estates and Banishing Certain Persons Therein Mentioned.

Virginia: Hening's Stats., vol. 9, 377, Oct. 1777, An Act for Sequestering British Property Enabling Those Indebted to British Subjects to Pay off Such Debts, and directing proceedings in suits where such subjects are parties; Acts 1779, ch.23, An Act to Secure the Movable Property of Those Who Have Joined, or Hereafter May Join the Enemy.

117. See, e.g., Massachusetts: Acts 1778, ch. 11 (agents to manage confiscated estates to be appointed in every county).New Hampshire: Acts 1779, June 26, 1779 (probate judge appoint trustee to manage confiscated estate).

New Jersey: Acts 1778, ch. 14, Dec. 10, 1778 (commissioners to take possession of forfeited estates).

New York: No express provisions.

North Carolina: Acts 1779, ch. 2 (commissioners to take possession of forfeited estates).

Pennsylvania: No statutory mandate for commissioners or trustees.

Rhode Island: Acts 1779, Oct. 1779 (attorney general files condemnation suit, real and personal property to be held by state).

South Carolina: Acts 1782, ch. 13, Feb. 26, 1782 (commissioners appointed by senate and house will manage confiscated property and sell same at public auction).

Virginia: Hening's Stats., vol. 9, 377, Oct. 1777 (commissioners appointed by governor will manage confiscated estates).

118. Connecticut: Acts 1778, 495, An Act for Confiscating the Estates of Persons Inimical to the Independence and Liberties of the United States, within this state, and for payment of their debts, and directing proceedings therein [act enforced by selectmen of the town].Massachusetts: Acts 1777, ch. 48, An Act to Prevent the Waste, Destruction and Embezzlement of the Goods or Estates of Such Persons Who Have Left the Same and Fled to Our Enemies for Protection; and also for the payment of their just debts out of their estates.

New Hampshire: Acts 1777, Nov. 29, 1777, An Act to Prevent the Transfer or Conveyance of the Estates and Property of All Such Persons Who Have Been or Shall Be Apprehended upon Suspicion of Being Guilty of Treason, misprision of treason or other inimical practices respecting this state, the United States, any or either of them, and also securing all lands within this state, as well of such persons as have traitorously deserted, or may hereafter desert the common cause of America, and have gone over to or in any way or manner joined our enemies, as of those who belong to, or reside in Great Britain.

Rhode Island put the duty of ferreting out the estates of disloyal persons and absentees on its attorney general. Acts 1779, Oct. 1779.

119. See, e.g., Georgia: Acts 1782, Aug. 5, 1782, An Act for Empowering a Less Number of Commissioners to Be a Board That Is Mentioned in the Act Passed at Augusta on the Fourth Day of May One Thousand Seven Hundred and Eighty-Two, for inflicting penalties on and confiscating the estates of such persons as have been guilty of treason against this state and for other purposes therein mentioned.New Jersey: Acts 1778, ch. 27, Apr. 18, 1778, An Act for Taking Charge of and Leasing the Real Estate, and for Forfeiting the Personal Estates of Certain Fugitives and Offenders, and for enlarging and continuing the powers of commissioners appointed to seize and dispose of such personal estates, and for ascertaining and discharging the lawful debts and

claims thereon [commissioners are to make return of property confiscated to a justice of peace in their counties. Justice to direct constable to execute a writ].

North Carolina: Acts 1779, ch. 2, An Act to Carry into Effect an Act Passed at Newbern in November in the Year One Thousand Seven Hundred and Seventy Seven Intitled An Act for Confiscating the Property of All Such Persons as Are Inimical to the United States, and of such persons as shall not, within a certain time therein mentioned, appear and submit to the state whether they shall be received as citizens thereof, and of such persons as fail to appear and shall not be admitted as citizens, and for other purposes therein mentioned [commissioners appointed to seize lands to be confiscated].

South Carolina: Acts 1782, ch. 13, Feb. 26, 1782, An Act for Disposing of Certain Estates and Banishing Certain Persons Therein Mentioned.

Virginia: Hening's Stats., vol. 9, 377, Oct. 1777, An Act for Sequestering British Property Enabling Those Indebted to British Subjects to Pay Off Such Debts, and directing proceedings in suits where such subjects are parties.

120. See, e.g., Delaware: Acts 1778, 151, An Act to Prevent the Inhabitants of This State from Dealing and Furnishing the Enemies Thereof with Supplies, and for Other Purposes Therein Mentioned.New Jersey: Acts 1780, ch. 5, Dec. 21, 1780, An Act More Effectually to Prevent the Inhabitants of This State from Trading with the Enemy, or going within their lines, and for other purposes therein mentioned.

121. See, e.g., Connecticut: Acts 1778, 495, An Act for Confiscating the Estates of Persons Inimical to the Independence and Liberties of the United States, within This State, and for Payment of Their Debts, and Directing Proceedings Therein.

122. Connecticut: Acts 1778, 495 [select men to report on lands subject to confiscation to justice of peace for bench trial condemnation hearing].Massachusetts: Acts 1777, ch. 38 [select men or committee of correspondence to report absent persons to the judge of probate court for confiscation of same].

New Hampshire: Acts 1777, Nov. 29, 1777 [select men to seize estates of persons who have been guilty of various offenses].

123. See, e.g., Massachusetts: Acts 1780, ch. 2; New Hampshire: Acts 1781, Mar. 25, 1781; New Jersey: Acts 1778, ch. 27, Apr. 18, 1778.

124. See, e.g., Massachusetts: Acts 1777, ch. 32, An Act against Treason and Misprision of Treason and for Regulating Trials in Such Cases and for Directing the Mode of Executing Judgments against Persons Attainted of Felony [alleged offenders to be tried in superior court before jury]; Acts 1779, ch. 3 [persons who are charged with treason to be tried before superior court].New Hampshire: Acts 1777, Jan. 17, 1777, An Act against Treason and Misprision of Treason, and for Regulating Trials in Such Cases, and for directing the mode of treason executing judgments against persons convicted of those crimes.

125. These states had confiscation acts directing commissioners appointed by the state to take possession of Tory real and personal property. There was no requirement that the commissioners prove their case before an independent judicial officer.

126. See, e.g., Delaware: Acts 1778, 161, An Act of Free Pardon and Obligation, and for Other Purposes. Individuals therein mentioned; Acts 1778, 1, An Act of Free Pardon and Oblivion, and for Other Purposes Therein Mentioned; Georgia: Acts 1781, Aug. 20, 1781, *Colonial Records of Georgia*, vol. 19, 142, An Act Declaring Certain Persons, Who Are Therein Described Citizens of This State, and for Burying in Oblivion Certain High Crimes and Misdemeanors; South Carolina: Acts 1782, ch. 14, Feb. 26, 1782, An Act for Pardoning the Persons Therein Described on the Conditions Therein Mentioned. The New England states, Connecticut, Massachusetts, New Hampshire, and Rhode Island, had no general pardon acts before the end of hostilities. New Jersey passed a general pardon act in 1777 relating to non-jurors and not to known Loyalists. See Acts 1777, ch. 34, June 5, 1777, An Act of Free and General Pardon, and for Other Purposes. North Carolina passed a post-war pardon act that did not restore confiscated property to pardoned Loyalists. See Acts 1783, ch. 6, An Act of Pardon and Oblivion. South Carolina also passed a postwar pardon act restoring the unsold portion of

former Loyalist estates to their owners, provided the owners returned to South Carolina. Acts 1784, Mar. 26, 1784, An Act for Restoring to Certain Persons Therein Mentioned Their Estates, Both Real and Personal, and for Permitting the Said Persons to Return to This State and for Other Purposes Therein Mentioned.

127. See, e.g., North Carolina: Acts 1781, ch. 4, An Act Directing the Sale of Confiscated Property [real and personal property of enumerated persons that are forfeit to the state will be sold at public auction].New York: Acts 1780, ch. 51, An Act for the Immediate Sale of Part of the Forfeited Estates [1779 act suspending forfeitures and sales is repealed. Commissioners of forfeiture shall offer real and personal property for sale at auction].

Pennsylvania: Acts 1778, ch. 97, Mar. 2, 1779, A Supplement to an Act Intitled An Act for the Attainder of Diverse Traitors, if They Render Not Themselves by a Certain Day and for Vesting Their Estates in This Common-Wealth; and for more effectually discovering the same; and for ascertaining and satisfying the lawful debts and claims thereupon.

South Carolina: Acts 1782, ch. 13, Feb. 26, 1782, An Act for Disposing of Certain Estates and Banishing Certain Persons Therein Mentioned.

Maryland was the last of the thirteen states to authorize sale of confiscated lands. See Acts 1782, ch. 59; Acts 1782, ch. 60.

128. See, e.g., Georgia: Acts 1778, Mar. 1, 1778, Oct. 30, 1778.Massachusetts: Acts 1777, ch. 38, An Act to Prevent the Waste, Destruction and Embezzlement of the Goods or Estates of Such Persons Who Have Left the Same and Fled to Our Enemies for Protection; and also for the payment of their just debts out of their estates.

New Jersey: Acts 1778, ch. 14, Dec. 10, 1778, An Act for Forfeiting and Selling, in the State of New Jersey, the Real Estates of Certain Fugitives and Offenders and for Directing the Mode of Determining and Satisfying the Lawful Debts and Demands Which May Be Due from, or Made against, Such Fugitives and Offenders, and for other purposes therein mentioned.

129. See, e.g., Georgia: Acts 1778, Nov. 25, 1778, *Colonial Records of Georgia*, vol. 19, 126. An act to compel non-residents to return within a certain time or in default thereof, that their estates be confiscated and for confiscating the estate of William Knox, formerly provost marshal of the then province now state of Georgia; Acts 1782, May 4, 1782, An Act for Inflicting Penalties on, and Confiscating the Estate of Such Persons as Are Therein Declared Guilty of Treason, and for other purposes therein mentioned [more than two hundred men listed by name are banished from Georgia due to collaborating with the British Crown]. Massachusetts: Acts 1779, ch. 9, An Act to Confiscate the Estates of Certain Notorious Conspirators against the Government and Liberties of the Inhabitants of the Late Province, Now State of Massachusetts-Bay [list of more than twenty named individuals whose real and personal property will be confiscated].

130. See, e.g., Delaware: Acts 1778, 151, An Act to Prevent the Inhabitants of This State from Dealing and Furnishing the Enemies Thereof with Supplies, and for Other Purposes Therein Mentioned [horses, teams, and goods of those apprehended trading with the enemy will be confiscated].

Massachusetts: Acts 1781, ch. 7, An Act in Addition to an Act Intitled An Act for Preventing All Commerce and Illegal Correspondence with the Enemies of the United States of America [reiterates authority to seize goods to be shipped to Great Britain or its other colonies. Goods seized will be condemned and sold].

New Jersey: Acts 1780, ch. 5, Dec. 21, 1780, An Act More Effectually to Prevent the Inhabitants of This State from Trading with the Enemy, or Going within Their Lines, and for other purposes therein mentioned [any person apprehended going to the enemy lines without a license or permission, or who attempts to convey or send goods to the enemy, who found guilty at trial, will forfeit his real and personal property to the state].

New York: Acts 1782, ch. 39, An Act More Effectually to Prevent Illicit Trade with the Enemy [all goods that were brought from places occupied by the enemy are declared contraband and will be seized, unless excepted by the act].

Rhode Island: Acts 1781, Mar. 1781, An Act More Effectually to Prevent Illicit Trade, Commerce, and Correspondence, with the Enemies of This and Other United States of America [any resident of Rhode Island who imports goods, wares, and merchandise from Great Britain will have the goods confiscated].

Virginia authorized punishment by fine for traders who boarded British vessels to transact business. See Hening's Stats., vol. 11, 136, ch. 16, Oct. 1782, An Act to Prohibit Intercourse with and the Admission of British Subjects into This State [no person may go aboard a vessel flying the colors of Great Britain without permission of the governor and counsel. Anyone who violates this statute may be fined $200 and given three months' imprisonment].

131. Calhoon, *The Loyalists in Revolutionary America*, 501.

132. Calhoon, *The Loyalists in Revolutionary America*, 501.

133. See Treaty of Paris, last accessed Jan. 30, 2017, http://www.ourdocuments.gov/doc.php?flash'true&doc'6&page'transcript.

134. Robert S. Lambert, "The Confiscation of Loyalist Property in Georgia, 1782–1786," *William and Mary Quarterly (Third Series)* 20 (1963): 91.

135. Lambert, "The Confiscation of Loyalist Property," 83.

136. Lambert, "The Confiscation of Loyalist Property," 84–85.

137. John Franklin Jameson, *The American Revolution as a Social Movement* (Princeton, NJ: Princeton University Press, 1967), 35.

138. Richard D. Brown, "The Confiscation and Disposition of Loyalists' Estates in Suffolk County," *William and Mary Quarterly (Third Series)* 21 (1964): 534.

139. Brown, "The Confiscation and Disposition of Loyalists' Estates," 538.

140. "Massachusetts Declaration of Rights," last accessed Jan. 30, 2017, http://www.malegislature.gov/Laws/Constitution. Article I was annulled by Amendments, Art. CVI, in 1976. The amendment changed *men* to *people* and added a second sentence reading, "Equality under the law shall not be denied or abridged because of sex, race, color, creed or national origin."

141. Brown, "The Confiscation and Disposition of Loyalist's Estates," 540.

142. . *List of Those Tories Who Took Part with Great-Britain in the Revolutionary War, and Who Were Attainted with Treason Commonly Called the Black List to Which Is Prefixed the Opinions of Attorneys McKean and Dallas* (Philadelphia, 1802; New York: privately printed, 1865.)

143. Harry B. Yoshpe, *The Disposition of Loyalist Estates in the Southern District of the State of New York* (New York: Columbia University Press, 1939).

144. Yoshpe, *The Disposition of Loyalist Estates*, 26–27 n. 41.

145. Calhoon, *The Loyalists in Revolutionary America*, 400–401.

146. Jameson, *The American Revolution as a Social Movement*, 35.

147. Yoshpe, *The Disposition of Loyalist Estates*, 27–30.

148. 1 N.C. 5 (1787).

149. Jeff Broadwater, "Bayard v. Singleton," last accessed Jan. 30, 2017, http://www.northcarolinahistory.org/encyclopedia/bayard-v-singleton.

150. *Bayard v. Singleton*, 1 N.C. 5.

151. *Bayard v. Singleton*, 1 N.C. 7.

152. *Bayard v. Singleton*, 1 N.C. 10.

153. *Bayard v. Singleton*, 1 N.C. 6–7.

154. *Bayard v. Singleton*, 1 N.C. 9.

155. *Bayard v. Singleton*, 1 N.C. 10.

156. *Bayard v. Singleton*, 1 N.C. 9–10.

157. Acts 1778, ch. 45, Oct. 8, 1778.

158. Acts 1778, ch. 45, § 6. This account is based on the original records of the court transcribed by Rutgers University and posted online, last accessed Jan. 30, 2017, http://njlegallib.rutgers.edu/hw/Minutes.html#1780_11. See also Daniel J. Hulsebosch, "A

Symposium on the People Themselves: Popular Constitutionalism and Judicial Review," and "A Discrete and Cosmopolitan Minority: The Loyalists, the Atlantic World, and the Origins of Judicial Review," *Chicago-Kent Law Review* 81 (2006): 825, 848–849.

159. *Holmes v. Walton*, petition for certiorari, last accessed Feb. 3, 2017, http://njlegallib.rutgers.edu/hw/Reasons_Nov_1779.html.

160. *Holmes v. Walton*, petition for certiorari, http://njlegallib.rutgers.edu/hw/Reasons_Nov_1779.html.

161. Acts 1779, ch. 7, § 1, Dec. 25, 1779.

162. *Holmes v. Watson*, minutes, last accessed Feb. 3, 2017, http://njlegallin.rutgers.edu/hw/Minutes.html.

163. New Jersey Const. 1776, Art. XXII.

164. Hulsebosch, "A Discrete and Cosmopolitan Minority," 849.

165. The account of *Rutgers v. Waddington* is taken from James B. Thayer, *Cases on Constitutional Law*, vol. 1 (Cambridge, MA: Charles W. Sever, 1895), 65–70. Thayer took his account from Henry B. Dawson, ed., *Rutgers v. Waddington* (New York: Samuel Loudon, 1784; repr. Morisiania, NY, 1866).

166. Treaty of Paris, Art. 5, last accessed Jan. 30, 2017, http://www.ourdocuments.gov/doc.php?flash'true&doc'6&page'transcript.

167. New York Const. 1777, Art. XXXV, last accessed Jan. 30, 2017, http://avalon.yale.edu/18th_century/ny01.asp. Emphasis added.

168. Hulsebosch, "A Discrete and Cosmopolitan Minority," 845–847.

169. Hulsebosch, "A Discrete and Cosmopolitan Minority," 846–847.

170. Hulsebosch, "A Discrete and Cosmopolitan Minority," 846–847.

171. *Rutgers v. Waddington*, in Thayer, *Cases on Constitutional Law*, 71–72.

172. *Rutgers v. Waddington*, in Thayer, *Cases on Constitutional Law*, 72.

173. "The United States in Congress assembled shall have the sole and exclusive right and power of determining on peace and war . . . of entering into treaties." Articles of Confederation, Art. IX, § 1.

174. Vattel, *The Law of Nations*, vol. 3, § 26.

175. Vattel, *The Law of Nations*, vol. 3, § 27.

176. Vattel, *The Law of Nations*, vol. 3, § 29.

177. Vattel, *The Law of Nations*, vol. 3, ch. 9, § 161.

178. Vattel, *The Law of Nations*, vol. 3, ch. 14, §§ 204–206.

179. Virginia Const. 1776, Declaration of Rights, Art. VIII.

180. "Bills of attainder are legislative acts passed for the special purpose of attainting particular individuals of treason, or felony, or to inflict pains and penalties beyond, or contrary to the common law. They are state-engines of oppression in the last resort, and of the most powerful and extensive operation, reaching to the absent and the dead, as well as to the present and the living. They supply the want of legal forms, legal evidence, and of every other barrier which the laws provide against tyranny and injustice in ordinary cases: being a legislative declaration of the guilt of the party, without trial, without a hearing, and often without the examination of witnesses, and subjecting his person to condign punishment, and his estate to confiscation and forfeiture. Instances of their application to these nefarious purposes occur in almost every page of the English history for a very considerable period: and very few reigns have passed in which the power has not been exercised, though, to the honour of the nation, I believe, no instance of the kind has occurred for more than half a century." William Blackstone, *Commentaries on the Common Law of England*, vol. 1, edited by St. George Tucker (Philadelphia: Birch & Small, 1803), 292–293. For the classic English definition and description of *attaint for treason*, see "Bill of Attainder," last accessed Feb. 17, 2017, http://www.reference.com/government-politics/.example-bill-of-attainder-7c1fe1ec834381e4?go=cdpArticles/htm.

181. Bills of attainder have been unconstitutional since 1789. See U.S. Const., Art. I, § 10.

182. "Whereas a certain Josiah Philips labourer of the Parish of Lynnhaven and county of Princess Anne together with diverse others . . . have levied war against this

Commonwealth . . . and whereas the delays which would attend the proceeding to outlaw the said offenders according to the usual forms and procedures of the courts of law would leave the said good people for a long time exposed to murder and devastation. Be it therefore enacted by the General assembly that if the said Josiah Philips his associates and confederates shall not on or before the last day of June in this present year render themselves to the Governor . . . then [they] shall stand and be convicted and attained of high treason, and shall suffer the pains of death." Acts 1778, ch. 12, An Act to Attaint Josiah Phillips and Others, unless they render themselves to justice within a certain time.

183. Colonial Williamsburg official history site, last accessed Jan. 30, 2017, http://www.history.org/foundation/journal/spring02/attainder.cfm.

184. 8 Va. (4 Call) 5 (1782).

185. Acts 1776, ch. 3, sec. 3: "The governor, or in case of his death, inability or necessary absence, the Councilor who acts as President shall in no wise have or exercise a right of granting pardon to any person or persons convicted in manner aforesaid, but may suspend the execution until the meeting of the general assembly who shall determine whether such person or persons are proper objects of mercy or not, and order accordingly."

186. *Caton*, 8 Va. 5.

187. *Caton*, 8 Va. 5.

188. Virginia Const., Art. II, § 9 (1776).

189. Hulsebosch, "Symposium on the People Themselves: Popular Constitutionalism and Judicial Review," 853–854.

190. *Caton*, 8 Va. 13.

191. *Caton*, 8 Va. 8.

192. *Martin v. Hunter's Lessee*, 11 U.S. (7 Cranch) 603 (1813).

193. Acts 1777, ch. 9, Oct. 1777.

194. Acts 1779, ch. 45, May 1779.

195. Acts 1779, ch. 45.

196. Acts 1779, ch. 14, Oct. 1779.

197. Acts 1779, ch. 14.

198. Treaty of Paris, last accessed Jan. 30, 2017, http://www.ourdocuments.gov/doc.php?Flash=true&doc=6&page=transcript.

199. Acts 1784, ch. 53.

200. Acts 1785, ch. 53, Oct. 1785.

201. Acts 1785, ch. 63, Oct. 1785.

202. Treaty of Paris, last accessed Jan. 30, 2017, http://www.ourdocuments.gov/doc.php?flash=true&doc=6&page=transcript.

203. *Hunter v. Fairfax's Devisee*, 15 Va. (1 Munf.) 218 (1810).

204. *Hunter v. Fairfax's Devisee*, 15 Va. 218.

205. *Martin v. Hunter's Lessee*, 11 U.S. (7 Cranch) 603, 618 (1813).

206. *Martin v. Hunter's Lessee*, 11 U.S. 619–620. Justice Story said that the common law allowed an alien to take title to land by will or deed, but not by intestate succession. He also held that it makes no difference under the law if the alien was an enemy alien.

207. *Martin v. Hunter's Lessee*, 11 U.S. 620–622.

208. *Martin v. Hunter's Lessee*, 11 U.S. 620.

209. *Martin v. Hunter's Lessee*, 11 U.S. 620.

210. Acts 1782, ch. 8, Oct. 14, 1782, An Act to Amend and Reduce into One, the Several Acts for Ascertaining Certain Taxes, establishing a permanent revenue sequestered quitrents due and payable to Lord Fairfax or his successor until the right of descent shall be more fully ascertained, and the general assembly shall make final provision thereon; and all quitrents thereafter to become due, shall be paid into the public treasury, under the operation of the laws of that session; for which quitrents, the inhabitants of the Northern Neck shall be exonerated from the future claim of the proprietor.

211. *Martin v. Hunter's Lessee*, 11 U.S. 623.

212. Acts 1782, ch. 33, § 3, Oct. 1782: "And whereas the death of the Right Honorable Thomas Lord Fairfax may occasion great inconvenience to those who may incline to make entries for vacant lands in the Northern Neck: Be it further enacted that all entries made with the surveyors of the counties within the Northern Neck and returned to the office formerly kept by Thomas Lord Fairfax, that be held, deemed, and taken as good and valid in law as those theretofore made under the direction of the said Thomas Lord Fairfax, until some mode shall be taken up and adopted by the General Assembly concerning the territory of the Northern Neck."
213. *Martin v. Hunter's Lessee*, 11 U.S. 625.
214. *Martin v. Hunter's Lessee*, 11 U.S. 628.
215. *Martin v. Hunter's Lessee*, 11 U.S. 628.
216. *Martin v. Hunter's Lessee*, 11 U.S. 629–630.
217. *Martin v. Hunter's Lessee*, 11 U.S. 630.
218. *Hunter v. Martin, Devisee of Fairfax*, 18 Va. (4 Munf.) 1 (1815).
219. Virginia's highest court rejected the doctrine that asserted the decisions of the U.S. Supreme Court were necessarily binding on lower state courts. The Virginia court treated the Supreme Court's decision in *Martin v. Hunter's Lessee* as advisory only. *Hunter v. Martin, Devisee of Fairfax*, 18 Va. 1.
220. *Martin v. Hunter's Lessee*, 14 U.S. (1 Wheat.) 304 (1816).
221. *Martin v. Hunter's Lessee*, 14 U.S. 328.
222. *Martin v. Hunter's Lessee*, 14 U.S. 327.
223. *Martin v. Hunter's Lessee*, 14 U.S. 332.
224. *Martin v. Hunter's Lessee*, 14 U.S. 340–341, 351.
225. *Martin v. Hunter's Lessee*, 14 U.S. 355.
226. *Martin v. Hunter's Lessee*, 14 U.S. 356.
227. *Martin v. Hunter's Lessee*, 14 U.S. 358.
228. *Martin v. Hunter's Lessee*, 14 U.S. 363.
229. Kennedy Hickman, "The Quasi-War: America's First Conflict," last accessed Jan. 30, 2017, http://militaryhistory.about.com/od/navalbattles1601800/p/quasiwar.htm.
230. 230. The Alien Enemies Acts, 1798, ch. 58, 1 Stats. at Large, 570, authorized summary executive deportation of dangerous enemy aliens. The Alien Enemies Acts, 1798, ch. 66, 1 Stats. at large, 577, authorized executive branch ex parte deportation of all enemy aliens, dangerous or otherwise. The Sedition Act, Acts 1798, ch. 74, 1 Stats. at Large, 596, made anti-government writings or utterances criminal.
231. The Alien Acts authorized the president to deport aliens suspected of "treasonable or secret machinations" against the United States without notice and hearing. The statute would automatically expire at the end of two years. See Acts 1798, ch. 59, 1 Stats. at Large, 570; Acts 1798, ch. 66, 1 Stats. at Large, 577. The statute titled "An Act in Addition to the Act, Entitled An Act for the Punishment of Certain Crimes against the United States" defined three new crimes. Section 1 made it a crime to "combine or conspire together" to oppose any measure of the government directed by proper authority or to impede the operation of any law of the United States, or advise or attempt to procure any insurrection, riot, or unlawful assembly, punishable by a fine of up to $5,000 and imprisonment from six months to five years. Section 2 made it a crime to write, print, utter, or publish or knowingly assist in writing, printing, uttering, or publishing any writing that attacked the Constitution of the United States, or advocated resistance to any statute of the United States, or to encourage, aid, or abet any hostile designs of any foreign nation on the United States, punishable by a fine of up to $2,000 and two years' imprisonment. Section 3 allowed a defendant to give evidence in his defense. Acts 1798, ch. 74, 1 Stats. at Large, 596. For the Sedition Act, see Acts 1798, ch. 66, 1 Stats at Large, 577.
232. See Virginia Resolution Dec. 24, 1798, last accessed Feb. 3, 2017, http://avalon.law.yale.edu/18th_century/virres.app. See Kentucky Resolution Dec. 3, 1799, last accessed Feb. 3, 2017, http://avalon.law.yale.edu/18th_century/kenres.app.

233. The Alien and Sedition Acts, last accessed Jan. 30, 2017, https://ourdocuments.gov/doc.php?flash+true&doc=16&pag=transcription#no.1.
234. See Jeffrey A. Smith, *Franklin and Bache: Envisioning the Enlightened Republic* (New York: Oxford University Press, 1990), 85–134.
235. Jack Lynch, "The Alien and Sedition Acts," last accessed Jan. 30, 2017, http://www.history.org/Foundation/journal/winter07/alien.cfm.
236. See U.S. Const., Art. I, § 8 (to declare war, to grant letters of marque, to raise and support an army and navy, to pass laws for the governance of the army and navy, to call up the militia, and to organize and train the militia. Art. 1, § 10, clause 3 forbade the states' raising a navy and engaging in war.
237. U.S. Const., Art. II, § 2.

TWO

The War Powers, Suspension of Civil Liberties, and Military Commissions during the Civil War

"Must I shoot a simple-minded soldier boy who deserts while I must not touch a hair of a wily agitator who induces him to desert?"
—Abraham Lincoln, letter to Erastus Corning

The Civil War brought the joint congressional/executive constitutional authority to suspend civil liberties in time of war into play. The Revolutionary War program to stifle Tory dissenters pre-dated the Constitution. It was a program carried on by state governments and only suggested that the national government might have the authority to suspend civil liberties in time of war. The 1787 Constitution, with one exception, did not speak to the issue of suppression of civil liberties in time of war.[1] In 1815, Gen. Andrew Jackson had declared martial law in New Orleans and adjacent parishes during the British invasion of Louisiana. Jackson had jailed a New Orleans state legislator for acting as a British spy.[2] Jackson attempted to arrest a U.S. district judge, but the judge summoned Jackson to answer for contempt of court and fined him $1,000.[3] After Jackson defeated the British at Chalmette, he returned authority to the state and city. In 1815, the Louisiana Supreme Court held that Jackson did not have the authority to declare martial law and suspend the operation of civil courts.[4]

During the First Seminole War in 1818, General Jackson ordered two British subjects, Alexander Arbuthnot and Robert Christy Ambrister, to be tried before a military commission for spying. The military tribunal convicted both men, but the tribunal commuted Ambrister's death sentence to corporal punishment because Arbuthnot was not found guilty of spying for the British government. Both men were, in Jackson's view, "pirates and outlaws" deserving the ultimate penalty.[5] General Jackson disregarded the tribunal's sentence: both men were shot. The House Military Affairs Committee issued a report in 1819 that was highly critical of Jackson's use of martial law and trial by military commission.

During the Mexican War, Gen. Winfield Scott instituted military commissions to try American soldiers and civilians, as well as Mexican civilians, for criminal offenses during the occupation of Mexico. Scott issued General Order 20 in February 1847, setting up military commission tribunals prior to his overland campaign to capture Mexico City. From February 1847 to July 1848, 117 offenders were tried by military commission. The 117 individuals consisted of 74 U.S. soldiers, 12 U.S. civilians, and 31 Mexican civilians. One U.S. citizen was convicted of rape and robbery, for which offenses he was sentenced to be hanged. According to contemporary sources, the conviction rate for Mexicans was slightly lower than that for U.S. citizens.[6] Neither Gen. Jackson's nor Gen. Scott's suspension of civil liberties presaged President Lincoln's suppression of civil liberties during the Civil War.

This chapter is a detailed examination of the Lincoln administration's history of suspension of civil liberties and the legal fallout from that suspension. After the Civil War ended, the U.S. Supreme Court tried to reverse the course of history in *Ex parte Milligan*[7] without making any real change in the relationship between the war power and the Bill of Rights. Federal authorities continued to use military rule during Reconstruction. Civilians were detained without charges, and several were tried by military commission when the U.S. and state courts were open.

LINCOLN'S APRIL 1861 SUSPENSION OF HABEAS CORPUS

In early April 1861, seven Southern states had passed secession ordinances and had declared themselves independent.[8] The Secessionists had seized U.S. property and had formed a new government in Montgomery, Alabama, with former U.S. senator Jefferson Davis as head of state.[9] Half the U.S. Army officer corps had resigned, leaving the army without competent leadership. In Washington, D.C., all telegraph communications with the North had gone dead. There were rumors that Maryland Secessionists had destroyed the bridges on the Philadelphia, Wilmington & Baltimore R.R. to block the travel of militia troops to Washington to protect the capitol from Secessionist attack.[10]

On the 14th, Secessionist artillery opened fire on Fort Sumter in Charleston, South Carolina. Lincoln issued a call for seventy-five thousand militia from the states that remained in the Union to put down the South Carolina insurrection.[11] By the 19th, the post had surrendered to the Secessionists. The U.S. capitol was defenseless. Across the Potomac, Virginia had called a convention to vote on seceding from the Union. The

Figure 2.1. Abraham Lincoln (Brady Handy Collection, Library of Congress).

District of Columbia was surrounded by slave states that threatened secession over the call-up of militia. The governor of Maryland seemed incapable of quelling pro-Secessionist guerrilla activities. The Maryland legislature was scheduled to meet to consider a secession ordinance that would take Maryland out of the Union and make Lincoln and his government a virtual prisoner in the District of Columbia.[12] Congress was not in session, and no declaration of war could be passed until it returned to the city. Maryland militia colonel Isaac Trimble organized pro-Secessionist militiamen into bridge-burning parties that destroyed the Philadelphia, Wilmington & Baltimore R.R. bridge over Big Gunpowder Falls, cutting off rail access to Baltimore and Washington from Philadelphia.[13]

This was the worst crisis the U.S. government ever faced. The Japanese sneak attack on Pearl Harbor and the terrorist attack of September 11, 2001, pale in comparison with the April 1861 crisis. Newly inaugurated President Abraham Lincoln, protected only by a corporal's guard of army regulars and civilian volunteers led by his friend Maj. David Hunter,[14] sat in the White House with his cabinet trying to save what was left of the United States. On the 19th, Lincoln asked Attorney General Edward N. Bates to look into the possibility of issuing a decree of martial law that would permit the United States to protect its lifeline with the North, the rail system from Washington through Annapolis Junction, Baltimore, and the Susquehanna Ferry to Wilmington and Philadelphia. Lincoln could put a strip of land on either side of the railroad right of way under military rule and use newly arrived militia units from Northern states to protect key railroad bridges and control the civilian population.

The next day Attorney General Edward N. Bates's chief assistant, Titian J. Coffey, turned in a memorandum of legal authority drawn from international law treatises, defining "martial law" and warning the president that Congress alone could suspend the writ of habeas corpus and declare martial law. This was not what Mr. Lincoln wanted to hear.[15] General Winfield Scott, the commanding general of the U.S. Army, wanted to order Maj. Gen. Benjamin F. Butler to arrest the Secessionist Maryland politicians in Annapolis, but Lincoln at first told him not to do so.[16] That afternoon, the 6th Massachusetts Militia Regiment, on its way to defend Washington from Southern aggression, crossed Baltimore from the Philadelphia, Wilmington & Baltimore station to the Baltimore & Ohio station in column of fours. An ugly crowd gathered: rocks were thrown, someone fired a shot from the crowd, and the 6th Massachusetts let go a volley into the mob, killing several Baltimoreans. Seven 6th Massachusetts solders were the first Union fatalities of the war.[17] The 6th Massachusetts troop train arrived at Washington National Depot on the 19th. They were dispatched to the Capitol and went into camp in and around the building.

Union militia units trickled into Washington to provide a defensive perimeter for the national capital. A Pennsylvania militia unit came in by train from Harrisburg on the 19th. Massachusetts militia Maj. Gen. Benjamin F. Butler landed the 8th Massachusetts and 7th New York at Annapolis and put them aboard the Baltimore & Ohio branch line railroad to Washington. These regiments joined the 6th Massachusetts quartered in and around the Capitol. These regiments provided some defense force for the capitol, relieving the regulars and Maj. Hunter's corporal's guard at the White House.[18] Next day, General Scott warned the president that Washington was still under the danger of imminent attack by Secessionists. Lincoln acted: on the 27th, he directed Secretary of State William H. Seward to issue an order to General Scott establishing martial law along the right of way of the Baltimore & Ohio and Philadelphia, Wilmington & Baltimore:

> The Commanding General of the Army of the United States:
> You are engaged in suppressing an insurrection against the laws of the United States. If at any point on or in the vicinity of any military line which is now or which shall be used between the City of Philadelphia, and the City of Washington you find resistance which renders it necessary to suspend the writ of *habeas corpus* for the public safety, you personally or through the officer in command at the point where resistance occurs, are authorized to suspend the writ.[19]

Article II, § 9, of the Constitution did provide for emergency suspension of the writ of habeas corpus. "The privilege of the Writ of Habeas Corpus shall not be suspended, unless when in Cases of Rebellion or Invasion the public Safety may require it." The attorney general and most legal authorities such as former Supreme Court justice Joseph Story believed that the writ could be suspended only by act of Congress.[20] But Congress was not in session and would not be recalled to Washington until July. Lincoln would act without waiting for congressional approval.

THE GREAT WRIT

The writ of habeas corpus is an ancient legal means for testing the legality of confinement. The writ requires the custodian of a person alleged to be unlawfully detained to show cause why a court order should not be issued to free the person unlawfully detained. The writ is initiated by filing a civil petition in a court having jurisdiction to hear such petitions, alleging that an individual is unlawfully confined, specifying the reasons, and identifying the person who by name is the custodian of the object of the writ. The presiding judge then sends notice of hearing to show cause to the custodian, permitting the custodian to be heard in open court as to why the confined person ought to remain confined. It was a writ often invoked in Royal courts in the seventeenth and eighteenth centuries to free political prisoners.[21] The "great writ" was imported as part of the common law. It was provided for in the U.S. Judicial Code of 1789 and was widely used in the nineteenth century to test the legality of confinement of prisoners before trial and to test the legality of induction or enlistment into the army or militia on active duty. The power of the writ of habeas corpus to prevent the unlawful detention and seizure of U.S.

citizens was a favorite Fourth of July speech topic. It was also a very practical legal tool that permitted the judicial branch of the U.S. government to review the conduct of the executive branch with respect to the detention of U.S. citizens.[22]

Secretary Seward's order also implicitly authorized General Scott and the department commander to invoke "martial law." In the mid-nineteenth century, "martial law" was widely thought to be some type of separate body of precedential law, although the great commentators such as Prof. Francis Lieber, who wrote General Order 100 for the Governance of the Army in the Field, correctly identified "martial law" as military rule for the sake of winning the conflict.[23]

There were no precedents for invoking martial law to protect a civilian rail system from saboteurs. President Lincoln was embarking on uncharted constitutional seas.

THE SECRETARY OF STATE CURTAILS CIVIL LIBERTIES

The Rights of the Accused in 1861

Although the law of criminal procedure has changed a great deal from what it was in Lincoln's time, the basic constitutional rights of an accused date all the way back to the adoption of the Bill of Rights. According to Prof. David Bodenhamer, the basic rights of the accused had become fixed by the end of the colonial period and the early American Revolution.[24] These rights were guaranteed by state bills of rights and by the Federal Bill of Rights. The Lincoln administration short-circuited the following basic rights of the accused from 1861 to 1865.

Probable Cause to Arrest

A state or federal peace officer needed probable cause to arrest any person. "Probable cause" was normally established by applying for an arrest warrant to a magistrate who passed on the information the peace officer had obtained to show the accused may have committed an offense. The magistrate would issue a warrant and require the peace officer to return the accused to the magistrate for a hearing.[25] As an emergency alternative, a peace officer could arrest without a warrant if an offense was committed in his presence or the peace officer had independent probable cause to believe the accused had committed a felony. A warrantless arrest was suspect, and the accused had to be produced before a magistrate within twenty-four hours for a hearing on whether there was probable cause to detain the accused. From 1861 to 1865, thousands of suspected disloyal persons were arrested without warrants. These individuals never appeared before a magistrate for any type of arraignment. Instead they were held by the military in close confinement.[26]

Freedom from Unreasonable Searches and Seizures

The Fourth Amendment and corresponding state constitutions guaranteed every citizen freedom from unreasonable searches and seizures.[27] A reasonable search and seizure was based on a warrant issued by a disinterested magistrate. Failure to obtain a warrant before searching the premises was unconstitutional, although the remedy for an unreasonable search had not evolved into the suppression sanction by 1860. Union soldiers routinely carried out warrantless searches of the homes and shops of suspected disloyal persons from 1861 through 1865 and never produced the evidence seized in a civilian court.

Bail in Non-Capital Cases

The Eighth Amendment and all state constitutions guaranteed the accused's right to bail that was not excessive.[28] The Federal Bill of Rights, however, did not provide for the right to bail in non-capital cases. The right to bail did not guaranty that the accused would be free until trial, because the accused still had to come up with cash or a pledge of property to secure bail. Persons apprehended by the provost marshal for the federal district, or by soldiers under his direction, were not given bail.

Notice and Hearing on Charges

The Sixth Amendment to the U.S. Constitution required that an accused in federal court was entitled to notice of the charges against him, the right to present a defense to those charges, and the right to legal counsel. State constitutions contained similar provisions. Neither the federal nor state criminal justice systems provided for free legal counsel. The accused could hire a lawyer to speak for him at the preliminary hearing and at trial.[29]

Habeas Corpus

The accused held as a prisoner could file a writ of habeas corpus in U.S. district or U.S. circuit court or a state court having jurisdiction if an accused believed he was wrongfully and unlawfully detained contrary to law. The court would order the authorities to produce the prisoner in court to show cause why the prisoner should not be released. This was an evidentiary hearing on the merits of probable cause to confine the accused. It was available before trial and after trial. All states had similar provisions for issuing a writ of habeas corpus. Although Article II, § 9, of the U.S. Constitution and most state constitutions permitted suspension of the privilege of habeas corpus in time of rebellion or invasion, the writ could not be suspended in ordinary times when the civilian courts were open for business.[30]

Trial by Jury

The Sixth Amendment and all state constitutions guaranteed that the accused would be tried before a jury of his peers. Secret proceedings and non-jury trials were unconstitutional. The Lincoln administration's use of military commissions to try disloyal persons precluded trial by jury.[31]

Speedy Public Trial

The Sixth Amendment and most state constitutions provided that all criminal trials were to be speedy and public (i.e., the accused would not be made to languish for years in custody before obtaining his day in court).[32] Appellate review of criminal convictions was provided for by statute in some states, but the U.S. judicial code did not provide for appellate review of federal convictions until 1879.[33] The thousands of prisoners of state arrested from 1861 to 1865 and confined in federal prisons or forts were not given a speedy public trial. Most prisoners of state were not tried before any tribunal. They were held without charges until released by taking the loyalty oath and posting bond for good behavior.

Procedural Due Process of Law

The Fifth Amendment guaranteed that no citizen would be deprived of life, liberty, or property except by due process of law.[34] All state constitutions in 1860 had similar due process clauses. In criminal cases, the due process clause reinforced the rights of the accused spelled out in the Sixth Amendment and corresponding state constitutional provisions. The accused was guaranteed a fundamentally fair process for determining guilt that required that the accused be given a meaningful right to defend himself in person and by counsel.[35] President Lincoln would ultimately suspend all these rights by the midpoint of the war throughout the nation for disloyal citizens and other undesirables.[36]

The State Department in Charge

President Lincoln assigned the task of administering the suspension of civil liberties to Secretary of State Seward.[37] The suspension of habeas corpus along the Philadelphia–Washington railroad line was followed by suspension of habeas in Key West, Florida.[38] The government established military rule in Key West and suspended the writ of habeas corpus after deposing the civilian authorities. Key West happened to be the main naval base for the Gulf Blockade Squadron.

Ex Parte Merryman

Seward's program of military arrest of civilians was tested by an irate Marylander, John Merryman, a militia captain suspected of burning some of the railroad bridges on the Philadelphia, Wilmington & Baltimore north of Baltimore.[39] He was arrested on May 25, 1861, by order of Maj. Gen. William H. Keim, a Pennsylvania militia officer, and turned over to Maj. Gen. George Cadwalader, commandant at Baltimore's Fort McHenry. Merryman hired a lawyer who immediately filed a petition for habeas corpus in the Circuit Court of Maryland. The petition was presented to Chief Justice Roger B. Taney, the circuit justice, who ordered Cadwalader to bring Merryman to the courthouse in Baltimore and show cause why he was detained. Cadwalader refused to appear in court, citing the president's suspension of habeas corpus along the railroad corridor. This caused the chief justice of the United States to write a scorching opinion chastising the president for illegal imposition of the suspension of the writ of habeas corpus.[40] Taney pointed out that the suspension of habeas corpus clause of the Constitution appeared in Article I, which enumerated the powers of Congress.[41] He agreed with Joseph Story that only Congress could suspend the great writ.[42] Taney criticized the president and his minions in the following language:

> But the comments before me show, that the military authority in this case has gone far beyond the mere suspension of the privilege of the writ of habeas corpus. He has, by force of arms, thrust aside the judicial authorities and officers to whom the constitution has confided the power and duty of interpreting and administering the laws, and substituted a military government in its place, to be administered and executed by military officers.[43]

Taney's rebuke was unenforceable: the president and the executive department alone had the power to compel obedience to Taney's writ.

By the time Lincoln sent a special message to Congress on July 4, 1861, justifying his extreme measures during the crisis that spring, three executive orders had suspended the writ of habeas corpus. Lincoln justified his actions as necessary to preserve the Union. Lincoln asked Congress rhetorically,

> To state the question more directly, are all the laws but one to go unexecuted, and the government itself go to pieces, lest that one be violated? Even in such a case, would not the official oath be broken, if the government should be overthrown, when it was believed that disregarding the single law, would tend to preserve it?[44]

Congress then ratified Lincoln's suspension of civil liberties by an interim resolution.

Arresting the Maryland Legislators

In August 1861, following the defeat of Brig. Gen. Irvin McDowell's Army of Virginia at Manassas and its ignominious flight to the safety of the Washington defenses, President Lincoln and Secretary Seward became worried that the Maryland legislature might vote the state out of the Union. Early in September, Maj. Gen. George B. McClellan, the new commander of the Union Army of the Potomac, and Secretary of War Cameron were brought into the discussion of how to handle the Maryland legislature. Cameron issued an order to Maj. Gen. John A. Dix, department commander at Baltimore, to prevent the Maryland legislature from passing a secession ordinance. Dix sent a list of legislators to Cameron and McClellan identifying pro-secession legislators. Cameron told Dix to order the arrest of six Maryland legislators who were whisked off by steamer to incarceration in New York City. Modern writers believe that these arrests were ordered by General McClellan, a "War Democrat," without first obtaining approval from the White House. Modern commentators also believe that neither man consulted Secretary Seward before making the arrests.[45] The arrest of the legislators was not part of Seward's plan for the suspension of civil liberties. In October 1861, Lincoln suggested to Gen. Winfield Scott that the writ should be suspended along a line running northeast from Washington, D.C., to Maine. Scott then issued an order to his subordinate commanders establishing martial law and suspension of habeas corpus.

Seward was responsible for the suspension of civil liberties, including the arrest of disloyal U.S. citizens in the railroad corridor. Most of the early arrests of alleged disloyal civilians were made outside the rail corridor in such far-off venues as Missouri and Illinois. Seward's detention of disloyal citizens was haphazard, partial, and incomplete. Frederick Bancroft, his biographer, believed that Seward had no intention of prosecuting any of the detainees for treason or other crimes; his aim was to take a few active, vociferous anti-government activists temporarily out of circulation.[46]

Local Military Commanders Declare Martial Law

Martial law was routinely declared by Union commanders for territory captured from the Confederacy and for Union territory invaded by Confederate forces (e.g., New Mexico and Arizona Territory).[47] Colonel E. R. S. Canby, commander of U.S. forces in New Mexico, suspended habeas corpus on his own initiative in August 1861.[48] The chief justice of Colorado Territory suspended the writ for one notorious Confederate sympathizer in October 1861.[49] Colorado Territory was also under martial law late in the war on account of continued unrest among Native American tribes in the region.[50]

Union military authorities in Missouri had taken the law into their own hands in 1861. Captain Nathaniel Lyon, a Regular officer, arrested dozens of Missouri militiamen assembled at Camp Jackson outside St. Louis. Emmett McDonald retained counsel who filed a writ of habeas corpus in U.S. District Court in St. Louis. Judge Samuel Treat issued the writ, but Lyon's commanding officer, Brig. Gen. William S. Harney, refused to honor the writ and to produce McDonald before Judge Treat for a hearing on the writ. Harney appealed to a law higher than the Constitution, military necessity.[51]

Brigadier General Ulysses S. Grant, without first obtaining authority from his department commander, Maj. Gen. John C. Fremont, ordered the arrest of civilians in or near Jefferson City who interfered with his troops' foraging parties.[52] General Fremont suspended the writ of habeas corpus and declared martial law in St. Louis, Missouri, on August 14, 1861, without authority from Gen. Scott or Secretary Cameron. On August 30, Fremont issued a proclamation extending martial law to the entire state of Missouri. He also ordered that all Missouri slaves be freed. President Lincoln canceled the portion of Fremont's order freeing Missouri slaves but not his declaration of martial law. Fremont's successor, Maj. Gen. Henry W. Halleck, reaffirmed Fremont's martial law declaration in December 1861.[53] In September 1863, Maj. Gen. John A. Schofield reissued a declaration of martial law

> against all persons who shall in any manner encourage mutiny, insubordination, or disorderly conduct or endeavor to create disaffection among troops and against all persons who shall publish or utter publicly words calculated to incite insurrection or lawless acts among the people, or who shall publish falsehoods or misrepresentations of fact calculated to embarrass or weaken the military authorities.[54]

Martial law was declared again during Maj. Gen. Sterling Price's raid on Missouri carried out in October 1864.[55]

Kentucky also fell under martial law. Kentucky was invaded by Confederate forces in May 1861 and in October 1862. Confederate cavalry units operated within Kentucky throughout the war. A series of declarations of martial law were issued for specific districts within the commonwealth.[56] President Lincoln suspended the writ of habeas corpus and declared martial law in Kentucky on July 19, 1864.[57] President Johnson terminated martial law in Kentucky on October 14, 1865.[58]

During the Gettysburg campaign, the city of Baltimore and Maryland's eastern shore were placed under martial law by Maj. Gen. Robert Schenk, commanding general, 8th Corps.[59] Schenk placed the entire state of Delaware under martial law on July 3, 1863.[60] Delaware and Maryland's eastern shore were placed under martial law again in May 1864 by Maj. Gen. Lew Wallace, commander, 8th Corps.[61] During Early's raid on Washington, martial law was declared again in Annapolis, Maryland.[62]

Camp Douglas, Chicago, Illinois, a prisoner-of-war camp, was placed under martial law on July 8, 1862.[63]

In the summer of 1863, Brig. Gen. John H. Morgan, CSA, invaded Indiana and Ohio. Martial law was declared during the invasion in several Indiana and Ohio towns.[64] Brig. Gen. Napoleon T. J. Dana declared martial law in Brownsville, Texas, in December 1863.[65] The East Tennessee Union commander decreed martial law in Sparta, Tennessee, in July 1864.[66] The secretary of the navy authorized imposition of martial law in Port Royal Sound in 1861.[67]

President Lincoln suspended the writ of habeas corpus throughout the loyal states on September 25, 1862, with respect to

> all rebels, their servants and agents and abettors within the United States, and all persons discouraging volunteer enlistments, resisting militia drafts, or guilty of any disloyal practice, affording aid and comfort to rebels against the authority of the United States.[68]

The writ of habeas corpus was also suspended for "all persons arrested, or who are now, or hereafter, during the rebellion imprisoned in any fort, camp, arsenal, military prison or other place of confinement by any military authority." Both classes of individuals would be subject to trial by military commission.[69]

Suppression of the Press

Seward made an attempt to censor newspapers friendly to the Democratic cause, ordering the arrest of the editor of the *Hagerstown Mail* for alleged disloyal publications. He was quickly released from custody by taking the loyalty oath, and Seward continued on his campaign of newspaper cleansing by ordering the New York postmaster not to accept five New York City newspapers for mailing.[70] Acting under the orders of Secretary Seward, Brig. Gen. John A. Dix authorized the suppression of the *Exchange*, a pro-Confederate newspaper in Baltimore published by F. Key Howard and W. W. Glenn. Glenn was held for months in Fort McHenry without charges before being released in the spring of 1862. Howard, transported to Fort Lafayette and Fort Warren, was discharged from custody in November 1862.[71] Seward's ad hoc campaign to restrict the freedom of the press put a prior restraint on political speech for allegedly disloyal newspaper editors.[72] The First Amendment to the U.S. Constitution and comparable state provisions guaranteed the inviolable freedom of the press to publish whatever it wished, subject to civil or criminal penalties for libel.[73]

THE SECRETARY OF WAR TAKES OVER SUSPENSION OF CIVIL LIBERTIES

Stanton's Coordinated Plan

In February 1862, President Lincoln shifted the responsibility from Seward to the Secretary of War. Simon Cameron, his initial appointee, was unable to separate the nation's interest from his need to take care of political cronies from Pennsylvania. Lincoln moved him out of the War Department by offering him the ambassadorship to Imperial Russia. Edwin M. Stanton, the new secretary, was a nationally famous trial lawyer and "War Democrat" with a justifiable reputation as a bulldog. He was exactly the kind of man to balance Lincoln's cabinet and clean up the corrupt War Department's allocation of choice defense contracts as political boodle. He was also the perfect man to run a comprehensive program of military rule wherever the president needed such rule.

The administration's plan for suspension of civil liberties matured under Stanton's guidance and expert management. The first step was Lincoln's issuance of Executive Order No. 1 Relating to Political Prisoners. After bashing the federal judiciary for failure to support his use of suspension of civil liberties, he directed that all political prisoners who took an oath of allegiance to the United States be freed. However, the order excepted those suspected of spying for the Confederacy and any person whose release would be "incompatible with public safety."[74]

The Militia Act of 1862 authorized a limited form of national draft. Congress provided that the president could draft any member of the militia not previously called to active duty to serve for nine months' time. Secretary Stanton followed with a War Department order suspending the writ of habeas corpus for persons resisting the draft and engaged in disloyal practices.[75] On the same day, Stanton issued an order directing all U.S. marshals and other law enforcement officers to arrest "any person or persons who may be engaged, by act, speech, or writing to discourage volunteer enlistments" and directing that the offenders arrested on these charges be tried by a military commission.[76] President Lincoln issued a second order suspending the writ of habeas corpus after the Battle of Antietam on September 24, 1862. This order instituted nationwide suspension of the writ.[77]

The Prize Cases

In 1863, the Supreme Court had to face up to the belligerent status of the Confederate States of America (CSA). President Lincoln had ordered a naval blockade of all Confederate seaports and outlets to the sea in April 1861 without a declaration of war. U.S. naval vessels captured a number of neutral foreign flag vessels attempting to run the blockade with cargos for the Confederacy. These vessels were taken to loyal U.S. ports, and a libel was filed against each vessel and its cargo by the U.S. attorney on behalf of the officers and men of the capturing vessel. The court would issue a decree of condemnation and order the captured ship and cargo put up for sale as prizes taken during time of war.

The owners of three neutral vessels challenged the libel against their vessels in admiralty court. The barque *Amy Warwick,* owned by David and William Currie, Abraham Warwick, and George W. Allen, was homeported in Richmond, Virginia. The ship's captain was unaware that war had broken out between the Confederate States and the United States and was still flying the U.S. colors. She was taken by the USS *Quaker City* on July 10, 1861, off Cape Hatteras loaded with a cargo of coffee. The *Crenshaw,* owned by David and William Currie, captured by the USS *Star* on May 17, 1861, at the mouth of the James River, was on her way to Liverpool with a cargo of tobacco from Richmond, Virginia. The owners admitted in court that they were aware that Virginia had seceded from the Union and was at war with the United States. She was condemned as a prize and ordered to be sold.

The third ship, *Hiawatha,* a British barque owned by Miller, Massman & Co. of Liverpool, was bound for Liverpool with a cargo of tobacco and was captured on May 20, 1861, by the USS *Minnesota.* Her owners opposed the condemnation on the ground that the notice of blockade was legally insufficient. The owners of the cargo also challenged the sale of their tobacco on the same ground. The *Brilliante,* a Mexican schooner, owned by Rafael Preciat and Julian Gual of Campeche, had just cleared New Orleans with a cargo of flour, partially owned by the shipowners and Senores Ybana and Donde, Mexican citizens. She was anchored in Biloxi Bay waiting for clearance from the blockading fleet when she was seized by the crew of the USS *Massachusetts.* She was taken to Key West, and a libel was filed against ship and cargo. The owners resisted the libel in district court on the illegality of the blockade under international law. All four libels were consolidated before the U.S. Supreme Court on writs of error.

The combined cases presented potential danger to the war effort: according to the best opinion of international law experts, a blockade could only be imposed on an enemy belligerent nation in a state of war. According to Vattel, a state of war between two nations requires that the decision to go to war was an act of a sovereign nation, accompanied by a demand for satisfaction by one belligerent against the other for wrongdoing.[78] The Civil War commenced without a formal declaration of war. The blockade would have been legitimate if the Confederate States was an "enemy" as defined by Vattel. He defined "enemy" in *Law of Nations,* vol. 3, § 70, as the whole body of the people whose sovereign has declared war. This rule would entitle U.S. naval vessels to detain any Confederate States shipping stopped on the high seas or in the waters of the Confederacy, provided that a state of war existed.

Recognition of the blockade's legitimacy could mean de facto recognition of the Confederate States of America as a separate, belligerent state. On the other hand, failure to recognize a state of war between the United States and the Confederate States would destroy the blockade and require that the United States permit neutral shipping to offload cargos and take out cargos of goods that would greatly aid the Confederate war effort. Second, if the blockade was illegal, and no state of war existed between the United States and the Confederate States, cargos and vessels belonging to citizens of neutral nations could not be lawfully seized and sold under judicial supervision.

Vattel had some further comments on blockades that affected the Union containment of Confederate ports. In section 111, he dealt with neutral powers trading with a belligerent party, pointing out that neutral shipping that carried on ordinary pre-war trade was protected. When a supposed neutral ship carried contraband, commodities useful in war, the blockading party had the right to stop that vessel, search it, and confiscate the contraband goods aboard the neutral vessel. In section 115, Vattel asserts that enemy goods found aboard neutral shipping may be seized. In section 294, Vattel notes that the common law of war should be observed during a civil war.[79] Prize money was one of the primary incentives to enlisted men and officers to join the navy. The navy would be severely handicapped in recruiting men for the blockade, which would be a "paper tiger" if the president had no right to impose a blockade.[80]

Justice Grier wrote the majority opinion. His opinion was to the point. He reduced all the legal arguments of opposing counsel to two issues:

> 1st. Had the President a right to institute a blockade of ports in possession of persons in armed rebellion against the Government, on the principles of international law, as known and acknowledged among civilized States?
>
> 2d. Was the property of persons domiciled or residing within those States a proper subject of capture on the sea as "enemies' property"?[81]

Grier answered the first issue favorably to the Lincoln administration. He held that a state of war did exist between the United States and the Confederate States.[82] Citing Vattel, Grier wrote that during a civil war, the belligerent parties "must necessarily be considered as constituting, at least for a time, two separate bodies. Having no common superior to judge between them, they stand in precisely the same predicament as two nations who engage in a contest and have recourse to arms."[83] Justice Grier held that Congress alone has the power to declare war and noted that Congress cannot declare war on any state of the Union. He said that the president, as commander in chief, has no power to declare war. The militia act of 1795 permits the president to call out the militia to suppress an insurrection.[84] When President Lincoln invoked the militia act on April 19, 1861, it was an acknowledgment that a de facto civil war had begun. Justice Grier also cited the English declaration of neutrality issued May 13, 1861, as evidence that a de facto state of civil war existed. He concluded that a citizen of any neutral state is estopped to deny that a state of war existed.[85] Carrying the argument of the defendants to its ultimate absurdity, Justice Grier pointed out that to argue that insurgents who have risen in rebellion against their sovereign, expelled her courts, established a revolutionary government, organized armies, and commenced hostilities are not enemies because they are traitors and that a war levied on the government by traitors, in order to dismember and destroy it, is not a war because it is an "insurrection" is absurd.[86]

Justice Grier also held that the question whether the United States is at war is a political question to be determined by the president. The acts of Congress since 1861 that support the conduct of the war constituted de facto recognition of a state of war. Congress has therefore ratified the state of war and the imposition of the blockade. Justice Grier concluded that the president had the authority to institute the blockade without a formal declaration of war.[87] On the second issue, Justice Grier concluded that seizure of cargos and ships owned by Confederate citizens, even those who did not support secession, was appropriate, since the term "enemy" according to admiralty law included any property moved by illegal means:

> Whether property be liable to capture as "enemies' property" does not in any manner depend on the personal allegiance of the owner. "It is the illegal traffic that stamps it as 'enemies' property.' It is of no consequence whether it belongs to an ally or a citizen. 8 Cr., 384. The owner, pro hac vice, is an enemy." 3 Wash. C.C.R., 183.[88]

Justice Grier concluded that "produce of the soil" from enemy territory was "enemy property" that could be seized. He concluded that only a portion of the cargo from *Crenshaw* owned by New York citizens was improperly seized during the fifteen-day grace period and should be returned to its owners. All other condemnations were affirmed.[89] Justice Nelson dissented in the case of the *Hiawatha*, believing that ship had been seized in the James River, its master having no intent to break the blockade.[90] He also challenged the majority's conclusion that the conflict between Union and Confederate forces was a war within the meaning of international law, since Congress did not issue a formal declaration of war.[91] Justice Nelson concluded that the president alone lacked the authority to declare war and that the seizures of the four vessels was illegal.[92]

The impact of the prize cases on suspension of civil liberties is not self-evident. By holding that a state of war rather than rebellion existed de facto between the Confederate States and the United States, the Court had supported the inference that the Civil War was subject to the international law of war. Therefore, any U.S. citizen who supported the Confederacy, a negotiated peace allowing the Confederacy to exist as a separate state on the North American continent, or doing anything that gave aid and comfort to the Confederacy was in fact acting treasonably. The Missouri trials by military commission routinely charged the defendant bushwhackers and bridge burners with treason. According to the U.S. Constitution, an allegation of treason had to be proved by the testimony of two eyewitnesses to the treasonable act. The military commissions did not always follow this rule. General Halleck disapproved of treason convictions by military commission in Missouri, stating that military commissions had no jurisdiction to try anyone for treason.[93]

Domestic suspension of civil liberties as a military necessity is consistent with the international law of war. The Constitution's division of authority over suspension of civil liberties, granting the power of suspension of habeas corpus to Congress but not forbidding the president to act as commander in chief in cases of military necessity, was resolved by the prize cases by sustaining the presidential blockade without congressional authority for the blockade.

The Habeas Corpus Act of 1863

In March 1863, Congress passed the habeas corpus act regularizing the suspension of the writ of habeas corpus in the United States.[94] The preamble stated that "during the present rebellion, the President of the United States, whenever, in his judgment, the public safety may require it, is authorized to suspend the privilege of the writ of habeas corpus in any case throughout the United States, or any part thereof."[95] The preamble also provided that any federal official could plead suspension of the writ in answer to any writ issues by any judge.[96] Section 2 of the act directed the secretaries of state and war to furnish a list of all persons held as prisoners of state in states "in which the administration of the laws has continued unimpaired"[97] to the district judge or circuit judge having jurisdiction over the prison or fort where the prisoners of state are held in confinement. The judge was directed to submit the names to the grand jury. If the grand jury failed to return an indictment against any prisoner, the prisoner would be discharged from custody. The judge could also require any prisoner who is discharged to post bond.[98] Section 4 allowed any government agent to raise a presidential order suspending the writ of habeas corpus an affirmative defense in any civil action brought by a prisoner of state for damages for false arrest, false imprisonment, or unlawful search and seizure. If the defendant pleaded the suspension of the writ, the court must dismiss the action. Section 5 permitted federal defendants to remove any such claim from state to federal court by filing a petition for removal in federal circuit or district court. Section 5 also permitted removal of writs of attachment associated with civil actions to federal court. The same section also carried a proviso that no appeal would lie from a judgment in favor of any defendant.[99] Section 7 placed a two-year statute of limitations on any civil action against any federal official for false imprisonment, any trespass, or wrongdoing.[100]

The habeas corpus act of 1863 immunized federal officials from liability for unlawful arrest, false imprisonment, or unlawful seizure of goods. The act also granted President Lincoln carte blanche for suspension of the writ of habeas corpus and, implicitly, any declaration of martial law made after the act had become law. The act did not validate any prior presidential suspension of habeas corpus or imposition of martial law. The commanders of military installations and prisons holding prisoners of state seldom complied with the provisions of section 2.[101] Judge Advocate General Holt held that the act's reporting provisions did not apply to men who were triable before a military commission.[102] The habeas corpus act of 1863 accomplished little more than ensuring that the president had the authority to suspend the writ and impose martial law in any part of the United States and insulating federal officials from civil liability for arrests, searches and seizures, confiscation of goods, and other measures designed to curb disloyalty. Meanwhile the state courts continued to issue writs of habeas corpus to military officials to discharge enlisted men who were underage or otherwise enlisted under false pretenses.

Ex Parte Vallandigham

Major General Ambrose E. Burnside had been the commanding general, Army of the Potomac, during the disastrous December 1862 Battle of Fredericksburg and the "mud march" of January 1863. Burnside was exiled to the Military District of Ohio, a peaceful backwater of the war. In April, Burnside issued General Order 38 pertaining to disloyal persons which promised that "declaring sympathies with the enemy will no longer be tolerated in this department. Persons committing such offenses will be at once arrested with a view to being tried [by military commission]."[103]

Burnside's department was the home base of anti-war Dayton congressman Clement L. Vallandigham, who made a fiery speech against the war in his home district in Ohio. General Burnside ordered Vallandigham arrested on May 2, 1863:

> On Tuesday morning last I caused the arrest of the Hon. C. L. Vallandigham. He is now in this city, undergoing trial before a military commission for uttering sedition. Some trouble was caused in Dayton on account of his arrest, but all is now quiet. I hope to maintain perfect order in other portions of this department. There is necessarily much

> excitement among his friends. We are all hoping to hear of the glorious and final success of General Hooker.[104]

Vallandigham was a very cagey politician: he allowed his supporters to spread rumors that he would file a petition for writ of habeas corpus in the Circuit Court of Ohio before Justice Noah G. Swain of the U.S. Supreme Court. Vallandigham was tried before a military commission in Cincinnati. He was charged with uttering disloyal remarks at the Mount Vernon rally against the government and inciting the population to resist Gen. Burnside's General Order 38.[105] Vallandigham disputed the jurisdiction of the commission. Nonetheless, the commission proceeded to try him, found him guilty, and sentenced Vallandigham to close confinement for the duration of the war. The incident was a political embarrassment to the Lincoln administration. Lincoln changed the sentence of confinement to banishment: Vallandigham was escorted to Confederate lines in Tennessee and turned over to the Confederacy.[106]

Vallandigham's lawyers file a habeas corpus petition with the U.S. Circuit Court for the Southern District of Ohio. Circuit Judge Leavitt held that Vallandigham's arrest was justified by military necessity and refused to issue the writ.[107] Vallandigham petitioned the U.S. Supreme Court for certiorari to challenge the jurisdiction of the military commission that convicted Vallandigham.[108] The certiorari petition was denied, even though trial of civilians by military commission was never authorized by Congress, let alone by the U.S. Constitution. Justice Wayne dodged the implications of Vallandigham's petition: that the Lincoln administration had instituted an unconstitutional system of military courts for civilian trials. Wayne examined the difference between the power of the English courts to issue writs of habeas corpus to free people unlawfully detained and the power to issue such writs granted by Article III of the U.S. Constitution and concluded that the U.S. Supreme Court had no power to issue a writ of habeas corpus to free a civilian held unlawfully by military authorities.[109]

Vallandigham eventually left the Confederacy for Canada on an outbound blockade runner where he instituted his 1863 campaign for the governorship of Ohio. Vallandigham won the Democratic nomination but lost the general election to a Republican.[110]

The Plan to Curb Copperheads and Draft Protesters

Secretary Stanton set out to develop a systematic plan for dealing with anti-war dissenters in the loyal Northern states. This was, he believed, necessary because the anti-war protesters would likely interfere with the direct draft of men from the states.

Prompt action was required because the United States was about to conduct a direct draft of men for the first time in U.S. history. Congress, acting on dubious constitutional grounds, passed the Enrollment Act of 1863 establishing a nationwide military presence.[111] Every congressional district had one or more provost marshals whose duty it was to supervise the draft. The provost marshal was enjoined to arrest deserters and enemy spies.[112] Section 24 of the Enrollment Act decreed that anyone who should "procure or entice, or attempt to procure or entice a soldier in the service of the United States to desert" was guilty of a felony.[113] Section 25 made a felon out of anyone who resisted the draft or counseled any drafted man not to appear for induction.[114] In both instances, the provost marshal was instructed to deliver these miscreants to the civil authorities for criminal prosecution.

Section 38 of the act opened up the prosecution of civilians by military authorities before military tribunals. It mandated that any person, during time of war, who "shall be found lurking or acting as spies, in or about any of the fortifications, posts, quarters or encampments of the United States, or elsewhere, shall be triable by a general court martial or military commission, and shall, upon conviction, suffer death."[115]

Secretary Stanton promptly appointed provost marshals for all congressional districts. The provost marshals became responsible for keeping a list of deserters who resided in their districts and thus put them in position to arrest the deserter and his family. The provost marshal's efforts were supplemented by detachments of soldiers who arrested suspected deserters and those who harbored them (e.g., their families) without obtaining an arrest warrant.

Draft resistance stiffened in June 1863, as the first day for selecting inductees approached. In July 1863, the first draft selection sparked riots throughout the Northeast, the most spectacular being the weeklong rampage in New York City, put down only with the assistance of combat troops sent from the field of Gettysburg. State judges complacently issued writs of habeas corpus to the provost marshal of the district demanding he bring newly inducted men before the state court to show cause why the man had been drafted.[116] President Lincoln would not put up with interference with the draft by state judges, although then-current legal authorities held that a state judge could issue a writ of habeas corpus to a federal official.[117] After a protracted discussion of the exact wording of the proclamation with his divided cabinet, President Lincoln issued a proclamation on September 15, 1863, suspending the writ of habeas corpus with respect to everyone serving in the military and all "prisoners of war, spies, and aiders or abettors" in U.S. custody.[118]

The Northern states began to experience military arrests of civilians without warrant and without preferring charges, much as the border state of Missouri had experienced it since 1861.[119] Civilians would be tried before military commissions rather than the U.S. District Court for whatever criminal acts the military thought were best punished by the military. Prior to mid-1863, the classes of civilians tried by military commission were limited to those engaged in guerilla activities, dishonest military contractors, and civilians employed by the army.[120] The Enrollment Act of 1863 added draft resisters, draft evaders, and those who counseled resistance to the draft to the groups that would be prosecuted by military commissions.[121] The best-known military trials of draft resisters occurred in Harrisburg, Pennsylvania, as a result of the "Fishing Creek Confederacy Conspiracy." Twenty-four eastern Pennsylvanians from Columbia County were tried by military commission for draft resistance. Fifteen were acquitted, and only three of the eight men convicted were sentenced to prison.[122]

Stanton's System for Controlling Dissenters

Stanton's system for controlling dissent in the final months of the war consisted of a nationwide chain of provost marshals reporting directly to his provost marshal general. First, the local provost marshals had statutory authority to arrest deserters and anyone who interfered with the draft. They also had authority to arrest persons suspected of disloyal activities without applying to a magistrate for a warrant. Second, the provost marshal could confine any disloyal person indefinitely without a hearing to let to bail before a magistrate and without charges being filed. Thousands of alleged disloyal citizens were arrested and confined in military prisons without any formal charges being preferred against them. Those who took the oath of allegiance were usually let go after posting a bond for good behavior.[123] Those who refused to take the oath were held until war's end. They were freed without any explanation for their detention.[124] Third, President Lincoln had suspended the power of U.S. judges to issue writs of habeas corpus to challenge the arrest. Fourth, any disloyal person whom the provost marshal believed was in fact guilty of disloyal activities would be tried before a military commission consisting of commissioned officers of the department. Trial by jury was not permitted. The verdict, judgment, and sentence of the military commission were reached according to the law of war (not according to U.S. criminal law and procedure), and punishment prescribed by the commission was not subject to judicial review by an independent judge. The president personally reserved the right to review all death sentences. Trial by military commission was a rare event outside of the border states of Kentucky and Missouri and conquered Southern territory. Neely found only 5 percent of all military commission trials were convened in the loyal Northern states.[125]

Justification

The Lincoln administration justified its policies as a matter of military necessity. Lincoln's best explanation of his motivation and of suppression of civil liberties occurs in a response to a letter signed by Erastus Corning and other anti-war Democrats in the spring of 1863. Lincoln explained to these people that the country was in a state of rebellion. Consequently, the provisions of the Constitution for suspension of habeas corpus were relevant to explain his actions.

> Ours is a case of Rebellion—so called by the resolutions before me—in fact, a clear, flagrant, and gigantic case of Rebellion; and the provision of the constitution that "The privilege of the writ of Habeas Corpus shall not be suspended, unless when in cases of Rebellion or Invasion, the public Safety may require it" is *the* provision which specially applies to our present case. This provision plainly attests the understanding of those who made the constitution that ordinary courts of justice are inadequate to "cases of Rebellion"—attests their purpose that in such cases, men may be held in custody whom the courts acting on ordinary rules, would discharge. Habeas Corpus, does not discharge men who are proved to be guilty of defined crime; and its suspension is allowed by the constitution on purpose that, men may be arrested and held, who cannot be proved to be guilty of defined crime, "when, in cases of Rebellion or Invasion the public Safety may require it." This is precisely our present case—a case of Rebellion, wherein the public Safety does require the suspension. Indeed, arrests by process of courts, and arrests in cases of rebellion, do not proceed altogether upon the same basis. The former is directed at the small percentage of ordinary and continuous perpetration of crime; while the latter is directed at sudden and extensive uprisings against the government, which, at most, will succeed or fail, in no great length of time. In the latter case, arrests are made, not so much for what has been done, as for what probably would be done. The latter is more for the preventive, and less for the vindictive, than the former. In such cases the purposes of men are much more easily understood, than in cases of ordinary crime. The man who stands by and says nothing, when the peril of his government is discussed, cannot be misunderstood. If not hindered, he is sure to help the enemy. Much more, if he talks ambiguously—talks for his country with "but" and "ifs" and "ands."[126]

Lincoln said that the Democrats' contention that military arrests were constitutional only in locations where the states were in rebellion was such that he could not see any distinction between the border states, the Southern Confederacy, and loyal Union states on the ground that arrests by military authorities without warrant were constitutional "wherever the public safety does require them, as well in places to which they may prevent the rebellion spreading . . . as well where they may restrain mischievous interference with the raising and supplying of armies."[127]

Lincoln's justification for his suppression of civil liberties included his explanation of the trial of Clement Vallandigham, Lincoln asserting that

> he was not arrested because he was damaging the political prospects of the administration, or the personal interests of the commanding general; but because he was damaging the army, upon the existence, and

> vigor of which, the life of the nation depends. He was warring upon the military; and this gave the military constitutional jurisdiction to lay hands upon him.[128]

Lincoln closed his letter with the phrase that heads this chapter, justifying his suspension of civil liberties. Lincoln cited no constitutional provision that supported his view, because none did. Lincoln was writing on a clean slate: he was explaining his decision to suspend civil liberties on the ground that as commander in chief, he was responsible for winning the war against the Confederacy.[129]

Lincoln's justification is not completely satisfactory. It stresses his view that winning the war is the ultimate justification of any measure that may be required to prevail against the Confederacy. Lincoln recognized no requirement that the means undertaken to achieve victory must be both proportionate to the end and lawful in themselves. He conceded that arrests without warrant or charges; incarceration without arraignment, bail, or trial by jury; and eventual trial by military commission were not lawful during peacetime, but Lincoln does not offer an explanation that justifies such extraordinary measures in peaceful Northern states not invaded by the Confederates.[130]

Suppression of the Press

In 1861, Secretary of State Seward appointed H. E. Thayer censor of telegraphic traffic in and out of Washington, D.C. Thayer was instructed to prevent the issue of all telegraphic messages from Washington relating to "'the civil or military operations of the government,' and it was understood that only a bare statement of the essential facts without extended comment would be allowed in the despatches."[131] In February 1862, the censorship of news was transferred from the Secretary of State's Office to the War Department. Secretary Stanton seized control of all telegraph lines in the United States shortly after assuming responsibility for censorship. Civilian telegraph companies willingly complied with Stanton's censorship directives.[132] The War Department's censorship program was marginally successful: frontline newspaper correspondents sent their copy to their home office by mail or by private courier to avoid censorship.[133]

According to David W. Bulla and Gregory A. Borchard, the Lincoln administration also suppressed more than three hundred newspapers considered disloyal during the period of Stanton's guidance.[134] Their list included the eleven Indiana newspapers suppressed by Brig. Gen. Milo Hascall, commanding general of the District of Indiana in the summer of 1863, for allegedly disloyal editorials and articles.[135] Major General Ambrose Burnside suppressed the anti-war *Chicago Times* in 1863. President Lincoln revoked Burnside's suppression order after one issue of the daily had been suppressed.[136] The U.S. War Department warned or suppressed a half dozen newspapers in 1863[137] and more than twenty newspapers in 1864.[138] Anti-war newspapers were often attacked and their presses destroyed by vigilante mobs.[139] In 1864, thirteen newspapers were wrecked by mobs.[140]

Democratic opponents accused Lincoln of using the suppression of civil liberties as a means of stifling opposition to the Lincoln administration, pointing to the high-profile case of arbitrary arrest of Congressman Vallandigham, editors of anti-administration newspapers, and the Camp Douglas conspirators, claiming that these men were simply anti-war Democrats who spoke out in mass meetings and in print about the evil of suppressing civil liberties.

The National Detective Police

Secretary Stanton also established a nationwide secret police, the National Detective Police, headed by Col. Lafayette Baker. Baker's men had nationwide authority to arrest and confine disloyal persons in Old Capitol Prison without charges for the duration of the war. Baker's detectives investigated claims relating to fraud upon the United States from 1862 through the end of hostilities. The National Detective Police also rounded up suspected Southern spies in the District of Columbia. Baker started his career as a civilian operative, then was commissioned as a provost marshal with the rank of captain of cavalry. Baker was promoted to colonel and later commissioned as a brigadier general of volunteers. Nominally, he was also the commanding officer of the 1st District of Columbia Cavalry Battalion. Baker was the principal agent behind the arrest and confinement of more than two hundred men and women believed to be implicated in the assassination of Lincoln in April–May 1865.[141]

The Statistics

The number of people arrested and detained from April 1861 to May 1865 is unclear. The *American Annual Encyclopaedia of Important Events of the Year 1865* cited the provost marshal general's records to support a figure of thirty-eight thousand military arrests during the war.[142] John A. Marshall's *American Bastille* estimated the number at "from ten to twenty thousand" in the original 1869 edition, according to Mark Neely, and raised the figure to "thirty thousand" in the 1885 revised edition.[143] The most commonly accepted figure, 13,535, was quoted by James G. Randall from a private War Department search made for him in the 1930s.[144] Neely challenged Randall's estimate after reviewing existing documents in the Turner–Baker papers held by the National Archives and not released to public review in 1951 when Randall completed his revised version of *Constitutional Problems of the Lincoln Administration*. Although Neely did not give his own estimate, he found records of 5,442 civilians arrested and imprisoned as prisoners of state in the Turner–Baker papers.

He noted that the provost marshal's files for Missouri listed 5,104 civilians arrested and incarcerated in the Gratiot Street prison in St. Louis. Neely found 2,331 persons tried by military commission outside of Missouri. He noted that records for Kentucky and Ohio's Camp Chase are missing. He concluded his analysis by asserting that the 13,535 arrests reported by Randall were far too low.[145]

Neely discovered records showing that 4,271 men were tried by military commission during the war.[146] Neely noted that the men tried by military commission included defaulting government contractors, pro-Confederate guerillas, draft evaders, and merchants.[147]

THE NORTHWEST CONSPIRACY: *EX PARTE MILLIGAN*

The Republican and Democratic Parties sponsored and used paramilitary organizations to break up rallies for the opposition and to protect their political events from the paramilitary organizations of the other side. During the 1860 election, the Republican Party had organized marching societies called the Wide Awakes to parade in support of Republican candidates throughout the North. The Wide Awakes were hardly military in organization or in character. They were replaced by 1862 by the Union League, a paramilitary organization that received military training and arms from state arsenals. The Indiana Union League supported Governor Oliver P. Morton's attempt to keep Indiana in the war in the face of a Democratically controlled Indiana General Assembly.[148] The anti-war pro-Confederate Democrats of the southern Midwest, had their own paramilitary force, consisting of members of a secret society called at various times the Knights of the Golden Circle, the Order of American Knights, and the Sons of Liberty.[149]

Partisan political violence characterized the 1862 congressional elections. Gangs of toughs broke up rival political meetings, and there were gun battles in Indiana and Illinois between Democrats and Republicans.[150] After the 1862 midterm congressional elections changed the political balance of power in the Illinois and Indiana state legislatures in favor of peace-at-any-price Democrats, Governor Yates of Illinois and Governor Morton of Indiana were moved to take action against Democratic acts of violence directed at Republicans. Since armed companies of Democrats were drilling and marching in order to protect the Democrats from pro-Republican armed gangs, the two governors, with the cooperation of the federal military commanders for the districts of Illinois and Indiana, began arming members of the Union League from state and federal arsenals to repel assaults by armed Democrats.[151]

The Democratic Party had two wings: "War" and "Anti-War." Antiwar Democrats were the dominant group in Ohio, Indiana, and Illinois because the lower half of these states had originally been settled by

Southerners, and Middle Western farmers had used the Ohio and Mississippi Rivers to ship their grain and hogs to market for thirty years before the war. The anti-war Democrats had been involved in the formation of secret societies, variously known as the Knights of the Golden Circle, the Order of American Knights, and the Sons of Liberty. These secret societies had been investigated by a state grand jury in Indiana and were said to have at least fifteen thousand members in the fall of 1862.[152] The Republican governors of Illinois and Indiana perceived these secret societies as threats to national security and to Republican control of the electoral process. Some action had to be taken to stop the growth of these groups.

In October 1864, the provost marshal for the Military District of Indiana arrested Lambdin Milligan, Samuel Bowles, and four other men suspected of conspiring to free Confederate prisoners at Camp Douglas in Chicago. The conspiracy involved funds sent in from Canada destined to buy arms for eight thousand Confederate prisoners of war in Camp Douglas, who would be freed by the Sons of Liberty during the Democratic National Convention. The plot was engineered by the Confederate Secret Service consisting of Clement C. Clay of Alabama, Jacob Thompson of Mississippi, and his aide Capt. Thomas Hines, a former member of Morgan's cavalry.[153] The Confederates enlisted Clement Vallandigham, the congressman-in-exile, who was living in Windsor, Ontario, and scheming to get back to Ohio to run for governor. Vallandigham contacted the state commanders of the Sons of Liberty from Illinois, Indiana, Ohio, Missouri, and New York who spent time with him in June 1864. The general plan was to create a Northwestern Confederacy of states that was neutral and would remain out of the fight. The state commanders were to organize armed bands to carry out the revolution against the central government. Vallandigham quickly bowed out as leader of the conspiracy, allowing the state commanders and the Confederate Secret Service to arrange the uprising.[154]

Harrison H. Dodd of Indianapolis was the strongest personality among the state commanders. The insurrection was planned to coincide with the Democratic National Convention in Chicago set for August 16, 1864. Confederate cavalry was positioned in western Kentucky to cooperate with the Sons of Liberty and to attempt to free Confederate prisoners of war.[155] The Confederate Secret Service supplied Dodd and his fellow state commanders with $75,000 to carry out the plan, which in its final phase was reduced to engineering a breakout of Confederate prisoners at Camp Douglas.[156]

Dodd enlisted other Hoosiers in the plan from the beginning. One of his most active helpers was Dr. William Bowles, proprietor of the French Lick Health Spa in southern Indiana. Bowles was involved in large-scale arms purchases made by the conspirators resulting crates of weapons being shipped to Dodd's office in Indianapolis. The August 29, 1864, deadline for the general uprising and prisoner freeing passed without a revolution; Confederate saboteurs started incendiary fires in Cairo, Illinois, and roamed about western Indiana probing for local support for the uprising. Union agent Felix Stidger had infiltrated the Sons of Liberty. He would be the government's star witness in the trial of the Northwest Conspirators. September waned, and in early October, U.S. authorities apprehended Andrew Humphrey in Sullivan County, Indiana. Swift military arrests brought in Dodd, Dr. Bowles, Lambdin Milligan, a Montgomery County lawyer, and many others. The U.S. military commander appointed a military commission to try William Bowles, Lambdin Milligan, Stephen Horsey, Andrew Humphreys, Horace Heffren, and J. J. Bingham in a seven-week-long state trial covered and given top billing by the national newspapers. Felix Stidger and other former Sons of Liberty gave testimony about the details of the conspiracy, the identification of its alleged membership, and the aid and comfort of the Confederacy to the conspirators. Predictably, the military commission sentenced all the convicted conspirators (there was no doubt that the commission would convict them all) to die.

Milligan's attorneys applied for a writ of habeas corpus from the Circuit Court of Indiana on the grounds that as the civil authorities were not overthrown and the civilian courts were in session, the military commission had no jurisdiction to try and convict Milligan. The circuit court issued a split decision, refusing to issue the writ. Under prevailing federal law, a split decision was automatically certifiable to the U.S. Supreme Court. The Court accepted the writ appeal in February 1866, and the case was immediately argued to the full Court.[157]

On April 3, 1866, the Court announced its decision. The majority ordered a writ of habeas corpus to be issued to the U.S. Army commanding general of the District of Indiana, freeing Milligan. Justice David Davis, Lincoln's 1860 campaign manager, an experienced trial lawyer and judge from Bloomington, Illinois, wrote the majority opinion. Justice Davis's approach to the Milligan case was strikingly different from Chief Justice Taney in *Merryman* and Justice Wayne in *Vallandigham*:

> The importance of the main question presented by this record cannot be overstated; for it involves the very framework of the government and the fundamental principles of American liberty. During the late wicked Rebellion, the temper of the times did not allow that calmness in deliberation and discussion so necessary to a correct conclusion of a purely judicial question. Then, considerations of safety were mingled with the exercise of power; and feelings and interests prevailed which are happily terminated. Now that the public safety is assured, this question, as well as all others, can be discussed and decided without passion or the admixture of any element not required to form a legal judgment. We approach the investigation of this case, fully sensible of the magnitude of the inquiry and the necessity of full and cautious deliberation.[158]

According to Davis, the Circuit Court for Indiana had jurisdiction under the Habeas Corpus Act of 1863 to grant a writ of habeas corpus and to certify any issue before it to the U.S. Supreme Court pertaining to the lawfulness of custody of any person detained by military authorities. He pointed out that Congress did not contemplate that men arrested by

Figure 2.2. Justice David Davis (Library of Congress).

military authorities would be held indefinitely, since the act provided that military authorities were to make lists of persons arrested and turn the cases over to the circuit courts of the United States for grand jury consideration of an indictment.[159] Justice Davis then dealt with the trial by military commission. Davis characterized trials by military commission as lacking almost all the safeguards of Article III of the U.S. Constitution and the Fifth and Sixth Amendments.[160]

> The controlling question in the case is this: Upon the facts stated in Milligan's petition, and the exhibits filed, had the military commission mentioned in its jurisdiction, legally, to try and sentence him? Milligan, not a resident of one of the rebellious states, or a prisoner of war, but a citizen of Indiana for twenty years past, and never in the military or naval service, is, while at his home, arrested by the military power of the United States, imprisoned, and, on certain criminal charges preferred against him, tried, convicted, and sentenced to be hanged by a military commission, organized under the direction of the military commander of the military district of Indiana. Had this tribunal the legal power and authority to try and punish this man?
>
> No graver question was ever considered by this court, nor one which more nearly concerns the rights of the whole people; for it is the birthright of every American citizen when charged with crime, to be tried and punished according to law. The power of punishment is, alone through the means which the laws have provided for that purpose, and if they are ineffectual, there is an immunity from punishment, no matter how great an offender the individual may be, or how much his crimes may have shocked the sense of justice of the country, or endangered its safety. By the protection of the law human rights are secured; withdraw that protection, and they are at the mercy of wicked rulers, or the clamor of an excited people. If there was law to justify this military trial, it is not our province to interfere; if there was not, it is our duty to declare the nullity of the whole proceedings.[161]

Justice Davis listed the Fifth and Sixth Amendment rights violated by the military when it tried Milligan by military commission. He noted that Milligan was deprived of an indictment by grand jury and of a speedy public trial by an impartial jury.[162] He ignored the U.S. solicitor general's argument that the military commission trials were justified by martial law due to the imminence of Confederate invasion or insurrection.

> It follows, from what has been said on this subject, that there are occasions when martial rule can be properly applied. If, in foreign invasion or civil war, the courts are actually closed, and it is impossible to administer criminal justice according to law, then, on the theatre of active military operations, where war really prevails, there is a necessity to furnish a substitute for the civil authority, thus overthrown, to preserve the safety of the army and society; and as no power is left but the military, it is allowed to govern by martial rule until the laws can have their free course. Because, during the late Rebellion it could have been

> enforced in Virginia, where the national authority was overturned and the courts driven out, it does not follow that it should obtain in Indiana, where that authority was never disputed, and justice was always administered. And so in the case of a foreign invasion, martial rule may become a necessity in one state, when, in another, it would be "mere lawless violence."[163]

Justice Davis held that so long as the civil courts were open for business, military commissions had no jurisdiction to hear such offenses.[164]

Chief Justice Chase wrote a minority opinion concurring in the result, but only to the extent that Congress had not authorized trial of the Northwest Conspirators by military commission.[165] Chase and his dissenting colleagues held that the Fifth and Sixth Amendments did not prevent Congress from authorizing trial of civilians engaged in treasonable acts by military commission. Chase said,

> We think that Congress had power, though not exercised, to authorize the military commission which was held in Indiana. It is not denied that the power to make rules for the government of the army and navy is a power to provide for trial and punishment by military courts without a jury. It has been so understood and exercised from the adoption of the Constitution to the present time.[166]

Chase declared that the Fifth Amendment did not restrict Congress's power to authorize trial by military commission because "cases arising in the land and naval forces, or in the militia in actual service in time of war are expressly excepted from the *fifth amendment.*"[167] Chase concluded that Congress failed to authorize trial of the Northwest Conspirators by military commission because it tacitly approved turning the conspirators over to the civil authorities for prosecution.[168] The rationale of Chase's dissent will resurface in the twenty-first century during the controversy over the Bush administration's development of rules for trial of alleged terrorists by military commission.[169]

The Lincoln Conspirators

While the case of Lambdin Milligan was pending before the Circuit Court of Indiana, President Lincoln was shot by John Wilkes Booth, supported by a conspiracy that reached from Washington across the Anacostia River into Charles County, Maryland. Within a week, seven alleged accomplices, Samuel Arnold, George Atzerodt, Dr. Samuel Mudd, Michael O'Laughlen, Lewis Paine (aka Lewis Powell), Edman Spangler, and Mrs. Mary Surratt were apprehended and lodged in the Old Capitol Prison. Shortly thereafter, Booth's faithful companion David Herold, son of a Washington Navy Yard employee, joined the others.

President Andrew Johnson appointed a military commission to try Booth's accomplices. The administration had concerns that had the seven been tried by a civilian court, some of them might be acquitted. The military commission's chairman, Maj. Gen. David Hunter, was the same individual who had guarded Lincoln's White House in April 1861. Hunter was the officer in charge of Lincoln's funeral and the journey taking Lincoln's remains to Springfield, Illinois, for burial. The other members of the commission were Maj. Gen. Lew Wallace, Maj. Gen. August Kautz, Brig. Gen. James Ekin, Brig. Gen. Robert S. Foster, Brig. Gen. Thomas M. Harris, Brig. Gen. Albion Howe, Col. Charles H. Tompkins, and Lt. Col. Daniel R. Clendenin.[170] Judge Advocate General Joseph H. Holt of Kentucky would be the government's chief trial counsel, assisted by Congressman John A. Bingham and Judge Advocate Henry Burnett.

The Hunter Commission was to try Booth's alleged accomplices for treason, conspiracy to murder President Lincoln, the attempted murder of Secretary of State Seward, and lying in wait to kill Vice President Andrew Johnson, Secretary of War Edwin Stanton, and Lt. Gen. Ulysses S. Grant. Clement C. Clay, William C. Cleary, President Jefferson Davis, George Harper, George N. Sanders, John Surratt, Jacob Thompson, Beverly Tucker, and George Young were listed as unindicted co-conspirators in the charges and specifications.[171]

The first sitting of the commission was on May 9, 1865. The commission received evidence up to June 30, 1865, when it retired for deliberation. The defendants were represented by counsel but were precluded by common law from taking the stand in their own behalf. The defense lawyers were a mixed lot. Mary Surratt's counsel, Senator Reverdy Johnson of Maryland, was assisted by his associates Frederick Aiken and John Clampit.[172] Senator Johnson withdrew as counsel in a huff just after proceedings commenced, leaving the very inexperienced Aiken and Clampit to fend for themselves as Mrs. Surratt's counsel. Former District of Columbia provost marshal William E. Doster represented Lewis Powell and George Atzerodt.[173] Frederick Stone tried to defend David Herold,[174] and Walter S. Cox was counsel for Sam Arnold and Michael O'Laughlen.[175] Brigadier General Thomas S. Ewing, one of the three famous Ewing brothers who were brothers-in-law to Maj. Gen. William T. Sherman, represented Dr. Mudd and Edman Spangler.[176]

The trial was held in the second story of the Washington Arsenal Penitentiary. The male prisoners were in shackles during the trial, although the protective hoods installed by the army over each prisoner's head were removed for trial. Three hundred seventy-one witnesses testified during the military commission trial. Benn Pittman prepared a shorthand transcript of each day's proceedings later published in *American State Trials*.[177] Other shorthand versions of the day's proceedings were published in the nation's newspapers, the most accurate being the question-and-answer transcript prepared by Ben Perley Poore.[178] The conspirators were convicted by the commission. Atzerodt, Herold, Powell, and Mrs. Surratt were sentenced to death; Arnold, Mudd, O'Laughlen, and Spangler were given long prison sentences eventually served out at Fort Jefferson, Dry Tortugas. President Johnson did not exercise his prerogative to commute Mrs. Surratt's sentence to avoid her death: the four sentenced to die were hanged in the Washington Arsenal Prison yard on a specially constructed four-bay scaffold.[179]

Within two years' time, the Hunter Commission's verdict and judgment was undone by the evidence that was received in the trial of John E. Surratt, one of the alleged conspirators, who had been hiding in the Papal States as a Papal Zouave until uncovered by a U.S. informer. Apprehended in Egypt after a near-miraculous escape from custody in Rome, Surratt was indicted by a U.S. grand jury in the District of Columbia and tried before a jury in the Supreme Court of the District of Columbia sitting as a criminal district court. The testimony of Sanford Conover, a self-appointed U.S. spy in Canada, had been one of the most important links in the conviction of the conspirators before the Hunter Commission. Despite information from Montreal and Toronto indicating that portions of Conover's testimony were perjurious, Holt believed in his witness and allowed the trial to continue after disclosure of Conover's perjury. Conover had connected Booth with the Confederate Secret Service and Jefferson Davis. Conover had testified to a secret meeting held in Ontario in late 1864 where Booth got his instructions from the Secret Service. Conover agreed to produce seven witnesses to the meeting that would implicate Clement Clay as the master of the assassination plot in Canada. In 1866, he brought down two of the seven supposed witnesses who turned out to be frauds whose stories had been written for them by Conover. Before the Surratt trial, this evidence was exposed as a complete fabrication, and Conover was indicted and convicted of perjury.[180] The jury could not agree on a verdict in the trial of John Surratt.[181] He was not retried, and he finished out his days as an obscure bookkeeper in Baltimore.

The Post-War Critique

In the 1870s, Rev. Isaac Handy, a Virginia Presbyterian preacher who had been imprisoned in Fort Delaware, published an autobiographical account of his imprisonment but avoided dealing with the larger issues.[182] In 1869, Democratic political publicist John A. Marshall published *American Bastille*, another collection of anecdotal accounts of individual experiences of some prisoners of state. It was also filled with virulent anti-Republican propaganda and was issued shortly before the Hayes-Tilden campaign. Again, Marshall made no attempt to explain the system of suspension of civil liberties and how it operated.

James Ford Rhodes, the premier Civil War historian of the nineteenth century, said little about the suspension of civil liberties. At the time he wrote *A History of the United States from the Compromise of 1850* in 1894, the subject of suspension of civil liberties was still sensitive, and some of those involved in that suspension were still living.

James G. Randall conducted a careful review of known sources in 1926 when writing *Constitutional Problems under Lincoln*[183] that dealt with the suppression of civil liberties by the Lincoln administration. Randall attempted to soften the impact of Lincoln's suspension of civil liberties. He acknowledged that suspension of habeas corpus, trial by military commission, and suppression of newspapers occurred but asserted that on the whole people arbitrarily arrested by the Union military authorities were fairly treated. Randall also praised the Supreme Court for the decision throwing out Lambdin Milligan's conviction by military commission and highlighted the other celebrity cases such as *Ex parte Merryman* and *Ex pane Vallandigham.*[184]

Frank Klement, who wrote the ultimate book debunking the existence of a Copperhead fifth column during the Civil War in the Midwest also contributed *The Limits of Dissent: Clement L. Vallandigham and the Civil War*[185] in which, in line with his thesis that there was no disloyal secret association out to derail the war effort, he decried Lincoln's support for Gen. Burnside's military commission that tried Vallandigham for conspiracy and sent him into exile into the Confederacy.

William Hanchett's *The Lincoln Conspiracies*[186] appeared in 1986. Doctor Hanchett intended to expose the weakness in the four major conspiracy theories that were put out by other authors to explain the assassination of Abraham Lincoln. Hanchett had to deal with the conspirators' trial by the Hunter Commission and the trial of John Surratt in 1867. Chapter 3 of his work dealt with the conspirators' trial and the disclosure in 1866 that the conspirators had been hanged on perjured testimony. Hanchett did not choose to comment on the suspension of civil liberties that permitted the conspirators to be tried by military commission. Chief Justice William Rehnquist followed Hanchett with his *All the Laws But One*[187] published in 1998. Relying on secondary source materials, the chief justice enunciated a theory of suspension of civil liberties consistent with Lincoln's own view in 1861: exigent circumstances warranted the suspension of civil liberties in time of war. Rehnquist surveyed the legal history of suppression of civil liberties from the time of the War between the States to World War II, justifying suspension of civil liberties by Lincoln, Wilson, and Franklin D. Roosevelt, despite serious adverse consequences. Thirteen chapters in his book were devoted to the legal history of Lincoln's suppression of civil liberties. He presented his view of the *Merryman* and *Vallandigham* decisions and somehow missed the vital fact that Sanford Conover's testimony was a collection of lies. The chief justice did not discuss the John Surratt trial and the fact that the Surratt jury could not reach a verdict against Surratt who was charged with being Booth's right-hand man in the assassination plot.

Mark Neely's *The Fate of Liberty*[188] won the Pulitzer Prize in 1992. Neely, curator of the Lincoln Museum in Fort Wayne, decided to find out if the Lincoln administration used suspension of civil liberties to persecute Democratic opponents of the war. Neely obtained the services of two graduate students to go to the National Archives and wade through the case files of prisoners of state and trials by military commission in the Old Wars Section. They read and digested one thousand cases which they believed broadly represented the more than 13,100 alleged Union prisoners of state.

Neely also personally read and examined the materials in the Turner–Baker microfilms, a series of letters between Judge Advocate General Turner and Col. Lafayette Baker, Lincoln's chief of security relating to disloyal persons. Baker had a partial list of prisoners of state held in the Old Capitol Penitentiary. The Turner–Baker papers also held records of trials by military commission not found elsewhere. Neely reexamined the reports of Missouri military commission trials that appear in the Official Record of the War of the Rebellion Series 11, Vol. 2, from 1861 to 1863.

No historian had made such an extensive examination of original source material pertaining to the suppression of civil liberties. Neely also gave a quick review of some major historians' viewpoints on the extent of military arrests of civilians and the number of trials by military commission that were contrary to his findings.

Neely came up with the following conclusions: The Lincoln administration arrested very few newspaper editors, politicians, or other dissenters. These cases received widespread publicity, and other historians greatly overstated the importance of these high-profile cases such as *Ex parte Milligan*, the Vallandigham episode, and the Camp Douglas Conspirators trials.[189]

The Lincoln administration suspended the writ of habeas corpus and tried civilians before military commissions principally in Missouri, where statewide Confederate guerrilla activities warranted severe measures to control insurrection.[190] Neely found evidence supporting the conclusion that the army conducted 4,271 trials by military commission, 55.5 percent of which were held in Missouri, Kentucky, and Maryland. More than 1,300 trials by military commission took place in occupied Confederate territory. Only a small number of trials by military commission were of the type of Vallandigham's trial in Cincinnati and the Northwest Conspirators trials in Indianapolis. The type of people arrested and tried by military commission consisted of marauding Confederate deserters, cotton speculators buying cotton without U.S. permits, and "blockade runners" who were smuggling contraband items to the Confederacy at great profit.[191]

Neely's third-largest group of military arrests and military commission trials came from Maryland and Kentucky and involved the same kind of individuals who were being arrested and tried in occupied territory: blockade runners.[192] The fourth major group of persons arrested and sometimes tried by military commission were advocates of draft resistance, to manage people who advocated draft resistance or draft evaders themselves, and against civilians who were smuggling goods and cash into the Confederacy. He believed that arbitrary arrest, suspension of habeas corpus, and trial by military commission were warranted as a means of controlling these kinds of activities, even though civilian courts were open and the North was invaded only four times during the war.[193]

According to Neely, *Ex parte Milligan* was irrelevant because it did not change the behavior of the U.S. government. The U.S. government continued to make military arrests of civilians and tried the offenders by military commission during Reconstruction for several years after the end of hostilities, despite Justice Davis's opinion that such conduct was unconstitutional when the civilian courts were open for business.[194]

CONCLUSION

Neely won the Pulitzer Prize in 1992, and the prize was well deserved. However, there are some disquieting notes in this work. Like so many historians, Neely falls into the fallacy of the ends justifying the means. The Lincoln administration faced the challenge of the United States splitting into two states, destroying the unity of the nation. In order to prevent destruction of the Union, Lincoln mobilized more than a million men to form an army and navy capable of coercing the Confederate states back into the Union. The means Lincoln chose and Congress ratified, ad hoc, as the situation changed included suppression of the free press, censorship, and arrests of civilians in the North thought to be disloyal without charges or judicial review. Lincoln asserted in his letter to Erastus Corning that the necessity of winning the war justified extraordinary means to quell anti-war, anti-administration journals and action groups such as the Sons of Liberty. Lincoln thought that the grave danger to the Union posed by Copperheads and draft resisters in the North and by guerrilla activity in the border states of Missouri and Kentucky justified suspending habeas corpus and disregarding the usual process of the criminal law, despite the clear provisions of the Habeas Corpus Act of 1863 requiring military officials to submit lists of prisoners of state to the appropriate U.S. circuit or district court for grand jury review for indictable offenses. Federal and state courts in the Northern states and in the border states were open, and routine prosecution of criminal offenders continued throughout the war. Neely correctly pointed out that the high-profile politically motivated arrests and trials of John Merryman, Clement Vallandigham, the Northwest Conspirators, and the Lincoln assassination conspirators were not representative of the usual kind of case tried by military commission. The Lincoln and Johnson administrations permitted these trials to be covered by the press, and their day-to-day reportage of the showcase trials validated the administration's resort to extreme measures to save the Union.

The fact that the high-profile cases are not statistically representative of the usual traffic of the program to suppress dissenters does not make them any less important. The U.S. Supreme Court put its seal of approval on trial by military commission in *Ex parte Vallandigham*. Chief Justice Taney's impotent rage at the executive in *Ex parte Merryman* showed that the Lincoln administration would not be bound by judicial review of its suspension of habeas corpus. Justice Davis's majority opinion in *Ex parte Milligan* left room for the suspension of civil liberties by the government in dicta indicating that there could be occasions when arrest without probable cause, incarceration without a bail hearing, and trial by military commission could be justified by exigent circumstances. The Lincoln administration's suppression of civil liberties spawned similar suppression of civil liberties by the Woodrow Wilson administration in an organized, deliberate program of suppression of dissent during World War I.

Few writers have understood just what the average American citizen lost during the Civil War when civil liberties were suspended. The military could arrest anyone it wanted to without any warrant or justification, search his person and belongings, throw him in prison, and never tell him what he was accused of doing that was criminal. If the military chose to try anyone for an offense against the nebulous "law of war," it could do so. It could deprive a citizen of the right to bail, to a grand jury indictment to support charges, and to a jury trial. The suppression of these rights and the waiver of the reasonable doubt rule for determining guilt made the risk of conviction and incarceration of innocent men and women much more likely than would be the case in a civilian court before a judge and jury. This observation was confirmed by the results in the trial of John Surratt in U.S. Circuit Court after the end of the war.

NOTES

1. Art. I, § 9, clause 2, describing the powers and duties of Congress, stated that "the privilege of the writ of habeas corpus shall not be suspended, unless when in cases of rebellion or invasion the public safety may require it." This clause indicated that the drafters of the 1787 constitution contemplated some curtailment of civil liberties during wartime.

2. See Charles E. Gayarré, William Beer, and Grace Elizabeth King, *History of Louisiana* (New Orleans: Pelican, 1905; repr. 1965), 602–615, for an account of the trial of Louvallier.

3. The story of Jackson's clash with Judge Duncan and his contempt citation comes from Zachary F. Smith, *The Battle of New Orleans, Including the Previous Engagements between the Americans and the British, the Indians, and the Spanish Which Led to the Final Conflict on the 8th of January, 1815*, Filson Club Publication 19 (Louisville, KY: John P. Morton, 1904), 145–146.

4. *Johnson v. Duncan*, 3 Mart. 530, 532–533 (LA, 1815).

5. Biographies of Alexander Arbuthnot and Richard Ambrister from Executed Today, last accessed Jan. 31, 2017, http://www.executedtoday.com/2008/04/29/1818-alexander-arbuthnot-Richard-ambrister-andrew-jackson-seminole-war.

6. Louis Fisher, "Military Commissions; Problems of Authority and Practice," *Boston University International Law Journal* 24, no. 1 (2006): 15–53.

7. 71 U.S. (4 Wall.) 2 (1866).

8. Alabama, Arkansas, Florida, Georgia, Louisiana, Mississippi, South Carolina, and Texas formed the original Confederate States of America at Montgomery in March 1861. Tennessee, North Carolina, and Virginia seceded after April 15, 1861. Although Missouri and Kentucky did not leave the Union, each state maintained a shadow government in exile that sent senators and representatives to the Confederate government.

9. "Journal of the Confederate Congress Friday Feb. 9, 1861," last accessed Jan. 31, 2017, http://memory.loc.gov/cgi-bin/query/r?ammem/hlaw:@field(DOCID+@lit(cc00110)).

10. Margaret Leech, *Reveille in Washington, 1860–1865* (New York: Harper, 1941).

11. William H. Rehnquist, *All the Laws but One: Civil Liberties in Wartime* (New York: Knopf, 1998), 17.

12. For background on Maryland's secession crisis, see Bradley T. Johnson, "Confederate Military History: Maryland," in *Confederate Military History: A Library of Confederate States History, in Twelve Volumes, Written by Distinguished Men of the South, and Edited by Gen. Clement. A. Evans of Georgia*, vol. 2, ed. Clement A. Evans (Atlanta, GA: Confederate Publishing, 1899; Secaucus, NJ: Blue & Grey Press, 1981), 22–27.

13. Johnson, "Confederate Military History: Maryland," 23. Johnson asserts that Gov. Thomas Hicks ordered Trimble to destroy the bridges.

14. Edward A. Miller Jr., *Lincoln's Abolitionist General* (Columbia: University of South Carolina Press, 1997), 54–57. See also Leech, *Reveille in Washington*, 71–73. Leech noted that Capt. Irvin McDowell also had a small detachment of regulars stationed at the capitol building, and DC militia had been mustered into service. Hunter's command consisted of the Frontier Battalion led by James G. Lane, an infamous Kansas jayhawker, and the Clay Battalion, led by Cassius M. Clay. The Frontier Guards went to the White House and the Clay Battalion remained at Willard's Hotel.

15. Mark E. Neely Jr., *The Fate of Liberty: Abraham Lincoln and Civil Liberties* (New York: Oxford University Press, 1991), 5.

16. Neely, *The Fate of Liberty*, 6–7.

17. Johnson, "Confederate Military History: Maryland," 20–22. See also "6th Massachusetts," last accessed Jan. 31, 2017, http://www.actonmemoriallibrary.org/civilwar/regiments/mass/6mvi.htm.

18. Leech, *Reveille in Washington*, 82.

19. Rehnquist, *All the Laws but One*, 25. Mark Neely quotes another version published by Roy P. Basler, the editor of *The Collected Works of Abraham Lincoln*, that describes the railroad route as the makeshift route through Perryville, Annapolis Junction, to Washington that bypassed the destroyed PW&B bridges in Harford County, Maryland. This more limited version was superseded by Seward's authorized version. See also John Sheldon Moody, Calvin Duvall Cowles, Frederick Caryton Ainsworth, Robert N. Scott, Henry Martyn Lazelle, George Breckenridge Davis, Leslie J. Perry, and Joseph William Kirkley, eds., *The War of the Rebellion: A Compilation of the Official Records of the Union and Confederate Armies*, series 2, vol. 1 (Washington, DC: Government Printing Office, 1880–1901), 567 (Abraham Lincoln to Winfield Scott), also known as *The Official Record of the War of the Rebellion*, hereafter "OR."

20. Joseph Story, *Commentary on the Constitution of the United States with a Preliminary Review of the Constitutional History of the Colonies and States before the Adoption of the Constitution*, 5th ed., vol. 3 (Boston: Willard, Gray; Cambridge, MA: Brown, Shattuck, 1833; Boston: Little, Brown, 1891), § 1342.

21. Although the writ existed before 1679, the English Habeas Corpus Act of 1679 authorized royal courts to issue the writ to test the legality of confinement.

22. Brian Farrell, "Habeas Corpus in Time of Emergency: A Historical and Comparative View," *Pace International Law Review Online Companion* (Apr. 2010), particularly 88–89, relating to President Lincoln's suspension of the writ.

23. Francis Lieber, "General Order 100 Instructions for the Government of Armies of the United States in the Field," Apr. 23, 1863, Sec. 1, Art. 4, defined *martial law* as "simply military authority exercised in accordance with the laws and usages of war." In Sec. 1, Art. 6, Lieber asserts that "all civil and penal law shall continue to take its usual course in the enemy's places and territories under Martial Law, unless interrupted or stopped by order of the occupying military power." Text taken from the Armed Forces Military Law Project, last accessed Jan. 31, 2017, http://au.af.mil/au/awcgate/law/liebercode.htm.yale.edu/19th_century/lieber.asp#sec1.

24. David Bodenhamer, *Fair Trial: Rights of the Accused in American History* (New York: Oxford University Press, 1992), 19. Bodehamer's list included the following:

1. No search or seizure without warrant.
2. Right to reasonable bail.
3. Confessions out of court invalid.
4. Right to have cause determined with reasonable speed.
5. Grand jury indictment in capital cases.
6. Right to know the charges.
7. Straightforward pleading with double jeopardy barred.
8. Right to challenge jurors.
9. Process to compel witnesses for the defense.
10. Right to confront accuser.
11. Trial by jury.
12. Limitation of punishment to the convict: no corruption of blood or forfeiture.
13. No cruel or unusual punishment.
14. Equal protection of the law: dependent classes—women, children, servants—have access to the courts.
15. Equal execution of the law: no capricious mitigation or application of penalties.
16. [Limited] Right of appeal.

25. "The right of the people to be secure in their persons . . . against unreasonable . . . seizures, shall not be violated, and no warrant shall issue but upon probable cause supported by Oath or affirmation." U.S. Const., Amend. IV. See also *Ex parte Burford*, 7 U.S. (3 Cr.) 448 (1806). For corresponding state constitutional provisions, see Alabama Const. 1819, Art. I, § 9; Arkansas Constitution, 1836 (none); California Const. 1849, Art. I, § 19; Connecticut Const. 1818, Art. I, § 8; Delaware Const. 1831, Art. I, § 6; Florida Const. 1838, Art. I, § 7; Georgia Const. (none); Illinois Const. 1848, Art. XIII, § 7; Indiana Const. 1851, Art. I, § 11; Iowa Const. 1857, § 8; Kansas Const. 1859, Bill of Rights (none); Kentucky Const. 1852, Art. XIII, § 11; Louisiana Const. 1852 (none); Maine Const. 1819, Art. I, § 5; Maryland Const. 1851, Art. XXIII (by implication); Massachusetts Const. 1780, Declaration of Rights, Art. XIV; Michigan Const. 1859, Art. III, § 26; Minnesota Const. 1857, Art. I, § 10; Mississippi Const. 1852, Art. I, § 9; Missouri Const. 1820, Art. XIII, § 13; New Hampshire Const. 1792, Art. I, § 19 (by implication); New Jersey Const. 1844, Art. I, § 6; New York Const. 1846 (none); North Carolina Const. 1776, Declaration of Rights, § 11; Ohio Const. 1851, Art. I, § 14; Oregon Const. 1857, Art. I, § 9; Pennsylvania Const. 1838, Art. IX, § 8; Rhode Island Const. 1842, Art. I, § 6; South Carolina Const. 1790 (none); Tennessee Const. 1834, Art. I, § 7; Texas Const. 1845, Art. I, § 7; Vermont Const. 1793, ch. 1, Art. XI; Virginia Const. 1851, Declaration of Rights, § 10. The law of arrest was summarized in William Blackstone, *Commentaries on the Laws of England: Treatise on Public Wrongs*, vol. 4 (1767; Boston: Beacon, 1962), 289–293.

26. See Bodenhamer, *Fair Trial: Rights of the Accused in American History*, 48–60.

27. "The right of the people to be secure in their persons, houses, papers, and effects, against unreasonable searches and seizures, shall not be violated, and no Warrants shall issue, but upon probable cause, supported by Oath or affirmation, and particularly describing the place to be searched, and the persons or things to be seized." U.S. Const., Amend. IV. For corresponding state constitutional provisions, see Alabama Const. 1819, Art. I, § 9; Arkansas Const. 1836 (none); California Const. 1849, Art. I, § 19; Connecticut Const. 1818, Art. I, § 8; Delaware Const. 1831, Art. I, § 6; Florida Const. 1838, Art. I, § 7; Georgia Const. 1798 (none); Illinois Const. 1848, Art. XIII, § 7; Indiana Const. 1851, Art. I, § 11; Iowa Const. 1857, § 8; Kansas Const. 1859, Bill of Rights (none); Kentucky Const. 1852, Art. XIII, § 11; Louisiana Const. 1852 (none); Maine Const. 1819, Art. I, § 5; Maryland Const. 1851, Art. 23 (by implication); Massachusetts Const. 1780, Declaration of Rights, Art. XIV; Michigan Const. 1859, Art. III, § 26; Minnesota Const. 1857, Art. I, § 10; Mississippi Const. 1852, Art. I, § 9; Missouri Const. 1820, Art. XIII, § 13; New Hampshire Const. 1792, Art. I, § 19 (by implication); New Jersey Const. 1844, Art. I, § 6; New York Const. 1846 (none); North Carolina Const. 1776, Declaration of Rights, § 11; Ohio Const. 1851, Art. I, § 14; Oregon Const. 1857, Art. I, § 9; Pennsylvania Const. 1838, Art. IX, § 8; Rhode Island Const. 1842, Art. I, § 6; South Carolina Const. 1790 (none); Tennessee Const. 1834, Art. I, § 7; Texas Const. 1845, Art. I, § 7; Vermont Const. 1793, ch. 1, Art. XI; Virginia Const. 1851, Declaration of Rights, § 10; Wisconsin Const. 1848, Art. I, § 11. The Massachusetts case of *Fisher v. Girr*, 67 Mass. 1, 31–32 (1854), overturned a civil judgment for defendants in a tort action against law enforcement officers for enforcing the liquor laws and conducting a search based on the statements of three witnesses, not resulting in a hearing before a disinterested magistrate. The Supreme Judicial Court of Massachusetts held that the non-judicial warrant was unconstitutional.

28. The U.S. Constitution did not specifically address the pre-conviction right to bail. Amend. VIII states that "excessive bail shall not be required," but the federal courts have consistently held that pre-trial detention and bail are included in the due process clause of Amend. V rather than the "excessive bail" requirement in Amend. VIII. See *Shah v. County of Los Angeles*, 797 F.2d 743 (9th Cir. 1986); *Meade v. Grubbs*, 841 F.2d 1512 (10th Cir. 1988). Most state constitutions contained a comprehensive bail provision in their bills of rights. See Alabama Const. 1819, Art. I, § 17; Arkansas Const. 1836, Art II., § 16; California Const. 1849, Art. I, § 7; Connecticut Const. 1818, Art. I, § 14; Delaware Const. 1831, Art. I, § 12; Florida Const. 1838, Art. I, § 11; Georgia Const. 1798 (none); Illinois Const. 1848, Art. XIII, § 10; Indiana Const. 1851, Art. I, § 17; Iowa Const. 1857 (none); Kansas Const. 1859, Bill of Rights, § 9; Kentucky Const. 1852, Art. XIII, § 18; Louisiana Const. 1852, Art. CIV; Maine Const. 1819, Art. I, § 10; Maryland Const. 1851 (none); Massachusetts Const. 1780, Declaration of Rights (none); Michigan Const. 1859 (none); Minnesota Const. 1857, Art. I, § 7; Mississippi Const. 1852, Art. I, § 17; Missouri Const. 1820, Art. XIII, § 11; New Hampshire Const. 1792 (none); New Jersey Const. 1844 (none); New York Const. 1846 (none); North Carolina Const. 1776, Declaration of Rights (none); Ohio Const. 1851, Art. I, § 9; Oregon Const. 1857 (none); Pennsylvania Const. 1838, Art. IX, § 14; Rhode Island Const. 1842, Art. I, § 9; South Carolina Const. 1790 (none); Tennessee Const. 1834, Art. I, § 15; Texas Const. 1845, Art. I, § 9; Vermont Const. 1793 (none); Virginia Const. 1851 (none); Wisconsin Const. 1848, Art. I, § 6.

29. "In all criminal prosecutions, the accused shall have the right to be informed of the nature and cause of the accusation." U.S. Const. Amend. VI. For corresponding state constitutional provisions, see Alabama Const. 1819, Art. I, § 10; Arkansas Const. 1836, Art. I, § 11; California Const. 1849 (none); Connecticut Const. 1818, Art. I, § 9; Delaware Const. 1831, Art. I, § 7; Florida Const. 1838, Art. I, § 10; Georgia Const. 1798 (none); Illinois Const. 1848, Art. XIII, § 9; Indiana Const. 1851, Art. I, § 13; Iowa Const. 1857, § 10; Kansas Const. 1859, Bill of Rights, § 10; Kentucky Const. 1852, Art. XIII, § 12; Louisiana Const. 1852 (none); Maine Const. 1819, Art. I, § 6; Maryland Const. 1851, Art. XIX; Massachusetts Const. 1780, Declaration of Rights, Art. XII (by implication); Michigan Const. 1859 (none); Minnesota Const. 1857, Art. I, § 6; Mississippi Const.

1852, Art. I, § 10; Missouri Const. 1820, Art. XIII, § 9; New Hampshire Const. 1792, Art. I, § 15; New Jersey Const. 1844, Art. I, § 8; New York Const. 1846 (none); North Carolina Const. 1776, Declaration of Rights, § 7; Ohio Const. 1851, Art. I, § 10; Oregon Const. 1857, Art. I, § 11; Pennsylvania Const. 1838, Art. IX, § 9; Rhode Island Const. 1842, Art. I, § 10; South Carolina Const. 1790 (none); Tennessee Const. 1834, Art. I, § 9; Texas Const. 1845 (none); Vermont Const. 1793, ch. 1, Art. X; Virginia Const. 1851, Declaration of Rights, § 8; Wisconsin Const. 1848, Art. I, § 7.

30. "The privilege of the writ of habeas corpus shall not be suspended, unless when in cases of rebellion or invasion the public safety may require it." U.S. Const. Art. II, § 9. For corresponding state constitutional provisions, see Alabama Const. 1819 (none); Arkansas Const. 1836 (none); California Const. 1849, Art. I, § 5; Connecticut Const. 1818 (none); Delaware Const. 1831, Art. I, § 13; Florida Const. 1838 (none); Georgia Const., 1798, Art. IV, § 9; Illinois Const. 1848 (none); Indiana Const. 1851, Art. I, § 27; Iowa Const. 1857 (none); Kansas Const. 1859, Bill of Rights, § 8; Kentucky Const. 1852 (none); Louisiana Const. 1852, Title VI, Art. CIII; Maine Const. 1819, Art. I, § 6; Maryland Const. 1851, Art. XIX; Massachusetts Const. 1780, Declaration of Rights, Art. XII (by implication); Michigan Const. 1859 (none); Minnesota Const. 1857, Art. I, § 6; Mississippi Const. 1852, Art. I, § 10; Missouri Const. 1820, Art. XIII, § 9; New Hampshire Const. 1792, Art. I, § 17 (by implication); New Jersey Const. 1844, Art. I, § 8; New York Const. 1846 (none); North Carolina Const., Declaration of Rights (none); Ohio Const. 1851, Art. I, § 10; Oregon Const. 1857, Art. I, § 11; Pennsylvania Const. 1838, Art. IX, § 9; Rhode Island Const. 1842, Art. I, § 10; South Carolina Const. 1790 (none); Tennessee Const. 1834, Art. I, § 9; Texas Const. 1845, Art. I, § 8; Vermont Const. 1793, ch. 1, Art. X; Virginia Const. 1851, Declaration of Rights, § 8; Wisconsin Const. (none). Most state constitutions made an exception for low-level offenses that could be heard by a justice of the peace.

31. "In all criminal prosecutions, the accused shall have the right to a speedy and public trial, by an impartial jury." U.S. Const. Amend. VI. For corresponding state constitutional provisions, see Alabama Const. 1819, Art. I, § 10; Arkansas Const. 1836, Art. I, § 11; California Const. 1849, Art. I, § 3; Connecticut Const. 1818, Art. I, § 9; Delaware Const. 1831, Art. I, § 7; Florida Const. 1838, Art. I, § 10; Georgia Const. 1798, Art. IV, § 5; Illinois Const. 1848, Art. XIII, § 9; Indiana Const. 1851, Art. I, § 13; Iowa Const. 1857, § 10; Kansas Const. 1859, Bill of Rights, § 10; Kentucky Const. 1852, Art. XIII, § 12; Louisiana Const. 1852, Title VI, Art. CIII; Maine Const. 1819, Art. I, § 6; Maryland Const. 1851, Art. 19; Massachusetts Const. 1780, Declaration of Rights (none); Michigan Const. 1859, Art. I, § 27; Minnesota Const. 1857, Art. I, § 6; Mississippi Const. 1852, Art. I, § 10; Missouri Const. 1820, Art. XIII, § 9; New Hampshire Const. 1792 (none); New Jersey Const. 1844, Art. I, § 8; New York Const. 1846 (none); North Carolina Const. Declaration of Rights, § 8; Ohio Const. 1851, Art. I, § 10; Oregon Const. 1857, Art. I, § 11; Pennsylvania Const. 1838, Art. IX, § 9; Rhode Island Const. 1842, Art. I, § 15; South Carolina Const. 1790, Art. IX, § 6; Tennessee Const. 1834, Art. I, § 9; Texas Const. 1845, Art. I, § 8; Vermont Const. 1793, ch. 1, Art. X; Virginia Const. 1851, Declaration of Rights, § 8; Wisconsin Const. 1848, Art. I, § 7.

32. "In all criminal prosecutions, the accused shall have the right to a speedy and public trial." U.S. Const. Amend. VI. For corresponding state constitutional provisions, see Alabama Const. 1819, Art. I, § 10; Arkansas Const. 1836, Art. I, § 11; California Const. 1849, Art. I, § 8 (by implication); Connecticut Const. 1818, Art. I, § 9; Delaware Const. 1831, Art. I, § 7; Florida Const. 1838, Art. I, § 10; Georgia Const. 1798 (none); Illinois Const. 1848, Art. XIII, § 9; Indiana Const. 1851, Art. I, § 13; Iowa Const. 1857, § 10; Kansas Const. 1859, Bill of Rights, § 10; Kentucky Const. 1852, Art. XIII, § 12; Louisiana Const. 1852, Title VI, Art. CIII; Maine Const. 1819, Art. I, § 6; Maryland Const. 1851, Art. 19; Massachusetts Const. 1780, Declaration of Rights, Art. XII (by implication); Michigan Const. 1859 (none); Minnesota Const. 1857, Art. I, § 6; Mississippi Const. 1852, Art. I, § 10; Missouri Const. 1820, Art. XIII, § 9; New Hampshire Const. 1792, Art. I, § 17 (by implication); New Jersey Const. 1844, Art. I, § 8; New York Const. 1846 (none); North Carolina Const. Declaration of Rights (none); Ohio Const.

1851, Art. I, § 10; Oregon Const. 1857, Art. I, § 11; Pennsylvania Const. 1838, Art. IX, § 9; Rhode Island Const. 1842, Art. I, § 10; South Carolina Const. 1790 (none); Tennessee Const. 1834, Art. I, § 9; Texas Const. 1845, Art. I, § 8; Vermont Const. 1793, ch. 1, Art. X; Virginia Const. 1851, Declaration of Rights, § 8; Wisconsin Const. 1848, Art. I, § 7.

33. David Rossman, "Criminal Law: 'Were There No Appeal'; The History of Review in American Criminal Courts," *Journal of Criminal Law & Criminology* 81 (1990): 518, 521–523.

34. U.S. Const. Amend. V.

35. For corresponding state constitutional provisions, see Alabama Const. 1819, Art. I, § 10; Arkansas Const. 1836, Art. I, § 10; California Const. 1849, Art. I, § 8; Connecticut Const. 1818, Art. I, § 9; Delaware Const. 1831, Art. I, § 7; Florida Const. 1838, Art. I, § 8; Georgia Const. 1798 (none); Illinois Const. 1848, Art. XIII, § 8; Indiana Const. 1851, Art. I, § 12; Iowa Const. 1857 (none); Kansas Const. 1859 (none); Kentucky Const. 1852, Art. XIII, § 12; Louisiana Const. 1852 (none); Maine Const. 1819, Art. I, § 6; Maryland Const. 1851, Art. XXI; Massachusetts Const. 1780, Declaration of Rights, Art. XII; Michigan Const. 1859, Art. III, § 32; Minnesota Const. 1857, Art. I, § 7; Mississippi Const. 1832, Art. I, § 10; Missouri Const. 1820, Art. XIII, § 9; New Hampshire Const. 1792, Art. I, § 15; New Jersey Const. 1844 (none); New York Const. 1846, Art. I, § 6; North Carolina Const., Declaration of Rights, Art. XII; Ohio Const. 1851, Art. I, § 10; Oregon Const. 1857, Art. I, § 10; Pennsylvania Const. 1838, Art. IX, § 9; Rhode Island Const. 1842, Art. I, § 10; South Carolina Const. 1790, Art. IX, § 2; Tennessee Const. 1834, Art. I, § 8; Texas Const. 1845, Art. I, § 16; Vermont Const. 1793, ch. 1, Art. X; Virginia Const. 1851, Declaration of Rights, § 8; Wisconsin Const. 148, Art. I, § 9.

36. See Neely, *The Fate of Liberty*, 84–86 (cotton traders, blockade runners), 86–90 (Confederate deserters), 94–105 (selling liquor to soldiers, fraud on the government).

37. For a good discussion of the State Department's management of suspension of habeas corpus, see James G. Randall, *Constitutional Problems under Lincoln*, 2nd ed. (Champaign-Urbana: University of Illinois Press, 1956 [1926]), 149–151.

38. The executive order may be found in Neely, *The Fate of Liberty*, 9–10.

39. Many years after the end of the war, the truth about bridge burning in Maryland came out. Governor Hicks feared another outbreak of mob violence like that which occurred when the 6th Massachusetts crossed Baltimore between the PW&B and Camden railroad stations. He had a conference with militia colonel Isaac Trimble, the outcome of which was an expedition led by Trimble to burn the PW&B bridges over Gunpowder Falls. This, Hicks thought, would discourage troop trains from passing through Baltimore and provoking another riot. See George L. P. Radcliffe, *Governor Thomas H. Hicks of Maryland and the Civil War* (Baltimore, MD: Johns Hopkins University Studies in Historical and Political Science, 1901), 56–57.

40. *Ex parte Merryman*, 17 F. Cas. 144 (C.Ct. Md. 1861).

41. *Ex parte Merryman*, 148.

42. *Ex parte Merryman*, 151–152.

43. *Ex parte Merryman*, 151.

44. Roy E. Basler, ed., *Collected Works of Abraham Lincoln*, vol. 4 (New Brunswick, NJ: Rutgers University Press, 1953), 449 (July 4, 1861).

45. Neely, *The Fate of Liberty*, 15–17.

46. Frederick A. Bancroft, *The Life of William A. Seward*, vol. 2 (New York: Harper, 1899), 276–277.

47. See, e.g., OR series 1, vol. 7, 654 (West Tennessee per John A. Rawlins AAG, Feb. 22, 1862); OR series 1, vol. 8, 547 (G.O. 17 Dept. of Kansas: entire state of Kansas); OR series 1, vol. 9, 561 (Proclamation for New Mexico by Col. James H. Carleton, 1st Cal. Vol. Cav. June 15, 1862, see also OR series 1, vol. 50 [part 1], 96); OR series 1, vol. 9, 680 (E. R. S. Canby to J. Chivington, martial law in New Mexico, dated June 27, 1862); OR series 1, vol. 50 (part 1), 96 (Col. James Carlton to E. R. S. Canby, dated June 15, 1862 [Arizona Territory]); OR series 1, vol. 50 (part 2), 49 (dated Aug. 4, 1862, amending previous order for Arizona); OR series 1, vol. 11 (part 2), 77 (Proclamation for Yorktown and vicinity by Maj. Gen Geo. B. McClellan, dated Apr. 1, 1862); OR series 1, vol.

14 (part 1) (G. O. 11 Dept. of the South declaring martial law in Florida, Georgia, and South Carolina, dated May 9, 1862); OR series 1, vol. 1 (part 2), 173 (Lt. Col. John Faskin to Maj. Gen. John E. Wool Baltimore placing Point of Rocks, MD, under martial law, dated Sept. 3, 1862); OR series 1, vol. 22 (part 2), 226 (G.O. 10 Dist. of Kansas, dated Apr. 18, 1862, martial law abolished for Leavenworth, Kansas); OR series 1, vol. 22 (part 2), 388 (Brig. Gen. Thomas Ewing to Lt. Col. C. W. Marsh AAG, dated July 22, 1863); OR series 1, vol. 47 (part 3), 623 (G.O. 22 Dist of Fla., dated May 24, 1865 [Jacksonville, FL]). Martial law was also declared for Round Valley California, due to a Native American uprising in November 1862. See OR series 1, vol. 50 (part 2), 218 (Proclamation, dated Nov. 10, 1862). Martial law was revoked for Round Valley on Feb. 11, 1863, OR series 1, vol. 50 (part 2), 310.

48. OR series 2, vol. 2, 40 (Proclamation of Aug. 8, 1861, Dept. of New Mexico).

49. OR series 2, vol. 2, 119–120 (Benjamin Hall to the President of the United States, Oct. 26, 1861).

50. OR series 1, vol. 48 (part 1), 763 (G.O. 10 Dist. Colorado, dated Feb. 6, 1865).

51. Neely, *The Fate of Liberty*, 32–33.

52. Neely, *The Fate of Liberty*, 33–34.

53. OR series 2, vol. 1, 221 (Proclamation of Martial Law, Dept. of Missouri, dated Aug. 30, 1861); OR series 2, vol. 2, 155 (G.O. 34, dated Dec. 26, 1861). See also OR series 2, vol. 2, 230 (Maj. Gen. Henry W. Halleck to Maj. Gen. George B. McClellan, Nov. 20, 1861); Abraham Lincoln to Maj. Gen. George B. McClellan, Nov. 21, 1861 (authorizing declaration of martial law in Missouri); OR series 1, vol. 8, 468 (G.O. 36, Dec. 26, 1861, all railroads in state of Missouri). See also OR series 2, vol. 1, 155 (G.O. 34 Dept. Of Missouri, dated Dec. 26, 1861) (same); OR series 2, vol. 1, 270 (G.O. 2 Dept. of the Mississippi, dated Mar. 13, 1862). Martial law in Missouri was terminated in 1865 piecemeal. See OR series 1, vol. 48 (part 2), 66 (Brig. Gen. C. Fiske to Maj. Gen. G. Dodge terminating martial law in district of northern Missouri, dated Apr. 10, 1865).

54. OR series 2, vol. 22 (part 2), 546 (G.O. 96 Dept. of the Missouri, dated Sept. 17, 1863).

55. OR series 1, vol. 41 (part 1) (G.O. 54 Dept. of Kansas, dated Oct. 10, 1864); OR series 1, vol. 41 (part 4), 118 (G.F.O. 6 Army of the Border, dated Oct. 19, 1864, Lafayette Co., MO).

56. OR series 1, vol. 52 (part 1), 277 (G.F.O. 2 Dept. of the Ohio, dated Sept. 2, 1862, Jefferson Co., KY); OR series 1, vol. 52 (part 1), 277 (Proclamation dated Sept. 5, 1861, Cincinnati, Louisville, and Covington); OR series 1, vol. 52 (part 1), 344 (G.O. 26 Dist. Cent. Ky., dated Mar. 25, 1863 (Fayette, Clark, Jessamine, Woolford, and Franklin Co. east of river; revoked Apr. 4, 1863, per G.O. 27 Dist of Cent. Ky., OR series 1, vol. 52 [part 1], 349); OR series 1, vol. 23 (part 2), 572 (G.O. 120 Dept. Of Ohio, dated July 31, 1863 [entire state of Kentucky declared under martial law]).

57. OR series 1, vol. 39 (part 2), 180 (G.O. 233 War Dept., dated July 19, 1864).

58. OR series 1, vol. 49 (part 2), 1116 (G.O. 149, dated Oct. 14, 1865).

59. OR series 1, vol. 27 (part 3), 437 (orders with attached proclamation, dated June 30, 1863).

60. OR series 1, vol. 27 (part 3), 504 (Proclamation of martial law, dated July 3, 1863).

61. OR series 1, vol. 37 (part 1), 375 (Maj. Gen. Lew Wallace to E. D. Townsend, dated May 3, 1864).

62. OR series 1, vol. 37 (part 2), 219 (S. B. Lawrence AAG 8th Corps to Col. A. R. Root, dated July 11, 1864).

63. OR series 2, vol. 4, 154 (Col. W. Hoffman, Comm. Gen. Prisoners, to Col. J. H. Tucker, dated July 8, 1862).

64. OR series 1, vol. 23 (part 1), 753 (Maj. Gen. A. Burnside to Col. P. McKinney, July 15, 1863, Portsmouth, OH); OR series 1, vol. 23 (part 1), 672 (Portsmouth, OH, report of Col. Peter Kinney, dated July 29, 1863); OR series 1, vol. 23 (part 1), 740 (Proclamation of Martial Law Butler Co., OH, dated July 13, 1863); OR series 1, vol. 23, 745 (G.O. 114 Dept. of Ohio, martial law declared in Cincinnati, Covington, and Newport, revoked S.O. 267 Dept. of Ohio, dated July 15, 1863, OR series 1, vol. 52 [part 1], 411).

65. OR series 1, vol. 26 (Brig. Gen. N. J. T. Dana to Brig. Gen. C. P. Stone, dated Dec. 11, 1863).

66. OR series 1, vol. 39 (part 1), 53 (Maj. T. H. Reeves to Lt. P.S. Abbott, dated July 20, 1864).

67. OR series 1, vol. 12, 438 (Gideon Welles to Flag Off. DuPont, dated Dec. 28, 1861). The navy also put St. Augustine, Florida, under martial law in April 1862. OR series 1, vol. 12, 753.

68. OR series 3, vol. 2, 587 (G.O. 141 War Dept., dated Sept. 25, 1862).

69. OR series 3, vol. 2, 587 (G.O. 141 War Dept., dated Sept. 25, 1862).

70. Neely, *The Fate of Liberty*, 45–47.

71. See OR series 2, vol. 2, 778–786 (Case of Howard and Glenn of the Baltimore Exchange newspaper).

72. Other journalists arrested pursuant to Seward's order include J. R. and F. D. Flanders of Malone, New York. OR series 2, vol. 2, 69. Seward ordered the suspension of U.S. mail delivery of the *Louisville Courier* in September 1861. OR series 2, vol. 2, 70 (William H. Seward to Montgomery Blair, dated Sept. 17, 1861). Secretary of War Cameron corresponded with the U.S. marshal for the District of Connecticut, instructing him to stop the circulation of the *New York Daily News* throughout Connecticut. Marshal David H. Carr complied with Cameron's order. OR series 2, vol. 2, 60 (David H. Carr to Simon Cameron, Sept. 11, 1861).

73. "Congress shall make no law abridging the freedom of speech, or of the press." U.S. Const. Amend. I. For comparable state constitutional provisions re freedom of the press, see Alabama Const. 1819, Art. I, § 8; Arkansas Const. 1836, Art. I, § 7; California Const. 1849, Art. I, § 9; Connecticut Const. 1818, Art. I, § 5; Delaware Const. 1831, Art. I, § 5; Florida Const. 1838, Art. I, § 5; Georgia Const. 1798, Art. IV, § 5; Illinois Const. 1848, Art. XIII, § 23; Indiana Const. 1851, Art. I, § 9; Iowa Const. 1857, Art. I, § 7; Kansas Const. 1859, Bill of Rights, § 11; Kentucky Const. 1852, Art. XIII, § 9; Louisiana Const. 1852, Title VI, Art. CVI; Maine Const. 1819, Art. I, § 4; Maryland Const. 1851, Art. XXXVIII; Massachusetts Const. 1780, Declaration of Rights, Art. XVI; Michigan Const. 1859, Art. II, § 42; Minnesota Const. 1857, Art. I, § 3; Mississippi Const. 1852, Art. I, § 6; Missouri Const. 1820, Art. XIII, § 16; New Hampshire Const. 1792, part 1, § 22; New Jersey Const. 1844, Art. I, § 5; New York Const. 1846, Art. I, § 8; North Carolina Const., Declaration of Rights, § 15; Ohio Const. 1851, Art. I, § 11; Oregon Const. 1857, Art. I, § 8; Pennsylvania Const. 1838, Art. IX, § 7; Rhode Island Const. 1842, Art. I, § 20; South Carolina Const. 1798 (none); Tennessee Const. 1834, Art. I, § 19; Texas Const. 1845, Art. I, § 5; Vermont Const. 1793, ch. 1, Art. XIII; Virginia Const. 1851, Declaration of Rights, § 12. While the First Amendment expressly limited congressional action to suppress free speech, such as the infamous Alien and Sedition Acts, the president and the executive department were not expressly limited by the Constitution. Prior to 1861, no president nor any member of the executive branch had attempted to put allegedly disloyal newspapers out of circulation.

74. OR series 2, vol. 2, 221–222 (Feb. 14, 1862).

75. OR series 2, vol. 4, 158–159 (Aug. 8, 1862).

76. OR series 2, vol. 4, 358.

77. Abraham Lincoln: "Proclamation 94—Suspending the Writ of Habeas Corpus," September 24, 1862; made available online by Gerhard Peters and John T. Woolley, The American Presidency Project, last accessed Jan. 31, 2017, http://www.presidency.ucsb.edu/ws/?pid'69783&st=8&st=.

78. Emmerich de Vattel, *The Law of Nations or the Principles of Natural Law in Four Books*, trans. Joseph Chitty (Philadelphia: 1858 [1758, 1833]), vol. 3, § 66, at 381–389. See also Vattel, *Law of Nations*, vol. 3, § 70.

79. See Vattel, *Law of Nations*, vol. 3, §§ 111–113.

80. For a good discussion of Civil War U.S. Navy recruiting practices, see Denis J. Ringle, *Mr. Lincoln's Navy* (Annapolis, MD: U.S. Naval Institute Press, 1998), 10–16.

81. *The Brig Amy Warwick* et al., 67 U.S. 635, 665–666 (1863).

82. *The Brig Amy Warwick*, 67 U.S. 668.

83. *The Brig Amy Warwick*, 67 U.S. 667. For the full text of this analysis, see Vattel, *The Law of Nations*, vol. 3, § 293.
84. *The Brig Amy Warwick*, 67 U.S. 667–668.
85. *The Brig Amy Warwick*, 67 U.S. 669.
86. *The Brig Amy Warwick*, 67 U.S. 670.
87. *The Brig Amy Warwick*, 67 U.S. 670–671.
88. *The Brig Amy Warwick*, 67 U.S. 675. Justice Grier was on sound international law grounds in asserting this proposition. See Vattel, *The Law of Nations*, vol. 3, § 70.
89. *The Brig Amy Warwick*, 67 U.S. 674–675 (Warwick), 675–677 (Hiawatha), 677–680 (Brilliante), 680–682 (Crenshaw).
90. *The Brig Amy Warwick*, at 684–686.
91. *The Brig Amy Warwick*, 688–691.
92. *The Brig Amy Warwick*, 697–699. Justice Nelson also characterized Congress's Aug. 6, 1862, act confirming and ratifying all of President Lincoln's proclamations and orders after March 4, 1861, as amounting to an unconstitutional ex post facto law. *The Brig Amy Warwick*, 697–698.
93. OR series 2, vol. 1, 405 (G.O. 20 Dept. of Missouri, dated Jan. 14, 1862, review of military commission Case of George Cunningham by direction of Gen. Halleck, J. R. Keaton, AAG). This represents Gen. Halleck's interpretation of Maj. Gen. John C. Fremont's G.O. 6 issued Aug. 30, 1861, preceded by Fremont's proclamation that contains the following language relating to treason: "All persons engaged in treasonable correspondence, in giving or procuring aid to the enemies of the United States, in fomenting tumults, in disturbing the public tranquility by creating and circulating false reports or incendiary documents, are in their own interest warned that they are exposing themselves to sudden and severe punishment." See OR series 1, vol. 1, 467–468.
94. 12 Stats. at Large, ch. 80, 755–758 (1863).
95. 12 Stats. at Large, ch. 80, 755–758.
96. 12 Stats. at Large, ch. 80, 755–758.
97. 12 Stats. at Large, ch. 80, 755–758, § 2.
98. 12 Stats. at Large, ch. 80, 755–758, § 2.
99. 12 Stats. at Large, ch. 80, 755–758, § 5.
100. 12 Stats. at Large, ch. 80, 755–758, § 7.
101. Randall, *Constitutional Problems under Lincoln*, 164–166.
102. Randall, *Constitutional Problems under Lincoln*, 167.
103. OR series 1, vol. 23/2, 237 (Apr. 14, 1863).
104. OR series 1, vol. 13/2, 135–316 (Burnside to Stanton, May 7, 1863).
105. *Ex parte Vallandigham*, 68 U.S. 243, 3–4 (preface by Wallace).
106. Rehnquist, *All the Laws but One*, 67.
107. *Ex parte Vallandigham*, 28 F. Cas. 874 (Cir. Ct. S.D. Ohio 1863).
108. *Ex parte Vallandigham*, 68 U.S. (1 Wall.) 243 (1863).
109. *Ex parte Vallandigham*, 68 U.S. 248–251. Justice Wayne said that Congress had granted appellate power to the U.S. Supreme Court, and Congress made no provision for the U.S. Supreme Court to review the action of a military commission because such a body was not a court. Wayne acknowledged that Congress had given the Court extraordinary writ power by section 14 of the Judiciary Act of 1789, but he denied that such writs could be issued against a military commission because it was not a court. By such specious reasoning, the face of the Court was saved.
110. See Rev. James L. Vallandigham, *The Life of Clement L. Vallandigham* (Baltimore, MD: Turnbull, 1872), for an uncritical biography by Vallandigham's brother. The best modern biography of Vallandigham is Frank L. Klement, *The Limits of Dissent: Clement L. Vallandigham and the Civil War* (New York: Fordham University Press, 1998).
111. 12 Stat. at Large, ch. 74 (1863).
112. 12 Stat. at Large, ch. 74, §§ 4–5, 7.
113. 12 Stat. at Large, ch. 74, § 24.
114. 114. 12 Stat. at Large, ch. 74, § 25.

115. 12 Stat. at Large, ch. 74, § 38.

116. See the discussion of state judges issuing writs of habeas corpus to federal military officers in Randall, *Constitutional Problems under Lincoln*, 428–432.

117. For relevant state case law see, e.g., *Wantlan v. White*, 19 Ind. 470 (1862), held: habeas corpus is appropriate remedy to free underage minor from military custody; *Commonwealth ex rel. Bressler versus Gane*, 3 Grant 447, 450 (Pa. 1863), held: federal suspension of habeas does not apply to states, writ to recover a soldier issued by state judge not blocked by federal law; *Commonwealth ex rel. M'Lain v. Wright*, 3 Grant 437, 446 (Pa. 1863), to same effect; but see *In re Spangler*, 11 Mich. 298, 308–309 (1863), held: habeas corpus will not lie to free a recruit from service state court deprived of jurisdiction by Act of Congress; *Ex parte Anderson*, 16 Iowa 595, 599 (1864), held: writ cannot be issued to free minor who enlisted under age, then deserted: he must first face court-martial for desertion then pursue habeas remedy; *In re Gregg*, 15 Wis. 479, 481 (1862), held: habeas corpus will not lie to free a minor over eighteen from military service against the wishes of his parent.

118. Basler, *Collected Works of Abraham Lincoln*, vol. 6, 451–452.

119. See Neely, *The Fate of Liberty*, 32–50.

120. Neely, *The Fate of Liberty*, 162–168.

121. Armed bands of draft resisters challenged the enrollers in Hancock County, Illinois, in June 1863. They visited the enrollers and threatened them with violent harm if they proceeded to enroll men for the draft. A Fulton County draft enroller was also threatened with retribution if he continued his work. In Shelby County, an armed band seized the enrollment records. In Olney, a mob of five hundred men made the enrollers stop their work by force. See Robert E. Sterling, *Civil War Draft Resistance in the Midwest* (De Kalb: Northern Illinois University Press, 1977), 255–258. No draft resisters were tried by military commission.

122. Sterling, *Civil War Draft Resistance*, 174. See also Arnold Shankman, "Draft Resistance in Civil War Pennsylvania," *Pennsylvania Magazine of History and Biography* 101 (1977): 190, for an extended account of Pennsylvania draft resisters and their activities in 1863–1865. Draft enrollers were murdered in Lancaster County. The Pennsylvania Supreme Court held the Enrollment Act of 1863 as unconstitutional and issued a preliminary injunction against the provost marshals and draft enrollers conducting the draft in Pennsylvania in *Kneedler v. Lane*, 45 Pa. 238 (1863). Several months later, one of the justices of the supreme court who had supported the injunction retired, and his replacement was a strong Unionist. The supreme court reversed itself and dissolved the injunction. See *Kneedler v. Lane*, 3 Grant 523 (Pa. 1864). In 1864, another trial by military commission was staged for a group of anti-war men in Cambria County. Three of the group were convicted; the rest were discharged from custody. Shankman, "Draft Resistance in Civil War Pennsylvania," 203.

123. Randall, *Constitutional Problems under Lincoln*, 156–157.

124. Randall, *Constitutional Problems under Lincoln*, 93–94.

125. Neely, *The Fate of Liberty*, 173.

126. Abraham Lincoln to Erastus Corning et al., dated June 12, 1863, OR series 2, vol. 6, serial 119, 8.

127. Abraham Lincoln to Erastus Corning, OR series 2, vol. 6, serial 119, 8.

128. Abraham Lincoln to Erastus Corning, OR series 2, vol. 6, serial 119, 8.

129. Abraham Lincoln to Erastus Corning, OR series 2, vol. 6, serial 119, 8.

130. Lincoln's ethics appear to be consequentialist—that is, the rightness or wrongness of any act or inaction is to be determined by the consequences of the act and not by any external standard. This ethical stance particularly appeals to many Americans. It is also the moral philosophy expounded by Jeremy Bentham and John Stuart Mill.

131. James G. Randall, "The Newspaper Problem in Its Bearing upon Military Secrecy during the Civil War," *American Historical Review* 23, no. 2 (1918): 303–304.

132. Randall, "The Newspaper Problem," 305.

133. Randall, "The Newspaper Problem," 306.

134. David W. Bulla and Gregory A. Borchard, *Journalism during the Civil War* (New York: Peter Lang, 2010), 159–160.
135. See the biographic sketch of Gen. Hascall in Ezra Warner, *Generals in Blue* (Baton Rouge: Louisiana State University Press, 1964), 213. David W. Bulla and Justyna Sempruch, *Lincoln's Censor Milo Hascall and Freedom of the Press in Civil War Indiana* (West Lafayette, IN: Purdue University Press, 2008), presents a complete picture of the suppression of Indiana Democratic newspapers.
136. Randall, *Constitutional Problems under Lincoln*, 321.
137. This list of newspapers suppressed by War Department orders is taken from D. Appleton and Co., eds., *The American Annual Cyclopaedia and Register of Important Events of the Year 1863* (New York: D. Appleton, 1864), 423–424.
138. This list of newspapers warned or suppressed by the War Department in 1864 is taken from D. Appleton and Co., eds., *The American Annual Cyclopaedia and Register of Important Events of the Year 1864* (New York: D. Appleton, 1865), 393–394.
139. This list of newspapers destroyed by mob violence in 1863 is taken from D. Appleton and Co., eds., *The American Annual Cyclopaedia and Register of Important Events of the Year 1863* (New York: D. Appleton, 1864), 423–424.
140. This list of newspapers destroyed by mob violence in 1864 is taken from D. Appleton and Co., eds., *The American Annual Cyclopaedia and Register of Important Events of the Year 1864* (New York: D. Appleton, 1865), 393–394.
141. See C. Wyatt Evans, "Lafayette Baker and Security in the Civil War North," *North & South: The Official Magazine of the Civil War Society* 11, no. 44, last accessed Jan. 31, 2017, http://connection.ebhost.com/c/articles/41525734/lafayette-baker-security-civil-war-north.
142. D. Appleton & Co., eds., *The American Annual Encyclopaedia and Register of Important Events of the Year 1865* (New York: D. Appleton, 1864; vol. 5, 1866), 414, cited in Neely, *The Fate of Liberty*, 113.
143. Neely, *The Fate of Liberty*, 114.
144. Neely, *The Fate of Liberty*, 115–116.
145. Neely, *The Fate of Liberty*, 118–133.
146. Neely, *The Fate of Liberty*, 129.
147. Neely, *The Fate of Liberty*, 167–173.
148. Gilbert Tredway, *Democratic Opposition to the Lincoln Administration in Indiana* (Indianapolis: Indiana Hist. Bureau, 1973), 122–125.
149. Tredway, *Democratic Opposition*, 124–131.
150. Tredway, *Democratic Opposition*, 71–80.
151. Tredway, *Democratic Opposition*, 122–124.
152. Tredway, *Democratic Opposition*, 115–117. The grand jury report lumped the Democratic Mutual Protection Societies with the alleged disloyal Order of American Knights.
153. Tredway, *Democratic Opposition*, 177–179.
154. Tredway, *Democratic Opposition*, 179.
155. Tredway, *Democratic Opposition*, 183.
156. Tredway, *Democratic Opposition*, 187–188.
157. Rehnquist, *All the Laws but One*, 117.
158. *Ex parte Milligan*, 71 U.S. (4 Wall.) 2, 109 (1866).
159. *Ex parte Milligan*, 71 U.S. 115–116.
160. *Ex parte Milligan*, 71 U.S. 119.
161. *Ex parte Milligan*, 71 U.S. 118–119.
162. *Ex parte Milligan*, 71 U.S. 122–123.
163. *Ex parte Milligan*, 71 U.S. 127.
164. *Ex parte Milligan*, 71 U.S. 127.
165. *Ex parte Milligan*, 71 U.S. 134–135. Justices Wayne, Swayne, and Miller joined the chief justice's partial dissent.
166. *Ex parte Milligan*, 71 U.S. 136–137.
167. *Ex parte Milligan*, 71 U.S. 137.

168. *Ex parte Milligan*, 71 U.S. 139.
169. See ch. 7.
170. The commission posed for a group picture with Holt and Bingham after the trial. See William C. Davis, ed., *The Images of War*, vol. 6 (New York: Doubleday, 1984), 377.
171. Rehnquist, *All the Laws but One*, 146–147.
172. Ben Perley Poore, *The Conspiracy Trial for the Murder of the President, and the Attempt to Overthrow the Government by the Assassination of Its Principal Officers, Edited with an Introduction by Ben Perley Poore*, vol. 1 (Boston: J. Tilton, 1865), 20.
173. Poore, *The Conspiracy Trial*, vol. 1, 20; Rehnquist, *All the Laws but One*, 156.
174. Poore, *The Conspiracy Trial*, vol. 1, 20.
175. Poore, *The Conspiracy Trial*, vol. 1, 20.
176. Dorothy Meserve Kunhardt and Philip B. Kunhardt Jr., *Twenty Days: A Narrative in Text and Pictures of the Assassination of Abraham Lincoln* (New York: Harper & Row, 1965; Career Press, 1985), 194.
177. John D. Lawson, ed., *American State Trials*, vol. 8 (St. Louis, MO: F. H. Thomas Law Books, 1914–1936), 25–656.
178. Poore, *The Conspiracy Trial*, vol. 1, 20; Meserve Kunhardt and Kunhardt, *Twenty Days*, 195.
179. Meserve Kunhardt and Kunhardt, *Twenty Days*, 179, 195, 203–205. Poore, *The Conspiracy Trial*, vol. 1, 20.
180. Hanchett, *The Lincoln Conspiracies*, 80–81.
181. For a full account of John Surratt's trial, see John D. Lawson, ed., *American State Trials*, vol. 9, 1–336.
182. Isaac W. P. Handy, *U.S. Bonds or Duress by Federal Authorities* (Baltimore, MD: Turnbull, 1874), was an account by a Union prisoner of state of fifteen months spent in Fort Delaware and futile attempts to gain release without taking a loyalty oath to the Union government. Although Handy tells stories about other prisoners of state and why they were confined, he does not talk about the suspension of civil liberties as a system.
183. Champaign-Urbana: University of Illinois Press, 1926.
184. James C. Randall's *Constitutional Problems under Lincoln* (1926) was the first systematic explanation of suspension of civil liberties during the Civil War. Randall dealt with suspension of habeas corpus and the famous cases *Ex parte Merryman* and *Ex parte Vallandigham*, mentioning the effect of trial of civilians by military commissions and *Ex parte Milligan*, as well as the Hunter Commission and the Lincoln conspirators. However, the general operation of the system as a means of controlling the civilian population was hinted at but not explained.
185. Fordham University Press, 1970.
186. 186. Champaign-Urbana: University of Illinois Press, 1986.
187. New York: Knopf, 1998.
188. New York: Oxford University Press, 1992.
189. "The only large group of arrests that appeared in any way to resemble what most Democrats complained about at the time, the sort that really disturbed historians and civil libertarians, were those that followed the August 8, 1862, orders. And those were sincerely meant to enforce conscription rather than stifle dissent, which explains their relaxation in one month's time after most draft quotas had been filled." Neely, *The Fate of Liberty*, 232–234.
190. Neely, *The Fate of Liberty*, 168–169.
191. Neely, *The Fate of Liberty*, 78–92, 168–169.
192. Neely, *The Fate of Liberty*, 75–77.
193. Neely, *The Fate of Liberty*, 170–171.
194. Neely, *The Fate of Liberty*, 175–184.

THREE

Wilson's War on Anti-War Protesters

> "There are citizens of the United States, I blush to admit, born under other flags but welcomed under our generous naturalization laws to the full freedom and opportunity of America, who have poured the poison of disloyalty into the very arteries of our national life. . . . Such creatures of passion, disloyalty and anarchy must be crushed out. . . . The hand of our power should close over them at once."
> —Woodrow Wilson, Third Annual Message to Congress, 1915

World War I began in late July 1914. President Woodrow Wilson issued his neutrality proclamation on August 2, 1914. Three weeks later, Wilson released his "Appeal to the American People" in a message to the Senate on August 19. Wilson asked the American people to "be neutral in fact as well as in name" and "impartial in thought as well as in action."[1]

THE UNITED STATES IS DRAWN INTO WAR

The United States remained neutral from August 1914 to April 1917. U.S. firms did business with Imperial Germany, England, France, Italy, and the Russian Empire. Most of the durable goods sold to the combatants were shipped aboard vessels belonging to the belligerents.

U.S. shipping carried a significant amount of war materials, however, under neutrality laws. Neutral vessels were not to be stopped, boarded, or sunk by the belligerents.

In April 1915, the German navy issued an ultimatum printed in the *New York Times* warning all passengers on British ships that these ships were liable to be sunk as an act of war.

> Notice! Travellers intending to embark on the Atlantic voyage are reminded that a state of war exists between Germany and her allies and Great Britain and her allies; that the zone of war includes the waters

> adjacent to the British Isles; that, in accordance with formal notice given by the Imperial German Government, vessels flying the flag of Great Britain, or any of her allies, are liable to destruction in those waters and that travellers sailing in the war zone on the ships of Great Britain or her allies do so at their own risk. Imperial German Embassy, Washington, D.C., April 22, 1915.[2]

The notice appeared shortly before the RMS *Lusitania* departed from New York for Queenstown and London. On May 6, 1915, U-20 sank the *Lusitania* carrying 1,959 souls, 1,265 passengers and 694 crew. One thousand one hundred ninety-five men and women drowned. One hundred twenty-eight American citizens died in the disaster.[3] President Wilson sent three notes to the German Empire condemning the sinking of unarmed passenger liners, trumpeting a call for freedom of the seas. The third note stated that any sinking of U.S. vessels would have serious consequences.[4] Germany backed away from its promise to sink passenger ships for more than a year before it returned to its old ways, drawing another message to Congress from President Wilson demanding protection for neutral citizens.[5]

Initially, President Wilson was an advocate for U.S. neutrality. He opposed the "Preparedness Movement" supported by pro-Allied Republicans (e.g., ex-president Theodore Roosevelt, Henry Stimson, and Gen. Leonard Wood, the chief of staff of the U.S. Army). After the sinking of the *Lusitania,* Roosevelt and his colleagues argued for increasing the size of the U.S. Army by instituting universal military training. The Preparedness Movement lobbied for an annual draft of six hundred thousand men for six months' military training followed by a reserve obligation. The Preparedness Movement also wanted to do away with the National Guard and replace it with a very large reserve force. This would require congressional action. Wilson opposed this program. In the spring of 1916, he made a national speaking tour advocating a buildup of the U.S. Navy equal to that of the Royal Navy. Wilson also advocated doubling the size of the regular army and increasing National Guard authorized strength to 440,000 by 1921.[6]

Woodrow Wilson ran for reelection on an anti-war platform in 1916. He won a narrow victory over Republican candidate Charles Evans Hughes.[7] On January 31, 1917, the German government announced that it would resume unrestricted submarine warfare, sinking any vessel under any flag heading for England, France, or Italy as of February 1, 1917.[8] President Wilson immediately severed all diplomatic relationships with Germany. Meanwhile, German foreign secretary Count Arthur Zimmerman sent a telegram to Heinrich von Eckardt, his ambassador to Mexico, before unrestricted submarine warfare would resume on February 1, 1917. Zimmerman instructed Eckardt to approach the Mexican government with a proposal for a Germano–Mexican alliance that would open a "third front" on the border of Mexico and the United States.

Zimmerman promised that if an attack on the United States was successful, Mexico would recover possession of Texas, New Mexico, and Arizona. Zimmerman also instructed Eckardt to urge Mexico to facilitate an alliance between Germany and the Japanese Empire. Mexico took no action on Zimmerman's proposed alliance and officially rejected the offer after the United States entered the war.[9]

President Wilson regarded the Zimmerman telegram as the last straw. He addressed Congress on April 2, 1917. Wilson said,

> The present German warfare against commerce is a warfare against mankind. It is a war against all nations. American ships have been sunk, American lives taken, in ways which it has stirred us very deeply to learn of, but the ships and people of other neutral and friendly nations have been sunk and overwhelmed in the waters in the same way. There has been no discrimination. The challenge is to all mankind. Each nation must decide for itself how it will meet it. The choice we make for ourselves must be made with a moderation of counsel and a temperateness of judgment befitting our character and our motives as a nation. We must put excited feeling away.
>
> Our motive will not be revenge or the victorious assertion of the physical might of the nation, but only the vindication of right, of human right, of which we are only a single champion.
>
> When I addressed the Congress on the 26th of February last I thought that it would suffice to assert our neutral rights with arms, our right to use the seas against unlawful interference, our right to keep our people safe against unlawful violence. But armed neutrality, it now appears, is impracticable. Because submarines are in effect outlaws when used as the German submarines have been used against merchant shipping, it is impossible to defend ships against their attacks as the law of nations has assumed that merchantmen would defend themselves against privateers or cruisers, visible craft giving chase upon the open sea.
>
> It is common prudence in such circumstances, grim necessity, indeed, to endeavor to destroy them before they have shown their own intention. They must be dealt with upon sight, if dealt with at all.
>
> The German Government denies the right of neutrals to use arms at all within the areas of the sea which it has proscribed, even in the defense of rights which no modern publicist has ever before questioned their right to defend. The intimation is conveyed that the armed guards which we have placed on our merchant-ships will be treated as beyond the pale of law and subject to be dealt with as pirates would be.[10]

Congress voted overwhelmingly to declare war on the Central Powers. There were dissenters. Progressive Republican senator Robert La Follette of Wisconsin was one of six senators who voted against the war. There was opposition in the House as well. Fifty representatives including Majority Leader Claude Kitchin and Rep. Jeanette Rankin voted against the declaration of war.[11]

Figure 3.1. Woodrow Wilson (Pach Bros., Library of Congress).

THE WILSON ADMINISTRATION'S PROGRAM TO SUPPRESS DISSENT

President Wilson, Congress, Secretary of War Newton Baker, Postmaster General Albert Burleson and Federal Bureau of Justice Chief A. Bruce Bielaski helped to devise a nationwide program to manage anti-war dissent. Wilson promoted suppression of those hyphenated Americans who might have ties to Germany and Austria-Hungary through his speeches and through the Committee on Public Information.

The Creel Commission

Wilson established the Committee on Public Information on April 13, 1917, by executive order. He appointed George Creel, a Colorado newspaper reporter, chairman. The committee consisted of Creel, Secretary of State Robert Lansing, Secretary of War Newton Baker, and Secretary of the Navy Josephus Daniels as ex officio members.[12] The Committee on Public Information, usually referred to as the Creel Committee, was responsible for creating a favorable public relations campaign for entering the war on the Allied side. The committee used newsprint, posters, radio, telegraph, cable, and movies to broadcast its message. It recruited about seventy-five thousand "Four Minute Men," volunteers who spoke about the war at social events for no longer than four minutes. Creel Committee experts considered that the average human attention span was no more than four minutes. The Four Minute Men's prepared talking points included the virtue of the draft, why food was rationed, the need to support the war bond drives, why citizens should plant victory gardens, and why America was fighting. Creel estimated that by the end of the war, the Four Minute Men gave more than 7.5 million speeches to 314 million people in 5,200 communities. The Four Minute Men were told to keep their message positive, always use their own words, and avoid "hymns of hate."

For ten days in May 1917, the Four Minute Men were expected to promote "Universal Service by Selective Draft" in advance of national draft registration on June 5, 1917. The high voluntary percentage of compliance with the Selective Service law can be attributed to the Creel Committee's successful propaganda efforts.[13]

At its apogee in 1918, the Creel Committee had over twenty staff sections working in Washington, D.C., and in nine overseas offices. The committee's news division produced a daily newspaper, the *Official Bulletin*, that circulated stories about U.S. and Allied heroism and German cruelty to newspapers in the United States. Copies of the *Official Bulletin* were also sent to all U.S. Army and Navy installations, government agencies, and every U.S. post office.[14]

The Poster Division allowed the publication of a crude image of slavering apelike German soldiers carrying a languishing female in its left hand labeled "Destroy this Mad Brute."[15] The division used the talents of Charles Dana Gibson and James Montgomery Flagg to design pro-Allied and anti-German posters. Flagg produced a poster derived from a British recruiting poster showing Lord Kitchener beckoning to the viewer, substituting Uncle Sam for Kitchener and using a similar slogan, "I Want

You for the U.S. Army," to spur recruiting. The purpose of the poster campaign was to provide a visual image of the German Empire as evil, and by association any pro-German sentiment as support for the evil empire, and to portray the Allied case as just and U.S. participation in the war as morally justified.

The Motion Picture Division produced feature-length propaganda films such as *Pershing's Crusaders* (May 1918), *America's Answer (to the Hun)* (August 1918), and *Under Four Flags* (November 1918). The Motion Picture Division used snippets of frontline footage that were considerably less sensational than Hollywood's depiction of life in the trenches. U.S. soldiers were portrayed as well fed, rested, and eager to fight the Hun.[16]

The Creel Committee "voluntary guidelines" for newspapers, magazines, and motion pictures worked as de facto censorship regulations. Reporters and moviemakers would not have access to official press releases and news conferences unless their parent companies followed the guidelines. The committee also produced propaganda in support of passage of the Espionage Act of 1917 and the Sedition Act of 1918. The committee officially opposed censorship, going on record that the media was free to publish anything on the war.[17] However, George Creel acknowledged that his voluntary guidelines were effective censorship devices in a letter to President Wilson in 1918.[18] The Creel Committee effectively curtailed anti-war news articles and editorials in the mainstream press and virtually shut off Socialist publications such as *Appeal to Reason* from publishing its anti-war and anti-business articles.

Another committee division produced events targeting recent immigrants from Ireland, Italy, and Poland. These events featured ethnic entertainers and speeches on how to be a good American by buying bonds and otherwise supporting the war effort.[19]

The committee's propaganda efforts were attacked by members of Congress and the media for spreading disinformation. Early in its existence, the committee generated a statement to be released by Secretary of the Navy Daniels describing a supposed attack on a U.S. convoy by several submarines, at least one of which was allegedly sunk by U.S. warships guarding the convoy. According to reliable eyewitnesses, only one submarine was sighted. It fired three or four torpedoes at a merchant ship, but the torpedoes missed the target. Several days later another convoy's escorts sank a U-boat. The statement combined the two events into a single day's action to increase the dramatic appeal of the United States' anti-submarine warfare tactics.[20] In March 1918, the Creel Committee was accused of exaggerating and distorting the number of U.S. aircraft produced by the infant U.S. aircraft industry. Senator Bois Penrose of Pennsylvania attacked the committee press release which stated that the United States had shipped hundreds of aircraft to France. The bitter truth was that the United States had sent over only one airplane.[21] These accusations are a small sampling of the U.S. media's attempts to discredit the Creel Committee. Despite repeated charges of exaggeration and downright lying to the public, the committee continued to conduct voluntary censoring of newspaper and magazine stories, plastering factories with pro-war posters, and sending its Four Minute Men out to justify the U.S. war effort.

During the Civil War, the Lincoln administration had sporadically attempted to control newspapers that were deemed disloyal. In 1863–1864, the War Department closed a number of anti-war newspapers. In World War I, the Wilson administration's campaign to enforce conformity to the war effort included an organized, meticulous pro-Allies, anti-German stream of propaganda designed to communicate the president's dislike and contempt for Germany and Austria-Hungary. De facto news censorship helped to control the anti-war press by denying access to government briefings to journals that would not follow the guidelines. By implication, the committee contributed to the prevailing domestic anti-German immigrant feelings that eventually encouraged vigilante acts committed by U.S. citizens against those suspected of disloyalty to the war effort.

The committee began to wind down its propaganda machine in July 1918. It ceased issuing press releases and other propaganda when the Armistice was signed. Although the committee continued to occupy office space, it no longer had any raison d'être. President Wilson terminated the committee on August 21, 1919, by Executive Order 3154.[22]

The Espionage Act of 1917

Lobbying the Congress for passage of the Espionage Act of 1917 was one of the early successful public relations programs of the Creel Committee. In 1915, the president called for extensive revision of then-existing statutes relating to espionage after the *Lusitania* incident. President Wilson's draft bill, prepared by the staff of the Department of Justice in 1915, proposed a form of press censorship that would allow the president to appoint an executive branch bureau to censor newspapers, magazines, and motion pictures. The Senate, controlled by the Democrats, passed Wilson's bill virtually unchanged on February 20, 1916. The Wilson administration was criticized by Hearst newspaper columnist Arthur Brisbane,[23] who wrote to the president asking if the proposed legislation would shield the president from criticism by the press. Wilson replied, "I can imagine no greater disservice to the country than to establish a system of censorship that would deny to the people of a free republic like ours their indisputable right to their own public officials."[24] Despite his fine words, President Wilson did not withdraw the censorship title from the bill.

Joseph Tumulty, Wilson's private secretary, urged Wilson to drop the press censorship provisions from the act because many people believed that the act was "really a gigantic machine, erected for the despotic control of the press."[25] Tumulty was a 1901 graduate of St. Peter's College who was elected as a Democrat to the New Jersey General Assembly in 1907. When Wilson ran for governor of New Jersey in 1910, Tumulty was one of his small circle of advisors. Wilson made Tumulty his private secretary (equivalent to today's White House chief of staff) in 1913. Tumulty tried to persuade President Wilson to postpone his marriage to Edith Bolling Galt, Wilson's second wife, until after the 1916 elections. Tumulty made an enemy of Edith Wilson, who objected to his presence in the White House because he was a Catholic. Col. Edward M. House, Wilson's advisor who had living quarters in the White House, also urged Wilson to sack Tumulty, which Wilson did. David Lawrence, a Princeton alumni and Wilson's former student, intervened and saved Tumulty's job for the balance of Wilson's second term.[26]

Wilson entered into a negotiating session with Senate and House leaders leading to a compromise bill version that had no express censorship provisions. The House passed the version without press censorship powers. The Senate quickly followed suit, and the bill became law on June 15, 1917. The Espionage Act was intended to replace the Defense Secrets Act of 1911. The main provisions in Title I of the act established heavy fines and long prison terms for any person convicted of obtaining confidential information on U.S. military bases, troops, weapons, warships, aircraft, and troop dispositions who transmitted those secrets to anyone. Title II authorized the secretary of the treasury, at that time the person responsible for management of the U.S. Coast Guard, to establish safe anchorages for vessels and to have the authority to manage the movement of vessels and to inspect vessels for contraband. Section 2 established a felony punishable by a fine of up to $10,000 and imprisonment up to two years for any ship captain or master who refused to obey an order to anchor or to submit to search ordered by the Treasury Department.[27] Title III established a felony punishable by a fine of up to $10,000 and imprisonment up to twenty years for burning a foreign flag vessel or its cargo.[28] Title IV established a felony punishable by a $10,000 fine and imprisonment for up to ten years for the obstruction of or destruction of goods intended to be exported to another nation.[29] Title V provided that during a war in which the United States was neutral, the United States could detain goods destined for any belligerent and seize ships built for any belligerent. Section 6 of Title V established a felony punishable by a fine up to $10,000 and imprisonment up to five years for anyone who attempted to take an armed vessel out of port to be turned over to one of the belligerents. Section 7 of Title V also provided for a felony punishable by a fine of up to $1,000 and imprisonment up to one year for any person who was interned as an agent or citizens of a belligerent nation who escaped from internment.[30]

Title VI established the right of the United States to seize arms and munitions on probable cause that the arms and munitions were destined to a foreign hostile nation.[31] Title VII covered unlawful exports to belligerent nations. Sections 1 and 2 established a felony punishable by a $10,000 fine and up to two years' imprisonment for anyone who exported or attempted to export goods to an enemy belligerent once a presidential proclamation had been issued stating that a foreign state was a belligerent opposed to the United States.[32] Title VIII dealt with a felony punishable by a fine up to $10,000 and up to five years' imprisonment for making false statements with intent to influence the conduct of the United States or foreign governments, or attempting to impersonate a foreign diplomat or consul.[33]

The provisions of the Espionage Act that threatened to impose federal controls over traditional freedom of speech were in Titles I and XII. Section 3 of Title I represented a radical limitation on constitutional freedom of speech. It made anyone who made a false report or statement with intent to interfere "with the operation or success of the military or naval forces of the United States or to promote the success of its enemies" guilty of a felony punishable by a fine of up to $10,000 and imprisonment up to twenty years, or both. Similarly anyone who "shall willfully cause or attempt to cause insubordination, disloyalty, mutiny, or refusal of duty, in the military or naval forces of the United States" or anyone who "shall willfully obstruct the recruiting or enlistment service of the United States" was also guilty of the same felony and liable to the same punishment.[34]

Title XII granted the postmaster general the authority to refuse to mail any publication that violated any provision of the act. It also provided that the postmaster general could refuse to mail "Every letter, writing, circular, postal card, picture, print, engraving, photograph, newspaper, pamphlet, book or other publication of any kind, containing any matter advocating or urging treason, insurrection, or forcible resistance to any law of the United States."[35]

Title I, § 3, of the Espionage Act provisions was vague, to say the least. It did not define "insubordination" or describe what "obstruct the recruiting or enlistment service of the United States" meant. "Obstruct . . . recruiting" could include a statement that the war was "a rich man's war and a poor man's fight,"[36] if the utterer intended to discourage voluntary enlistments. The statute could be stretched to include a statement that the 1917 Selective Service Act was unconstitutional or an unwise legislative act that ought to be repealed. A "false report" that was intended to interfere with the "operation or success" of military operations could be construed to include exaggerated reports of U.S. Air Expeditionary Force casualties or atrocities committed by U.S. soldiers and marines. Enforcement of Title I was in the hands of individual U.S. attorneys in every judicial district of the United States. The attorney general's office had no national espionage section overseeing prosecutions under the act.

Title XII did not define "advocating or urging treason." Conceivably, the postmaster general could order newspapers and books printed by or for U.S. Socialist Party members to be refused all mailing privileges, since one wing of U.S. Socialists were opposed to the war on ideological grounds, and standard socialist ideology called for a war of the working class against the capitalist class in some form. The International Workers of the World also had an anti-war wing that opposed the war and the draft. Union membership campaign materials could be refused by the postmaster general under the rubric that any anti-war or anti-draft publication was "advocating or urging treason" by implication. Anything from traditional German American organizations that contained something complimentary about German heritage, music, clothing, beer, or foods could be construed as "advocating or urging treason" because it cast Germany in a favorable light.

The Sedition Act of 1918

President Wilson was not satisfied with the provisions of Title I, § 3, and Title XII. He sent up an amendment to the Espionage Act in 1918 that increased federal control over freedom of expression and the press. It added (1) false statements intended to obstruct the sale of war bonds or of making loans to the United States; (2) willful printing, writing, or publishing of "any disloyal, profane, scurrilous, or abusive language about the form of government of the United States or the Constitution of the United States, or the military or naval forces of the United States, or the flag of the United States, or the uniform of the Army or Navy of the United States or any language intended to bring the form of government of the United States, or the Constitution of the United States, or the military or naval forces of the United States or the flag of the United States, or the uniform of the Army or Navy of the United States into contempt, scorn, contumely, or disrepute"; (3) to "willfully utter, print, write, or publish any language intended to incite, provoke, or encourage resistance to the United States, or to promote the cause of its enemies"; (4) to "display the flag of any foreign enemy"; (5) to "willfully by utterance, writing, printing, publication, or language spoken, urge incite or advocate any curtailment of production in this country any thing or things, product or products, necessary or essential to the prosecution of the war. . . . With intent by such curtailment to cripple or hinder the United States in the prosecution of the war"; and (5) to "willfully advocate, teach, defend, or suggest the doing of any of the acts or things in this section enumerated, and whoever shall by word or act support or favor the cause of any country with which the United States is at war or by word or act oppose the cause of the United States."[37]

The new section 3 expanded the potential for prosecution under the Espionage Act. Making a false statement about a war bond was now a felony. Writing or publishing any language that could be construed as "disloyal, profane, scurrilous or abusive" or any language with intent to cast "scorn, contumely or disrepute" relating to the Constitution, the form of the government, the flag, the armed forces of the United States, or the uniform of service members was a felony. Any statement that could be construed as a willful utterance or printing of any matter that would put Germany or Austro-Hungary in any kind of favorable light was a felony. Finally, inciting any person to reduce production (i.e., to strike at a defense plant) was a felony.

The sedition act also added a new section 4 to Title XII requiring individual postmasters to stamp mailing rejected by the postmaster general with a return stating, "Mail to this address undeliverable under Espionage Act plainly written or stamped upon the outside" of the rejected mailing.[38] This provision was intended to keep newspapers, periodicals, and other mailings that were prohibited by Title XII from accumulating in the dead letter section of the post offices of the United States.

Thousands of men and women were investigated by the U.S. Marshal's Service, the Justice Department Bureau of Investigation, and vigilantes for alleged disloyal speech and writings. Nearly two thousand men and women were prosecuted for violations of the Espionage Act or the Sedition Act from 1917 to 1919.[39] The Wilson administration targeted anti-war Socialists for prosecution. The stories of the prosecution of Eugene V. Debs, Emma Goldman, and other Socialists appear below, showing how these acts were used to eliminate the U.S. Socialist Party as a viable third-party movement.[40] These acts were also turned on the leaders of the Marxist-oriented International Workers of the World, causing the collapse of the most powerful single labor union in the United States.[41] The United States prosecuted Jehovah's Witnesses under the espionage act. Hundreds of men and women who were of German or Austro-Hungarian descent were also prosecuted for disloyal utterances against the United States and the Allies or remarks favorable to the Central Powers. Post-war, during the 1919–1920 "Red Scare," the act was turned on men and women who supported the Bolshevik revolution in Russia, who denounced the use of U.S. troops to put down the 1917 Revolution.

The American Protective League

The American Protective League was a private non-governmental organization established by Chicago businessman Albert M. Briggs as a civilian adjunct to the Department of Justice's Bureau of Investigation.[42]

Prior to the United States' entry into the war, the Bureau of Investigation had less than 250 field agents throughout the United States who lacked statutory authority to carry firearms and authority to make arrests.[43] Bureau Chief A. Bruce Bielaski[44] welcomed the assistance of private volunteer investigators. Attorney General Thomas W. Gregory,[45] who favored a broad construction of Title I, § 3, of the Espionage Act, encouraged Briggs and his friends who promptly enlisted thousands of volunteers across the United States. American Protective League members were given silver badges that marked the badge wearer as an "auxiliary to the U.S. Department of Justice."[46] American Protective League letterhead stationery contained the words "Organized with the Approval and Operating under the Direction of the United States Department of Justice, Bureau of Investigation."[47] Attorney General Gregory requested a $275,000 appropriation to pay for the league's expenses.[48]

The American Protective League's local chapters assisted the Bureau of Investigation by conducting surveillance of suspected disloyal persons. In August 1917, Attorney General Gregory wrote to Francis H. Weston. Gregory stated, "I have today several hundred thousand private citizens: some as individuals, most of them as members of patriotic bodies engaged in . . . assisting the heavily overworked Federal authorities in keeping an eye on disloyal individuals and making reports of disloyal utterances."[49] League members considered themselves "agents" of the Bureau of Investigation. Connecticut league members collected information on Seventh-Day Adventists' activities in their home state.[50] League members routinely burglarized the homes and the offices of suspected disloyal people in the course of their investigations.[51] No league members were prosecuted for burglary.

The most notable American Protective League project was the September 3, 1918, slackers roundup in New York City. Teams of league members button-holed men between eighteen and thirty-five on the streets of New York City and invaded office buildings and theaters, demanding that every young man produce his draft card. The league members, assisted by Bureau of Investigation agents and local police, arrested every man who was 1-A and every man who did not have his draft card on his person.[52] The detainees, numbering about sixty thousand,[53] were taken to the 69th New York Infantry Armory in Manhattan or to local jails in the boroughs such as the Tombs in Manhattan and the Raymond Street Jail in Brooklyn. Men detained in northern New Jersey were held in local armories awaiting review by a federal magistrate. The alleged draft evaders were brought before federal judges over the next several days. Most of the detainees were released. One thousand five hundred detainees were held for prosecution.[54]

The New York raid was the culmination of a series of league raids in other major cities. A slacker raid in Chicago resulted in twenty-seven thousand detainees, about 5 percent of which turned out to be draft evaders and military deserters.[55] The American Protective League and the Bureau of Investigation detained eight thousand men during the Detroit slacker raid.[56] The slacker raids resulted in arrest and detainment of U.S. citizens and resident aliens without probable cause to suspect that these men had committed any crime. Most of the arrests were carried out by league members or by soldiers, Bureau of Investigation agents and local police not being present to make an arrest. Senators Hiram Johnson[57] of California and Reed O. Smoot[58] of Utah called for an investigation by the Senate Military Affairs Committee into the slacker raids because soldiers and sailors had assisted in the roundup of alleged slackers. A prolonged debate on the floor of the Senate on the resolution on September 6, 1918, failed to resolve the matter.[59] Attorney General Gregory sent a letter to President Wilson defending the raids and at the same time disavowing the participation of the American Protective League in the raids.[60] Gregory said,

> Contrary to my express instructions, however, instructions which I have repeated over and over again and contrary to law, certain members of the investigating force of this department, without consultation with me or with any law officer of the department, used soldiers and sailors and certain members of the American Protective League, I am satisfied, in making arrests. I am convinced by the inquiries which I have made that they were led into this breach by an excess of zeal for the public good. While this extenuates, it does not excuse their action.[61]

Gregory's disavowal of support for the league's participation in the slacker raids was halfhearted at best. In 1918, the only remedy available to a man who was detained by the league in one of the slacker raids would have been suit for false arrest against the league. The United States was immune from suit. No record of any suits filed by detainees against the league have been found. The American Protective League was officially disbanded in 1919, but the organization provided volunteers to conduct investigations of suspected Communists in 1919–1920 during the Red Scare.[62]

Vigilantes

Vigilante groups throughout the United States sprang up after Congress declared war on the Central Powers. The vigilantes enforced support for the war, the draft, and the liberty loan drives and suppressed anti-war organizations and speakers. The vigilantes were opposed to Socialist Party events and to the IWW on the ground that these organizations were anti-war and unpatriotic. The vigilantes also exhibited virulent nativist tendencies, targeting German Americans in Washington and Idaho and even in the Teutonic strongholds of Illinois and Wisconsin for flag kissing, tarring and feathering, and other humiliating forms of intimidation.[63] Some of these groups, such as the American Defense League and the National Security League, were organized bodies bent on denouncing disloyal citizens and turning them over to the authorities.[64] The American Defense League and the National Security League were not officially sponsored by the U.S. Attorney General or by any other federal agency. Most vigilantism was spontaneous and related to local incidents that appeared to vigilantes to represent disloyal conduct. Vigilante attacks on African Americans increased sharply during the war because of the mass migration of African Americans to the industrial north to take jobs in factories expanding to meet the war effort. Many white workers were hostile to African Americans, who were perceived as taking a white man's job away.

The East St. Louis Riot

In July 1917, white people rioted in East St. Louis, Missouri, burning the houses of African Americans who had recently migrated from the Deep South to take jobs in local factories due to the need for more workers to aid in the war effort. African Americans had been hired in February 1917 to replace striking white workers at the Aluminum Ore Company. White workers went to the city council to lobby for a "no migrants" ordinance in May 1917. A rumor that an African American had held up a white man caused the angry workers to spill out on the street and stop streetcars, taking out African American passengers and beating them. Illinois governor Frank Lowden called in the National Guard to put down the violence. The July riot was incited when a carload of East St. Louis police officers was shot up by African Americans, mistaking the police car for another carload of whites who had opened fire on African Americans. The white rioters shot down African Americans fleeing a fire. They also lynched an unknown number of males.[65]

The Offensive against the IWW

Vigilantes also attacked members of the Industrial Workers of the World and their labor organizers on the ground that IWW membership was disloyal to the war effort. The IWW enlisted African Americans, Asian Americans, women, and recent immigrants into its ranks.[66]

The IWW was not a traditional craft union. The IWW organized entire industries without regard to craft. Second, the IWW advocated class warfare and the overthrow of "Wall Street capitalists." According to IWW ideologues, industrial plants should be managed by workers' committees for the good of the working class and not for the good of shareholders.[67]

The Bisbee Strike

Two examples of vigilante attacks on Wobblies will show why the anti-labor violence was related to the Wilson administration's program to curb dissent. Arizona had two governors in 1917: Republican Thomas P. Campbell had apparently been elected by thirty votes and was sworn in as governor in 1917. Democratic challenger George W. P. Hunt claimed that Campbell had been elected because of fraud. Hunt petitioned for a recount and demanded that Campbell give up the governorship, which Campbell refused to do. State government almost stopped functioning in early 1917 until a recount showed that Hunt had won the governorship. Hunt finally broke the stalemate and assumed the governorship in December 1917.[68] Arizona was in a state of anarchy for nine months. The state was powerless to act if a major civil disturbance occurred.

About half the miners at the Phelps Dodge copper mine in Bisbee chose to go out on strike on June 27, 1917. Two unions represented Bisbee's miners: the International Union of Mine, Mill & Smelter Workers represented about 1,800 Bisbee miners. The Industrial Workers of the World represented about 800 workers, many of whom were Mexicans and southern Europeans excluded from the International Union of Mine, Mill & Smelter Workers ranks due to racial prejudice. On June 24, the IWW presented Phelps Dodge with a list of demands relating to safety and working conditions, ending unequal treatment of minority miners, and a flat wage system to replace the Phelps Dodge sliding wage scale. Phelps Dodge refused to listen to the IWW's demands, and the IWW called a strike on June 27.

Someone spread a rumor that the IWW had been infiltrated by pro-German agents.[69] Another rumor circulated that the IWW had a cache of weapons and dynamite to sabotage Phelps Dodge. Phelps Dodge had established a vigilante group known as the Citizens' Protective League during a prior labor dispute. The league was called into action to put an end to the strike. Dissident miners formed the Workman's Loyalty League, another vigilante group that promised to stop the strike. Both groups worked under the direction of county sheriff Harry Wheeler, a former member of Teddy Roosevelt's Rough Riders. Wheeler decided to round up the IWW strikers and their friends and deport them from Bisbee. The vigilantes went to work at 4:00 a.m. Wheeler deputized members of both protective leagues, armed those who came to help with the roundup with revolvers if they showed up without sidearms, and instructed them to round up the strikers and take them to the local baseball field. By 6:30 a.m., they began rounding up miners. Miner James Brew shot Loyalty Leaguer Orson McRea and was in turn shot and killed by McRea's Loyalty League teammates. The roundup was completed within two hours. At 11:00 a.m., a train of boxcars was backed up to the baseball field, and the 1,186 men who were rounded up were loaded into the boxcars without food or water.[70] Sheriff Wheeler issued a proclamation stating that the miners were arrested on charges of vagrancy, treason, and disturbing the peace. The train pulled out of Bisbee and stopped across the border with New Mexico at Columbus. Columbus officials turned the train of deportees away on the grounds that they could not be accommodated in Columbus, and the train backed down the tracks to Hermanas where the deportees were marched off the boxcars and detained without adequate food or shelter until the U.S. Army's trainload of supplies arrived on July 14.[71] President Wilson officially deplored the deportation of the mine workers. He appointed a blue-ribbon committee headed by Felix Frankfurter to investigate the Bisbee deportation. The Frankfurter committee determined that no federal statutes had been violated by the vigilantes and turned their findings and information over to Arizona officials for possible criminal prosecution of the vigilante ringleaders.

Frank Little's Murder

In August 1917, IWW organizer Frank Little was forcibly removed from his boardinghouse, tied to an automobile, and dragged through the streets of Butte, Montana, behind a car, tearing off the skin from both knees. His assailants then hanged him from a railroad trestle. Little was the son of an Oklahoma doctor who joined the Western Federation of Miners shortly after 1900. In 1903, Little became an organizer for the WFM. Two years later, his union became part of the International Workers of the World. Little then became an IWW organizer. He was responsible for organizing miners at Bisbee, Arizona, before they were deported to Mexico. He was opposed to U.S. involvement in the war and to the draft. He was in Butte, Montana, during the 1917 Anaconda copper mine workers' strike, acting as a union organizer. Little gave daily speeches at Finlandia Hall next to his rooming house. Little antagonized local loyalists and the Anaconda company. At that time, the IWW was rumored to be funded with German money to sabotage the war effort. Little's July 19 speech at Finlandia Hall was chock-full of incendiary language. He called U.S. Army soldiers "Uncle Sam's scabs in uniform." He also said that "if the mines are taken under federal control, we will make it so hot for the government that it will not be able to send any troops to France."[72] The men who lynched Little hung a card from his body carrying the statement "Others Take Notice First and Last Warning," bearing the vigilante numbers 3-7-77, a number used by Virginia City Montana vigilantes in the 1870s.[73] U.S. attorney and future U.S. senator Burton K. Wheeler condemned the lynching. Wheeler had sent a letter to the attorney general inquiring if Little should be prosecuted under the Espionage Act for his anti-war rant. County Attorney Joseph Jackson said, "It is a cold blooded murder and every effort will be used to apprehend the men who did it. If they are caught they will be prosecuted to the full extent of the law."[74]

Robert Prager's Lynching

Robert Prager, a coal miner living in Collinsville, Illinois, was born in Dresden, Germany, around 1886. He immigrated to the United States in 1905 and drifted from place to place until 1918. Prager had spent a year in the Indiana Reformatory at Pendleton sometime between 1905 and 1917 when he showed up in Collinsville. At the outbreak of U.S. participation in World War I, Prager tried to enlist in the U.S. Navy but was rejected because he was blind in one eye. Prager arrived in Collinsville in early June 1917. He worked in a local bakery for several months, then took a job with a St. Louis bakery for a few months. In 1918 he left the St. Louis job and applied for membership in the United Mine Workers in order to go to work in the coal mine at Maryville, Illinois. The local refused to issue Prager a card because he was deemed to be "unmarried, stubbornly argumentative, given to Socialist doctrines, blind in one eye," and he looked "like a spy."[75] On April 3, 1918, a group of miners ran Prager out of town. Prager took a room in a rooming house in Collinsville. Moses Johnson and James Fornaro, two United Mine Worker union leaders at Maryville, thought that Prager's life was in danger. They called the Collinsville Police Department and requested that Prager be taken into protective custody. The police refused to act. The next day, Prager went back to Maryville with his typewritten personal attack on Fornaro. He put up carbon copies in several locations in Maryville.

That night, a group of miners in Collinsville were drinking in a local saloon. They resolved to find Prager and run him out of Collinsville. The miners dragged Prager out of his house and paraded him down Main Street in his underwear draped in a U.S. flag.[76] Collinsville police officer Fred Frost rescued Prager and took him to city hall. Prager hid in the basement. A miner named Joe Riegel persuaded the police to allow him to have a look at Prager. Wesley Beaver, who crowded into city hall with Riegel, discovered Prager's hiding place. Riegel rallied a mob outside city hall that dragged Prager out of the basement and marched him outside the city limits of Collinsville, where Prager was hanged shortly after midnight, April 5, 1918.[77]

The Collinsville police disclaimed any responsibility for investigating Prager's murder or for arresting any of the mob members. After the coroner's April 8, 1918, inquest, the Illinois attorney general assumed responsibility for investigating the lynching.[78]

Riegel admitted that he was the leader of the mob at the coroner's inquest. He told the coroner that the mob forced Prager to kiss the flag. Prager was interrogated by mob members about his German sympathy. The mob led Prager to a "hanging tree." When he refused to tell the mob who else was working with him as a German spy, several teenagers grabbed a rope and tied a hangman's knot around Prager's neck and threw the rope over a tree branch. The boys pulled Prager up, but they had forgotten to tie his hands, and Prager saved his life by holding on to the hanging rope. He was let down, his hands were tied, and Riegel took the rope and hanged Prager.[79] Riegel later repudiated his confession to the coroner. The coroner's jury issued a verdict of death by violent and external means and ordered that Riegel and four other men be indicted for murder.[80]

On April 25, Riegel and ten other Collinsville and Maryville men[81] were indicted for murder. The defendants did not show any signs of remorse or fear. They acted as if the town and all prospective jurors would support them. This turned out to be the case. Their trial convened on May 1. The prosecution witnesses had trouble identifying any of the eleven defendants as participants in the hanging. Riegel's confession had been repudiated. On June 1, the jury returned a unanimous verdict of "not guilty." The crowd in the courtroom broke into a wild demonstration of support for the defendants. Defense counsel had argued to the jury that the defendants should be acquitted because the miners who had hanged Prager were obedient to the unwritten law that was provoked by the war.[82]

The death of Robert Prager and the acquittal of the eleven men accused of his murder provoked a mixed reaction in the press. The *New York Times* editorial condemned the lynching and acquittal as a gross miscarriage of justice.[83] The *Collinsville Herald*'s editorial stated that "the whole city is glad" that the eleven men were acquitted.[84] The *Washington Post* editorial said, "In spite of excesses such as lynching, it is a healthful and wholesome awakening in the interior of the country."[85]

Pastor Schumann

Vigilantes also hounded suspected pro-German sympathizers in the Midwest. The case of Rev. Wilhelm Schumann, pastor of the Evangelical Synod Church in the small town of Pomeroy, Iowa,[86] will serve as an example of vigilantism at work. Pastor Schumann was born in Germany, and between August 1914 and April 1917, he expressed his personal support for the German war effort. Pomeroy had a substantial population of German-born citizens. Before U.S. entry into the war, the stationmaster at Pomeroy wrote to the U.S. secretary of state to complain that local Germans gathered at the end of the railroad station to engage in what the stationmaster believed to be furious anti-Allied, pro-German diatribes.[87] The stationmaster did not speak German. In November 1917, Werner Hanni, an undercover operative for the Bureau of Investigation, reported that Rev. Schumann was a disloyal person who should be arrested. Hanni provided his own translation of Rev. Schumann's last sermon. Hanni swore that Schumann had denounced England and Russia, whom he said started the war in order to rule all of Europe. Hani said Rev. Schumann also asserted that "this war is for the capitalist only and the Liberty Loan is a humbug." Schumann was arrested on December 1, 1917, by a Bureau of Investigation agent.[88] Two days later, a mob of about 150 men and boys gathered at Schumann's house demanding that Shumann salute the U.S. flag. The local newspaper published a warning that if the authorities did not prosecute Schumann for his disloyalty, the citizens of Pomeroy would take the law into their own hands and drive Schumann out of town.[89] On December 31, 1917, Schumann's church burned to the ground. The cause of the fire was never established. On January 8, 1918, a crowd cornered Rev. Schumann in a store warning him to leave town. A county sheriff's deputy came to Pomeroy and escorted Rev. Schumann out of town through a mob, some of whom carried weapons. Schumann returned to Pomeroy in the spring of 1918 before his trial commenced in June. Hanni was the principal witness against the pastor. Schumann took the stand in his own behalf, stating that in 1914 he was pro-German but had reluctantly sided with the United States later on in the war. The jury gave a verdict of guilty, and Schumann was sentenced to five years in prison and ordered to pay a $250 fine. Schumann appealed his conviction and went back to Pomeroy to rebuild his church. The town postmaster Edin Wattonville and a man named Hans Weygant appeared at the construction site and got into a row with Schumann, who tossed a brick at his tormentors. Schumann was arrested again and found guilty of assault with intent to do bodily injury. In November 1919 after his appeal was turned down, Rev. Schumann headed to the Leavenworth Penitentiary where he remained for two years until pardoned by President Warren Harding.[90]

These vigilante episodes, a sampling out of hundreds of cases in which American citizens and resident aliens were bullied, humiliated, and subjected to physical harm, loss of job, and other forms of personal harm, illustrate the widespread resort to private vengeance by U.S. citizens. Otherwise sober and responsible members of the upper class were swept up in denouncing disloyalty and encouraging violence against anti-war citizens.[91] Former secretary of state Elihu Root said that there were men walking the streets of New York who should be shot for treason. Episcopal bishop George Herbert Kinsolving of Texas declared that Chicago mayor William "Big Bill" Thompson, a notorious anglophobe who opposed the war, "was guilty of treason and ought to be shot. There is only one way to punish treason: that is by death to the man that is guilty. I am in favor of the firing squad and a stone wall as the proper means of combating treachery to the United States. What the country needs is a few first-class hangings."[92]

The media also encouraged vigilante action. Two examples show the media's attitude toward vigilante justice. A 1917 *Wall Street Journal* editorial brayed, "We are now at war, and militant pacifists are earnestly reminded that there is no shortage of hemp or lamp posts."[93] In November 1917, *Time* magazine published a three-panel cartoon, the first panel depicting an agitator haranguing a crowd under a lamppost, the second panel showing someone placing a noose around the agitator's neck from behind, and the third showing the agitator hanging from the lamppost.[94]

A contemporary analyst would want to know whether the vigilantes had any legal justification for "enforcing" loyalty in 1917–1918. In short, is there any legal justification for private citizens to enforce the criminal law (i.e., arrest, trial, and conviction of alleged evildoers)? U.S. history had many instances where private citizens acting in concert rounded up prostitutes, robbers, and other wrongdoers when the machinery of the state was too rudimentary to deal with masses of criminals preying on the public. Vigilantes cleared the streets of San Francisco of robbers, murderers, and other criminals in the 1850s when the city's law enforcement was unable to cope with rampant street crime.[95] Vigilantes cleaned up Virginia City and Nevada City, Montana, in the 1860s, hanging cheating gamblers, flogging confidence men, and running prostitutes out of town.[96] The premise for private citizens to enforce the criminal laws of the jurisdiction in both of these best-known incidents of vigilantism in the United States was the same: local law enforcement failed to respond to the needs of law-abiding citizens. During World War I, prevailing public opinion held that disloyal citizens were encouraging opposition to the war, interfering with the draft, spying for Germany, or discouraging the purchase of Liberty bonds. Law enforcement was powerless to take action against them. Therefore, private action was the only means of enforcing the law.[97]

The vigilante tradition extended back to colonial times and is a blend of the common-law hue and cry and the posse comitatus. English common law recognized that private citizens were obliged to call out their neighbors if a crime was committed in their presence. Men serving on the hue and cry could detain an alleged perpetrator.[98] The posse comitatus was normally summoned by a law enforcement officer to assist the officer in carrying out his duties.[99] Posse members also possessed authority to arrest a perpetrator.[100] In 1917–1918, most of the United States was sparsely populated.[101] Until 1920 more than half of all U.S. citizens lived on farms or in small towns.[102] Organized police departments existed only in large cities. Law enforcement in rural or small-town America was in the hands of the county sheriff or the town constable, a peace officer with limited armament and no professional training, because none existed in the United States before 1916.[103] The county prosecutor in the early twentieth century was a lawyer who was elected to a position whose salary was paid from fines and other money collected from wrongdoers.[104] The prosecutor had unfettered discretion to have a grand jury called to consider indicting someone for commission of a crime. The prosecutor controlled witnesses and demonstrative evidence that the grand jury reviewed in reaching a verdict. The judiciary consisted of justices of the peace, with limited jurisdiction over misdemeanors, and county circuit judges who could convene criminal jury trials, provided the county prosecutor got a grand jury to issue an indictment. It is no surprise that in stressful times, the primitive law enforcement machinery in rural counties would be overtaxed. During World War I, German agents engaged in sabotage.[105] Labor trouble broke out in key industries such as the copper mines and the railroads that impeded the war effort. The Industrial Workers of the World were blamed for these strikes and for committing sabotage.[106] Anti-war citizens interfered with the draft and preached class warfare and resistance to federal authority.[107] People of German descent were unwilling supporters of the United States.[108] People felt threatened by disloyal fellow citizens.[109] It was the first experience of involvement in a major twentieth-century international war.

Vigilantes took the law into their own hands, greatly extending their activities beyond the traditional posse comitatus. They were not legally justified in committing acts of violence against alleged disloyal people. They had no authority to arrest, search, or detain anyone. Vigilantes were virtually immune from prosecution by the law because of the primitive character of rural law enforcement. David Kennedy contends that the Wilson administration encouraged vigilante action through George Creel's propaganda efforts portraying disloyal people as evil monsters.[110] Creel's committee did attack disloyalty and slackers and urged that these people be brought to justice. The United States had been inundated by millions of immigrants from Russia, Poland, Hungary, and Italy from 1880 to 1917.[111] The public reaction to the new immigrants was to retreat into nativism. During the war, hundreds of thousands of African Americans from the Deep South migrated to Chicago, Detroit, and other northern industrial cities to take jobs in war industries.[112] White Anglo-Saxon Protestants perceived these groups as threats to their way of life. Post-war nativism would get further impetus from the pseudoscience of eugenics that supported a claim that people of British, French, and German descent were biologically superior to people of eastern and southern European descent.[113]

There is no compelling evidence that President Wilson or any cabinet member deliberately encouraged vigilante attacks on disloyal citizens, but Wilson did nothing to discourage these attacks. That said, vigilante terrorism supported Wilson's campaign to deal with anti-war dissenters.

State Sedition and Criminal Syndicalism Statutes

President Wilson's program was supplemented by state laws and state extra-legal non-governmental organizations. Most states had a committee of public safety appointed by the governor empowered to coordinate statewide activities in support of the war effort.[114] This delegation of authority did not include law enforcement. In one or two instances, state committees of public safety worked with the American Protective League in conducting surveillance of alleged disloyal people.[115]

In 1917, Idaho[116] and Minnesota[117] passed criminal syndicalism acts[118] aimed at the IWW's organizational activities. These acts were copied by many states in 1919 during the Red Scare to deal with homegrown IWW organizers.[119] Some of these acts are still on the state statute books. One wartime prosecution for criminal syndicalism eventually reached the U.S. Supreme Court, where the Court affirmed that states could pass laws against speaking against the draft.[120] Joseph Gilbert was one of three speakers at an August 1917 Nonpartisan League rally in Kenyon, Minnesota. According to agents who had infiltrated the crowd, Gilbert did "unlawfully and wilfully teach and advocate by word of mouth and oral speech that men should not enlist in the military and naval forces of the United States, and that the citizens of the State of Minnesota should not assist the United States in prosecuting and carrying on war with the public enemies of the United States."[121] He was indicted for violating the 1917 criminal syndicalism law and was convicted. The Minnesota Supreme Court sustained the conviction against Gilbert's argument that the criminal syndicalism statute was unconstitutional.[122] Gilbert's petition for certiorari was granted, and the Supreme Court sustained the lower court.

Justice McKenna wrote the opinion for the court. He acknowledged Gilbert's main constitutional argument: the power to pass statutes limiting anti-war and anti-draft speech was an exclusive power of the United States to "provide for the common defense" and to "raise and support armies" and could not be exercised by any state.

> Undoubtedly, the United States can declare war and it, not the States, has the power to raise and maintain armies. But there are other considerations. The United States is composed of the States, the States are constituted of the citizens of the United States, who also are citizens of the States, and it is from these citizens that armies are raised and wars waged, and whether to victory and its benefits, or to defeat and its calamities, the States as well as the United States are intimately concerned. And whether to victory or defeat depends upon their morale, the spirit and determination that animates them—whether it is repellent and adverse or eager and militant; and to maintain it eager and militant against attempts at its debasement in aid of the enemies of the United States, is a service of patriotism; and from the contention that it encroaches upon or usurps any power of Congress, there is an instinctive and immediate revolt. Cold and technical reasoning in its minute consideration may indeed insist on a separation of the sovereignties and resistance in each to any cooperation from the other, but there is opposing demonstration in the fact that this country is one composed of many and must on occasions be animated as one and that the consti-

> tuted and constituting sovereignties must have power of cooperation against the enemies of all. Of such instance, we think, is the statute of Minnesota and it goes no farther.[123]

Gilbert's second argument, that the criminal syndicalism statute was a prior restraint on free speech, also got short shrift from the Court. It sustained the constitutionality of the Minnesota act relying on *Schenck v. United States,*[124] the case in which Justice Holmes asserted that "the most stringent protection of free speech would not protect a man in falsely shouting fire in a theater and causing a panic."[125] Gilbert's conviction under the criminal syndicalism act was sustained.

Gilbert did not settle for all time the power of states to pass laws regulating activity that was arguably the subject of earlier federal legislation based on congressional power to declare war and raise an army. *Gilbert* stands for the general principle that a state may regulate speech directed at undermining the war effort because Congress did not preempt state legislation by passing the Espionage Act of 1917.

Connecticut's Home Guard overstepped its boundaries in December 1917 when its members forcibly evacuated families of German descent from their homes near the Winchester Arms Company Plant.[126] In April 1918, Home Guard members and the American Protective League's Hartford chapter broke up a Socialist Party meeting in Hartford, demanding that the Socialists pledge allegiance to the flag and lecturing the Socialists on their patriotic duty to support the war effort.[127]

The Kansas Home Guard, armed with obsolete "trapdoor" Springfield Model 1873 single-shot rifles left over from Spanish–American War discards, helped to sell Liberty bonds, provided honor guards for veterans' funerals, and guarded strategic bridges and factories. Some companies also rounded up slackers and spied on allegedly pro-German citizens, hoping to turn them in for prosecution.[128]

Home Guard companies in most states operated semi-independently of the governor's supervision and control. The temptation for some Home Guard units to hound disloyal citizens was too great to prevent the Home Guards from becoming an instrument in the program to suppress anti-war dissent.

THE ANTI-WAR OPPOSITION

Thousands of U.S. citizens and resident aliens opposed the United States' entry on the side of the Allies. The opposition consisted of the traditional pacifist groups, the Socialist Party, the International Workers of the World, and pro-German American citizens and resident aliens. Prior to the declaration of war, these anti-war groups had conducted a vigorous debate with those who advocated the United States' entry into the war on the Allied side.

Pacifists

The Society of Friends, Amish, Mennonites, German Baptists (Dunkards), Seventh-Day Adventists, and Jehovah's Witnesses (commonly known as Russellites) opposed all forms of armed combat. These traditional pacifist groups objected to all warfare on moral grounds. After the 1917 conscription act became law, pacifist men between seventeen and thirty-five had to register for the draft and were subject to being called to serve in non-combatant duties. Unofficially, 3,989 men primarily from the Amish, Mennonite, and other traditional peace churches claimed to be conscientious objectors after registration and drafting. Of this group, 1,300 men chose non-combatant service, 1,200 were given farm furloughs, 99 went to Europe to do reconstruction work for the American Friends Service Committee (AFSC), 450 were court-martialed and sent to prison, and 940 remained in camps until after the Armistice.[129] The latter two categories included men whose traditional religious confessions did not recognize universal pacifism.

The case of Ben Salmon illustrates how non-traditional conscientious objectors were treated during World War I. Salmon, a Roman Catholic born in Denver in 1889, gradually adopted total pacifism as a moral imperative from his interpretation of the Gospels. He was a clerk for the Colorado & Southern Railroad and was active in organized labor. His agitation for labor reform eventually cost him his job in 1915.[130] Salmon was an exponent of Henry George's single-tax theory of wealth distribution. He ran for a seat in the Colorado state legislature as a Single Tax candidate and lost. When war broke out, Cardinal James Gibbons of Baltimore issued a statement in support of the declaration of war. Gibbons's statement read in pertinent part:

> In the present emergency it behooves every American citizen to do his duty and to uphold the hands of the President and the legislative department in the solemn obligation that confronts us. The primary duty of a citizen is loyalty to his country. This loyalty is manifested more by acts than words; by solemn service rather than empty declamation. It is exhibited in absolute and unreserved obedience to his country's call. Both houses of Congress, with the executive, are charged and sworn to frame those laws that are demanded by the present crisis. Whatever, therefore, Congress may decide should be unequivocally complied with by every patriotic citizen. The members of both houses of Congress are the instruments of God in guiding us in our civic duties. It behooves all of us, therefore, to pray that the Lord of Hosts may inspire our national legislature and executive to frame such laws in the present crisis as will redound to the glory of our country, to righteousness of conduct, and to the future permanent peace of the nations of the world.[131]

The official U.S. Catholic position required loyalty to the United States and support of the war effort.[132] Ben Salmon did not accept the official position of his church. He registered for the draft on June 5, 1917, complying with the federal mandate that all men seventeen to thirty-five register on that date or be subject to criminal prosecution.[133] Salmon then sent a letter to President Wilson that stated his views on waging war:

> Regardless of nationality, all men are brothers. God is "our Father who art in heaven." The commandment "Thou shalt not kill" is unconditional and inexorable. . . . The Lowly Nazarine taught us the doctrine of non-resistance, and so convinced was he of the soundness of that doctrine that he sealed his belief with death on the cross. When human law conflicts with Divine Law, my duty is clear. Conscience, my infallible guide impels me to tell you that prison, death or both are infinitely preferable to joining any branch of the Army.[134]

Salmon gave up campaigning for the single tax and transferred his energy to the pacifist movement. He became the Denver secretary of the Peoples' Council for America for Democracy and Peace.[135]

The Selective Service Administration sent Salmon a questionnaire which he refused to complete. In January 1918 two Denver police officers arrested Salmon for refusal to complete the questionnaire. Salmon was released on bond and stood trial for this misdemeanor charge on March 30, 1918.[136]

Salmon argued that the questionnaire violated his First Amendment right to free exercise of his religion. This argument was not enough to prevent a conviction and sentence to nine months in the Denver jail. Salmon's friends put up bond, and he was released pending an appeal to the Colorado Supreme Court. The Denver Selective Service Board issued a draft notice to Salmon on May 16, 1918. Salmon refused to report for induction, claiming that his state court misdemeanor charge was under appeal and he had a dependent wife and mother. The board ordered him to report for induction on May 20, 1918.[137] When he failed to report, the Denver police rearrested him and carted him off to Fort Logan, Colorado. The army put Salmon in solitary confinement.[138]

After spending three days in solitary confinement, the army put Salmon on a train for Camp Funston, Kansas. The army told Salmon he would be tried by general court-martial for "desertion and propaganda." Salmon was not served with charges under the Articles of War at Camp Funston. Instead he was transferred to Camp Pawnee, Kansas, and then to Camp Dodge, Iowa. Salmon appeared before a board of officers charged with reviewing conscientious objector claims. The board ruled that Salmon was a "sincere" conscientious objector. The board recommended that he be placed in alternative farmwork in lieu of reporting for duty in the army. The board also offered to recommend that his Colorado misdemeanor conviction be commuted to time served. There was a catch, however. In order to receive conscientious objector status, Salmon had to agree to cooperate with the army by allowing himself to be inducted into the army. Salmon refused again.

The army then convened a general court-martial to try Salmon for desertion. Salmon asserted that he had never been inducted into the U.S. Army, essentially a plea of lack of jurisdiction. He also claimed that he had a dependent wife and child, exempting him from service under the act. Finally, Salmon argued, without benefit of counsel, that the Selective Service law was an unconstitutional statute contrary to the freedom of religion clause of the First Amendment and the due process clause of the Fifth Amendment.[139] The court-martial voted unanimously to convict Salmon and sentenced him to death. The court then recommended that Salmon's sentence be commuted to twenty-five years at hard labor.[140] The army offered another "deal" to Salmon to serve as a non-combatant clerk. If Salmon accepted this offer, the court-martial verdict and judgment would be rescinded. Salmon refused again. He was then transferred to the federal penitentiary at Leavenworth, Kansas, to serve his sentence.[141] When the prison guards ordered the absolutist conscientious objectors to work, Salmon refused. He was put in solitary confinement for five months in the dead of winter. In June 1919, Salmon and other absolute conscientious objectors imprisoned at Leavenworth were transferred to Fort Douglas, Utah. Salmon again refused to work and was again put into solitary confinement. Salmon went on a hunger strike and was force-fed for 135 days before he was moved to St. Elizabeth's Hospital in Washington, D.C., where he remained until pardoned and freed. Salmon's older brother applied for clemency for his brother. The application was rejected by Attorney General Palmer and by President Wilson.

Salmon was eventually released from confinement by a general amnesty issued by President Harding and issued a dishonorable discharge from the U.S. Army on Thanksgiving Day 1920. Salmon returned to obscurity and Colorado for twelve more years before his untimely death.[142]

The Supreme Court held that the Selective Service Act of 1917 was a constitutional exercise of congressional authority under Article I, § 8, of the Constitution in the *Draft Law Cases*.[143] Consequently, Ben Salmon was required to comply with the act by registering, completing an induction form, and reporting for induction. Moreover, once an order to report for induction was issued, Ben Salmon was obliged to report to his local board for induction. If he failed to report, he would be automatically inducted into the army and would be subject to the Articles of War. Failure to report would be considered desertion in time of war, a charge that could result in the death penalty.[144] Ben Salmon's court-martial and imprisonment were imposed by the army when the army believed it had jurisdiction to try Salmon for desertion and other crimes under the Articles of War. Article 12 of the 1916 version of the Articles of War stated that a general court-martial has jurisdiction to try "any person subject to military law . . . or any other person who by statute or by the law of war is subject to trial by military tribunals."[145] Article 2 defined "persons subject to military law" to include all officers and soldiers belonging to the armies of the United States."[146] Modern commentators have insisted that Salmon was not a member of the armed forces of the United States. Since 1940, men who refused to report for induction have been tried by civilian courts for failure to report for induction.[147] That was untrue in May 1918 when Ben Salmon was ordered to report for induction.

In 1918, the judge advocate general of the army issued a formal opinion relating to conscientious objectors who failed to report for induction. He said,

> A conscientious objector is under the same duty as other drafted men to obey the order of the local board to appear and submit to physical examination and to report for duty. If he was, in fact, inducted into the military service by the local board through proper order and failed to report for duty as ordered, he became a deserter and may be proceeded against and punished as such.[148]

The judge advocate general treated any man who received written notice to report for induction as a member of the army and subject to the Articles of War. The judge advocate's opinion was supported by several later federal lower court decisions. Ben Salmon would not have prevailed had he filed a habeas corpus petition. The Second Circuit decided *United States ex rel. Feld v. Bullard*[149] in 1923, which turned on the issue of the status of a person who had registered for the draft, failed to complete his questionnaire, and failed to report for induction. The New Jersey order to report for induction sent to Feld's last known address stated, "Unless, upon your so reporting to this office, orders rescinding the present order are issued, then from and after the date just specified you shall be in the military service of the United States."[150] Feld was living and working in Brazil at the time he was ordered to report. After returning to the United States post-war, he was arrested by the army and tried for desertion. He filed a habeas corpus petition alleging that, as he had never reported for induction, he was not subject to the Articles of War. The court said that:

> Thus, after the induction, a registrant becomes subject to military law and must be tried for an offense against it by the military authorities. *Franke v. Murray*, 248 Fed. 865, 160 C.C.A. 623, L.R.A. 1918E, 1015, Ann. Cas. 1918D, 98. If a court-martial has jurisdiction, its proceedings are not subject to review by the civil tribunals, except for the purpose of ascertaining whether a military court has jurisdiction of the person or subject-matter, and whether, though having such jurisdiction, it had exceeded its powers in the sentence pronounced. *Carter v. Roberts*, 177 U.S. 496, 20 Sup. Ct. 713, 44 L. Ed. 861; *Carter v. McClaughry*, 183 U.S. 365, 22 Sup. Ct. 181, 46 L. Ed. 236.[151]

In *Franke v. Murray*,[152] the Eighth Circuit held that section 2 of the Selective Service Act made every man who received notice to report for induction a member of the army. It rejected a lower court decision freeing a conscientious objector, holding that a man ordered to report for induction was not a member of the army until sworn in. The Franke Court said,

> There is therefore no room for doubt that, under the Selective Draft Act and the Articles of War, the appellant having been drafted into the service of the United States, he became from the date of said draft, and certainly after acceptance and notice, subject to the laws and regulations governing the regular army, including the Articles of War. The laws governing voluntary enlistments cannot be applied to involuntary enlistments by draft or conscription.
>
> It is also claimed that the time when he became a soldier, within the meaning of the law, is regulated by article 109 of the Articles of War. But that article only refers to voluntary enlistments. It reads, "At the time of his enlistment every soldier shall take the following oath or affirmation," and then follows the form of the oath. But as the petitioner did not enlist, but was drafted under the Selective Draft Act, this article does not apply.[153]

The construction put on section 109 of the Articles of War by *Franke* and *Feld* never reached the Supreme Court during World War I or within ten years after the end of hostilities. During World War II, both cases were overruled sub silencio in 1944 by the U.S. Supreme Court. The Court reviewed the conviction and confinement by court-martial of Billings, a Jehovah's Witness who reported for induction but refused to take the oath administered to all enlistees and draftees. Billings was arrested and held for trial by the army. The army followed the 1918 judge advocate general's opinion and tried Billings by general court-martial. Billings claimed that the army did not have jurisdiction over his person because he had not taken the oath and was not inducted. Billings filed a petition for writ of habeas corpus. The district court agreed with Billings's contention and ordered him discharged from army custody. The Tenth Circuit disagreed and reversed the district court[154] without citing *Franke* or other World War I draft cases supporting the construction that "induction" into the army occurred before any oath was administered to the draftees. Billings sought certiorari, and the Supreme Court reinstated the district court judgment. The Court said,

> Moreover, it should be remembered that he who reports at the induction station is following the procedure outlined in the *Falbo* case for the exhaustion of his administrative remedies. Unless he follows that procedure he may not challenge the legality of his classification in the courts. But we can hardly say that he must report to the military in order to exhaust his administrative remedies and then say that if he does so report he may be forcibly inducted against his will. That would indeed make a trap of the *Falbo* case by subjecting those who reported

> for completion of the Selective Service process to more severe penalties than those who stayed away in defiance of the board's order to report. These considerations together indicate to us that a selectee becomes "actually inducted" within the meaning of § 11 of the Act when in obedience to the order of his board and after the Army has found him acceptable for service he undergoes whatever ceremony or requirements of admission the War Department has prescribed[155]

Billings was set free from military custody. He was not cleared of any wrongdoing. The United States was free to indict Billings in U.S. District Court and seek punishment for his transgressions in civilian courts.

Sections 2, 5, and 6 of the 1917 Selective Service Act relate to military jurisdiction over inductees who fail to report for induction. The corresponding provisions of sections 2 and 11 of the 1940 Selective Service Act are different. The 1917 act made no provision for civilian jurisdiction over individuals who refused to report for induction, although it did provide for civilian jurisdiction over those men who were required to register for the draft. It did not contain an express proviso relating to the trial of men who refused to report for induction.[156]

The 1940 act contained a proviso that stated,

> No person shall be tried by any naval or military court martial in any case arising under this Act unless such person has been actually inducted for the training and service prescribed by this Act.[157]

The Billings decision construed section 11 that contained the proviso. Although the Billings interpretation of military jurisdiction under the 1940 act could apply to the 1917 act, the court could very well have refused to do so because the 1917 act did not contain an express statement that refusal to report for induction could be tried in a civilian court. "Induction" for those called to serve in World War I meant service of a letter ordering the draftee to report for induction. Ben Salmon would have been subject to the Articles of War in 1918. He was not entitled to be tried by a civilian judge and jury in district court.

The United States initiated prosecution of Judge Rutherford and eight other members of the International Bible Students Society, a religious group founded by Charles Taze in the 1870s. In 1916, Judge Joseph Franklin Rutherford became the presiding officer of the International Bible Students Society (known today as the Jehovah's Witnesses). The organization published a magazine known as the *Watchtower* to spread its doctrines.[158] One of the core tenets of the Society was opposition to all war and refusal to accept induction into the military. In 1917, the United States prosecuted Judge Rutherford and seven other members of the Society under the Espionage Act. The prosecution was based on articles appearing in a book called *The Finished Mystery* published by the Watchtower and distributed in U.S. military training camps. The government considered the following passages violations of the Espionage Act:

> Standing opposite to those Satan has placed three great untruths, human immorality, the Antichrist and a certain delusion which is best described by the word Patriotism, but which is in reality murder, the spirit of the very Devil. * * * Under the guise of Patriotism the civil governments of earth demand of peace-loving men the sacrifice of themselves and their loved ones and the butchery of their fellows, and hail it as a duty demanded by the laws of heaven. Page 247.
>
> If you say that this war is a last resort in a situation which every other method, patiently tried, has failed to meet, I must answer that this is not true—that other ways and means of action, tried by experience and justified by success, have been laid before the administration and willfully rejected.
>
> In its ultimate causes, this war is the natural product of our unchristian civilization. * * * There is not a question raised, an issue involved, a cause at stake, which is worth the life of one blue-jacket on the sea or one khaki-coat in the trenches. Page 251.[159]

The district court convicted the Russellites, but their convictions were reversed in 1920 by the Second Circuit.[160]

The Socialists

The Socialist Party, formed in 1895 by a group of labor activists that included Eugene V. Debs of the American Railway Union and William (Big Bill) Haywood of the Western Miners Federation and by eastern intellectuals such as Morris Hilquit, based its political ideology on the teachings of Karl Marx. The party opposed all international wars on the ground that such wars were provoked by the capitalist class due to market disputes, and the working class should not aid capitalists by fighting their wars for them. The Socialists also prophesied the eventual takeover of the means of production by peaceful means, primarily by electing Socialist candidates to public office. The Socialists did succeed in electing Victor Berger to Congress representing Wisconsin's Fifth Congressional District in 1910. The Socialists also won local mayoral races in Milwaukee and other cities.[161] The Socialists also put up a presidential ticket. Eugene V. Debs was the Socialist presidential candidate in 1904, 1908, 1912, and 1920.[162]

In April 1917, delegates from most local Socialist Party organizations met in St. Louis to consider what to do about U.S. entry into World War I. The majority of party delegates passed a resolution later ratified by most Socialist state committees expressing disapproval of U.S. entry into the war and condemning U.S. intervention on the Allied side.[163] The party called the declaration of war "a crime against the people of the United States" and pledged "continuous, active opposition to the war" and to conscription.[164] The party adopted a resolution stating that U.S. entry into the war "was instigated by the predatory capitalists in the United States who boast of the enormous profit of $7,000,000,000 from the manufacture and sale of munitions and war supplies and from the exportation of American foodstuffs and other necessaries."[165]

The St. Louis Resolution immediately placed loyal Socialist Party members in jeopardy because the resolution's language appeared to be the kind of public statement of principle that the Espionage Act made criminal. The more conservative members of the Socialist Party, including Charles Edward Russell, dropped out of the party because they supported U.S. entry into the war.[166] The Socialist Party remained divided over U.S. entry into the war. The Socialists who supported the St. Louis declaration and tried to implement it with political action faced prosecution under the Espionage Act.

The Case of Charles Schenck

Charles Schenck was the secretary of the Socialist Party of America. He was a Philadelphia resident and managed the party's business office located at 1326 Arch Street in Philadelphia. Shortly after the adoption of the St. Louis Resolution, he returned to Philadelphia and ordered fifteen thousand leaflets printed to be distributed to men who registered for the draft. The leaflets followed the St. Louis Resolution and urged the recipients not to report for induction.

> In exempting clergymen and members of the Society of Friends (popularly called Quakers) from active military service the examination boards have discriminated against you.
>
> If you do not assert and support your rights you are helping to "deny or disparage rights" which it is the solemn duty of all citizens and residents of the United States to retain.
>
> In lending tacit or silent consent to the conscription law, in neglecting to assert your rights, you are (whether knowingly or not) helping to condone and support a most infamous and insidious conspiracy to abridge and destroy the sacred and cherished rights of a free people. You are a citizen: not a subject! You delegate your power to the officers of the law to be used for your good and welfare, not against you.[167]

The Socialist Party headquarters were searched by Bureau of Investigation agents who seized the leaflets that had not been mailed by the party. Schenck and Ms. Elizabeth Baer, a member of the executive committee who made the minutes of the executive committee's approval of payment for the leaflets, were arrested and charged with violating the Espionage Act.[168]

Schenck and Baer were tried in the Eastern District of Pennsylvania. Judge J. Whittaker Thompson presided. Defense counsel argued that the Espionage Act was an unlawful restriction on the right of freedom of speech. Defense counsel filed a demurrer to the indictment. The trial judge overruled the defense demurrer to the indictment, and the trial went forward. The leaflet was introduced as a government exhibit, as were the minutes of the executive committee. On December 17, 1917, the jury returned a verdict of guilty of conspiracy to violate the Espionage Act against both defendants, and Schenck was convicted of one count of violating the act.[169] Defense counsel petitioned for writ of error, which the Supreme Court granted. The Schenck case was argued on January 9 and 10, 1919, and the Court's decision was issued on March 3, 1919.[170]

Justice Oliver Wendell Holmes wrote the decision for a unanimous court upholding the Espionage Act against the First Amendment challenge raised by defense counsel. Holmes correctly concluded that Schenck and Baer had violated the Espionage Act by publishing and ratifying the publication of an anti-war, anti-draft leaflet.[171] Holmes then dealt with the free speech defense raised by Schenck and Baer:

> But it is said, suppose that that [anti-draft action] was the tendency of this circular, it is protected by the First Amendment to the Constitution. Two of the strongest expressions are said to be quoted respectively from well-known public men. It well may be that the prohibition of laws abridging the freedom of speech is not confined to previous restraints, although to prevent them may have been the main purpose, as intimated in *Patterson v. Colorado*, 205 U.S. 454, 462. We admit that in many places and in ordinary times the defendants in saying all that was said in the circular would have been within their constitutional rights. But the character of every act depends upon the circumstances in which it is done. *Aikens v. Wisconsin*, 195 U.S. 194, 205, 206. The most stringent protection of free speech would not protect a man in falsely shouting fire in a theater and causing a panic. It does not even protect a man from an injunction against uttering words that may have all the effect of force. *Gompers v. Bucks Stove & Range Co.*, 221 U.S. 418, 439. The question in every case is whether the words used are used in such circumstances and are of such a nature as to create a clear and present danger that they will bring about the substantive evils that Congress has a right to prevent. It is a question of proximity and degree. When a nation is at war many things that might be said in time of peace are such a hindrance to its effort that their utterance will not be endured so long as men fight and that no Court could regard them as protected by any constitutional right. . . . The statute of 1917 in §4 punishes conspiracies to obstruct as well as actual obstruction. If the act, (speaking, or circulating a paper,) its tendency and the intent with which it is done are the same, we perceive no ground for saying that success alone warrants making the act a crime. *Goldman v. United States*, 245 U.S. 474, 477. Indeed, that case might be said to dispose of the present contention if the precedent covers all *media concludendi*. But as the right to free speech was not referred to specially, we have thought fit to add a few words.[172]

Patterson was a writ of error to the Colorado Supreme Court, which upheld Patterson's conviction for criminal contempt of court. Patterson, a newspaper editor, had published a newspaper article and cartoon critical of the entire Colorado Supreme Court. He was cited for direct contempt of court, convicted, and fined by the judges, whom Patterson ridiculed. The issue was whether a written citation and trial for criminal contempt was required by due process of law. The court held that it was not. It affirmed Patterson's contempt conviction. Justice Holmes wrote the opinion.[173] He included in dicta the following passage:

> We leave undecided the question whether there is to be found in the *Fourteenth Amendment* a prohibition similar to that in the First. But even if we were to assume that freedom of speech and freedom of the press were protected from abridgment on the part not only of the United States but also of the States, still we should be far from the conclusion that the plaintiff in error would have us reach. In the first place, the main purpose of such constitutional provisions is "to prevent all such *previous restraints* upon publications as had been practiced by other governments," and they do not prevent the subsequent punishment of such as may be deemed contrary to the public welfare.[174]

Aikens involved a Wisconsin prosecution for malicious interference with property rights. The *Milwaukee Journal* had announced that it was increasing its advertising space prices. Aikens and other editors of competing journals allegedly agreed to bar any advertiser from their papers if the advertiser had agreed to pay the *Journal*'s new advertising rates. The Wisconsin attorney general prosecuted the editors under a Wisconsin statute that said "any two or more persons who shall combine . . . for the purpose of wilfully or maliciously injuring another in his reputation, trade, business or profession by any means whatever" are guilty of a crime.[175] The prosecution resulted in a conviction and fine against the editors who sought a writ of error from the U.S. Supreme Court on Fourteenth Amendment due process grounds. Justice Holmes wrote the opinion sustaining the convictions. In another passage of dictum, Holmes said,

> When the acts consist of making a combination calculated to cause temporal damage, the power to punish such acts, when done maliciously, cannot be denied because they are to be followed and worked out by conduct which might have been lawful if not preceded by the acts. No conduct has such an absolute privilege as to justify all possible schemes of which it may be a part. The most innocent and constitutionally protected of acts or omissions may be made a step in a criminal plot, and if it is a step in a plot neither its innocence not the Constitution is sufficient to prevent the punishment of the plot by law.[176]

These two cases were the rocks upon which the Court sustained Schenk's and Baer's convictions under the Espionage Act against a First Amendment free speech challenge. *Patterson* stood for the proposition that the First Amendment guarantee of free speech applied only to prior restraints on freedom of speech and did not forbid criminal prosecution for speech after its utterance. *Aikens* justified conviction for a conspiracy, even if some acts in furtherance of the conspiracy were "innocent and constitutionally protected."[177] Holmes threw in *Gompers v. Buck Stove & Range Co.*,[178] a labor case involving an injunction to stop a secondary boycott of goods made by Buck Stoves. The injunction also forbade the American Federal of Labor from issuing any statements that Bucks Stoves was unfair to labor or issuing "we don't patronize" lists to members. Gompers and two other labor leaders were charged with contempt of court and given jail sentences. The Court set aside the convictions on the ground that civil contempt proceedings could not impose criminal sentences. The Court never reached freedom of speech and freedom of the press issues raised by Gompers and his AFL colleagues.

The conclusions implied from *Patterson* and *Aiken* were that (1) Schenck and Baer could print anti-draft leaflets without fear of being enjoined from doing so because the First Amendment forbade prior restraints on speech, and that (2) once the leaflets were printed, though the printing was constitutionally protected and therefore innocent, the people responsible for conspiring to publish the leaflets could be prosecuted under a statute making it unlawful to say or print any matter attacking the draft. This was permissible because in time of war or national emergency, Congress and the executive branch could place restrictions on otherwise constitutionally protected speech in furtherance of the war effort. Holmes and the Court justified restriction on civil liberties guaranteed by the Constitution in aid of the war effort, implying that the power to wage war, jointly held by Congress and the president, could override the guarantees of the Bill of Rights.

Schenck became ruling precedent for the next thirty-five years. It has not been overturned as of 2015, although its force has been blunted by *Brandenburg v. Ohio*,[179] which held that a Ku Klux Klan leader could not be convicted of violating Ohio's criminal syndicalism statute by advocating racial intolerance and government action to expel Jews and African Americans from the United States because the Klan leader's speech was not immediately "inciting or producing imminent lawless action [or] likely to incite or produce such action." The Klansmen had held a recruiting meeting in Ohio, and Brandenburg had harangued the new recruits using vitriolic, racially hateful language with no possibility of carrying out the threat to expel Jews and African Americans from the United States.[180] One must assume that no one is free in 2015 to shout "fire" in a theater when there is no fire and set off a panic because the false cry of fire still constitutes a clear and present danger to human life.

Schenck illustrates the best legal argument for extraordinary governmental power jointly exercised by the president and Congress during time of war to suspend constitutional guaranties including the First Amendment's free speech and freedom of the press guaranties. When the president and Congress deem it expedient to the war effort to place post-publication restraints on the content of speech and printed matter in order to curb dissent from the stated aims of the government, the courts will uphold the curtailment of civil rights. The Supreme Court gave its support to this extraordinary power by ratifying Schenck's conviction.

Jacob Frowerk and the *Missouri Staats Zeitung*

Jacob Frowerk was the editor of a Kansas City German-language newspaper, the *Missouri Staats Zeitung*. Frowerk wrote a series of editorials from July 6 through December 7, 1917, that condemned the United States' involvement on the Allied side of the war. Frowerk asserted that the draft was unconstitutional. He also argued that the prevailing U.S. view of the German Empire was wrong: that Germany was not the epitome of all evil. These statements were the kind of anti-war, anti-draft speech punishable under the Espionage Act. Frowerk and his publisher, Carl Gleeser, were arrested and indicted for conspiring to violate section 3 of the Espionage Act, a violation of section 4. The defendants demurred to the indictment on the ground that the Espionage Act was contrary to the First Amendment guaranty of free speech. The demurrer was overruled, and the case proceeded to trial in U.S. District Court, resulting in a guilty verdict and ten-year prison sentences for Frowerk and Gleeser. The defendants filed a petition for writ of error with the Supreme Court, which was granted.[181]

The Supreme Court agreed with the district court that section 3 of the Espionage Act was constitutional. Justice Holmes wrote the opinion for a unanimous court. He started his opinion with a commentary on conspiracy and the necessity of an overt act in furtherance of the conspiracy, which Holmes said was provided by the newspaper articles.[182] Holmes was disturbed by the absence of a bill of exceptions spelling out alleged errors committed by the trial court, but he was able to craft an opinion affirming the trial court without resort to proof of exceptions to the lower court's rulings.[183] Holmes continued:

> It may be that all this might be said or written even in time of war in circumstances that would not make it a crime. We do not lose our right to condemn either measures or men because the Country is at war. It does not appear that there was any special effort to reach men who were subject to the draft; and if the evidence should show that the defendant was a poor man, turning out copy for Gleeser, his employer, at less than a day laborer's pay, for Gleeser to use or reject as he saw fit, in a newspaper of small circulation, there would be a natural inclination to test every question of law to be found in the record very thoroughly before upholding the very severe penalty imposed. But we must take the case on the record as it is, and on that record it is impossible to say that it might not have been found that the circulation of the paper was in quarters where a little breath would be enough to kindle a flame and that the fact was known and relied upon by those who sent

> the paper out. Small compensation would not exonerate the defendant if it were found that he expected the result, even if pay were his chief desire. When we consider that we do not know how strong the Government's evidence may have been we find ourselves unable to say that the articles could not furnish a basis for a conviction upon the first count at least. We pass therefore to the other points that are raised.[184]

Holmes's statement can be interpreted as an endorsement of the still-developing idea that the trial court was in a better position to evaluate the evidence of a conspiracy to violate the Espionage Act than the Supreme Court. Holmes gave due deference to the trial court, even though his opinion implies that he might have differed on the characterization of the evidence.

In 1917–1918, the law of conspiracy was essentially the same as it is today. A conspiracy was a combination among two or more individuals to commit a felony. It was necessary to allege and prove one or more overt acts in furtherance of the conspiracy to convict the conspirators, and any substantive crime committed by one conspirator was imputed to all members of the conspiracy.[185] Holmes never addressed the demurrer on First Amendment grounds.

Frowerk followed *Schenck*, and Holmes mentioned *Schenck* when he evaluated the evidence of anti-war, anti-draft statements. This decision added nothing to the law of free speech.

The Case of Victor Berger

Victor H. Berger was a native of Austria-Hungary who immigrated to the United States in 1878 with his parents. The Bergers settled in Bridgeport, Connecticut. Victor decided to go west to Milwaukee, Wisconsin, in 1881. Initially he was a schoolteacher teaching German in the Milwaukee public school system. Berger was one of the founders of Social Democracy of America in 1897 and later the Social Democratic Party of America. Eugene Debs traced his conversion to Socialism to reading Berger's writings while Debs was imprisoned for his labor activities. Victor Berger was the editor of three succeeding Socialist newspapers published in Milwaukee, the *Vorwarts* (German language, 1892–1911), the *Social Democratic Herald* (1901–1913), and the *Milwaukee Leader* (1911–1929). Berger ran for Congress in the Fifth District of Wisconsin (Milwaukee and Milwaukee County) in 1904 and lost. He ran again in 1910 and won, the first Socialist elected to Congress.[186] Berger supported the St. Louis Resolution, writing anti-war editorials in the *Leader* that were reported to the Department of Justice. Berger was indicted for multiple violations of the espionage act in February 1918. He was tried before Judge Kenesaw Mountain Landis in Chicago with three other men.

Kenesaw Mountain Landis was one of the most colorful judicial characters ever to occupy the federal bench. Landis was the eighth child of

Dr. Abraham Hoch Landis, whose ancestors had emigrated from Alsace in the nineteenth century. Dr. Landis was a Union veteran who was wounded at the Battle of Kennesaw Mountain, Georgia, in the summer of 1864. When he could not come up with a name for his newborn son, his wife suggested Dr. Landis christen his son for the battle in which he was wounded. Kenesaw Mountain Landis's family moved to Delphi, Indiana, then to Logansport, Indiana, in the 1880s. Landis attended school until age fifteen, then dropped out to work as a clerk. His administrative skills and his active role in local Republican politics led to an appointment as court reporter. Landis was very proud of his skill as a shorthand reporter. Landis was admitted to his county bar in 1890 and then attended two law schools, receiving a bachelor of laws degree from Northwestern University in 1891. Landis stayed in Chicago and opened a law office. President Cleveland appointed Walter Q. Gresham to the federal bench in 1893, and Gresham hired Landis as his secretary. When Judge Gresham died in office, Landis returned to private practice until he was appointed to the federal bench in 1905. Landis was a very short man with piercing brown eyes and a shock of white hair hanging over his left eye. His courtroom style was exceedingly informal. He often stepped down from the bench and sat in the witness box or on the steps of the bench during trials. He was a showman who formulated unforgettable quotations for his newspaper reporter friends on the issues of the day. Landis presided in several major corporate cases relating to anti-trust violations, the most notable being the trial of Standard Oil Co. in which he forced John D. Rockefeller to testify. In 1920, after the Berger trials, Judge Landis was appointed the first commissioner of baseball, a post he held until his death in 1944. Judge Landis banned Shoeless Joe Jackson and seven other members of the Chicago White Sox from baseball for conspiring to throw the 1919 World Series at the request of gamblers.[187]

Berger's defense counsel filed an affidavit of prejudice against Judge Landis, citing the following direct quotation:

> If anybody has said anything worse about the Germans than I have I would like to know it so I can use it. . . . One must have a very judicial mind, indeed, not to be prejudiced against the German Americans in this country. Their hearts are reeking with disloyalty. This defendant is the kind of a man that spreads this kind of propaganda and it has been spread until it has affected practically all the Germans in this country. This same kind of excuse of the defendant offering to protect the German people is the same kind of excuse offered by the pacifists in this country, who are against the United States and have the interests of the enemy at heart by defending that thing they call the Kaiser and his darling people. You are the same kind of a man that comes over to this country from Germany to get away from the Kaiser and war. You have become a citizen of this country and lived here as such, and now when this country is at war with Germany you seek to undermine the coun-

> try which gave you protection. You are of the same mind that practically all the German-Americans are in this country, and you call yourselves German-Americans. Your hearts are reeking with disloyalty. I know a safeblower, he is a friend of mine, who is making a good soldier in France. He was a bank robber for nine years, that was his business in peace time, and now he is a good soldier, and as between him and this defendant, I prefer the safeblower.[188]

Judge Landis refused to recuse himself from the Berger trial. In due course, the government put on its witnesses and the jury returned a verdict of "guilty." Berger was sentenced to twenty years in prison.[189] Berger's appeal from his conviction was certified to the Supreme Court in 1919, resulting in the Court's overturning Berger's conviction. The Court chose the safe ground, Judge Landis's failure to abide by section 21 of the judicial code that required him to step down when an affidavit of bias or prejudice is filed.[190] Berger was not retried.

While Berger was under indictment, he was elected to Congress a second time. In 1919, Berger was barred from Congress on the ground that he was disloyal. A special election was called in the Fifth District, and Berger was reelected. Congress held a second hearing and excluded Berger from Congress again on the same grounds. His seat was not filled until 1921.[191]

Victor Berger was tried for writing editorials critical of the United States' involvement in World War I and critical of the draft. The *Milwaukee Leader* was also denied second-class mailing privileges by Postmaster General Burleson for its alleged disloyal content.[192] The third assistant postmaster general held a hearing in September 1917 and concluded that the *Leader* contained matter inimical to the war effort. Berger filed an extraordinary writ petition in the District of Columbia to overturn the decision. Eventually, Berger's petition, denied by the circuit court, was reviewed by the U.S. Supreme Court. The Court held that the provisions of the Espionage Act allowing the postmaster general to discontinue second-class mail privileges for any publication considered disloyal was constitutional because second-class mail privileges were not a right but a privilege that could be terminated for cause after notice and hearing. The Court also thought that the *Leader*'s editorial staff could get the publication reinstated by changing its editorial line such that its editorials and articles were not critical of the war or the draft. The Court did not pass on whether revocation of second-class mail privileges for a periodical on grounds of disloyal content constituted an impermissible direct regulation of the content of speech rather than a regulation as to time and manner of presentation. The denial of second-class mail privileges was not a direct prior restraint on free speech. Lawyers for the *Milwaukee Leader* raised denial of free speech as their sixth count of mandamus[193] and argued at length in their brief to the Supreme Court that denial of second-class privileges to a periodical was a direct restraint on free speech.[194] The government did not respond to this argument,[195] and the Court ignored the free speech issue in its decision.

The Case of Eugene V. Debs

Eugene V. Debs consistently supported the anti-war resolution adopted in St. Louis in 1917. Debs, a native of Terre Haute, Indiana, was a railroader and labor organizer for the Brotherhood of Railroad Firemen in the 1870s. The Brotherhood was a typical craft-based union for railroad firemen only. The engineers, conductors, and trainmen had their own craft unions. Debs also served as Terre Haute city clerk from 1879 to 1883 and was elected to the Indiana General Assembly in 1884, serving until 1887. In the 1890s he quit his post as grand chairman of the Brotherhood of Railroad Firemen and organized the first industry-wide union in the United States, the American Railway Union. The American Railway Union struck the Pullman plant in Chicago in 1894, calling for a nationwide boycott, refusing to move Pullman's railroad cars anywhere in the country. Debs opposed the boycott but supported it anyhow.[196] President Grover Cleveland obtained an injunction against the Pullman strikers, which he enforced by sending the U.S. Army to the Pullman plant. The soldiers confronted the strikers, breaking the strike. Eugene Debs was charged with criminal contempt of court for his part in the strike. He was convicted and sent to prison for three months. Debs began to read Socialist literature in prison and came out of the federal prison at Woodstock, Illinois, a convinced Socialist.[197] Debs persuaded the American Railway Union's surviving leadership to amalgamate with the Brotherhood of the Cooperative Commonwealth, forming the nucleus of the Social Democratic Party. Debs was the Socialist nominee for president of the United States in 1904, 1908, and 1912. In the 1912 election, Debs garnered 901,551 votes but won no electoral college delegates.

Debs found time to organize another nationwide labor union, the Industrial Workers of the World, in 1905. William (Big Bill) Haywood, president of the Western Federation of Miners, became one of the board of governors of the IWW. Eventually, Haywood, an anarchist, fell out with other Socialist Party leaders and was expelled from the Socialist Party. The IWW continued its program of industrial sabotage and of calling general strikes to overturn capitalist control of the means of production, while the Socialists continued to win local elections in Milwaukee and elsewhere.

Debs quickly became a target for the U.S. Department of Justice. Having refused to repudiate the St. Louis Resolution, Bureau of Investigation agents followed the aging Socialist leader from city to city, taking notes on his public statements. Debs was careful not to make a public statement that could be construed as supporting resistance to the draft. In June 1918, Debs made a visit to Canton, Ohio. He visited three Socialists held

Figure 3.2. Eugene V. Debs (Library of Congress).

in the local jail for alleged anti-war, anti-draft statements. Debs was scheduled to make a speech at Nimisilla Park that afternoon. The speakers' stand was not draped in red, white, and blue bunting. Debs's speech started with a disclaimer that by implication referred to the party's anti-war, anti-draft stand.[198]

The speech was standard Socialist fare for the most part, including Debs's expression of sympathy and solidarity with Rose Pastor Stokes, convicted of Espionage Act violations for advocating an end to U.S. involvement in the war. Midway through his speech, Debs uttered the words that would lead to his prosecution under the Espionage Act:

> They have always taught and trained you to believe it to be your patriotic duty to go to war and to have yourselves slaughtered at their command. But in all the history of the world you, the people, have never had a voice in declaring war, and strange as it certainly appears, no war by any nation in any age has ever been declared by the people.
>
> And here let me emphasize the fact—and it cannot be repeated too often—that the working class who fight all the battles, the working class who make the supreme sacrifices, the working class who freely shed their blood and furnish their corpses, have never yet had a voice in either declaring war or making peace. It is the ruling class that invariably does both. They alone declare war and they alone make peace. . . .
>
> If war is right let it be declared by the people. You who have your lives to lose, you certainly above all others have the right to decide the momentous issues of war or peace.[199]

Debs went on to defend Rose Pastor Stokes and to state that he personally abhorred war. Debs did not tell his audience to refuse to report for induction or to discourage others from complying with the draft. *Cleveland Plain Dealer* reporter Clyde Miller was in the crowd. He had taken down the speech, and as soon as Debs was finished, Miller called in his story and then telephoned U.S. attorney Edwin Wertz in Cleveland. Wertz contributed a sidebar to Miller's article stating that "no man even though four times the candidate of his party for the highest office in the land, can violate the basic law of the land." Wertz also told Miller that he would have Debs arrested.[200] On July 1, 1918, Debs was arrested in Cleveland by U.S. marshals and charged with violating the Espionage Act.[201]

Debs's trial in the Northern District of Ohio began September 9, 1918. Debs's legal team demurred to the indictment on the ground that the Espionage Act placed an unconstitutional prior restraint on free speech. The trial judge overruled the demurrer.[202] During voir dire, most prospective jurors expressed negative opinions about Socialism and Socialist political positions. Judge Westenhaver denied defense motions to excuse jurors for cause because they had preconceived notions about Socialism and Socialists.[203]

The prosecution's transcription of the speech was a poorly done partial transcript by an inexperienced stenographer. Ironically, the Socialist Party had hired a stenographer who produced the speech in its entirety, only to end up being used by the prosecution to prove its case against Debs. Clyde Miller testified for the government, recounting an interview he had with Debs before his speech in which Debs affirmed his support of the St. Louis Resolution.[204]

The government called Charles Ruthenberg, already imprisoned for making disloyal statements at the time of Debs's speech. Ruthenberg was forced to testify that Debs was a member of the Socialist Party who supported the St. Louis Resolution. "I have been accused of obstructing the war. I admit it. Gentlemen, I abhor war. I would oppose the war if I stood alone." The government also called Joe Triner, who was a confidential informant for the Bureau of Naval Intelligence who pretended to be a Socialist in order to get evidence on Socialist Party members' anti-war activities. Triner told the jury he went to a Socialist meeting in Chicago in August 1918 and heard Debs say, "They may call me a disloyalist and brand me a traitor, but I shall stick to my principles. The master class pretends to wage this war for democracy, but by persecuting us, they have branded this pretension a lie. . . . There is only one war in which I have any interest, and that is for the workers of the world against the capitalists."[205] The jury convicted Debs on two of four counts of violation of the Espionage Act.

Debs's legal team looked forward to the U.S. Supreme Court to overturn Debs's conviction and his ten-year prison sentence. They filed a petition for writ of error which the Supreme Court granted. The Court acknowledged that most of Debs's speech had been standard Socialist Party line, but Justice Holmes writing for a unanimous court said that the Socialist doctrinal statements were unimportant to the case. He itemized the statements from the Canton speech that supported conviction, that is, Debs's disclaimer, his defense of Rose Pastor Stokes, and the passage quoted above.[206] Holmes did not address the free speech argument made by Debs's lawyer; he simply cited *Schenck* for the general proposition that the Espionage Act prohibition against disloyal speech was not an invasion of Debs's First Amendment right to freedom of speech.[207] Debs's conviction was sustained. Debs was sent to the West Virginia State Penitentiary in Moundsville to begin his ten-year sentence. A few months later, Debs was transferred to the Atlanta Federal Penitentiary, where he was incarcerated in 1920 when the Socialist Party nominated him for president again. Debs and his running mate polled more than 913,000 votes in the 1920 election, demonstrating widespread sympathy for Debs among non-Socialist liberals. President Harding commuted Debs's sentence to time served on December 23, 1921, allowing Debs to be freed in time for Christmas. Debs did not make a political comeback. Debs died in 1926 at the Limdlahr Sanitarium in Elmhurst, Illinois, from congestive heart failure.

Abrams v. United States

On the morning of August 23, 1918, hundreds of leaflets fluttered down from a New York City factory building to the streets below. People on the sidewalks gathered the leaflets: one set was in Yiddish, the other in

English. The leaflets attacked President Wilson's decision to send U.S. troops to the Russian Empire to put down the Bolshevik takeover of the Russian government. The leaflet said that it was a crime for the workers of America, Germany, and Japan to fight the workers' republic of Russia and followed with a disclaimer that "we hate and despise German militarism more than do your hypocritical tyrants. We have more reasons for denouncing German militarism than has the coward in the White House."[208] The leaflets did not advocate resisting the draft, nor did they call upon U.S. soldiers to desert the colors. The leaflets did not enjoin readers to stop buying war bonds. The leaflets asserted that workers had only one enemy, the capitalist class throughout the world. The leaflet called for a general strike in opposition to making war on the workers' republic. The leaflets had been printed up by a group of Russian émigrés, including Jacob Abrams, and distributed by Abrams's confederates. Abrams and his friends were arrested and charged with conspiracy with the German government to violate the Espionage Act. They were tried and convicted in the Southern District of New York and given long prison terms. The Supreme Court granted the defendants' writ of error. The Court affirmed the convictions 7 to 2, Justices Holmes and Brandeis dissenting.[209]

Justice Clarke wrote the majority opinion. After reciting the contents of the leaflets, Clarke said,

> These excerpts sufficiently show, that while the immediate occasion for this particular outbreak of lawlessness, on the part of the defendant alien anarchists, may have been resentment caused by our Government sending troops into Russia as a strategic operation against the Germans on the eastern battle front, yet the plain purpose of their propaganda was to excite, at the supreme crisis of the war, disaffection, sedition, riots, and, as they hoped, revolution, in this country for the purpose of embarrassing and if possible defeating the military plans of the Government in Europe. . . .
>
> The language of these circulars was obviously intended to provoke and to encourage resistance to the United States in the war, as the third count runs, and, the defendants, in terms, plainly urged and advocated a resort to a general strike of workers in ammunition factories for the purpose of curtailing the production of ordnance and munitions necessary and essential to the prosecution of the war as is charged in the fourth count. . . . The judgment of the District Court must be affirmed.[210]

Justice Clarke did not discuss issues respecting free speech. He cited Holmes's *Schenck* opinion as foreclosing any issues relating to freedom of speech.[211] Justices Holmes and Brandeis joined in a dissenting opinion. Holmes wrote the opinion, which traditional constitutional scholarship has considered a retreat from *Schenck*. Holmes said,

> No argument seems to me necessary to show that these pronunciamentos in no way attack the form of government of the United States, or that they do not support either of the first two counts. What little I have to say about the third count may be postponed until I have considered the fourth. With regard to that it seems too plain to be denied that the suggestion to workers in the ammunition factories that they are producing bullets to murder their dearest, and the further advocacy of a general strike, both in the second leaflet, do urge curtailment of production of things necessary to the prosecution of the war within the meaning of the Act of May 16, 1918, c. 75, 40 Stat. 553, amending §3 of the earlier Act of 1917. But to make the conduct criminal that statute requires that it should be "with intent by such curtailment to cripple or hinder the United States in the prosecution of the war." It seems to me that no such intent is proved.[212]

Holmes and Brandeis believed that Abrams lacked specific intent to hinder the war effort because Abrams was addressing U.S. involvement in the Russian Revolution and not the war against Germany and Austria-Hungary. Holmes reaffirmed his *Schenck* opinion that Congress could act to prevent a clear and present danger to U.S. security, but denied that Abrams's leaflets contained any matter that constituted such danger.[213]

Abrams really does not have any impact on *Schenck*. The majority thought that Abrams's leaflets constituted a violation of the Espionage Act and some kind of danger to the war effort because the leaflets called for a general strike and were distributed with intent to disrupt war production so far as it affected U.S. involvement in the Russian Revolution. Holmes and Brandeis believed that Abrams lacked specific intent to interfere with the war effort.

Other Prosecutions under the Sedition Act of 1918

Hundreds of men and women were prosecuted under the Espionage Act from 1917 to 1919. The War Department issued a *Statement Concerning the Treatment of Conscientious Objectors* in June 1919. According to the War Department, 64,693 men claimed conscientious objector status before their local draft board; 56,830 (87.8 percent) were recognized by the draft, and 20,873 (32.2 percent) were drafted. Only 3,989 draftees claimed conscientious objector status at training camp; 1,978 draftees were considered "sincere" and awarded conscientious objector status by the army boards interviewing draftees claiming that status. Most of the "sincere" conscientious objectors were furloughed to do farmwork or were assigned to the Society of Friends reconstruction details in France. Five hundred four draftees were court-martialed. Only one draftee was acquitted. Seventeen were sentenced to death, 142 to life in prison, 73 to twenty-year prison sentences, and 218 to lesser terms in prison. Considering that more than two million men were drafted in 1917–1918, the 504 conscientious objectors who were court-martialed were a minuscule percentage of American citizens.

The number of Espionage Act prosecutions is still open to debate. Steven Kohn lists 520 men and women who served a minimum of one year in jail for alleged Espionage Act violations. His list omits such individuals as Victor Berger, who was given a long sentence but successfully set aside his Espionage Act conviction on appeal.[214] Kohn's list includes sixty-four IWW members detained in Omaha in 1918 who never went to trial who spent more than a year in pre-trial detention. Other authorities state that more than two thousand prosecutions were initiated under the Espionage Act, but without citing their sources.[215] The probable source for this figure is Zechariah Chaffee, *Freedom of Speech Appendix II Index of Reported Cases under the Espionage Acts of 1917 and 1918.*[216] Chaffee states that "the Attorney General's Reports for 1918 and 1919 show that there were 988 cases commenced in 1917–1918, and 968 in 1918–1919. Out of these 1,956 cases only a small fraction are reported anywhere."[217]

A LEXIS search produced 152 hits for "Espionage w/2 Act." One hundred twenty-four were prosecutions for violating section 3 or 4 of the Espionage Act. Two cases involved the postmaster general's prohibition against second-class postal service for allegedly anti-war newspapers, including *The Masses* case. Thirty-four cases involved search warrants for alcoholic beverages, and two were unclassifiable. Chaffee's 1,956 prosecutions appears to be the conservative estimate of the number of prosecutions under the act.[218]

Space simply precludes discussing each and every case such as *O'Hare v. United States,*[219] the prosecution of Kate Richards O'Hare for violating the Espionage Act in a North Dakota speech advocating Socialism and refusal to support the draft, or *Herman v. United States,*[220] a case involving letters from a local Socialist Party leader to fellow party members concurring in anti-war, anti-draft statements made by them, or the many cases brought against German Americans for uttering pro-German statements after April 1917, such as *Dierkes v. United States,*[221] the case of a Socialist of German descent who declared, "The poor slob—I feel sorry for him. I would rather serve a term in the penitentiary than wear a uniform in Wilson's Wall Street war. Mohr would look like hell toting a gun in Wilson's Wall Street war," and for interfering with the draft, such as *Hinkhouse v. United States,*[222] the case of a Washington State farmer who was opposed to the war and counseled resident alien neighbors to give up their first citizenship papers in order to escape the draft.[223]

More than one hundred officers of the IWW were tried and convicted of violating the Espionage Act in a mass trial conducted by Judge Kenesaw Mountain Landis in Chicago in 1918. William (Big Bill) Haywood was among those who were convicted of advocating resistance to the draft.[224] Federal agents raided the Chicago IWW headquarters in 1917 and seized what were believed to be incriminating documents advocating resistance to the draft and anti-war sentiments. One hundred fifteen union officers and rank-and-file members were indicted and tried together.[225] The IWW defendants' petition for certiorari was denied by the Supreme Court.[226]

Postmaster General Burleson used the authority granted to him by the Espionage Act to suspend mailing privileges for a number of journals, including *The Masses*. The publisher filed an equity action in the Southern District of New York to enjoin the postmaster general from refusing to deliver the paper by second-class mail. The district court refused to grant the injunction, citing section 12 of the act, despite the complainant's argument that deprivation of mailing was unlawful. The Second Circuit decision upholding the denial of an injunction forced the magazine to shut down. *The Masses* was a Socialist magazine located in Greenwich Village that published political articles, poetry, drama, and literary criticism pieces from 1912 to 1917. Max Eastman was its editor. Contributors included world-class literary people such as Jack London, Sherwood Anderson, Carl Sandburg, and Louis Untermeyer. Dorothy Day, the Catholic pacifist, also contributed articles to the magazine. After the magazine was shut down, Max Eastman and contributors John Reed, Floyd Dell, Josephine Bell, H. J. Glintenkamp, Art Young, and Merrill Rogers were indicted for violating sections 2 and 4 of the espionage act. Judge Learned Hand presided at the first 1917 trial. The jury could not agree, and Hand granted a mistrial. The second, 1918 trial also ended in a hung jury. The defendants were not retried.[227]

The United States also commenced Espionage Act prosecution against anarchists Emma Goldman and Alexander Berkman.[228] They were tried and convicted and given long prison terms. Following their release in 1921, the United States prosecuted the two under the Anarchist's Exclusion Act,[229] and they were deported to the Soviet Union.[230]

CONCLUSION

Abraham Lincoln and his cabinet developed an ad hoc program for curbing dissenters during the Civil War. Lincoln, assisted by Secretary of State Seward and Secretary of War Stanton, tried to limit dissent without seeking a general sedition act from Congress. They accomplished suppression of the Copperheads and anti-draft protestors by suspending habeas corpus, arresting and confining known anti-war activists without arraignment and proffer of criminal charges, and ensuring that certain classes of anti-war activists were tried before military commissions without the right to trial by jury. During the war, the Supreme Court cooperated with the Lincoln administration and sustained Lincoln's policies in the prize cases and in *Ex parte Vallandigham*. *Ex parte Milligan* cast some doubt on the legitimacy of the Lincoln administration's modes of suppressing dissent. President Wilson and his cabinet did not follow Lincoln's path.

President Wilson, his attorney general Thomas Watts Gregory, his secretary of war Newton Baker, and Postmaster General Burleson concocted a plan to suppress dissent before U.S. entry into the war. The Wilson administration had a favorable Democratically controlled House and Senate that would pass any legislation that held any promise of aiding the war effort. The Espionage Act and the Sedition Act were the backbone of Wilson's plan to suppress anti-war dissent. On the whole, the program accomplished the mission. Postmaster General Burleson put Socialist and anarchist newspapers and magazines out of business by refusing to accord the publications mailing privileges. Attorney General Gregory, his Bureau of Investigation, the U.S. Marshal's Service, and civilian members of the American Protective League kept Socialists, IWW leaders, pacifists, German Americans who favored their Vaterland, and anarchists under surveillance, and Gregory's U.S. attorneys prosecuted hundreds of individuals for Espionage Act violations. Most prosecutions were successful, thanks to the willing cooperation of the U.S. Supreme Court. The Court ensured that the First Amendment catalog of rights (i.e., freedom of speech, freedom of the press, and freedom of assembly for the purpose of redress of grievances) did not block Espionage Act prosecutions. The Court countenanced post-speech punishment for the contents of speeches and news media, which had a substantial chilling effect on the anti-war opposition. The Court enunciated a litmus test for punishing speech and the press: if the speech constituted a "clear and present danger" to the internal security of the United States, it was punishable. Various verbal formulae have been added to this litmus since 1919, but the decisions of the Court have never been overruled.

The Supreme Court helped to perpetuate an implicit principle of constitutional law: in time of war or national emergency, constitutional liberties may be suspended to preclude interference with the war effort. The decision to suspend constitutional civil liberties guaranties is to be made by the executive and legislative branches, reflecting public opinion relating to the potential danger to U.S. security posed by anti-war dissenters. Hopefully, constitutional liberties would be restored after the end of hostilities. All three branches of the government helped to formulate this principle: Congress passed legislation authorizing suppression of constitutional liberties to aid the war effort, the executive branch used its prosecutorial system to enforce limits, and the courts ratified both branches' decision to annul constitutional liberties.

NOTES

1. See *New York Times*, Aug. 7, 1914, 1 (neutrality proclamation), and Aug. 18, 1914 (appeal to the American people). See Woodrow Wilson's "Appeal to the People for Assistance in Maintaining Neutrality during the Onset of WWI," 1914, last accessed Feb. 13, 2017, http://www.shafr.org/teaching/draft/-classroom-documents/woodrow-wilsons-appeal-to-the-peopler-for-assistance-in-maintaining-neutrality-during-the-onset-of-wwi.

2. See "Imperial German Embassy Note of Apr. 22, 1915," last accessed Feb. 13, 2017, http://www.historywiz.com/lusitanianote.htm.

3. Sam Greenhill, "Arms Find Challenges Allied Claims It Was Solely a Passenger Ship," last accessed Feb. 13, 2017, http://www.dailymail.co.uk/news/article-1098904/Secret-Lusitania-Arms-challenges-Allied-claims-solely-passenger-ship.html#ixzz3oOsbGtVy. The *Lusitania* carried a cargo of munitions in defiance of its status as an unarmed passenger vessel. The Admiralty and the First Sea Lord knew that the *Lusitania* carried munitions, accounting for the second explosion that brought the ship down within eighteen minutes of the torpedo explosion. This was hidden from the public and not disclosed. See also Jesse Greenspan, "Remembering the Sinking of RMS *Lusitania*," last accessed Feb. 13, 2017, http://www.history.com/news/the-sinking-of-rms-lusitania-100-years-ago.

4. The first note affirmed the right of Americans to travel as passengers on merchant ships and called for the Germans to abandon submarine warfare against commercial vessels, whatever flag they sailed under. Three U.S. vessels were sunk: the *Falaba*, *Cushing*, and *Gulflight*. In the second note, Wilson rejected the German arguments that the British blockade was illegal and was a cruel and deadly attack on innocent civilians and their charge that the *Lusitania* had been carrying munitions. William Jennings Bryan considered Wilson's second note too provocative and resigned in protest after failing to moderate it, to be replaced by Robert Lansing, who later said in his memoirs that following the tragedy he always had the "conviction that we would ultimately become the ally of Britain." The third note, of July 21, issued an ultimatum, to the effect that the United States would regard any subsequent sinkings as "deliberately unfriendly."

5. Woodrow Wilson, "Address to a Joint Session of Congress on German Violations of International Law, Apr. 16, 1916," in The American Presidency Project, Papers of Woodrow Wilson, ed. John Wooley and Gerhart Peters, last accessed Feb. 3, 2017, http://www.presidency.ucsb.edu/woodrow_wilson.php.

6. William L. Genders, "Woodrow Wilson and the Preparedness Tour of the Midwest January–February 1916," *Australasian Journal of American Studies* 9 (1990): 75–77.

7. "1916 Presidential Election," last accessed Feb. 3, 2017, http://www.270towin.com/1916_Election. Hughes, the governor of New York, was a progressive Republican. Theodore Roosevelt said that the only thing different between Hughes (who wore a mustache) and Wilson was a shave. The November 1916 presidential election was extraordinarily close. Wilson won California by 3,773 votes out of almost a million votes cast and New Hampshire by 54 votes. Hughes won Minnesota by 393 votes out of over 358,000. In the final count, Wilson had 277 electoral votes versus Hughes's 254. Wilson may have benefitted from the weak Socialist candidate, who did not have the vote-getting power of the charismatic Eugene V. Debs.

8. See the note severing diplomatic relations in Woodrow Wilson, *Why We Are at War 1917*, 2003, Project Gutenberg, last accessed Feb. 3, 2017, http://www.gutenberg.org/dirs/etext04/whwar10h.htm#4.

9. See "Zimmerman Message," last accessed Feb. 3, 2017, http://www.archives.gov/education/lessons/zimmermann. British cryptographers from Room 40 broke the telegram and forwarded a copy to the United States.

10. Woodrow Wilson, address to Congress, Apr. 2, 1917, last accessed Feb. 3, 2017, http://www.gutenberg.org/dirs/etext04/whwar10h.htm#4.

11. In the Senate, the declaration of war passed 82 to 6, with Senators Lane, Stone, Vardaman, Gronna, La Follette, and Norris voting against it. In the House, the declaration passed 373 to 50, with Kitchin, a senior Democrat, notably opposing it. Most of the opposition came from the West and the Midwest. See Frances Wickware, *The American Year Book*, vol. 8 (New York: D. Appleton, 1918), 10.
12. Executive Order 2594, Apr. 14, 1917, reprinted in the American Presidency Project, last accessed Feb. 3, 2017, http://www.presidency.ucsb.edu/ws/index.php?pid=75409.
13. Christopher Eric Howard, "Propaganda against Propaganda: Deconstructing the Dominant Narrative of the Committee on Public Information" (master's thesis, Appalachian State University, 2014).
14. Howard, "Propaganda against Propaganda."
15. "The Committee on Public Information," Propaganda Critic, last accessed Feb. 3, 2017, http://www.propagandacritic.com/articles/ww1.cpi.html.
16. "The Committee on Public Information."
17. *New York Times*, Aug. 1, 1917, 1.
18. *New York Times*, Feb. 3, 1918, 1. On February 23, 1918, the committee sent a circular to all book and magazine publishers requesting that the publishers submit proposed articles on the war to the committee for review prior to publication to avoid breaking military secrecy. *New York Times*, Feb. 22, 1918, 3.
19. The committee hired John McCormack, the Irish tenor, to sing patriotic tunes at Mt. Vernon to a largely Irish American audience in 1917. George Creel, *How We Advertised America: The First Telling of the Amazing Story of the Committee on Public Information That Carried the Gospel of Americanism to Every Corner of the Globe* (New York: Harper, 1920), 204, 207.
20. *New York Times*, July 17, 1917.
21. *New York Times*, Mar. 28, 1918, 4.
22. List of presidential executive orders compiled by WPA Historical Records Survey 1:267 (New York: Archives Publishing Company, 1944).
23. Arthur Brisbane (b. December 12, 1864, d. December 25, 1936) was one of the most renowned twentieth-century U.S. newspaper editors and columnists. "Biography of Arthur Brisbane," *Encyclopaedia Britannica Online*, last accessed Feb. 3, 2017, http://www.britannica.com/EBchecked/topic/79721.
24. Edward Robb Ellis, *Echoes of Distant Thunder: Life in the United States, 1914–1918* (New York: Coward, McCann & Geoghegan, 1975), 435.
25. Ellis, *Echoes of Distant Thunder*, 435; John Morton Blum, *Joe Tumulty and the Wilson Era* (New York: Houghton Mifflin, 1951), 135–136.
26. See Blum, *Joe Tumulty and the Wilson Era*, 116–122.
27. 40 Stat. 220, §§ 1–4.
28. 40 Stat. 221, § 1.
29. 40 Stat. 221, § 1.
30. 40 Stat. 221–223, §§ 1–11.
31. 40 Stat. 223–225, §§ 1–8.
32. 40 Stat. 225–226, §§ 1–3.
33. 40 Stat. 226, §§ 1–4.
34. 40 Stat. 219, § 3.
35. 40 Stat. 230, § 2.
36. This phrase was first used during the Civil War because the Enrollment Act of 1863 contained a provision that any man drafted could pay a $300 commutation fee or hire a substitute to serve in his place. See Camillo Mac Betha, "Rich Man's War and a Poor Man's Fight," Truthout, Feb. 13, 2011, last accessed Feb. 3, 2017, http://truth-out.org/archive/component/k2/item/94447:rich-mans-war-and-a-poor-mans-fight.
37. P.L. 65-150, 40 Stat. 553.
38. 40 Stat. 554.

39. Thomas I. Emerson, "Freedom of Expression in Wartime," Faculty Scholars Series, paper 2801, 1968, last accessed Feb. 3, 2017, http://digitalcommons.law.yale.edu//fss_papers/2801.

40. See Ernest Freeberg, *Democracy's Prisoner: Eugene V. Debs, the Great War and the Right to Dissent* (Cambridge, MA: Harvard University Press, 2008), for the prosecution of Eugene Debs for a speech given in Canton, Ohio, June 16, 1918.

41. More than one hundred IWW leaders, including union president William (Big Bill) Haywood, were convicted in a mass trial in U.S. District Court for the Northern District of Illinois in 1919. The convictions of these IWW leaders were affirmed by the Seventh Circuit. See *Haywood v. United States*, 268 F. 795 (7th Cir. 1920).

42. David M. Kennedy, *Over Here: The First World War and American Society* (New York and London: Oxford University Press, 1979), 81–83.

43. Kennedy, *Over Here*, 83.

44. Alexander Bruce Bielaski, son of a Methodist minister, received an LL.B. from George Washington University in 1904 and went to work in the Department of Justice. He was assistant to Stanley Finch, the head of the Bureau of Investigation (forerunner of the FBI from 1909 to 1912). He replaced Finch in 1912. Bielaski's new first assistant was J. Edgar Hoover, who replaced Bielaski's successor, William Stanley Allen, in 1924. See biography of Alexander B. Bielaski, last accessed Feb. 3, 2017, http://www.fbi.gov/about-us/history/directors/bielaski; and "The Lithuanian FBI Boss and His Famous Sister," Vilnews, last accessed Feb. 3, 2017, http://vilnews.com/2012-04-the-lithuanian-fbi-boss-and-his-famous-sister.

45. Thomas Watt Gregory received his LL.B. from the University of Texas in 1884. He practiced law in Austin from 1885 until he was appointed attorney general of the United States in 1914. Thomas W. Gregory was a friend of Col. Frank House, Wilson's closest advisor, and was an ardent Progressive. Gregory served as attorney general from 1913 to 1919. Kennedy, *Over Here*, 78–79; biography of Thomas Watt Gregory, from the Texas State Historical Association, last accessed Feb. 3, 2017, http://www.tshaoline.org/handbook/online/articles/fgr53.

46. See APL badge display, last accessed Feb. 14, 2017, http://www.policeguide.com/Police_Photo_Galleries/Badge_Gallery_/American_Protective_League/american_protective_league-badges.html.

47. Kennedy, *Over Here*, 81.

48. Kennedy, *Over Here*, 81–82.

49. Thomas W. Gregory to Frank H. Weston, Aug. 10, 1917, Gregory Papers, quoted in Kennedy, *Over Here*, 82.

50. Kennedy, *Over Here*, 62.

51. Emerson Hough, *The Web: The Authorized History of the American Protective League* (Chicago: Reilly & Lee, 1919), 163–165.

52. *New York Times*, Sept. 6, 1918.

53. *New York Times*, Sept. 4, 1918; Sept. 18, 1918. See also Hough, *The Web*, 141–147.

54. Hough, *The Web*, 141–147.

55. Christopher Capozzola, *Uncle Sam Wants You: World War I and the Making of the Modern American Citizen* (New York: Oxford University Press, 2008), 44–45.

56. *New York Times*, Sept. 3, 1918.

57. See biography of Hiram Johnson in the biographical directory of the U.S. Congress, last accessed Feb. 3, 2017, http://bioguide.congress.gov/scripts/biodisplay.pl?index=j000140; Lewis Francos Byington, *History of San Francisco*, vol. 2 (Chicago: S. J. Clarke, 1931), 347–350.

58. See biography of Reed O. Smoot in the biographical directory of the U.S. Congress, last accessed Feb. 23, 2017, http://bioguide.congress.gov/scripts/biodisplay.pl?index=S000644. Smoot was the first member of the Church of Jesus Christ of Latter Day Saints to be elected to the U.S. Senate.

59. *New York Times*, Sept. 7, 1918.

60. *New York Times*, Sept. 11, 1918.

61. *New York Times*, Sept. 12, 1918.

62. See Hough, *The Web*, 13–14.

63. William H. Thomas Jr., *Unsafe for Democracy: World War I and the U.S. Department of Justice's Covert Campaign to Suppress Dissent* (Madison: University of Wisconsin Press, 2008), 265–284.

64. Christopher Capozzola, "The Only Badge You Need Is Your Patriotic Fervor: Vigilance, Coercion and the Law in World War I America," *Journal of American History* 88 (2002): 1354, 1360–1361.

65. John Cobb and Elliott Rudwick, "East St. Louis Race Riot 1917," last accessed Feb. 4, 2017, http://www.eslarp.uiuc.edu/ibex/archive/nunes/esl%20history/race_riot.htm.

66. IWW leadership included an Italian immigrant, Carlo Tresca; Mary "Mother" Jones, born in Ireland; and Joe Hill, a Swedish immigrant and folk singer. See Dean Dempsey, "The IWW and the Other Campaign Part II," Industrial Workers of the World, last accessed Feb. 5, 2017, http://www.iww.org/node/2773, and biographies of Mother Jones and Joe Hill from "IWW Biography," Industrial Workers of the World, last accessed Feb. 5, 2017, http://www.iww.org/history/biography. The IWW was particularly appealing to Finns. Between five thousand and ten thousand IWW members were Finnish. There were two important Finnish-language newspapers, the *Industrialisti*, a daily published in Duluth, Minnesota, which had a circulation of ten thousand copies, and the monthly *Tie Vapauteen* ("Road to Freedom"), which had a large circulation as well. Finnish IWW educational programs included the Work People's College in Duluth and the Finnish Labour Temple in Port Arthur, Ontario. See Auvo Kostianen, "Policies of the Left and Right," in *Finns in the United States: A History of Settlement, Dissent, and Integration*, ed. Auvo Kostianen (Lansing: Michigan State University Press, 2014), 131–156. African American Ben Fletcher was head of Philadelphia Longshoremen's Local 8, which had more than five thousand members. See the biography of Ben Fletcher from "IWW Biography," Industrial Workers of the World, last accessed Feb. 5, 2017, http://www.iww.org/history/biography.

67. "The I.W.W.—a Brief History," Industrial Workers of the World, last accessed Feb. 14, 2017, http://www.iww.org/about/official/StJohn/1,3,4,5; "The Original I.W.W. Preamble," Industrial Workers of the World, last accessed Feb. 14, 2017, http://www.iww.org/about/official/StJohn/2.

68. "The Bisbee Deportation," last accessed Feb. 14, 2017, http://www.library.arizona.edu/exhibits/bisbee/history/whoswho/george_hunt.html.

69. The treasurer of the IWW issued a categorical denial that any German payoff to the union to cause labor trouble was ever undertaken. *New York Times*, July 14, 1917.

70. *New York Times*, July 13, 1917.

71. *New York Times*, July 14, 1917.

72. *New York Times*, Aug. 2, 1917.

73. *New York Times*, Aug. 2, 1917.

74. *New York Times*, Aug. 2, 1917.

75. Edward A. Schwartz, "The Lynching of Robert Prager, the United Mine Workers and the Problems of Patriotism in 1918," *Illinois Historical Society Journal* 95 (2002): 414–415.

76. *New York Times*, Apr. 6, 1918.

77. Schwartz, "The Lynching of Robert Prager," 415. The mob allowed Prager to write a short note to his parents that read, "Dear Parents Carl Henry Prager, Dresden, Germany: I must, on this the 4th day of April, 1918, die. Please pray for me, my dear parents. This is my last letter and testament. Your son, Robert Paul Prager." *New York Times*, Apr. 6, 1918.

78. *New York Times*, Apr. 9, 1918.

79. *New York Times*, Apr. 11, 1918.

80. The other men named by the grand jury were Wesley Beaver, Richard Dukes Jr., Enid Elmore, and William Brockmeier. *New York Times*, Apr. 12, 1918; Lancaster, Ohio, *Eagle*, Apr. 12, 1918.

81. The defendants were coal miners Riegel, William Brockmeier, James De Matties, Richard Dukes Jr., Enid Elmore, Frank Flannery, John L. Hallsworth, and Cecil Larramore; hotel porters Wesley Beaver and Charles Cranmer; and Calvin Gillmore a plumber. *New York Times*, June 2, 1918.

82. *New York Times*, June 2, 1918.

83. *New York Times*, June 3, 1918.

84. Quoted in Schwartz, "The Lynching of Robert Prager," 419.

85. Quoted in Schwartz, "The Lynching of Robert Prager," 416.

86. Pomeroy had survived an 1893 tornado that wrecked the town and killed seventy-one people. See "Pomeroy, Iowa," *Stormstalker*, July 6, 1893, last accessed Feb. 5, 2017, http://stormstalker.wordpress.com/2013/03/09/pomeroy. In 1920, the town had a population of 874. See Iowa Data Center, "Population of Incorporated Places," p. 20, last accessed Feb. 5, 2017, http://data.iowadatacenter.org/datatables/PlacesAll/plpopulation18502000.pdf.

87. Thomas, *Unsafe for Democracy*, 12.

88. Thomas, *Unsafe for Democracy*, 13–14.

89. Thomas, *Unsafe for Democracy*, 15.

90. Thomas, *Unsafe for Democracy*, 16–23.

91. Ellis, *Echoes of Distant Thunder*, 428–429.

92. Ellis, *Echoes of Distant Thunder*, 429.

93. Ellis, *Echoes of Distant Thunder*, 429.

94. Thomas, *Unsafe for Democracy*, 276.

95. See Michelle Jolly, "Sex, Vigilantism, and San Francisco in 1856," last accessed Feb. 5, 2017, http://www.common-place.org/vol-03/no-04/san-francisco; "VIPs on San Francisco's Waterfront," *Maritime Heritage Project*, last accessed Feb. 17, 2017, http://www.maritimeheritage.org/vips/vigilance.html. For an in-depth review of the 1851 Vigilance Committee, see Mary Floyd Williams, *History of the San Francisco Vigilance Committee of 1851: A Study of Social Control on the California Frontier in the Day of the Gold Rush*, vol. 12, ed. Herbert E. Bolton (University of California Publications in History, 1921).

96. "Montana Legends: Virginia City—A Lively Ghost Town," last accessed Feb. 5, 2017, http://www.legendsofamerica.com/mt-virginiacity.html.

97. Thomas, *Unsafe for Democracy*, 272–273. Thomas cites newspaper editorials and statements by Sen. George Chamberlain that civil authorities were inadequate to enforce the law.

98. Sir William Blackstone, *Commentaries on the Common Law of England*, 3rd ed., ed. Thomas M. Cooley (Chicago: Callahan, 1884), vol. 4, 292–293.

99. The following states still recognize the existence of the posse comitatus:

Alabama: Ala. Code § 9-12-2.
Arizona: Ariz. Rev. Stats. § 11-441 (powers of the sheriff).
Arkansas: Ark. Code Ann. § 12-63-203.
California: Cal. Gov. Code § 26604.
Colorado: Colo. Rev. Stat. § 30-10-516.
Florida: Fla. Stat. § 30.071.
Georgia: Ga. Code Ann. § 17-4-24.
Idaho: Idaho Code § 18-707.
Illinois: 55 ILCS 5/3-6022.
Kentucky: Ky. Rev. Stat. § 70.060.
Louisiana: La. C.Cr.P. Art. 219.
Maine: 30-A Me. Rev. Stat. § 382 (special deputies in time of emergency).
Maryland: *City of Baltimore v. Silver*, 263 Md. 439, 452, 283 A.2d 788, 794–795 (1971) (conservator of the peace may call on citizens for assistance); Maryland Const., Art. IV, § 6.
Missouri: Mo. Rev. Stat. Ann. § 84.200 (St. Louis County).
Montana: Mont. Code § 7-32-2121 (duties of sheriff).

Nebraska: Remington Rev. Stat. § 23-704 (sheriff may call on citizens for assistance).
Nevada: Nev. Rev. Stat. Ann. § 248.090 (sheriff may call on citizens for assistance).
New York: N.Y. County Law § 55 (special deputies).
North Carolina: N.C. Gen. Stat. § 17–22 (serving attachments).
North Dakota: N.D. Cent. Code, § 29-06-03.
Ohio: Oh. Rev. Code Ann. 311.07 (power of sheriff).
Oklahoma: 19 Okl. Stat. § 516 (power of sheriff).
Oregon: Or. Rev. Stat. § 206.050 (service of process).
Pennsylvania: Mayors of third-class cities can summons a posse comitatus. *Jenkins Sportswear v. City of Pittston*, 22 Pa. D. & C.2d 566 (CCP Luzerne Co., 1960).
South Carolina: S.C. Code Ann. § 23-15-70.
South Dakota: S.D. Codified Laws § 7-12-1 (duties of sheriff).
Tennessee: Tenn. Code Ann. § 8-8-213 (conservator of the peace); Tenn. Code Ann. § 38-3-112 (governor may call out posse).
Texas: *Hughes v. State*, 612 S.W.2d 581 (Tex. Crim. App. 1981) (posse member made arrest).
Virginia: Va. Code Ann. § 18.2-463 (refusal to assist police is misdemeanor).
Washington: Wash. Rev. Code § 36.28.010 (duties of sheriff).
Wisconsin: Wis. Stat. § 59.28 (duties of sheriff).
Wyoming: Wyo. Stat. § 18-3-606 (duties of sheriff).

100. Blackstone, *Commentaries on the Common Law of England*, vol. 1, 343 (powers of the sheriff include summoning the posse comitatus).

101. Capozzola, "The Only Badge You Need Is Your Patriotic Fervor," 1357. Capozzola also notes that labor relations were policed by private police forces hired by businesses to suppress labor organization, labor sabotage, and other acts of rebellion against the owners of businesses.

102. "Population Characteristics 1900 to 2000," in *Statistical Abstract of the United States*. In 1900, 30,215,000 people lived in cities, and 45,997,000 lived in rural areas. In 1910, 42,064,000 Americans lived in cities, and 50,164,000 lived in rural areas. The great shift in population due to World War I migration from rural to urban areas is reflected in the 1920 census: 54,253,000 Americans were city dwellers while 51,768,000 were rural dwellers.

103. Berkeley, California, police chief August Vollmer established the first police training school in 1916. See August Vollmer and Albert Schneider, "The School for Police as Planned at Berkeley," *Journal of the American Institute of Criminal Law and Criminology* 7 (1917): 877.

104. Will Reller served as the progressive prosecutor of Wayne County, Indiana, from 1913 through 1917. His compensation came from fine money and rewards for successful convictions. After leaving the prosecutor's office in 1917, he founded a law firm that still exists today, the largest in the county seat of Richmond, Indiana. The author spent seven years in the Reller firm and collected stories from Will Reller about his years as a Bull Moose prosecutor.

105. The Black Tom explosion that occurred on July 30, 1916, on a manmade island that was part of Jersey City, New Jersey, was the most serious German sabotage act of the war. "Black Tom Explosion," last accessed Feb. 5, 2017, http://www.state.nj.us/dep/parksamdforests/parks/liberty_state_park/liberty_blacktomexplosion.html012.html.

106. Most of the vigilante acts were directed at IWW members and organizers. The IWW professed to believe in industrial sabotage as a means of fomenting the class war that would allow workers to take over entire industries to be managed by workers' councils. See "History of the IWW," last accessed Feb. 5, 2017, http://www.iww.org/en/history/myths/5.

107. The anti-war movement included Jane Addams of Hull House, Helen Keller, and other long-term pacifists as well as immigrant anarchists and labor organizers such as Emma Goldman. One wing of the Socialist Party led by Eugene V. Debs also

opposed the war and preached against the draft. See Alpha History, "Opposition to World War I," last accessed Feb. 5, 2017, http://alphahistory.com/worldwar1/opposition-to-world-war-I. See also Howard Zinn, *A People's History of the United States* (New York: Harper & Row, 1980), ch. 14. Chapter 14 is Zinn's account of the World War I anti-war movement.

108. See Thomas, *Unsafe for Democracy*, 55–61.

109. Thomas, *Unsafe for Democracy*, 51–52. Thomas reprinted the *Providence Journal*'s 1917 warning to frightened citizens:

> Keep your eyes and ears open. Whenever any suspicious act or disloyal word comes to your notice, communicate at once with the Bureau of Investigation of the Department of Justice. We are at war with the most merciless and inhuman nation in the world. Hundreds of thousands of its people in this country want to see America humiliated and beaten to her knees, and they are doing, and will do, everything in their power to bring this about. Take nothing for granted. Energy and alertness in this direction may save the life of your son, your husband or your brother.

110. Kennedy, *Over Here*, 72–73.

111. Approximately twenty-four million men, women, and children emigrated to the United States during the thirty-seven years prior to United States' entry into World War I from eastern and southern Europe. These immigrants could not speak English and tended to concentrate in the ghettos of New York, Philadelphia, Boston, and Chicago.

112. See U.S. House of Representatives, "World War I and the Great Migration," last accessed Feb. 5, 2017, http://history.house.gov/Exhibitions-and-Publications/BAIC/Exhibitions-and-Historical-Essays/Temporary-Farewll/World-War-I-And-Great-Migration-Historical.

113. See Encyclopedia of the American Nation, "Nativist, WW I and the 1920's," last accessed Feb. 5, 2017, http://www.americanforeignrelations.com/E-N/Nativism-World-war-and-the-1920s.html.

114. The Pennsylvania Council of National Defense and Committee of Public Safety was established in March 1917 as a civilian organization to provide safety for the Commonwealth of Pennsylvania. It later became a cooperative agency of the Federal Council of National Defense. This group advised Governor Martin Brumbaugh, promoted civilian affairs, and assisted businessmen in the war effort. Philadelphia lawyer George Wharton Pepper served as chairman. See Pennsylvania Council of National Defense and Committee of Public Safety Records, Collection 1551, 1917–1921, last accessed Feb. 5, 2017, http://www2.hsp.org/collections/manuscripts/p/PCND1551.html.

115. The Minnesota Committee of Public Safety worked with a private group formed by local manufacturers and businessmen called the Citizens' Alliance. Together the Citizens' Alliance and the CPS ferreted out alleged disloyal men and women from 1917 through the end of the war. Minnesota also had a Home Guard, which the CPS used to conduct a campaign to stamp out the Socialist Party. See MNopedia, "Home Guard," last accessed Feb. 5, 2017, http://www.mnopedia.org/group/minnesota-home-guard.

116. Act of Mar. 14, 1917, ch. 145, 1917 Idaho Sess. Laws 459.

117. Act of Apr. 13, 1917, ch. 215, 1917 Minn. Laws 311.

118. Minn. Laws 1917, ch. 215, p. 311. By 1919, twenty-five states had adopted similar criminal syndicalism statutes. The states were Rhode Island, Connecticut, New Hampshire, Vermont, New York, Pennsylvania, South Carolina, Arkansas, Oklahoma, New Mexico, West Virginia, Ohio, Indiana, Michigan, Illinois, Iowa, Minnesota, South Dakota, Montana, Utah, Wyoming, Idaho, California, Washington, and Oregon. F. G. Franklin, "Preserving the Honor of the Flag: Anti-Syndicalist Legislation in Several States: Penalties Provided for Desecration of the Flag, League of American Municipalities," *Modern City* 5 (July 1920): 20.

119. The states enacting criminal syndicalism statutes from 1917 to 1919 were Alaska Territory (1919), Arizona (1918), California (1919), Colorado (1919), Hawaii Territory (1919), Idaho (1917), Indiana (1919), Iowa (1919), Kansas (1920), Kentucky (1919), Michigan (1919), Minnesota (1917), Montana (1918), Nebraska (1919), Nevada (1919), Ohio (1919), Oklahoma (1919), Oregon (1919), South Dakota (1918), Utah (1919), Washington (1919), West Virginia (1919), and Wyoming (1919). Eldridge Foster Dowell, *A History of Criminal Syndicalism Legislation in the United States*, Johns Hopkins University Studies in Historical and Political Science 57, no. 1 (Baltimore, MD: Johns Hopkins University Press, 1939): appendix 1, p. 147.

120. *State v. Gilbert*, 141 Minn. 263, 169 N.W. 790 (1918), aff'd sub nom. *Gilbert v. Minnesota*, 254 U.S. 325 (1920).

121. *State v. Gilbert*, 141 Minn. 264, 168 N.W. 790.

122. *State v. Gilbert*, 168 N.E. 792.

123. 254 U.S. 328–329.

124. 249 U.S. 47 (1919).

125. *Schenck*, 249 U.S. 52.

126. Capozzola, "The Only Badge You Need Is Your Patriotic Fervor," 1362–1364.

127. Capozzola, "The Only Badge You Need Is Your Patriotic Fervor," 1363.

128. See "The Kansas State Guard in World War I," last accessed Feb. 6, 2017, https://web.archives.org/web/20110216031026/www.kansasguardmuseum.org/disunit.php?id=33.

129. Ann Yoder, "World War I Conscientious Objectors," last modified Sept. 13, 2013, last accessed Feb. 5, 2017, http://www.swarthmore.edu/library/peace/conscientiousobjection/WWI.COs.coverpage.htm.

130. This account of the life of Ben Salmon is taken from *National Catholic Reporter*, last accessed Feb. 5, 2017, https://ncronline.org/blogs/road-peace/ben-salmon-and-army-peace.

131. Allen Sinclair Will, *Life of Cardinal Gibbons, Archbishop of Baltimore* (New York: E. P. Dutton, 1922), 815.

132. Gibbons prepared a resolution for approval by the U.S. archbishops at their annual meeting held Apr. 18, 1917, at Catholic University of America. Will, *Life of Cardinal Gibbons*, 815.

133. Congress passed the first Selective Service Act in April 1917 (P.L. 65-12, 40 Stat. 76). All males aged twenty-one to thirty were required to register on June 5, 1917. Willful failure to register on the day appointed by the president was deemed a misdemeanor punishable by imprisonment up to one year. See § 5.

134. Ben Salmon to President Wilson, June 5, 1917, last accessed Feb. 5, 2017, http://www.bensalmon.org/uploads/8/2/5/7/8257/wilsonconscription.pdf.

135. John Dear, "Ben Salmon and the Army of Peace," *National Catholic Reporter*, Feb. 23, 2010, last accessed Feb. 5, 2017, https://ncronline.org/blogs/road-peace/ben-salmon-and-army-peace.

136. Dear, "Ben Salmon and the Army of Peace."

137. P.L. 65-12, 40 Stat. 76. The U.S. Supreme Court had sustained the validity of the Selective Service Act under Art. 1, § 8, of the Constitution, even though those men drafted would be serving overseas and no foreign power had invaded the continental United States or any of its dependents. *Cox v. Wood*, 247 U.S. 3 (1918). Earlier the Supreme Court had held in the Selective Draft Law Cases, 245 U.S. 366 (1918) that Art. 1, § 8, permitted a direct draft of citizens and did not limit military service to repelling an invasion only.

138. Dear, "Ben Salmon and the Army of Peace."

139. Dear, "Ben Salmon and the Army of Peace."

140. Dear, "Ben Salmon and the Army of Peace."

141. Dear, "Ben Salmon and the Army of Peace." Salmon's wife wrote her husband after the deal was offered in early September 1918, urging him to accept the offer for the good of his family. Salmon persisted in refusing to cooperate in any way with the war effort or with his induction. The Seventh Circuit would later hold in *Ex parte*

Kerekes, 274 F. 870 (7th Cir. 1921) that a citizen of Austria-Hungary who did not desire to become a U.S. citizen, specifically exempted from the Selective Service Act of 1917, who nonetheless allowed himself to be inducted under a misapprehension of the law could not be freed from military arrest for desertion by a writ of habeas corpus. The court conceded that once the military had obtained control over the inductee, even if wrongfully so, it had jurisdiction to try him for a military offense.

142. Dear, "Ben Salmon and the Army of Peace." In 1919 Salmon went on a hunger strike at Camp Douglas that nearly cost him his life in protest over inhumane treatment of conscientious objector prisoners by camp prison guards. Salmon died in 1932 from pneumonia. During his incarceration, Salmon wrote a two-hundred-page manuscript challenging the prevailing Roman Catholic theory of a "just war." Salmon argued that the state does not have the authority to determine if a war is just or unjust.

143. 245 U.S. 356 (1918). In pertinent part Art. I, § 8, reads, "[Congress shall have the power] . . . to declare war; . . . to raise and support armies, but no appropriation of money to that use shall be for a longer term than two years; . . . to make rules for the government and regulation of the land and naval forces." Chief Justice White also invoked the "necessary and proper," clause of Art. I, § 8, in support of the unanimous decision of the court sustaining the constitutionality of the draft.

144. Provost Marshal General Crowder issued a ruling in August 1917 that anyone who failed to report for induction would be automatically accepted for induction, enrolled in the army, and court-martialed if the inductee continued to absent himself from the army. *New York Times*, Aug. 19, 1917.

145. Articles of War § 12 (1916).

146. Articles of War § 2. No provision was made for including draftees not reporting for induction because the draft did not exist in 1916.

147. P.L. 65-12, 40 Stat. 76. The 1917 act made no provision for trying men who refused to report for induction in civilian courts. Section 5 stated that failure to register for the draft was a misdemeanor concurrently triable in state and federal court. It did not provide for civilian prosecution of refusal to report for induction.

148. *Opinions of the Judge Advocate General of the United States*, vol. 2 (Washington, DC: Government Printing Office, 1919), 249.

149. *United States ex rel. Feld v. Bullard*, 290 F. 704 (2d Cir. 1923).

150. *United States ex rel. Feld v. Bullard*, 290 F. 707.

151. *United States ex rel. Feld v. Bullard*, 290 F. 708.

152. 248 F. 865 (8th Cir. 1918).

153. Franke, 248 F. 865, 868–869.

154. *Billings v. Truesdale*, 135 F.2d 505–506 (8th Cir. 1943).

155. *Billings v. Truesdale*, 321 U.S. 542, 559 (1944).

156. Compare P.L. 65-12, 40 Stat. 76–77 (1917) and P.L. 76-720, 54 Stat. 885, 894–895.

157. P.L. 76-720, 54 Stat. 895.

158. See "A Short History of the Watchtower Organization," last accessed Feb. 5, 2017, http://www.bible/ca/jw-history.htm.

159. These statements were quoted by the Second Circuit opinion. See *Rutherford v. United States*, 258 F. 855, 864 (2d Cir. 1920).

160. *Rutherford*, 258 F. 855, 863.

161. Milwaukee citizens elected Socialist Emil Seidel in 1910, followed by Socialist Daniel Hoan in 1916. Mayor Hoan served until 1940. See Wisconsin Historical Society Historical Essay, "Milwaukee Sewer Socialism," last accessed Feb. 5, 2017, http://www.wisconsinhistory.org/turning-points/tp-043?action=more_essay. Socialist Frank Zeidler served as Milwaukee's mayor from 1949 to 1961. Zeidler co-founded the reconstituted Socialist Party in 1972. See Wisconsin Historical Society, "Frank P. Zeidler, the Last Socialist to Run a Major City," last accessed Feb. 5, 2017, http://www.wisconsinhistory.org/Content.aspx?dsNav=Ny:True,Ro:0,N:4294963828-4294963805&dsNavOnly=Ntk:All%7c%7c3%7c%2c&dsRecordDetails=R:CS346&dsDimensionSearch=D:Socialist+Party,Dxm:All,Dxp:3&dsCompoundDimensionSearch=D:Socialist+Party,Dxm:All,Dxp:3.

162. "Debs Biography," Eugene V. Debs Foundation, last accessed Feb. 5, 2017, http://debsfoundation.org/idex.php/landing/debs-biography.
163. "The Socialist Party of America (1897–1946)," last accessed Feb. 4, 2017, http://www.marxists.org/history/usa/eam/spa/socialistparty.html.
164. Quoted in James Weinstein, "Anti-War Sentiment and the Socialist Party," *Political Science Quarterly* 74, no. 2 (June 1959): 219.
165. Thomas, *Unsafe for Democracy*, 162, quoted from the Socialist Party platform of 1917.
166. Ellis, *Echoes of Distant Thunder*, 434.
167. *Schenck v. United States*, 249 U.S. 47 (1919), record of proceedings below exhibit no.
168. *New York Times*, Mar. 4, 1919, 10.
169. "Schenck v. United States," last accessed Feb. 5, 2017, http://www.answers.com/topic/schenck-v-united-states.
170. *Schenck v. United States*, 249 U.S. 47, 49 (1919).
171. *Schenck v. United States*, 249 U.S. 47.
172. *Schenck v. United States*, 249 U.S. 52.
173. *Patterson v. Colorado*, 205 U.S. 454, 458–459 (1907).
174. *Patterson v. Colorado*, 205 U.S. 454, 462 (1907).
175. Wis. Stat. 1898, § 4466a, quoted in *Aikens v. Wisconsin*, 195 U.S. 194, 201 (1904).
176. *Aikens v. Wisconsin*, 195 U.S. 194, 205–206.
177. *Aikens v. Wisconsin*, 195 U.S. 194, 206.
178. 221 U.S. 418 (1911).
179. 395 U.S. 444 (1969). The Brandenburg court said, "The constitutional guarantees of free speech and free press do not permit a State to forbid or proscribe advocacy of the use of force or of law violation except where such advocacy is directed to inciting or producing imminent lawless action and is likely to incite or produce such action." *Brandenburg v. Ohio*, 395 U.S. 447.
180. *Brandenburg v. Ohio*, 395 U.S. 447.
181. *Frowerk v. United States*, 249 U.S. 204, 206 (1919).
182. *Frowerk v. United States*, 249 U.S. 205.
183. *Frowerk v. United States*, 249 U.S. 205, 209.
184. *Frowerk v. United States*, 249 U.S. 208–209.
185. See Francis Wharton, *A Treatise on the Criminal Law by Francis Wharton, LL.D. Author of Treatise on "Criminal Evidence," "Medical Jurisprudence," Eleventh Edition with Large Additions by James M. Kerr*, 11th ed. (San Francisco: Bancroft Whitney; Rochester, NY: Lawyers Cooperative, 1912), §§ 1600–1624.
186. Peter Drier, "Berger: One of the Greatest Americans," *Milwaukee Journal Sentinel*, May 5, 2012, last accessed Feb. 5, 2017, http://www.jsonline.com/news/opinion/berger-one-of-the-greatest-americans-kb57psj-150305515.html. In 1912, Berger was one of the leaders who expelled William (Big Bill) Haywood, the president of the IWW, from the Socialist National Executive Committee. The IWW never forgave Berger for leading the opposition to Haywood.
187. "Biography of Kenesaw Mountain Landis," U-S-History.com, last accessed Feb. 5, 2017, http://www.u-s-history.com/pages/h2074.html; see also David Pietruza, *Judge and Jury: The Life and Times of Judge Kenesaw Mountain Landis* (South Bend, IN: Diamond Communications, 1998); Edwin Wildman, *Famous Leaders of Character in America from the Latter Half of the Nineteenth Century* (Boston: Page, 1922), 299–312.
188. *Berger v. United States*, 255 U.S. 22, 28–29 (1921).
189. *Berger v. United States*, 255 U.S. 35.
190. *Berger v. United States*, 255 U.S. 35.
191. Peter Drier, "Berger: One of the Greatest Americans."
192. *United States ex rel. Milwaukee Social Democratic Publishing Co. v. Burleson*, 255 U.S. 407, 413–414 (1921). These same editorials written by Berger were the basis for his Espionage Act indictment.

193. *Record United States ex rel. Milwaukee Social Democratic Publ. Co. v. Burleson*, plea of relator, dated Nov. 19, 1917.

194. Brief of appellant, 12–17.

195. Brief of appellee. The government stressed the lawfulness of the Espionage Act and the lawfulness of the postmaster general's regulation of the mails.

196. Stephen Marion Reynolds, "Biography of Eugene V. Debs," last accessed Feb. 5, 2017, http://www.marxists.org/archive/debs/bio/bio.htm; "Biography of Eugene V. Debs," Eugene V. Debs Foundation, last accessed Feb. 14, 2017, http://debsfoundation.org/index.php/landing/debs-biography.

197. Victor Berger visited Debs in jail to convince Debs that Socialism was the only possible path toward obtaining labor's rights in the industrial world. "Biography of Eugene V. Debs," Eugene V. Debs Foundation, last accessed Feb. 14, 2017, http://debsfoundation.org/index.php/landing/debs-biography.

198. Ernest Freeberg, *Democracy's Prisoner: Eugene V. Debs, the Great War, and the Right to Dissent* (Cambridge, MA: Harvard University Press, 2008), 72–73.

199. Eugene V. Debs, "The Canton, Ohio Speech Anti-War Speech," reported from *The Call*, June 17, 1918, republished online, last accessed Feb. 5, 2017, http://www.marxists.org/archive/debs/works/1918/canton.htm. See also Freeberg, *Democracy's Prisoner*, 76–77.

200. Freeberg, *Democracy's Prisoner*, 78.

201. Freeberg, *Democracy's Prisoner*, 79.

202. *Debs v. United States*, 249 U.S. 211, 212 (1919).

203. Freeberg, *Democracy's Prisoner*, 84.

204. Freeberg, *Democracy's Prisoner*, 93.

205. Freeberg, *Democracy's Prisoner*, 95. Freeberg believes that the government called Ruthenberg for the purpose of associating Debs with Ruthenberg, a local radical whom the public in Cleveland despised.

206. *Debs v. United States*, 249 U.S. 213.

207. *Debs v. United States*, 249 U.S. 214.

208. Zechariah Chafee Jr., "A Contemporary State Trial: The United States v. Jacob Abrams et al.," *Harvard Law Review* 33 (1920): 747, reprinted in Edward D. Re, ed., *Freedom's Prophet: Selected Writings of Zechariah Chafee, Jr., University Professor, Harvard Law School* (New York: Oceana Publications, 1981), 85–86.

209. *Abrams v. United States*, 250 U.S. 616 (1919).

210. *Abrams v. United States*, 250 U.S. 623–624.

211. *Abrams v. United States*, 250 U.S. 619–620.

212. *Abrams v. United States*, 250 U.S. 626.

213. *Abrams v. United States*, 250 U.S. 627–628. Holmes said,

> I never have seen any reason to doubt that the questions of law that alone were before this Court in the cases of Schenck, Frohwerk and Debs, 249 U.S. 47, 204, 211, were rightly decided. I do not doubt for a moment that by the same reasoning that would justify punishing persuasion to murder, the United States constitutionally may punish speech that produces or is intended to produce a clear and imminent danger that it will bring about forthwith certain substantive evils that the United States constitutionally may seek to prevent. The power undoubtedly is greater in time of war than in time of peace because war opens dangers that do not exist at other times.

214. See Stephen M. Kohn, *American Political Prisoners: Prosecutions under the Espionage and Sedition Acts* (Westport, CT: Prager, 1994), ch. 12.

215. See "Sedition and Domestic Terrorism," last accessed Feb. 5, 2017, http://law.jrank.org.pages/2025/Sedition-Domestic-Terrorism-Espionage-Acts1917-1918.html.

216. New York: Harcourt, Brace (1920).

217. Zechariah Chaffee, *Freedom of Speech Appendix II Index of Reported Cases under the Espionage Acts of 1917 and 1918* (New York: Harcourt, Brace, 1920), 125–127.

218. See Stephen M. Kohn, *American Political Prisoners*, ch. 12. "Sedition and Domestic Terrorism"; Chaffee, *Freedom of Speech*.

219. 253 F. 538 (8th Cir. 1918).

220. 257 F. 601 (9th Cir. 1919).

221. 274 F. 75 (6th Cir. 1921).

222. 266 F. 977 (9th Cir. 1920).

223. For other prosecutions of German Americans under the Espionage Act, see, for example, *Kirchner v. United States*, 255 F. 301 (4th Cir. 1918) (admitting pre-April 1917 statements of pro-German sympathy); *Albers v. United States*, 263 F. 27 (9th Cir. 1920).

224. *Haywood v. United States*, 268 F. 795 (7th Cir. 1920). One hundred sixty-six members of the IWW were indicted in Chicago; 104 were convicted. See Kohn, *American Political Prisoners*, 14–16. Two other mass trials of the IWW leadership were held in Wichita, Kansas, for fifty IWW members, twenty-five being convicted, and in Sacramento, California, for fifty-three West Coast IWW leaders, forty-six of whom stood trial. All were convicted. Sixty-four IWW leaders were detained in Omaha and held in jail for more than a year but were never tried. Kohn, *American Political Prisoners*, 16–18.

225. See "The IWW, Post World War I Hysteria and the Red Scare," last accessed Feb. 5, 2017, http://www.originalcurse1918.com/chicago/iww.html.

226. *Haywood v. United States*, 256 U.S. 689 (1921).

227. *Masses Pub. Co. v. Patten*, 246 F. 24 (2d Cir. 1917). See also John Simkin, "The Masses," last accessed Feb. 18, 2017, http://spartacus.educational.com.

228. See Lance Selfa, "Emma Goldman: A Life of Controversy," *International Socialist Review* 34 (March–April 2004), last accessed Feb. 13, 2017, http://www.isreview.org/issues/34/emmagoldman.shtml.

229. The act required the Immigration Bureau to deny immigration to the United States for four classes: anarchists, epileptics, beggars, and importers of prostitutes. The act barred anyone "who disbelieves in or who is opposed to all organized government, or who is a member of or affiliated with any organization entertaining or teaching such disbelief in or opposition to all organized government." The law also limited the deportation of non-citizen anarchists to the first three years of their residency in the United States. Congress amended the act in 1918.

230. See "American Experience People & Events: Emma Goldman," PBS, last accessed Feb. 5, 2017, http://www.pbs.org/wgbh/amex/goldman/peopleevents/p_goldman.html.

FOUR

Franklin Roosevelt and Military Necessity

> If the Japs are released, no one will be able to tell a saboteur from any other Jap. We don't want to have a second Pearl Harbor in California. We don't propose to have the Japs back in California during this war if there is any lawful means of preventing it.
> —Attorney General Earl Warren, press conference, 1943

In September 1, 1939, Germany invaded Poland. German Panzer divisions crossed the Polish border from East Prussia and Germany in the north and Silesia and Slovakia in the south. The advance of German armored units was supported by more than one thousand German air force (Luftwaffe) aircraft. On September 3, 1939, Britain and France declared war on Germany. The chief German objective was Warsaw, which surrendered on September 27, 1939. Meanwhile Soviet armor divisions and supporting infantry occupied the eastern half of Poland pursuant to the non-aggression pact. In October 1939, Germany directly annexed those former Polish territories along German's eastern border: West Prussia, Poznan, Upper Silesia, and the former Free City of Danzig. The remainder of German-occupied Poland (including the cities of Warsaw, Krakow, Radom, and Lublin) was organized as the so-called Generalgouvernement (General Government) under a civilian governor general, the Nazi party lawyer Hans Frank.[1]

WAR ENGULFS THE WORLD

France and Great Britain were committed to declare war on Germany if Germany attacked Poland. The Soviet Union had agreed not to attack Germany. The United States was neutral and remained officially neutral until December 7, 1941. Nazi Germany overwhelmed Denmark and Norway in April 1940. In a matter of a few weeks, German forces had conquered both states and installed puppet governments headed by pro-Nazis.[2]

Hitler's armed forces attacked Belgium, the Netherlands, and France on May 10, 1940, overrunning Belgium's fixed defenses and small army, continuing on into France through the Ardennes forest west of the end of the Maginot Line. German armored divisions supported by Luftwaffe Stuka dive-bombers destroyed French armored divisions, opening the road to Paris. Hitler's army entered Paris on June 1940. Meanwhile, the British Expeditionary Force that had been supporting the Belgians and the left flank of the French army was pushed back into a perimeter around Dunkirk, from which the British army was evacuated in 1940. France signed an armistice with Germany ceding the north and west part of France to Germany and establishing a pro-German government at Vichy headed by retired French marshal Henri Petain.[3]

At the end of June 1940, England alone had survived German conquest. The English Channel, barely twenty-two miles wide at its narrowest point between England and France, proved to be a greater challenge to German forces than the Royal Air Force. The situation was further complicated by President Roosevelt's attempts to get around the Neutrality Acts of 1935, 1936, 1937, and 1939. The 1935 Neutrality Act imposed an embargo on shipments of arms and ammunition to any state participating in a war. The act also established the Munitions Control Board to oversee the embargo.[4] The 1936 act amended the 1935 act by forbidding loans to belligerents and extended its life for fourteen months.[5] The 1937 act extended coverage of the 1935 and 1936 acts embargo to civil wars. The 1937 act also prohibited U.S. ships from transporting arms and munitions, passengers, or articles to any belligerent. Belligerent nations could purchase arms and munitions from U.S. suppliers so long as the belligerent arranged for shipping and paid for the arms and munitions in cash.[6] The 1939 act repealed the earlier Neutrality Acts. The 1939 act continued the cash-and-carry arms and munitions sales to belligerents. The National Munitions Control Board, held over from the prior neutrality acts, was empowered to issue licenses for arms exports and imports. Importing or exporting arms without a license was a felony.[7] The neutrality act was not repealed until March 1941. By that date, Congress and the president were ready to aid Great Britain and other allied belligerents despite the isolationist movement in the United States.

DOMESTIC ANTI-WAR MOVEMENTS AND THE ROOSEVELT ADMINISTRATION

Domestic Opposition to Involvement in a European War

Although President Roosevelt and many members of Congress sympathized with England and its stand, public opinion in the United States was sharply divided. In the mid-1930s a majority of its citizens and of both houses of Congress believed that the United States should not become involved in any foreign war, particularly in any war between England, France, the Soviet Union, and Germany.[8]

The anti-war movement was an uneasy alliance between Socialist and Communist groups and a growing, well-organized German American ethnic organization known as the German American Bund. The Socialists and Communists opposed any war on the grounds that were quite similar to the Socialist opposition to World War I: any shooting war between European belligerents would pit the working class against itself in the service of the bourgeois class.[9] Father Charles Coughlin spewed anti-war and pro-fascist propaganda during his weekly radio programs.[10] The German American Bund, an organization made up of German immigrants and first-generation German Americans, preached that Hitler and Germany were destined to conquer Europe and put Hitler's program of racial purity into effect all over Europe.[11] The Bund leader was photographed with Hitler at the 1936 Olympics.[12] The post-World War I revulsion against involvement in foreign wars led to the formation of the America First Committee in September 1940 by R. Douglas Stuart Jr., a Yale University law student. His New Haven supporters included future president Gerald Ford, future Peace Corps director Sergeant Shriver, and future U.S. Supreme Court justice Potter Stewart.[13] America First's spokesman was Charles Lindbergh. America First opposed entry into the European war on the grounds that the quarrel between Hitler and Great Britain was not the business of the United States.[14] December 7, 1941, halted the massive efforts of America First to manipulate U.S. public opinion. The organization officially dissolved shortly after Pearl Harbor.

The Japanese Problem: Detention of Resident Aliens and U.S. Citizens of Japanese Descent

Prelude

Japan had its own notion of "manifest destiny." The Japanese Empire emerged from the middle ages in 1857 when Commodore Matthew C. Perry's U.S. Navy task force entered Tokyo Bay. The Meiji Restoration brought Japan into the industrial age. In 1905, the Japanese navy decisively defeated the Imperial Russian Fleet at the Battle of the Tsushima

Straits. Japanese army units also surrounded and captured Port Arthur. The Russo–Japanese war ended in major concessions from the Russian Empire in favor of Japanese hegemony on the Asian continent. In 1910, Japan annexed the Korean Peninsula.[15] Japan was one of the allied nations during World War I, seizing Germany's Pacific colonies and later establishing a League of Nations–sanctioned protectorate over the Mariana Islands. The Japanese Empire expanded its military and naval forces in the 1930s. In 1931–1932, Japan seized control of Manchuria and set up a puppet government.[16] By 1937, Japan had provoked an Asian continental war with the Republic of China. Japanese troops were responsible for mass killing of civilians in Nanking, an atrocity that shocked the United States and President Roosevelt, who favored the Chinese in the Sino–Japanese conflict.[17] Japan also had envisioned acquiring the Dutch East Indies and the oil reserves that would allow its air force and fleet to operate independently of foreign control of petroleum resources. The empire invented the "Greater East Asian Co-prosperity Sphere," a program of gradual acquisition of the Indies and Southeast Asia by conquest and diplomacy to support the empire. The Vichy government permitted Japan to take control of rubber-rich Indochina in 1940.[18] Japan, already exercising control over Taiwan, coveted the Philippines Islands, a U.S. protectorate since 1898.

Only two naval powers could derail the empire's plans: the United States and England. The Royal Navy presence in eastern Asia was substantially reduced by England's naval commitment to the home fleet due to the war with Germany. The United States' Pacific Fleet was home based on the U.S. mainland prior to 1940 when the fleet was sent to Pearl Harbor on an extended training exercise. President Roosevelt became wary of Japanese aggression after the Japanese started a war with China in 1937. President Roosevelt felt that the presence of the fleet in Hawaiian waters would influence the Japanese to back away from their plans to acquire more territory by conquest. The fleet would be based in Pearl Harbor permanently. The Roosevelt administration imposed sanctions including a partial embargo of strategic including sanctions on exports to Japan, barring all oil exports in 1940 and restricting the sale of machine tools and other crucial equipment. He was considering an embargo on scrap metal. The Japanese Imperial General Staff believed that the United States was marshaling its naval resources in order to block Japanese expansion to the Dutch East Indies and the Philippines, due to be free of its U.S. protectorate in 1946.

The United States and Japan attempted to negotiate a settlement of Japan's grievances against the United States arising from the U.S. embargo. Japanese ambassador Nomura came to Washington early in 1941 to conduct negotiations, not knowing that the Imperial General Staff had already decided on a preemptive strike against the U.S. Pacific Fleet at Pearl Harbor. Nomura was not notified of the planned attack on Pearl

Harbor until the morning of December 7. The Japanese ultimatum, a fourteen-part radiogram, was not translated and delivered to Secretary of State Cordell Hull and President Roosevelt until after the first wave of Japanese planes had attacked the Pacific Fleet.[19]

Pearl Harbor

At 7:55 a.m., Sunday, December 7, 1941, the U.S. naval base at Pearl Harbor, Oahu, was attacked by aircraft of the Imperial Japanese Navy. The attack came in two waves: the first wave eliminated almost all the U.S. Army Air Corps fighters assigned to protect Oahu. Japanese bombs and torpedoes killed 2,335 soldiers, sailors, and marines, along with sixty-eight civilians, and wounded 1,178.

The U.S. Pacific Fleet line of battle lost the USS *Arizona* sunk, the USS *Oklahoma* capsized and sunk, the USS *West Virginia* severely damaged, the USS *Utah* sunk, the USS *Maryland*, the USS *Pennsylvania* severely damaged in dry dock,[20] the USS *Tennessee* damaged, the USS *Nevada* damaged and grounded in shallow water, and the USS *California* beached in shallow water.[21] Eleven cruisers, destroyers, and service vessels were sunk or badly damaged.

On Monday, December 8, 1941, a joint session of the House and Senate was convened in Washington. President Roosevelt addressed the Congress and requested a declaration of war against Japan, which was promptly voted by both houses.[22] Japan had signed the Tri-Partite Pact with the Third Reich and Italy in 1940. Germany and Italy declared war on the United States on December 11, 1941. German submarines, already deployed off the U.S. east coast sank the first U.S. merchantman in February 1942.[23]

Roosevelt Reacts to Public Opinion

The first Japanese immigrants to the United States landed in San Francisco in 1869. Japanese laborers had been imported by the Kingdom of Hawaii to furnish labor for its sugar plantations in 1835.[24] The Issei, the Japanese who migrated to the United States from 1869 up to 1924, were subject to discrimination on the state and federal level. In 1924, Congress passed an act barring all Japanese immigrants from naturalization.[25] California placed restrictions on land ownership by Issei and also demanded that Japanese American children attend segregated schools.[26] Despite discrimination, Japanese immigrants and their children established truck farms on leased land in California and set up small businesses, allowing members of this ethnic group to attend colleges and universities by the 1930s. Anti-Japanese prejudice still dogged the second-generation Nissei born in the United States.[27]

The Japanese attack on Pearl Harbor led to hysteria and panic in California and Oregon in December 1941 that continued into the early

Figure 4.1. Franklin D. Roosevelt (Library of Congress).

months of 1942. Public anxiety was heightened during early 1942 by a series of Japanese nuisance raids on British Columbia, California, and Oregon shore targets.[28] The white majority population of these two states harbored latent racism directed at oriental immigrants and their descendants, particularly those of Japanese heritage. In 1942, more than one hundred thousand Japanese resident aliens and native-born U.S. citizens of Japanese heritage lived in California, Oregon, and Washington. California Attorney General Earl Warren's exacerbated the hysteria by public announcements that persons of Japanese heritage were threats to the security of California. Warren and several California congressmen pressured U.S. West Coast Army commander Lt. Gen. John DeWitt to "do something" about the alien presence on the West Coast. Early in 1942, the Joint Immigration Committee of the California legislature sent a manifesto to all California media outlets asserting that ethnic Japanese could never be truly American because their heritage required all people of Japanese heritage to be loyal subjects of the emperor. The manifesto also asserted that California's Japanese-language schools taught their students that the Japanese race was superior to the white race. The California Department of the American Legion and the Native Sons of the Golden West supported the manifesto. The American Legion also demanded that any U.S. citizen who held dual citizenship in Japan be interned in a concentration camp. Attorney General Earl Warren and California senator Hiram Johnson pressured the federal government to intern three classes of persons with Japanese heritage: (a) Issei, resident aliens who immigrated to the United States prior to 1924 who were barred from seeking U.S. citizenship by law; (b) Nissei, native-born U.S. citizens of Japanese ancestry, and (c) Kibei, native-born U.S. citizens of Japanese ancestry who had been brought up in Imperial Japan. Warren and Johnson would incarcerate any person with as little as one-sixteenth Japanese ancestry.

President Roosevelt issued Presidential Proclamations 2525, 2526, and 2527 on December 7, 1941, designating Japanese, German, and Italian nationals as enemy aliens. General DeWitt advocated internment of every German and Italian resident alien, as well as internment of Japanese aliens. Thousands of Japanese, German, and Italian resident aliens were interned under these three proclamations subject to a later hearing on the status of internment.[29]

Shortly after Pearl Harbor, President Roosevelt received a report from Curtis Munson on the Japanese American population of Hawaii. Munson concluded that the vast majority of Issei and Nissei were loyal to the United States and would not assist Japan by spying or sabotage. Munson remarked that the Hawaiian Japanese ethnic population was as loyal as the mainland Japanese ethnic population.[30] Shortly after December 7, Secretary of the Navy Frank Knox charged that local Japanese ethnics were engaged in sabotage and spying for Japan prior to the attack on Pearl Harbor. He recommended that all Issei and Nissei be relocated to a detention camp on one of the Hawaiian Islands. Knox's information from Hawaii was wrong. The espionage program run from the Japanese consulate used Japanese intelligence operatives and a paid German citizen, not local talent. Munson's December 22, 1941, follow-up report stated that Hawaiian Japanese ethnics were not involved in espionage activities emanating from the Honolulu Japanese consulate.[31] Munson and navy lieutenant commander Kenneth Ringle proposed an alternative to Knox's relocation: Nissei in Hawaii would take over stores and other property of Issei, and Nissei would be allowed to volunteer for Red Cross service and, after a security investigation, work in defense industries. This plan was neither accepted nor endorsed by Secretary Knox or the White House.[32]

General DeWitt sent messages to the War Department stating that West Coast Japanese ethnics were communicating with Imperial Japanese agents. DeWitt accepted an FBI report, which later proved to be a false report invented by a single agent, that twenty thousand Japanese ethnics were planning an uprising against the United States. DeWitt's G-2 staff reported that local Japanese ethnics were communicating with Japanese fleet units offshore by radio.[33] General DeWitt at first resisted demands for relocation, then changed his mind and insisted that local Japanese ethnics should be relocated away from the West Coast.[34] DeWitt designated exclusionary sites and zones along the Pacific coast from which all Japanese ethnics would be excluded and relocated. Attorney General Francis Biddle opposed wholesale relocation of native-born citizens of Japanese heritage on constitutional grounds: he was unsure that U.S. citizens could be summarily confined without notice and hearing and removed from their homes.[35] DeWitt lobbied the War Department to authorize a military relocation program bypassing the Department of Justice. The media reported that West Coast Japanese ethnics were in danger of violent reprisals after Pearl Harbor. Damon Runyon claimed that Japanese Americans were enemy agents with radio transmitters; *Readers' Digest* ran a piece "exposing" the treacherous plans of Japanese Americans in California to sabotage California industries.[36] Powerful agricultural trade organizations (e.g., the Western Growers Protective Association, the Growers-Shippers Vegetable Association, and the White American Nurserymen of Los Angeles) demanded that Japanese ethnics be removed from California.[37] President Roosevelt was bombarded by letters from California, Oregon, and Washington citizens and organizations demanding that all Issei and Nissei be ejected from the West Coast.[38]

Attorney General Warren was unsatisfied with the limited internment of a few hundred Japanese nationals in California. California congressman Leland Ford wrote to Secretaries Knox and Stimson and Attorney General Biddle demanding that the War Department or Navy Department evacuate all Japanese Americans from the West Coast.[39] On January 12, 1942, the Dominion of Canada issued an evacuation order for all Japanese national males aged eighteen to forty-five who resided in British Columbia.[40] Supreme Court justice Owen Roberts, chair of the presidential commission appointed to investigate the sneak attack on Pearl Harbor, had a confidential meeting with President Roosevelt on January 18, 1942, followed by a second meeting on January 24. According to Secretary Stimson's diary, Justice Roberts told the president that the Japanese Issei and Nissei in Hawaii were "a great potential danger in the islands in case a pinch came in our fortunes."[41] The Roberts Committee Report was then made public. It contained no indictment of any Japanese resident aliens or Japanese Americans, but it did mention that the Japanese consulate in Honolulu was engaged in systematic spying for Imperial Japan. This set off a wave of media outrage. The *Los Angeles Times* switched its position from support for Issei and Nissei to one of clamor for immediate evacuation of all Issei and Nissei from the West Coast.[42] California governor Culbert Olson met with General DeWitt on January 27. He informed DeWitt that the people of California wanted the Japanese removed. Two days later, Attorney General Warren released a statement supporting Governor Olson.[43] DeWitt in turn submitted his concurrence to Karl Bendetsen, a War Department official, who in turn met with a West Coast congressional delegation headed by Congressman Ford. Justice Department lawyers James Rowe and Edward Ennis also attended the meeting. Bendetsen told the congressmen that General DeWitt agreed that all people of Japanese heritage should be evacuated and that the War Department was prepared to take over the Enemy Alien Program. The congressional delegation sent a document containing policy recommendations for evacuation without notice and hearing to President Roosevelt. Attorney General Biddle was on record as reporting to the president at a cabinet meeting on January 30, 1942, that the Department of Justice was engaged in wiretap surveillance of Japanese Americans on the West Coast without congressional authorization.[44] Two days later, the attorney general sent a memo to President Roosevelt recommending that if Nissei were to be evacuated without notice and hearing, the president should suspend the writ of habeas corpus for Nissei.[45] General DeWitt, assisted by Deputy Attorney General Tom C. Clark, drafted a report justifying removal of Issei and Nissei on the ground of military necessity. Attorney General Warren met with 150 California law enforcement officers on February 2, 1942. Warren spoke to the group, demanding that Japanese ethnics be evacuated as soon as possible to avoid racial violence directed at Japanese ethnics.[46] Secretary Stimson, believing that evacuation was a civil and military necessity, sent a memo to the president recommending immediate action to evacuate more than one hundred thousand Japanese ethnics from the West Coast on February 11.[47] President Roosevelt left word that he did not have time for a meeting: Stimson called Roosevelt on the afternoon of February 15. The president agreed to authorize the War Department to conduct the evacuation of all Japanese ethnics, resident aliens, and citizens alike. He would issue an executive order to that effect within the next few days.[48] Executive Order 9066 would be issued on February 19, 1942.[49]

Executive Order 9066

Executive Order 9066 occupied two columns in the Federal Register for February 19, 1942. The president authorized the War Department and its military commanders to designate military areas from which persons should be excluded. The secretary of war was authorized to provide food, water, blankets, and other necessities to those who were evacuated from those areas for national security purposes. The proclamation authorized military commanders to take such other precautions as they deemed necessary. All other federal executive departments were directed to cooperate with the War Department and to furnish assistance such as medical aid to the evacuees.[50]

Executive Order 9066 is particularly important for what it does not say. It says nothing with respect to identification of allegedly disloyal persons or of any hearing before a disinterested magistrate to establish that any person slated to be evacuated was disloyal. Like the Enemy Alien Act, the executive order allowed the War Department to detain anyone without any determination of probable cause, even though the sweep of the executive order would include resident enemy aliens and anyone else, including native-born U.S. citizens. The order authorized any military commander to carry out evacuation upon a War Department order to do so. The order placed restrictions on travel and assembly, subject to the whim of the military commander imposing evacuation on any population. Although not specifically directed at Japanese ethnics who were native-born U.S. citizens, the Enemy Alien Act already allowed the Department of Justice to round up enemy aliens and deport them or detain them in concentration camps. It would be surplusage with respect to rounding up Issei under the Enemy Alien Act who could not become naturalized citizens. The due process guaranties of the U.S. Constitution would ordinarily protect a U.S. native-born citizen from an ex parte arrest and incarceration. The order was overly broad on its face, authorizing military commanders to exclude people from designated zones without any cause to believe that the excluded people were a menace to national security. Executive Order 9066 was invoked only against Japanese ethnics on the Pacific Coast. Although Gen. DeWitt requested permission to evacuate German and Italian ethnics from the same area, the War Department denied permission to do so.[51]

Most Japanese ethnics, in order to prove their loyalty to the United States, submitted to Gen. DeWitt's evacuation order in the spring of 1942.[52] The evacuees had to leave behind most of their personal property and their real estate without any federal protection for their property. "Relocation centers" were hastily put together in California and other western states to receive the evacuees. The War Department set up a civilian sub-agency known as the Wartime Civil Control Administration to find temporary quarters for the evacuees. The War Department appropriated stables and fairground facilities to house the evacuees temporarily while final arrangements for relocation centers were made.[53] President Roosevelt established a new alphabet agency to handle the evacuation, the War Relocation Authority. Milton Eisenhower, brother of Gen. Dwight D. Eisenhower, was appointed to head the new agency.[54] Eventually relocation centers were constructed and opened in Arizona, California, Kansas, Utah, and Wyoming with barracks to house the evacuees.[55] More than 110,000 Japanese ethnics were relocated from 1942 through 1945.[56]

Some daring Nissei resisted evacuation[57] and generated a lawsuit that would eventually submit Executive Order 9066 and an act of Congress imposing fine and imprisonment on any person who failed to obey an evacuation order[58] to the scrutiny of the U.S. Supreme Court.

Hirabayashi v. United States

Gordon Hirabayashi was born in Seattle, Washington, in April 1918. He was educated in Seattle's public schools and at the time of his arrest was a senior at the University of Washington. He was ordered to report to a civil control station for evacuation registration on May 11 or May 12, 1942. Hirabayashi failed to report. He also violated the curfew imposed on Japanese ethnics by being absent from his place of residence after 8:00 p.m. on May 9, 1942.[59] Hirabayashi's counsel moved to dismiss the indictment against his client on the ground that Hirabayashi was a U.S. citizen who had never been a subject of the Japanese Empire, and the act of March 21, 1942, making any Japanese ethnic who failed to report for registration and removal guilty of a misdemeanor was a denial of due process of law and an unconstitutional delegation of legislative power. The district court overruled the demurrer. The district judge based his decision on military necessity, citing the Japanese nuisance attacks on Santa Barbara, Seaside, and Vancouver as well as the landing on Kiska Island in the Aleutians and the air attack on Dutch Harbor. The court opined that Japanese saboteurs and parachutists constituted a danger to California.[60] Therefore, Japanese ethnics should be removed from the West Coast to prevent them giving aid to their former countrymen. The district judge enlarged on his theme of exigent circumstances. Citing and quoting from *Ex parte Kanai,*[61] he said,

> Rights of the individual, under our federal Constitution and its amendments, are not absolute. When such rights come into conflict with other rights granted for the protection and safety and general welfare of the public, they must at times give way.[62]

Hirabayashi's case was tried to a jury, and he was convicted of failure to report and of a curfew violation. He appealed to the Ninth Circuit, which never entertained an argument on the merits. Instead, the Ninth Circuit

Figure 4.2. Japanese Internment Camp (Peter Croty, Library of Congress).

certified a question to the U.S. Supreme Court relating to Hirabayashi's conviction:

> The questions for our decision are whether the particular restriction violated, namely that all persons of Japanese ancestry residing in such

> an area be within their place of residence daily between the hours of 8:00 p. m. and 6:00 a. m., was adopted by the military commander in the exercise of an unconstitutional delegation by Congress of its legislative power, and whether the restriction unconstitutionally discriminated between citizens of Japanese ancestry and those of other ancestries in violation of the Fifth Amendment.[63]

Chief Justice Stone wrote the Court's opinion, confined to answering this certified question, ignoring the due process challenge Hirabayashi's counsel raised to the statute. Since Hirabayashi's sentences on both counts were to run concurrently, the Court did not have to decide the due process issue of the evacuation order if the curfew violation conviction was sustained.[64]

The Court noted that the curfew had been ordered by Gen. DeWitt based on President Roosevelt's Executive Order 9066. DeWitt's Public Proclamation 3, issued March 27, 1942, pursuant to Executive Order 9066, said,

> The present situation within these Military Areas and Zones requires as a matter of military necessity the establishment of certain regulations pertaining to all enemy aliens and all persons of Japanese ancestry within said Military Areas and Zones. . . . [Effective March 27, 1942] all alien Japanese, all alien Germans, all alien Italians, and all persons of Japanese ancestry residing or being within the geographical limits of Military Area No. 1 . . . shall be within their place of residence between the hours of 8:00 P.M. and 6:00 A.M., which period is hereinafter referred to as the hours of curfew.

The proclamation also stated that curfew violators would be subject to the criminal penalties provided by the Act of Congress of March 21, 1942. That statute established a misdemeanor punishable by fine and imprisonment for anyone who failed to obey a War Department evacuation order.[65]

The Court adopted a description of presidential and congressional war power that was broad enough to permit the executive branch of government to undertake any action to suppress dissent or active cooperation with the enemy without probable cause:

> We are immediately concerned with the question whether it is within the constitutional power of the national government, through the joint action of Congress and the Executive, to impose this restriction as an emergency war measure. The exercise of that power here involves no question of martial law or trial by military tribunal. . . .
>
> The war power of the national government is "the power to wage war successfully." See Charles Evans Hughes, War Powers Under the Constitution, 42 A. B. A. Rep. 232, 238. It extends to every matter and activity so related to war as substantially to affect its conduct and progress. The power is not restricted to the winning of victories in the field and the repulse of enemy forces. It embraces every phase of the

> national defense, including the protection of war materials and the members of the armed forces from injury and from the dangers which attend the rise, prosecution and progress of war. [citations omitted] Since the Constitution commits to the Executive and to Congress the exercise of the war power in all the vicissitudes and conditions of warfare, it has necessarily given them wide scope for the exercise of judgment and discretion in determining the nature and extent of the threatened injury or danger and in the selection of the means for resisting it. [citations omitted] Where, as they did here, the conditions call for the exercise of judgment and discretion and for the choice of means by those branches of the Government on which the Constitution has placed the responsibility of war-making, it is not for any court to sit in review of the wisdom of their action or substitute its judgment for theirs.[66]

The Court abdicated judicial review of decisions made by President Roosevelt and the War Department ratified by Congress that affected the civil liberties of U.S. citizens. The Court also rationalized that the executive branch could take into account the "sociology" of the Issei and Nissei who maintained a separate ethnic identity and did not "melt" in the proverbial melting pot for immigrants from all other nations. The Court opined that "the association of influential Japanese residents with Japanese Consulates has been deemed a ready means for the dissemination of propaganda and for the maintenance of the influence of the Japanese Government with the Japanese population in this country."[67] The implication of this speculation was that the Roosevelt Administration could classify all U.S. citizens into "loyal" (not Japanese) and potentially disloyal (Japanese heritage) and restrict the civil liberties of Nissei because of their race.[68]

The Court answered the Ninth Circuit's certified question negatively and affirmed Hirabayashi's conviction.[69] Hirabayashi was put on probation and ordered to proceed to an internment camp, paying his own transportation costs. Post-war, Hirabayashi finished his undergraduate education at the University of Washington, staying on to complete an M.A. and Ph.D. in sociology. He taught at the American University in Beirut and Cairo and accepted an appointment to an associate professorship at the University of Alberta, where he remained until retirement in 1983. Hirabayashi's conviction was overturned by the Ninth Circuit in 1987. Law Professor Peter Irons "discovered" that the United States' justification of military necessity for the imposition of evacuation and curfew regulations was not supported by the evidence and "fraudulent." He filed a writ of error coram nobis in the Ninth Circuit and successfully overturned the 1943 conviction.[70] Hirabayashi's counsel produced an original copy of Gen. DeWitt's 1942 report, a report that was altered by the War Department before its submission to the district court in Hirabayashi's original 1942 prosecution. Hirabayashi contended that the original report showed that the evacuation and curfew orders were based on race prejudice rather than military necessity. Two years earlier, Fred Korematsu's 1953 conviction was overturned in a similar proceeding on that ground. DeWitt's unedited report indicated that Japanese ethnics were to be evacuated because of their race and the supposed loyalty to the Emperor that overrode loyalty to the United States. DeWitt's final report stated,

Because of the ties of race, the intense feeling of filial piety and the strong bonds of common tradition, culture and customs, this population presented a tightly-knit racial group. It included in excess of 115,000 persons deployed along the Pacific Coast. Whether by design or accident, virtually always their communities were adjacent to very vital shore installations, war plants, etc. While it is believed that some were loyal, it was known that many were not. It was impossible to establish the identity of the loyal and the disloyal with any degree of safety. It was not that there was insufficient time in which to make such a determination; it was simply a matter of facing the realities that a positive determination could not be made, that an exact separation of the "sheep from the goats" was unfeasible.[71]

Korematsu v. United States

Fred Korematsu, the third of four sons born to an Issei couple who ran a nursery in Oakland, California, was twenty-three years old when war broke out. He was turned down when he tried to enlist in the U.S. Coast Guard and the California National Guard because he was a Japanese ethnic. He was working as a welder in an Oakland shipyard in the early spring of 1942 when he was served with a notice to report to the union office. He was fired because of his ancestry. Shortly after he was let go, the War Department issued a Japanese evacuation order for Oakland and vicinity. Korematsu tried to evade relocation. He changed his name and had plastic surgery on his eyes to look less oriental and tried to pass as Hawaiian. He was arrested on May 30, 1942, in San Leandro, California, and jailed in San Francisco. The San Francisco ACLU office asked Korematsu if he would be willing to be a test case to challenge the constitutionality of Japanese ethnic relocation. Korematsu was prosecuted for refusing to comply with the evacuation order promulgated under the authority of Executive Order 9066. The U.S. District Court for the Northern District of California refused to rule on his constitutional objections and convicted him. Korematsu was sentenced to five years' probation and sent to an assembly center in San Bruno, then relocated forcibly to Topaz, Utah, where the government had set up one of ten incarceration camps for Japanese Americans. Meanwhile, his ACLU attorneys appealed his conviction to the Ninth Circuit, which affirmed. The U.S. Supreme Court accepted certiorari and set Korematsu's case for argument in the October 1943 term.

Justice Hugo Black wrote the opinion for the Court, affirming Korematsu's conviction. He noted that Korematsu had knowingly violated General DeWitt's Civilian Exclusion Order 34, requiring that all ethnic Japanese were to be evacuated from the Oakland area. Black conceded that there was no question relating to Korematsu's loyalty to the United States.[72] Black also reaffirmed the traditional rule of the Court that any restriction based on race was subject to strict scrutiny by the Court.[73] Relying on the majority opinion in *Hirabayashi,* Black argued that Hirabayashi's conviction was upheld because the war power justified a curfew imposed on Japanese ethnics in an area threatened by Japanese attack. He went on in this vein:

> In the light of the principles we announced in the *Hirabayashi* case, we are unable to conclude that it was beyond the war power of Congress and the Executive to exclude those of Japanese ancestry from the West Coast war area at the time they did.[74]

The Court rejected Korematsu's argument that at the time of his arrest, any danger of a Japanese invasion of California had passed. If the Court had accepted that argument, then Order 34 would have been moot and would no longer affect any Japanese ethnic in the Oakland area. Again, the Court refused to substitute its judgment for that of the War Department in military affairs.[75]

Justice Black went on to state that:

> Like curfew, exclusion of those of Japanese origin was deemed necessary because of the presence of an unascertained number of disloyal members of the group, most of whom we have no doubt were loyal to this country. It was because we could not reject the finding of the military authorities that it was impossible to bring about an immediate segregation of the disloyal from the loyal that we sustained the validity of the curfew order as applying to the whole group.[76]

The Court again abdicated its power to review the actions of the War Department, granting exceptional deference to the War Department's perception of a Japanese menace on the West Coast, even though the War Department knew that Japanese ethnics were not disloyal and did not cooperate with the enemy. Justice Frankfurter concurred in the result. Frankfurter said,

> The provisions of the Constitution which confer on the Congress and the President powers to enable this country to wage war are as much part of the Constitution as provisions looking to a nation at peace. And we have had recent occasion to quote approvingly the statement of former Chief Justice Hughes that the war power of the Government is "the power to wage war successfully." *Hirabayashi v. United States, supra* at 93; and see *Home Bldg. & L. Assn. v. Blaisdell,* 290 U.S. 398, 426.

> Therefore, the validity of action under the war power must be judged wholly in the context of war. That action is not to be stigmatized as lawless because like action in times of peace would be lawless. To talk about a military order that expresses an allowable judgment of war needs by those entrusted with the duty of conducting war as "an unconstitutional order" is to suffuse a part of the Constitution with an atmosphere of unconstitutionality.[77]

Justices Roberts, Murphy, and Jackson dissented. Justice Roberts went through a detailed analysis of the chronology of Gen. DeWitt's various orders in order to show that the orders were inconsistent:

> The predicament in which the petitioner thus found himself was this: He was forbidden, by Military Order, to leave the zone in which he lived; he was forbidden, by Military Order, after a date fixed, to be found within that zone unless he were in an Assembly Center located in that zone. General DeWitt's report to the Secretary of War concerning the programme of evacuation and relocation of Japanese makes it entirely clear, if it were necessary to refer to that document—and, in the light of the above recitation, I think it is not—that an Assembly Center was a euphemism for a prison. No person within such a center was permitted to leave except by Military Order.[78]

Justice Roberts proposed the following dilemma:

> As I have said above, the petitioner, prior to his arrest, was faced with two diametrically contradictory orders given sanction by the Act of Congress of March 21, 1942. The earlier of those orders made him a criminal if he left the zone in which he resided; the later made him a criminal if he did not leave.
>
> I had supposed that if a citizen was constrained by two laws, or two orders having the force of law, and obedience to one would violate the other, to punish him for violation of either would deny him due process of law. And I had supposed that under these circumstances a conviction for violating one of the orders could not stand.[79]

Justice Murphy wrote a second dissenting opinion. He argued that Korematsu and other Japanese ethnics were imprisoned in concentration camps because of their race without justification.[80]

> This exclusion of "all persons of Japanese ancestry, both alien and non-alien," from the Pacific Coast area on a plea of military necessity in the absence of martial law ought not to be approved. Such exclusion goes over "the very brink of constitutional power" and falls into the ugly abyss of racism.
>
> In dealing with matters relating to the prosecution and progress of a war, we must accord great respect and consideration to the judgments of the military authorities who are on the scene and who have full knowledge of the military facts. . . .
>
> At the same time, however, it is essential that there be definite limits to military discretion, especially where martial law has not been

> declared. Individuals must not be left impoverished of their constitutional rights on a plea of military necessity that has neither substance nor support. Thus, like other claims conflicting with the asserted constitutional rights of the individual, the military claim must subject itself to the judicial process of having its reasonableness determined and its conflicts with other interests reconciled.[81]

Justice Murphy's refusal to abdicate judicial supervision of the internment orders did not sway his colleagues, who were willing to allow the executive and legislative branches a free hand in determining the means employed to fight World War II.

Fred Korematsu served his five years' probation in an internment camp. He became one of the principal activists among the ethnic Japanese for federal recognition and payment of reparation for the internment of ethic Japanese. In 1983, Prof. Peter Irons and Aiko Herzig-Yoshinaga discovered Curtis B. Munson's original November 1941 report to John Franklin Carter followed by three later updates indicating that there was no overt threat to security arising from the ethnic Japanese in Hawaii or on the West Coast. The report had been rewritten and doctored by the War Department to support internment. General DeWitt had already admitted in the course of recommending Japanese ethnic internment that "no sabotage has taken place to date." Irons and a group of California lawyers filed a petition for writ of error coram nobis to set aside Korematsu's 1943 conviction on the ground that the conviction was predicated on an error of fact concerning the threat of widespread Japanese ethnic spying and sabotage in support of the Japanese Empire's war against the United States. The district court agreed with the petitioner's contention that Korematsu's conviction was based on factual errors and set it aside in 1984.[82] In 1986, the conviction of Minoru Yasui was also set aside in a similar writ action in U.S. District Court for the District of Oregon.[83] In 1987, the Ninth Circuit set aside the conviction of Gordon Hirabayashi.[84] Congress passed an appropriation for payment of reparation to every living Japanese ethnic who was interned during World War II in 1988, supplementing that appropriation in 1992.[85]

Ex parte Endo

Korematsu and *Hirabayashi* were not the last word on the suppression of civil liberties for Americans of Japanese heritage: Mitsuye Endo, a native-born citizen of Japanese ancestry, was forced to leave her workplace and her Sacramento, California, home in 1942 to relocate to the Tule Lake Relocation Center because of her heritage. Ms. Endo was solicited by attorney James Purcell to become a test application. Her brother was in the U.S. Army, and she had no connections to the Japanese government. Purcell believed she would be the perfect petitioner to test the legality of confinement in the relocation centers.[86] In July 1942, Ms. Endo filed a petition for habeas corpus in the Northern District of California. The court denied her application, and she appealed to the Ninth Circuit. The Ninth Circuit certified a question of law to the U.S. Supreme Court before deciding *Endo.*[87]

The War Relocation Authority issued a handbook describing the conditions under which interned civilians would be able to move out of internment centers and live in the general civilian population. Administrative Instruction 22 stated that a U.S. citizen of Japanese heritage who had never lived in Japan nor attended any Japanese schools was eligible to apply for permission to leave the relocation center, provided that the applicant could show the War Relocation Agency that he or she had a specific job at a location that was not in the Western Defense Command area of responsibility. The War Relocation Agency regulations stated that citizens released under this program were still in the "constructive custody" of the military commander in whose jurisdiction the relocation center was located. A later regulation provided for indefinite leave from the relocation center.[88] The War Relocation Board would allow a detainee to take indefinite leave for employment or education under the following circumstances: (1) the War Relocation Authority must have investigated and approved an offer of employment or support for the detainee; (2) the applicant does not intend to work but has "adequate financial resources to take care of himself" and a relocation officer has investigated and approved "public sentiment at his proposed destination"; (3) the applicant has made arrangements to live at a hotel or in a private home approved by a relocation officer while arranging for employment; (4) the applicant proposes to accept employment by a federal or local governmental agency; or (5) the applicant is going to live with designated classes of relatives.[89]

The War Relocation Agency also laid a general condition on indefinite leave: if "community sentiment is unfavorable" or when the applicant plans to go to an area which has been closed by the WRA to the issuance of indefinite leave. Nor will such leave issue if the area where the applicant plans to reside or work is one which has not been cleared for relocation.[90] Ms. Endo applied for leave clearance on February 19, 1943. She did not apply for indefinite leave. Instead she filed an application for writ of habeas corpus alleging that she was wrongfully and unconstitutionally detained. Justice Douglas writing for the majority said,

> It is conceded by the Department of Justice and by the War Relocation Authority that appellant is a loyal and law-abiding citizen. They make no claim that she is detained on any charge or that she is even suspected of disloyalty. Moreover, they do not contend that she may be held any longer in the Relocation Center. They concede that it is beyond the power of the War Relocation Authority to detain citizens against whom no charges of disloyalty or subversiveness have been

> made for a period longer than that necessary to separate the loyal from the disloyal and to provide the necessary guidance for relocation.[91]

The Court rejected the government's argument that loyal citizens should continue to be detained because orderly relocation would require personal supervision of the detainees released on leave. If the War Relocation Authority, now a component of the Department of the Interior, simply released people who were loyal, "there might have been a dangerously disorderly migration of unwanted people to unprepared communities";[92] this argument was a more sophisticated version of "failure to exhaust administrative remedies," since Ms. Endo failed to apply for indefinite leave and was never denied indefinite leave.

Justice Douglas then concluded:

> First. We are of the view that Mitsuye Endo should be given her liberty. In reaching that conclusion we do not come to the underlying constitutional issues which have been argued. For we conclude that, whatever power the War Relocation Authority may have to detain other classes of citizens, it has no authority to subject citizens who are concededly loyal to its leave procedure.[93]

The Court reversed the district court's denial of habeas corpus relief. Ms. Endo was shortly allowed to leave the Utah Relocation Center and take a job in Chicago.[94] The three internment cases left the Court with a confusing jurisprudence. According to the *Endo* decision, a loyal American citizen who was native born and never educated in Japan should be freed from internment and allowed to settle wherever she could obtain work outside the West Coast. According to *Korematsu*, failure to leave a restricted area and report to a relocation center as directed by the army was a felony, despite the evidence establishing that Mr. Korematsu was a loyal native-born American citizen, even though *Endo* would be precedent for his immediate release if Korematsu had filed a petition for writ of habeas corpus instead of appealing his conviction. According to *Hirabayashi*, a loyal native-born American citizen was guilty of a curfew violation, even though the curfew applied only to U.S. citizens of Japanese descent and, according to *Endo*, Hirabayashi would have been instantly freed from custody if he had reported to a relocation center. Hirabayashi was still required to comply with the curfew as if he was a disloyal person.

INTERNMENT OF U.S. CITIZENS AND RESIDENT ALIENS OF GERMAN AND ITALIAN ORIGIN

German Internment

Resident aliens who were German citizens were also interned during World War II. Unlike the Japanese evacuation and internment orders, U.S. citizens who had German heritage were not rounded up and interned. The number of individuals of German heritage was so high that a general internment was palpably impossible. General DeWitt had originally requested that German and Italian nationals living in the West Coast exclusionary zones be evacuated with the Japanese ethnics, but the War Department vetoed that request, using the Alien Enemy Act's provisions to round up German citizens in the United States for whom some semblance of probable cause could be put together. Arthur Jacobs, coeditor of *World War Two Experiences: The Internment of German-Americans*, stated that European Americans accounted for 56 percent of those people interned under the Alien Control Act. Some 10,905 Germans, 3,278 Italians, 53 Hungarians, 25 Rumanians, 5 Bulgarians, and 161 other aliens were interned without notice and hearing by the Immigration and Naturalization Service.[95] This total does not include ethnic Germans from Latin America who were interned in the United States.[96] German resident aliens interned under the 1798 act were, according an administrative hearing, without right of counsel after initial internment. There were no appeals from the decision of the administrator on the status of a particular individual. Habeas corpus actions filed to free German aliens were not successful. Only those individuals who could prove that they were not German citizens were granted their freedom. The most significant case, *United States ex rel. Schwartzkopf v. Uhl*,[97] decided in 1943, granted habeas corpus to a German Jew who was interned and held indefinitely after an administrative hearing officer determined that he was a "German national." At one time he had been a naturalized German citizen although he was born in Prague, the capital of the Austrian province of Bohemia. He returned to Austria in 1927 and was naturalized. He immigrated to the United States in 1936 before Hitler's Anschluss, the seizure of Austria and most of Czechoslovakia and their annexation into the Third Reich. The administrator determined that Schwartzkopf's homeland as of 1942 was part of the Third Reich, making Schwartzkopf de facto a German alien.[98] The administrator's determination could not be appealed, so Schwartzkopf filed a writ of habeas corpus to test his detention. The district court dismissed his petition, and he appealed to the Second Circuit. The United States contended that Schwartzkopf was a de facto German citizen because of the Anschluss, even though the United States never recognized the legitimacy of the seizure of Austria and Czechoslovakia and Hitler issued an executive order depriving all Jews in the Third Reich of German citizenship.[99] The court homed in on the issue of "citizen of Germany."

> In determining who are "citizens" of a foreign nation our courts must consider not only the municipal law of the foreign nation but also the accepted rules and practices under international law. If the relator's citizenship be tested by the municipal law of Germany—disregarding for the moment the cancellation of his German citizenship by the November 1941 "Executive Order"—the claim that he is a citizen of Germany must be based upon the conquest and annexation of Austria and the decree of July 3, 1938, granting German citizenship to all citizens of Austria. But under generally accepted principles of international law Germany could impose citizenship by annexation (collective naturalization) only on those who were inhabitants of Austria in 1938.[100]

Since Schwartzkopf had left Austria two years before Hitler seized the country and annexed it, he was not a "German citizen" and could go free.

> We cannot doubt therefore that the word "citizen" as used in the statute must be construed in the light of this accepted right of election. So construed the appellant is not a citizen of Germany within the meaning of the Act. More than a year before the German conquest he fled from Austria and came to this country for permanent residence, and nothing is shown to indicate that he has ever consented to accept the sovereignty of the invader.[101]

Other detainees who could establish citizenship in some other country were also freed, even though their country of origin had been incorporated into Hitler's Third Reich.[102] Those who could not do so were subject to deportation to Nazi Germany, and post-war to the German Federal Republic.

The post-war case of *Ludecke v. Watkins*[103] illustrated how German nationals were treated by the courts. Ludecke, a former Nazi and German citizen, had been sent to a concentration camp by Hitler as part of the purge of Ernst Roehm's brownshirts from the party. He escaped and fled to the United States where he wrote and published an anti-Hitler book excoriating Hitler as a treacherous monster. His application for U.S. citizenship was denied in 1938. Shortly after Pearl Harbor, he was detained, and his administrative hearing determined that he was a dangerous German national. He was interned for the duration of hostilities and was scheduled for post-war deportation to Germany when he filed his habeas corpus petition. The district court dismissed the petition and the circuit court affirmed.[104] The Supreme Court accepted certiorari and also affirmed the dismissal. Justice Frankfurter, writing for the majority, held that the executive decision to intern German nationals under the 1798 act and to deport them even after the end of hostilities was not a fit subject for judicial review.[105]

Italian Internment

According to 1940 census data, more than six hundred thousand U.S. residents were natives of Italy. Many had never applied for U.S. citizenship. Mussolini's regime was part of the original Tri-Partite Pact and joined Germany in attacking Albania and southern France in 1940. More than three thousand Italian citizens were interned from December 1941 under the 1798 act. Attorney General Biddle announced that restrictions on Italian nationals including internment would end effective October 12, 1942.[106] When Italy capitulated in 1943 and joined the Allies, the remaining detainees were released over a period of a year's time.[107] There is no record that any Italian detainee filed a habeas corpus petition to test the lawfulness of the detention order.

GERMAN ESPIONAGE AND DOMESTIC SPIES

Background

The United States had been penetrated by German espionage agents operating from German consulates and the German embassy in Washington as early as 1936.[108] Two rival agencies conducted the German intelligence program affecting the United States. The first agency was organized under the German [Armed Forces] High Command (OKW) known as the *Amt Auslands und Abwehr* ("Abwehr"). The Abwehr was an independent branch of the service commands. The German Wehrmacht (army), Kriegsmarine (navy), and Luftwaffe (air force) also had their own intelligence sections. The military intelligence sections conducted no secret intelligence activities themselves. They depended on the Abwehr for intelligence information. The Abwehr also furnished strategic intelligence to the OKW. The Abwehr had three divisions ("Abteilung"). Abt I was responsible for offensive intelligence, including espionage; Abt II for sabotage and subversion; and Abt III for counterintelligence and security. Abt I was divided into separate sections for military, naval, air, and economic intelligence, plus certain technical sections. Each section was broken down into geographical subsections. The Abwehr had its headquarters in Berlin and field offices throughout Germany and occupied countries known as *Abwehrstellen* (Asts). The Asts had branch offices known as *Nebenstellen* (Nests). German intelligence operatives in neutral countries like the United States were known as *Kriegsorganisations* (KO), working out of the German embassy or consulate office. Ast Hamburg and Nest Bremen were responsible for wartime espionage against the United States, but another Ast or KO could send agents to the United States. Abwehr offices were staffed by active, reserve, or retired officers of the army, navy, and air force and by civilians recruited by the Abwehr.[109]

Germany had a second intelligence agency, the Sicherheitsdienst (SD), which was the Nazi Party's intelligence and security service. In September 1939, the SD was merged with the Gestapo and other police agencies to form the Reichssicherheitshauptamt (RSHA), the central security service of the Reich. The SD, whose staff were almost all Nazi Party members, established section Amt VI as its foreign intelligence section and trained and sent its own agents to the Allied nations and neutrals. The SD agents at first collected only political intelligence. By the beginning of 1944, SD had its own espionage programs in Spain, Argentina, and elsewhere.[110]

The SD plotted to take over the Abwehr. The SD's takeover was backed by the SS's commander, Heinrich Himmler,[111] and Ernst Kaltenbrunner, the head of RSHA.[112] In the spring of 1944, the RSHA took over the Abwehr. The Abwehr was the predominant sabotage and espionage agency from 1939 to 1944, and the SD predominated in the latter stages of the war.[113] The Abwehr dispatched agents to the United States before and after December 7, 1941. Many were inept and were quickly apprehended by the FBI and local police.

German Espionage Agents

Four German agents landed from a German U-boat at Amagansett, Long Island, in the wee hours of June 13, 1942.[114] The agents were armed with explosives and primers in order to sabotage U.S. defense industries. Four days later, four more German agents were put ashore from a second U-boat at Ponte Vedra Beach, near Jacksonville, Florida.[115] All eight German agents were apprehended by June 27, 1942, and were taken into military custody. President Roosevelt authorized trial by military commission for the eight agents. The military commission met in the Justice Department building in downtown Washington from July 8 to August 4, 1942. Attorney General Francis Biddle was lead prosecutor, supported by Judge Advocate General Myron C. Cramer. The German agents were defended by Col. Kenneth C. Royall (later secretary of war under President Truman) and Maj. Lausen H. Stone.[116] The commission convicted all eight men and sentenced them to be hanged. Attorney General Biddle petitioned President Roosevelt to commute the death sentences for George Dash and Ernest Peter Berger. The president sentenced Dash to thirty years, and Berger drew a life sentence.[117]

Ex parte Quirin

On July 2, 1942, President Roosevelt ordered that the German saboteurs be tried by military commission according to the law of war and the Articles of War. He directed the commission to try petitioners for offenses against the law of war and the Articles of War and prescribed regulations for the procedure on the trial and for review of the record of the trial and of any judgment or sentence of the commission. On the same day, by proclamation, the president declared that

> all persons who are subjects, citizens or residents of any nation at war with the United States or who give obedience to or act under the direction of any such nation, and who during time of war enter or attempt to enter the United States . . . through coastal or boundary defenses, and are charged with committing or attempting or preparing to commit sabotage, espionage, hostile or warlike acts, or violations of the law of war, shall be subject to the law of war and to the jurisdiction of military tribunals.[118]

The judge advocate general preferred charges on July 3, 1942, charging the German saboteurs with the following:

1. violation of the law of war;
2. violation of Article 81 of the Articles of War, defining the offense of relieving or attempting to relieve, or corresponding with or giving intelligence to, the enemy;
3. violation of Article 82, defining the offense of spying; and
4. conspiracy to commit the offenses alleged in charges 1, 2, and 3.[119]

Richard Quirin, one of the six men condemned to death, received legal help from appointed military defense counsel Col. Kenneth C. Royall, assisted by Col. Cassius M. Dowell. Royall filed a petition for leave to file a writ of habeas corpus in the U.S. District Court for the District of Columbia. The petition was denied.[120] Royall then petitioned the U.S. Supreme Court for leave to file habeas corpus. After filing the writ petition, Royall also pursued an appeal to the D.C. Circuit which was denied. Royall filed a writ of certiorari from the D.C. Circuit's order denying habeas.[121]

The petitioners' grounds for seeking release from custody were as follows: (a) Article 82 of the Articles of War providing for trial of spies and saboteurs by military commission applied only to acts committed in connection with actual military operations on or near military installations; the German agents were apprehended outside the zone of any military installation and not subject to trial by military commission; and (b) trial before a military commission when the civilian courts were open and able to conduct business was a violation of the Fifth Amendment. The Court set up the issue so that it could decide the case without issuing the writ and holding a return on writ hearing. The Court said that "it may without issuing the writ consider and determine whether the facts alleged by the petition, if proved, would warrant discharge of the prisoner."[122]

The Court concluded that the presidential order directing them to be tried by military commission under the Articles of War was not a denial of any of the saboteurs' Fifth and Sixth Amendment rights to a fair trial. The Court said that setting aside a presidential order and proclamation in time of war when the president was acting as commander in chief of the army was impossible unless the court had "the clear conviction that they are in conflict with the Constitution or laws of Congress constitutionally enacted."[123]

The Court noted that the Constitution provided Congress with the authority to "provide for the common Defence," "to raise and support Armies," "to provide and maintain a Navy," and "to make Rules for the Government and Regulation of the land a naval forces."[124] The Court identified the grant of power to the president of "executive Power," the presidential duty to "take Care that the Laws be faithfully executed," the president's status as "the Commander in Chief of the Army and Navy," and the grant of power to "appoint and commission officers of the United States.[125] The Court concluded that these general grants of power authorized the president to appoint military commissions for the purpose of trying enemy saboteurs, whether or not any were U.S. citizens.[126] The Court noted that the law of war is part of the law of nations and that Congress has provided for trial of offenders against the law of war through enacting Article 15 of the Articles of War.[127] The Court noted that the president chose to exercise the authority established by Article 15 to set up a military commission to try the saboteurs. The Court said,

> It is unnecessary for present purposes to determine to what extent the President as Commander in Chief has constitutional power to create military commissions without the support of Congressional legislation. For here Congress has authorized trial of offenses against the law of war before such commissions. We are concerned only with the question whether it is within the constitutional power of the National Government to place petitioners upon trial before a military commission for the offenses with which they are charged. We must therefore first inquire whether any of the acts charged is an offense against the law of war cognizable before a military tribunal, and if so whether the Constitution prohibits the trial.[128]

The Court's analysis of Article 15 involved stretching the elasticity of statutory construction almost to the breaking point. The Court then concluded that the Articles of War did not offend against the Fifth and Sixth Amendments to the Constitution because the charges and specifications of the judge advocate general alleged offenses against the law of war.[129] The Court identified the saboteurs as "unlawful combatants" and "spies," citing Winthrop's Precedents and sections 4 and 5 of General Order 100.[130] The Court distinguished the saboteurs from *Ex parte Milligan* on the ground that Lambdin Milligan was a longtime citizen of Indiana, and the saboteurs who were U.S. citizens were, with one exception, naturalized citizens.[131] The dicta relating to *Milligan* substantially reduced the constitutional power of the *Milligan* decision.

Quirin was an important source of precedent for President Bush's executive order setting up military commissions to try Guantanamo detainees and the follow-up act of Congress used by the Bush and Obama administrations to authorize trial by military commission. If *Quirin* represents the state of the law, it is authority for the president to set up a tribunal that will not be subject to judicial review to try alleged offenders against the law of war. Post-war, *Quirin* provided support for the trial of Japanese war criminals by an international military commission.[132] *Quirin* will appear in the twenty-first century as one of the primary cases cited in support of President Bush's establishment of military commissions to try Guantanamo detainees, the Supreme Court carefully distinguishing *Quirin* from the facts involved in *Boumedienne v. Bush* and *Hamdi v. Rumsfeld*.[133]

Gimpel and Colepaugh

Nazi spies and saboteurs, including native-born U.S. citizens, were tried by military commission after the *Quirin* decision. The best-known prosecution was the trial of Erich Gimpel and William Colepaugh, a native U.S. citizen, for espionage in the winter of 1945. Gimpel and Colepaugh were trained Nazi spies. Gimpel was a Peruvian resident alien who was interned shortly after hostilities broke out and later transferred to a U.S. detention center in Texas before he was shipped back to Germany in 1941. Colepaugh, an MIT graduate, was so pro-German that he got in trouble with his local draft board. Colepaugh's mother was a German national. Colepaugh fled the United States, serving as a seaman on a Swedish ship, then to Germany where he was recruited as a spy.[134] On October 24, 1944, the two spies boarded U-1230 headed for the U.S. East Coast. Gimpel and Colepaugh left U-1230 on November 29, 1944, in Frenchman's Bay, Maine. Anticipating the possibility that an enemy submarine, estimated westbound in Canadian waters late in November, might enter the Gulf of Maine, the commander of the Eastern Sea Frontier ordered precautionary air sweeps in that area. Daylight air patrols were flown on several days beginning on November 23, when weather permitted. Coordinated with these flights were Royal Canadian Air Force flights made on November 26 and 27, three hours before first light. No contacts were reported.[135] The two spies, wearing light overcoats, were spotted by civilians as they tramped down a local highway. The two were picked up by a local taxi driver and a train ride to Portland, Maine. The spies left Portland by train to New York City where they set up a spy headquarters at a New York City hotel.[136] Colepaugh came down with a case of cold feet and left the hotel with all the cash and the suitcases. He told a friend in Connecticut that he was a German spy. The FBI was called in, and Gimpel was arrested the next day.[137]

Gimpel and Colepaugh were tried by military commission in February 1945. Both men were convicted and sentenced to death. Before their sentences could be executed, President Roosevelt died, and all executions were suspended. President Truman commuted their sentences to life; Gimpel was deported in 1955, and Colepaugh was freed in 1962. At last report, Colepaugh was living in Florida in a rest home.[138] Neither man challenged the legality of the military commission trial by seeking habeas corpus review. A reviewing court would probably have refused the writ based on *Ex parte Quirin*.

MARTIAL LAW AND TRIAL BY MILITARY COMMISSION

Martial Law in Hawaii

On the afternoon of December 7, 1941, Hawaiian territorial governor Joseph B. Poindexter declared martial law and suspended the writ of habeas corpus in Hawaii. On the 8th, Lt. Gen. Walter C. Short, commanding general of all army forces in Hawaiian forces, issued a proclamation declaring that he was taking over the government and assuming the military governorship of Hawaii.[139] During the period of martial law, ordinary civilians were prosecuted by military commissions for petty civilian offenses. Side by side with these military tribunals, the U.S. District Court for Hawaii continued to operate. The military governor ordered that no criminal jury trials were to be conducted. That ban was lifted in 1944.[140]

In 1944, two men convicted of ordinary civilian crimes by military commissions sitting in Hawaii challenged their convictions in U.S. District Court for the Territory of Hawaii by filing habeas corpus applications. Harry White, a Honolulu stockbroker, was arrested for embezzlement by military police on August 20, 1942.[141] Civilian courts were not allowed to conduct jury trials by the military governor. White was tried by a military commission called a "provost court" over his lawyer's objection to military jurisdiction. White's trial was held on August 25, resulting in his conviction and sentencing to five years' imprisonment, later reduced to four years.[142]

Lloyd C. Duncan was a civilian shipfitter employed in the navy yard at Honolulu. On February 24, 1944, Duncan had an altercation with two armed marine sentries at the navy yard. He was arrested by the military authorities. In early 1944, the civilian courts were open and conducting criminal jury trials. Duncan was tried by military commission for violating paragraph 8.01, Title 8, of General Order No. 2, forbidding assault on military or naval personnel with intent to resist or hinder them in the discharge of their duty. Duncan was convicted and sentenced to six months' imprisonment.[143]

Both men filed applications for writs of habeas corpus. The District Court for the Territory of Hawaii granted the writ. The court determined that civilians could not be tried by military commission for these civilian offenses and ordered the men freed, but the Ninth Circuit reversed, holding that a state of emergency in Hawaii testified to during the hearing on the habeas corpus petition by Adm. Chester Nimitz, commander of the U.S. Pacific Fleet, and Gen. Robert C. Richardson, area army commander, justified trying both men by military commission, citing *Ex parte Milligan* and *Korematsu* as authority for imposing military jurisdiction on the applicants during a state of emergency.[144] The applicants sought certiorari, which was granted by the Supreme Court in 1945.

The U.S. Supreme Court reversed the Ninth Circuit. The petitioners contended that on the dates when they were convicted, Hawaii was no longer under threat of enemy attack or invasion. They asserted that the justification for imposing martial law had ceased and the civilian courts should have been allowed to function and to decide their fates.[145]

The Court first determined that at the time White and Duncan were arrested "the dangers apprehended by the military were not sufficiently imminent to cause them to require civilians to evacuate the area or even to evacuate any of the buildings necessary to carry on the business of the courts."[146] The Court said that Congress authorized the governor of Hawaii to declare martial law under section 67 of the Organic Act, but the meaning of "martial law" was not defined. "The language of §67 thus fails to define adequately the scope of the power given to the military and to show whether the Organic Act provides that courts of law be supplanted by military tribunals."[147] The Court concluded that section 67 did not incorporate prior Hawaiian national law with respect to such decisions as *In re Kalanianaole*,[148] which sustained the power of the Hawaiian president to try civilians for any crime by military commission during the insurrection of 1895.[149] Even if Congress intended to incorporate Hawaiian case law in the Organic Act, *Kalanianaole* was concerned with acts in furtherance of an armed rebellion and not ordinary civilian crimes. Section 5 of the Organic Act guaranteed that the U.S. Constitution "shall have the same force and effect within the said Territory as elsewhere in the United States."[150] The petitioners were entitled to the rights of the accused under the Fourth, Fifth, and Sixth Amendments.[151]

The Court then conducted a general review of the history of martial law in England and the United States from the seventeenth century to 1944. It concluded that "our system of government clearly is the antithesis of total military rule."[152] White and Duncan were not subject to military jurisdiction by reason of being members of the armed forces, and they were not enemy belligerents or civilians living within temporary military governments established in enemy territory occupied by friendly forces.[153] Therefore, the petitioners could not be subjected to military trial because no state of rebellion existed in 1942 and 1944.[154]

The majority opinion did not hold that *Ex parte Milligan* required the result reached in *Duncan*, although Justice Murphy's concurring opinion asserts that *Milligan* compelled the result in *Duncan*.[155] The Court left the door open to congressional acts that authorized military rule and the closing of civilian courts under conditions of imminent invasion or rebellion.

PREACHERS OF VIOLENT OVERTHROW OF THE GOVERNMENT

The Smith Act

During World War II, Congress passed a statute directed at current and former Communist Party members and "fellow travelers" and not at German or Japanese spies or U.S. citizens who committed treasonable acts on behalf of Germany or Japan. Some members of Congress believed that the Alien Registration Act of 1918 did not adequately provide for deportation of aliens who were members of the Communist Party and other allied Socialist groups. Under the 1918 act, an alien could be deported only on the grounds that the alien was a member of an organization advocating violent overthrow of the government at the time the alien immigrated to the United States. The 1918 sedition act had expired after the end of World War I. A new "get tough" act drafted and sponsored by Virginia congressman Howard Smith sailed through Congress.[156] Title I related to alleged subversive activities. A person found guilty of selling or publishing any written or printed matter "advocating, advising, or teaching the duty, necessity, desirability, or propriety of overthrowing or destroying any government in the United States by force or violence," or attempts to publish such matter, or "organizes or helps or attempts to organize any society, group, or assembly of persons who teach, advocate, or encourage the overthrow or destruction of any such government by force or violence; or becomes or is a member of, or affiliates with, any such society, group, or assembly of persons, knowing the purposes thereof" would be guilty of a felony punishable by fine and imprisonment up to twenty years.[157]

Harry Bridges

Title II stated that any alien who at any time was a member of any organization advocating violent overthrow of the government would be subject to deportation. The act was aimed at left-wing labor leader Harry Bridges of the International Brotherhood of Longshoremen who was an ex-Communist and a thorn in the side of the government, leading strikes that interfered with the war effort. Bridges was prosecuted under Title II for deportation. He had been previously prosecuted for deportation in 1939, but the proceedings were dismissed because he was not a member of the Communist Party at the time he immigrated to the United States. Bridges was then prosecuted under the Smith Act in June 1941. The Immigration Service special examiner who heard the evidence found that Bridges had advocated violent overthrow of the government on the date of his entry into the United States and recommended Bridges's deportation. Bridges appealed to the Board of Immigration Appeals (BIA), who reversed the examiner on the grounds that the government's two key witnesses were unreliable. Despite the BIA findings, Attorney General Biddle ordered Bridges deported in 1942. Bridges filed a petition for writ of habeas corpus, but the district court denied his application in May 1942. The Ninth Circuit affirmed and Bridges sought certiorari, which the Supreme Court granted.[158] The Court reversed the Ninth Circuit. The majority held that Bridges was not "affiliated with" any organization that advocated the violent overthrow of the government.[159] The majority said,

> The associations which Harry Bridges had with various Communist groups seem to indicate no more than cooperative measures to attain objectives which were wholly legitimate. The link by which it is sought to tie him to subversive activities is an exceedingly tenuous one, if it may be said to exist at all.[160]

The Court noted that the courts below relied on a hearsay statement from O'Neill, a sometime co-worker with Bridges, that violated the ordinary rules of evidence. The government asked O'Neill on direct examination about an unsigned, unsworn statement he gave to investigators. The government offered the statement as evidence of Bridge's "affiliation" with the Communist Party. An Immigration Service officer later testified that O'Neil had repeated the statements to him and to other witnesses. These statements were that O'Neil joined the Communist Party in December 1936, that he walked into Bridges's office one day in 1937 and saw Bridges pasting assessment stamps in a Communist Party book, and that Bridges reminded O'Neil that he had not been attending party meetings. O'Neil admitted making statements to the investigating officers but denied making those particular statements.[161] Harry Bridges would be threatened with deportation again after World War II. He became a naturalized citizen in 1945. The Justice Department brought criminal and civil charges against Bridges for obtaining citizenship under false pretenses and for perjuring himself on his application for naturalization by stating that he was not a member of the Communist Party. Bridges moved to dismiss the indictment, but the district court overruled his motion[162] and the Ninth Circuit affirmed.[163] Bridges sought certiorari, and the Supreme Court overturned the revocation on the grounds that the statute of limitations relating to perjury and fraud had run before Bridges was indicted.[164]

The Socialist Labor Party

The FBI raided the Minneapolis and St. Paul offices of the Socialist Workers Party (SWP), a Trotskyist splinter party that controlled Teamsters Local 544, on June 27, 1941. A U.S. grand jury indicted twenty-nine men who were either members of the SWP or Teamsters Local 544 on a charge of plotting to overthrow the government of the United States under the sedition act of 1861 and the Smith Act. The defendants included James P. Cannon, the SWP's national secretary, Farrell Dobbs, and Albert Goldman.[165] The case against the SWP members went to trial in the fall of 1941. Five defendants were acquitted by the Court for lack of evidence. The government introduced evidence showing that the remaining twenty-three defendants (one defendant had committed suicide during the trial) had armed themselves with rifles and pistols and held target practice sessions. Some of the defendants had gone to Mexico to meet with Leon Trotsky before Trotsky's assassination. The jury convicted eighteen defendants of violations of the Smith Act, acquitting five. Dunne and the convicted party members appealed to the Eighth Circuit. That court affirmed the Smith Act convictions. The Eighth Circuit recognized that the provisions of the Smith Act were limitations on freedom of speech but agreed with the trial court and the government that the defendants were not entitled to a jury instruction that invoked the "clear and present danger" test for political speech advocating the overthrow of the U.S. government enunciated in *Schenck v. United States*.[166] The circuit court agreed with the trial court that the Smith Act prosecutions were governed by *Gitlow v. New York*,[167] the case involving convictions of Communist Party leaders for violating the New York State criminal anarchy act by issuing a manifesto that advocated immediate, violent overthrow of the U.S. government. The *Gitlow* decision had stated that "utterances of a certain kind involve such danger of substantive evil that they may be punished.[168] "The 8th Circuit stated that the *Gitlow* decision articulated a standard limiting allegedly free speech in cases where the speech forbidden was likely to cause the evil (i.e., the overthrow of the government) that applied to the SWP defendants.[169] The SWP defendants were given two-year prison sentences. The last defendant was released in February 1945.

Pro-Nazi Groups

President Roosevelt pushed Attorney General Francis Biddle to prosecute fascist sympathizers and anti-Semites under the Smith Act in the winter of 1942. Biddle responded by initiating prosecution of George W. Christians, founder of the Crusader White Shirts, specifying that he had attempted to spread dissent in the armed forces in March 1942. The Crusader White Shirts were a small ultra-right-wing, neo-fascist organization.[170] Christians was convicted and sentenced to five years' imprisonment.

The Washington, D.C., Trials

The government indicted thirty men and women in July 1942 for Smith Act violations. The defendants were alleged to be pro-fascists and dedicated isolationists who fomented opposition to the U.S. military's recruiting efforts. Some of the defendants were well known: George Sylvester Viereck, a poet and author and a publicist for the German government as far back as World War I; Lawrence Dennis, a former American diplomat and economist who had been advising some of the congressmen who were highly critical of the Roosevelt administration; Mrs. Elizabeth Dilling of Chicago, an anti-Communist author and lecturer with a national reputation for opposing the Roosevelt administration; and Rev. Gerald Winrod. Reverend Winrod had a national following that included young Rev. Billy Graham. Winrod ran for and almost won a Kansas U.S. Senate seat in 1938. The last prominent defendant, William Griffin, was a New York–based publisher and a Roman Catholic with ties to the hierarchy and clergy who was a strong anti-Communist.

Most of the defendants were people who were not nationally prominent and had no influence on the war effort, such as a sign painter who was almost totally deaf, a factory worker from Detroit, a waiter, and a maid. They were charged with conspiring to undermine the morale of the armed forces by circulating pro-German propaganda.[171] The trial of these individuals plus three additional defendants was delayed until April 17, 1944. When trial opened, federal prosecutor O. John Rogge's strategy was to introduce written and spoken statements made by the defendants and comparing those statements with Nazi propaganda, in an attempt to show that the defendants were likewise attempting to stir up opposition to the war.[172] Judge Edward C. Eicher, who presided over the trial, died in November 1944, resulting in a mistrial. The Justice Department agonized over prosecutor Rogge's plea to retry the defendants. In 1946, Attorney General Tom Clark fired Rogge, and the government then moved to dismiss all charges against the remaining defendants.

A discussion of the post-war Smith Act prosecution of Communist Party members is outside the scope of this chapter, since the Cold War anti-Communist crusade belongs to a period after the end of World War II. The Department of Justice prosecuted 140 Communist Party members for conspiring to advocate the violent overthrow of the government between 1949 and 1956. Ten party members including William Dennis were convicted of Smith Act violations in 1949. The convictions were upheld by the Supreme Court in *Dennis v. United States* decided in 1951.[173] The Court had before it two issues: was the Smith Act provision for punishing combinations or conspiracies to overthrow the government an unlawful prior restraint on free speech, and did the defendants receive a constitutionally fair trial? The majority opinion held that the Smith Act requires proof of intent to overthrow the government by force and violence.[174] The majority also held that the Smith Act was not an unlawful prior restraint on free speech. The Court looked to the *Schenck* decision that enunciated the "clear and present danger" test for prior restraints on speech advocating resistance to the war and the draft.[175] The Dennis Court said,

> The rule we deduce from these cases is that where an offense is specified by a statute in nonspeech or nonpress terms, a conviction relying upon speech or press as evidence of violation may be sustained only when the speech or publication created a "clear and present danger" of attempting or accomplishing the prohibited crime, e.g., interference with enlistment. The dissents, we repeat, in emphasizing the value of speech, were addressed to the argument of the sufficiency of the evidence.[176]

The court concluded that the Communist Party members' propaganda constituted a clear and present danger of an impending Communist revolution, activities not protected by the First Amendment.[177] The Smith Act prosecutions ended by 1961, when the Supreme Court affirmed the conviction of Scales for membership in the Communist Party.[178]

CONCLUSION

Prior to December 7, 1941, a sizable minority of U.S. citizens and resident aliens opposed U.S. involvement in World War II. President Roosevelt and his top advisors were convinced that Hitler had to be stopped before he conquered all of Europe including England. Roosevelt was able to deal with the isolationist, pro-German dissenters without resort to prosecutions under the 1917 Espionage Act. Father Coughlin's pro-Nazi propaganda was driven off the airwaves by informal pressure on his bishop to muzzle him. The German American Bund was harassed by law enforcement, but the Bund merged with America First, an isolationist organization that contained a surfeit of prominent Ivy Leaguers and politicians and had Charles Lindbergh as its spokesperson. America First died on December 7, 1941. The Japanese attack on Pearl Harbor set off a wave of public outrage that made anti-war activity highly unpopular.

The Roosevelt administration had no concerted plan to suppress dissenters. Roosevelt, Attorney General Biddle, and other close advisors responded to individual crises ad hoc with ill-conceived plans to deal with potential traitors. Anti-Japanese sentiment on the West Coast forced Roosevelt to agree with General John DeWitt that U.S. citizens of Japanese heritage were potential traitors and needed to be confined to concentration camps. The Supreme Court reacted to public sentiment by supporting the confinement of citizens of Japanese heritage when habeas corpus cases reached the court in 1942–1944. None of the thousands of Japanese-heritage detainees were given any kind of hearing before incarceration. The Supreme Court accepted the Roosevelt administration's assertion of military necessity without requiring any proof showing that U.S. citizens of Japanese heritage were a collective danger to national security. The Court extended unusual deference to executive branch decisions to ignore due process of law because of irrational public anxiety over the Imperial Japanese Navy's surprise attack on Pearl Harbor. The Court was also inconsistent. After the public outcry against all Japanese subsided, the Court held that civilians could not be tried by military commission in Hawaii when the civil courts were open and the immediate threat of Japanese invasion had passed. It is impossible to reconcile *Duncan* and *Endo* with *Korematsu* and *Hirabayashi*. Imposition of martial law in Hawaii shortly after Pearl Harbor, when the threat of a Japanese invasion of Hawaii was a likely possibility, and maintenance of martial law until 1944 until all possibility of invasion had passed was initially supported by Gen. Short's conception of military necessity. When Duncan was arrested for brawling with marine sentries at Pearl Harbor, military necessity no longer existed. Moving more than one hundred thousand U.S. citizens and resident Japanese aliens from their homes on the California mainland in 1942, when no serious threat of Japanese invasion existed, was an act consistent with martial law and inconsistent with ordinary civil process for dealing with any alleged security threats. General DeWitt's reaction to civilian pressure to force people of Japanese heritage from their homes and businesses because the United States was at war with Imperial Japan depended on the false premise that a U.S. citizen or resident alien was "disloyal" on account of the birthplace of their ancestors. The evacuation and detention orders were not driven by military necessity to prepare the West Coast for a possible invasion.

At the same time, thousands of resident aliens of Japanese, German, and Italian heritage were confined under the auspices of the 1793 enemy alien act. These detainees were given a preliminary hearing before an Immigration Service administrator before incarceration. Appeals from the Immigration Service rulings on enemy aliens went in favor of continued incarceration and deportation, if feasible. If any of the resident Japanese aliens living on the West Coast posed any serious threat to internal security in 1942, they could have been confined and deported under the enemy alien act after pre-incarceration hearings with a right of appeal. The 1793 act was sufficient to deal with the handful of known or suspected pro-Japanese U.S. citizens who might be spies or quislings. Congress also participated in the internment of U.S. citizens of Japanese stock by authorizing President Roosevelt's designation of areas of the Pacific coast as "No Japanese" enclaves to protect the war effort. The courts were willing to validate the interment of U.S. citizens as a form of "military necessity" to be determined by the executive and legislative branches of the government without judicial interference. The Supreme Court at first sustained the confinement of U.S. citizens in *Korematsu* and *Hirabayashi,* then reversed itself and allowed Ms. Endo to leave an internment camp because the government admitted that she was a loyal native-born citizen.

Congress and President Roosevelt were also engaged in witch-hunting prior to Pearl Harbor. President Roosevelt signed the Smith Act in 1940, originally designed to ensnare Communists. Only a handful of Trotskyites and pro-Axis citizens were ever prosecuted under the Smith Act during World War II. The case against the thirty-three Washington, D.C., defendants collapsed for want of proof of specific intent to overthrow the government. The Trotskyites were not as fortunate, since their propaganda called for a revolution that the small splinter group could never have fomented. Post-war, the Smith Act allowed the Justice Department to prosecute suspected Communist Party members for plotting to overthrow the government. The Smith Act fell out of favor with the Justice Department when the Supreme Court imposed a specific intent requirement on the elements of a Smith Act violation in the 1950s.

President Roosevelt extended the authority of the executive branch to try spies and saboteurs by military commission. Congress had not provided legislation calling for military commissions, and the old Articles of War originally enacted shortly after the United States was formed and last revised after World War I contained an unclear provision for trial by military commission of persons engaged in spying or sabotage on behalf of a foreign belligerent. It was unclear that this clause applied to U.S. citizens. Despite the lack of express delegation of authority, the eight German saboteurs who landed in 1942 and the two German spies who were landed in 1944 were tried, convicted, and sentenced to die by military commission, although four of the defendants were U.S. citizens. The Supreme Court ignored the provisions of the Treason Act of 1790 and the protection afforded criminal defendants by the Fifth and Sixth Amendments that arguably were the rights of the U.S. citizens accused of treasonable activity. The Roosevelt administration invoked the "law of war" as the legal support for trial of U.S. citizens by military commission when engaged in activities on behalf of the enemy. The Court, in *Ex parte Quirin,* came perilously close to supporting a claim that the specific guaranties of the Bill of Rights were trumped by a general body of international law that was not even embodied in a treaty or other international pact.

Judicial review of the executive and legislative branches did nothing to strengthen the rights of U.S. citizens under the Bill of Rights. The Japanese internment cases, the Smith Act prosecutions, and the espionage cases simply cannot be reconciled by any line of principled jurisprudence. Each case was an ad hoc decision turning on matters not openly discussed by the courts: U.S. public opinion and the war aims of the executive and legislative branches of the federal government.

NOTES

1. Gerhardt L. Weinberg, *A World at Arms* (New York: Cambridge University Press, 1994), 43, 48–59.

2. Weinberg, *A World at Arms*, 113–121; Nizkor Project, "Invasion of Denmark and Norway," last accessed Feb. 5, 2017, http://www.nizkor.org/hweb/imt/tgmwc/judgment/j-invasion-denmark-norway-01.html; Earl. F. Ziemke, *The German Decision to Invade Norway and Denmark*, last accessed Feb. 5, 2017, http://www.history.army.mil/books/70-7_02.htm.

3. Weinberg, *A World at Arms*, 122–132, 514–515; See Gary Sheffield, "The Fall of France," BBC, last accessed Feb. 5, 2017, http://www.bbc.co.uk/history/worldwars/wwtwo/fall_france_01.shtml. The German invasion of the Netherlands and Belgium on May 10, 1940, was designed to draw the small British Expeditionary Force northward away from the French static defense line. This operation succeeded beyond expectation. See also "Battle of France," *New World Encyclopedia*, last accessed Feb. 5, 2017, http://www.newworldencyclopedia.org/entry/Battle_of_France.

4. Joint Resolution 49 Stat. 1081 (Aug. 31, 1935); 22 U.S.C. 441 note.

5. Public Resolution 74-74/Chapter 106, 74th Cong., 2nd Sess. Joint Resolution: Extending and Amending the Joint Resolution (Public Resolution Numbered 67, Seventy-Fourth Congress), approved Aug. 31, 1935, Extending and Amending the Joint Resolution (Public Resolution Numbered 67, Seventy-Fourth Congress), approved Aug. 31, 1935. 49 Stat. 1152 (Feb. 29, 1936).

6. Public Resolution No. 1, 75th Cong., 50 Stat. 3 (May 1, 1937).

7. Joint resolution to preserve the neutrality and the peace of the United States and to secure the safety of its citizens and their interests. P.L. 459, 77th Cong., ch. 104t (Nov. 4, 1939).

8. See David Gordon, "America First: The Anti-War Movement, Charles Lindbergh and the Second World War, 1940–1941. Originally Presented at a Joint Meeting of the Historical Society and the New York Military Affairs Symposium on September 26, 2003," *Veterans Today Military & Foreign Affairs Journal*, Apr. 16, 2010, last accessed Feb. 6, 2017, http://www.veteranstoday.com/2010/04/16/david-gordon-america-first-the-anti-war-movement-charles-lindbergh-and-the-2nd-world-war. According to Gordon, as late as November 1941 only 25 percent of those polled favored intervention in the world war.

9. Dissent in World War I and World War II, last accessed Feb. 5, 2017, http://www.galegroup.com/whic/ReferenceDetailsPage/ReferenceDetailsWindow?failOverType=&query=&prodid=windowstat.

10. Michael Sayers and Albert E. Kahn, *Sabotage! The Secret War against America* (New York: Harper, 1942), 151. Coughlin was interviewed by Dale Kramer in 1936. He told Kramer that "democracy is doomed. . . . It is Fascism or Communism, take your choice. . . . Take the road to Fascism."

11. See Jim Bredemus, "American Bund: The Failure of American Nazisim; The German American Bund," last accessed Feb. 6, 2017, http://www.traces.org/americanbund.html.

12. Bredemus, "American Bund: The Failure of American Nazism."

13. Gordon, "America First: The Anti-War Movement, Charles Lindbergh and the Second World War, 1940–1941." America First claimed to have more than eight hundred thousand members in 650 chapters, most located in the Midwest. The movement was supported by Gen. Robert Wood, CEO of Sears Roebuck; Charles Lindbergh; Sinclair Lewis; and Col. Robert McCormick, publisher of the *Chicago Tribune*.

14. Gordon, "America First: The Anti-War Movement, Charles Lindbergh and the Second World War, 1940–1941."

15. See "Brief History of Japan," last accessed Feb. 18, 2017, http://www.facts-about-japan.com/brief-history.html.

16. Greg Robinson, *By Order of the President: FDR and the Internment of Japanese Americans* (Cambridge, MA: Harvard University Press, 2001), 46.

17. Robinson, *By Order of the President*, 59.

18. See Walter A. MacDougall, "International Relations," *Encyclopaedia Britannica Online*, last accessed Feb. 6, 2017, http://www.britannica.com/topicinternationalrelations.

19. Gordon W. Prange, *At Dawn We Slept: The Untold Story of Pearl Harbor* (New York: McGraw-Hill, 1981), 502.

20. Prange, *At Dawn We Slept*, 536–537.

21. Prange, *At Dawn We Slept*, 507–516, 567.

22. See Franklin D. Roosevelt, "Speech to Joint Session of Congress, December 8, 1941," last accessed Feb. 6, 2017, http://docs.fdrlibrarymarist.edu/tmirhdee.html. His address to Congress was one of the greatest presidential speeches in U.S. history.

23. Michael Gannon, *Operation Drumbeat: The Dramatic True Story of Germany's First U-Boat Attacks along the American Coast in World War II* (New York: Harper & Row, 1990).

24. Gannon, *Operation Drumbeat*.

25. 43 Stats. 153 (1924). See Stanley E. Easton and Lucien Ellington, "Japanese Americans," *Gale Encyclopedia of Multicultural America*, 2000, last accessed Feb. 6, 2017, http://www.encyclopedia.com/history/united-states-and-canada/us-history/Japanese-Americans.

26. Easton and Ellington, "Japanese Americans."

27. Easton and Ellington, "Japanese Americans."

28. See, e.g., bombardment of Ellwood oil field near Santa Barbara, Feb. 23, 1942; bombardment of Estevan Point Light House, Vancouver, B.C., June 20, 1942; bombardment of Fort Stevens, Oregon, June 21–22, 1942; and the sole air attack on the U.S. mainland executed by a single Japanese float plane launched from the submarine aircraft carrier I-25 that dropped a bomb near Mount Emily, Oregon. These nuisance attacks were not as frightening as the torpedoing of ten U.S., Canadian, and Soviet vessels within sight of Los Angeles, Santa Barbara, San Diego, and Santa Monica.

29. Internment was authorized by the Alien Enemy Act of 1798, 1 Stat. 577 (1798). Portions of this act have never been repealed.

30. Robinson, *By Order of the President*, 75–76.

31. Robinson, *By Order of the President*, 78.

32. Robinson, *By Order of the President*, 78–79.

33. Robinson, *By Order of the President*, 84.

34. Robinson, *By Order of the President*, 84–85.

35. Robinson, *By Order of the President*, 86–87.

36. Robinson, *By Order of the President*, 90.

37. Robinson, *By Order of the President*, 90.

38. Robinson, *By Order of the President*, 91.

39. Robinson, *By Order of the President*, 92.

40. Robinson, *By Order of the President*, 93.

41. Quoted in Robinson, *By Order of the President*, 95.

42. Robinson, *By Order of the President*, 96.

43. Robinson, *By Order of the President*, 96.

44. Robinson, *By Order of the President*, 98.

45. Robinson, *By Order of the President*, 99.

46. Robinson, *By Order of the President*, 101–102.

47. Robinson, *By Order of the President*, 105.

48. Robinson, *By Order of the President*, 106.

49. Robinson, *By Order of the President*, 108.

50. 7 Fed. Reg. 1407 (Feb. 19, 1942).
51. Robinson, *By Order of the President*, 128.
52. Allen W. Austin, "Eastward Pioneers: Japanese American Resettlement during World War II and the Contested Meaning of Exile and Incarceration," *Journal of American Ethnic History* 26 (2007): 59–60.
53. Robinson, *By Order of the President*, 129.
54. See Executive Order 9102, Mar. 18, 1942, last accessed Feb. 6, 2017, http://www.presidency.ucsb.edu/ws/?pid'16239.
55. "Japanese Internment in U.S. History Pre-Columbian to the New Millennium," USHistory.org, last accessed Feb. 6, 2017, http://www.ushistory.org/us/51e.asp.
56. "Japanese Internment Camps," last accessed Feb. 6, 2017, http://www.historyonthenet.com/WW2/japan_internment_camps.htm.
57. Austin, "Eastward Pioneers," 60.
58. 56 Stat. 173 P.L. 503 provided that anyone who remained in a military area who knowingly remained in the exclusionary area would be punished by one year in jail and a fine of up to $5,000.
59. *Hirabayashi v. United States*, 320 U.S. 81, 84 (1943). See also Karen Sparks, "Gordon Kiyoshi Hirabayshi American Civil Disobedience Advocate," *Encyclopaedia Britannica Online*, last accessed Feb. 18, 2017, http://www.britannica.com/biography/Gordon-Hiribayshi.
60. *United States v. Hirabayashi*, 46 F. Supp. 657, 659, 661 (D. Wash. 1942).
61. 46 F. Supp. 286 (D.Wis. 1942).
62. 46 F. Supp. 660.
63. *Hirabayashi v. United States*, 320 U.S. 83.
64. *Hirabayashi v. United States*, 320 U.S. 86.
65. 56 Stat. 173 (1942).
66. *Hirabayashi v. United States*, 320 U.S. 93.
67. *Hirabayashi v. United States*, 320 U.S. 98.
68. *Hirabayashi v. United States*, 320 U.S. 98–99.
69. *Hirabayashi v. United States*, 320 U.S. 104–105.
70. *Hirabayashi v. United States*, 828 F.2d 591 (9th Cir. 1987).
71. See *Final Report: Japanese Evacuation from the West Coast 1942 Headquarters Western Defense Command and Fourth Army Office of the Commanding General Presidio of San Francisco, California* (1943).
72. *Korematsu v. United States*, 323 U.S. 214, 216 (1944).
73. *Korematsu v. United States*, 323 U.S. 234.
74. *Korematsu v. United States*, 323 U.S. 235.
75. *Korematsu v. United States*, 323 U.S. 218.
76. *Korematsu v. United States*, 323 U.S. 218–219.
77. *Korematsu v. United States*, 323 U.S. 224–225.
78. *Korematsu v. United States*, 323 U.S. 230.
79. *Korematsu v. United States*, 323 U.S. 233.
80. *Korematsu v. United States*, 323 U.S. 325–326.
81. *Korematsu v. United States*, 323 U.S. 333–334.
82. 584 F. Supp. 1406 (N.D. Cal. 1984).
83. The District Court first denied the petition. Yasui's appeal was filed six days late, and the Ninth Circuit remanded his appeal to allow the district court to determine if there were reasonable circumstances precluding the filing of his timely appeal. *Yasui v. United States*, 772 F.2d 1496 (9th Cir. 1985).
84. See *Hirabayashi v. United States*, 828 F.2d 591 (9th Cir. 1987).
85. 50a U.S.C. § 1989b et seq. (2012). Section 1989b-4 provided for a $20,000 reparation payment to every known internee.
86. See "Ex Parte Endo," *Densho Encyclopedia*, last accessed Feb. 18, 2017, http://encyclopediadensho.org/WEx_parte_Endo, for details relating to Ms. Endo's personal life. After the war, she married and moved to Chicago where she worked as a secretary. Ms. Endo died in 2006.

87. *Ex parte Endo,* 323 U.S. 283, 285 (1944).
88. See 7 Fed. Reg. 7656, Sept. 26, 1942, regulations. Administrative Instruction No. 22 was revised on Nov. 6, 1942, and was superseded by the handbook of July 20, 1943. The Sept. 26, 1942, regulations were revised January 1, 1944. See 9 Fed. Reg. 154.
89. See 9 Fed. Reg. 154, § 5.3(c).
90. Handbook, § 60.6.6. Nine factors are specified, each of which is "regarded by intelligence agencies as sufficient to warrant a recommendation that leave clearance be denied unless there is an adequate explanation" (§ 60.10.2). These include, among others, a failure or refusal to swear unqualified allegiance to the United States and to forswear any form of allegiance to the Japanese Emperor or any other foreign government, power, or organization; a request for repatriation or expatriation whether or not subsequently retracted; military training in Japan; employment on Japanese naval vessels; three trips to Japan after the age of six, except in the case of seamen whose trips were confined to ports of call; an organizer, agent, member, or contributor to specified organizations that intelligence agencies consider subversive.
91. *Ex parte Endo,* 323 U.S. 295.
92. *Ex parte Endo,* 323 U.S. 296–297.
93. *Ex parte Endo,* 323 U.S. 298.
94. See biography of Misuye Endo, last accessed Feb. 6, 2017, http://ww1.cuny.edu/portal_ur/conent/womens_leaderhship/mitsuye_endo.html.
95. Deborah McCarty Smith, "Years of Silence: The Untold Story of German-American Internment," last accessed Feb. 6, 2017, http://www.foitimes.com/internment/udq.htm.
96. More than 4,500 ethnic Germans from Latin America were interned at one of the fifty U.S. internment camps for German nationals. U.S. resident German aliens were interned along with wives and children who were natural-born U.S. citizens. For an extended history of German internment, see German American Internee Coalition, "U.S. Department of Justice Internment Facilities," last accessed Feb. 6, 2017, http://www.gaic.info/internment-camps/u-s-department-of-justice-internment-facilities.
97. 137 F.2d 898 (2d Cir. 1943).
98. *United States ex rel. Schwartzkopf v. Uhl,* 137 F.2d. 899 (2d Cir. 1943).
99. *United States ex rel. Schwartzkopf v. Uhl,* 137 F.2d. 900.
100. *United States ex rel. Schwartzkopf v. Uhl,* 137 F.2d. 901.
101. *United States ex rel. Schwartzkopf v. Uhl,* 137 F.2d. 903.
102. See, e.g., *United States ex rel. Umeker v. McCoy,* 54 F. Supp. 679 (D. North Dakota 1944). Umeker was born in Alsace when it was part of the First Reich, later ceded to France by the Treaty of Versailles in 1919. He immigrated after 1919 to the United States as a French citizen. The administrative officer classified him as a dangerous German citizen because Hitler reincorporated Alsace into the Third Reich. The Court granted habeas and freed him.
103. *Ludecke v. Watkins,* 335 U.S. 160 (1948).
104. *Ludecke v. Watkins,* 355 U.S. 162–165.
105. *Ludecke v. Watkins,* 355 U.S. 166. Frankfurter went on to state that a state of war did not cease when a cease-fire had occurred and that the president's congressionally approved power to detain and deport enemy aliens was not affected by the May 1945 surrender of the Third Reich.
106. U.S. Department of Justice, *Report to the Congress of the United States: A Review of the Restrictions on Persons of Italian Ancestry during World War II,* November 2001, appendix B: "Chronology of Events Surrounding the Evacuation, Relocation, and Internment of Persons of Italian Ancestry during World War II."
107. See "The Story of Italian American Internment during WW II," ItalianHistorical.org, last accessed Feb. 6, 2017, http://www.italianhistorical.org/page19a.html.
108. "German Espionage and Sabotage against the United States in World War II," 3, last accessed Feb. 6, 2017, http://www.patriotfiles.com/index.plp?name=Section=viewarticle&artid=1075&allpagaes=1&theme=Printer.
109. "German Espionage and Sabotage against the United States in World War II," 2.

110. "German Espionage and Sabotage against the United States in World War II," 3–4.

111. See the BBC History profile of Heinrich Himmler, last accessed Feb. 6, 2017, http://www.bbc.co.uk/history/historic_figures/himmler_heinrich.shtml.

112. "Biography of Ernst Katlenbrunner," *Encyclopaedia Britannica Online*, last accessed Feb. 6, 2017, http://www.britannica.com/biography/Ernst-Kaltenbrunner.

113. FBI Handout, *German Espionage and Sabotage against the U.S. in World War II: George John Dasch and the Nazi Saboteurs* (Washington, DC: U.S. Dept of Navy, Navy Historical Center), 2–3.

114. The agents were George John Dasch, age thirty-nine; Ernest Peter Burger, thirty-six; Heinrich Harm Heinck, thirty-five; and Richard Quirin, thirty-four, an American citizen in Nazi service. FBI Handout, *German Espionage and Sabotage against the U.S. in World War.*

115. The agents were Edward John Kerling, age thirty-three; Werner Theil, thirty-five; Herman Otto Neubauer, thirty-two; and Herbert Hans Haupt, twenty-two. FBI Handout, *German Espionage and Sabotage against the U.S. in World War II.*

116. Royall later served as President Truman's secretary of defense; Maj. Stone was the son of Chief Justice Harlan Fisk Stone. FBI Handout, *German Espionage and Sabotage against the U.S. in World War II.*

117. Ernst Burger was a naturalized American citizen. Haupt was naturalized as a minor when his father was naturalized in 1930. George Dasch served as a clerk in the kaiser's army during World War I near the end of the war. In 1927, he enlisted in the U.S. Army and received an honorable discharge in 1928. FBI Handout, *German Espionage and Sabotage against the U.S. in World War II.* In April 1948, President Truman granted executive clemency to Dasch and Burger on condition of deportation. They were transported to the American Zone of Germany and were freed.

118. For the order establishing the military commission, see 7 Fed. Reg. 5103. For the accompanying resolution, see U.S. Presidential Library Public Papers and Addresses of Franklin D. Roosevelt, 297 (1942).

119. *Ex parte Quirin*, 317 U.S. 22 (1942).

120. *Ex parte Quirin*, 47 F. Supp. 431 (D.D.C. 1942).

121. *Ex parte Quirin*, 317 U.S. 1, 2 (1942).

122. *Ex parte Quirin*, 317 U.S. 24.

123. *Ex parte Quirin*, 317 U.S. 26.

124. U.S. Const., Art. I, §§ 8, cl. 1, 12, 13, 14. The court also noted U.S. Const., Art. I, § 8, cl. 18: "To make all Laws which shall be necessary and proper for carrying into Execution the foregoing Powers, and all other Powers vested by this Constitution in the Government of the United States, or in any Department or Officer thereof."

125. U.S. Const., Art. II, § 2, cl. 1; § 3, cl. 1.

126. *Ex parte Quirin*, 317 U.S. 27–29 (citing Art. 1, 2, 12, 15, 38, and 46 of the Articles of War as authority for the president to set up rules for military commissions).

127. *Ex parte Quirin*, 317 U.S. 28. Article 15 reads as follows:

> ART. 15. JURISDICTION NOT EXCLUSIVE.—The provisions of these articles conferring jurisdiction upon courts-martial shall not be construed as depriving military commissions, provost courts, or other military tribunals of concurrent jurisdiction in respect of offenders or offenses that by statute *or by the law of war* may be triable by such military commissions, provost courts, or other military tribunals. (Emphasis added.)

128. *Ex parte Quirin*, 317 U.S. 29.

129. *Ex parte Quirin*, 317 U.S. 30–31, 38–40.

130. *Ex parte Quirin*, 317 U.S. 31. The court cited the trial of Maj. John Andre by a commission appointed by General Washington, the trial of Mexicans during the War with Mexico, and the trials of T. O. Hogg, John Y. Beall, and Robert C. Kennedy by military commission during the Civil War among other examples as precedent for

trying the saboteurs by military commission under the law of war rather than domestic law.

131. *Ex parte Quirin*, 371 U.S. 45–46.

132. See, e.g., *In re Yamashita*, 327 U.S. 1, 10 (1946) (without citation, same argument); *Hirota v. MacArthur*, 338 U.S. 197, 202 (1948) (concurring opinion of Douglas, J).

133. See, e.g., *Boumedienne v. Bush*, 553 U.S. 723 (2008); *Hamdi v. Rumsfeld*, 378 F.3d 426 (4th Cir. 2004) reversed 542 U.S. 507 (2004).

134. Richard Sassaman, "Nazi Spies Come Ashore," last accessed Feb. 6, 2017, http://www.americainwwii.com/articles/nazi-spies-come-ashore.

135. *Eastern Sea Frontier War Diary* (College Park, MD: Modern Military Branch, National Archives and Records Administration, 1944), ch. 2.

136. Sassaman, "Nazi Spies Come Ashore."

137. Sassaman, "Nazi Spies Come Ashore."

138. Sassaman, "Nazi Spies Come Ashore."

139. Hawaii Guide, "Martial Law and the Japanese American Dilemma," last accessed Feb. 6, 2017, http://hawaii-guide.info/past-and-present/history/world.war.II. Hawaiian civilian police, the army, and the FBI arrested alleged dangerous persons. Some were citizens and resident aliens of Japanese heritage, but the resident population of Japanese heritage was too large to incarcerate. A curfew was imposed and a territory-wide blackout was instituted. All Hawaii residents were fingerprinted and required to carry an identification card at all times. Civilians could have no more than $200 in cash on their person. Martial law lasted until October 24, 1944.

140. *Ex parte Duncan*, 146 F.2d 576 (9th Cir. 1944).

141. *Ex parte Duncan*, 146 F.2d 576, 577.

142. *Duncan v. Kahanamoku*, 327 U.S. 304, 309–310 (1946).

143. *Duncan v. Kahanamoku*, 327 U.S. 311.

144. *Ex parte Duncan*, 146 F.2d 576, 583–584.

145. *Duncan v. Kahanamoku*, 327 U.S. 312–313.

146. *Duncan v. Kahanamoku*, 327 U.S. 313.

147. *Duncan v. Kahanamoku*, 327 U.S. 315–316.

148. *In re Kalanianole*, 10 Haw. 29 (1895).

149. *Duncan v. Kahanamoku*, 327 U.S. 316.

150. *Duncan v. Kahanamoku*, 327 U.S. 317–318.

151. *Duncan v. Kahanamoku*, 327 U.S. 318.

152. *Duncan v. Kahanamoku*, 327 U.S. 322.

153. *Duncan v. Kahanamoku*, 327 U.S. 313–314.

154. *Duncan v. Kahanamoku*, 327 U.S. 324.

155. *Duncan v. Kahanamoku*, 327 U.S. 327.

156. See "Smith Act," last accessed Feb. 6, 2017, http://www.bc.edu/bc_org/avp/cas/comm/free_speech/smithactof1940.html.

157. 18 U.S.C. § 2385.

158. *Bridges v. Wixom*, 326 U.S. 235, 139–140 (1945).

159. *Bridges v. Wixom*, 326 U.S. 142–143.

160. *Bridges v. Wixom*, 326 U.S. 145.

161. *Bridges v. Wixom*, 326 U.S. 151–152.

162. *United States v. Bridges*, 86 F. Supp. 922 (N.D. Cal. 1949).

163. *Bridges v. United States*, 199 F.2d 811 (9th Cir. 1952), motion for rehearing en banc denied, 201 F.2d 254 (1952).

164. *Bridges v. United States*, 346 U.S. 209 (1953); see also *New York Times*, June 17, 1950, sec. 1, p. 1.

165. *Dunne v. United States*, 138 F.2d 137, 150–151 (8th Cir. 1943).

166. *Schenck v. United States*, 249 U.S. 47 (1919).

167. *Gitlow v. New York*, 268 U.S. 652 (1925).

168. *Gitlow v. New York*, 268 U.S. 670.

169. *Dunne v. United States*, 138 F.2d 145.

170. Dave Tabler, "George W. Christians, American Fascist," Jan. 6, 2011, last accessed Feb. 6, 2017, http://www.appalacianhistory.net/2015/03/george-w-christians-american-fascist.html.

171. L. A. Rollins, "Book Review of Lawrence Dennis and Maximilian St. George, a Trial on Trial: The Great Sedition Trial of 1944," Institute for Historical Review, 1984, last accessed Feb. 6, 2017, http://www.ihr.org/jhr/v06/v06p123_Rollins.html.

172. See Michael R. Belknap, *Cold War Political Justice* (Westport, CT: Greenwood, 1977), 40–41, and Michael Collins Piper and Ken Hoop, "A Mockery of Justice: The Great Sedition Trial of 1944," last accessed Feb. 6, 2017, http://www.thebirdman.org/Index/Others-Doc-History/+Doc-History-WW2period/SeditionTrialOf1944.htm.

173. *Dennis v. United States*, 341 U.S. 494 (1951).

174. *Dennis v. United States*, 341 U.S. 349.

175. See *Schenck v. United States*, 249 U.S. 47 (1919).

176. *Dennis v. United States*, 341 U.S. 505.

177. *Dennis v. United States*, 341 U.S. 504–505.

178. *Scales v. United States*, 367 U.S. 203 (1961).

FIVE

The Cold War

"Today we are engaged in a final all out battle between communistic atheism and Christianity. The modern champions of communism have selected this as the time, and ladies and gentlemen, the chips are down, they are truly down."
—Sen. Joseph R. McCarthy, speech at Wheeling, West Virginia, February 9, 1950

"Let us not assassinate this lad further, senator. You've done enough. Have you no sense of decency, sir? At long last, have you left no sense of decency?"
—Joseph Welch, attorney for the U.S. Army, Army–McCarthy Hearings, June 9, 1954

From 1946 through 1989, the United States and the Soviet Union were locked in a power struggle for predominance among the nations. This struggle generated an arms race that pitted the technology and industrial capacity of the two states in a head-to-head competition for military supremacy. This period was called the Cold War because both sides developed massive military forces to deal with a threatened attack by their opponent, as if a formal declaration of war had been voted by Congress and the Supreme Soviet.[1] The Soviet Union claimed to be the mother of revolution against the capitalist economic system, taking responsibility for and credit for communist revolutions in Latin America, notably in Cuba in 1956–1959. The Soviet Union also used its military presence in Eastern Europe after the end of World War II to set up puppet communist regimes in Bulgaria, Czechoslovakia, East Germany, Lithuania, Latvia, Estonia, Poland, Romania, and Yugoslavia. The Soviets supported the successful local Communist revolution in China led by Mao Zedong that overthrew the Nationalist regime of Chiang Kai-shek, driving the Nationalists off the mainland into Taiwan. The Soviets also set up a puppet state in the northern half of Korea and installed Kim Il Sung as president of a Communist North Korean government. Newspapers, radio, and the infant television medium helped to fuel a domestic anti-Communist crusade.[2]

In 1945, the United States manufactured and exploded three nuclear devices. Two devices were dropped by Army Air Force B-29 bombers on the Japanese cities of Hiroshima and Nagasaki. Thousands of Japanese civilians were killed or injured by these detonations. From August 1945 until the summer of 1950, the United States was the only state that possessed nuclear devices. In the summer of 1950, the Soviet Union announced that it had detonated a nuclear device. In April 1950, the National Security Council issued a top-secret document that worked a fundamental change in the organization and aims of the United States. NSC 68 turned the United States from a peacetime footing to a permanent state of siege in order to deal with the continuing menace of the Soviet Union. NSC 68 set out a background statement describing the Soviet Union as a state seeking to control the entire world, using local Communist parties as agents in its quest for world domination and the imposition of slavery to the Soviet Union upon all the world.[3] NSC 68 described the Soviet Union's competitive position as strong because the economy and the military forces of the Soviet Union were less costly than those of the United States and the civilian population was used to a much lower standard of living.[4] NSC 68 constructed a scenario for a global war with the Soviet Union, predicting a Soviet invasion of Scandinavia and Spain and air attacks on Britain, Canada, and the United States.[5] The report assumed that the Soviet Union had ten to twenty nuclear devices in its stockpile that it would not hesitate to use on Britain and the United States.[6] The paper urged that the president adopt a policy of containment, that is, prevent the emergence of new Communist states outside the Soviet Union and its satellites.[7] Noting that a democratic society, such as the United States, lacks the single-minded will to power of a dictatorship, the report said that the United States needed to mobilize all its capabilities and all the capabilities of the non-Communist nations to defeat the Soviet Union.[8] According to NSC 68, "the integrity and vitality of our system is in greater jeopardy than ever before in our history. . . . The risks we face are a new order of magnitude commensurate with the total struggle in which we are engaged."[9] The report proposed three alternative courses of action: (a) continuation of current policies, (b) isolationism, or (b) a shooting war.[10] Rejecting all of these proposals, NSA 68 set out a fourth alternative calling for a rapid buildup of U.S. armed forces with respect to achieving rough parity with the Soviet Union.[11] Recommendation (18) dealt with the internal threat posed by the Communist Party. The report stated,

> 18. The capability of the United States either in peace or in the event of war to cope with threats to its security or to gain its objectives would be severely weakened by internal developments, important among which are:
>
> a. Serious espionage, subversion and sabotage, particularly by concerted and well-directed communist activity.

NSC 68 described all Communists as agents of the Soviet Union and set the framework for a perpetual state of preparation for nuclear war with respect to the Soviet Union in which domestic Communists would be treated as undesirables. It set the tone for action to reduce the internal Communist menace and branded all Communists as potential enemies of the state.

By the time NSC 68 was issued, the Soviet Union had manufactured and exploded a nuclear device, arguably assisted by documents stolen by U.S. and British members of the Communist Party. The Soviet Union possessed a weapon capable of killing many thousands of people.

The Republican Party led the anti-Communist crusade, blaming the collapse of Chiang Kai-shek's Nationalist government on the U.S. State Department's alleged pro-Communist policies. It was widely held that the tiny U.S. Communist Party was fomenting a revolution against the government and at the same time had infiltrated the Truman administration in order to spy on the United States. The attorney general published a list of organizations that were deemed to be "Communist front" groups. Any individual who maintained membership in or cooperated with a Communist front group's programs was considered a security risk.

The Truman administration required that federal employees take loyalty oaths and extended background checks on employees to investigating their association with Communist front organizations.[12] Thousands of federal employees lost their jobs due to feared disloyalty. Thousands of educators, scientists, journalists, writers, and actors were "blacklisted" because they had perceived ties to Communist front organizations.[13] Self-appointed anti-Communists screened individuals for disloyalty and brought pressure on employers not to hire "disloyal" individuals.[14]

The House Un-American Activities Committee held public hearings to attack entertainers, academics, and professional people for alleged pro-Communist activities and sympathies.[15] Wisconsin's junior senator Joseph R. McCarthy took advantage of public fear of a domestic Communist revolution by using a Senate committee to investigate alleged Communist infiltration of the State Department and the army. In 1954, Senator McCarthy's attacks on the army were displayed on television. McCarthy's reputation went into a tailspin at the conclusion of his investigation of the army, and the Senate censured him for improper conduct in 1954. The damage done to individuals who were innocent of any wrongdoing was incalculable.[16] During the height of the anti-Communist crusade, the Justice Department arrested Julius and Ethel Rosenberg, who were tried for treason and sentenced to death.[17] State Department official Alger Hiss was accused of pro-Communist activity in the State Department by Whittaker Chambers, an acknowledged former Communist secret agent. He appeared before the House Un-American Activities Committee and swore that Hiss had passed classified information to him to deliver to Moscow.[18] Hiss appeared and swore he was not a Communist and did not pass secret information to any Communists.[19]

In June 1950, North Korean dictator Kim Il Sung's army, equipped with Soviet tanks, aircraft, and artillery, invaded the southern half of the Korean Peninsula. U.S. forces commanded by Gen. Douglas MacArthur joined contingents from other nations under a UN resolution to stop North Korean aggression. Initially, the North Koreans were able to drive UN forces into a small perimeter around the seaport of Pusan in southeast Korea. General MacArthur orchestrated one of the greatest military feats of the twentieth century by landing marines at the seaport of Incheon a few miles from Seoul on September 15, 1950, causing the collapse of the North Korean offensive and a quick North Korean withdrawal across the 38th parallel. MacArthur pushed Kim's solders back north of Pyongyang, the North Korean capital, almost to the Chinese border. He overplayed his hand, leading to the intervention of the People's Republic of China in support of Kim's regime. The UN forces retreated to a line along the 38th parallel, taking heavy casualties. A bloody stalemate set in until the warring parties signed an armistice agreement in late July 1953.[20]

Meanwhile the hunt for suspected Communists and fellow travelers went on. Most states adopted some form of loyalty oath requirement for government employees,[21] and self-appointed anti-Communists screened public libraries for books that were Communist oriented or espoused Marxist doctrine.[22]

The anti-Communist crusade was launched before World War II by a Congressional Special Committee on Un-American Activities, commonly called the Dies Committee and revived shortly after the end of World War II when the media and key Republican politicians were engaged in finding out who was to blame for the collapse of democratic regimes in Poland, Czechoslovakia, and Hungary and the installation of pro-Soviet puppet governments in these vassal states.[23] A debate over the accountability of the Truman administration for these losses was exacerbated in 1949 when Chiang Kai-shek's Chinese Nationalist regime collapsed. News commentators and newspaper editors claimed that domestic Communists had infiltrated the State Department and had crippled U.S. foreign policy under Secretary of State Dean Acheson.[24] The discovery of a Communist spy ring in 1950 that included physicist Klaus Fuchs, who fed secrets pertaining to the construction of the atom bomb to a chain of U.S. citizens who were Communist Party members, who in turn passed these secrets on to Moscow, helped to ignite fear and a demand for punishment of domestic Communists and their sympathizers.[25] The prime movers behind the crusade included Col. Robert McCormick, publisher of the *Chicago Tribune*; the Hearst newspaper empire headed by William Randolph Hearst; and newspaper columnists Fulton Lewis Jr., Westbrook Pegler, and George Sokolsky.[26] The Republican Senate leadership also joined the crusade because it was politically advantageous to accuse the Democrats of being "soft on Communism." Senate majority leader, Ohio senator Robert Taft, was one of the key people behind the crusade.[27]

Professor Robert Griffith asserted that the anti-Communist crusade was rooted in social and political conservatism and opposition to the change in the U.S. economy and the U.S. government brought about by the New Deal and Fair Deal. Griffith also claimed that the anti-Communist crusade was related to the long-standing phenomenon of nativism and xenophobia.[28]

EXECUTIVE ANTI-COMMUNISM

President Truman's Loyalty Oath Program

President Truman was concerned about Communist infiltration of the executive branch of the government long before Klaus Fuchs and his spy ring were discovered. The Soviet Union, a World War II ally, a nation that lost twenty million men and women to the Nazi invasion of the western USSR, had become a rival and an enemy by 1946. Fear of Communist infiltration of the executive branch of the U.S. government had existed since the establishment of the Dies Committee on Un-American Activities in 1938. In 1943, two years before the end of World War II, Congress passed section 304 of the Urgent Deficiency Appropriation Act, which stated,

> No part of any appropriation, allocation or fund shall (1) which is made available under or pursuant to this act or (2) which is now, or which is hereafter made, available under or pursuant to any other Act, to any department, agency or instrumentality of the United States, shall be used, after November 15, 1943, to pay any part of the salary of Goodwin B. Watson, William E. Dodd, Jr., and Robert Morse Lovett , unless prior to such date such person has been appointed by the President with the advice and consent of the Senate.[29]

Robert Lovett was a former University of Chicago English literature professor and editor of the *New Republic* magazine. He was the secretary of the Virgin Islands and had been acting governor in 1940–1941. Doctor Dodd was an FCC administrator with a long history of involvement with labor unions suspected of being Communist front groups.[30] Doctor Watson also worked in the FCC as chief of the analysis division. These three men were denounced by Rep. Martin Dies on the House floor as part of a

Figure 5.1. President Harry S. Truman (Library of Congress).

group of thirty-nine disloyal individuals on February 1, 1943. The House appointed a specials subcommittee of the Appropriations Committee to review the thirty-nine individuals who were permitted to testify without benefit of counsel in closed-door hearings. The special committee recommended that Dodd, Lovett, and Watson be barred from federal employment by cutting off their salaries.[31]

The three men continued to work for the United States for several months until they were terminated in 1944. Lovett, Dodd, and Watson all filed suits in the court of claims to recover back pay and allowances, alleging that section 304 was an unconstitutional ex post facto law. The court of claims allowed their claims, and the United States took certiorari to the Supreme Court. Section 304 did not survive the Supreme Court's review.[32] The court quickly rejected the contention that the intent of section 304 was merely to cut off compensation, not to bar the three men from government service. The Court held up a permanent bar to continued employment for the three claimants, noting that the purpose of enacting section 304 was to purge Lovett, Dodds, and Watson from government service for disloyalty.[33]

> Any other interpretation of the section would completely frustrate the purpose of all who sponsored 304, which clearly was to purge the then existing and all future lists of government employees of those whom Congress deemed guilty of "subversive activities" and therefore unfit to hold a federal job. What was challenged, therefore, is a statute which, because of what Congress thought to be their political beliefs, prohibited respondents from ever engaging in any government work, except as jurors or soldiers.[34]

The Court described section 304 as a bill of attainder because it inflicted punishment on the three claimants by depriving them of their federal positions. The Court supported its analysis by reference to two post–Civil War decisions, *Cummins v. Missouri*[35] and *Ex parte Garland*.[36]

Cummins was a writ of error brought by a Roman Catholic priest who was convicted of practicing his profession without taking Missouri's loyalty oath required by the state constitution. That oath required a member of the affected professional classes (i.e., lawyers, clergymen, and teachers) to swear that they had never borne arms against the United States nor given aid or comfort to persons engaged in hostility to the United States and had never been a member of, or connected with, any order, society, or organization inimical to the government of the United States. Cummins refused to take the oath. He continued to say mass and give sermons. Father Cummins was arrested and convicted of violating the penalty clause of the Missouri constitution's loyalty oath sections.[37] He sought writ of error to the Supreme Court. The Court held that the Missouri constitution's oath requirement was a bill of attainder, punishing Cummins without benefit of Sixth Amendment rights. The Court also held that the Missouri oath was an ex post facto law, making an act not originally criminal into a crime.[38]

Garland, an Arkansas lawyer who had served in the Confederate Congress, filed an application for readmission to the U.S. Supreme Court, having been admitted before the Civil War. In order to be readmitted, Garland was required to take an oath that he had never borne arms against the United States nor given aid and comfort to its enemies.[39] The Court granted his petition for readmission without his taking the oath, invalidating the act of Congress that imposed the oath as a bill of attainder and ex post facto law.[40] The Court considered the imposition of loss of office or position, or exclusion from an office previously held, to be punishment, though in *Garland* the petitioner was not subject to imprisonment or fine for failing to take the oath of office. After discussing

Cummins and *Garland*, the Court held that section 304 was an ex post facto law punishing the three claimants for an act that was lawful.

> Section 304 was designed to apply to particular individuals. Just as the statute in the two cases mentioned, it "operates as a legislative decree of perpetual exclusion from a chosen vocation." *Ex parte Garland*, supra, at 377. This permanent proscription from any opportunity to serve the Government is punishment, and of a most severe type. It is a type of punishment which Congress has only invoked for special types of odious and dangerous crimes, such as treason, 18 U. S. C. 2; acceptance of bribes by members of Congress, 18 U. S. C. 199, 202, 203; or by other government officials, 18 U. S. C. 207; and interference with elections by Army and Navy officers, 18 U. S. C. 58.[41]

The Supreme Court affirmed the court of claims and ordered that back salary and benefits be paid to the three men.[42]

President Truman issued Executive Order 9835 in March 1947 requiring all federal employees to take a loyalty oath.[43] All applicants for federal jobs would be subjected to a background investigation by the Civil Service Commission or an agency investigative group before a hiring decision could become permanent.[44] Current federal employees were to be subjected to a background investigation.[45] The executive order instructed all departments to turn over a list of names of all employees to the FBI.[46] Any employee accused of disloyalty after his name had been turned over to the FBI and other federal agencies for clearance could not be discharged without an administrative hearing before a department loyalty board. The Civil Service Commission was directed to establish a three-person Loyalty Review Board to act as a clearinghouse for information on loyalty and to coordinate all executive department loyalty programs.[47] The Loyalty Review Board's power to recommend dismissal of disloyal employees was tested in *Bailey v. Richardson*.[48]

Dorothy Bailey had a non-sensitive federal job covered by the classified civil service from 1939 to June 1947 when she was separated due to reduction in force. In March 1948, she applied for her old position and was given a temporary appointment, and she was reinstated on May 28, 1948.[49] Ms. Bailey was reappointed under the Truman loyalty screening program. She was investigated by the Regional Civil Service Commission that sent her an interrogatory asking her to admit or deny that:

> the Commission has received information to the effect that you are or have been a member of the Communist Party or the Communist Political Association; that you have attended meetings of the Communist Party, and have associated on numerous occasions with known Communist Party members.
>
> The Commission has received information to the effect that you are or have been a member of the American League for Peace and Democracy, an organization which has been declared by the Attorney General to come within the purview of Executive Order 9835.[50]

Bailey's answer denied that she had ever been a member of the Communist Party and admitted she had briefly belonged to the American League for Peace and Democracy. The regional board recommended her dismissal for disloyalty. She requested a personal hearing before the Loyalty Review Board. No evidence showing any Communist Party membership or any subversive activities was presented at the hearing. The board refused to identify the person who had made the accusation that she was a Communist and disloyal. Ms. Bailey testified that she was a loyal American. The board nonetheless sustained the finding of the regional board, and she was dismissed.[51]

Executive Order 9835 permitted an employee to be disqualified when reasonable grounds for belief existed showing that the employee was disloyal.[52] Bailey filed a declaratory judgment action in the U.S. District Court for the District of Columbia. Both sides moved for summary judgment, and the district court granted the government's summary judgment motion. Bailey appealed. She was represented by Thurman Arnold, with Abe Fortas, Paul A. Porter, and Milton V. Freeman on the brief to the court.[53] The D.C. Circuit issued an extensive opinion, making two distinct findings:

> 1. The part of the Civil Service Loyalty Review Board's order that barred Miss Bailey from federal service for three years was constitutionally invalid by reason of Article I §9, holding that a bar to federal employment on account of prior association with a Communist or Communist front organization was an ex post facto law, following the Supreme Court's decision in *United States v. Lovett;*[54]
>
> 2. However, the decision to discharge Miss Bailey due to her suspected disloyalty was neither punishment nor an ex post facto law. She was not entitled to the range of rights stated in the Sixth Amendment.[55]

The majority opinion closed with the following dicta:

> It is our clear opinion that the President, absent congressional restriction, may remove from Government service any person of whose loyalty he is not completely convinced. He may do so without assigning any reason and without giving the employee any explanatory notice. If, as a matter of policy, he chooses to give the employee a general description of the information which concerns him and to hear what the employee has to say, he does not thereby strip himself of any portion of his constitutional power to choose and to remove. We conclude that the Executive Order before us and the proceedings under it violated no congressional limitation upon the executive power of removal; that no constitutional right was involved in this non-appointment or dismissal; and that, in so far as the circumstances imposed hardship upon the individual, the exigencies of government in the public interest under current conditions must prevail, as they always must when a similar clash arises.[56]

Judge Edgerton dissented, pointing out that Miss Bailey was deprived of her livelihood without trial by jury, without evidence, and without the opportunity to confront her accusers.[57] He pointed out that Miss Bailey produced abundant evidence in the form of affidavits attesting to her loyalty from bankers and federal officials, and no evidence indicating that she had engaged in any disloyal acts was presented during her hearing before the Loyalty Review Board. Her file contained unsworn statements from unidentified informants in Miss Bailey's FBI file stating that she was a Communist as early as 1935.[58]

Judge Edgerton pointed out that Executive Order 9835 guaranteed the right of cross-examination to employees who were investigated for disloyalty. He quoted from the order that the standard for dismissal "shall be that, on all the evidence, reasonable grounds exist for belief that the person involved is disloyal to the Government of the United States." Judge Edgerton noted,

> Dismissal for disloyalty is punishment and requires all the safeguards of a judicial trial. Most dismissals, including among others dismissals for colorless or undisclosed reasons and dismissals for incompetence, are plainly not punitive. They do not require a judicial trial or even a full administrative hearing. They are within the authority of the executive. Likewise most tax laws are within the authority of the legislature. It does not follow that all legislative taxation is constitutional or that all executive dismissals are constitutional. Punishment is infliction of harm, usually for wrong conduct but in appellant's case for wrong views.[59]

Judge Edgerton, citing *Lovett*, asserted that the majority's distinction between dismissal and eligibility as a punishment contradicted *Lovett* and had no basis in reason. He concluded that Miss Bailey was entitled to all the rights of the accused under the Sixth Amendment. Having received no Sixth Amendment rights before the Loyalty Review Board,[60] as well as punishing her for her ideas, a violation of the First Amendment free speech clause.[61]

The *Bailey* majority opinion placed a seal of approval on executive branch dismissals of alleged disloyal employees via an administrative hearing in which the employee accused of disloyalty had no right of cross-examination or confrontation. In Miss Bailey's case, the executive branch dismissed her on suspicion of disloyalty, contrary to the weight of the evidence, giving greater weight to the anonymous unsworn statements of informants than to sworn affidavits from Miss Bailey's employers. The Supreme Court denied certiorari, making the *Bailey* decision the last word on administrative disloyalty proceedings during the Truman era.

Congress passed the National Security Act of 1950 over President Truman's veto. Section 4(a) forbade any person to conspire to "perform any act which would substantially contribute to . . . the establishment of a totalitarian dictatorship" within the United States.[62] Section 2(b) made a crime out of communicating any classified information to anyone whom a government officer or employee knows or has reason to know is a Communist or fellow-traveler.[63] Section 2(c) made a crime out of any Communist receiving classified information from a government officer or employee.[64] Violators of section 2 would be punished by a fine not greater than $10,000 or a jail term of up to ten years, or both.[65] The same act also required Communist Party members to register with the United States.[66] The executive branch did little to enforce the act during President Truman's final term.

The Truman loyalty program ended in 1953. The departmental loyalty boards heard cases involving 16,503 individuals. Five hundred sixty individuals were denied employment or removed on account of disloyalty.[67]

President Eisenhower's Disloyalty Program

The Eisenhower administration employed the same techniques to ferret out disloyal persons from 1953 through 1961. President Eisenhower approved of Senator Richard M. Nixon as his 1952 vice-presidential running mate on the strength of his record as a congressman on the House Un-American Activities Committee.[68] Nixon took credit for ferreting out Alger Hiss and exposing his alleged membership in an espionage ring passing secret information to Whittaker Chambers. Dwight Eisenhower ran on a platform in 1952 that promised to expose and deal with Communists in government.[69] President Eisenhower revoked Executive Order 90835 and instituted a new loyalty program designating each department of the federal government as the proper agency for loyalty investigations.[70] The Loyalty Review Board was disbanded, and its register of suspected disloyal persons was to be turned over to the Office of Personnel Management.[71] The criteria for dismissal or refusal to employ on account of disloyalty were redefined by Executive Order 10450 as follows:

> Should there develop at any stage of investigation information indicating that the employment of any officer or employee of the Government may not be clearly consistent with the interests of the national security, the head of the department or agency concerned or his representative shall immediately suspend the employment of the person involved if he deems such suspension necessary in the interests of the national security and, following such investigation and review as he deems necessary, the head of the department or agency concerned shall terminate the employment of such suspended officer or employee whenever he shall determine such termination necessary or advisable in the interests of the national security.[72]

The criteria established by the president allowed a department head to dismiss an employee after investigation if the employee had a drinking problem, suffered from mental illness, or had engaged in espionage. An employee who knowingly belonged to any organization that advocated the use of force to prevent other citizens from exercising their civil rights or that sought to overthrow the government by unlawful means, or who intended to further the aims of that organization, could be dismissed.[73] The criteria also allowed dismissal for an employee who had a friend or relative who was a member of any such group. An employee could be dismissed for unauthorized disclosure of classified information. An employee who was called before a congressional committee investigating disloyalty as a witness who claimed the protection of the Fifth Amendment could also be discharged.[74] The Eisenhower loyalty program was much more tightly drawn than its predecessor and interfered with First Amendment freedom of association and the protection of the Fifth Amendment, something that the Truman program did not envision.[75]

The Attorney General's List of Subversive Organizations and the FBI

President Truman authorized the Department of Justice to furnish a list of totalitarian, fascist, Communist, or subversive organizations to his Loyalty Review Board in 1947.[76] The original list contained forty-eight organizations deemed to be subversive.[77] Attorney General Herbert Brownell issued a much longer list in 1955 that included 298 organizations, inflated by including numerous fascist, pro-German, and pro-Japanese organizations and the Ku Klux Klan.

The attorney general continued to pursue suspected Communist front organizations.[78] The attorney general and the FBI pursued the National Lawyers Guild from 1948 to 1958 in an unsuccessful attempt to find evidence showing that the guild was a Communist front organization. The National Lawyers Guild, formed in 1936, had a number of Communist attorneys on its membership rolls. The FBI burglarized the guild's offices in 1940 in order to obtain copies of its membership rolls and organizational minutes. Post-war, in 1947, the guild was targeted by the FBI as a subversive organization. The FBI put an unauthorized wiretap on the guild headquarters phones in November 1947.[79] The FBI burglarized the guild s offices again early in 1948, searching for documents showing ties to the Communist Party. Despite J. Edgar Hoover's urging, the attorney general did not include the Guild in its 1948 list of subversive organizations.[80] The FBI continued its wiretap on guild phone lines after 1948, searching for evidence of subversive activities. During the trial of Judith Coplon for espionage, an eight-hundred-page FBI report on the guild and many of its members surfaced. The guild threatened to make public the FBI invasion of its members' privacy by illegal wiretaps.[81]

Meanwhile, Congressman Richard Nixon requested that the House Un-American Activities Committee investigate the guild's alleged Communist ties.[82] HUAC held a hearing on the guild's relationship to Communists and Communist causes, concluding with a report issued in September 1950 supporting the subversive nature of the guild.[83] Attorney General McGrath prevailed on the American Bar Association in 1950 to pass a resolution that each state board of bar examiners impose a loyalty oath on top of the usual oath of an attorney to uphold and defend the Constitution. The resolution was aimed at guild members.[84] The ABA appointed Austin Canfield as head of a special committee to investigate Communist tactics as affecting the decorum of the courtroom.[85] Canfield's committee was in regular contact with the FBI and came up with a series of recommendations to the ABA, including a resolution stating that a lawyer who took the Fifth Amendment was unfit to practice law.[86]

Pressure from the FBI and the ABA caused Attorney General Brownell to place the guild on the list of subversive organizations. He announced his decision before the guild had been notified. By law, the guild had a right to an administrative hearing before the Justice Department before it was listed. The guild went ahead with a request for hearing, postponing the addition of the guild to the list. The attorney general eventually withdrew his proposed listing, and the guild was never put on the attorney general's list, although newspaper, radio, and television stories repeated the falsehood that the guild had been listed through 1958.[87]

Judicial Limitation on the Loyalty Programs

The Supreme Court put substantial limitations on the scope of Executive Order 10450 and its enabling legislation in *Cole v. Young*,[88] decided in 1956. Cole was a civil service worker in the New York office of the Federal Food and Drug Administration. He was suspended without pay in November 1953 while under investigation for alleged disloyalty. Cole refused to request a hearing on his alleged disloyalty and was dismissed. He tried to appeal to the Civil Service Commission because he was hired under the veterans' preference act, but the commission found it lacked jurisdiction to hear his appeal.[89] This decision was based on the 1950 act authorizing suspension or discharge for national security reasons without regard to any other act of Congress, including the veterans' preference act.[90]

The Court chose to define "national security" very narrowly as it related only to those activities which are directly concerned with the nation's safety, as distinguished from the general welfare. The Court noted that the Department of Health, Education, and Welfare had not made a determination that Cole's position was associated with the national security; therefore his dismissal under the auspices of Executive Order

10450 and the 1950 act was illegal and violated the Veterans' Preference Act.[91] Cole's case was reversed and remanded.[92]

Vitarelli v. Seaton,[93] handed down in 1959, further curbed executive authority to dismiss employees for disloyalty. Vitarelli was a Department of the Interior non–civil service specialist stationed in Guam in 1954, when he was suspended from his duties for alleged disloyalty. The Department of the Interior disclosed that it possessed information that Vitarelli had a "sympathetic association" with three named persons alleged to have been members of or in sympathetic association with the Communist Party and that he had concealed from the government the true extent of these associations at the time of a previous inquiry into them, and that he had registered as a supporter of the American Labor Party in New York City in 1945, had subscribed to the *USSR Information Bulletin*, and had purchased copies of the *Daily Worker* and *New Masses*.

Vitarelli requested a hearing and presented evidence of his loyalty to the United States. The Department of the Interior called no witnesses and presented no evidence showing that the events alleged in its suspension letter were correct. Vitarelli was dismissed as a security risk. He filed an action for declaratory judgment and reinstatement in the District Court for the District of Columbia. The United States then filed an amended statement of discharge removing any reasons based on a security risk and moved for summary judgment because a Department of Interior non–civil service employee could be discharged without cause. The district court granted the government's motion for summary judgment, and the D.C. Circuit affirmed.[94] Vitarelli's certiorari petition was granted.

The Supreme Court refused to allow the Interior Department to get away with shifting the grounds for Vitarelli's dismissal from disloyalty to "no cause." It reversed the D.C. Circuit, granting Vitarelli full relief.[95] *Vitarelli* put some limits on dismissal of federal employees accused of being an alleged security risk. At minimum, an employee accused of being a security risk was entitled to a constitutionally valid administrative hearing.[96] The executive department as moving party was required to establish disloyalty by the greater weight of the evidence, not relying solely on statements from alleged confidential informants who were not disclosed to the employee or employee's counsel and were unavailable to testify at the hearing. The employee's right to cross-examination meant nothing if his or her accusers were not produced at the hearing. The government could not substitute a discharge without cause for non–civil service employees after serving notice of intent to suspend and discharge on account of disloyalty. The Eisenhower loyalty program lost momentum after 1958. The administration began to back away from militant anti-Communism after the decline and fall of Sen. Joseph McCarthy in 1954.[97]

CONGRESSIONAL ANTI-COMMUNISM

The Cold War produced a new approach to suppressing dissent: congressional initiatives to use the committee process to harass and threaten dissenters. From 1946 through the end of the 1950s, congressional reaction to media demands for action against Communists in government led to committee investigations of alleged Communist infiltration of the executive branch of government. Congressional attention was focused on the threat of Communist infiltration of public and private entities, starting sometime in 1947. Two congressional committees were the primary vehicles used to root out Communist influence in government and in the private sector: the House Un-American Activities Committee and the Senate Government Operations Committee Special Subcommittee.

House Un-American Activities Committee: Motion Picture Industry Investigation

The House Un-American Activities Committee was the direct lineal descendant of a Special Congressional Committee on Un-American Activities chaired by Texas congressman Martin Dies, authorized in 1938. The Dies Committee was charged with investigation of Communist infiltration inside the Work Projects Administration. It summoned known Communist Party leaders such as Earl Browder to testify in public.[98] A series of hearings were held relating to Communists in the Federal Theater Project, a branch of the WPA. Hallie Flanagan, the project director, was grilled on the alleged Communist content of plays produced by the project. One representative demanded to know if Christopher Marlowe or "Mr. Euripides" were Communist playwrights.[99] The Dies Committee deferred investigating the Ku Klux Klan but did issue a report on the menace to security arising from U.S. citizens of Japanese ancestry.[100]

Congressman Dies retired in 1945, and Congress then turned the Un-American Activities Committee into a standing committee initially chaired by Congressman J. Parnell Thomas of New Jersey. HUAC initiated a probe into Communist infiltration of the motion picture industry in 1947. In 1946, the *Hollywood Reporter* had published a list of writers and actors who were reported to be Communist Party members or fellow travelers. HUAC used this list to prepare a witness list for subpoena purposes. The committee devoted nine days of hearings to Communist infiltration of the entertainment industry. It first brought in a group of witnesses who agreed that Communists posed a serious threat to the motion picture industry. Walt Disney and Ronald Reagan, president of the Screen Actors Guild, testified that the threat of Communist infiltration and manipulation of motion pictures to portray the party line and to attack the U.S. way of life was real and should be taken seriously.[101] The committee called a list of executives and producers who were publicly anti-Communist, including studio heads Louis B. Mayer and Jack Warner.[102] HUAC also called a list of actors, including Gary Cooper, Adolph Menjou, George Murphy, Ronald Reagan, and Robert Taylor.[103] Menjou declared, "I am a witch hunter if the witches are Communists. I am a baiter. I would like to see them all back in Russia."[104] HUAC's witness list consisted of forty-three men and women thought to have Communist ties. Nineteen refused to give evidence to the committee. Eleven of the nineteen potential witnesses were subpoenaed as witnesses to appear on October 27, 1947.[105] Bertolt Brecht, one of the eleven, finally agreed to answer questions about his alleged Communist past.[106] Ten refused to answer questions concerning their alleged Communist Party affiliation.[107] Rather than seeking the shield of the Fifth Amendment privilege against self-incrimination, these ten Hollywood screenwriters and directors asserted that questions directed at their Communist Party affiliation violated the First Amendment rights to freedom of assembly and speech. Tactically, this was a poor choice. The principal question that each refused to answer, "Are you now or have you ever been a member of the Communist Party?" did not call for an answer that would have curtailed any of these ten's right to speak on political issues, nor would it have implicated them in any sort of criminal activity. The Hollywood Ten tried to read statements into the record condemning the motion picture probe as unconstitutional: they were thwarted in this attempt.[108]

HUAC continued to call more Hollywood witnesses, including Eric Johnston, president of the Motion Picture Association of America, who testified that he proposed a three-point program to the association that would bar hiring any proven Communists or retaining any Communists. The association did not adopt his proposed anti-Communist resolution.[109]

On November 24, the House of Representatives voted to cite all of the Hollywood Ten for contempt of Congress. On November 25, Eric Johnson issued a press release from a meeting of motion picture executives at the Waldorf Astoria hotel in New York City. The press release asserted that the Hollywood Ten would be fired or suspended without pay and not reemployed until they were cleared of contempt charges and had sworn that they were not Communists. It read as follows:

> Members of the Association of Motion Picture Producers deplore the action of the 10 Hollywood men who have been cited for contempt by the House of Representatives. We do not desire to prejudge their legal rights, but their actions have been a disservice to their employers and have impaired their usefulness to the industry. We will forthwith discharge or suspend without compensation those in our employ, and we will not re-employ any of the 10 until such time as he is acquitted or has purged himself of contempt and declares under oath that he is not a Communist.

> On the broader issue of alleged subversive and disloyal elements in Hollywood, our members are likewise prepared to take positive action. We will not knowingly employ a Communist or a member of any party or group which advocates the overthrow of the government of the United States by force or by any illegal or unconstitutional methods. In pursuing this policy, we are not going to be swayed by hysteria or intimidation from any source. We are frank to recognize that such a policy involves danger and risks. There is the danger of hurting innocent people. There is the risk of creating an atmosphere of fear. Creative work at its best cannot be carried on in an atmosphere of fear. We will guard against this danger, this risk, this fear. To this end we will invite the Hollywood talent guilds to work with us to eliminate any subversives: to protect the innocent; and to safeguard free speech and a free screen wherever threatened. The absence of a national policy, established by Congress, with respect to the employment of Communists in private industry makes our task difficult. Ours is a nation of laws. We request Congress to enact legislation to assist American industry to rid itself of subversive, disloyal elements. Nothing subversive or un-American has appeared on the screen, nor can any number of Hollywood investigations obscure the patriotic services of the 30,000 loyal Americans employed in Hollywood who have given our government invaluable aid to war and peace.[110]

Meanwhile, director John Huston and actors Humphrey Bogart and Lauren Bacall organized the Committee for the First Amendment to resist congressional probes into the political affiliations of Hollywood writers, directors, and actors. Committee members flew to Washington for the October 1947 hearings.[111] HUAC had failed to find any evidence that Communists in the motion picture industry were secretly disseminating Communist propaganda. HUAC did terrify the motion picture industry, which depended on public popularity for its profits. The industry reacted to the probe by instituting its own loyalty programs. When Howard Hughes purchased RKO pictures in May 1948, he fired most of the older employees and closed the studio for six months while he investigated the loyalty of the remaining employees.[112]

The Hollywood Ten were indicted for contempt of Congress in 1948 and were convicted of contempt by the U.S. District Court for the District of Columbia in 1948. John Howard Lawson and Dalton Trumbo were tried by jury, and the rest had bench trials. Lawson and Trumbo appealed their convictions. The District of Columbia Circuit affirmed, resting its conclusions on *Barsky v. United States*,[113] a case involving the refusal to turn over books and records of the Joint Anti-Fascist Committee to the House Un-American Activities Committee. Barsky was cited by the House for conspiring to refuse to produce the committee's books and records as subpoenaed, and he was convicted of contempt of Congress. He appealed his contempt conviction, which was affirmed. The *Barsky* court said,

> The problem thus presented is difficult and delicate. In it we have not only the frequent "real problem of balancing the public interest against private security," but in this instance we must do so in the midst of swirling currents of public emotion in both directions. We are presented with extreme declarations in respect to Communists and equally extreme declarations in respect to the Congressional Committee. The duty of the courts is no less than to render judgment with utter detachment.[114]

The Court held that HUAC had the right to ask the witnesses and the committee about the alleged Communist affiliation of the committee.[115] The *Barsky* court also held that the government was not required to wait until Communists constituted a clear and present danger to the government of the United States to ask people about their Communist affiliation.[116] The *Lawson* court followed *Barsky,* holding that the First Amendment rights of free speech and free association were not involved in answering the committee's questions.[117] At the time, membership in the Communist Party of the United States, or failure to register as a party member, was not against the law. This eliminated a good-faith claim of protection under the Fifth Amendment privilege against self-incrimination. Trumbo and Lawson filed a petition for certiorari, accompanied by an amicus curia brief signed by 204 Hollywood writers, rectors, and actors.[118] The Supreme Court denied certiorari.[119]

House Un-American Activities Committee: Three Former Communists

HUAC followed up its probe into the entertainment industry with testimony from three admitted former Communists, Elizabeth Bentley, Louis Budenz, and Whittaker Chambers. Elizabeth Bentley, a Vassar graduate who once held a fellowship to study art at the University of Florence, joined the American League against War and Fascism, a Communist front group, while finishing her work at Columbia University. She eventually joined the Communist Party and acted as an espionage agent working with a secret cell of U.S. government employees called the Silvermaster Ring.[120] She also supervised a second spy ring headed by Victor Perlo.[121] In 1945, Bentley had a falling-out with the secret police when she failed to turn over the members of her two spy rings to her Russian handler.[122] She then defected because she feared the NKVD would "liquidate" her or that she would be arrested by the FBI. Bentley chose to turn herself in to the FBI office in Hartford, Connecticut.[123] Bentley was debriefed and later testified before HUAC. She identified William Remington; William Gold, the go-between for atomic scientist Klaus Fuchs; Lauchlin Currie, a former assistant to President Roosevelt; and Harry Dexter White as Communists and cell members.[124] Gold was to prove to be the link between Julius and Ethel Rosenberg and the theft of top-secret documents relating to the making of nuclear devices by Dr.

Klaus Fuchs. Bentley was a witness for the prosecution at the Rosenberg trial. She was cross-examined about her drinking problem and psychiatric issues. She also published her autobiography, converted to Catholicism, and had a series of short-term college teaching positions. She died of heart disease in 1963.[125]

Louis Budenz, an Indianapolis native educated by the Jesuits, was the director of the Catholic Social Bureau.[126] Budenz then became a labor organizer, leading a number of strikes for the unions that supported *Labor Age* and was jailed twenty-one times for his union activities.[127] He became a Communist Party member in 1935.[128] Because he was a talented journalist, the Communist Party made him labor editor of the *Daily Worker*, and in 1940 the editor of the *Daily Worker*. In 1945, Budenz defected from the party and returned to his Catholic roots.[129] He was a prodigious writer, publishing four major books and more than one hundred articles relating to the Communist threat. Budenz testified before HUAC for the first time in 1946.[130] Budenz identified Gerhard Eisler as the chief controller for Soviet espionage in the United States.[131] Eisler tried to leave the United States for Germany but was detained, indicted, and convicted for contempt of Congress and making a false official statement in order to obtain a temporary visa.[132] Budenz became a favorite source for information on Communist espionage and Communist infiltration of the executive branch of the government delivered by testimony before HUAC. He returned in August 1948, giving evidence that Alger Hiss was known to be a Communist.[133] Later, in August 1951, Budenz would appear before the Senate Internal Security Subcommittee to give testimony that in his opinion, Owen Lattimore was a Communist and member of a party cell in the Institute for Pacific Relations.[134] Budenz was a government witness in the 1952 trial of twenty-six Communist Party members in New York City.[135] In January 1953, Budenz appeared before a House special subcommittee investigating tax-exempt foundations, testifying that twenty-eight academicians were Communist Party members. Columbia Law School Professor Walter Gelhorn and Dr. Ira Reid of Swarthmore College testified the next day, denying that they had anything to do with the Communist Party.[136] Budenz's identification of former fellow Communists was not supported by corroborative documentary evidence nor by other witnesses. As anti-Communism faded from public concern in the 1960s, he retired from Fordham and moved to Providence, Rhode Island, where he died in April 1972.[137]

Jay Vivian Chambers, better known under his assumed name of David Whittaker Chambers, was born in 1901 in Philadelphia and grew up on Long Island. He graduated from high school and left home, going to Baltimore to find work under the assumed name of Charles Adams. Chambers eventually ended up broke in New Orleans and came home to work briefly for his father's newspaper under a second alias, "Charles Whittaker." In 1920, he enrolled in Columbia University. Chambers made friends with two youthful Communists, David Zabladowsky and Irving Kaplan.[138] Chambers quit Columbia, moved in briefly with his grandfather Chambers, and then left for Europe in the summer of 1923. Chambers had contact with Marxist thinkers in Europe but had no active association with the Communist Party.[139] By 1925, Chambers had drifted into Communist Party membership.[140]

Chambers was tapped for a role as a Communist underground agent in 1932. He was assigned courier duties, making trips to Washington to pick up documents that had been copied or photographed by Soviet agents working in the executive branch of the federal government and conveying them to his Soviet handlers in New York City. The spy network for whom Chambers worked was headed by a man known as "J. Peters," an NKVD officer. Meanwhile he kept his wife and children in a separate compartment of his life. Chambers continued to deliver stolen documents to Peters. Chambers used several aliases during this time: "Karl" and "George Crosley."[141]

Sometime in 1934, Chambers met Alger Hiss, a Harvard-educated lawyer working the Agricultural Adjustment Agency. A group of left-wing intellectuals working for the federal government in New Deal letter agencies met regularly to talk about political issues and Marxist theory. The group was sponsored by Harold Ware and included several men who were involved in espionage on behalf of the Soviet Union.[142] The "regulars" included Lee Pressman, an AAA attorney who was Hiss's Harvard classmate and friend.[143] Chambers was introduced to the Ware group in 1934 by J. Peters.[144] When Ware was killed in an auto accident in 1935, Peters took over his place as group leader. Whittaker Chambers met with the Ware group from 1934 until he defected from the Communist Party in 1938.[145] In the summer of 1934, Chambers met Alger Hiss and his wife Priscilla through John Herrmann, a Communist who lived in Washington.[146]

Chambers was instructed to form a second espionage group in Washington, with Hiss as its leader. At that time, Hiss had been "loaned" to Congress to act as special assistant to the Nye Committee.[147] Chambers, Hiss, and their spouses also formed a social relationship that lasted for about four years. Their association terminated sometime in 1936.[148] Two years later, Chambers renounced the Communist Party and joined the *Time* magazine staff as an editor.

In 1939, Chambers gave a series of statements to the FBI identifying Communists who were engaged in espionage during the 1930s. His accusations included most of the Ware group members and Alger Hiss.[149] In early 1948, the FBI knew that Chambers had accused Hiss of being a Communist Party member and an espionage agent, and Igor Gouzenko and Elizabeth Bentley had heard from other Communists that Hiss was a party member and spy.

HUAC demonstrated the power of a congressional committee to destroy the reputation of U.S. citizens in 1948 when it called Whittaker Chambers as a witness. On August 3, 1948, Chambers was sworn and gave his story to HUAC.[150] Chambers testified about the members of the Ware group and told the committee that Alger Hiss was a member of the Ware group and an avowed Communist.[151]

Hiss promptly sent a telegram to HUAC denying his involvement in the Communist Party and requesting that he be allowed to appear before HUAC to clear his name. Hiss claimed that he had never laid eyes on Whittaker Chambers.[152] The committee scheduled Hiss for Thursday, August 5. Hiss immediately said,

> I am not and never have been a member of the Communist Party. I do not and never have adhered to the tenets of the Communist Party. I am not and never have been a member of any Communist-front organization. I have never followed the Communist Party line, directly or indirectly. To the best of my knowledge, none of my friends is a Communist.[153]

Hiss also denied knowing Whittaker Chambers. He denied that Chambers had come to his home to plead with him to defect from the Communist Party.[154] Congressman Richard Nixon suggested that Hiss and Chambers be summoned before HUAC a second time so that Hiss could confront Chambers.[155] Prior to the scheduled confrontation, Chambers appeared again and reiterated his testimony that Alger Hiss was a Communist and his friend.[156]

Chambers returned to give testimony on August 7. Congressman Nixon questioned Chambers about the private life of Alger Hiss. Chambers told the committee about Hiss's cocker spaniel, about his stepson Timothy Hobson's summer camp on Maryland's eastern shore, and that Alger and Priscilla Hiss were amateur bird watchers who were thrilled one day when they observed a warbler on the banks of the Potomac.[157] On August 16, Hiss returned to HUAC where Congressman Nixon questioned him closely on his assertion that he knew no man by the name of Whittaker Chambers in the 1930s.[158] Hiss denied knowing anyone using the first name "Carl" as well.[159] Hiss then began to backpedal on his former denial.[160] Hiss admitted that he would probably be able to identify Chambers if Chambers were to appear in person before him.[161] Hiss then recalled that he had meetings with a freelance writer named George Crosley at the time that Hiss was working on a munitions investigation with the Nye Committee. Crosley wanted to do a story on the disclosure of war profiteering. Crosley and his family stayed with the Hiss family for several days and later took over the Hiss apartment. Hiss admitted selling Crosley his Model A roadster as well.[162] Congressman Nixon then trapped Hiss. One day when the Chambers were with the Hisses as overnight guests, the Hisses returned from a bird-watching trip excited about seeing a rare prothonotary warbler along the banks of the Potomac. Hiss fell into the trap, admitting to the sighting of the rare warbler known only to Hiss, his wife, and Whittaker Chambers.[163]

On August 17, Hiss confronted Chambers before HUAC. Chambers was brought into the hearing room for purposes of identification only. Hiss admitted he recognized Chambers, who had used the name "Crosley" in the 1930s.[164] Hiss then denied that he was a Communist and also that he knew George Crosley to be a Communist.[165] Chambers then repeated his earlier accusation that Hiss was a Communist.[166] Hiss got out of his chair and approached Chambers, baiting him to make the accusation that Hiss was a Communist outside the protection of the committee room so Hiss could sue him for libel.[167]

Whittaker Chambers appeared on *Meet the Press* on August 27, 1948. When pressed by *Washington Post* reporter Edward Folliard, one of the panel members, Chambers said, "Alger Hiss was a Communist and may still be one."[168] Hiss responded by filing a libel suit against Chambers and NBC in U.S. District Court for the District of Maryland in September 1948.[169] The defamation suit was eventually dismissed with prejudice after Hiss was convicted of perjury before Congress.

Chambers planned his defense with Semmes, Bowen & Semmes's Richard Cleveland, son of former president Grover Cleveland. During preparation for his deposition, Chambers disclosed that he had shielded Hiss from accountability for his espionage activities before HUAC.[170] Hiss's attorney, William Marbury, made an oral request for production of documents during Chambers's deposition that pertained to or affected Hiss. That request was routine, but the results were not. Chambers contacted his wife's nephew Nathan Levine in New York City. Levine met Chambers and his wife at Mrs. Chambers's mother's house. Levine had secreted an envelope containing documents including memos signed by Hiss and two rolls of microfilm in an air shaft in the second-floor bathroom. Chambers had forgotten that he had entrusted microfilm rolls to his nephew for safekeeping.[171] Chambers allowed his lawyers to examine the documents. The documents were taken to Semmes, Bowen & Semmes's offices, photostated, and locked in the firm's vault.[172] Chambers was scheduled for his deposition on November 17, 1948. He entered the Piper & Marbury conference room carrying the sheaf of photostats showing Hiss's signature. Marbury concealed his emotions, asked for a brief recess, and then stepped out to take a phone call. When he returned, Marbury's associate wound up Chambers's deposition. The next day, Marbury and Cleveland jointly agreed to turn over Chambers's documents to the Justice Department. The attorney general took no action with respect to any espionage charges against Hiss. All the events occurred in 1934–1938, and the statute of limitations had run on any spying that Hiss may have done. Chambers, taking no chances, took one of the pumpkins growing on his Westminster, Maryland, farm, carved out the insides, and inserted the microfilm rolls in the pumpkin for safekeeping.[173]

Meanwhile, the Justice Department processed the Hiss documents while the FBI gathered information that could lead to Chambers's indictment for perjury.[174] Eventually, the investigation changed direction and a grand jury indicted Hiss for perjury in 1949. Chambers became a key prosecution witness in the two Hiss perjury trials. After Hiss was convicted, Chambers wrote *Witness*, his autobiography, which was a best seller. Chambers left *Time* and became one of the editors of William F. Buckley's *National Review*. Chambers suffered from coronary artery disease. He had three non-fatal heart attacks. His fourth attack brought on his death in 1961.[175]

SENATOR JOSEPH R. MCCARTHY

In 1946, an obscure Wisconsin county judge from Appleton, Joseph R. McCarthy, ran a successful campaign to obtain the Republican nomination for Senate. His primary opponent, Robert M. La Follette Jr., son of the Progressive Party leader "Fighting Bob" La Follette, who had been elected to the Senate as a Republican in 1925 and 1928 and reelected as a Progressive in 1934 and 1940, conducted a lackluster campaign and lost the primary to McCarthy. Joseph McCarthy campaigned on the current issues dividing Republicans from Democrats: the New Deal's enlarged bureaucratic interference in private enterprise, socialized health care, and very occasionally echoing Republican Party leaders such as Robert M. Taft that the United States faced an external Communist threat to national security and an internal subversive Communist Party bent on destroyed U.S. freedoms. McCarthy easily defeated his Democratic opponent, Howard McMurray, in November, running on the same anti–New Deal, anti–big government platform that got him the nomination. Nationally, the Republican Party made significant gains in both houses of Congress, and the Eightieth Congress, seated in January 1947, was solidly Republican.[176]

Senator McCarthy, a very junior member of the Senate club, had made friends with Col. Robert R. McCormick, publisher of the *Chicago Tribune* that would later help him rise to the position of superstar after 1950. His initial committee assignments were minor. He developed a reputation for conscious disregard of the club rules of the Senate, which did not endear him to senior senators in either party.[177] The one notable experience during his first two years in office was the Senate Armed Services Committee subcommittee investigation into the Malmedy massacre, a German wartime atrocity in which 150 captured U.S. soldiers were executed by soldiers from the 1st SS Panzer Division. Seventy-three German soldiers were convicted of war crimes by a war crimes tribunal, forty-three being

Figure 5.2. Senator Joseph R. McCarthy (U.S. Senate Historical Office).

sentenced to death. The defendants lost a habeas corpus petition in the U.S. Supreme Court, but two separate investigations were launched into the defendants' charges that they were tortured during interrogation by U.S. authorities. Delaware County, Pennsylvania, Orphans Court Judge Van Roden testified before the subcommittee on May 4, 1949, that the Nazi SS men were convicted on "improper evidence" obtained by coercion, including mock trials and other coercive techniques.[178] McCarthy intervened in the Senate investigation, claiming that the SS soldiers were denied a fair trial. He also attacked Connecticut Republican senator Raymond E. Baldwin. McCarthy latched on to the fact that a member of Baldwin's law firm had been one of the prosecutors at the war crimes trial of the Malmedy defendants. McCarthy then took over the subcommittee hearing, using his senatorial privilege to abuse Baldwin, the prosecutors, and the U.S. Army. His accusations of "whitewash" grabbed headlines. He called the war crimes judges "morons" and made accusations that army witnesses were liars. He demanded that the U.S. prosecutors be given lie detector tests, and when Sen. Baldwin denied his request, he stormed out of the subcommittee hearing.[179] Two months after the hearing ended, McCarthy made a speech on the Senate floor accusing Senator Baldwin of whitewashing the torture of the German soldiers to protect his law partner.[180]

McCarthy came out of obscurity in February 1950. He was asked by the local Republican women of Wheeling, West Virginia, to be the speaker at their 1950 Lincoln Day dinner. Wheeling was a prosperous steel town ruled by Republicans, but not a focal point in national politics. McCarthy woke up the crowd by waving a sheaf of papers, claiming that he had a list of 205 Communists in the State Department. McCarthy based his charges on a 1946 letter from Secretary of State Byrnes to Congressman Adolph Sabath that was put in the Congressional Record stating that a screening of three thousand temporary government employees in the State Department resulted in a recommendation that 285 employees not be retained. By 1950, seventy-nine had been terminated. McCarthy charged that all those who were not recommended for retention were Communists.[181] This accusation found its way into the newspapers, and when McCarthy's plane landed in Salt Lake City the next day, he was mobbed by reporters demanding to see the names on his list. McCarthy told the press that Secretary of State Acheson would call him, and he would read the names over the telephone to him.[182] On February 11, McCarthy sent a telegram to President Truman demanding that he waive his executive order forbidding disclosure of executive branch loyalty reviews for State Department employees.[183] Senator McCarthy continued to repeat his charge that there were anywhere from 57 to 205 disloyal employees working in the State Department. The low figure was based on his assertion that there were "57 card-carrying Communists" employed in the State Department.[184]

Senator McCarthy then called for a resolution authorizing Senate investigation of Communist infiltration of the State Department. The Democratic leadership put out a resolution that would authorize investigation by the Committee on Foreign Relations, and the Republican leadership arranged for the resolution to exclude any specific charges against State Department employees.[185] The Foreign Relations Committee established a special subcommittee chaired by Maryland senator Millard Tydings, who had served his state as senator since 1926. His Senate colleagues on the subcommittee consisted of Democrats Bryan McMahon of Connecticut and Theodore Green of Rhode Island and Republicans Henry Cabot Lodge of Massachusetts and Bourke Hickenlooper of Iowa.[186]

The Tydings Subcommittee hearings got off to a rocky start, the members disagreeing about the issue of public versus executive sessions and Senator Tydings demanding that McCarthy present evidence showing that "Case 14" was a Communist before any testimony was taken.[187] Senator McCarthy was allowed to state his case for a Communist presence in the State Department in his own fashion: he proceeded to use information contained in appendix 9 of the Dies Committee's report to show that lawyer Dorothy Kenyon, who was not a State Department employee but who had briefly served as a U.S. delegate to the UN Commission on the Status of Women, belonged to twenty-eight different Communist front organizations.[188] McCarthy carefully structured his "revelation" of Ms. Kenyon's alleged pro-Communist sympathy by associating her with known Communists who also worked for the same causes she did.[189] McCarthy's next presentation was an indictment of Prof. Philip C. Jessop, a diplomat and widely respected authority on international law. Jessop was serving at the time of the Tydings hearing as ambassador-at-large. McCarthy charged that Jessop was "soft on Communism." Jessop had been a character witness for Alger Hiss in his perjury prosecution and had a major role in shaping U.S. far eastern foreign policy.

Senator McCarthy's bombshell was dropped on March 21, 1950, in executive session. He accused Johns Hopkins University professor Owen Lattimore of being the top Soviet espionage agent in the United States. Lattimore was not a State Department employee. He had worked for the Office of War Information during World War II and was a renowned expert on Chinese affairs who gave seminars to State Department employees on China. He was a member of the Institute of Pacific Relations and had been editor of its publication *Pacific Affairs*. Professor Lattimore had urged the United States to withdraw support from Chiang Kai-shek's regime and later argued that the United States should withdraw from South Korea. The Chiang Kai-shek lobby led by Chinese fabric importer Alfred Kohlberg denounced Lattimore. Senator McCarthy based his accusation on a magazine article by Father James F. Kearney, S.J., and statements made by Louis Budenz in some of his articles and a *Washington Times-Herald* editorial.[190] He had no investigative report on Lattimore's alleged pro-Communist activities, only opinion from right-wing commentators unsupported by any facts. He concluded his denunciation as follows:

> Let me repeat that. Here is the man shaping our Asiatic policy. He said this in his own book. No one else has said this for him. Owen Lattimore

has said, in his book entitled "Solution in Asia," "that among the people of Asia, the Soviet Union has a great power of attraction: it stands for democracy." I submit that the background of Mr. Lattimore, his close collaboration and affiliation with numerous Communist organizations; his friendship and close cooperation with pro-Communist individuals, leaves absolutely no doubt that he is an extremely bad security risk under Secretary of State Acheson's yardstick of loyalty or under any other yardstick you could apply, and in fact, his wide knowledge of far eastern affairs and his affinity for the Soviet cause in that area might well have already done this Nation incalculable and irreparable harm.

So much for Mr. Lattimore.[191]

Louis Budenz later testified before the subcommittee and stated that although he never met Prof. Lattimore, he was aware from hearsay that he was a member of a Communist cell on the editorial staff of *Amerasia* magazine and staff from the Institute for Pacific Relations.[192] Frederick Vanderbilt Field, identified by Senator McCarthy as a Communist, appeared and testified that he was a co-worker with Prof. Lattimore at the Institute for Pacific Relations, but he invoked his Fifth Amendment privilege against self-incrimination when he was questioned about his own Communist Party involvement.[193] The Tydings Subcommittee's hearings resulted in no findings respecting identification of any known Communist in the U.S. State Department, nor were any of the State Department's consultants in the private sector identified as Communists or as spies. It did provide Senator McCarthy a platform for accusing people of Communist sympathies based on very weak evidence supplied to him by Adolph Kohlberg from Hearst newspaper editorials and other sources equally weak. The subcommittee's majority report did denounce Senator McCarthy for his tactics before the subcommittee for perpetrating a fraud and a hoax on the American people.[194]

Senator McCarthy made a speech on the Senate floor on March 30, 1950, reiterating his charge that Lattimore was pro-Communist, but he backed away from accusing Lattimore of being a spy.[195] Lattimore spent years trying to clear his name, even though the Tydings Subcommittee failed to find that he had pro-Communist opinions or was a Communist Party member. Lattimore was called before the Senate Internal Security Committee in 1952 and grilled for days on his alleged association with known Communists. He was indicted for perjury on the ground that his answers to questions put to him by Sen. Pat McCarran, the committee chair, were contrary to facts stated in the papers of the Institute for Pacific Relations. The perjury case was dismissed by the court because the government's allegations of perjury were too vague to make out an indictable offense.[196]

Senator McCarthy was solicited by the Republican Party as a campaign speaker in favor of candidates in fifteen states, including speeches in support of Maryland senator Tydings's opponent, Republican John M. Butler.[197] McCarthy's speeches consisted of an indictment of the Democratic Party and a call to drive from the Senate "those small-minded men who have compromised country for party—who have covered up treachery and incompetence." Drive from the government "Communists, dupes and fellow travelers who have plotted the Communist victory in Asia." McCarthy became a valuable asset to the Republican Party because the defeat of Senator Tydings and Senator Scott Lucas was attributed to McCarthy's anti-Communist rhetoric. Although several Republican senators privately deplored Senator McCarthy's tactics, they publicly supported his subcommittee's work to ferret out Communists in government because it was a politically profitable issue with which to drub the Democrat incumbents.[198]

Senator McCarthy had the Senate floor as a theater for his accusations of Communism in government from 1951 through the end of 1952. He was also able to pursue allegedly disloyal members of the executive branch through the committee structure. Senator McCarthy caught Swiss ambassador John Carter Vincent in his crosshairs, characterizing Vincent as one of the culprits of the United States' failed China policy. Vincent had a naval intelligence file containing an accusation that he was a Communist. Louis Budenz testified before the Senate Internal Security Committee chaired by Nevada senator Pat McCarran that an unidentified navy officer filed a report stating that Vincent was a Communist. Budenz also said that it was known among other Communists that Vincent was a party member. The White House refused to authorize the turnover of Vincent's file to the McCarran Committee. Vincent was repeatedly cleared by various loyalty review agencies. In 1952, following Budenz's testimony, he was cleared by the Loyalty Review Board. The Eisenhower administration dropped Vincent as an ambassadorial candidate for Costa Rica. He was posted instead to the mission in Tangiers. Later, Secretary of State John Foster Dulles asked Vincent to resign.[199] Vincent complied and disappeared from public view, living in Cambridge, Massachusetts, until his death in 1972.[200]

Senator McCarthy gave a major speech denouncing Gen. George C. Marshall as an appeaser based on material supplied to him by outside sources, principally Hanson Baldwin's *Great Mistakes of the War*, which dealt with the Chinese problem at length. Senator McCarthy threw in some gratuitous slurs, stating that Gen. Marshall "had an affinity for Chinese Reds."[201] Next, Senator McCarthy opposed the nomination of Phillip C. Jessup as a delegate to the UN General Assembly. Jessup had already withstood an attack on his loyalty by HUAC. Professor Jessop was responsible for a State Department white paper on U.S.–China relations that was unfavorable to Chiang Kai-shek's regime. Senator McCarthy appeared at Jessup's confirmation hearing, denouncing him as associated with six Communist front organizations and noting that he had failed to support aid to England in 1940–1941. McCarthy's frontal assault on Jessup was assisted by a flank attack by former Minnesota governor Harold Stassen, who testified before the Senate Internal Security Committee subcommittee investigating the Institute of Pacific Relations. Governor Stassen said that Jessup had proposed cutting off all aid to Nationalist China in 1949 and had supported diplomatic recognition of the People's Republic of China.[202] Jessop's nomination failed to clear the subcommittee, and he also disappeared from the limelight. He returned to his law professorship until President John F. Kennedy put Jessup on the International Court of Justice.[203]

In January 1951, Senator McCarthy was the ranking Republican member of the Senate Committee on Expenditures for the Government. He made sure that newly elected senator Richard Nixon was assigned to his committee, bumping Maine senator Margaret Chase Smith from the committee.[204] McCarthy was, in turn, was bumped from the Appropriations Committee.[205] He was not assigned to any other first-tier Senate committee. From 1951 through the end of 1952, the committee conducted routine investigations of executive branch waste and inefficiency. Following the 1952 election in which Dwight D. Eisenhower was elected president and Senator McCarthy was reelected, Senator McCarthy was able to use his committee as a platform for investigating the executive branch of the government with regard to Communist infiltration using the ploy that his committee, renamed the Senate Committee on Government Operations, had a permanent investigative subcommittee that McCarthy was able to use to investigate Communism in government as a waste of government resources.[206]

In 1953, Senator McCarthy decided to investigate the U.S. Information Service libraries in Europe to see whether the library books contained any communistic publications. His subcommittee had probed the Voice of America for suspected Communists and Communist sympathizers without success.[207] The senator sent two of his staff members, Roy Cohn and G. David Schine, to Europe to visit USIS libraries and take stock of the publications offered to explain the American way of life to Europeans.[208] Cohn and Schine itemized a number of publications that they considered to contain objectionable matter (e.g., advocating programs consistent with Communist views, degrading the United States and criticizing its social structure).[209] McCarthy's subcommittee held a series of hearings on USIS libraries in the spring of 1953, subpoenaing *New York Post* editor James Wechsler to explain the contents of books he had authored that were deemed anti-American.[210] As usual, McCarthy's investigation produced headlines but did not result in a formal report or in legislation dealing with USIS libraries.

Senator McCarthy then decided to investigate Communists in the U.S. Army. In September 1953, he brought in a low-ranking army employee whom he cross-examined on loyalty issues. The senator found a book used by the Army Intelligence School called *Psychological and Cultural Traits of Soviet Siberia,* which he damned as pro-Communist, followed by berating Army Chief of Intelligence Maj. Gen. Richard C. Patridge as "completely incompetent."[211] Senator McCarthy followed up by digging into supposed Communist infiltration of the top-secret Signal Corps Laboratory at Forth Monmouth, New Jersey.[212] This probe led to Dr. Irving Peress, an army dentist drafted in late 1952 who had answered his military loyalty oath questionnaire by claiming the privilege against self-incrimination. The army initiated an administrative separation against Dr. Peress, who requested G-1 for promotion to major, which was granted while Peress was under investigation by G-2 for alleged disloyalty. The loyalty proceedings resulted in a recommendation for administrative separation with an honorable discharge to be granted March 31, 1954.[213]

Senator McCarthy's investigative staff got wind of Dr. Peress in late fall 1953. He was brought in before the senators' investigative subcommittee on January 30, 1954. Doctor Peress refused to answer questions about Communist Party membership or any pro-Communist activities, asserting his right to avoid self-incrimination.[214] On February 18, 1954, Senator McCarthy's investigative committee met in New York City in executive session to take the testimony of a New York Police Department undercover officer who had infiltrated the Communist Party. She identified Dr. Peress and his wife as known party members. She was followed by Brig. Gen. Ralph Zwicker, the commanding officer at Camp Kilmer. General Zwicker was questioned by Roy Cohn and Senator McCarthy about the Communist presence at Camp Kilmer and what his duty was to ferret out and discharge Communists. Zwicker and McCarthy became hostile, and Senator McCarthy threatened to continue interrogating the general until he answered the senator's questions honestly. McCarthy proposed a hypothetical question: if John Jones was an army major against whom there was sworn testimony that he was a Communist, and he took refuge in the Fifth Amendment when questioned about his party affiliation, should that major get an honorable discharge? General Zwicker said he was all for getting rid of Communists, but when pushed by Senator McCarthy, Gen. Zwicker said he didn't think the officer should be removed from the army.[215] Senator McCarthy then lost his temper:

> Then, general, you should be removed from any command. Any man who has been given an honor of being promoted to general and who says, "I will protect another general who protected Communists" is not fit to wear the uniform, General. I think it is a tremendous disgrace to the Army to have this sort of thing given to the public. I intend to give it to them. I have a duty to do that. I intend to repeat to the press exactly what you said. So that you know that. You will be back here, General.[216]

The senator's outburst precipitated retaliation by the army. On March 11, 1954, the Department of the Army released its chronology of the attempts made by McCarthy's chief investigator, Roy Cohn, to obtain a commission and special favors for investigator G. David Schine, who had been drafted, including weekends off during boot camp.[217] Cohn protested the accusations of special favoritism for Schine, citing that Schine had to wrap up investigations for the Senate subcommittee when he was called up to serve. Pressure from fellow senators as well as from the media led to a lengthy hearing before McCarthy's investigative subcommittee on the charges against Roy Cohn. Senator McCarthy stepped down from the chair, turning over proceedings to Sen. Carl Mundt so that he could act as chief defense counselor for Cohn.[218] The Army–McCarthy hearings were televised in June and July 1954. Over a period of nearly sixty days, witnesses appeared before the subcommittee. Senator McCarthy requested the privilege of cross-examining every witness, which he used to embarrass and discredit the army. Senator McCarthy insisted that the investigation he launched into Communist penetration in army installations exposed the lax security measures taken by the army to protect itself from Communist infiltration. The senator also did his best to clear his investigator of any wrongdoing in seeking special favors for G. David Schine.[219] The army, ably represented by Joseph Welch of Hale & Dore, one of the top Boston law firms, produced evidence showing that Cohn had browbeaten army officials and inveigled Secretary of the Army Robert Stevens to grant special favors to Schine. Welch produced a photo of Secretary Stevens and Cohn that also included Schine, which he claimed had been doctored by McCarthy's staff. Democratic senator Stuart Symington had antagonized Senator McCarthy throughout the early days of the hearings. Symington had been arrested as a juvenile with three friends for unauthorized use of a motor vehicle. Senator McCarthy draped his arms around Senator Symington and asked him if he had stolen any cars recently.[220] The hearings were trivialized by such instances. Both sides were guilty of playing to the television audience.

The public had an opportunity to sample Senator McCarthy's method of exposing people who may have had some tie to a pro-Communist organization. Midway through the hearings, Senator McCarthy confronted army chief counsel Joseph Welch with the disclosure that one of the associates in his law firm was guilty of pro-Communist activities. His accusation was based on the false premise that any lawyer or law student who joined the National Lawyers Guild was a Communist or Communist sympathizer. Cohn had reached an agreement with the army not to mention that Frederick Fisher, a Hale & Dorr associate originally assigned to the hearing task force, had once briefly belonged to the National Lawyers Guild. Welch had sent Fisher back to Boston before the start of the hearing. Contrary to agreement, Senator McCarthy chose to bring up Fisher's National Lawyers Guild membership on television.[221]

The public reaction to the hearings was unfavorable to Senator McCarthy and to Roy Cohn.[222] Cohn resigned his position shortly after the close of the hearings and returned to private practice in New York City.[223] For more than a year, other Senate members and a dedicated crew of lobbyists had explored ways to curb Senator McCarthy's attacks on suspected pro-Communists.[224] Vermont senator Ralph Flanders made a speech on the Senate floor on June 11, 1954, during the Army–McCarthy hearings, denouncing Senator McCarthy's tactics and repeated violations of Senate procedures. He introduced a resolution to censure Senator McCarthy. The anti-McCarthy lobbyists intensified their campaign to punish Senator McCarthy. Ultimately the Democratic and Republican leadership acquiesced in the resolution.[225] The censure resolution was adopted by the Senate on August 2, 1954.[226] Senator McCarthy's power to ferret out Communists was lost. The media no longer paid attention to his diatribes against Communists in government. McCarthy's loss of face contributed to his drinking problem and health issues that took over his life. He remained in the Senate until his death in May 1957.[227]

In some respects, Senator McCarthy was a victim of the anti-Communist crusade, as well as the instigator of the destruction of the reputation of dozens of decent people. Senator McCarthy did not invent the climate of fear of internal Communist subversion. From 1950 through 1954, he was the principal public spokesperson for that fear. The Republican leadership used McCarthy as a "heavy" to attack the Truman administration. The more conservative Republican supporters of Senator Robert Taft were willing to allow McCarthy to attack the Eisenhower administration, which they mistrusted. His subcommittee attacks on government officials based on inadequate hearsay from dubious witnesses and documents were not the only instances of congressional use of hearsay and rumor to destroy the reputation of government employees. HUAC and the McCarran Committee also did their fair share of abuse. McCarthy's demise did not end the campaign to find Communists in government, labor unions, and the media. The anti-Communist crusade went on with diminished force until President John F. Kennedy, a former supporter of Senator McCarthy, took office in January 1961.

STATE ANTI-COMMUNIST PROGRAMS

State Loyalty Oath Statutes

More than twenty states adopted some form of loyalty oath requirement for government employees and teachers between 1946 and 1956.[228]

Loyalty oaths had been required before: in post–Civil War Missouri the state constitution had imposed a loyalty oath on all learned professions, requiring prospective lawyers, ministers, priests, and rabbis to swear that they had never borne arms against the United States. Failure to take the oath would result in the rejection of a license to practice the profession. The Supreme Court held that the Missouri oath was an ex post facto law and a bill of attainder in *Cummins v. Missouri.*[229] The Supreme Court also held that a federally imposed loyalty oath requiring applicants for admission to the U.S. Supreme Court to swear that they had never borne arms for the Confederacy or given aid to the Confederacy also amounted to an ex post facto law and a bill of attainder.[230] One might suppose that an oath relating to past association with the Communist Party or Communist front groups might also be an ex post facto law and, if punishment was prescribed for refusing to take the oath, a bill of attainder. The twentieth-century courts generally took a different view of anti-Communist oaths. State governments and the courts adopted the position that government employment was not a right but a privilege that the state was free to regulate by imposing a loyalty oath on state employees. Therefore, a state employee who refused to take the oath could be fired. Prospective new hires who refused to take the oath would not be hired.

State Loyalty Oath Cases

In the early 1950s, state-imposed loyalty oaths were repeatedly challenged in court. Almost all judicial decisions on the constitutionality of such oaths went in favor of the state-imposed loyalty oath requirement, even if failure to take the oath would result in the involuntary termination of a state or local employee.

State loyalty oath requirements were challenged in the court system on constitutional grounds with indifferent success. Two state loyalty oath cases made their way to the U.S. Supreme Court by 1951. *Garner v. Board of Public Works*[231] reviewed a challenge to the Los Angeles County loyalty oath requirement. *Adler v. Board of Education*[232] examined a challenge to the Feinberg Law, a New York statute that imposed a loyalty oath requirement on all public school teachers.

The charter of the City of Los Angeles was amended in 1941 to provide that any person who advises, advocates, or teaches the violent overthrow of the U.S. or California government within five years prior to 1941, or who belonged to any organization that advises, advocates, or teaches the violent overthrow of the government during the same five-year period was ineligible for any public job in the City of Los Angeles. The City of Los Angeles passed an ordinance in 1948 requiring every city officer or employee to take an oath stating that the employee had not advised, advocated, or taught the violent overthrow of the government within five years prior to 1948 and would not do so while working for the

City of Los Angeles.[233] Garner and sixteen other city employees refused to take the oath or the accompanying affidavit. All were discharged after a civil service board hearing. The seventeen recusants filed an action in superior court to be reinstated with back pay. The superior court dismissed their suit, and they appealed to the California Court of Appeals, which affirmed the dismissal.[234] The U.S. Supreme Court accepted certiorari in 1951.[235]

Garner argued that the loyalty oath and affidavit constituted an ex post facto law and a bill of attainder, because failure to take the oath would result in dismissal. The Court rejected the ex post facto law argument on the ground that the Los Angeles Charter had been amended to require all employees to refrain from advocating or teaching violent overthrow of the government many years before the ordinance requiring the oath went into effect. Hence, failure to take the oath resulting in dismissal was consistent with the earlier charter amendment and not an ex post facto law.[236] The Court characterized employment as a privilege, not a right, following its analysis in the *Lovett* decision discussed above.[237] The Court noted that the statute in *Lovett* specifically referred to three named individuals who were to be discharged and was not a general statute affecting all federal employees.[238] It followed, then, that the privilege of city employment was conditioned on loyalty to the United States and to the State of California and on a declaration not to engage in advocating or teaching the violent overthrow of the government.[239] The Court affirmed the California courts.[240] Justice Douglas's dissenting opinion argued that the loyalty oath and affidavit were unconstitutional bills of attainder and ex post facto laws. Justice Douglas said,

> Deprivation of a man's means of livelihood by reason of past conduct, not subject to this penalty when committed, is punishment whether he is a professional man, a day laborer who works for private industry, or a government employee. The deprivation is nonetheless unconstitutional whether it be for one single past act or a series of past acts.[241]

This point did not persuade the majority to void the Los Angeles loyalty oath and affidavit.

Adler involved similar issues. The New York Feinberg Law, an amendment to section 3022 of the New York Education Law, mandated that the New York Board of Regents make a rule that any teacher who is a member of any organization listed as subversive by the regents was ineligible for retention in the public schools of the State of New York. Any teacher ineligible to be retained for such membership would be removed under section 12-a of the New York Civil Service Act.[242] Adler, a public school teacher subject to the Feinberg Act, filed a declaration judgment and injunction action in Kings County, New York, seeking to overturn section 3022 and dependent regulations of the Board of Regents as a violation of the First Amendment rights of freedom of speech and association. Adler also argued that the statute was a denial of due process of law under the Fourteenth Amendment. The trial term agreed with Adler and granted judgment on the pleadings for the plaintiff. On motion for judgment on the pleadings, the court held that subdivision (c) of section 12-a, the Feinberg Law, and the rules of the State Board of Regents issued by virtue of the statute violated the Fourteenth Amendment due process clause.[243] The appellate division reversed,[244] and the court of appeals affirmed.[245]

The U.S. Supreme Court accepted Adler's appeal under 28 U.S.C. §1257. The Court found that no one has the right to work for the New York state educational system, pigeonholing all of Adler's constitutional issues as claims relating to a privilege granted by New York. The Court concluded that the provisions of section 3022 did not deprive Adler or anyone else seeking relief of any First Amendment freedoms.[246] The Court enunciated that:

> A teacher works in a sensitive area in a schoolroom. There he shapes the attitude of young minds towards the society in which they live. In this, the state has a vital concern. It must preserve the integrity of the schools. That the school authorities have the right and the duty to screen the officials, teachers, and employees as to their fitness to maintain the integrity of the schools as a part of ordered society, cannot be doubted. One's associates, past and present, as well as one's conduct, may properly be considered in determining fitness and loyalty. From time immemorial, one's reputation has been determined in part by the company he keeps. In the employment of officials and teachers of the school system, the state may very properly inquire into the company they keep.[247]

The Court implicitly endorsed "guilt by association" as the criterion for loss of a teaching position in New York. It refused to budge on its guilt by association holding in *Garner*.[248] Justices Black, Douglas, and Frankfurter dissented.[249]

A few representative state decisions show how loyalty oaths were upheld during the Cold War. A taxpayer lawsuit initiated in the Cuyahoga County, Ohio, Court of Common Pleas challenging the Cleveland School Board's requirement that all employees take a non-Communist loyalty oath was dismissed on an agreed statement of facts by the Court of Common Pleas in a lengthy opinion filled with patriotic rhetoric. Dworken, the plaintiff, challenged the loyalty oath on the ground that it violated the First Amendment rights of freedom of speech and assembly, as well as the Declaration of Independence.[250] The court did not engage in a penetrating analysis of the fact that failure to take the oath would result in dismissal of the employee as an ex post facto law or bill of attainder. The opinion did not mention *Cummins v. Missouri* or *Garland*.

In 1952, California dealt with the challenge to its loyalty oath, section 3102 California Government Code, in *Pockman v. Leonard*.[251] Professor

Pockman, an associate professor at San Francisco State College, brought a mandamus writ to direct his employer to certify his name on the public payroll and pay his salary, which the college administration had stopped because Prof. Pockman had failed to take the loyalty oath mandated by section 3100-3109 of the California Government Code (the Levering Law).[252] All public employees were classified as "civil defense employees" without regard to their actual occupations. The California Supreme Court sustained the dismissal of Prof. Pockman's mandamus writ, finding that the legislature acted within the scope of its authority in designating all employees, including college professors, as "civil defense employees."[253] The court also rejected Prof. Pockman's argument that he was exempted from taking the Levering Act oath because he had taken a similar oath in 1946 when he joined the faculty.[254] The court refused to take up Prof. Pockman's constitutional arguments that included assertions that the Levering Act oath and affidavits constituted an ex post facto law and bill of attainder, relying on *Adler v. Board of Education*[255] and *Garner v. Board of Public Works*[256] to sustain the constitutionality of the Levering Act.[257]

Hirschman v. Los Angeles County,[258] also decided in 1952, did raise these issues. Hirschman and several other civil service employees were fired by Los Angeles County for refusal to execute an affidavit relating to subversive activity, part of a package that included a loyalty oath and affidavit relating aliases that closely matched the required Levering Law affidavit. The text of the oath and affidavit read as follows:

> I do further swear (or affirm) that I do not advocate, nor am I now a member, nor have I been since December 7, 1941, a member of any political party or organization that advocates the overthrow of the Government of the United States or State of California, or County of Los Angeles, by force or violence, except those specified as follows: (the organizations here to be listed embrace all organizations advocating the overthrow of government by force or violence including any of the hereinafter named if they should ever be determined by a court of law to advocate the overthrow of government by force or violence); and that during such time as I am an officer or employee of the County of Los Angeles, I will not advocate nor become a member of any political party or organization that advocates the overthrow of the Government of the United States, or State of California, or County of Los Angeles, by force or violence.
>
> C. Affidavit re Aliases
>
> I do further swear (or affirm) that I have never used or been known by any names other than those listed as follows: . . .
>
> D. Membership in Organizations
>
> I do further swear (or affirm) that I have never been a member of, or directly or indirectly supported or followed any of the hereinafter listed organizations, except those that I indicate by an X mark. [Next follows a list of 142 organizations which were selected from those men-

tioned in one or more of the reports of the Joint Fact-Finding Committee of the California Legislature on Un-American Activities in California.][259]

Hirschman was discharged after a hearing before the County Civil Service Commission on the ground that failure to take the oath and affidavit was insubordination. The county had its oath and affidavits that matched the form adopted for state employees under the Levering Act.[260] The California Supreme Court failed to examine the issue raised by punishment of Hirschman and others similarly situated (i.e., loss of job for insubordination, for refusing to sign the anti-Communist affidavits). It is unclear if Hirschman's attorney raised the bill of attainder/ex post facto law issue before the first-level appellate court or the Supreme Court.

The District of Columbia approved of the eviction of a couple from its Lincoln Heights housing project on the ground that they belonged to an organization listed on the attorney general's list.[261] No anti-Communist oath or affidavit was required as part of the application process for public housing in the District of Columbia. However, a 1952 amendment to the Housing Act of 1937 provided that "no housing unit constructed under the United States Housing Act of 1937, as amended, shall be occupied by a person who is a member of an organization designated as subversive by the Attorney General." The District Housing Authority sent a certificate of non-membership to Mr. and Mrs. Rudder, together with the attorney general's list of subversive organizations. They refused to sign the certificate and were noticed to quit their apartment. The court sustained the validity of the certificate and the Rudders' eviction, even though the Rudders were being punished for not signing a statement that they had never belonged to an organization listed on the attorney general's list.[262]

VIGILANTE ACTION

Pressure Group Anti-Communism

The crusade against Communists and Communist influence was not confined to government entities. Newspapers, television, and radio stations, civic groups, and special interest groups also joined up and initiated their own anti-Communist programs. The National Association of Manufacturers issued a pamphlet during World War II called "Freedom from Victory," reporting on the "menace of socialism" in Europe.[263] The Knights of Columbus published five reports on the Communist menace, two of which were written by Father John F. Cronin focusing on what local citizens and parishioners could do about the Communist menace.[264] In 1947, Attorney General Tom Clark urged the Advertising Council to form the Heritage Foundation to educate the American public on the dangers of Communism and the importance of the free enterprise system.[265] The U.S. Chamber of Commerce published a booklet called *A Program for Community Anti-Communist Action* in 1948. The booklet was intended to be used by local chambers of commerce. Local chambers were to organize anti-Communist community groups. The pressure group thus formed would take on the mission of informing the public of the danger of Communism in their midst. The community group was to include a subcommittee on community action that was to engage in a program of rooting out the Communist menace. Using intelligence collected by the information subcommittee identifying local Communists and Communist front groups, the community action subcommittee was instructed to monitor local radio and newspapers and immediately report any pro-Communist comments or articles to the radio station or newspaper publishers and request that the media stop publishing pro-Communist matter.[266] Local subcommittees were advised that "pro-Communist influence in the lecture field is very great," and local organizations should screen lecturers for their views on Communism. If a local group brought in a pro-Communist lecturer, the subcommittee should take action to counter the pro-Communist speaker.[267] The subcommittee should attend the lecture, take notes, and report the pro-Communist lecture to *Counterattack.* The subcommittees were also told to be on the lookout for Communist front groups in almost every calling or profession.[268] Communist front group fund-raising activities should be reported to the Better Business Bureau to warn the public.[269]

The local subcommittee was instructed to be especially alert for pro-Communist teachers in the public school system. "It is coming to be a recognized principle that Communists should be denied federal employment," the pamphlet said, while instructing subcommittee members to root out pro-Communist teachers and librarians and see to it that they were fired.[270] Library materials relating to Communism ought also to be screened for subtle pro-Communist matter. Subcommittees were advised that anti-Communist materials should not be outweighed by pro-Communist materials, although keeping a copy of the works of Marx and Lenin was not an offense.[271] Self-appointed anti-Communists screened public libraries for books that were Communist oriented or espoused Marxist doctrine from that date until the late 1950s.[272]

The Blacklists

The nine members of the Hollywood Ten who did not recant and admit their Communist ties were barred from Hollywood until the late 1960s. Dalton Trumbo and Ring Lardner Jr. wrote screenplays under assumed names to get around the blacklist. Trumbo managed to win an Academy Award for Best Screenplay in 1953 for *Roman Holiday* under the name of Ian Hunter, a friend who was not blacklisted.[273] Motion picture industry executives did not publish their own blacklist of suspected

Communists. Instead they relied on private vigilantes such as J. B. Matthews, former counsel to HUAC, who had access to appendix 9, a document originally generated by HUAC listing more than three thousand suspected Communists. The document had been destroyed by committee order and was never filed in the Library of Congress, but copies had been made and distributed to key individuals before the destruction order.[274]

Blacklists had been produced by the California Un-American Activities Committee chaired by Senator Jack Tenney and supplied to be included in appendix 9. Eighty-four of the 204 men and women who signed the amicus brief in *Lawson v. United States* would be blacklisted in "Red Channels," a publication produced by *Counterattack*. The American Legion produced its own blacklist in 1949 containing 128 suspected Communists. The American Legion's list of potential Communists and fellow travelers was vetted whenever anyone on the list wrote to a prospective employer denying any association with the Communist Party. The employer would forward the letter to the Legion, which passed judgment on the entertainer's status as a non-Communist or reformed Communist. The Legion referred difficult cases to Hearst columnist George Sokolsky, who would periodically consult Roy Brewer and Ward Bond, past presidents of the anti-Communist Motion Picture Alliance for the Preservation of American Ideals.

In May 1947, Alfred Kohlberg, an importer of Chinese fabrics, provided funds for the start-up of an anti-Communist information service called American Business Consultants Inc. Three former FBI agents, John G. Keenan, company president; Kenneth M. Bierly; and Theodore C. Kirkpatrick, managing editor, formed the corporation and editorial board of a newsletter called *Counterattack*. They retained former army intelligence officer Maj. Francis J. McNamara as the primary editor of *Counterattack*. *Counterattack* exposed suspected Communists in movies, radio, television, and newspapers. *Counterattack* produced a pamphlet called "Red Channels" identifying more than three hundred television actors, directors, writers, and producers who were suspected of Communist tendencies. Many of the people on the "Red Channels" blacklist lost their livelihoods and were shunned by producers, directors, and sponsors as potential liabilities. The blacklist worked, according to Prof. Schwartz, because "Red Channels" and other anti-Communist groups threatened to boycott the sponsoring companies' products if a radio or television show or a motion picture had someone on the blacklist in the cast.[275]

People who appeared on the "Red Channels" blacklist could become eligible for employment if they were "cleared." In order to be cleared, the blacklisted person presented evidence that their listing on the blacklist was a mistake (e.g., two people with the same name, the person had renounced former pro-Communist ties and was now a dedicated anti-Communist). Witnesses summoned to hearings were expected to identify other Communists and Communist sympathizers in the entertainment industry. These people would be added to the blacklist. Unless cleared by AWARE; or by Sokolsky, Brewer, or Bond; or by the security chief of the Batten, Barton, Durstine & Osborne advertising agency; or by CBS security officers Daniel T. O'Shea and Alfred Berry, they would not appear on television or radio, on the stage, or in motion pictures. These men claimed they were performing a beneficial service, did so without remuneration, and typically made themselves easily available to listed individuals. Such "clearance men" were known for their strong anti-Communist sentiments, and certification from the clearance men could make listed individuals acceptable to the organizations that had cited them and thereby render them eligible for reemployment.

The clearance men met with listed people to learn their side of the story and, where possible, to work out a mutually acceptable ritual of atonement. Edward Dmytryk, one of the Hollywood Ten who, after reversing his 1947 position, atoned by naming twenty-six names to HUAC in 1951, convinced Brewer that "the people who had broken with the Party had to be helped, both because it was the right thing to do and because it hurt the Communist Party." Brewer concurred and signaled Dmytryk's rehabilitation by arranging a favorable article, "What Makes a Hollywood Communist," in the *Saturday Evening Post* on May 17, 1951. The director returned to work shortly thereafter. Brewer likewise arranged for John Garfield to publish an article titled "I Was a Sucker for a Left Hook" as part of a rehabilitation process that was cut short by the actor's death. (Garfield's friends maintained that his fatal heart attack resulted from the stress caused by his blacklisting and his efforts to clear himself.) Brewer also arranged for the clearances of Gene Kelly, José Ferrer, and John Huston.

Brewer, Sokolsky, and most of the other prominent clearance men pointed out that they had never blacklisted anyone, and they regarded their activity as a humanitarian service that gave employment to people who otherwise would not be permitted to work. On the other hand, anyone who failed to meet their personal standards of political correctness was doomed to unemployment. For instance, Brewer turned down one scriptwriter cited by the American Legion. Although the writer had written the requisite letter answering the charges against him, described his anti-Communist activities, and publicly stated anti-Communist sentiments, Brewer claimed that his letter was not sufficiently penitent or humble. Even after the writer filed a sixty-four-page document with the FBI listing his political activities, Brewer failed to clear him, and he remained out of the film industry from 1951 to 1955.[276]

The clearing process sometimes required listed individuals to hire the organization that blacklisted them to perform an investigation in order to certify that they were "clean." There were people who made a profit from clearing suspected disloyal entertainment figures. Kenneth Bierly, former editor of *Counterattack*, started a public relations business clearing blacklisted entertainers. Bierly would be in the awkward position of having blacklisted someone and then taking money to clear that person. Bierly cleared Judy Holliday, who was blacklisted by "Red Channels." Laurence A. Johnson, a Syracuse grocery chain owner, and Vincent Hartnett, one of the five original *Counterattack* members who wrote the introduction to "Red Channels," founded an organization called AWARE for the purpose of issuing clearances to the entertainment industry when requested by media executives. John Henry Faulk, a well-respected radio show host and humorist, was blacklisted, and AWARE put out newsletters stating that he was a Communist. AWARE had confused Faulk with another person with a similar name. Faulk lost his radio show and was unemployed for a number of years after he sued Johnson and Hartnett for libel. Faulk hired Louis Nizer as his attorney. The Faulk case went to trial, and the jury returned a verdict for Faulk for $3,500,000, later reduced to $550,000. Nizer's account of the trial in his 1966 book *The Jury Returns* details Faulk's case.[277]

In 1960, Dalton Trumbo was acknowledged as the author of the script for *Spartacus*, a film directed by Stanley Kubrick and produced by Kirk Douglas. The blacklist had expired, and others of the Hollywood Ten could come out of the closet. Otto Preminger announced in 1960 that Trumbo had written the script for *Exodus*. The blacklist no longer kept talented people out of work on account of their politics.[278]

THE COMMUNIST TRIALS

There were three state trials relating to Communist espionage and conspiracies to overthrow the government during the Cold War. *United States v. Rosenberg* resulted in the execution of the second woman sentenced to death by the federal government. *United States v. Dennis* was a mass trial of the U.S. Communist Party leadership for violating the Smith Act. *United States v. Hiss* indirectly attacked Communist infiltration of the State Department and espionage activities conducted during the 1930s.

United States v. Rosenberg

In 1950, the British loaned nuclear physicist Klaus Fuchs to the United States for its Manhattan Project, the building of the first nuclear explosive device, and the preliminary data on a nuclear fusion device. Fuchs was recruited by the Communist Party in Great Britain and by the Soviet secret police as an espionage agent. Fuchs passed top-secret scientific documents to an American courier, Harry Gold,[279] who in turn gave the documents to David Greenglass, who handed off the documents to Julius Rosenberg. Most of the important material relating to Fuchs's espionage, his 1950 depositions, is classified and still unavailable to the public.[280]

The secret police also had another mole in the Manhattan Project, army sergeant David Greenglass, who was recruited as an espionage agent by his brother-in-law Julius Rosenberg. Sergeant Greenglass and his wife were members of the Young Communist League in 1943 when Greenglass joined the army. Greenglass took highly classified documents from the Manhattan Project to his apartment where he and his wife made microfilm copies of the documents. He returned the originals to the project offices each morning.[281] Initially, the Greenglasses passed the microfilms to Julius Rosenberg. Rosenberg had a civilian position with the Signal Corps.[282] When Rosenberg was removed from his position because his Communist Party membership was discovered by the Army Signal Corps, Greenglass took his microfilms to Harry Gold.[283] According to Greenglass's testimony at the Rosenberg trial, Harry Gold visited Greenglass at Los Alamos when Gold came to pick up secret documents from Klaus Fuchs. Greenglass gave Gold a detailed description of experiments using implosion to detonate the atomic bomb, sketches of lens molds, and a list of prospective recruits for Soviet espionage. Sergeant Greenglass went on leave to New York City in September 1945 and presented Julius Rosenberg with another list of Los Alamos scientists and possible recruits for espionage. Greenglass also furnished his brother-in-law with a highly detailed description of the nuclear device dropped on Nagasaki, together with a cross-section drawing of the bomb.[284] Greenglass exited his role as a Communist espionage agent in February 1946.[285] Greenglass and Gold went about their lives from 1946 to 1950. When Klaus Fuchs identified Gold as his espionage courier, the FBI arrested Gold, and Gold identified Greenglass as one of his espionage contacts. Greenglass was arrested, and the FBI notified the Atomic Energy Commission. The commission told the FBI that Greenglass's sketch of the Nagasaki bomb was a top-secret security breach.[286] Meanwhile, the FBI had arrested Julius Rosenberg in July 1950. In August, Ethel Rosenberg was arrested.[287]

The FBI also arrested Alfred Slack, a Rochester, New York, chemical plant supervisor, who allegedly turned over data on explosives from a Kingsport, Tennessee, plant to Harry Gold during World War II.[288] The next people rounded up in the FBI net were Harry Gold's former employer, Abraham Brothman, and his business partner, Miss Miriam Moskowitz. Brothman had a small industrial design company in New York City and had allegedly turned over unclassified documents relating to synthetic rubber manufacturing techniques to a Soviet handler. Harry Gold also claimed that Brothman was a Communist.[289] Morton Sobel was the last to be arrested after being kidnapped in Mexico and returned to the United States. Sobel had fled to Mexico when the "atom spy ring" scandal broke with the arrest of Klaus Fuchs. Eventually, he would be indicted for espionage along with David Greenglass, Julius and Ethel Rosenberg, and their Soviet Handler, Anatoli Yackovlev. Meanwhile, the newspapers, newsmagazines, and radio and television broadcasts published wildly speculative accounts about the "atomic spy ring" members. The FBI's evidence did not support any espionage indictment against Brothman or Moskowitz. Morton Sobel was not involved in any of the espionage connected with nuclear devices emanating from Los Alamos.

The Justice Department treated the accused spies differently, according to the willingness of the accused agents to plead guilty. Julius and Ethel Rosenberg refused to admit any wrongdoing and denied any knowledge of any atomic spy ring. David Greenglass traded his testimony against his brother-in-law and sister for a plea bargain in which he would be given a fifteen-year sentence and his wife would not be prosecuted. Harry Gold traded a guilty plea for a thirty-year sentence.[290] Greenglass and Gold would be part of the all-star government witness cast that also included perennial favorite Elizabeth Bentley.[291]

The Rosenberg espionage trial began March 6, 1951, before a jury with Judge Irving Kauffman presiding. Greenglass[292] and Gold[293] testified that Julius Rosenberg and his wife had been the conduit between the U.S. espionage ring at Los Alamos and Feslikov and Anatoli Yakovlev, the Soviet secret police officers who forwarded the nuclear device documents to Moscow.[294]

Julius and Ethel Rosenberg testified in their own behalf. Both denied any involvement in an espionage ring. They were cross-examined about their membership in the Communist Party. Both took advantage of the privilege against self-incrimination to refuse to answer any questions relating to their Communist Party connection.[295] Morton Sobel did not testify. The jury returned a guilty verdict against all three defendants. Judge Kauffman sentenced Sobel to thirty years' imprisonment. The Rosenbergs received the death sentence.

On appeal to the Second Circuit, the Rosenbergs' counsel argued that the crime of espionage should be treated as a form of treason. If so, then under the 1793 act, the government would have been required to prove at least one treasonable act by testimony of two eyewitnesses. The Rosenbergs were not convicted of any overt treasonable act before two eyewitnesses. David Greenglass testified about two document deliveries to Julius Rosenberg, but no one else was privy to that act. Harry Gold testified to one transaction with Julius Rosenberg that did not involve a treasonable act. No witness put forth any evidence showing that Ethel Rosenberg committed a treasonable act in their presence. Judge Frank also acknowledged the Rosenbergs' second argument that the jury was entitled to receive the treason instruction in this case, which was not included in Judge Kauffman's charge to the jury. Therefore, the defense argued on a motion for rehearing; if espionage is to be treated as a form of treason, the Rosenbergs were not guilty.[296] Judge Frank made a false analogy to *Ex parte Quirin*, holding that espionage was a crime distinct from treason and not subject to the two-witness rule.[297]

Third, the defense counsel asserted that imposition of the death penalty for espionage was a cruel and unusual punishment. Judge Frank said that this argument was a variation of the first argument that an act of espionage is in substance an act of treason. He said,

> This argument, we think, involves an unfounded assumption, e.g., that Congress will always authorize the death sentence for treason. Without that assumption the argument would compel the strange conclusion that, if Congress, in its discretion, authorized a maximum twenty-year penalty for treason, no greater punishment could be given for espionage, sedition or a similar crime without its becoming "cruel and unusual." Moreover, as the *Quirin* case had the unavoidable consequence of permitting death sentences to be imposed upon the citizen-saboteurs for crimes other than treason, the Supreme Court must there have implicitly rejected the "cruel and unusual" argument. As, however, the Supreme Court did not specifically discuss it, that Court may well think it desirable to review that aspect of our decision in this case.[298]

If this case had been brought in the 1970s at the time the Court decided *Furman v. Georgia*,[299] the result would have been different because the Court by 1972 was ready to set aside the death penalty as cruel and unusual punishment if imposed by a judge alone without a jury review of the aggravating and mitigating circumstances of the crime. Rosenberg's petition for certiorari came up at a time when the Court was loath to examine the constitutionality of the death penalty's imposition. After multiple applications for a stay, the Rosenbergs were executed on June 19, 1953.[300]

Scholars and researchers since 1953 have reevaluated the evidence for and against conviction in an endless series of books. The liberally oriented Monday-morning quarterbacks have unanimously agreed that Julius and Ethel Rosenberg were not guilty of espionage, and even if they were, the death sentence imposed on them was cruel, unusual, and unduly harsh.[301] Some liberal critics have adopted the Soviet party line accusation that the Rosenbergs were sentenced to death because of prevailing U.S. anti-Semitism. That claim is factually unsupported. Judge Kauffman and the U.S. attorneys assigned to the Rosenberg case were Jews.

The conservative commentators have concurred that the evidence against the Rosenbergs was sufficient to prove them guilty beyond a reasonable doubt. They also concluded that the death sentence had to be considered part of the national hysteria over Communist espionage in the government, especially the stealing of nuclear secrets.[302] President Eisenhower said as much when he refused to commute the Rosenbergs' sentence in 1953.

Much material relating to Communist penetration of the Los Alamos complex and the Manhattan Project has never been declassified. After sixty years' time, it is impossible to assess the Rosenberg case other than what it appeared to be in 1951: a case founded on the oral evidence of paid informant Elizabeth Bentley and the testimony of David Greenglass and Harry Gold given as a trade-off for a favorable plea bargain.

Smith Act Prosecutions

In 1950, the Justice Department pursued an indictment against eleven men known as the top leadership of the Communist Party of America. All were indicted under section 3 of the Smith Act, charged with "willfully and knowingly" conspiring to organize the Communist Party of the United States as a group to "teach and advocate the overthrow and destruction of the government by force and violence," and "knowingly and willfully to advocate and teach the duty and necessity of overthrowing and destroying" the government by "force and violence."[303] All the defendants were officials at some time between 1945 and 1948. The prosecution introduced documentary evidence consisting of Communist Party leaflets and booklets calling for violent overthrow of the capitalist system and the government. The defendants contended that the Smith Act was an unconstitutional violation of the First Amendment free speech clause. The trial judge, former Columbia law professor Harold Medina, was a new Truman appointee to the bench. The Communists' strategy was to engage in disruptive tactics during trial to demonstrate the evils of the capitalist system. Eugene Dennis, representing himself, set the tone for the trial in his opening statement:

> The allegation of crime rests on the charge that we Communist leaders used our inalienable American rights of free speech, press, and association, and sought to advance certain general political doctrines which the indictment falsely says teach and advocate the duty and necessity to overthrow the Government of the United States by force and violence. . . .
>
> We 11 defendants will prove that the very time when we allegedly began this menacing conspiracy we were in fact advocating and organizing all-out support to the Government of the United States. . . .
>
> We will prove that all of us . . . taught the duty of upholding the United States Government and of intensifying the anti-Axis war effort . . . and we defendants will put in evidence the honorable war record of the 15,000 American Communists who, in accord with what we taught and advocated, served with the armed forces in the military defense of our country. . . .
>
> We Communist leaders will show that in June and July of 1945 we thought that labor and the people could not rely on the Truman Administration to curb the greedy monopolists. . . . We will establish that everything we did teach and advocate was in the interests of the American people and in accord with their understanding of achieving a Government of, by, and for the people. . . .
>
> My co-defendants and I will show that we put into practice the real principles of Marxism-Leninism, by teaching that labor and the people

> should intervene to defend their living standards, their democratic rights, and world peace.[304]

The prosecution submitted Communist pamphlets and writings advocating the violent overthrow of the U.S. government. The parade of government witnesses included former Communist Party members Garfield Herron and Herbert Philbrick, paid FBI operatives who infiltrated the party. Herron testified about the instruction he was given in a school for new Communist Party members in Chicago. The government's position was that the school was a preparatory school for immediate revolutionary action. During cross-examination, counsel for one of the defendants tried to introduce the entire text of writings by Marx and Lenin that Herron had mentioned during direct examination, for the purpose of rebutting the government's position that the Communist Party advocated violent overthrow of the government. Judge Medina excluded the proffer but consented to allow counsel to read relevant portions into the record. At that point, the judge invoked a pre-trial ruling denying both sides the privilege of arguing the admissibility of evidence and told counsel to stop arguing. Dennis broke into a pro se argument that the prosecution was an attempt to destroy his right to free speech. Judge Medina left the bench until defense counsel cooled down. When he returned, defense counsel read portions of *Das Kapital* into the record.[305]

The government called Louis Budenz, former *Daily Worker* editor on March 30. Budenz testified that Communist Party leaders held secret meetings in 1939 to plan ways and means to disrupt U.S. defense production after the Soviet Union and the German Reich had concluded a non-aggression pact allowing Germany to invade Poland. Defense lawyers and the defendants sneered at Judge Medina when Budenz testified that the U.S. Communist Party used the writings of Marx and Lenin as guides to action in secret Communist leadership schools. Defense counsel objected to Budenz's testimony because the government "was putting books on trial." Budenz went on to explain that the Communist Party was not a political party but a conspiracy organized to carry out orders from Moscow with respect to the Soviet Union's policies. Budenz told the jury that the Politburo, to which every defendant belonged, exercised dictatorial control over all Communist Party members. Budenz said that he attended secret meetings in Chicago and Milwaukee in which Dennis told party members to prepare for a revolution turning U.S. participation in World War II into a civil war. Defense counsel continued to break up Budenz's testimony with objections and comments, causing Judge Medina to warn counsel and the defendants about their grimacing and laughing during Budenz's testimony.[306]

The trial took nine months. Defense counsel attempted to prove that the U.S. Communist Party advocated peaceable transition to a socialist economy and government rather than violent overthrow. Some of the defendants took the stand to try to prove the peaceful nature of the party's dogmas. The government conducted a learned treatise cross-examination of the defendants to show that the writings of Marx and Lenin advocated violent overthrow of the government.[307] Judge Medina charged the jury on October 12, and the jury returned a verdict of guilty. Judge Medina then fined and sentenced the defense lawyers for continued direct contempt of court. The Second Circuit affirmed the convictions of the eleven Politburo members, and they sought certiorari.[308] The U.S. Supreme Court accepted only two issues: (1) whether either section 2 or 3 of the Smith Act, inherently or as construed and applied in the instant case, violates the First Amendment and other provisions of the Bill of Rights; and (2) whether either section 2 or 3 of the act, inherently or as construed and applied in the instant case, violates the First and Fifth Amendments because of indefiniteness.[309]

The first issue was the more important of the two. The Court assumed that the massive evidence assembled during trial amply supported the jury's verdict that the eleven defendants conspired to advocate the overthrow of the U.S. government by violent means.[310] The Court concluded that the Smith Act did not violate the free speech clause of the First Amendment. The Court supported Judge Medina's instruction to the jury that the eleven defendants had the specific intent to overthrow the U.S. government.[311] The Court concluded that Congress had the authority to enact restrictions on freedom of speech as part of its effort to protect the United States from armed rebellion. The Court emphasized that the Smith Act would not interfere with academic discussions of Marxism and Leninism; it applied only to advocacy, that is, incitement to action.[312] Nonetheless, the Court warned, the advocacy of a Communist takeover had an element of First Amendment protected political speech content that required explanation. The Court said, "An analysis of the leading cases in this Court which have involved direct limitations on speech, however, will demonstrate that both the majority of the Court and the dissenters in particular cases have recognized that this is not an unlimited, unqualified right, but that the societal value of speech must, on occasion, be subordinated to other values and considerations."[313] Following the "clear and present danger" litmus established in *Schenck v. United States*,[314] the Court said the issue boils down to "whether the words used are used in such circumstances and are of such a nature as to create a clear and present danger that they will bring about the substantive evils that Congress has a right to prevent."[315] Applying the clear and present danger test, the Court found that:

> The rule we deduce from these cases is that where an offense is specified by a statute in nonspeech or nonpress terms, a conviction relying upon speech or press as evidence of violation may be sustained only

> when the speech or publication created a "clear and present danger" of attempting or accomplishing the prohibited crime.[316]

The Court mentioned that neither Justice Holmes nor Justice Brandeis thought that the clear and present danger test would become a dogmatic rule.[317]

In concluding that the Smith Act did not violate the First Amendment, the Court said,

> Speech is not an absolute, above and beyond control by the legislature when its judgment, subject to review here, is that certain kinds of speech are so undesirable as to warrant criminal sanction. Nothing is more certain in modern society than the principle that there are no absolutes, that a name, a phrase, a standard has meaning only when associated with the considerations which gave birth to the nomenclature. . . . Overthrow of the Government by force and violence is certainly a substantial enough interest for the Government to limit speech. Indeed, this is the ultimate value of any society, for if a society cannot protect its very structure from armed internal attack, it must follow that no subordinate value can be protected.[318]

The Court was engaged in balancing the limitation on Communists' freedom of speech with respect to Marxist principles, including overthrow of the capitalist regime, against the evidence that Communists were inciting their membership and others to engage in the violent overthrow of the government. The interest of preservation of the existing order was greater than the interest of the Communists in declaiming their doctrine. The convictions were affirmed.

Yates and thirteen other mid-level Communist leaders were indicted in U.S. District Court in California in 1952 for violating section 3 of the Smith Act (i.e., conspiring to advocate the violent overthrow of the government). The defendants were tried before a jury and were convicted and sentenced. Their appeal to the Ninth Circuit resulted in an affirmance of their convictions. The fourteen sought certiorari, which was granted. The case turned on the Warren Court's literal adoption of the *Dennis* case. The Court first dealt with the meaning of "organize" in section 3 of the Smith Act. The petitioners argued that "organize" was equivalent to "found" or "bring into existence." If so, the statute of limitations had run in 1951 because the Communist Party was organized from the Communist Association in 1945. The government argued that "organize" included continuous activities in support of the party. Nothing in the legislative history of the Smith Act shed any light on what Congress meant by "organize." The Court chose to use the ordinary, plain meaning of "organize" applied to section 3 of the Smith Act (i.e., the initial organization of the Communist Party in 1945). It held that the "organized" portion of the indictment should have been withdrawn from the jury.[319]

The Court also sustained the defendants' contention that the Smith Act requires proof of advocating and teaching forcible overthrow as an abstract principle with evil intent.[320] The Court distinguished the *Dennis* holding by stating that in *Dennis*, a group of Communists were indoctrinated in the necessary action to overthrow the government, but Yates and his fellow Communists were not engaged in indoctrinating anyone in action steps to overthrow the government.[321] The trial judge did not distinguish between advocacy urging the hearer to do something rather than to believe in something. The first type of speech was prohibited by *Dennis*; the second was not prohibited.[322] The Court concluded that none of the fourteen defendants engaged in advocacy speech sufficient to meet *Dennis*.[323] The Court reversed and remanded nine of the defendants for a potential second trial, excusing five defendants whose convictions were reversed.[324]

The Smith Act has not been used to prosecute dissidents in more than forty years, although it remains on the statute books. Although *Yates* did not overrule *Dennis*, the Justice Department lost interest in prosecuting Communists under the act.

Perjury: Alger Hiss

In 1950, Alger Hiss was indicted for perjury and stood trial in New York City. Hiss was accused of lying to the House Un-American Activities Committee in 1948 under oath about two matters: (1) testifying that he did not hand over secret State Department documents to Whittaker Chambers in February and March 1938; and (2) testifying that he had not seen or conversed with Whittaker Chambers in February and March 1938.[325] The documents and microfilms produced by Chambers in a discovery response to Hiss's slander suit were an important part of the prosecution's case. The government also introduced the typewriter upon which Mrs. Hiss had typed some of the documents that Chambers had collected. The typewriter, which the Hisses had given to the Catletts, their maid's family, turned up in a collection of used equipment owned by Washington junk dealer Ira Lockey.[326] Hiss's brother Donald, assisted by Mike Catlett, son of Alger Hiss's maid, discovered the typewriter well before the FBI could track it down. He turned over his information to Alger Hiss's defense team about three months after locating the machine. Defense counsel bought the machine from Lockey for fifteen dollars. Defense experts analyzed the typed documents and compared them to typed materials from the Woodstock, concluding that all the notes had been typed on the Hiss Woodstock. Defense counsel then turned over the typewriter to the FBI for evaluation.[327] FBI experts also concluded that the typed documents had been typed on Hiss's Woodstock.[328] Defense counsel wisely chose not to call their experts at trial, leaving the FBI's expert opinion evidence unchallenged. Defense counsel then explored the hypothesis that Whittaker Chambers had borrowed the Woodstock from Hiss to type the incriminating notes.

Hiss's first trial was dismissed because the jury could not agree.[329] The prosecution put Whittaker Chambers and his wife on the stand to prove that Alger Hiss had passed State Department secret documents to him in early 1938. Mrs. Chambers testified that Chambers and Hiss had been friends from 1934 through the end of 1937, often visiting one another in the Hisses' apartments in Washington and once spending part of a summer in the Poconos with Priscilla Hiss. Defense counsel was unable to discredit her testimony.[330] Chambers testified that he had received documents from Hiss which were passed on to another Communist agent to be microfilmed for transmission to Chambers's Soviet contact.[331] Lloyd Paul Stryker, Hiss's leading defense counsel, cross-examined Chambers for three days. He made Chambers admit that he had lied under oath to HUAC and to the grand jury when he told these bodies that Hiss had not been engaged in espionage. Defense counsel had hired a psychiatrist to sit in on Chambers's testimony to look for mental abnormalities. During the defense case, the psychiatrist testified that Chambers was mentally ill and a psychopathic liar.[332] Defense counsel also presented a long parade of favorable character witnesses, including Supreme Court Justices Frankfurter and Reed and Illinois governor Adlai Stevenson.[333] Hiss took the stand and denied passing documents to Chambers and also denied meeting him in early 1938. Hiss was forced to admit that the handwritten notes turned over by Chambers to the FBI were in his handwriting. Hiss's testimony consisted of a series of very sharp recollections of facts favorable to his case and failure or lapse of memory about giving his Woodstock typewriter to the Catletts, loaning Chambers $400, and transferring title to his 1929 Ford Model A roadster to Chambers.[334]

Defense counsel Lloyd Stryker summed up his version of the case on July 6–7, 1950. His emotional plea to acquit Hiss was premised on the argument that Whittaker Chambers was the real liar who made up the story about Hiss passing documents to him.[335] Chief prosecutor Murphy's summation was an unemotional exposition of the evidence showing that Hiss passed documents to Chambers, as evinced by expert testimony that the pages of documents and summaries had been typed on Hiss's Woodstock typewriter and by Whittaker Chambers's testimony. Judge Kauffman charged the jury with respect to the law of perjury, which required either two witnesses to the lie or one witness supported by documentary evidence to convict. The jury split, eight for conviction and four to acquit. The U.S. Attorney's Office rescheduled the Hiss case for a second trial in the autumn of 1950.

By November 1950, the United States had signed the North Atlantic Treaty, obligating the United States to defend Britain, France, West Germany, Belgium, and Luxembourg from Soviet invasion. The Chinese Nationalists had lost the civil war with Mao Zedong's Communists and were driven off the Chinese mainland to Taiwan Island. The Soviet Union had exploded its first nuclear device. Public opinion solidified against the Soviet Union and all Communists. It would prove hard to get the kind of jury that was unable to convict Hiss at his first trial. Prosecutor Murphy retried his case without major changes in witnesses or in tactics. Lloyd Paul Stryker was replaced by Boston attorney Claude Cross, who was retained because defense counsel had moved for a change of venue to Vermont.[336] The motion was denied, and the case went on in the Southern District of New York. Judge Kauffman did not preside at Hiss's second trial. Judge Henry W. Goddard was the no-nonsense presiding judge.[337] The evidence was essentially the same as that given in the first trial, although defense counsel learned that Chambers had made a passport application using a fictitious name in 1935, a fact used to hammer away at Chambers's credibility.[338] Doctor Carl Binger, the psychiatrist who was barred from testifying at the first trial, returned and was permitted to express his opinion as to Chambers's mental state. He stated that Chambers was a psychopathic personality, the outstanding characteristics of such a person being an amoral, asocial, or delinquent nature. Doctor Binger reeled off a collection of symptoms that included lying, stealing, and acts of deception. He characterized Chambers as a pathological liar.[339] Prosecutor Murphy's cross-examination included an admission by Dr. Binger that Chambers's personality disorder did not account for Chambers having possession of the State Department documents from Hiss's office. Otherwise, he was unable to undo Binger's opinion evidence.[340] Doctor Henry A. Murray from Harvard Medical School also gave an expert opinion backing up that of Dr. Binger. Murray opined that Chambers was a psychopathic personality and congenital liar. Murray's opinion was based on a random sampling of Whittaker Chambers's writings that did not include any of Chambers's *Time* or *Life* magazine stories written since 1939.[341] Despite the opinions of Hiss's experts, the jury chose to believe Chambers and the government's case. Prosecutor Murphy relied on the documentary evidence to show Hiss's perjury. Hiss was convicted, spending forty-four months in a U.S. penitentiary.[342]

Alger Hiss spent the rest of his very long life attempting to clear his name. The Second Circuit affirmed his conviction. The Supreme Court declined to take certiorari.[343] Hiss spent most of his prison time at the Lewisburg Federal Penitentiary. His closest friends in Lewisburg were convicted Mafia mobsters.[344] Hiss filed a new trial motion. Hiss's attorneys had found technicians who were willing to execute affidavits that another Woodstock typewriter could be configured to be a close match for the keystrokes and dropped characters of the Woodstock identified as the machine owned by the Hisses in 1938. Hiss claimed that this was newly discovered scientific evidence that should precipitate a new trial. Judge Goddard denied the new trial motion in July 1952.[345] The Second

Circuit sustained the trial judge, and the Supreme Court declined to take certiorari.[346]

Whittaker Chambers's autobiography *Witness* appeared in 1952 and was an immediate best seller.[347] Chambers stuck to his story that Alger Hiss, a good friend, had passed State Department documents to him as part of his Communist spy ring. Hiss made a living selling stationery after his release from prison. He left his wife and produced his own story of the Chambers-Hiss trials called *In the Court of Public Opinion*, published in 1957.[348] Hiss was partially rehabilitated in 1968, the left-wing supporters of Vice President Hubert Humphrey claiming that Hiss was a victim of Richard Nixon's persecution. Alger Hiss became a regular lecturer on college campuses in the early 1970s. In 1977, he was readmitted to the Massachusetts Bar, although by that time, he was in his seventies. Hiss continued to try to clear his name up to the time of his death in 1996.

CONCLUSION

One view of the Cold War asserts that from 1945 to 1989, the United States and the Soviet Union were engaged in a slow-paced sub-nuclear world war struggle for ultimate power.[349] This viewpoint supports the analysis of the treatment of Communists and Communist sympathizers as conspirators and outcasts that threaten the continued existence of the United States as agents of the Soviet Union. Presidents Truman and Eisenhower developed a concerted plan to deal with domestic Communists. Although the executive branch loyalty oath program cost thousands of federal employees' jobs on suspicion of left-wing affiliation, it did not halt espionage. Congress led the way to impose loyalty oaths as conditions for private employment by establishing a loyalty oath for labor leaders in the Taft–Hartley Act. The state legislatures that passed loyalty oath statutes that affected state and local government employees and teachers were following the leader. The United States had embarked on an anti-Communist crusade that could not be stopped by opposition from the tiny minority of left-wing citizens who were affected adversely by the crusade. Robert Griffith pointed out that the rush to adopt loyalty oaths for employees was based on fear. The ad hoc attempts to control internal dissent resulted in a pile of court cases that gave no guidance respecting the exercise of the war power when no formal declaration of war was issued by Congress. President Truman received congressional authorization to use military forces in Korea without a formal declaration of war. President Truman also pushed the executive power to act as commander in chief to its ultimate limit when he seized the Youngstown Sheet and Tube factory to avert a strike that might affect war production.[350] While the *Youngstown Sheet and Tube* case does not speak directly to the issue of suppression of dissent in time of war, it did establish judicial parameters for the president's invocation of his authority to conduct the war that have lasting implications for today. In particular, Justice Jackson's separate opinion laid down a ladder for measuring the executive branch's authority under the war power jointly held by the executive and legislative branches:

1. When the President acts pursuant to an express or implied authorization of Congress, his authority is at its maximum, for it includes all that he possesses in his own right plus all that Congress can delegate. In these circumstances, and in these only, may he be said (for what it may be worth) to personify the federal sovereignty. If his act is held unconstitutional under these circumstances, it usually means that the Federal Government as an undivided whole lacks power. A seizure executed by the President pursuant to an Act of Congress would be supported by the strongest of presumptions and the widest latitude of judicial interpretation, and the burden of persuasion would rest heavily upon any who might attack it.
2. When the President acts in absence of either a congressional grant or denial of authority, he can only rely upon his own independent powers, but there is a zone of twilight in which he and Congress may have concurrent authority, or in which its distribution is uncertain. Therefore, congressional inertia, indifference or quiescence may sometimes, at least as a practical matter, enable, if not invite, measures on independent presidential responsibility. In this area, any actual test of power is likely to depend on the imperatives of events and contemporary imponderables rather than on abstract theories of law.
3. When the President takes measures incompatible with the expressed or implied will of Congress, his power is at its lowest ebb, for then he can rely only upon his own constitutional powers minus any constitutional powers of Congress over the matter. Courts can sustain exclusive presidential control in such a case only by disabling the Congress from acting upon the subject. Presidential claim to a power at once so conclusive and preclusive must be scrutinized with caution, for what is at stake is the equilibrium established by our constitutional system. [Citations omitted.][351]

Justice Jackson's litmus test for the reach of the war power would grant the maximum authority under the U.S. Constitution to the executive branch to enforce the Smith Act and dismissal of federal employees for failure to take the loyalty oath. The Jackson test would also support the indictment and conviction of Alger Hiss for lying to a congressional committee. The litmus test would establish a presumption of authority under the war power for these jointly conceived programs. Neither President

Truman nor President Eisenhower established programs for suppression of dissent without congressional assent.

Congress, with substantial support from the media, started the anti-Communist crusade. The crusade involved conservative newspapers and television stations, private citizens, veterans' groups, and state governments, all of whom were working to show that they were loyal Americans who hated Communists. Congress used its power to conduct investigations to expose Communists and former Communists and fellow travelers, leaving it to public opinion, channeled through the media, to destroy the reputation and livelihood of the "outed" Communists. If that was the intent of HUAC and the McCarthy Committee from 1948 through 1954, the congressional investigators were indifferent to the damage done to those men and women falsely and wrongfully accused of membership in or affiliation with the Communist Party. The destruction of Owen Lattimore, an innocent non-Communist federal employee, is an example of the effectiveness of a casual mention by a paid informant that listed Lattimore as a Communist based on hearsay and not on the informant's firsthand knowledge. Louis Budenz was particularly adept at identifying supposed Communists based on the past passive phrase, "I was told that X was a Party member." The multiple hearsay testimony could only have been admitted at a congressional hearing; it would not pass muster as evidence in any court proceeding. The informants never identified the source of the hearsay they repeated, but it was sufficient for media exploitation.

The exposure of supposed Communists in federal, state, and local government based on unreliable hearsay reports was consistent with public opinion during the early Cold War when U.S. politics were driven by fear of the Soviet Union's undertaking a hostile military adventure against the United States or one of its allies. The crusade failed to eliminate espionage by agents of the Soviet Union, although the crusade's Smith Act prosecutions reduced the U.S. Communist Party to a handful of diehards. The crusade had little to do with the United States' involvement in the Korean War other than providing a predicate to the resolution authorizing President Truman to support the UN condemnation of North Korea's attack on South Korea.

Vigilante actions during the Cold War, unlike World War I vigilantes, were peaceful. Some vigilantes blacklisted suspected Communists and fellow travelers in the entertainment industry until they repented their ways and endorsed the anti-Communist crusade. Some of the vigilantes were out to make a profit from clearing suspected Communists and Communist sympathizers in the entertainment industry. Despite the non-violent character of private anti-Communism, the blacklists in the entertainment industry and in academia injured hundreds of innocent people whose only association with Communism was limited to attending functions of a front group, or worse yet, belonging to a group listed by the attorney general.

The great anti-Communist crusade was politically inspired, and its results were political rather than legal. Conservative Republicans were able to push less-conservative Democratic politicians into a battery of programs that acted as purges of the far left wing of U.S. politics. The crusade resembled the Wilson administration's attacks on Wobblies and Socialists during World War I. A tiny minority of the U.S. populace with little or no public following was purged then as well as during the first decade of the Cold War. If that was the purpose of the anti-Communist crusade, it was highly successful. The purge came with a high price tag: many thousands of non-Communists were wrongfully purged along with a handful of Communists. The courts cooperated with the White House and Congress, supporting the Cold War trials of Communists for organizing the Communist Party and the firing of employees after an administrative board raised a doubt about their loyalty.

NOTES

1. According to Amy Knight, the Cold War anti-Communist crusade was touched off not by Stalin's repudiation of the Yalta agreement, nor by the 1946 Westminster College speech of Winston Churchill, but by the September 1945 defection of an obscure Soviet cryptology clerk stationed at the USSR's Canadian embassy. Igor Gouzenko gave a statement to the Royal Canadian Mounted Police describing a Soviet espionage ring operating in the Dominion of Canada with tentacles reaching into Washington, D.C., and into the Los Alamos Manhattan Project. Gouzenko's story was passed on to Washington to FBI director J. Edgar Hoover, who immediately notified President Truman of the existence of a Soviet espionage ring in the U.S. government. Canadian prime minister MacKenzie King flew to Washington on September 29, 1945, to Gouzenko's information with President Truman. Shortly after Gouzenko's defection, Elizabeth Bentley, a former Communist Party member and federal employee, voluntarily went to the FBI and gave a statement implicating Harry Dexter White and Alger Hiss as part of the Gouzenko ring. See Amy Knight, *How the Cold War Began: The Igor Gouzenko Affair and the Hunt for Soviet Spies* (New York: Carroll, 2005), 1–7.
2. 2. Robert Griffith, *The Politics of Fear* (Amherst: University Massachusetts Press, 1970; rev. ed., 1987), xix.
3. "A Report to the National Security Council—NSC 68," *Truman Library*, Apr. 12, 1950, 4–8, last accessed Feb. 6, 2017, http://www.trumanlibrary.org/whistlestop/study_collections/coldwar/documents/pdf/10-1.pdf.
4. "A Report to the National Security Council—NSC 68," 15. The report also notes that the greatest weakness of the Soviet system is the internal climate of fear, suspicion, and distrust.
5. "A Report to the National Security Council—NSC 68," 17–18.
6. "A Report to the National Security Council—NSC 68," 20.
7. "A Report to the National Security Council—NSC 68," 21.
8. "A Report to the National Security Council—NSC 68," 24.
9. "A Report to the National Security Council—NSC 68," 34.
10. "A Report to the National Security Council—NSC 68," 52–58.
11. "A Report to the National Security Council—NSC 68," 54.
12. Executive Order 9835, 12 Fed. Reg. 1935, Mar. 27, 1947.
13. Griffith, *The Politics of Fear*, xix.

14. Richard A. Schwartz, "How the Film and Television Blacklists Worked" (published in a slightly different form in *Film & History Annual for 1999* [CD-ROM]), last accessed Feb. 6, 2017, http://comptalk.fiu.edu/blacklist.htm.

15. Griffith, *The Politics of Fear*, 32–33.

16. See Griffith, *The Politics of Fear*, 54–60, for the rise of Sen. McCarthy.

17. See Robert Samuel Theodore Chorley, "Inquest on the Rosenberg–Sobell Case," *Modern Law Review* 33, no. 2 (1970): 121.

18. See Allen Weinstein, *Perjury: The Hiss–Chambers Case* (New York: Knopf, 1978), 5–7.

19. Weinstein, *Perjury: The Hiss–Chambers Case*, 11.

20. See Allen R. Millett, "Korean War," *Encyclopaedia Britannica Online*, last accessed Feb. 6, 2017, http://www.britannica.com/event/Korean-War, and "Korean War," History.com, last accessed Feb. 6, 2017, http://www.history.com/topics/korean.war.

21. See, e.g., Kit Oldham, "U.S. Supreme Court Strikes Down Loyalty Oaths for Washington State Employees on June 1, 1964," last accessed Feb. 18, 2017, http://www.historylink.org/index.cfm. Forty-two states and more than two thousand counties, cities, and towns passed loyalty oath statutes and ordinances between 1947 and 1956.

22. For the American Legion's role in purging libraries, see M. J. Heale, *American Anti-Communism: Purging the Enemy Within* (Baltimore, MD: Johns Hopkins University Press, 1990), 173–174.

23. Griffith, *The Politics of Fear*, 32.

24. This charge was repeated as a Republican mantra in the late 1940s. Griffith, *The Politics of Fear*, 31; Heale, *American Anti-Communism*, 146.

25. See Heale, *American Anti-Communism*, 147–148.

26. Griffith, *The Politics of Fear*, 62–63.

27. Heale, *American Anti-Communism*, 152, 156–157. Indiana senator William Jenner and Michigan senator Homer Ferguson were also outspoken critics of the Democratic regime's lack of zeal in rooting out Communists.

28. Griffith, *The Politics of Fear*, 30–31.

29. 57 Stat. 430, 450 (1943).

30. Obit., *New York Times*, Oct. 19, 1952, 87. Dodd was assistant editor of the *Dispatch*, a journal published by the International Longshoreman's and Warehouseman's Union, associated with Harry Bridges. Dodd had a Ph.D. from the University of Berlin. He was a news monitor for the FCC.

31. 78th Cong., 1st Sess., p. 5 (1943). The subcommittee found that Watson, Dodd, and Lovett were guilty of having engaged in "subversive activity within the definition adopted by the committee." H. Rep. No. 448, 78th Cong., 1st Sess., pp. 5, 7, 9. The full committee accepted the subcommittee report and submitted section 304 to the House for adoption. The committee reported that Dr. Watson's organizational affiliations and writings "constitute subversive activity within the definition adopted by your committee, and that he is, therefore, unfit for the present to continue in Government employment." H. Rep. No. 448, 78th Cong., 1st Sess., p. 6. As to Lovett, the committee further reported that it had rejected a "strong appeal" from the secretary of the interior for permission to retain Lovett in government service, because as the committee stated, it could not "escape the conviction that this official is unfit to hold a position of trust with this Government by reason of his membership, association, and affiliation with organizations whose aims and purposes are subversive to the Government of the United States."

32. *United States v. Lovett*, 328 U.S. 303 (1946).

33. *United States v. Lovett*, 328 U.S. 313–314.

34. *United States v. Lovett*, 328 U.S. 315.

35. 71 U.S. 277 (1867).

36. 71 U.S. 333 (1867).

37. *Cummins v. Missouri*, 71 U.S. 277. See 1866 U.S. LEXIS 885 *** 1–7. See also Missouri Const. 1865, Art. II, §§ 3, 6–7, 9, 14.

38. *Cummins v. Missouri*, 71 U.S. 325 (bill of attainder), 327–328 (ex post facto law).

39. *Ex parte Garland,* 71 U.S. 375. Garland received a presidential pardon for his service to the Confederate States in 1866. For the oath required, see 12 Stats. 502 (July 2, 1862). The penalty for false swearing was deprivation of office.

40. *Ex parte Garland,* 71 U.S. 377–378. The court also allowed Garland's admission to its bar because he had been pardoned, removing any of the stigma of service to the Confederacy and restoring his rights as a U.S. citizen. *Ex parte Garland,* 71 U.S. 380–381.

41. *United States v. Lovett,* 328 U.S. 316.

42. *United States v. Lovett,* 328 U.S. 317.

43. 12 Fed. Reg. 1935, Mar. 27, 1947.

44. 12 Fed. Reg. 1935.

45. 12 Fed. Reg. 1937.

46. 12 Fed. Reg. 1938.

47. 12 Fed. Reg. 1938.

48. *Bailey v. Richardson,* 182 F.2d 46 (D.C. Cir. 1950) aff'd per curiam 341 U.S. 918 (1951).

49. *Bailey v. Richardson,* 182 F.2d 48.

50. *Bailey v. Richardson,* 182 F.2d 49–50.

51. *Bailey v. Richardson,* 182 F.2d 50.

52. Executive Order 9835, 12 Fed. Reg. 1935, 1938.

53. For information on Thurman Arnold, former dean of the School of Law at the University of West Virginia; professor of law, Yale University Law School; former federal appellate judge; and founder of the megafirm of Arnold & Porter, see "Thurman Arnold Wesley Arnold Facts," YourDictionary.com, last accessed Feb. 8, 2017, http://biography.yourdictionary.com/thurman-wesley-arnold; for information on Abe Fortas, a future justice of the U.S. Supreme Court and advisor to President Lyndon Johnson, see "Biography of Abe Fortas," Biography.com, last accessed Feb. 8, 2017, http://www.biography.com/people/abe-fortas-9299311#synosis; for information on Paul Porter, co-founder of Arnold & Porter, former chair of the Federal Communications Commission, see "Biography of Paul Porter," Liquisearch.com, last accessed Feb. 8, 2017, http://www.liquisearch.com/paul_a_porter/biography; for information on Milton Freeman, another Arnold & Porter partner who previously worked at the Securities Exchange Commission, the drafter of SEC rule 10B-5 respecting offering statements, see his obituary in the *New York Times,* http://www.nytimes.com/2000/06/09/business/milton-freeman-88-wrote-securities-fraud-law.html.

54. *Bailey v. Richardson,* 182 F.2d 54–55.

55. *Bailey v. Richardson,* 182 F.2d 56–57.

56. *Bailey v. Richardson,* 182 F.2d 65.

57. *Bailey v. Richardson,* 182 F.2d 66 (Edgerton, J. dissenting).

58. *Bailey v. Richardson,* 182 F.2d 67.

59. *Bailey v. Richardson,* 182 F.2d 69.

60. *Bailey v. Richardson,* 182 F.2d 71.

61. *Bailey v. Richardson,* 182 F.2d 71–22 (freedom of speech).

62. 64 Stat. 987 § 4(a).

63. 64 Stat. 987 § 4(b).

64. 64 Stat. 987 § 4(c).

65. 64 Stat. 987 § 4(d).

66. 64 Stat. 987–988 (1950). The act's long preamble identified the Communist Party as part of a worldwide movement directed by the Soviet Union.

67. Lloyd Garrison, "Some Observations on the Loyalty-Security Program," *University of Chicago Law Review* 23, no. 1 (1955): 4n7 (quoting Civil Service Commission Report for 1953, pp. 29–32).

68. "Biography of Richard M. Nixon," U.S. Senate, last accessed Feb. 8, 2017, http://www.senate.gov/artandhistory/history/common/generic/VP_Richard_Nixon.htm.

69. "Republican Party Platform of 1952," last accessed Feb. 8, 2017, http://www.presidency.ucsb.edu, § 25837 (Communism).

70. Executive Order 10450, 2, 18 Fed. Reg. 2489, Apr. 27, 1953.

71. Executive Order 10450, 2.
72. Executive Order 10450, § 6.
73. Executive Order 10450, § 6.
74. Executive Order 10450, § 8(a)6. Section 7 barred reinstatement or reemployment of any person who had been dismissed for reasons of national security. Section 8(a) established criteria for the determination that a person would be deemed a security risk.
75. See, e.g., *Peters v. Hobby*, 349 U.S. 331 (1955), held: a consultant twice cleared by HEW's internal investigation into supposed pro-Communist activities could not be discharged for disloyalty. The Department of Health and Welfare had no authority to appeal its internal decision to the Loyalty Review Board.
76. Executive Order 9835, § III.
77. For some reason, Wikipedia published an incorrect list. Wikipedia erroneously included the National Lawyers Guild, which was never listed by the attorney general as a Communist front organization. See "Communist Front Organizations," *Wikipedia*, http://en.wikipedia.org/wiki/Communist_front05/08/13.
78. See "Attorney General's List of Subversive Organizations," taken from *Scope of Soviet Activities in the United States 84th Cong. Sess. Hearings before the Subcommittee to Investigate the Administration of the Internal Security Act and Other Internal Security Laws of the Committee of the Judiciary*, 722, U.S. Congress, Senate, *On Scope of Soviet Activity in the United States*, 84th Cong., 2nd Sess., Apr. 10, 11, and 12, 1956, part 13.
79. Percival R. Bailey, "The Case of the National Lawyers Guild, 1939 to 1958," in *Beyond the Hiss Case: The FBI, Congress and the Cold War*, ed. Athan G. Theoharis (Philadelphia: Temple University Press, 1982), 134.
80. Bailey, "The Case of the National Lawyers Guild," 134–135.
81. Bailey, "The Case of the National Lawyers Guild," 142.
82. Bailey, "The Case of the National Lawyers Guild," 141–142.
83. Bailey, "The Case of the National Lawyers Guild," 145–147.
84. Bailey, "The Case of the National Lawyers Guild," 146.
85. Bailey, "The Case of the National Lawyers Guild," 153–154.
86. Bailey, "The Case of the National Lawyers Guild," 155.
87. Bailey, "The Case of the National Lawyers Guild," 159–162.
88. *Cole v. Young*, 351 U.S. 536 (1956).
89. *Cole v. Young*, 351 U.S. 539–541.
90. *Cole v. Young*, 351 U.S. 541–542.
91. *Cole v. Young*, 351 U.S. 543.
92. *Cole v. Young*, 351 U.S. 558.
93. *Vitarelli v. Seaton*, 359 U.S. 535 (1959).
94. *Vitarelli v. Seaton*, 253 F.2d 338 (D.C. Cir. 1958).
95. *Vitarelli v. Seaton*, 359 U.S. 536–537.
96. *Vitarelli v. Seaton*, 359 U.S. 546. The court also noted that Vitarelli was not given notice of the names of the individuals who allegedly were his pro-Communist acquaintances and had no opportunity to cross-examine his accusers, rights guaranteed by Executive Order 10450. *Vitarelli v. Seaton*, 359 U.S. 544–545.
97. For a general review of the Eisenhower administration's anti-Communist initiatives, see Jeff Broadwater, *Eisenhower and the Anti-Communist Crusade* (Chapel Hill: University of North Carolina Press, 2010).
98. Griffith, *The Politics of Fear*, 31–32.
99. U.S. Congress, House of Representatives, Special Committee on Un-American Activities, *On H. Res. 282 to Investigate (1) the Extent, Character and Objects of Un-American Propaganda Activities in the United States (2) the Diffusion within the United States of Subversive and Un-American Propaganda That Is Instigated from Foreign Countries or of a Domestic Origin and Attacks the Principles of the Form of Government as Guaranteed by Our Constitution, and (3) All Other Questions in Relation Thereto That Would Aid Congress in Considering any Remedial Legislation*, 75th Cong., 3rd Sess., vol. 4, p. 2856 (Marlow), vol. 4, p. 2858 (Euripides) (testimony of Ms. Hallie Flanagan, Dec. 16, 1938).

100. U.S. Congress, House of Representatives, Special Committee on Un-American Activities, *Report on Japanese Activities*, 77th Cong., 2nd Sess., 1942, app. 6, last accessed Feb. 8, 2017, https://archives.org/details/investigationoffu194114unit.

101. U.S. Congress, House of Representatives, Committee on Un-American Activities, *Hearings Regarding the Communist Infiltration of the Motion Picture Industry*, 80th Cong., 1st Sess., Oct. 20, 21, 22, 23, 24, 27, 28, 29, and 30, 1947, P.L. 601, § 121, subsection Q (2), 280–289 (Disney), 213–216 (Reagan).

102. See *Hearings Regarding the Communist Infiltration of the Motion Picture Industry*, 4 (H. A. Smith, committee investigator), 5 (A. B. Leckie), 6 (Louis J. Russell), 7–53 (Jack L. Warner), 54–68 (Samuel Grosvenor Wood), 69–81 (Louis Burt Mayer, statement at 70–71). Author and philosopher Ayn Rand also gave a statement to HUAC at the end of the first day. She was appalled at the pro-Communist orientation of the wartime movie *Song of Russia*. See *Hearings Regarding the Communist Infiltration of the Motion Picture Industry*, 82–90.

103. See *Hearings Regarding the Communist Infiltration of the Motion Picture Industry*, 219–224 (Cooper), 208–212 (Murphy), 91–107 (Menjou), 164–170 (Reagan), 213–218 (Taylor).

104. *Hearings Regarding the Communist Infiltration of the Motion Picture Industry*, 100.

105. "Hollywood Ten," *Encyclopaedia Britannica Online*, 2013, last accessed Feb. 8, 2017, http://www.britannica.com/topic/Hollywood-Ten.

106. *Hearings Regarding the Communist Infiltration of the Motion Picture Industry*, 491–504.

107. The Hollywood Ten were Alvah Bessie, screenwriter Herbert Biberman, screenwriter and director Lester Cole, screenwriter Edward Dmytryk, director Ring Lardner Jr., screenwriter John Howard Lawson, screenwriter Albert Maltz, screenwriter Samuel Ornitz, screenwriter and producer Adrian Scott, and screenwriter Dalton Trumbo. For excerpts from testimony of several of the ten, see Jeffrey Linder, ed., "Hollywood Ten," last accessed Feb. 8, 2017, http://law2.umkc.edu/faculty/projects/ftrials/hollywood10/hollywoodtendoc.html. See also *Hearings Regarding the Communist Infiltration of the Motion Picture Industry*, 383–385 (Alvah Bessie), 412–414 (Herbert Beiberman), 489–490 (Lester Cole), 459–461 (Edward Dmytryk), 479–482 (Ring Lardner Jr.), 290–295 (John Howard Lawson), 363–365 (Albert Maltz), 402–404 (Samuel Ornitz), 466–467 (Adrian Scott), 329–440 (Dalton Trumbo).

108. "Hollywood Ten."

109. *Hearings Regarding the Communist Infiltration of the Motion Picture Industry*, 312–313.

110. This statement is available online. See Donald M. Nelson, "Waldorf Conference Statement," last accessed Feb. 8, 2017, http://cobbles.com/simpp_archive/huac_nelson1947.htm.

111. Jeffrey Meyers, *John Huston: Courage and Art* (New York: Crown, 2011), 121–122.

112. Charles Higham, *Howard Hughes: The Secret Life* (New York: St. Martin's, 1993; repr., 2004), 131–133.

113. *Lawson v. United States*, 176 F.2d 49 (D.C. Cir. 1949). See also *Barsky v. United States*, 167 F.2d 241 (D.C. Cir. 1948).

114. *Barsky v. United States*, 167 F.2d 244.

115. *Barsky v. United States*, 167 F.2d 245.

116. *Barsky v. United States*, 167 F.2d 246–447.

117. *Lawson v. United States*, 176 F.2d 53–54.

118. *John Howard Lawson, Petitioner, v. the United States of America*. Amicus brief (P)/G Leslie Field/1948/334/335 U.S. 861/69 S.Ct. 135/93 L.Ed. 408/11-5-1948.

119. *Lawson v. United States*, 339 U.S. 934.

120. Kathryn S. Olmstead, *The Red Spy Queen: A Biography of Elizabeth Bentley* (Chapel Hill: University of North Carolina Press, 2002), 1–19. See also "Red Spy Queen: The Story of Elizabeth Bentley," last accessed Feb. 8, 2017, http://scandalouswoman.blogspot.com/2008/07/elizabeth-bentley-red-spy-queen.html.

121. "Red Spy Queen: The Story of Elizabeth Bentley."

122. Olmstead, *The Red Spy Queen*, 63–65.
123. "Red Spy Queen: The Story of Elizabeth Bentley."
124. Olmstead, *The Red Spy Queen*, 134.
125. "Red Spy Queen: The Story of Elizabeth Bentley."
126. See Louis Budenz, *This Is My Story* (New York: McGraw-Hill, 1947), 2–27.
127. "Biography of Louis Budenz," last accessed Feb. 8, 2017, http://www.documentstalk.com/wp/budenz-louis-francis-1891-1972.
128. "Biography of Louis Budenz."
129. *New York Times*, Oct. 12, 1945, 15.
130. Walter Goodman, *The Committee: The Extraordinary Career of the House Committee on Un-American Activities* (New York: Farrar, Straus & Giroux, 1968), 184.
131. *New York Times*, Oct. 19, 1946, 9; *New York Times*, Nov. 23, 1946, 1. Budenz contended that the Communist Party was "a conspiracy to set up a worldwide dictatorship under the control of the dictatorship of the Kremlin . . . a quisling movement . . . to set up a Soviet dictatorship which means overthrow of the United States Government."
132. *Eisler v. United States*, 170 F.2d 273 (1948) cert. granted, 355 U.S. 857 (1948) cert. dismissed, 338 U.S. 883 (1949). See also *New York Times*, May 22, 1949, E4; Feb. 5, 1947, 1.
133. Bentley–Chambers hearing, 1035; *New York Times*, Oct. 27, 1948, 1.
134. *New York Times*, Aug. 23, 1951, 7.
135. *New York Times*, Apr. 16, 1952, 10.
136. *New York Times*, Dec. 31, 1952, 3.
137. *New York Times*, Apr. 28, 1972, 44.
138. Weinstein, *Perjury: The Hiss–Chambers Case*, 86–87.
139. Weinstein, *Perjury: The Hiss–Chambers Case*, 89–91.
140. Weinstein, *Perjury: The Hiss–Chambers Case*, 94–96.
141. Weinstein, *Perjury: The Hiss–Chambers Case*, 112–117.
142. Weinstein, *Perjury: The Hiss–Chambers Case*, 127.
143. Pressman identified other Ware group members during his 1950 HUAC testimony as John Abt, Charles Kramer, and Nathan Witt. He claimed to have met Chambers in 1936. Weinstein, *Perjury: The Hiss–Chambers Case*, 133.
144. Weinstein, *Perjury: The Hiss–Chambers Case*, 131.
145. Weinstein, *Perjury: The Hiss–Chambers Case*, 139.
146. Weinstein, *Perjury: The Hiss–Chambers Case*, 139. The evidence supporting the first meeting of Chambers and Hiss comes from Chambers's own account and was corroborated by Josephine Herbst, the former wife of Herrmann.
147. Weinstein, *Perjury: The Hiss–Chambers Case*, 142.
148. Weinstein, *Perjury: The Hiss–Chambers Case*, 145–153.
149. Weinstein, *Perjury: The Hiss–Chambers Case*, 5.
150. Bentley–Chambers hearing, 563–586.
151. Bentley–Chambers hearing, 565.
152. Bentley–Chambers hearing, 585–586.
153. Bentley–Chambers hearing, 643.
154. Bentley–Chambers hearing, 646–647. Hiss also stated that he did not recognize Chambers from the news photos appearing after his testimony. Hiss volunteered that he did not want to take the oath and that he had never seen the man.
155. Bentley–Chambers hearing, 651.
156. Bentley–Chambers hearing, 661–662.
157. Bentley–Chambers hearing, 665 (dog), 666 (warbler).
158. Bentley–Chambers hearing, 913–933.
159. Bentley–Chambers hearing, 938.
160. Bentley–Chambers hearing, 940.
161. Bentley–Chambers hearing, 948.
162. Bentley–Chambers hearing, 955–956. Hiss acknowledged that he had sublet his apartment to Crosley and his wife in the summer of 1935. He gave a brief physical

description of Crosley and his wife and mentioned that he sold Crosley "an old Ford" that he had retained after buying a new Plymouth.

163. Bentley–Chambers hearing, 961–662. See also Whittaker Chambers, *Witness* (New York: Random House, 1952; Washington, D.C.: Regnery, 1987), 580, 582; Weinstein, *Perjury: The Hiss–Chambers Case*, 32.

164. Bentley–Chambers hearing, 979.

165. Bentley–Chambers hearing, 987.

166. Bentley–Chambers hearing, 988.

167. Bentley–Chambers hearing, 989.

168. Chambers, *Witness*, 711.

169. Chambers, *Witness*, 722; Weinstein, *Perjury: The Hiss–Chambers Case*, 162–164.

170. Chambers, *Witness*, 730.

171. Chambers, *Witness*, 737–738.

172. Chambers, *Witness*, 738.

173. Chambers, *Witness*, 750–751 (Justice Dept.), 752–753 (pumpkin). See also Weinstein, *Perjury: The Hiss–Chambers Case*, 174–176.

174. Weinstein, *Perjury: The Hiss–Chambers Case*, 178–181.

175. For an account of Chambers's life post-Hiss, see Lee Chambers, "Whittaker Chambers: Man of Courage and Faith," last accessed Feb. 8, 2017, http://www.heritage.org/research/reports/2001/04/whittaker-chambers-man-of-courage-and-faith.

176. See Griffith, *The Politics of Fear*, 5–11.

177. Griffith, *The Politics of Fear*, 14–19.

178. *New York Times*, May 5, 1949, 8.

179. Griffith, *The Politics of Fear*, 20–24; *New York Times*, May 21, 1949, 3. See also Michael Reynolds, "Massacre at Malmédy during the Battle of the Bulge," *World War II* magazine, published online June 12, 2006, last accessed Feb. 8, 2017, http://www.historynet.com/massacre-at-malmedy-during-the-battle-of-the-bulge.htm#sthash.HN7abNh.dpuf.

180. Griffith, *The Politics of Fear*, 25. McCarthy charged that Sen. Baldwin was criminally responsible for a miscarriage of justice.

181. Griffith, *The Politics of Fear*, 49–50. The Wheeling speech was never fully transcribed.

182. Roy Cohn, *McCarthy* (New York: New American Library, 1968), 2–3.

183. Cohn, *McCarthy*, 3.

184. Griffith, *The Politics of Fear*, 51.

185. Griffith, *The Politics of Fear*, 59–60. See also U.S. Congress, Senate, Subcommittee of the Committee on Foreign Relations, *A Resolution to Investigate Whether There Are Employees in the State Department Disloyal to the United States*, 81st Cong., 1st Sess., 1950, part 1, p. 1. (hereafter "Tydings Subcommittee Report").

186. Griffith, *The Politics of Fear*, 65.

187. Griffith, *The Politics of Fear*, 66.

188. Tydings Subcommittee Report, 18–19; Griffith, *The Politics of Fear*, 67–68. Only six of the twenty-eight organizations were actually listed by the attorney general. Ms. Kenyon's affiliation with the six pre-dated the 1948 list.

189. Tydings Subcommittee Report, 18; Griffith, *The Politics of Fear*, 68.

190. Griffith, *The Politics of Fear*, 76–77. See also Tydings Subcommittee Report, 92–94.

191. Tydings Subcommittee Report, 104.

192. Tydings Subcommittee Report, 490–492.

193. Tydings Subcommittee Report, 710–713. Field also denied being an espionage agent for the Soviet Union.

194. *New York Times*, July 21, 1950, 1.

195. *New York Times*, Mar. 31, 1950, 1.

196. *United States v. Lattimore*, 127 F. Supp. 405 (D.D.C. 1955). Judge Youngdahl granted the defendant's motion to dismiss with prejudice. *United States v. Lattimore*, 127 F. Supp. 407–408.

197. *New York Times*, Oct. 20, 1950, 18.

198. Griffith, *The Politics of Fear*, 122–123. See also *New York Times*, Aug. 7, 1950, 17.
199. Griffith, *The Politics of Fear*, 133–135.
200. Obit., *New York Times*, Dec. 5, 1972, 50.
201. Griffith, *The Politics of Fear*, 145–146.
202. Griffith, *The Politics of Fear*, 148–149. See also *New York Times*, Aug. 10, 1951, 7.
203. Obit., *New York Times*, Feb. 1, 1986, 13.
204. Griffith, *The Politics of Fear*, 131. McCarthy bumped Maine senator Margaret Chase Smith from the committee.
205. Griffith, *The Politics of Fear*, 132.
206. Griffith, *The Politics of Fear*, 208–210.
207. Griffith, *The Politics of Fear*, 213–214. The subcommittee report settled for a conclusion that VOA was guilty of waste and inefficiency in broadcasting its propaganda messages to the world. It also hinted that VOA employed some people who were "not dedicated to the American way of life."
208. Cohn, *McCarthy*, 77–91.
209. Cohn, *McCarthy*, 78–79, set forth excerpts from books he considered to be anti-American or pro-Communist.
210. Cohn, *McCarthy*, 214–215. See also *New York Times*, May 8, 1953, 14.
211. Griffith, *The Politics of Fear*, 217.
212. Griffith, *The Politics of Fear*, 228.
213. Cohn, *McCarthy*, 57–59.
214. Cohn, *McCarthy*, 99–102.
215. Cohn, *McCarthy*, 105–106.
216. Cohn, *McCarthy*, 106.
217. Cohn, *McCarthy*, 125–126; Griffith, *The Politics of Fear*, 249.
218. Griffith, *The Politics of Fear*, 252–253.
219. Griffith, *The Politics of Fear*, 254–261.
220. Griffith, *The Politics of Fear*, 257.
221. "The Army–McCarthy Hearings, 1954," in *On Trial: American History through Court Proceedings and Hearings*, ed. Robert D. Marcus and Anthony Marcus (St. James, NY: Brandywine Press, 1998), vol. 2, 36–51, last accessed Feb. 8, 2017, http://historymatters.gmu.edu/d/6444.
222. Griffith, *The Politics of Fear*, 263n57.
223. Cohn, *McCarthy*, 218.
224. See Griffith, *The Politics of Fear*, 224–228. The opposition to McCarthy coalesced around former Connecticut senator William Benton. Griffith called the amalgamation of former senators and lobbyists who were out to curb Senator McCarthy the "clearing house."
225. Griffith, *The Politics of Fear*, 288–290. The text of Senate Resolution 301 read, "Resolved: that the conduct of the Senator from Wisconsin, Mr. McCarthy, is unbecoming a Member of the United States Senate, is contrary to senatorial traditions, and tends to bring the Senate into disrepute, and such conduct is hereby condemned."
226. Griffith, *The Politics of Fear*, 290.
227. Griffith, *The Politics of Fear*, 319–320.
228. See Arnold A. Rogow, "Loyalty Oath Issue in Iowa, 1951," *American Political Science Review* 55 (1961): 861. Rogow (861n1) stated that twenty-one states required loyalty oaths for teachers. The Fund for the Republic, *Digest of the Public Record of Communism in the United States* (New York, 1955). But in Walter Gellhorn, *The States and Subversion* (Ithaca, NY: Cornell University Press, 1952), 410, it is stated that twenty-seven states have "prescribed teacher's oaths of various types."
229. *Cummins v. Missouri*, 71 U.S. 277 (1867).
230. *Ex parte Garland*, 71 U.S. 333.
231. *Garner v. Board of Public Works*, 341 U.S. 716 (1951).
232. *Adler v. Board of Education*, 342 U.S. 485 (1952).
233. *Garner v. Board of Public Works*, 341 U.S. 717, 717–719.
234. See *Garner v. Board of Public Works*, 220 P.2d 958 (1950).

235. *Garner v. Board of Public Works*, 340 U.S. 941 (1951).
236. *Garner v. Board of Public Works*, 341 U.S. 721.
237. *Garner v. Board of Public Works*, 341 U.S. 722.
238. *Garner v. Board of Public Works*, 341 U.S. 723.
239. *Garner v. Board of Public Works*, 341 U.S. 722.
240. *Garner v. Board of Public Works*, 341 U.S. 724. Justice Frankfurter filed a long dissenting opinion. He agreed that municipal governments had the right to inquire into current and prospective employees' relationship to the Communist Party and to discharge Communists. He held that the two employees who refused to sign the non-Communist affidavit after taking the oath were rightfully discharged but felt that the employees who refused to take the oath came under a different classification. The oath contained no language, he said, that would limit its impact to affiliation with a known Communist organization with knowledge of its teaching. Without that proviso, he said, the oath ordinance was unconstitutional. *Garner v. Board of Public Works*, 341 U.S. 728.
241. *Garner v. Board of Public Works*, 341 U.S. 735.
242. See N.Y. Civil Service Law § 12-a (McKinney 1948).
243. *Lederman v. Board of Education*, 95 N.Y.S. 2d 114 (N.Y. Supr. 1949).
244. *Lederman v. Board of Education*, 96 N.Y.S. 2d 466 (N.Y. App. Div. 1950).
245. *Thompson v. Board of Education*, 95 N. E. 2d 806 (N.Y. 1950).
246. *Adler v. Board of Education*, 342 U.S. 485, 492 (1952).
247. *Adler v. Board of Education*, 342 U.S. 493.
248. *Garner v. Board of Public Works*, 341 U.S. 720.
249. *Adler v. Board of Education*, 342 U.S. 496–511. The dissents were similar to the same three justices' dissents in *Garner*. Justice Black complained that section 3022 of the Education Law was vague and did not allow the court to pass on constitutional issues. Justice Douglas continued to assert that Cummins and Garland controlled the outcome of the case. *Adler v. Board of Education*, 342 U.S. 508–509.
250. *Dworken v. Board of Education*, 94 N.E.2d 18 (Oh. Ct. Comm. Pleas 1950).
251. *Pockman v. Leonard*, 249 P.2d 267 (1952).
252. Acts 1950, 3rd Extraordinary Sess., ch. 7.
253. *Pockman v. Leonard*, 249 P.2d 680.
254. *Pockman v. Leonard*, 249 P.2d 684–686.
255. *Adler v. Board of Education*, 342 U.S. 485 (1952).
256. *Garner v. Board of Public Works*, 341 U.S. 716 (1951).
257. *Pockman v. Leonard*, 249 P.2d 686.
258. *Pockman*, 249 P.2d 287 (Cal. 1952).
259. The text of the oath and affidavit read as follows:

> I do further swear (or affirm) that I do not advocate, nor am I now a member, nor have I been since December 7, 1941, a member of any political party or organization that advocates the overthrow of the Government of the United States or State of California, or County of Los Angeles, by force or violence, except those specified as follows: (the organizations here to be listed embrace all organizations advocating the overthrow of government by force or violence including any of the hereinafter named if they should ever be determined by a court of law to advocate the overthrow of government by force or violence); and that during such time as I am an officer or employee of the County of Los Angeles, I will not advocate nor become a member of any political party or organization that advocates the overthrow of the Government of the United States, or State of California, or County of Los Angeles, by force or violence.
>
> C. Affidavit re Aliases
>
> I do further swear (or affirm) that I have never used or been known by any names other than those listed as follows: . . .
>
> D. Membership in Organizations

> I do further swear (or affirm) that I have never been a member of, or directly or indirectly supported or followed any of the hereinafter listed organizations, except those that I indicate by an X mark. [Next follows a list of 142 organizations that were selected from those mentioned in one or more of the reports of the Joint Fact-Finding Committee of the California Legislature on Un-American Activities in California.]

260. Cal. Gov. Code §§ 3100–3109. Laws, 1950, 3rd Extraordinary Sess., ch. 7.
261. *Rudder v. Housing Authority*, 105 A.2d 741 (D.C. App. 1954).
262. *Rudder v. Housing Authority*, 105 A.2d 745.
263. Larry Ceplair, *Anti-Communism in Twentieth-Century America: A Critical History* (Santa Barbara, CA: ABC-CLIO/Praeger, 2011), 78.
264. Ceplair, *Anti-Communism in Twentieth Century America*, 78.
265. Ceplair, *Anti-Communism in Twentieth Century America*, 78.
266. U.S. Chamber of Commerce, *A Program for Community Anti-Communist Action* (Washington, D.C.: U.S. Chamber of Commerce 1948), 21–22.
267. *A Program for Community Anti-Communist Action*, 23.
268. *A Program for Community Anti-Communist Action*, 24.
269. *A Program for Community Anti-Communist Action*, 25.
270. *A Program for Community Anti-Communist Action*, 26.
271. *A Program for Community Anti-Communist Action*, 27.
272. Wendy Wall, "Anti-Communism in the 1950's," last accessed Feb. 8, 2017, http://www.gilderlehrman.org/history-by-era/fifties/essays/anti-communism-1950s; Heale, *American Anti-Communism*, 188. John Steinbeck's *Grapes of Wrath* and *The Tales of Robin Hood* were often removed from local libraries because of alleged pro-Communist content.
273. Howard Suber, "Dalton Trumbo's Real Role in 'Roman Holiday,'" *Los Angeles Times*, Aug. 19, 1991, 3.
274. On July 29, 1946, William R. Wilkerson, publisher and founder of the *Hollywood Reporter*, published a "TradeView" column titled "A Vote for Joe Stalin." It named as Communist sympathizers Dalton Trumbo, Maurice Rapf, Lester Cole, Howard Koch, Harold Buchman, John Wexley, Ring Lardner Jr., Harold Salemson, Henry Meyers, Theodore Strauss, and John Howard Lawson. In August and September 1946, Wilkerson published other columns containing a larger number of alleged Communists and sympathizers. They became known as "Billy's List" and "Billy's Blacklist." Richard A. Schwartz, "How the Film and Television Blacklists Worked" (published in a slightly different form in *Film & History Annual for 1999* [CD-ROM], last accessed Feb. 8, 2017, http://comptalk.fiu.edu/blacklist.htm).
275. Wilkerson, "A Vote for Joe Stalin." Only thirty men and women failed the Legion's clearance requirements.
276. Sokolsky and his assistants received no compensation for their work. See Ellen Schrecker, *The Age of McCarthyism: A Brief History with Documents* (New York: Bedford St. Martin's, 2002), 244–249.
277. See Louis Nizer, *The Jury Returns* (New York: Doubleday, 1966), for a full account of the lawsuit.
278. Suber, "Dalton Trumbo's Real Role in 'Roman Holiday.'"
279. The short career of Harry Gold as an espionage courier is described in Ronald Radosh and Joyce Milton, *The Rosenberg File: A Search for the Truth* (New York: Vintage, 1984), 33–44.
280. See FBI FIOA, "Julius & Ethel Rosenberg File AQ," last accessed Feb. 8, 2017, http://vault.fbi.gov/rosenberg-case/klaus-fuchs/part-01-of-11.
281. Walter Schneir and Miram Schneir, *Invitation to an Inquest: Reopening the Rosenberg "Atom Spy" Case*, 3rd ed. (Baltimore, MD: Penguin, 1973), 70–75 (identification of Harry Gold), 77–81 (David Greenglass).
282. Schneir and Schneir, *Invitation to an Inquest*, 81–88 (Rosenberg).
283. Roger M. Anders, "The Rosenberg Case Revisited: The Greenglass Testimony and the Protection of Atomic Secrets," *American Historical Review* 83 (1978): 388–391.

See biography of David Greenglass as part of the University of Missouri–Kansas City Law School's Famous Trials program, last accessed Feb. 8, 2017, http://law2.umkc.edu/faculty/projects/ftrials/rosenb/ROS_BDGR.HTM.

284. Transcript, *United States v. Rosenberg et al.*, U.S. Dist. Ct., S.D. N.Y.C., 134–245.

285. Anders, "The Rosenberg Case Revisited," 389.

286. Anders, "The Rosenberg Case Revisited," 390.

287. Anders, "The Rosenberg Case Revisited," 390.

288. Schneir and Schneir, *Invitation to an Inquest*, 76–77.

289. Schneir and Schneir, *Invitation to an Inquest*, 83, 105.

290. *New York Times*, Jan. 11, 1953, E4.

291. Douglas Linder, ed., "The Rosenberg Trial," University of Missouri–Kansas City Law School's Famous Trials, http://law2.umkc.edu/faculty/projects/ftrials/rosenb/ROS_BDGR.HTM.

292. Linder, "The Rosenberg Trial" (excerpt of testimony of David Greenglass).

293. Linder, "The Rosenberg Trial" (excerpt of testimony of Harry Gold).

294. *New York Times*, Jan. 11, 1953, E4.

295. Linder, "The Rosenberg Trial" (testimony extracts Julius and Ethel Rosenberg).

296. *Rosenberg v. United States*, 195 F.2d. 583, 609–611 (2d Cir. 1952). See William Cohen, "Justice Douglas and the Rosenberg Case: Setting the Record Straight," *Cornell Law Review* 70 (1985): 211 (suggesting that Justice Douglas's vote not to accept certiorari for the Rosenberg case was based on lack of a significant legal issue, ignoring the defense argument relating to the treason act).

297. *Rosenberg v. United States*, 195 F.2d 583, 610–611 (1952). Judge Frank practically begged the Supreme Court to review the case because of the seriousness of this issue.

298. *Rosenberg v. United States*, 195 F.2d 583, 611 (1952).

299. *Furman v. Georgia*, 408 U.S. 238 (1972).

300. Radosh and Milton, *The Rosenberg File*, 414, 417–418.

301. See, e.g., Schneir and Schneir, *Invitation to an Inquest*, 416–424 (finding that the evidence against the Rosenbergs was insufficient to support conviction); Radosh and Milton, *The Rosenberg File*, 450–453 (same finding, with a special note that Ethel Rosenberg was arrested, tried, and convicted in order to pressure Julius Rosenberg to give the names of other spies). See also Alvin Goldstein, *The Unquiet Death of Julius and Ethel Rosenberg*, Lawrence Hill, video production (1975); Robert Meeropol and Michael Meeropol, *We Are Your Sons* (Urbana: University of Illinois Press, 1986); Robert Meeropol, *An Execution in the Family* (New York: St. Martin's, 2003).

302. See, e.g., Louis Nizer, *The Implosion Conspiracy* (New York: Doubleday, 1973); Alexander Feklisov and Sergei Kostin, *The Man behind the Rosenbergs* (New York: Enigma, 2001).

303. *Dennis v. United States*, 183 F.2d 201 (1950).

304. Opening statement of William V. Dennis in *United States v. Dennis* available at http://historymatters.gmu.edu/d/6446.

305. *New York Times*, Apr. 26, 1949, 1, 12.

306. *New York Times*, Mar. 31, 1949, 1, 7.

307. *New York Times*, June 9, 1949, 1.

308. *Dennis v. United States*, 183 F.2d 201 (2d Cir. 1950).

309. *Dennis v. United States*, 341 U.S. 494, 495–496 (1951).

310. *Dennis v. United States*, 341 U.S. 497.

311. *Dennis v. United States*, 341 U.S. 499–500.

312. *Dennis v. United States*, 341 U.S. 501–502.

313. *Dennis v. United States*, 341 U.S. 502.

314. 249 U.S. 47 (1919).

315. *Dennis v. United States*, 341 U.S. 503–504.

316. *Dennis v. United States*, 341 U.S. 506.

317. *Dennis v. United States*, 341 U.S. 508.

318. *Dennis v. United States*, 341 U.S. 508–509.

319. *Yates v. United States*, 354 U.S. 298, 312 (1957).

320. *Yates v. United States*, 354 U.S. 319.
321. *Yates v. United States*, 354 U.S. 322.
322. *Yates v. United States*, 354 U.S. 325.
323. *Yates v. United States*, 354 U.S. 327.
324. *Yates v. United States*, 354 U.S. 334.
325. Weinstein, *Perjury: The Hiss–Chambers Case*, 300.
326. Weinstein, *Perjury: The Hiss–Chambers Case*, 390.
327. Weinstein, *Perjury: The Hiss–Chambers Case*, 389–395.
328. Weinstein, *Perjury: The Hiss–Chambers Case*, 407–408.
329. Weinstein, *Perjury: The Hiss–Chambers Case*, 467–468.
330. Weinstein, *Perjury: The Hiss–Chambers Case*, 426–431.
331. Weinstein, *Perjury: The Hiss–Chambers Case*, 416–418.
332. Weinstein, *Perjury: The Hiss–Chambers Case*, 438–439. Dr. Binger was to respond to a long hypothetical question posed by Stryker, but Judge Kauffman ordered the question stricken from the record and excused the witness.
333. Weinstein, *Perjury: The Hiss–Chambers Case*, 447–448.
334. Weinstein, *Perjury: The Hiss–Chambers Case*, 449–456.
335. Weinstein, *Perjury: The Hiss–Chambers Case*, 460–461.
336. Weinstein, *Perjury: The Hiss–Chambers Case*, 470–471.
337. Weinstein, *Perjury: The Hiss–Chambers Case*, 470.
338. Weinstein, *Perjury: The Hiss–Chambers Case*, 475. Chambers had applied for a passport as "David Breen" using the name of a dead baby.
339. Weinstein, *Perjury: The Hiss–Chambers Case*, 486.
340. Weinstein, *Perjury: The Hiss–Chambers Case*, 487–491.
341. Weinstein, *Perjury: The Hiss–Chambers Case*, 492–493.
342. Weinstein, *Perjury: The Hiss–Chambers Case*, 470, 497.
343. *Hiss v. United States*, 185 F.2d 822 (2d. Cir. 1950) cert. denied, U.S. 340 U.S. 948 (1951).
344. Weinstein, *Perjury: The Hiss–Chambers Case*, 526–527.
345. *Hiss v. United States*, 107 F. Supp. 128 (S.D. N.Y. 1952).
346. *Hiss v. United States*, 201 F.2d 372 (2d Cir. 1953) cert. denied 345 U.S. 942. This was a one-sentence per curiam affirmation with no opinion.
347. Weinstein, *Perjury: The Hiss–Chambers Case*, 535.
348. Weinstein, *Perjury: The Hiss–Chambers Case*, 528, 530.
349. William W. Wiecek, "The Legal Foundations of Domestic Anticommunism: The Background of *Dennis v. United States*," *Supreme Court Review 2001* (2001): 417.
350. During World War II, President Roosevelt used the seizure power to take over industries threatened with strikes, including seizure of Montgomery Ward & Co., engaged in retail merchandising, operating only three production facilities. The Seventh Circuit supported the president's right to seize Montgomery Ward & Co. on the ground that "production" also included retailing. See *United States v. Montgomery Ward & Co.*, 150 F.2d 369 (7th Cir. 1945).
351. *Youngstown Sheet & Tube Co. v. Sawyer*, 343 U.S. 579, 637–638 (1952).

SIX

The Treatment of Vietnam Anti-War Activists and Draft Resisters

The guns and the bombs, the rockets and the warships, are all symbols of human failure.
—President Lyndon B. Johnson, 1964

As the senior commander in Vietnam, I was aware of the potency of public opinion—and I worried about it.
—Gen. William Westmoreland

THE VIETNAM WAR: ITS BEGINNINGS

A civil war started in 1946–1947 in what was then known as French Indo-China, comprising the historic Asian kingdoms of Laos, Cambodia, and Vietnam. A Vietnamese Communist, Ho Chi Minh, who had been a guerilla leader in the war against Japan, led a resistance movement against France when the French Republic reasserted control over the three kingdoms in 1946.[1] By 1954, the French had lost the will to commit more men and supplies to the struggle to contain Ho's forces, having been defeated in the field during the siege of Dien Bien Phu. Following the Korean solution, the kingdom of Cambodia was allowed to set up an independent government headed by Prince Sihanouk. Laos also had its own government. Vietnam was divided into a northern half controlled by Ho and a southern half controlled by a coalition pro-Western government. Ho renewed his effort to control all of Vietnam in the late 1950s. By early 1959, the United States was involved in sending armaments and military advisors to South Vietnam to assist the coalition in resisting a Communist putsch. President Kennedy instituted a policy of military aid to prop up the Diem regime in South Vietnam that was ultimately overthrown in

1963 by a military coup.[2] Dong Van Minh, "Big Min," became prime minister and strongman. In January 1964, a second military coup resulted in further chaos in South Vietnam. Mihn was deposed and replaced by another general, Nguyen Khanh. Meanwhile the Vietnamese armed forces were racked by desertions and ineffective leadership. Khanh was not able to halt the disintegration of the Republic of South Vietnam. The Army of the Republic of Vietnam (ARVN), more than five hundred thousand strong, could not isolate and defeat the local revolutionary resistance movement, the National Liberation Front.[3]

In August 1964, the United States claimed that North Vietnamese gunboats had attacked a U.S. destroyer, the USS *Maddox*, in the Tonkin Gulf on August 2.[4] The Department of Defense reported a second attack on *Maddox* on August 4, precipitating a congressional resolution authorizing President Johnson to use military force to protect U.S. forces in Southeast Asia.[5] In February 1965, the United States sent in two battalions of U.S. Marines that landed at Da Nang to prevent the collapse of the coalition government.[6] This commitment escalated throughout 1965 and 1966, eventually involving six U.S. Army divisions, two marine divisions, supporting U.S. Air Force, Marine, and naval aviation units, and field commands from Australia, New Zealand, and Thailand. The U.S. involvement in South Vietnam generated a prodigious anti-war movement on college campuses and among the general public from 1965 through 1972.[7]

Presidents Lyndon Johnson and Richard Nixon had no concerted plan to deal with the anti-war movement. The ad hoc attempts to control internal dissent resulted in a pile of court cases that gave no guidance respecting the exercise of the war power when no formal declaration of war was issued by Congress. President Johnson requested and received congressional authorization to use military forces in Vietnam without a formal declaration of war.[8] No war had more domestic opposition than the Vietnam War. The legal history of suppression of dissenters for this period is muddled beyond recognition.

Television brought the Vietnam War into the homes of U.S. citizens every night. Television made everyone a spectator of the countless demonstrations and sit-ins and the handful of self-immolations that marked the anti-war movement. Government by reaction to public opinion polls began in the 1960s. President Lyndon Johnson pored over the *New York Times* and the *Washington Post* every day to see how his programs were received by the public.[9] Increasingly, executive and congressional decisions were based on public opinion polls, the premise being that the national government should honor the wishes of the majority of citizens. Government by opinion polls was augmented by a hot and cold policy with regard to the Vietnam War. A period of ground offensives and intensive bombing of North Vietnam would be followed by "stand-downs" and backroom attempts to negotiate a cease-fire resulting in very public cease-fire talks held in Paris from 1968 through 1973. The Vietnam

War simply lasted too long for the U.S. electorate to tolerate. By 1968, public opinion swung from support for military intervention in Vietnam to opposition to the long-drawn-out war that cost fifty-eight thousand U.S. military deaths and the deaths of untold thousands of Vietnamese civilians caught between the warring factions of North and South.[10] The anti-war movement that challenged the Johnson and Nixon administrations' conduct of the war was part of the social upheaval of the mid- to late 1960s that included riots in African American ghettos in major cities; the rise of counter-culture, drug-using hippies in San Francisco's Haight-Ashbury and New York's East Village; student uprisings on campus against repressive paternalism by university administrators; a revolution in sexual conduct among the young and not so young; and women's liberation from male domination. These movements used tactics learned from Rev. Martin Luther King Jr.'s civil rights protests (i.e., popular demonstrations, cultivation of the media, exaggerating the popular support for demonstrations, spokespersons making non-negotiable demands on "the Establishment," and direct-action programs, normally non-violent in character, to provoke police retaliation and violence against the demonstrators).[11]

Anti-war dissenters were spied upon by the FBI because director J. Edgar Hoover considered all anti-war protest to be Communist inspired. The federal government moved slowly toward an ad hoc suppression of the dissenters, prosecuting anti-war activists. The most famous anti-war activist trial was the Chicago Seven trial in 1968, following dismal attempts to suppress anti-war demonstrators in Lincoln Park in Chicago during the 1968 Democratic National Convention.[12]

Thousands of men evaded the draft during the Vietnam War. Some fled the country to avoid military service, ending up in Canada or Sweden on a claim of political asylum. Many hundreds were tried, convicted, and sentenced to prison for refusal to report for induction. The world heavyweight champion, Muhammad Ali, was tried and convicted despite his plea that he was a minister and exempt from service. Ali's conviction was eventually thrown out because the United States used tainted wiretap evidence to convict him.[13] Hundreds of less notable draft evaders were convicted, served their time, and return to civilian life without notice.

FEDERAL SURVEILLANCE PROGRAMS

FBI Wiretaps and Burglaries

The Cold War mentality that dominated Washington in the 1950s did not disappear in 1965. The FBI had persistently engaged in unlawful wiretaps, burglaries, and other extra-legal tactics in pursuit of alleged

Figure 6.1. J. Edgar Hoover (William Smith Associated Press).

Communists, disclosed after J. Edgar Hoover's death when his personal files were discovered in his desk drawer and former FBI agents came forward acknowledging the FBI's illegal surveillance practices.[14] Hoover instituted a clandestine anti-Communist program in the 1950s referred to as COINTELPRO (counter-intelligence program) which carried through to 1971.[15] At least 130,000 first-class letters were opened and photographed by the FBI between 1940 and 1966 in eight U.S. cities. COINTELPRO also consisted of unauthorized wiretaps on the telephone lines of left-wing organizations and prominent left-wing activists. According to Marilyn Bardsley, COINTELPROs were initiated against radical groups such as the Student Non-Violent Coordinating Committee (SNCC); black nationalist organizations such as the Black Panther Party; New Left groups such as Students for a Democratic Society (SDS), and eventually every major anti–Vietnam War group. Bardsley details how Hoover used information derived from his illegal wiretap program to destroy people. Actress Jean Seberg was carrying a child fathered by a Black Panther Party member. She had contributed funds to the Black Panthers, and Hoover deemed her to be a security risk. The FBI leaked her story to Hollywood gossip columnists. When her pregnancy was revealed in Hollywood, Seberg attempted suicide. Her baby died in infancy, and she was institutionalized. She finally succeeded in killing herself in 1979.[16]

According to the Church Report, the FBI targeted Dr. Martin Luther King Jr. from 1963 to his death in 1968. Doctor King's famous "I Have a Dream" speech was the incentive for Hoover to order extraordinary and illegal surveillance of Dr. King's movements. His bureau's Domestic Intelligence Division reported that the speech made Dr. King a dangerous person because of his influence over African Americans. *Time* magazine named Dr. King "Man of the Year" for 1963. Hoover planned to destroy Dr. King's influence so that he could be replaced by an African American leader who was acceptable to the FBI.

FBI agents collected information on the private life of Dr. King and his principal associates in order to discredit Dr. King. King received a tape recording from the FBI made from several instances of alleged meetings between Dr. King and women in his hotel rooms. The tape came with a letter advising Dr. King that it would be made public unless King committed suicide.[17]

Hoover also authorized burglaries to obtain documentary evidence showing that left-wing organizations were really Communist front groups.[18] Hoover directed his Chicago agents to spy on comedian and anti-war activist Dick Gregory and may have ordered his execution.[19]

Hoover's agents had a special operation to destroy the Black Panther Party in the late 1960s. While the Black Panther Party was committed to a platform involving a revolution against white racism, item 8 of its ten-point program statement demanded an immediate end to all wars of aggression, including the Vietnam War.[20] The FBI put unauthorized wiretaps on Black Panther Party headquarters, sent fictitious letters to Panther Party families accusing their loved ones of infidelity, and made pretext phone calls to Stokely Carmichael's mother in order to terrorize and divide the Black Panthers into warring factions.[21] First, the FBI engineered a "shootout" with Black Panther Party leaders Fred Hampton and Mark Clark in which the Cook County State's Attorney men and Chicago Police fired ninety-eight rounds into the Black Panther headquarters on December 3, 1969. Only one shot was fired by someone in the headquarters during the 4:00 a.m. raid. Hampton and Clark were killed. The seven surviving Black Panthers living in the apartment were indicted for attempted murder and weapons violations by a Cook County grand jury. All charges were later dropped in a plea deal involving State's Attorney Hanrahan's men, who were cleared of any wrongdoing by federal prosecutors.[22]

Actress Jean Seberg was a major financial supporter of the Black Panther Party. Hoover's men executed a plot to send a forged letter falsely asserting that actress Jean Seberg's pregnancy was the result of an alliance with a Black Panther member. Seberg was mentally unstable. Hoover knew this and wanted to break her. He was successful. Her acting career failed, and she was hospitalized after trying to kill herself.[23] The FBI was particularly hard on the anti-war dissident group known as the Weathermen, deemed to be a threat to national security. FBI agents grew long hair and beards in order to infiltrate anti-war groups. One FBI agent became a personal bodyguard for Yippie leader Jerry Rubin during the 1968 demonstrations in Chicago.[24]

The results of COINTELPRO's illegal wiretaps and burglaries never reached the FBI file room. In 1971, a group of people calling themselves the Citizens Commission to Investigate the FBI broke into the FBI office in Media, Pennsylvania, and removed hundreds of documents relating to COINTELPRO, including reports on burglaries and wiretaps. The burglars went to the media with their "find," resulting in exposure of the FBI's activities by the *Washington Post* and the *New York Times*.[25] Most of the documents were turned over to Sen. George McGovern of South Dakota and Rep. Parren J. Mitchell of Maryland.[26] Director Hoover terminated COINTELPRO in 1971 because its surreptitious activities were exposed by the media. Eventually, Sen. McGovern and Congressman Mitchell turned over the documents to the Senate Select Committee to Study Governmental Operations with Respect to Intelligence Activities of the United States chaired by Sen. Frank Church in 1976.

The CIA

According to the Church Committee report, the CIA conducted an internal intelligence program known as "Operation Chaos" that involved opening first-class mail without notice to the sender or recipient. Nearly a quarter of a million first-class letters were opened and photographed in the United States by the CIA between 1953 and 1973, producing a CIA computerized index of nearly one and a half million names. The CIA maintained a computer index on three thousand people, and 7,200 separate files on U.S. citizens were established by the CIA as part of Operation Chaos. The CIA also kept files on domestic organizations it thought to be potential security risks.[27]

None of these nationwide illegal surveillance programs were ever challenged in court, and none were made public until 1971, when COINTELPRO became public knowledge through the Media burglary. The FBI and CIA engaged in unlawful searches and seizures contrary to the Fourth Amendment because their wiretaps were not authorized by a disinterested magistrate. The FBI and CIA opened personal mail without a search warrant. Although at least one scholar has suggested that surreptitious searches without warrant or probable cause may meet the criteria of the Fourth Amendment so long as the search was based on exigent circumstances,[28] the more commonly held view is that wiretaps and break-ins are Fourth Amendment violations.[29]

COINTELPRO was designed to destroy alleged subversive groups and activities. It was remarkably successful in exposing anti-war activities during the Vietnam War, which the FBI considered Communist inspired. If the surreptitious wiretaps and burglaries were exposed by reason of resort to a judicial officer for a warrant, the anti-war groups and individuals would have been forewarned, and the destruction of the anti-war movement would not have been possible. It is not clear whether the FBI promoted the division of the Students for a Democratic Society into two warring groups using information derived from its unlawful wiretaps and burglary of the Chicago headquarters of the SDS. Since much of COINTELPRO's files are still classified after more than forty years, it is impossible to discern FBI influence in the SDS debacle of 1969.

DRAFT RESISTANCE

The Vietnam War had a very ugly domestic problem: the number of men claiming conscientious objection to military service on purely moral rather than religious grounds was astounding.[30] During the nine years of the Vietnam War, twenty-seven million men reached draft age. Almost nine million men enlisted in the four armed services. Approximately 2.2 million of the remaining eighteen million men were drafted. Approximately seven hundred thousand men refused to report for induction or deserted shortly after being inducted. The Justice Department identified 570,000 men who violated the draft laws. The Justice Department referred 206,775 men who refused to be drafted to the U.S. attorneys in the fifty states for prosecution. Local grand juries indicted twenty-five thousand men. More than nine thousand were convicted, and 3,250 were sentenced to prison. The selective service local draft boards granted conscientious objector status to about 172,000 of the 570,000 men who refused to report for induction.[31] Untold thousands of men fled the United States to avoid the draft. Most of the draft fugitives were granted asylum in Canada or in Sweden. Draft avoidance and resistance of this magnitude had never occurred during any prior time in U.S. history.

The Johnson and Nixon administrations prosecuted draft resisters as ordinary criminals. The Supreme Court had held during World War II that an individual who refused to report for induction was not a member of the military and not subject to court-martial jurisdiction.[32] Given the time needed to convene a grand jury, initiate investigation, and proceed to trial, little more could have been expected from civilian trials of draft resisters.

Men resisted the draft by claiming conscientious objection to war on religious grounds, the traditional plea of the peace churches. Men also claimed moral conscientious objection not tied to a religious denomination. Some asserted that they were religiously or morally opposed to the Vietnam War but could serve in the armed forces in a just war. These claims were at first met with a dash of cold water in the district courts but were later recognized by some local draft boards. Other men claimed to be homosexual or mentally unsound in order to avoid induction. Many men claimed to be ministers, producing licenses from their states based on a mail-order period of instruction by a ministerial diploma mill. Members of the Nation of Islam asserted that all men were ministers and should be granted conscientious objector deferments based on ministerial status.[33]

Draft Resister Trials

Twenty-five thousand young men were indicted for willful refusal to report for induction from 1963 to 1972, when the draft was suspended by executive order. About nine thousand were convicted, and twenty-five thousand were sent to jail. A number of these defendants appealed their convictions, and of that group, a few cases stand out.

United States v. Seeger

In 1965, after the Tonkin Gulf Resolution and the first retaliatory bombings had been unleashed against North Vietnam, three draft cases were accepted by the U.S. Supreme Court. They were consolidated in order to decide the basis for conscientious objector status.[34] In the first case, Donald Seeger had appealed from his conviction of willful refusal to report for induction in the Southern District of New York. Seeger had a 2-S student deferment until he was reclassified 1-A in 1958. Seeger had claimed conscientious objector status in 1957, asserting that he declared that he was conscientiously opposed to participation in war because of his "religious" belief, although he professed to be skeptical about the existence of God. Seeger called on Plato, Aristotle, and Spinoza to support his ethical belief in intellectual and moral integrity "without belief in God, except in the remotest sense." The draft board found that Seeger's belief was sincere, honest, and made in good faith and was based upon individual training and belief, both of which included research in religious and cultural fields. The board denied his conscientious objector claim because he did not believe in a supreme being. Section 6(j) of the Selective Service Act required that any conscientious objector applicant show that his belief was based on a Supreme Being. Seeger was convicted and appealed to the Second Circuit, which reversed.[35] Two other conscientious objector appeals were consolidated with Seeger. Jakobson was also convicted in the Southern District of New York on a charge of refusing to submit to induction. Jakobson had a complex series of moral beliefs founded on his conception of a supreme being that fit no recognized religious faith.[36] His conviction was also overturned by the Second Circuit. Forest Britt Peter's claim for conscientious objector status was rejected by his California local board. He neither affirmed nor denied belief in a Supreme Being but admitted that "some power manifest in nature—the supreme expression" existed that helped the human race in ordering one's life. When Peter refused to be inducted, he was indicted for refusal to submit for induction and was tried and convicted in the Northern District of California. The Ninth Circuit affirmed his conviction.[37] The Court was interested in a single issue: was a registrant eligible to be classified as a conscientious objector under the Selective Service Act when his belief that serving in the military was contrary to his conscience based on ethical and moral principles that recognized a power greater than himself as ordering his beliefs, but not on the belief in an orthodox Supreme Being.

The court declared,

> Our question, therefore, is the narrow one: Does the term "Supreme Being" as used in §6(j) mean the orthodox God or the broader concept of a power or being, or a faith, "to which all else is subordinate or upon which all else is ultimately dependent"? Webster's New International Dictionary (Second Edition). In considering this question we resolve it solely in relation to the language of §6(j) and not otherwise.[38]

The Court reviewed the history of compulsory military service from the Civil War to World War II and Korea. The Court noted that the Selective Service Act of 1940 included a conscientious objector classification for those who professed to believe that military service was against the dictates of God, which could include the credo of a religious denomination or one's personal religious beliefs. The Court also said that Congress amended section 6 in 1948 to state that "religious training and belief" was to be defined as "an individual's belief in a relation to a Supreme Being involving duties superior to those arising from any human relation, but [not including] essentially political, sociological, or philosophical views or a merely personal moral code."[39] The Court also commented that any registrant who objected to military service on the basis of "a merely personal moral code" could not be classified as a conscientious objector.[40]

The Court faced a dilemma: section 6 of the Selective Service Act required belief in some sort of Supreme Being, and the three registrants were not able to profess belief in an orthodox God or set of gods. They were sincere that some higher power ordered their beliefs about war.

After exhausting the subject of belief in a Supreme Being, including a passage from Paul Tillich's *Systematic Theology*,[41] the Court concluded that a definition of belief in a Supreme Being was exceedingly diverse. The Court said,

> While the applicant's words may differ, the test is simple of application. It is essentially an objective one, namely, does the claimed belief occupy the same place in the life of the objector as an orthodox belief in God holds in the life of one clearly qualified for exemption?[42]

The court sustained the Second Circuit's decision and reversed the Ninth Circuit.[43]

Seeger, decided at a time when the anti-war movement was gathering steam and adherents, particularly among draft-age men on college campuses, offered a way out of compulsory service: a sincere belief that all war was immoral based on a personal religious belief supported by a vague conception of a higher power. No one knows how many men called up for induction met the *Seeger* test between 1965 and 1972. It offered intelligent agnostic men a way to avoid service that was far too sophisticated to be of much use to men of less-than-average intelligence and limited formal education. Seeger did not help Muhammad Ali's claim to conscientious objector classification.

Gillette v. United States

In 1970, the Supreme Court agreed to review the conviction of Guy P. Gillette for failure to report for induction. Gillette was classified 1-A and did not apply for conscientious objector status. He refused to report for induction and was indicted and tried in the Southern District of New York. Gillette argued that he should have been reclassified as a conscientious objector because his moral philosophy forbade him to take part in an unjust war. Gillette argued that the Vietnam War was unjust. The trial court excluded Gillette's evidence purporting to show testimony from Gillette stating that he had a belief that American intervention in Vietnam was unconstitutional, illegal, or immoral.[44] Gillette was convicted, and the Second Circuit affirmed his conviction[45]

Gillette's case was consolidated with another similar case, that of Louis Negre, who filed a habeas corpus petition to be discharged from the army due to Negre's moral and spiritual opposition to the war in Vietnam. Negre, a draftee, was sworn in on August 30, 1967. He never raised the issue of conscientious objection prior to taking the enlistment oath. Negre completed basic training and received orders to Vietnam. In February 1968, Negre started an administrative separation for conscientious objection. Ultimately, the army held that Negre was not entitled to a discharge as a conscientious objector because his objections were only to the Vietnam War. Negre had no other administrative remedy, so he filed an extraordinary writ petition in the Southern District of California. Negre's application was dismissed, and he appealed. The Ninth Circuit affirmed the dismissal in a short per curiam opinion.[46]

The Supreme Court affirmed Gillette's conviction and the dismissal of Negre's habeas corpus petition. The Court noted that both men based their conscientious objection on the grounds that the Vietnam War was an unjust war. Both men asserted that they had a religious and conscientious duty to avoid serving in an unjust war.[47] Gillette and Negre also argued that the First Amendment free exercise clause required the military and the courts to recognize their claim that they could not serve in an unjust war. The Court said,

> In line with religious counseling and numerous religious texts, Negre, a devout Catholic, believes that it is his duty as a faithful Catholic to discriminate between "just" and "unjust" wars, and to forswear participation in the latter. His assessment of the Vietnam conflict as an unjust war became clear in his mind after completion of infantry training, and Negre is now firmly of the view that any personal involvement in that war would contravene his conscience and "all that I had been taught in my religious training."[48]

The Court pointed to section 6(j) of the Selective Service Act that granted the privilege of conscientious objector classification to anyone who opposed participation in all war. It held that the statute made no provision for selective moral opposition to a particular war.[49]

The Court turned to the argument raised on appeal that any interference with the practice of Gilbert's and Negre's religious beliefs by forced service in the Vietnam War violated the free exercise clause and the establishment clause of the First Amendment. The Court easily disposed of the argument that the draft constituted the establishment of a state religion by noting that granting conscientious objector status to certain members of religious bodies was not overreaching of secular purposes and was not an undue involvement of government in religious activities.[50] Section 6(j) of the Selective Service Act did not discriminate against anyone on account of religious affiliation or belief. It stated neutral criteria for granting conscientious objector status to anyone who opposed all war based on religious training and belief.[51] The Court explained that the central interests involved in administering the Selective Service Act were to make the draft fair, evenhanded, and uniform.[52] Honoring objections to service in a particular war deemed to be unjust would be based on political principles rather than religious scruple. The Court also opined that it would be difficult for draft boards to sort out the truly religious opposition to a single unjust war and politically based objections to a single war.[53] The Court declared,

> To view the problem of fairness and evenhanded decision-making, in the present context, as merely a commonplace chore of weeding out "spurious claims," is to minimize substantial difficulties of real concern to a responsible legislative body. For example, under the petitioners' unarticulated scheme for exemption, an objector's claim to exemption might be based on some feature of a current conflict that most would regard as incidental, or might be predicated on a view of the facts that most would regard as mistaken. The particular complaint about the war may itself be "sincere," but it is difficult to know how to judge the "sincerity" of the objector's conclusion that the war *in toto* is unjust and that any personal involvement would contravene conscience and religion.[54]

The Court adopted the government's argument that objections to a particular war were "political and particular." The Court noted that an objection to service in a particular war could also be "rooted in religion and conscience," entangling the government in decisions about the dogmas of religious faith.[55] The Court affirmed both decisions.[56]

The *Seeger* and *Gillette* cases sent different messages: *Seeger* gave a window of opportunity to agnostics to obtain conscientious objector status so long as the agnostic acknowledged some kind of power greater than himself. *Gillette* took away the liberty of conscience of selective service draftees based on religious teachings that require the draftee to object to serving in an unjust war. The Supreme Court's plunge into theology was awkward at best. Both decisions played a part in the saga of Muhammad Ali.

Muhammad Ali

In 1960, Louisville, Kentucky, native Cassius M. Clay won the Olympic light heavyweight title.[57] Clay turned professional and eventually worked his way up the boxing ladder to a heavyweight title fight with reigning champion Sonny Liston in 1964. Following his victory over Liston, Clay announced that he had become a member of the Nation of Islam.[58] The Honorable Elijah Muhammad, leader of the Nation of Islam, gave Clay the new name of Muhammad Ali. In January 1967, Ali, then twenty-five years old, received notice that he was reclassified 1-A and to report for induction.[59] Ali quickly applied for conscientious objector status on the grounds that he was a Nation of Islam minister. His draft board rejected his application.[60] Ali defeated Zorah Foley in March 1967. It would be his last fight for three years.[61] He reported to the Houston, Texas, selective service office but refused to be sworn in, citing that the teachings of the Nation of Islam made all male members, including himself, ministers that were exempt from service.[62]

Ali was indicted for refusal to accept induction by the U.S. District Court for the Southern District of Texas. Meanwhile, Ali unsuccessfully pushed a civil suit to enjoin his induction based on the lack of African American membership on the local draft board in Houston.[63] The World Boxing Association and the New York Boxing Commission, not waiting for a verdict in his case, took away Ali's heavyweight title.[64] The criminal trial resulted in his conviction and a five-year sentence. The Fifth Circuit sustained his conviction.[65] Judge Ainsworth's opinion emphasized that Ali had been afforded all the administrative due process to which he was entitled with respect to his claim of conscientious objection. He itemized in detail all the administrative proceedings that Ali used prior to his refusal to be inducted. Ali had appealed his 1-A classification to the Kentucky State Selective Service Board, then to the Presidential Appeal Board, both agencies finding that he was not entitled to conscientious objector status.[66] Ali's second civil suit in Texas and his application under the All Writs Act to block his criminal prosecution also failed.[67]

Judge Ainsworth noted that there were four issues in Ali's appeal:

> 1) Was the selective service induction order to appellant invalid because of alleged systematic exclusion of Negroes from draft boards? 2) Did the District Court err in refusing to grant appellant's request for the production of certain documentary and other evidence? 3) Was there a basis in fact for the denial to appellant of a ministerial exemption? 4) Was there a basis in fact for the denial to appellant of conscientious objector status? 5) Did the proceedings as a whole, selective service and judicial, constitute a prohibited bill of attainder?[68]

Proceeding to the Fifth Amendment due process claim that selective service boards and their decisions were invalid due to exclusion of African Americans from selective service boards, Judge Ainsworth noted that no precedent existed in support of Ali's claim that African Americans were systematically excluded from service on draft boards. He acknowledged that African Americans were statistically under-represented on local selective service boards, citing the Marshall Commission report.[69] He concluded that local boards should be truly representative of the civilian population but noted that President Johnson had instructed Gen. Louis Hershey, selective service director, to take action to broaden the diversity of representation on local boards in March 1967.[70] Judge Ainsworth rejected Ali's characterization of the draft as a form of incarceration generating constitutional issues such as would come up in criminal cases. Judge Ainsworth noted that military service was a privilege, not a punishment, and Fifth Amendment due process issues could not be analogized to criminal procedure.[71]

Judge Ainsworth then rejected Ali's contention that he was entitled to take the depositions of Gen. Hershey, Congressman Mendel Rivers, and President Johnson and to discover Department of Justice documents and Selective Service Administration documents under Fed. R. Crim. Pro. 16. He characterized the discovery request as a "fishing expedition" and did not find that Ali was prejudiced by the refusal to grant such a broad discovery request.[72] Ali's third issue challenged the denial of exemption on the basis that all male members of the Nation of Islam were ministers and his full-time job was minister, supported by earnings from professional boxing. Judge Ainsworth said that the scope of review of a final decision of a selective service board was exceedingly narrow: a classification decision could not be overturned unless the court found that the registrant was denied basic procedural fairness or the board classification decision was without any basis in fact.[73] The Selective Service Act of 1940 provided for a general exemption for all regular or duly ordained ministers.[74] Judge Ainsworth noted that "regular minister of religion" was defined by Congress as "one who as his customary vocation preaches and teaches the principles of religion of a church, a religious sect, or organization of which he is a member, without having been formally ordained as a minister of religion, and who is recognized by such church, sect, or organization as a regular minister.[75] Ainsworth said that

> the test, therefore, is whether a registrant, as a vocation, regularly, not occasionally, teaches and preaches the principles of his religion. There must be regularity of religious activities, a ministerial vocation rather than an avocation, and a recognized standing as a minister to a congregation or leader of a group of lesser members of his faith.[76]

Judge Ainsworth noted that Ali had the burden of proof on the issue of his ministerial exemption. He also noted that Ali consistently gave his occupation as "professional boxer" on his correspondence with the Selective Service Commission, undercutting his argument that he was a full-time minister and part-time boxer.[77]

Addressing Ali's final issue, denial of conscientious objector status based on the religious teachings of the Nation of Islam, Judge Ainsworth noted that Ali had put his case for exemption as a minister four times to local boards, twice to statewide review boards in Kentucky and Texas, and finally to the Presidential Review Board. All the proceedings had been fair and reasonable, following selective service regulations and procedures.[78] Judge Ainsworth cited Ali's statement to his local board that "his religion teaches them not to take part in any way with infidels or any nonreligious group. They fight only in self-defense, not war."[79] The Department of Justice investigation preceding the Presidential Board's decision quoted by Judge Ainsworth opined that "It seems clear that the teachings of the Nation of Islam preclude fighting for the United States not because of objections to participation in war in any form, but rather because of political and racial objections to policies of the United States as interpreted by Elijah Muhammad."[80] The judge discussed Ali's testimony before a Kentucky selective service hearing officer asserting that his religious convictions forbade his participation in the Vietnam War. Ali's testimony on his anti-war convictions was published in the *Chicago Daily News* on February 18, 1966:

> I am a member of the Muslims and we don't go to no war unless they are declared by Allah himself. I don't have no personal quarrel with those Vietcongs. Let me tell you, we Muslims are taught to defend ourselves when we are attacked. Those Vietcong are not attacking me. These Vietcong are fighting a very nasty war over there. There is a lot of people getting killed. Why should we Muslims get involved? Besides, I am fighting for the government every day. I am laying my life on the line for the government. Nine out of ten soldiers would not want to be in my place in the ring. It is too dangerous.[81]

The Court held that the finding that a belief was "truly held" was a finding of fact to be made by the local board.[82] Judge Ainsworth held that there was more than adequate evidence that Ali did not hold any general belief that non-participation in all warfare was part of his personal credo.[83] Judge Ainsworth also rejected Ali's contention that induction was a bill of attainder, that is, punishment for an act that was not criminal in the first instance when done.[84] Ali's conviction was upheld.

Ali was not knocked out. His attorneys filed a petition for certiorari which was granted. Judge Ainsworth did not rule on evidence obtained from wiretaps on Ali's telephones. Ali raised an objection that evidence used against him was obtained by illegal wiretaps for the first time on petition for certiorari. The Supreme Court consolidated his case with several other cases challenging illegal wiretap evidence, and his conviction was reversed.[85] Ali's case was sent down to the district court for an evidentiary hearing on whether conviction was affected by illegal FBI wiretaps. The district court held a four-day hearing in June 1969 taking evidence from both sides on four wiretap conversations obtained without a warrant.[86] The telephones of Elijah Muhammad and Dr. Martin Luther King Jr. were illegally tapped by the FBI in 1964–1965. The four tap logs came from these sources: there was no tap on Ali's in each case. The wiretap was placed on the phone of Elijah Muhammad. Log 1 showed that a man named "Herbert" called Ali on April 22, 1965, and chatted with him about an upcoming boxing match. Log 2 was a call from Elijah Muhammad to Ali on March 24, 1964, in which Elijah Muhammad told

Ali that he wanted to see him about making a minister out of him when "he quit thinking of fighting all the time" and that Clay would make a better minister than a fighter. Log 3 was from Elijah Muhammad's phone calls of October 22, 1964, made by John Ali to Ali relating to a talk with Messenger.[87] Log 4 was taken from an illegal wiretap on the phone of Dr. Martin Luther King Jr., dated September 4, 1964. According to the Court, Log 4 was taken on September 4, 1964, in Atlanta in connection with surveillance of the telephone of Dr. Martin Luther King Jr. MLK (ostensibly Dr. King) exchanged greetings with defendant Clay, wished him well on his recent marriage, and in turn was invited to attend the defendant's next championship fight. Clay also told MLK to take care of himself, that he is known worldwide, and admonished him that he "should watch out for them whities," etc.[88]

The Court held that a fifth wiretap conversation was lawfully obtained because the attorney general authorized the FBI to make the tap for the purpose of gathering foreign intelligence.[89] The district court ruled that Ali had suffered no unfair prejudice due to the four illegally obtained wiretap conversations. The Fifth Circuit affirmed, both courts calling the tape logs "innocuous."[90] The Fifth Circuit also ruled that Ali was not entitled to discover wiretap conversations about Ali between third parties, Ali not being a party to the call.[91] The Court also examined the fifth wiretap log in camera and concluded that the call was in relation to obtaining foreign intelligence and would prejudice the security of the United States if released.[92] The Court noted that the fifth log played no part in Ali's trial and conviction, and therefore Ali was not prejudiced by the subject matter of the fifth log conversation.[93] Finally, the Court rejected reconsideration of its original decision.[94]

Ali filed a second certiorari petition, and the Supreme Court agreed to hear his case. According to information from Supreme Court law clerks gathered by Bob Woodward and Scott Armstrong published in *The Brethren* in 1979, Justice Thurgood Marshall recused himself from sitting on the Ali case because he was solicitor general when the case was first brought before the Court. His seven colleagues voted 5 to 3 to affirm Ali's conviction. Justice John M. Harlan was assigned to write the majority opinion. He sent his clerk out to gather material on the Nation of Islam. Harlan read Elijah Muhammad's statements to the Nation and concluded that Ali was sincere in his belief that his religion forbade him from fighting in any war that was not approved by Elijah Muhammad. Harlan concluded that the Justice Department's recommendation to the Presidential Board was a misrepresentation. Harlan notified his colleagues that he was changing his vote to reverse the court below. Justice Stewart arranged for a compromise decision that would not leave the court deadlocked.[95]

The Ali decision was announced on June 28, 1971.[96] The court's per curiam opinion, arranged by Justice Stewart, reversed Ali's conviction.

The Court noted that the Kentucky State board hearing officer had concluded that Ali was sincere in his opposition to any war not approved by Elijah Muhammad, based on the teachings of the Nation of Islam.[97] The Justice Department then advised the appeal board that Ali's claim should be denied, and the Kentucky board denied Ali's conscientious objector application without comment.[98] Applying the three-pronged test for conscientious objector classification set out in *Gillette v. United States*,[99] the Court held that Ali had to show that he conscientiously opposed war in any form, that his opposition to war was based on religious training and belief, and that his opposition was sincere.[100] The Court rejected the United States' characterization of Ali's anti-war conviction as selective opposition because it was going to dispose of the case on different grounds.[101] The United States conceded that Ali's anti-war beliefs were based on religious training and belief as required by *United States v. Seeger*.[102] The United States conceded that Ali's beliefs were sincere as well.[103] Noting that the appeal board gave no reason for denying Ali's claim, the Court found that the Justice Department's advisory memo was wrong as a matter of law when it asserted that Ali's opposition to war was not religiously based or sincerely held. Since the appeal board's decision was based on the FBI report, the decision could not be sustained because it was not clear that the board relied on any legitimate ground for denying Ali's appeal. The Court reversed his conviction.[104]

Ali had not had a boxing match since he defeated Zora Folley in March 1967. Ali's passport was taken, and all his boxing licenses were canceled. Ali made money during the three years he was barred from boxing by speaking at colleges. He was the first national figure to speak out against the war in Vietnam. Eventually in 1970, even before the Supreme Court threw out his conviction, Ali was able to get his boxing license restored. Ali made a lightning comeback, defeating Jerry Quarry and Oscar Bonavena. Ali then signed to fight the reigning heavyweight champion, Joe Frazier, at Madison Square Garden on March 8, 1971. Ali defeated Frazier and regained the heavyweight title. He lost the title in 1974, then regained it a third time before retiring from the ring.[105]

The Kentucky Draft Board's denial of Ali's application for conscientious objector classification was as much a political act as an act intended to enforce the Selective Service Act. The FBI report that caused the board to overrule its own hearing officer was neither an objective appraisal of Ali's sincerity nor of the teachings of Elijah Muhammad. Ali, despite his celebrity status, was not afforded a fair review of his classification. His prosecution served two purposes: to discourage other members of the Nation of Islam from seeking exempt status and to make an example of an African American celebrity who was an anti-war activist.

The sheer number of prosecutions, the thousands of draft-age men who married and fathered a child to avoid the draft, and the thousands of men who fled the United States to avoid the draft indicated that middle-class U.S. males were engaged in an unorganized protest against the Vietnam War. When President Nixon terminated the draft in 1972, the anti-war movement began its long, slow decline.

THE ANTI-WAR MOVEMENT

Members of the Society of Friends, Mennonites, and Amish Anabaptists, the traditional peace churches, had always opposed participation in any war, drawing no distinction between just and unjust wars. Their position was based on scripture, and conscientious objector status for their male members had been recognized as early as the American Revolution. Like all quietist religions, these churches did not proselytize. The governments of the thirteen states granted conscientious objector status to members of the peace churches.[106] Peace church members were draft exempt in the Civil War and World War I.[107] During World War I, homegrown Socialists opposed U.S. involvement in the European war because the true war for workers was the war against capitalists, not against other workers. The Wilson administration, as explained in detail in chapter 3, systematically drove Socialist anti-war opposition into the ground by arresting and convicting party leaders under the 1917 Espionage Act.

Non-religiously based anti-war opposition surfaced again during the 1950s, primarily aimed at nuclear warfare, arguing that nuclear warfare meant the destruction of all human life forms on the planet. In 1955, a loosely associated group of liberal internationalists emerged to oppose all nuclear warfare. The anti-war group included Annalee Stewart, a former member of the Women's International League for Peace; Socialist Party chair Norman Thomas; Joseph P. Warburg, a New York capitalist; journalist I. E. Stone; Norman Cousins, editor of the *Saturday Review*; and Quaker pacifist Clarence Pickett.[108] Albert Einstein and eight other scientists released a letter calling attention to the dangers of nuclear fallout and blaming the government for downplaying the danger to life from fallout.[109] A. J. Muste, a World War I pacifist Christian who abjured all forms of war; the War Resisters League (WRL); and Dorothy Day of the Catholic Worker movement, among others, advocated total pacifism. The Fellowship of Reconciliation, founded in 1915, advocated abstinence from all forms of violence, as did the American Friends Service Committee.[110] These tiny splinter groups went about renewing U.S. pacifism during the Eisenhower era.[111]

Yale graduate David Dellinger, who had been prosecuted for draft evasion during World War II, started a newsletter called *Liberation* in order to publicize a program of pacifism achieved through revolutionary non-violence. Dellinger and a small group of associates considered that the United States was responsible for inequality and instability throughout the world. Dellinger wished to empower the disadvantaged peoples of the world so that they could restructure the distribution of wealth and power.[112] The radical wing of the anti-war movement had a program and an advocate.

The 1956 presidential campaign gave the anti-war movement an issue: a treaty banning nuclear tests. Democratic Presidential candidate Adlai E. Stevenson proposed that the United States and the Soviet Union execute a bilateral treaty banning aboveground nuclear testing. Stevenson cited the danger to all due to nuclear fallout from testing and striving "to end the madness" of the balance of terror tactics of the Eisenhower administration. President Eisenhower said he would continue aboveground tests. Vice President Richard Nixon characterized Stevenson's proposal as "treason."[113] An anti-nuclear fiction work, Neville Shute's *On the Beach*, foretold a grim future in which all human life on the planet would be wiped out by nuclear fallout from a U.S.–Soviet Union exchange of nuclear weapons attacks.[114] Concerned citizens, including many traditional anti-war constituencies, organized to ban all forms of nuclear testing. Two action groups, the Committee for Non-violent Action and the Committee for a Sane Nuclear Policy, popularly known as SANE, engaged in demonstrations at the Nevada nuclear test site. Borrowing the modus operandi of civil rights groups, eleven SANE members "sat in" at the main gates of the Nevada test site.[115] SANE had its national headquarters in New York City, with 130 local branches and 125,000 members by the time the Soviet Union launched *Sputnik* in 1957.[116] In 1958, the anti–nuclear war peace movement hit the nation's college campuses with the formation of the Student Peace Union.[117] At its height in the early 1960s, SPU had about two thousand members. The founders, University of Chicago students Kenneth and Ele Calkins, eventually set up a commune on Chicago's South Side for SPU members.[118] The SPU sponsored demonstrations at the White House in 1961 and 1962, and a full-fledged confrontation with the New York City Police Department during the Cuban missile crisis in 1962. Internal bickering led to the dissolution of SPU in 1964.

In 1960, Al Haber, a student at the University of Michigan who belonged to a young Socialist club, decided to launch a new left-wing, nonviolent student group called Students for a Democratic Society (SDS). SDS was the campus wing of the League for Industrial Democracy, a Socialist group that had authors Jack London and Upton Sinclair as members during World War I. Michael Harrington, a New York Socialist, revived the league late in the 1950s as a forum for laborers, African Americans, and intellectuals. In June 1962, the United Auto Workers sponsored a conference at Port Huron, Michigan, for SDS members. Tom Hayden wrote down a leftist manifesto that is commonly known as the Port Huron Statement, the statement of the SDS's political beliefs. The statement is sixty-four pages long, and most of the statement is devoted to ending segregation, working to eradicate poverty, and radicalization of U.S. college campuses to move the projects of SDS from the campus to the larger, outside world. Hayden did address the Cold War and the nuclear arms race. The statement portions relating to SDS's anti-war position were as follows:

> How to end the Cold War? How to increase democracy in America? These are the decisive issues confronting liberal and socialist forces today. To us, the issues are intimately related, the struggle for one invariably being a struggle for the other. What policy and structural alternatives are needed to obtain these ends?
>
> 1. Universal controlled disarmament must replace deterrence and arms control as the national defense goal. The strategy of mutual threat can only temporarily prevent thermonuclear war, and it cannot but erode democratic institutions here while consolidating oppressive institutions in the Soviet Union. Yet American leadership, while giving rhetorical due to the ideal of disarmament, persists in accepting mixed deterrence as its policy formula: under Kennedy we have seen first-strike and second-strike weapons, counter-military and counter-population inventions, tactical atomic weapons and guerilla warriors, etc. The convenient rationalization that our weapons potpourri will confuse the enemy into fear of misbehaving is absurd and threatening. Our own intentions, once clearly retaliatory, are now ambiguous since the President has indicated we might in certain circumstances be the first to use nuclear weapons. We can expect that Russia will become more anxious herself, and perhaps even prepare to "preempt" us, and we (expecting the worst from the Russians) will nervously consider "preemption" ourselves. The symmetry of threat and counter-threat lead not to stability but to the edge of hell.[119]

SDS was committed from 1962 until its dissolution to nuclear disarmament and to opposing all U.S. involvement in nuclear or conventional wars.[120] This organization was poised to become the primary instrument of anti-war activism on college campuses after 1965.

Domestic Opposition to the Vietnam War and Operations in the Dominican Republic

The retaliatory air raids on North Vietnam in August 1964 provoked the first wave of campus anti-war direct action programs. SDS decided to hold an Easter march for peace on Easter Sunday 1965.[121] President Johnson's decision to send U.S. ground troops to Vietnam in February 1965 was widely supported.[122] When U.S. Marines were attacked at Pleiku on February 6, 1965, President Johnson ramped up the air war against North Vietnam to daily bombing raids.[123] The University of Michigan hosted a "teach-in," which involved thousands of faculty and student participants. The Michigan teach-in was imitated on many college campuses during the spring of 1965. President Johnson, on the recommendations of General Westmoreland and the Joint Chiefs of Staff, continued to send men and equipment to Vietnam to prevent the government of South Vietnam from collapsing. At first, the Vietnam incursion had widespread public support. In August 1965, 61.5 percent of those polled in a Gallup survey said that the United States did not make a mistake by sending troops to fight in Vietnam.[124] Johnson's decision, based on the recommendations of the Joint Chiefs of Staff to increase U.S. involvement early in 1966, led to the commitment of more than two hundred thousand U.S. soldiers, airmen, and marines to support the independence of the Republic of South Vietnam. Public opinion continued to support the war effort through 1966.[125]

The anti-war movement, a collection of loosely allied, quarrelsome groups from the New Left and traditional liberal peace advocates, took shape by the end of 1965. The movement had no head and no coordinating body; each group did what it thought best. SDS and other New Left groups staged their own anti-war rallies and marches. SANE and more traditional liberal peace groups did the same. The self-immolations began in November 1965 when Quaker anti-war activist Norman Morrison doused himself with kerosene while kneeling in front of the Pentagon, holding his daughter, aged eighteen months, in his arms. When Morrison set fire to himself, passersby rescued his child. Morrison left a letter to his wife telling her that he set fire to himself after reading a French priest's account of U.S. bombing of his village parishioners.[126]

Figure 6.2. Draft Resisters Marching (University of Wisconsin).

Congress took a hand in the anti-war movement in 1965–1966. Senators Wayne Morse and Ernest Greuning had voted against the Tonkin Gulf Resolution in 1964, but they were marginalized members of the Senate. The April 1965 invasion of the Dominican Republic provoked Senator J. William Fulbright, chair of the Senate Foreign Relations Committee, to launch an investigation into the Dominican Republic crisis. The committee could reach no consensus on the legitimacy of the landing of twenty thousand U.S. soldiers and marines in that Caribbean nation. Fulbright concluded that the Johnson administration's claim that the Dominican revolution of 1965 was inspired by Fidel Castro and dominated by Communists was spurious. Senator Fulbright characterized the Dominican Republic adventure as a U.S. policy failure. Fulbright issued his personal report in September 1965, while the Dominican operation was ongoing and U.S. Army troops were sporadically under attack by Dominican revolutionaries.[127] Fulbright generalized from the results of the Dominican probe to the situation in Vietnam. He became an opponent of the Vietnam War, joining Senators Greuning and Morse in opposition to the calls for increased troops, equipment, and funding for Vietnam. Eventually more senators would join Fulbright's opposition to further escalation in Vietnam.[128]

The SDS Easter 1966 march turned out thousands of supporters. SANE, not to be outdone by SDS, sponsored an international day of protest that turned out close to one hundred thousand participants in eighty cities.[129] Increased military operations in Vietnam during 1966 and 1967 and the increase in draft calls raised the tempo of anti-war opposition throughout the United States. By December 1967, less than half of those polled by Gallup favored the war.[130]

In February 1968, during the Vietnamese New Year celebrations known as Tet, North Vietnam's regular army and the Viet Cong launched a series of attacks on major population centers, including Saigon and Hue, the ancient capital of Vietnam. Viet Cong soldiers were able to penetrate the U.S. embassy grounds until driven out by the embassy guard. U.S. Army forces besieged Hue and routed the remainder of the North Vietnamese Army that had captured the city after destroying many of the city's ancient temples that were North Vietnamese strongpoints. Although U.S. troops defeated the North Vietnamese Army and the Viet Cong, inflicting many thousands of casualties on these commands, the public's perception of Tet was very negative. Post-Tet public opinion polls showed that support for the war was eroding.[131] Just how much of the loss of support was due to the constant anti-war rallies, draft card burnings, and protest marches will never be known. Since the anti-war demonstrations were covered by television and spilled over vicariously into the living rooms of ordinary people every night along with the nightly gloom-and-doom accounts of U.S. military action in Vietnam, the movement had some impact on the millions of U.S. citizens who were not part of the counter-culture and not engaged in anti-war activities. Since the media made it appear that the United States was not going to win a total victory à la World War II, nor quickly negotiate a face-saving stand-down and withdrawal, the collective patience of the public was wearing thin. President Johnson's decision not to seek a second term was followed by an attempt to grab the power vacuum in the Democratic Party by Sen. Robert F. Kennedy. The Kennedy campaign was marginally successful, winning the California primary on an anti-war negotiated peace platform when Sirhan Sirhan shot Sen. Kennedy, destroying the Democratic anti-war campaign in midstream.

Vice President Hubert H. Humphrey was nominated by the Chicago Democratic Convention in August 1968 amid protests and violence waged by demonstrators and the Chicago police force. Anti-war protestors targeted the convention, sending thousands of demonstrators to Chicago in early August 1968. A small splinter group of anti-war activists, the Youth International Party, nicknamed the "Yippies," put a pig named Pigasus up as their presidential candidate, turning the animal loose in the Chicago Civic Center.[132] Mayor Richard J. Daley put his police force on high alert by August 20. Six thousand Illinois National Guard soldiers were activated for anti-riot duties in Chicago on the same date.[133] The anti-war demonstrators camped out in Lincoln Park about four miles from the convention site. On the night of August 25, Chicago Police using tear gas, mace, and billy clubs broke up the camp at Lincoln Park. The next night the anti-war protestors counter-attacked the police cordon around Lincoln Park. On August 27, the protestors staged an un-birthday party for President Johnson. Chicago police in plain clothes attacked demonstrators and media people indiscriminately, injuring several newsmen in the process.[134]

Meanwhile, the Democratic Convention ground on, rejecting a platform provision for an immediate halt to the bombing of North Vietnam and a withdrawal from Vietnam. Vice President Humphrey was nominated on August 29. The main public figures for the anti-war demonstrators, Bobby Seale of the Black Panthers, SDS member Tom Hayden, and Yippie Jerry Rubin, tried to stage a protest in Grant Park. Chicago's finest attacked the Grant Park gathering with the usual weapons. Tear gas floated up to the Hilton Hotel's twenty-fifth floor, and Vice President Humphrey's eyes were red with tear gas fumes. Meanwhile, the police arrested hundreds of demonstrators, eight of whom would eventually be prosecuted under federal law for crossing state lines to start a riot.[135]

The Republican Party had nominated Richard Nixon earlier that summer. Candidate Nixon promised to end the war if elected. He won a narrow victory over Vice President Humphrey in November 1968. Nixon proposed to wind down U.S. involvement in Vietnam and to reach a negotiated settlement between North and South Vietnam at the Paris Peace Conference that had begun in 1968 after Tet. By November 1969,

Nixon's program had succeeded in reducing U.S. operations in Vietnam, and serious negotiations in Paris were stalled. President Nixon addressed the United States by television on November 3, 1969, arguing that his way of ending the Vietnam conflict would eventually be successful.[136] Nixon's secretary of state, Henry Kissinger, relentlessly pursued the negotiated settlement despite Vietnamese stalling and obfuscation.

Meanwhile, the anti-war protests continued unabated. Loosely coordinated by a group known as the "New Mobilization," which replaced the Rubin–Hayden "Mobilization" that had failed to manage the 1968 Chicago convention demonstrations effectively, the New Mobe organized more anti-war coalition protests.[137] In November 1969, forty-five thousand people marched from Arlington National Cemetery to the capitol, each marcher bearing the name of a U.S. serviceman killed in Vietnam or the name of a Vietnamese village wiped out by bombing. The next day, around five hundred thousand anti-war protestors marched up Pennsylvania Avenue and filled the mall to hear speakers and musicians attack the war.[138] An anti-war protest movement infiltrated the U.S. Army in Vietnam and at home. More than one thousand soldiers signed a petition to attend the national Moratorium in 1969. Soldiers in Pleiku fasted during Thanksgiving 1969 to protest the war.[139] Despite the spread of discontent among military personnel, the New Mobe was unable to coordinate anti-war activities, and it too fragmented over policy issues.[140]

When President Nixon let the public know that U.S. troops had invaded Cambodia on April 30, 1970, the anti-war movement was revitalized. The New Mobe leadership tried to patch up their ideological differences to challenge President Nixon's latest foray in Southeast Asia. In early May 1970, student anti–Cambodian invasion demonstrations started at Yale and spread across campuses from coast to coast.[141]

On May 4, 1970, students at Kent State University gathered on the campus lawn to protest the Cambodian invasion and the continuation of the Vietnam War.[142] On May 1, a student rally had been held on this lawn, known as the commons. The U.S. Constitution was symbolically buried, and the rally ended peaceably. That evening, students confronted local police in downtown Kent. Some students threw bottles at the police. Bonfires were started in city streets. The Kent mayor believed his police could not control the demonstrators and asked Ohio governor James Rhodes for help. Rhodes activated an Ohio National Guard infantry battalion and sent it to Kent on the night of May 2. When the guardsmen arrived, the campus ROTC building was on fire, and over one thousand student demonstrators surrounded the building. The crowd dispersed without incident that night, although tear gas was lobbed at isolated groups of demonstrators elsewhere on campus. Sunday, May 3, passed without any further confrontation between students, the police, and the guard.[143] Governor Rhodes went to the Kent State campus and threatened to initiate court proceedings to enjoin the student protest. Students had called for another rally for Monday, May 4, at noon on the commons. President White of Kent State assumed that the National Guard was in charge on campus (i.e., a state of martial law existed), and the university administration and the guard assumed that all further demonstrations on campus were banned. About twelve thousand leaflets were run off by the university notifying students that the noon rally was banned. Students began to gather at the bell on the campus commons around 11:00 a.m. Several hundred onlookers lined the walkways alongside the commons. One hundred guardsmen armed with M14 rifles occupied a position on the commons.[144]

A university employee with a bullhorn ordered the students to disperse. He was standing in a jeep, and the jeep drove around the commons repeating the order to disperse. Some students threw rocks at the jeep. Ohio National Guard general Canterbury ordered his troops to clear the commons, and the guardsmen advanced across the commons toward the bell. Protesters retreated up Blanket Hill, then down the hill to the practice football field. The confrontation between national guardsmen leveling their rifles at students yelling and pitching rocks lasted about ten minutes before the guardsmen retreated back up Blanket Hill. Upon reaching the crest, some of the guardsmen, apparently without orders, turned and fired into the ranks of the students below. Four students were killed and nine were wounded.[145] No one determined why the guardsmen opened fire. The guardsmen claimed they fired because they feared for their lives, a position supported by Gov. Rhodes and the National Guard high command. Demonstrators claimed, unsuccessfully, that the guardsmen opened fire without cause.[146]

The immediate result of the Kent State incident was a national student boycott of classes that shut down several university campuses. On May 9, more than one hundred thousand people gathered in Washington to protest the shootings and the Cambodian invasion. The demonstration disintegrated without leadership by New Mobe. President Nixon came out to talk to demonstrators, carefully avoiding any reference to U.S. policy in Cambodia and Vietnam.[147] Similar demonstrations were held across the United States.[148] On May 14, a dormitory at Jackson State College was attacked by Mississippi state police and national guardsmen. Two students were killed. On the same day at the University of California–San Diego campus, student George Winnie Jr. doused himself with gasoline and lit a match.[149]

The anti-war movement's radical wing began invading local draft boards in the summer of 1970. Bombs went off at recruiting offices. In Madison, Wisconsin, a bomb blast at the Army Mathematics Research Center killed a researcher.[150] Counter-demonstrations by New York City hard hats and office workers broke out in May 1970. The hard hats went after anti-war demonstrators, pummeling some and injuring bystanders.[151] Social commentators described the hard-hat demonstrations as a reaction to the elitist anti-war groups of college-educated, well-off people.[152]

The U.S. public was growing war weary: Vietnam had gone on for seven years without a resolution. Senators McGovern and Hatfield introduced a resolution in 1970 calling for cutting off funding for the Vietnam War by the end of 1970.[153] The resolution never passed both houses, but it foretold later legislative action to force the Nixon administration to end the war with or without a negotiated settlement in Paris. The White House staff concocted a plan to use unauthorized wiretaps and burglaries against anti-war protestors. Although FBI director J. Edgar Hoover disagreed with the White House plan, he stepped up COINTEL operations, authorizing field offices with greater discretion in placing wiretaps and lowering the age of confidential informants to eighteen. By the fall of 1970, FBI political investigations accounted for 40 percent of FBI fieldwork.[154] Meanwhile, the May 1970 public opinion polls showed that only 36 percent of those polled approved of the Vietnam War.[155] Eventually, Congress passed a resolution cutting off funds for further military expansion in Vietnam, forcing the Nixon administration to begin to withdraw U.S. forces from Cambodia and continue a drawdown of forces in Vietnam in 1970–1972, the target date for withdrawal of all forces being mid-1973.[156] President Nixon ended the draft for the class to be called up in 1973. The two Vietnams and the United States eventually signed peace accords in Paris on January 27, 1973, and U.S. airmen held captive in Hanoi were repatriated in February 1973. The anti-war movement lost its raison d'être and slowly faded away after the end of the draft.

Prosecution of Anti-War Activists

The United States prosecuted some notable anti-war activists during the Vietnam War era. These trials ended up backfiring on the U.S. Department of Justice and the Johnson and Nixon administrations. In almost every case, trial court convictions of anti-war activists were overturned on appeal, showing only that the Justice Department had the power to indict and try activists, thus interfering with their lives and their anti-war activities. The showcase trials included those of Dr. Benjamin Spock, the Berrigan brothers, the Chicago Seven, and the futile action to suppress the printing of the Pentagon papers.

United States v. O'Brien

Draft card burning was a popular outdoor exercise in anti-war free speech during the Vietnam War era. Congress was so incensed about burning draft cards that it passed a statute making knowing destruction of a draft card a federal felony in 1965.[157] David O'Brien and three friends went to the South Boston courthouse with their draft cards and set the cards on fire in front of a crowd of onlookers that included FBI agents. O'Brien and his friends were arrested, indicted, tried, and convicted of violation of the Selective Service Act. O'Brien argued at trial that the 1965 amendment served no purpose other than to directly prohibit freedom of speech and was therefore unconstitutional. O'Brien appealed to the First Circuit. That court agreed with O'Brien and overturned his conviction.[158] Judge Aldrich, writing for the court, noted that the 1948 act made a crime of knowingly parting with possession of a draft card, making the 1965 amendment redundant.[159] The Court continued to explain why it was about to strike down the 1965 amendment:

> We would be closing our eyes in the light of the prior law if we did not see on the face of the amendment that it was precisely directed at public as distinguished from private destruction. In other words, a special offense was committed by persons such as the defendant who made a spectacle of their disobedience. In singling out persons engaging in protest for special treatment the amendment strikes at the very core of what the First Amendment protects. It has long been beyond doubt that symbolic action may be protected speech. Speech is, of course, subject to necessary regulation in the legitimate interests of the community, *Kovacs v. Cooper,* infra, but statutes that go beyond the protection of those interests to suppress expressions of dissent are insupportable. We so find this one.[160]

The United States sought certiorari, and the Supreme Court agreed to hear the case in 1966. The Supreme Court reversed the First Circuit and reinstated O'Brien's conviction under the 1965 amendment. Chief Justice Warren, for the majority, noted that O'Brien asserted that burning a draft card was communicating an idea by conduct and was thus protected by the First Amendment. The chief justice stated that the Court could not accept a "limitless variety of conduct" as speech.[161] He noted that the Court had held that when speech and non-speech elements co-occur, a "significantly important governmental interest in regulating the non-speech element can justify incidental limitations"[162] He then found that the Selective Service Administration's interest in ensuring that every registrant carry a draft card was such an important and substantial interest as to outweigh the free speech interest of O'Brien. The chief justice argued that Congress's 1965 amendment was a rational exercise of the war power, designed to implement the draft because the draft card was essential to the orderly processes of local draft boards.[163] The chief justice said,

> The regulatory scheme involving Selective Service certificates includes clearly valid prohibitions against the alteration, forgery, or similar deceptive misuse of certificates. The destruction or mutilation of certificates obviously increases the difficulty of detecting and tracing abuses such as these. Further, a mutilated certificate might itself be used for deceptive purposes.[164]

The chief justice opined that the 1965 amendment furthered a substantial governmental interest, noting that he could "perceive no alternative means that would more precisely and narrowly assure the continued availability of Selective Service certificates."[165] The chief justice also disposed of O'Brien's contention that Congress had an unlawful purpose in enacting the 1965 amendment, restriction of otherwise protected speech. The chief justice said that "this Court will not strike down an otherwise constitutional statute on the basis of an alleged illicit legislative motive."[166] Congress's motivation was immaterial because a rational justification for the amendment could be concocted to support the 1965 amendment.

Justice Douglas's dissent was based on the Court's refusal to entertain an argument not made below: given the essential public purpose of the 1965 amendment, did that incidentally place too great a burden on an individual speaker's words or acts? Justice Douglas thought that the majority should have considered that argument. He urged reargument embracing that issue. He did not express any opinion on the constitutionality of the 1965 amendment.

Draft card burnings continued up to the end of the draft calls in 1972. A number of men were indicted, convicted, and fined or imprisoned for destroying their draft cards after 1965. Others turned in their draft cards in protest against the war. David Gutknecht was denied conscientious objector status by his local board and appealed the denial. While his appeal was pending, he was reclassified delinquent and 1-A and called up for induction. Gutknecht refused induction and was indicted, tried, and convicted of willful failure to report for induction. His conviction was affirmed by the circuit court, and the Supreme Court took certiorari and overturned his conviction. The Court held that reclassifying Gutknecht as "delinquent" because of his anti-war activities was an impermissible criminal penalty and unlawful.[167]

It is exceedingly difficult to reconcile cases such as *O'Brien*, *Crosson*, *Berrigan*, and *Moylan* relating to acts combining symbolic speech with a prohibited act and *Tinker*. All these cases involved an anti-war protester making a public statement by some physical act. When the perpetrators of the anti-war act were of draft age such as O'Brien and Crosson, the courts could look at the Selective Service Act as a valid exercise of congressional war power that overrode the First Amendment in the interest of preserving national security. The courts refused to go behind the congressional choice of means to further the Vietnam War. In the case of men beyond draft age such as Dr. Spock and the Berrigan brothers, the Court was unable to establish a doctrinal synthesis that satisfied anyone. Doctor Spock's conviction for advocating resistance to the draft was overturned; the Berrigans and their accomplices were convicted, and the Supreme Court refused to review their convictions.

Tinker v. Des Moines School District

In December 1965, three Des Moines teenagers decided to wear black armbands to school to protest the Vietnam War. John Tinker, fifteen, and Chris Eckhardt, sixteen, were high school students; Mary Beth Tinker was a thirteen-year-old middle school student. School officials discovered the planned protest several days before December 16, 1965, the day set by the young members of the Society of Friends for the protest. The school board adopted a rule on December 14, 1965, banning black armbands from all schools. When the Tinkers and Eckhardt showed up on December 16 wearing armbands, they were suspended from school and were not allowed in until they removed their armbands.[168] The children's parents filed a civil rights action in U.S. District Court for the District of Iowa, asking for a permanent injunction against the school board for enforcing the anti-armband policy and for damages. The district judge dismissed the complaint on the ground that the school board rule was a reasonable regulation designed to prevent disturbance of school discipline.[169] The Eighth Circuit heard the *Tinker* case en banc and was equally divided, resulting in an affirmance by default. The Supreme Court accepted certiorari and reversed the lower courts.

The material difference between the *Tinker* case and the other protester action cases was the basis for the original lawsuit, the Civil Rights Act of 1875, which permitted citizens of the United States to sue state officials acting under color of law for depriving U.S. citizens of life, liberty, or property without due process of law. *O'Brien*, *Crosson*, *Berrigan*, and *Spock* were criminal prosecutions under the federal Selective Service Act.

Dr. Benjamin Spock

Doctor Benjamin Spock, a pediatrician, was the author of several books on infant and child care that were the scriptures by which most baby boomers were raised. Spock's *Baby and Child Care* was the ultimate handbook for child rearing. Doctor Spock, a graduate of Yale College and Columbia Medical School, was the first pediatrician to study psychoanalysis. He used his knowledge of Freudian psychology to study children in his extensive practice and included psychological insights into child behaviors in *Baby and Child Care*. Spock was a World War II Navy Medical Corps veteran. He was an anti–nuclear war activist who joined SANE in 1962 and campaigned against nuclear fallout.[170] When the Vietnam War broke out, he joined the early anti-war demonstrations and campaigns, often accompanied by Yale chaplain William Sloane Coffin.[171] In 1967, Spock, Coffin, Mitchell Goodwin, Michael Ferber, and Marcus Raskin drafted and circulated a petition called "A Call to Resist Illegitimate Authority."[172] The call asserted that U.S. involvement in Vietnam was a violation of the 1945 Geneva Accords and the United Nations Charter. It called on all citizens, particularly young men, to stop aiding and abetting the unjust Vietnam War. The call also contained the following language relating to the draft:

> 6. We believe that each of these forms of resistance against illegitimate authority is courageous and justified. Many of us believe that open resistance to the war and the draft is the course of action most likely to strengthen the moral resolve with which all of us can oppose the war and most likely to bring an end to the war. 7. We will continue to lend our support to those who undertake resistance to this war. We will raise funds to organize draft resistance unions, to supply legal defense and bail, to support families and otherwise aid resistance to the war in whatever ways may seem appropriate.[173]

Spock and his colleagues were indicted in the District of Massachusetts for violating section 12 of the Selective Service Act, which made conspiracies to obstruct the draft criminal offenses.[174] All were convicted and sentenced to long prison terms. They appealed to the First Circuit. The appellants contended that the evidence was insufficient to convict them of conspiracy to impede the draft, and prosecution for issuing the proclamation was prohibited by the First Amendment freedom of speech clause.[175] The court reversed all convictions and ordered only Rev. Coggin and Goodman to be retried.[176] Judge Aldrich, writing for the majority, first dealt with the defendants' First Amendment claims. He used the traditional balancing of public versus private interest in freedom of speech:

> Admittedly, the First Amendment rights of free speech and free association are of such importance that they must prevail if the government's interest in deterring substantive crimes before they take place is insubstantial, or there is a "less restrictive alternative" by which the substantive evil may be prevented. This calls for a weighing. In *Aptheker* the Court struck down the broad Congressional proscription against issuing passports to Communists only after considering the availability and adequacy of other security measures, one actually proposed by the President. In defendants' much emphasized case of *New York Times Co. v. Sullivan,* 1964, 376 U.S. 254, 279–283, 84 S. Ct. 710, 11 L. Ed. 2d 686, not all public discussion was held protected; immunity was denied speakers motivated by "actual malice."
>
> In comparing the present private and public interests we start with the assumption that the defendants were not to be prevented from vigorous criticism of the government's program merely because the natural consequences might be to interfere with it, or even to lead to unlawful action.[177]

The court recognized that the government's interest in preventing interference with the draft was not diminished by the assertion that the draft card burnings were not an incitement to illegal action but an expression of sympathy or support, which would have been protected by the

First Amendment.[178] The court also noted that the defendants were not charged with giving moral support to draft evaders but were in fact accused of counseling and abetting evasion of the draft.[179] The court asserted that Spock and his co-defendants were engaged in activities that were "bifarious," that is, some lawful protected speech and speech forbidden by the Selective Service Act.[180] The court adopted the standard used in *Scales v. United States*[181] to evaluate the requirement that the prosecution show the defendant's specific intent to commit an act forbidden by the Selective Service Act:

> When the alleged agreement is both bifarious and political within the shadow of the First Amendment, we hold that an individual's specific intent to adhere to the illegal portions may be shown in one of three ways: by the individual defendant's prior or subsequent unambiguous statements; by the individual defendant's subsequent commission of the very illegal act contemplated by the agreement; or by the individual defendant's subsequent legal act if that act is "clearly undertaken for the specific purpose of rendering effective the later illegal activity which is advocated."[182]

The court found no persuasive evidence to support Dr. Spock's conviction.[183] It noted that the trial judge allowed statements of co-conspirators to be admitted against all defendants when the issue was the specific intent of the perpetrator.[184] The court noted that all four defendants had either signed the call or participated in the news conference in which the call became public, which was enough evidence to support their membership in a conspiracy.[185] The court noted that words in the call urging resistance to the draft were sufficient to constitute a "call for unlawful refusal"[186] to submit to induction. It found that Rev. Coffin and Goodman had signed the call, and their cases were remanded for a new trial. Spock and Ferber were acquitted.

Spock shows how a provision in the Selective Service Act could be used to corner and suppress dissenters by indicting them for conspiracy to advocate draft resistance. Had this case come up in 1918 or 1919, it would have been decided differently, the judiciary in those times having repeatedly refused to interfere with the executive branch's interpretation of the law relating to the draft. Since *Spock* did not reach the Supreme Court, it stands for the law in Boston and vicinity and may not hold in other circuits.

The Berrigan Brothers: The Baltimore Four Trial and the Catonsville Eight Trial

Philip and Daniel Berrigan were Catholic priests. Daniel was a member of the Society of Jesus, and Philip was a member of the Josephite order, formed especially to serve African Americans.[187] The Berrigans were born in Minnesota to a mother of German descent and a father of

Irish descent who was a railroad engineer and labor organizer. The Berrigans moved to Syracuse, New York, with their mother in the late 1920s. Older brother Dan Berrigan finished high school and college at Holy Cross and was accepted into the Society of Jesus, being ordained in 1952.[188] Father Berrigan went to France after his ordination and made contact with priests involved in the French worker-priest movement.[189] He returned to the United States, and the Society of Jesus sent him to Le Moyne College, Syracuse, New York, as an instructor. Later Father Berrigan taught at secular universities Cornell and Yale. He was a published poet, whose poetry reflected the Cold War concerns with nuclear holocaust and the immorality of war.[190]

Younger brother Phil Berrigan played semi-pro baseball before he was drafted in 1943. Phil went to army boot camp, encountering segregation for the first time in his life. Phil was commissioned a second lieutenant and was shipped off to Europe. Phil at first did not follow in his brother's footsteps, but in the late 1940s he was accepted into the Josephite Order and was ordained in 1955.[191] His first assignment was to a parish in Washington, D.C., located in the Anacostia neighborhood in Washington's east end. The order then moved him to an African American high school in New Orleans and finally to St. Peter Clavier Church, a Baltimore parish where he remained until he was laicized. Phil Berrigan published *The Catholic Church and the Negro* in 1962, the first of his six books on the mistreatment of African Americans and later on nuclear disarmament and pacifism. Phil Berrigan was a Freedom Rider in the early 1960s and participated in a number of African American civil rights protests in the South.

In the mid-1960s, Phil Berrigan founded Peace Mission, an anti–nuclear warfare program that used civil rights–type tactics against the military industrial complex. The Peace Mission was opposed to the Vietnam War, labeling it as immoral. The Berrigan movement escalated from sit-ins in front of Robert MacNamara's Washington residence to direct action in 1967. On October 17, 1967, Phil Berrigan, Tom Lewis, Dave Eberhardt, and Rev. James Mengel (the "Baltimore Four") broke into the Baltimore Selective Service Commission office and poured their own blood mixed with animal blood over draft files. This escapade led to their indictment and conviction for interfering with the draft. While out on bail from this incident, Phil and Dan Berrigan, joined by Tom Lewis, David Darst, Thomas Melville, Marjorie Melville, Mary Moylan, George Mische, and John Hogan (the "Catonsville Eight" invaded the Catonsville, Maryland, Selective Service Office in broad daylight. The eight activists seized a pile of files, lugged them out into the parking lot, and burned them. The eight were indicted for interfering with the draft.

The Baltimore Four were indicted for causing willful injury to United States property valued in excess of $100,[192] willful mutilation of United States public office records, and willfully hindering the administration of the Military Selective Service Act.[193] The Baltimore Four appealed to the Fourth Circuit, which affirmed their conviction. The defendants asserted that they objected to the Vietnam War as immoral and that U.S. participation in that war was illegal.[194] Defense counsel also raised a diminished intent issue. Defendants argued that their religiously based belief that the Vietnam War was immoral somehow overrode traditional mens rea and entitled them to a diminished intent defense. The Court dismissed that assertion, citing *United States v. Moylan*,[195] the companion case for the Catonsville Eight. The Court also dismissed defense arguments that the trial should have been postponed until the end of the Vietnam War due to prejudice against anti-war protestors in Maryland. At trial the defendants put on Dr. Peter Rossi, who told the trial court that public opinion polls showed an ambivalent attitude toward protestors. The trial court held that jury selection should go forward and a jury should be selected in the normal fashion.[196] The Fourth Circuit affirmed.[197]

The appellant's second assignment of error was novel: the appellants complained that the district court should have instructed the jury that the jury could acquit the defendants, even if the defendants were guilty as charged. The phenomenon of jury nullification, present in state and federal courts since 1787, if not before, is the principle that the jury can ignore the court's instructions and acquit an obviously guilty defendant on moral grounds (i.e., the law that the defendant violated was a bad law). The Fourth Circuit held that the Catonsville Eight were not entitled to a jury instruction on jury nullification. It reasoned that although jury nullification is acknowledged, it is wrong to encourage nullification via a specific instruction.[198] The court went forward to comment on the appellant's argument that they were motivated by a moral objection to the Vietnam War, which they believed was outrageously evil. The Catonsville Eight also argued that the Vietnam War was illegal and immoral, justifying their destruction of draft board records. The court did not agree with these contentions. Granting the Catonsville Eight credit for a sincere belief that the Vietnam War was illegal, it said:

> It implies no disparagement of their idealism to say that society will not tolerate the means they chose to register their opposition to the war. If these defendants were to be absolved from guilt because of their moral certainty that the war in Vietnam is wrong, would not others who might commit breaches of the law to demonstrate their sincere belief that the country is not prosecuting the war vigorously enough be entitled to acquittal? Both must answer for their acts.[199]

The Supreme Court denied certiorari for the Baltimore Four and the Catonsville Eight.[200]

The Berrigan brothers did not show up to be escorted to a federal prison. Instead, they went underground to escape confinement. They were located within a few months' time and taken to prison. Father Philip

Berrigan received a three-and-one-half-year sentence. Father Dan Berrigan drew a six-year prison term.

Father Philip Berrigan was laicized in order to marry Elizabeth McAlester, an anti-war activist who was a Catholic nun. In January 1971, *Time* magazine put the Berrigan brothers on the cover of the January 25 issue.[201] Phil Berrigan and Elizabeth McAlester were indicted for conspiracy to kidnap Secretary of State Henry Kissinger in 1971.[202] The jury was unable to reach a verdict on the conspiracy charge; Berrigan and McAlester were convicted of sending and receiving unauthorized mail while incarcerated.[203]

Philip Berrigan and Elizabeth McAlester founded the intentional community Jonah House in Baltimore after his release from prison. The Berrigans had three children: Frida in 1974, Jerry in 1975, and Kate in 1981. Philip and his brother organized the Plowshare Movement to carry on anti-war activities and anti-nuclear protests in 1980. In September of 1980, the Berrigan brothers, WRL's Elmer Maas, Dean Hammer, Father Carl Kabat, Sister Anne Montgomery, Molly Rush, and John Schuchardt entered King of Prussia, Pennsylvania, General Electric plant and symbolically disarmed two nose cones, beating them, they said, into plowshares.[204] The eight were indicted and convicted of burglary, criminal mischief, and conspiracy in the Montgomery County Court of Common Pleas.[205] The Pennsylvania Supreme Court affirmed their conviction but did order the court below to resentence the defendants because the sentence awarded was excessive.[206] Philip Berrigan and his associates held five more Plowshare events between 1982 and 2003. Philip Berrigan took part in a 1999 Plowshare operation at Middle River, Maryland, against depleted uranium used in making armor plate for tanks and warheads. Phil Berrigan was again arrested, tried, and convicted of malicious destruction of property and conspiracy to maliciously destroy property. Phil Berrigan spent thirty months in prison. Within weeks after his release, he received a diagnosis of cancer that took his life on December 6, 2002.[207] His widow survived him and is living at Jonah House in Baltimore.

Defense counsel did not raise any First Amendment free speech issues and did not argue that pouring blood over draft board files was a constitutionally protected non-verbal act of free speech. Perhaps that argument was not made because of the Supreme Court's 1968 ruling that sustained criminal sanctions for burning draft cards in *United States v. O'Brien*.[208] Perhaps counsel read *United States v. Crosson*[209] that supported conviction for flag burning. Flag burning would not reach the Supreme Court again until 1989 when the Court overturned the Texas flag desecration statute as an unlawful interference with free speech in *Texas v. Johnson*.[210] Since neither the trial court nor the Fourth Circuit was forced to consider pouring blood over draft files and burning draft files as physical "free speech" protected by the First Amendment, the Vietnam era passed without a major decision on non-verbal action serving as free speech, if one excepts the *Tinker* decision as implicit recognition of non-verbal free speech.

The Chicago Seven Trial

The National Mobilization Committee to End the War in Vietnam, known as the "Mobe," was an exceptionally loosely organized steering committee for several anti-war groups. Tom Hayden of Students for a Democratic Society was one of the principal organizers of the Mobe. The Mobe identified the 1968 Democratic Party convention in Chicago as a target for demonstrations against the war. By August 1968, Vice President Hubert Humphrey was almost certain to be the party's nominee.[211] Senator Robert Kennedy had been murdered by Sirhan Sirhan in Los Angeles in June 1968 after a victory party for him at the Ambassador Hotel.[212] Senator Eugene McCarthy's candidacy was languishing for lack of funds and organization. In January 1968, Jerry Rubin and Abbie Hoffman formed a group known as the Youth International Party (Yippies) that had for its purpose a counter-cultural comic attack on the Vietnam War.[213] The Yippies planned to turn up in Chicago during the Democratic Convention to spoof the convention process by nominating a pig as their candidate for president. The idea of a mass anti-war, anti-violence protest in Chicago spread from the Yippies to the Mobe. In June 1968, Tom Hayden, Rennie Davis, Robert Greenblatt, and David Dellinger, the Mobe's leadership, held a press conference in late June 1968 announcing that the Mobe would hold marches and demonstrations in Chicago during the convention in August.[214] The call to come to Chicago went out to all the member groups in the Mobe: by August 24, anti-war, anti–white supremacy demonstrators were rolling into Chicago, setting up a temporary camp in Lincoln Park, about five miles north of the convention site. Chicago mayor Richard J. Daley put his twelve-thousand-man police force on full alert well before the opening date. The governor of Illinois mobilized six thousand National Guard troops and sent them to Chicago on August 20 to help keep the peace.[215]

The City of Chicago turned down parade permit requests submitted by the Mobe coalition and also denied permission to use Lincoln Park as a tent camp for protestors.[216] Mayor Daley's police descended on Lincoln Park on August 25, 1968, using clubs, tear gas, and mace to break up the tent camp. Rennie Davis and Tom Hayden led a march to the Chicago Hilton where most delegates were staying. Chicago's police confronted the marchers and clubbed some of the demonstrators. Jerry Rubin, according to testimony from undercover police informants, urged the demonstrators to attack the police. Two police officers saw Tom Hayden letting the air out of the tires of their police car. He was arrested for this act.[217] Fugitives from Lincoln Park ran through the streets of Chicago looking for safe haven. Chicago was under an 11:00 p.m. curfew.

On August 26, 1968, Abbie Hoffman called Deputy Mayor Stahl, protesting the Daley administration's decision to storm Lincoln Park. According to undercover informants, Abbie Hoffman and Jerry Rubin told the demonstrators not to let the police drive them out of Lincoln Park. Davis allegedly told the crowd, "Don't let the pigs take the hill [high ground near a statue in the park]." A crowd of demonstrators estimated to be at least three thousand strong stayed in Lincoln Park chanting, singing songs, and talking. Chicago Police started clearing them from the park at 11:00 p.m. using tear gas and clubs.[218]

Beat Generation poet Allan Ginsberg led a sunrise service on August 27 that included chanting, prayers, and meditation. Four thousand demonstrators gathered at an afternoon rally at the Chicago Coliseum. The event was billed as an un-birthday party for President Johnson. The featured speakers included David Dellinger, Abbie Hoffman, folksinger Phil Ochs, novelist William Burroughs, and others. Later that evening, Bobby Seale spoke to about two thousand protesters in Lincoln Park. Chicago undercover officer Robert Pierson took notes on Seale's speech. The police cleared Lincoln Park twenty minutes after curfew with clubs and gas. Some of the demonstrators went into the Loop and smashed windows and street lights. Another confrontation between police and demonstrators near Grant Park turned ugly when police cleared the park with gas and nightsticks.[219] The police, sans badges, broke up the party with clubs and gas. The police targeted newspaper reporters and television crews, driving them away from the scene using clubs and tear gas.[220]

On the morning of August 28, Abbie Hoffman was arrested at breakfast for having the word "Fuck" on his forehead. The Democratic Convention at the Chicago International Amphitheater duly avoided a coalition anti-war platform plank and nominated Vice President Humphrey on August 28. Protestors milled around in Grant Park adjacent to convention delegates' downtown hotels. The Mobe used the Grant Park band shell as a stage for a series of speakers, including David Dellinger, Bobby Seale, Rennie Davis, and Tom Hayden. The crowd was estimated to be between ten thousand and fifteen thousand. After Vice President Humphrey was nominated that evening, Dellinger told the crowd that he would lead a march to the amphitheater. The police obstructed the marchers at Balbo and Michigan just outside the Loop. The police used clubs and gas to drive the demonstrators off Michigan Street. Meanwhile other confrontations were occurring at other downtown intersections. The Mobe leadership was powerless to direct the protests. Chicago police swarmed Grant Park, using clubs and gas on the demonstrators. A National Guard wire barrier was breached, and protestors poured into the Loop. Tear gas floated up to the upper stories of the Hilton Hotel, gassing the guests along with protestors on the street below.[221] The tumult finally subsided early on August 30, and the protestors drifted away to go home. One hundred ninety-two police officers were injured, and more than one thousand protestors were treated for head wounds and gas attacks. The police arrested 662 demonstrators, including the Mobe leadership.[222]

Rennie Davis, David Dellinger, Tom Hayden, Abbie Hoffman, Jerry Rubin, John Froines, and Bobby Seal were indicted for violating 18 U.S.C. § 1821, which made travel across state lines to incite a riot a federal felony.[223] The defendants were jointly tried by jury. Judge Julius Hoffman was the presiding judge. The defendants had able counsel, William A. Kunstler and Leonard Weinglass.[224] The prosecutors were veteran deputy U.S. attorneys Richard Schultz and Thomas Foran.[225] The trial lasted from September 4, 1969, to February 18, 1970. The defendants were found guilty and sentenced to long prison terms by Judge Hoffman.[226]

Bobby Seale was an intractable defendant. Judge Hoffman refused to grant a motion permitting Fred Hampton, Chicago Black Panther Party leader, visitation rights with Seale.[227] Seale interrupted proceedings by asserting the right to defend himself, since Charles Garry, his lawyer of choice, was unavailable due to illness. When the judge told him to sit down, he called Judge Hoffman a racist.[228] Judge Hoffman repeatedly denied Seale's request to defend himself, insisting that William Kunstler, who had initially appeared for Seale, whom Seale had fired, was Seale's attorney of record, barring Seale from representing himself.[229] Seale made a formal motion to represent himself on October 20, which Judge Hoffman denied.[230] Seale had a law student from Garry's law firm at the defense table that Garry used to advise Seale on law and tactics. Judge Hoffman ordered the law student away from the defense table because she was not admitted to the bar.[231] The judge refused to allow Seale to cross-examine prosecution witness, undercover officer Frapolli. Seale told the judge that he was violating Seale's constitutional rights. Judge Hoffman had enough of Seale's contempt and ordered him to be bound and gagged.[232] The courtroom held several Black Panther members who erupted in a near riot when prosecutor Schultz accused Seale of speaking to his followers before trial resumed, exhorting them to attack the judge. Seale called Shultz a liar and a fascist pig. The U.S. marshals assigned to the courtroom pinioned Seale in his chair, led him away from the courtroom, and chained him to a chair.[233] The next day, bound and gagged, Seale was at the defense table. The marshals grabbed him and punched him, believing that he was working his bindings loose. Seale was able to work his gag out of his mouth and began shouting at the judge and denouncing the trial. He was removed from the courtroom by force.[234] Two days later, Seale was brought in unbound and ungagged. Two uneventful days of trial went by; then Seale repeated his claim to be able to represent himself and called the judge a fascist pig again. On November 5, Seale got up from his chair and went to the lectern to cross-examine a prosecution witness. Judge Hoffman ordered him to return to his seat; Seale refused and again called Judge Hoffman a fascist. The next day,

Hoffman told the audience, the participants, and the jury that Seale would be tried separately.[235]

Hoffman and Rubin had their own method of dealing with the evidence. Following the basic premise behind Yippie politics, they cracked jokes and one-liners during the trial. Their clown routine included wearing judicial robes at a February session of the trial. The government put on a parade of undercover Chicago police officers and FBI agents who swore that the Chicago Seven had egged on the demonstrators, particularly those in Grant Park. Officer Robert Pierson testified that he let his hair grow long and allowed his beard to grow. Pierson told the jury that he dressed like a motorcycle gang member. Pierson became a bodyguard for Jerry Rubin. He repeated statements attributed to Rubin and Rennie Davis that could have been interpreted as incitement to riot.[236] Chicago detective Frank Riggio was assigned to keep an eye on Rennie Davis during the August 25–28 period. Riggio said he saw Tom Hayden let the air out of police car tires.[237] On October 15, 1969, the defendants brought U.S. and National Liberation Front flags into the courtroom to observe the Vietnam moratorium. Judge Hoffman ordered the defendants to put their flags away.[238] Undercover officer William Frapolly testified that he attended Northeastern Illinois State College and joined SDS as an undercover officer early in 1968. Frapolly volunteered to be a marshal for the upcoming demonstrations in July 1968. He testified that John Froines had gasoline and a stench chemical to use against police on August 28.[239] Officer Irwin Bock, another undercover operative, told the court that he had joined Veterans for Peace and was a member of the New Mobe's steering committee. Bock said that he attended an August Mobe meeting in which David Dellinger, Tom Hayden, and Chicago coordinator Rennie Davis planned a series of disruptive demonstrations starting August 24.[240] Very little evidence from the undercover officers was relevant to the charge of crossing state lines to engage in a riot. Many of the supposed inflammatory statements from Tom Hayden and other Mobe leaders turned out to be cautions to marshals and demonstration leaders to avoid a violent confrontation with the police.

The defendants called witnesses from the entertainment world (e.g., Arlo Guthrie, Judy Collins, Phil Ochs) and other celebrities (e.g., Rev. Jesse Jackson, Dr. Timothy Leary) to give testimony relating to the antiwar movement and the presence of the Chicago Seven in Chicago during the convention. Most of this evidence was only marginally relevant to the crime charged.[241] Judge Hoffman held Rubin, Hoffman, and the other defendants, as well as their attorneys, in direct contempt of court after the jury verdict and sentencing.[242]

The Seventh Circuit looked with extreme disfavor on Judge Hoffman's abuse of the contempt power, overturning the original convictions and remanding the contempt accusations for trial. The government conceded that the defendants who were not attorneys were wrongfully punished for direct contempt by Judge Hoffman. The Seventh Circuit held that the two defense lawyers cited for contempt were also wrongfully punished. The court relied on *Mayberry v. Pennsylvania,*[243] which held that a sitting trial judge who had been the object of personal attacks should not preside at a criminal contempt hearing. On retrial before another judge, the government introduced the entire trial transcript of the Chicago Seven trial. The district judge acquitted John Froines and Lee Weiner and dismissed several contempt specifications against the remaining defendants in a November 7, 1973, unreported memorandum opinion. The defendants' renewed motion to dismiss was denied in the same opinion. The remaining defendants testified in their own behalf. In rebuttal, the government offered evidence to refute testimony of a defense witness that the "defense camp" had been subjected to surveillance by military intelligence officers during the Anti-Riot Act trial. The district court then acquitted Leonard Weinglass, Rennie Davis, and Tom Hayden. The district court also acquitted portions of the contempt charges against David Dellinger, Abbie Hoffman, Jerry Rubin, and William Kunstler.[244] The district judge did find Dellinger, Hoffman, Rubin, and Kunstler guilty of criminal contempt but did not impose a sentence on the four defendants.[245] On appeal, the Seventh Circuit affirmed their convictions. The circuit court also held that government electronic surveillance logs discovered on a Brady motion were irrelevant to the contempt conviction.[246]

The Seventh Circuit also disapproved of the convictions for violating the anti-riot act. The court embarked on a lengthy discussion of the Anti-Riot act and its impact on freedom of speech. The court also considered that the statute could be construed as overly broad in its sweeping classification of forbidden acts. The court zeroed in on the definition of "to incite a riot, or to organize, promote, encourage, participate in, or carry on a riot," concluding that the statute described activities that were not protected by the First Amendment.[247] The court noted that when speech presented a clear and present danger to public order (e.g., inciting a riot) it was not protected by the First Amendment.[248] The court held that the indictment was not vitiated because it failed to identify the exact time and date of the alleged incitement to riot. The court also said that a bill of particulars was not mandatory.[249] The appellants also argued that the trial jury was improperly selected because prospective jurors were taken from the voter registration lists, excluding African Americans, young people, and those who were politically alienated, an anticipation of current practice drawing prospective jurors from voter lists and lists of licensed drivers.[250] The court held that using voter lists for prospective jurors did not constitute an improper selection method.[251]

The court examined voir dire questioning and concluded that Judge Hoffman failed to put a question to every prospective juror: "Did the prospective juror have relatives or close friends who were employees of any law enforcement agency?" He put this question to the first venire of twelve and did not repeat it. The court said, "However satisfactory this limited examination might be in some trials, under the circumstances of this case, the court's severe restriction of the voir dire may well have curtailed defendants' challenges for cause and failed to provide them with reasonable guidance in exercising peremptory challenges."[252] The court also focused on Judge Hoffman's refusal to ask prospective jurors about exposure to press coverage of the Chicago convention disturbances. The government insisted that the general question put to every juror asking them whether any reason existed that would prevent them from serving made jury selection constitutionally fair.[253] The court did not accept the government's argument. It analogized Judge Hoffman's handling of voir dire to the inadequate voir dire in *Irwin v. Doud,*[254] holding that Judge Hoffman had a duty to inquire into the effect of pre-trial publicity whether or not the government or the defendants moved to put questions about pre-trial publicity to the jury.[255] The court concluded that Judge Hoffman committed error by failing to voir dire jurors on pre-trial publicity.[256] The court also noted that Judge Hoffman and one of the marshals had communicated with the jury without informing defense counsel. One of those communications had to do with inability to reach a verdict. The court held that failure to take the jury communications in open court in the presence of defendants and counsel was reversible error.[257]

Turning to the evidence supporting conviction, the court held that Judge Hoffman committed error in not allowing defendants to put in evidence written statements made by several defendants, particularly memoranda prepared for the purpose of conducting demonstrations in Chicago, because the memos were relevant to the defendants' motivation to go to Chicago and were not barred as hearsay.[258] The defendants were not retried, and the Chicago Seven trial ended without a decisive conclusion relating to the August demonstrations.

The Chicago Seven trial was in one respect a low farce and travesty of justice due to the continual hijinks of Hoffman, Rubin, and other defendants, who made fun of the judge and of the trial for weeks. Judge Hoffman was unable to control the trial, and his periodic repression of the defendants and their counsel only served to encourage the defendants' act.

The Pentagon Papers

Daniel Ellsberg was a civilian employee working for RAND Corporation on DOD projects in 1967. Ellsberg was a Chicago native and former marine officer with an undergraduate degree and Ph.D. in economics from Harvard. He had been a RAND analyst from 1959 to 1964, when he became a civilian employee of the Department of Defense. In 1965 he transferred to the State Department and spent two years as a staff officer at the U.S. embassy in Saigon. Following his State Department tour, he returned to RAND and was assigned to work on a study on the history of U.S. involvement in Vietnam ordered by Secretary of Defense Robert McNamara. Ellsberg made an unauthorized copy of the completed study in 1970. Ellsberg sent copies of the study, formally known as *History of U.S. Decision-Making Process on Vietnam Policy*, to Sen. Mike Gravel of Alaska, chair of the Senate Foreign Relations Committee, and to the *New York Times* and *Washington Post*.[259]

The Nixon administration tried to suppress publication of the study, now known as the "Pentagon Papers," by the *Post* and the *Times*. The Justice Department filed suit to enjoin publication in the Southern District of New York. The Justice Department's theory was based on the danger to national security that would ensue if the study, classified top secret, was put into the hands of the enemies of the United States. A similar suit was filed in the District of Columbia. The district courts refused to issue an injunction, and the United States appealed. The D.C. Circuit affirmed the trial court,[260] but the Second Circuit reversed and remanded the *New York Times* case for an additional hearing in district court on the merits of the suit.[261] The Supreme Court accepted certiorari in both cases and held emergency oral argument to settle the case as soon as possible. The Supreme Court sustained the dismissal of the government's suit in a short per curiam opinion.[262]

Justices Douglas and Black joined in a concurring opinion reiterating Justice Black's long-held view that no prior restraint on free speech passed muster under the First Amendment, no matter how sensitive the matter was that would be published to the detriment of the objectives of the executive branch of government.[263] The concurring opinion of Justice Brennan also supported a fundamentalist interpretation of the First Amendment precluding any prior restraints on publication.[264]

Ellsberg was then indicted on 173 counts of espionage shortly after the Pentagon Papers were published. In August 1971, Nixon staffers Egil Crowe and David Young met with E. Howard Hunt and Gordon Liddy to plan a secret covert operation directed at discrediting Ellsberg's mental status. They planned a burglary at the offices of Dr. Lewis Fielding, Ellsberg's psychiatrist, to obtain and copy Ellsberg's patient files. The burglary, approved by John Ehrlichman, occurred on September 3, 1971, carried out by Hunt, Liddy, and CIA officers Eugenio Martínez, Felipe de Diego, and Bernard Barker. The burglars did not find Ellsberg's patient file.

The case of *United States v. Ellsberg* went to trial on January 3, 1973, Judge William M. Byrne Jr. presiding. The first weeks of the trial consisted of a parade of generals and government agency heads who explained to the jury that the Pentagon Papers were vital to U.S. security. Unfortunately, the defense undercut much of this testimony by cross-examining government witnesses and forcing them to admit that much of what was contained in the Pentagon Papers had already been disclosed to the media before the publication of the Pentagon Papers.[265] On April 26, 1973, Judge Byrne received a memo describing the burglary of Dr. Fielding's office. Judge Byrne provided the memo to the defense counsel. A defense motion for a mistrial was denied.

Judge Byrne also revealed that he personally met twice with John Ehrlichman, who offered him directorship of the FBI. Byrne said he refused to consider the offer while the Ellsberg case was pending, though he was criticized for even agreeing to meet with Ehrlichman during the case.

On May 9, Judge Byrne received a memo from former Nixon aide Egil Kroghe detailing the planning of the burglary of Dr. Ellsberg's psychiatrist.[266] Judge Byrne then learned about undisclosed, unlawful FBI wiretaps. The FBI had placed a wiretap without a warrant on Morton Halperin and recorded numerous conversations between Halperin and Ellsberg prior to trial. The government failed to disclose the wiretaps to defense counsel at any time prior to or during trial. Judge Byrne dismissed the remaining counts of the indictment against Ellsberg and Russo on May 11, 1973. Byrne ruled, "The totality of the circumstances of this case which I have only briefly sketched offend a sense of justice. The bizarre events have incurably infected the prosecution of this case."[267]

The Pentagon Papers cases demonstrated that the Nixon administration was unable to come to grips with what was at the time the greatest security breach in U.S. history. The Pentagon Papers had been classified top secret to prevent the public from finding out that presidents from Harry Truman through Lyndon Johnson lied to the public with respect to U.S. involvement in Vietnam. The anti-war movement claimed that President Johnson had lied to the public about the Tonkin Gulf incident in 1964, but no one was aware that his predecessors had been covertly aiding the Saigon government and involving the United States in Vietnam's internal affairs.

The Kent State Shootings Cases

The Kent State shootings provoked a series of criminal and civil actions against the State of Ohio, Governor James Rhodes, and the twenty-eight guardsmen who opened fire on the students. The Ohio guardsmen who opened fire on the Kent State students were exonerated by a state grand jury.[268] The State of Ohio prosecuted several student leaders and non-students for various crimes connected with the shooting and the burning of the ROTC building.[269]

Attorney General John Mitchell refused to convene a federal grand jury to look into the acts of the guardsmen as violations of the Civil Rights Act.[270] His successor, Attorney General Elliott Richardson, did order a grand jury to investigate the shootings in 1974.[271] The grand jury returned indictments against eight guardsmen for violating the civil rights of the dead and wounded students.[272] The indictments were later dismissed with prejudice by the U.S. District Court in November 1974.[273]

The families of the four dead students and the nine wounded survivors sued Ohio governor James Rhodes, the Ohio adjutant general and assistant adjutant general, and the twenty-eight soldiers who allegedly fired into the crowd under the federal Civil Rights Act of 1875 for wrongful death and personal injuries. The district court dismissed the complaint.[274] The plaintiffs had alleged that the named defendants, state officials in their representative capacities acting under color of law, had conspired to deprive the plaintiffs and plaintiffs' decedents of their civil rights.[275] The defendants' motion to dismiss was based on Governor Rhodes's May 2, 1970, proclamation[276] and on the complaint itself, which sued Governor Rhodes, the adjutant general and other state officials, and the guardsmen in their representative capacities and not individually. Since the State of Ohio had not consented to be sued, the district court held that the Eleventh Amendment barred the plaintiffs' suits.[277] The plaintiffs appealed to the Sixth Circuit, which affirmed the dismissal.[278]

The Supreme Court accepted certiorari. It reversed the courts below, establishing a foundation for civil actions against state officials in their representative capacities under 42 U.S.C. § 1983. Chief Justice Burger's opinion noted that some of the plaintiffs had pendent state law claims for personal injuries, and two plaintiffs, citizens of different states, had asserted diversity of citizenship jurisdiction in their complaints.[279] The chief justice stated that the issue was "whether the District Court properly dismissed the complaints."[280] Conventional review of motions to dismiss would begin with the premise that the facts pled would be accepted as true only for purposes of establishing jurisdiction. The complaints alleged that Governor Rhodes and the other defendants had "intentionally, recklessly, willfully and wantonly" caused the Ohio National Guard to be deployed at Kent State and to commit the shootings.[281] The chief justice moved immediately to the consideration of the Eleventh Amendment and its effect on suits against state officials. He noted that suits against the state are barred when the state is a named party or when the state is in fact a party although not named.[282] The chief justice asserted that since the Court's decision in *Ex parte Young*,[283] the Eleventh Amendment does not protect a state official who is alleged to have deprived a citizen of the United States of any federally protected right under color of law.[284] The Court also decided that the Ohio officials were not immune from suit in district court. The Court embarked on a summary discussion of the development of official immunity from suit, noting that members of both houses of Congress were given immunity from any act or omission made during debate or voting on legislation. The Court also noted that the state claimed that its officials were absolutely immune from suit.[285] Chief Justice Burger said,

> For present purposes we need determine only whether there is an absolute immunity, as the Court of Appeals determined, governing the specific allegations of the complaint against the chief executive officer of a State, the senior and subordinate officers and enlisted personnel of that State's National Guard, and the president of a state-controlled university. If the immunity is qualified, not absolute, the scope of that immunity will necessarily be related to facts as yet not established either by affidavits, admissions, or a trial record. Final resolution of this question must take into account the functions and responsibilities of these particular defendants in their capacities as officers of the state government, as well as the purposes of 42 U.S.C. §1983. In neither of these inquiries do we write on a clean slate. It can hardly be argued, at this late date, that under no circumstances can the officers of state government be subject to liability under this statute.[286]

That disposed of the main contention of Governor Rhodes and other state officials. The Court reversed and remanded the case for trial on the merits. *Scheuer* stands for the proposition that state officials ostensibly acting under law are not immune from federal Civil Rights Act suits based on the theory that these state officials deprived the plaintiff of life, liberty, or property without due process of law. Pointedly, Governor Rhodes did not declare martial law over the Kent State campus or the town of Kent. The Supreme Court had decided that a state declaration of martial law did not bar federal suits challenging acts of state governors and their minions that deprived citizens of life, liberty, or property during strikes when a state proclamation of martial law was in effect. *Sterling v. Constantine*,[287] decided in 1932, had upheld an injunction against Texas governor Sterling and the Texas Railroad Commission, which had imposed limitations on oil production at the wellhead. Governor Sterling insisted that his martial law declaration was made to control a virtual state of war in the drilling fields.[288] The Supreme Court held that the state declaration of martial law was not the real issue and that the federal courts were not deprived of jurisdiction by a martial law declaration. The Court affirmed the district court, holding that the state officials had acted under color of law to deprive plaintiffs of property without due process of law, a conclusion made by the district court based on evidence taken at the injunction hearing.[289]

Following remand, a protracted civil trial resulted in a verdict for the defendants.[290] The verdict was overturned by the Sixth Circuit.[291] The case was settled out of court by payment of $675,000 to the plaintiffs, estimated to have been a figure equal to the state's costs in retrying the case.[292]

CONCLUSION

The ten years from 1965 to 1975 are not easy to characterize or to understand after forty years' time. The Vietnam anti-war movement was plagued by surreptitious FBI and CIA intelligence activities. The anti-war movement was related to the civil rights movement, the sexual revolution, and drug culture as part of a generalized revolt against the uptight conformist moral standards of the 1950s. It was the only time in U.S. history when a tiny minority of activists from the left of the political and social spectrum was able to involve thousands of men and women who did not share their political and social goals in a movement to force Congress and the president to halt U.S. involvement in the Vietnamese civil war. The president did not openly exercise any of his war powers to suppress anti-war dissent. There were no arrests without probable cause and no trial of civilians before military commissions. The writ of habeas corpus was never suspended anywhere in the United States.

The executive branch did infiltrate anti-war groups and surreptitiously spy on their leaders for the purpose of disrupting the anti-war movement. Some of the covert operations against the anti-war movement were marginally successful, but the Johnson administration halfheartedly exploited illegal FBI and CIA wiretaps and burglaries. The Nixon administration's Espionage Act prosecution of Daniel Ellsberg and Anthony Russo floundered and eventually was ignominiously dismissed by the trial judge for numerous Brady violations. The executive branch never really took charge of any concerted program to control the anti-war movement and was eventually overwhelmed by the anti-war movement and war weariness.

NOTES

1. Charles De Benedetti and Charles Chatfield, *An American Ordeal: The Antiwar Movement of the Vietnam Era* (Syracuse, NY: Syracuse University Press, 1990), 80–85. For background on the French protectorate of Indo-China and French withdrawal, see also George C. Herring, "The Cold War and Vietnam," *OAH Magazine of History* 18 (2004): 18.

2. De Benedetti and Chatfield, *An American Ordeal*, 91. Diem and his brother were assassinated.

3. De Benedetti and Chatfield, *An American Ordeal*, 99.

4. See John Prados, "Essay: The Fortieth Anniversary of the Gulf of Tonkin Incident," last accessed Feb. 10, 2017, http://www.gwu.edu/~nsarchiv/NSAEBB/NSAEBB132/essay.htm.

5. See Prados, "Essay: The Fortieth Anniversary of the Gulf of Tonkin Incident."

6. For the history of U.S. Marine Corps involvement in the Vietnam War, see Allan R. Millett, *Semper Fidelis: The History of the United States Marine Corps* (New York: Macmillan, 1980), 559–606.

7. See De Benedetti and Chatfield, *An American Ordeal*, for a description of the anti-war movement.

8. De Benedetti and Chatfield, *An American Ordeal*, 32.

9. De Benedetti and Chatfield, *An American Ordeal*, 167–168.

10. For representative analysis of public opinion, see Harlan Hahn, "Correlates of Public Sentiments about War: Local Referenda on the Vietnam Issue," *American Political Science Review* 64 (1970): 1186, on Vietnam involvement from 1966–1968 referenda correlated with educational and socioeconomic indicia.

11. This characterization of the 1960s was taken from William O'Neill, *Coming Apart: An Informal History of America in the 1960's* (New York: Times Books, 1971), chs. 5–9. See also David Farber, "The Counterculture and the Peace Movement," in *Give Peace a Chance: Exploring the Vietnam Anti-War Movement*, ed. Melvin Small and William D. Hoover (Syracuse, NY: Syracuse University Press, 1992), 3–6.

12. See John Schultz, *The Chicago Conspiracy Trial* (Chicago: University of Chicago Press, 1970; 3rd ed., 1992), for a detailed account of the 1969 conspiracy trial.

13. See *Clay v. United States*, 403 U.S. 698 (1971).

14. For an account of Hoover's widespread unauthorized wiretaps during Vietnam, see Curt Gentry, *J. Edgar Hoover: The Man and the Secrets* (New York: Norton, 1991); Marilyn Bardsley, "The Life and Career of J. Edgar Hoover," last accessed Feb. 10, 2017, http://www.trutv.com/library/crime/gangsters_outlaws/cops_others/hoover/12.html.

15. Anthony Summers, *Official and Confidential: The Secret Life of J. Edgar Hoover* (New York: Putnam, 1993), 167, 380–383. COINTELPRO was initiated in 1956, and Hoover carried on the program until 1969–1970. Bardsley, "The Life and Career of J. Edgar Hoover," ch. 9.

16. Bardsley, "The Life and Career of J. Edgar Hoover," ch. 11. See also Church Report, vol. 2, 11.

17. Bardsley, "The Life and Career of J. Edgar Hoover," ch. 11. See also Church Report, vol. 2, 11.

18. Bardsley, "The Life and Career of J. Edgar Hoover," ch. 12; see also Summers, *Official and Confidential*, 385.

19. Summers, *Official and Confidential*, 383–384.

20. See "The Ten Point Plan," originally issued in 1966 by party chair Bobby Seale, last accessed Feb. 10, 2017, http://www.blackpantherparty/blogspot.com/p/founding-and-10-point-program.html. Item 8 read as follows: "8. WE WANT AN IMMEDIATE END TO ALL WARS OF AGGRESSION. We believe that the various conflicts which exist around the world stem directly from the aggressive desire of the United States ruling circle and government to force its domination upon the oppressed people of the world. We believe that if the United States government or its lackeys do not cease these aggressive wars it is the right of the people to defend themselves by any means necessary against their aggressors."

21. Gentry, *J. Edgar Hoover*, 617–619.

22. Gentry, *J. Edgar Hoover*, 620–621. See also Hans Bennett, "The Black Panthers and the Assassination of Fred Hampton," 2009, last accessed May 11, 2016, http://www.phillyimc.org/en/black-panthers-and-assassination-fred-hampton.

23. Gentry, *J. Edgar Hoover*, 647–648; Summers, *Official and Confidential*, 382–383. See also the biography of Jean Seberg, last accessed Feb. 10, 2017, http://www.saintjean.co.uk/menu2.htm. The website contains scans of FBI memos documenting Hoover's program to break her. Hoover noted at the foot of a memo directing the use of the forged letter: "Jean Seeberg [*sic*] has been a financial supporter of the BPP and should be neutralized. Her current pregnancy by (blacked out) while still married affords an opportunity for such effort." *Neutralized* in FBI argot meant to eliminate someone by death or other means from the political scene.

24. Schultz, *The Chicago Conspiracy Trial*, 133.

25. Gentry, *J. Edgar Hoover*, 674–676. The Media burglary disclosed Hoover's COINTELPRO system and the FBI's wholesale violations of federal law.

26. Allan M. Jalon, "A Break-in to End All Break-ins," *Los Angeles Times*, Mar. 8, 2006, last accessed Feb. 10, 2017, http://articles.latimes.com/2006/mar/08/opinion/oe-jalon8.

27. Report of Senate Select Committee to Study Governmental Operations, S. Rep 94-755 (Washington, D.C.: Government Printing Office, 1976) (hereafter "Church Committee"), vol. 2, 6. The CIA was not alone; the National Security Agency, the Department of the Army, and the Internal Revenue Service also maintained secret intelligence files on suspected subversives.

- Millions of private telegrams sent from, to, or through the United States were obtained by the National Security Agency from 1947 to 1975 under a secret "arrangement" with three U.S. telegraph companies.
- An estimated one hundred thousand Americans were the subjects of U.S. Army intelligence files created between the mid-1960s and 1971.
- Intelligence files on more than eleven thousand individuals and groups were created by the Internal Revenue Service.

28. See Akill Reed Amar, "Fourth Amendment First Principles," *Harvard Law Review* 107 (1994): 757, 802–804.

29. In 1928, the Supreme Court held in *Olmstead v. United States*, 277 U.S. 438 (1928), that use of a wiretap to intercept a private telephone conversation was not a "search" for purposes of the Fourth Amendment. In 1967, the Court overruled *Olmstead*, holding in *Katz v. United States*, 389 U.S. 347 (1967), that recording a telephone conversation from a phone booth was an invasion of privacy that required Fourth Amendment protection by warrant and probable cause.

30. Jessica Kindig, "Draft Resistance in the Vietnam Era," Antiwar and Radical History Project, University of Washington, last accessed Feb. 10, 2017, http://depts.washington.edu/antiwar/vietnam_draft.shtml.

31. Andy Mager, "We Ain't Marchin Any More," *Nonviolent*, Mar.–Apr. 2000, last accessed Feb. 10, 2017, http://www.warresisters.org/nva/nva0300-3.htm.

32. See *Billings v. Truesdell*, 321 U.S. 542 (1944), held: a person who has been ordered to report for induction under the 1940 Selective Service Act is not a member of the armed forces if he refused to report for induction and does not take the enlistment oath.

33. See "Draft Resistance in the Vietnam Era," last accessed Feb. 10, 2017, http://www.seas.upenn.edu/~pws/60s/types.html. According to the anonymous author, there were four ways to evade the draft: "Ethical Deferment, Un-Ethical Deferment, Conscientious Objection and Full Resistance—'Hell no, we won't go!' they would yell as they burned their draft cards. Some would go to jail; some would disappear 'underground' or some would flee to Canada."

34. See *United States v. Jakobson*, on certiorari to the same court, and *Peter v. United States*, on certiorari to the U.S. Court of Appeals for the Ninth Circuit. All three cases arose well before the Tonkin Gulf Resolution, and all the local board and administrative appeal decisions were rendered before August 1964.

35. *United States v. Seeger*, 380 U.S. 163, 166–167 (1965).

36. Jakobson was originally classified 1-A in 1953 and intermittently had a student classification until 1956. He made his conscientious objector claim in April 1958 for non-combatant classification (1-A-O) as a conscientious objector. He stated on the Selective Service System form that he believed in a "Supreme Being" who was "Creator of Man" in the sense of being "ultimately responsible for the existence of man" and who was "the Supreme Reality," of which "the existence of man is the *result*."

37. *Peter v. United States*, 324 F.2d 173 (9th Cir. 1963). Peter explained his ethical and moral philosophy. He attached a statement to his conscientious objector request, stating that he felt it a violation of his moral code to take human life and that he considered this belief superior to his obligation to the state. Despite a local board finding that Peter was sincere, he was denied conscientious objector status and refused to report for induction. *Peter v. United States*, 324 U.S. 174–177.

38. *United States v. Seeger*, 380 U.S. 174.

39. *United States v. Seeger*, 380 U.S. 178.

40. *United States v. Seeger*, 380 U.S. 172–173.

41. The Court also quoted Dr. John Robertson and the scheme on faith of the Second Vatican Council. *United States v. Seeger*, 380 U.S. 180 (direct quote), 181–182.
42. *United States v. Seeger*, 380 U.S. 184.
43. *United States v. Seeger*, 380 U.S. 187–188.
44. *Gillette v. United States*, 420 F.2d 298 (2d Cir. 1970).
45. *Gillette v. United States*, 420 F.2d 300.
46. *Negre v. Larson*, 418 F.2d 908 (9th Cir. 1969).
47. *Gillette v. United States*, 401 U.S. 440–441. (1971).
48. *Gillette v. United States*, 401 U.S. 440–441.
49. *Gillette v. United States*, 401 U.S. 443.
50. *Gillette v. United States*, 401 U.S. 449–450.
51. *Gillette v. United States*, 401 U.S. 450–451.
52. *Gillette v. United States*, 401 U.S. 455.
53. *Gillette v. United States*, 401 U.S. 455–456.
54. *Gillette v. United States*, 401 U.S. 456–457.
55. *Gillette v. United States*, 401 U.S. 458.
56. *Gillette v. United States*, 401 U.S. 463.
57. See the Official Muhammad Ali website, last accessed Feb. 10, 2017, http://www.ali.com, particularly http://www.ali.com/legend_boxer_beginning.php, for Clay's rise as an Olympic star.
58. *New York Times*, Mar. 7, 1964, 15. See also http://www.ali.com/legend_boxer_controversy.php.
59. Clay had been classified 4-F in 1964. See *New York Times*, Mar. 21, 1964, 18.
60. *New York Times*, Jan. 13, 1967, 50.
61. See http://www.ali.com/legend_boxer_exile.php.
62. *New York Times*, Apr. 29, 1967, 1. Ali issued a statement at the Selective Service Center: "I have searched my conscience and I find I cannot be true to my belief in my religion by accepting the call."
63. *New York Times*, Apr. 29, 1967, 34. See also *Clay v. United States*, 397 F.2d 907 (5th Cir. 1968). A stay of injunction pending appeal was refused. *Muhammad Ali v. Breathitt*, D.C., W.D. Ky., 1967, 268 F. Supp. 63. Registrant petitioned the Sixth Circuit for leave to appeal and for temporary restraining order pending appeal, which was denied, the court taking cognizance of the district judge's denial of a certification that immediate appeal was warranted and the denial of an order staying proceedings. (Unpublished opinion, 6th Cir., Docket No. 17787, Mar. 28, 1967.) The Sixth Circuit, on April 17, 1967, denied registrant's application for an order staying orders of the district court and for an injunction pending appeal. (Unpublished opinion, 6th Cir., Docket No. 17834.) On the same day, the Supreme Court denied registrant's application for stay of the order of the U.S. District Court for the Western District of Kentucky, for injunction pending appeal, and denied leave to file a petition for mandamus. *Muhammad Ali v. Gordon*, 386 U.S. 1002 (1967). Rehearing was denied by the Supreme Court on Apr. 24, 1967, 386 U.S. 1027 (1967). On the same day, the Supreme Court also denied petition for writ of certiorari to the Sixth Circuit. *Muhammad Ali v. Gordon*, 386 U.S. 1018 (1967).
64. *New York Times*, June 20, 1967, 25. The jury was all white, but *Batson v. Kentucky*, which would have invalidated such a jury selection, was still many years in the future.
65. *Clay v. United States*, 397 F.2d 901 (5th Cir. 1968).
66. *Clay v. United States*, 397 F.2d 905–907.
67. *Clay v. United States*, 397 F.2d 907–908.
68. *Clay v. United States*, 397 F.2d 908–909.
69. According to the report of the National Advisory Commission on Selective Service (the Marshall Commission), "In Kentucky, only 0.2% of 641 local board members is Negro, though 7.1% of the total population is Negro. In Texas, only 1.1% of local board members is Negro, though 12.4% of the total population is Negro. In the City of Louisville, the total population (1964) is 389,044, of which the white population is 310,717 and the Negro population 78,245, or 21% of the total population. The Jefferson County, Kentucky, total population (1960) number 610,947, of which there are 532,057

whites and 78,350 Negroes, or 12.8% of the total population. In Harris County, Texas, of a total population of 1,243,158, 19.81%, or 246,351, is Negro." *Clay v. United States*, 397 F.2d 909 (citations omitted).

70. *Clay v. United States*, 397 F.2d 910.

71. *Clay v. United States*, 397 F.2d 910–911.

72. *Clay v. United States*, 397 F.2d 915.

73. "Congress gave the courts no general authority of revision over draft board proceedings, and we have authority to reverse only if there is a denial of basic procedural fairness or if the conclusion of the board is without any basis in fact." *Clay v. United States*, 397 F.2d 916.

74. 50 U.S.C. App. § 456(g) (1967).

75. 50 U.S.C. App. § 456(g). See *Clay v. United States*, 397 F.2d 16.

76. *Clay v. United States*, 397 F.2d 917.

77. *Clay v. United States*, 397 F.2d 917–918.

78. *Clay v. United States*, 397 F.2d 917–919.

79. *Clay v. United States*, 397 F.2d 918. Ali also stated that he had no quarrel with the Viet Cong.

80. *Clay v. United States*, 397 F.2d 919n17. The DOJ report quoted the findings in *Sostre v. McGinnis*, 334 F.2d 906 (2d Cir. 1964), cert. denied 379 U.S. 892 (1964), appearing in note 16.

81. *Clay v. United States*, 397 F.2d 920.

82. *United States v. Seeger*, 380 U.S. 163, 183–185 (1965).

83. *Clay v. United States*, 397 F.2d 920–921.

84. *Clay v. United States*, 397 F.2d 922–924. Ali contended that he was entitled to trial by jury during the induction process.

85. *Giordano v. United States*, 394 U.S. 310 (1969).

86. *Clay v. United States*, 430 F.2d 165 (5th Cir. 1970), rehearing denied Aug. 19, 1970.

87. *Clay v. United States*, 430 F.2d 167–168.

88. *Clay v. United States*, 430 F.2d 167–168.

89. *Clay v. United States*, 430 F.2d 165, 166–167 (1970).

90. *Clay v. United States*, 430 F.2d 167.

91. *Clay v. United States*, 430 F.2d 169.

92. *Clay v. United States*, 430 F.2d 170.

93. *Clay v. United States*, 430 F.2d 171–172.

94. *Clay v. United States*, 430 F.2d 172. This short statement would open the door to the U.S. Supreme Court's reversal of Ali's conviction.

95. Bob Woodward and Scott Armstrong, *The Brethren: Inside the Supreme Court* (New York: Simon & Schuster, 1979), 157–158.

96. *Clay v. United States*, 403 U.S. 698 (1971).

97. *Clay v. United States*, 403 U.S. 699–700.

98. *Clay v. United States*, 403 U.S. 700.

99. *United States v. Gillette*, 401 U.S. 437 (1971). Gillette claimed conscientious objection to the Vietnam War alone as an unjust war contrary to his moral conviction. His case was consolidated with another similar case, and the court affirmed Gillette's conviction, holding that moral opposition to the Vietnam War alone did not qualify any registrant for conscientious objector status under the Selective Service Act. Justices Douglas dissented, citing John T. Noonan's analysis of the religious duty to avoid aiding and abetting an unjust war.

100. *Clay v. United States*, 403 U.S. 700.

101. *Clay v. United States*, 403 U.S. 701.

102. *Clay v. United States*, 403 U.S. 703, citing *United States v. Seeger*, 380 U.S. 163 (1965). The court said, "There is no dispute that petitioner's professed beliefs were founded on the basic tenets of the Muslim religion."

103. *Clay v. United States*, 403 U.S. 703.

104. *Clay v. United States*, 403 U.S. 704. The Court explained that whenever the Court could not determine if a criminal conviction was based on valid or invalid grounds, the Court had the duty to overturn the conviction.

105. See http://www.ali.com/legend_boxer_exile.php.

106. See Ellis M. West, "The Right to Religion-Based Exemptions in Early America: The Case of Conscientious Objectors to Conscription," *Journal of Law and Religion* 10 (1993): 367, 373–380, for Revolutionary War exemption, disagreeing with the majority historical view that the thirteen states recognized draft exemption.

107. See Francis Heisler, "The Law versus the Conscientious Objector," *University of Chicago Law Review* 20 (1953): 441, for the background on exemption for the peace church members in the 1917 and 1940 draft laws.

108. De Benedetti and Chatfield, *American Ordeal*, 13, 16–17.

109. De Benedetti and Chatfield, *American Ordeal*, 17.

110. De Benedetti and Chatfield, *American Ordeal*, 22.

111. De Benedetti and Chatfield, *American Ordeal*, 20–23.

112. De Benedetti and Chatfield, *American Ordeal*, 24.

113. De Benedetti and Chatfield, *American Ordeal*, 28.

114. De Benedetti and Chatfield, *American Ordeal*, 30.

115. De Benedetti and Chatfield, *American Ordeal*, 31.

116. De Benedetti and Chatfield, *American Ordeal*, 33.

117. De Benedetti and Chatfield, *American Ordeal*, 33. The SPU, though small, used tactics from Martin Luther King's toolbox: sit-ins and demonstrations against nuclear testing.

118. The commune and national SPU headquarters were located at 5504 S. Woodlawn. See the Student Peace Union 1961 trifold brochure, last accessed Feb. 10, 2017, http://www.peacebuttons.info/PDF/SPU%20flyer.pdf.

119. Thomas Hayden, "Port Huron Statement" (unpaginated), last accessed Feb. 10, 2017, http://coursesa.matrix.msu.edu/~hst306/documents/huron.html.

120. Mark Barringer, "The Anti-War Movement in the United States," last accessed Feb. 10, 2017, http://www.english.illinois.edu/maps/vietnam/antiwar.html.

121. De Benedetti and Chatfield, *American Ordeal*, 100–101.

122. See Gallup Poll, Aug. 27, 1965, last accessed Feb. 10, 2017, http://www.gallup.com/poll/2299/americans-look-back-vietnam-war.aspx: 61 percent of the public believed that Johnson's escalation of the Vietnam conflict was not a mistake; 34 percent thought that it was a mistake.

123. De Benedetti and Chatfield, *American Ordeal*, 104.

124. Gallup Poll, Aug. 27, 1965, http://www.gallup.com/poll/2299/americans-look-back-vietnam-war.aspx.

125. The Gallup Poll answers for March, May, September, and November 1966 showed that the percent of support for the war slowly declined from 59 percent in March to 51 percent in November. See "Explorations: The Vietnam War as History," last accessed Feb. 19, 2017, http://www.digitalhistory.uh.edu/learning_history/vietnam/vietnam_pubopinion.cfm.

126. De Benedetti and Chatfield, *American Ordeal*, 129.

127. See remarks of Sen. Fulbright, Congressional Record (Senate), Sept. 15, 196523855-61.

128. De Benedetti and Chatfield, *American Ordeal*, 124. Fulbright felt that President Johnson had used and manipulated him into supporting the Vietnam War.

129. De Benedetti and Chatfield, *American Ordeal*, 125.

130. Gallup Poll, Dec. 1967, last accessed Feb. 10, 2017, http://www.digitalhistory.uh.edu/learning_history/vietnam/vietnam_pubopinion.cfm. In February 1967, a majority of those polled (52 percent) still thought the Vietnam intervention was no mistake. By December, support had shrunk to 46 percent. Popular support continued its steady decline from December 1967 to May 1971.

131. In March 1968, while the siege of Hue was still in progress, 41 percent polled supported the war. By October only 37 percent supported the war. Gallup Poll, 1968,

last accessed Feb. 10, 2017, http://www.digitalhistory.uh.edu/learning_history/vietnam/vietnam_pubopinion.cfm.

132. De Benedetti and Chatfield, *American Ordeal*, 226–227.
133. De Benedetti and Chatfield, *American Ordeal*, 226.
134. De Benedetti and Chatfield, *American Ordeal*, 227.
135. De Benedetti and Chatfield, *American Ordeal*, 228.
136. "Biography of Richard M. Nixon," last accessed Feb. 10, 2017, http://www.nixonlibrary.gov/Thelife/apolitician/thepresident/index.php.
137. De Benedetti and Chatfield, *American Ordeal*, 248.
138. De Benedetti and Chatfield, *American Ordeal*, 262–263.
139. De Benedetti and Chatfield, *American Ordeal*, 264–265.
140. De Benedetti and Chatfield, *American Ordeal*, 270–272.
141. De Benedetti and Chatfield, *American Ordeal*, 279.
142. Jerry M. Lewis and Thomas R. Hensley, "The May 4 Shootings at Kent State: The Search for Historical Accuracy" (unpaginated), last accessed Feb. 10, 2017, http://dept.kent.edu/sociology/lewis/lewihen.htm.
143. Lewis and Hensley, "The May 4 Shootings at Kent State."
144. Lewis and Hensley, "The May 4 Shootings at Kent State."
145. Lewis and Hensley, "The May 4 Shootings at Kent State."
146. Lewis and Hensley, "The May 4 Shootings at Kent State."
147. De Benedetti and Chatfield, *American Ordeal*, 280–281.
148. De Benedetti and Chatfield, *American Ordeal*, 280.
149. De Benedetti and Chatfield, *American Ordeal*, 280.
150. De Benedetti and Chatfield, *American Ordeal*, 281–282.
151. De Benedetti and Chatfield, *American Ordeal*, 283.
152. De Benedetti and Chatfield, *American Ordeal*, 283.
153. De Benedetti and Chatfield, *American Ordeal*, 286.
154. De Benedetti and Chatfield, *American Ordeal*, 288.
155. Gallup Poll, May 1970, last accessed Feb. 10, 2017, http://www.digitalhistory.uh.edu/learning_history/vietnam/vietnam_pubopinion.cfm. In May 1970, a post–Kent State poll showed that only 36 percent of those polled still thought the Vietnam intervention was no mistake.
156. De Benedetti and Chatfield, *American Ordeal*, 291.
157. 50 U.S.C. App. § 462(b)(3) (6) (1965), 32 C.F.R. § 1617.1 (1962) required all men who were registered for the draft to keep their draft cards in their personal possession at all times.
158. *O'Brien v. United States*, 376 F.2d 538 (1st Cir. 1967).
159. *O'Brien v. United States*, 376 F.2d 540.
160. *O'Brien v. United States*, 376 F.2d 541. The court held that O'Brien was properly convicted of knowing non-possession of his draft card under 50 U.S.C. App § 462(b)(6) as a lesser included offense.
161. *United States v. O'Brien*, 391 U.S. 375 (1968).
162. *United States v. O'Brien*, 391 U.S. 376.
163. *United States v. O'Brien*, 391 U.S. 376–377, 378–379, 381.
164. *United States v. O'Brien*, 391 U.S. 379–380.
165. *United States v. O'Brien*, 391 U.S. 381.
166. *United States v. O'Brien*, 391 U.S. 383.
167. *Gutknecht v. United States*, 396 U.S. 295 (1970).
168. See First Amendment Schools, *Tinker v. DesMoines School Dist*, 393 U.S. 503 (1969), last accessed Feb. 19, 2017, http://www.firstamendmentschools.org/freedom/case.aspx?id=404.
169. *Tinker v. Des Moines Independent School District*, 258 F. Supp. 971 (D. Iowa 1966).
170. Biography of Dr. Benjamin Spock, *Encyclopedia of World Biography*, last accessed Feb. 19, 2017, http://www.notablebiographies.com/Sc-St/Spock-Benjamin.html.

171. See Jessica Mitford, *The Trial of Dr. Spock, the Rev. William Sloane Coffin, Jr., Michael Ferber, Mitchell Goodman, and Marcus Raskin* (New York: Knopf, 1969), for a detailed account of the Spock trial.

172. Profile of Dr. Benjamin Spock, last accessed Feb. 10, 2017, http://www.pbs.org/opb/thesixties/topics/war/newsmakers_3.html.

173. "A Call to Resist Illegitimate Authority," last accessed Feb. 10, 2017, http://content.wisconsinhistory.org/cdm/ref/collection/p15932coll8/id/55255. Spock and the other defendants then went on to participate in a draft card burning at the Arlington Street Church in Boston.

174. 50 App. U.S.C. § 462(a) (1967). The statute made it unlawful to conspire to "counsel, aid and abet diverse Selective Service registrants to . . . neglect, fail, refuse and evade service in the armed forces of the United States and all other duties required of registrants under the Universal Military Training and Service Act . . . and the rules, regulations and directions duly made pursuant to said Act . . . to . . . fail and refuse to have in their personal possession at all times their registration certificates [and] . . . valid notices of classification 3 [and conspire to] . . . unlawfully, willfully and knowingly hinder and interfere, by any means, with the administration of the Universal Military Training and Service Act."

175. *United States v. Spock*, 416 F.2d 165, 168–169 (1st Cir. 1969).

176. *United States v. Spock*, 416 F.2d 183.

177. *United States v. Spock*, 416 F.2d 170.

178. *United States v. Spock*, 416 F.2d 171–172.

179. *United States v. Spock*, 416 F.2d 171.

180. *United States v. Spock*, 416 F.2d 172. The court did not define *bifarious* but described it as activities that were in part lawful and in part unlawful.

181. *United States v. Scales*, 367 U.S. 203, 234 (1961). Scales was convicted under the Smith Act of knowing membership in the Communist Party of the United States. He challenged his conviction on the grounds that the Smith Act made membership in an organization a crime, which impinged on the free association clause of the First Amendment. The court affirmed Scales's conviction and in so doing set up the test for balancing First Amendment rights versus national security interests.

182. *United States v. Spock*, 416 F.2d 173.

183. *United States v. Spock*, 416 F.2d 179. The court noted that Spock did not attend the Arlington Street Church draft card burning and was peripherally involved in the Washington anti-draft protest march. The court noted that Rev. Coffin and Goodman had planned the demonstration. The court also stated that Ferber, who did not attend the Washington protest and only signed the call, was also not guilty by reason of failure of proof of specific intent.

184. *United States v. Spock*, 416 F.2d 173. The court noted that co-conspirators' declarations are not evidence of an individual actor's specific intent under the Scales standard.

185. *United States v. Spock*, 416 F.2d 175.

186. *United States v. Spock*, 416 F.2d 175. "The Call had a double aspect: in part it was a denunciation of governmental policy and, in part, it involved a public call to resist the duties imposed by the Act." This explains what the court meant by *bifarious*.

187. "Biography of Philip Berrigan," last accessed Feb. 10, 2017, http://www.americanswhotellthetruth.org/portraits/philip-berrigan.

188. "Biography of Daniel Berrigan, S.J.," last accessed Feb. 10, 2017, http://www.spiritualityandpractice.com/teachers/teachers.php?id'284.

189. The worker-priest movement involved priests living alone as fellow workers in factories and going to work with lay workers, engaging in strikes, boycotts, and other non-violent protests over wages, hours, and working conditions. Eventually, the Vatican imposed strict discipline on the worker-priests, ordering them to stop living alone and avoid any taint of Marxism in their approach to ministering to workers. For a good explanation of this movement, see Dorothy Day, "French Worker Priests and the Little Brothers of de Foucauld," *Catholic Worker*, Mar. 1954, 2–4, last accessed Feb. 10,

2017, http://www.catholicworker.org/dorothyday/daytext.fm?extID'174&earchTerm'jail.

190. "Biography of Daniel Berrigan, S.J."

191. Obit of Philip Berrigan, published in *Nonviolent Activist*, Jan.–Feb. 2003, last accessed Feb. 10, 2016, http://www.warresisters.org/nva/nva0103-5.htm.

192. 18 U.S.C. § 1361 (1967).

193. 50 App. U.S.C. § 462(a).

194. The Catonsville Eight also raised these issues and argued to the Fourth Circuit that they were entitled to a jury nullification instruction. See *United States v. Moylan*, 417 F.2d 1002 (4th Cir. 1969).

195. *United States v. Moylan*, 417 F.2d 1002 (4th Cir. 1969).

196. *United States v. Berrigan*, 417 F.2d 1014 (4th Cir. 1969).

197. *United States v. Berrigan*, 417 F.2d 1015. The court remanded the Baltimore Four case to the district court for resentencing only.

198. *United States v. Moylan*, 417 F.2d 1006.

199. *United States v. Moylan*, 417 F.2d 1009.

200. *United States v. Berrigan; United States v. Moylan*, 397 U.S. 910 (1970).

201. See *Time*, Jan. 25, 1971, cover, last accessed Feb. 10, 2017, http://content.time.com/time/magazine/0,9263,7601710125.00.html. According to the *Eugene, Oregon Register-Guard* of Aug. 30, 1973, 7D, Father Phil and Sr. McAlester were married "in trust and gratitude" in 1969. In 1972, their marriage was solemnized at Danbury Prison.

202. *New York Times*, Jan. 13, 1971, 1. Father Dan Berrigan and Sr. Elizabeth McAlester were also indicted and acquitted.

203. *New York Times*, May 29, 1973, 7.

204. *New York Times*, Sept. 10, 1980, A16.

205. *Commonwealth v. Berrigan*, 501 A.2d 226 (Pa. 1985). See also *Commonwealth v. Berrigan*, 535 A.2d 91 (Pa. Super. 1987) (on remand).

206. *Commonwealth v. Berrigan*, 501 A.2d 226 (Pa. 1985).

207. Obit., *New York Times*, Dec. 8, 2002, 58.

208. *United States v. O'Brien*, 391 U.S. 367 (1968).

209. *United States v. Crosson*, 462 F.2d 96 (9th Cir.), cert. denied 409 U.S. 964 (1972).

210. *United States v. O'Brien*, 491 U.S. 397 (1989). The court tried to distinguish *Crosson* because the statute under which Crosson was prosecuted was not directly aimed at prohibiting flag burning as an act of free speech, that is, not a direct restraint on the First Amendment freedom of speech.

211. *New York Times*, Aug. 25, 1968, 1. A pre-convention poll of delegates showed Humphrey only sixty-three votes short of nomination.

212. Jennifer Rosenberg, "Robert F. Kennedy Assassination," last accessed Feb. 10, 2017, http://history1900s.about.com/od/1960s/a/Robert-Kennedy-Assassination.htm.

213. De Benedetti and Chatfield, *American Ordeal*, 223.

214. De Benedetti and Chatfield, *American Ordeal*, 224.

215. De Benedetti and Chatfield, *American Ordeal*, 226–227.

216. De Benedetti and Chatfield, *American Ordeal*, 227.

217. The chronology of the Chicago Seven Trial is from Douglas Linder, ed., "Chicago Seven Trial," University of Missouri–Kansas City Great Trials Project, last accessed Feb. 10, 2017, http://law2.umkc.edu/faculty/projects/ftrials/Chicago7/CHI7_BIOG.html(hereafter "Chicago Seven Trial Chronology").

218. Chicago Seven Trial Chronology.

219. Chicago Seven Trial Chronology.

220. De Benedetti and Chatfield, *American Ordeal*, 227.

221. Chicago Seven Trial Chronology.

222. De Benedetti and Chatfield, *American Ordeal*, 228.

223. Section 1821 is now compiled as 18 U.S.C. § 2101.

224. Chicago Seven Trial Chronology.

225. Chicago Seven Trial Chronology. See also John Schultz, *The Chicago Conspiracy Trial* (New York: Da Capo Press, 1993; Chicago: University of Chicago Press, 2009), 18, 30–31.
226. Chicago Seven Trial Chronology.
227. Schultz, *The Chicago Conspiracy Trial*, 38.
228. Schultz, *The Chicago Conspiracy Trial*, 42–43.
229. Schultz, *The Chicago Conspiracy Trial*, 46–48.
230. Schultz, *The Chicago Conspiracy Trial*, 56.
231. Schultz, *The Chicago Conspiracy Trial*, 59.
232. Schultz, *The Chicago Conspiracy Trial*, 60.
233. Schultz, *The Chicago Conspiracy Trial*, 62–63.
234. Schultz, *The Chicago Conspiracy Trial*, 68–69.
235. Schultz, *The Chicago Conspiracy Trial*, 74–75.
236. See the testimony of Robert Pierson in Douglas Linder, ed., "Chicago Seven Trial," University of Missouri–Kansas City Great Trials, last accessed Feb. 10, 2017, http://law2.umkc.edu/faculty/projects/ftrials/Chicago7/Pierson.html. According to Pierson, Rubin said "that we have got to create little Chicagos everywhere, that we've got to have riots in every city. I told him that he could count on my being wherever he wanted me to go and to protect him from being arrested by the pigs." This statement if true could have been an inciting statement, if it had been made to a crowd, but Pierson said Rubin spoke to him alone.
237. See the testimony of Det. Riggio in Douglas Linder, ed., "Chicago Seven Trial," University of Missouri–Kansas City Great Trials, last accessed Feb. 10, 2017, http://law2.umkc.edu/faculty/projects/ftrials/Chicago7/riggio.html. Riggio testified that a crowd of demonstrators prevented him from arresting Hayden at the scene of the incident on August 25. A day later, Riggio did arrest Hayden. Riggio was shadowing Rennie Davis at Michigan and Balbo the night of the 28th and repeated profane remarks made by bystanders when he arrested Hayden again. Direct examination did not show any probable cause for the second arrest. Kunstler's cross-examination gave Riggio a chance to accuse Froines of instigating the riot at Michigan and Balbo.
238. See the testimony of Det. Riggio in Linder, "Chicago Seven Trial."
239. See the testimony of Off. William Frapolly in Linder, "Chicago Seven Trial."
240. See the testimony of Irwin Bock in Linder, "Chicago Seven Trial."
241. For a taste of defense evidence, see the testimony of Judy Collins in Linder, "Chicago Seven Trial." Judy Collins was called as a defense witness. She began to sing "Where Have All the Flowers Gone?" before Judge Hoffman managed to stop her. She testified that she had communicated with Abbie Hoffman about coming to Chicago to take part in the demonstrations but decided not to do so when the City of Chicago refused to grant permits to use the parks.
242. *In re Dellinger*, 502 F.2d 815 (7th Cir. 1974). The Seventh Circuit affirmed the conviction. Abbie Hoffman, David Dellinger, and Jerry Rubin were convicted, and the court affirmed their conviction as well.
243. *Mayberry v. Pennsylvania*, 400 U.S. 455 (1971).
244. *In re Dellinger*, 502 F.2d 813, 815 (7th Cir. 1974).
245. *In re Dellinger*, 502 F.2d 815.
246. *In re Dellinger*, 502 F.2d 818–819.
247. *United States v. Dellinger*, 472 F.2d 340 (7th Cir. 1972), cert. denied sub nom. *Dellinger v. United States*, 410 U.S. 970 (1973).
248. *United States v. Dellinger*, 472 F.2d 360.
249. *United States v. Dellinger*, 472 F.2d 364.
250. In *Taylor v. Louisiana*, 419 U.S. 522 (1975), the Supreme Court held that systematic exclusion of women from the juror lists violated the Fourteenth Amendment. States chose to pull jurors from voter lists and from lists of licensed drivers in order to broaden the type of people who would be called for jury duty.
251. *United States v. Dellinger*, 472 F.2d 365–366.
252. *United States v. Dellinger*, 472 F.2d 370.

253. *United States v. Dellinger*, 472 F.2d 372. The government also contended that the defendants waived any objections to voir dire interrogation because they did not submit any questions to Judge Hoffman and did not request inquiry into pre-trial publicity before the trial began. The government also argued that the defendants made no preemptory challenges, thus waiving any objections. The court did not agree.

254. *Irwin v. Doud*, 366 U.S. 717 (1961). The Supreme Court overturned Irwin's conviction, finding that there was clear and convincing evidence that there was "deep and bitter prejudice" against the accused and carefully examined voir dire questions and answers, finding that two-thirds of the prospective jurors had already made their mind up that the defendant was guilty.

255. *United States v. Dellinger*, 472 F.2d 374.

256. *United States v. Dellinger*, 472 F.2d 377.

257. *United States v. Dellinger*, 472 F.2d 380.

258. *United States v. Dellinger*, 472 F.2d 381–382.

259. "Biography of Daniel Ellsberg," last accessed Feb. 10, 2017, http://www.ellsberg.net/bio.

260. *United States v. Washington Post*, 446 F.2d 1327 per curiam (D.C. Cir. 1971); *Near v. Minnesota*, 283 U.S. 697 (1931), held that a Minnesota statute stating that anyone who was engaged in the publication, "regularly and customarily producing, publishing," and so on, "a malicious, scandalous and defamatory newspaper, magazine or other periodical," was guilty of a "nuisance, and authorizes suits, in the name of the State, in which such periodicals may be abated," to be an unlawful prior restraint on free speech and void. Both judges suggested that an injunction in the interest of national security would be an unlawful prior restraint. The D.C. Circuit imposed a stay pending Supreme Court review.

261. *United States v. New York Times*, 444 F.2d 544 (2d Cir. 1971).

262. *New York Times v. United States*, 403 U.S. 713 (1971).

263. *New York Times v. United States*, 403 U.S. 714–724.

264. *New York Times v. United States*, 403 U.S. 725–728.

265. See *New York Times*, Feb. 23, 1973, 196.

266. *New York Times*, May 6, 1973, 44.

267. *Washington Post*, Jan. 15, 2006, C09.

268. *Pittsburgh Post-Gazette*, Oct. 17, 1970, 1, 4.

269. *New York Times*, Nov. 23, 1971, 20. Non-student Jerry Rupe was the first to be tried for interfering with the firefighters trying to put out the ROTC fire.

270. *New York Times*, Nov. 24, 1971, 34. Attorney General Mitchell called the shootings "unnecessary, unwarranted and inexcusable" but refused to order a federal inquiry into the shootings.

271. *New York Times*, Aug. 4, 1973, 57.

272. *New York Times*, Mar. 30, 1974, 65. See also *New York Times*, Nov. 14, 1973, 11.

273. *New York Times*, Nov. 9, 1974, 1.

274. *Krause v. Rhodes*, 471 F.2d 430, 433 (6th Cir. 1972). Kent State University president White was also a named defendant. The pleadings alleged that he was reckless, willful, and wanton in failing to take action to control the guardsmen on the Kent State campus.

275. *Krause v. Rhodes*, 471 F.2d 433. The conspirators were also alleged to have committed intentional torts against the victims. The conspirators were also alleged to have been negligent insofar as the guardsmen were not properly trained for riot control techniques, and additionally, the complaint alleged that the conspirators negligently supplied the guardsmen with live ammunition.

276. *Krause v. Rhodes*, 471 F.2d 455.

277. *Krause v. Rhodes*, 471 F.2d 450–451. The Eleventh Amendment states, "The Judicial power of the United States shall not be construed to extend to any suit in law or equity, commenced or prosecuted against one of the United States by Citizens of another State, or by Citizens or Subjects of any Foreign State."

278. *Krause v. Rhodes*, 471 F.2d 430 (6th Cir. 1972).

279. *Scheuer v. Rhodes*, 416 U.S. 232, 234 (1974).
280. *Scheuer v. Rhodes*, 416 U.S. 235.
281. *Scheuer v. Rhodes*, 416 U.S. 235.
282. *Scheuer v. Rhodes*, 416 U.S. 237.
283. *Ex parte Young*, 209 U.S. 123 (1908). Young was an appeal from denial of a habeas corpus application by Minnesota attorney general Young, who refused to obey a court order to cease enforcing Minnesota's lower railroad fees against the Northern Pacific R.R. The Northern Pacific and other carriers filed suit in U.S. District Court to enjoin enforcement of the state fee charges, alleging that the state fee structure deprived them of property without due process of law. Young defended on the ground that he was immune from suit and the State of Minnesota could not be sued because the Eleventh Amendment barred a suit against the state by corporate citizens of other states in federal court. The Supreme Court decided that Young and the State of Minnesota were alleged to be depriving corporate citizens of their property without due process of law. Therefore, Young was a state official acting under color of law to deprive a U.S. citizen of property without due process of law, not immune from suit under the Eleventh Amendment.
284. *Scheuer v. Rhodes*, 416 U.S. 237.
285. *Scheuer v. Rhodes*, 416 U.S. 241.
286. *Scheuer v. Rhodes*, 416 U.S. 242–243.
287. *Sterling v. Constantine*, 278 U.S. 378 (1932).
288. *Sterling v. Constantine*, 278 U.S. 392–393.
289. *Sterling v. Constantine*, 278 U.S. 404.
290. *New York Times*, Aug. 28, 1975, 69.
291. *New York Times*, Sept. 13, 1977, 16.
292. *New York Times*, Sept. 13, 1977, 16.

SEVEN

The War on Terrorism and Suspension of Civil Liberties

> "I'm the commander—see, I don't need to explain—I do not need to explain why I say things. That's the interesting thing about being president."
> —President George W. Bush, as quoted in Bob Woodward's *Bush at War*

> "If fine speech-making, appeals to reason, or pleas for compassion had the power to move them, the terrorists would long ago have abandoned the field."
> —Vice President Richard Cheney

"Terrorism," according to the Merriam-Webster online dictionary, is "the use of violent acts to frighten the people in an area as a way of trying to achieve a political goal."[1] The *Encyclopedia Britannica* describes "terrorism" as

> the use or threat of violence and seeks to create fear, not just within the direct victims but among a wide audience. The degree to which it relies on fear distinguishes terrorism from both conventional and guerrilla warfare. . . . Terrorism proper is thus the systematic use of violence to generate fear, and thereby to achieve political goals, when direct military victory is not possible.[2]

HISTORY OF TERRORISM IN THE UNITED STATES

U.S. citizens, United States corporations, and United States governmental institutions have been attacked by terrorists for more than one hundred years prior to the destruction of the World Trade Center. A group of Tennessee Confederate veterans formed a social club called the Ku Klux

Klan shortly after the end of the Civil War in 1866. The Klansmen dressed up in hooded robes and conducted rides through the countryside. The riders noticed that African Americans were frightened by the procession of hooded horsemen. Politics in the newly repatriated southern states was controlled by an alliance between northern Republican politicians who went south to take advantage of the general disenfranchisement of all ex-Confederate soldiers and newly franchised African American freedmen. The Klan spread to most southern states and quickly evolved into organized suppression of newly franchised African American freedmen, enforced by hooded night riders burning the homes and barns of African Americans and occasional lynchings and murder of African Americans and white carpetbagger politicians. Congress launched an investigation into the antics of the Klan in the late 1860s, resulting in the passage of a civil rights statute in 1871 that made a felony punishable by a fine of up to $5,000 and imprisonment from six months to six years out of going about in hoods on the public highway and causing disorder and mayhem.[3]

The South Carolina Reconstruction government prosecuted hundreds of alleged Klansmen under the act.[4] The writ of habeas corpus was suspended in nine South Carolina counties by the United States.[5] Similar prosecutions occurred in Alabama, Mississippi, and Tennessee, curtailing Klan operations by the mid-1870s. The Hayes-Tilden compromise of 1876 ended Reconstruction, and federal enforcement of anti-Klan laws ceased.[6]

In 1882, anarchist Johann Most, an exponent of using assassinations and bombings to accomplish the destruction of the state, became the first anarchist terrorist in the United States.[7] Most helped to organize an anarchist association, the International Working Peoples Association, which had about six thousand members nationwide. The tiny group of anarchists became infamous after the Haymarket bombing in Chicago in 1886. A rally in support of the striking employees of the McCormick Reaper Company was called for May 2, 1886, in Chicago's Haymarket. The rally was the joint effort of the Knights of Labor and local anarchists. The rally was breaking up when a phalanx of Chicago police officers descended on the Haymarket and ordered the crowd to disperse. Someone threw a dynamite bomb, and the police retaliated by firing into the crowd. Some of the crowd returned fire. Eight anarchists were arrested, prosecuted, and convicted of the murder of the police officers.[8] Emma Goldman, a twenty-year-old Russian Jewish immigrant, joined Johann Most in New York City in 1889. In 1892, Goldman and her boyfriend, Alexander Berkman, journeyed from Worcester, Massachusetts, to Pittsburgh during the Carnegie Steel Homestead Steel Works strike. Henry Clay Frick managed the Homestead Works. Goldman and Berkman plotted to kill Frick as an incentive to destruction of the capitalist state. Berkman went to Frick's office alone, armed with a revolver, on July 22, 1892.

Berkman fired at the industrialist three times, wounding him once. Carnegie Steel security men subdued Berkman and packed him off to jail.[9] Berkman was convicted of assault and carrying a concealed weapon and sentenced to twenty years' imprisonment.[10] Emma Goldman was convicted of inciting a riot in 1893 after making a fiery speech during the Panic of 1893 urging the crowd to demand that the rich people in New York City give the starving unemployed workers and their families work or bread.[11] Goldman and Berkman were deported to the USSR shortly after the end of World War I.[12]

In 1901, Leon Czolgosz, a confirmed anarchist, attended the Pan-American Exposition in Buffalo, New York. President William McKinley was scheduled to address the crowd. Prior to his speech, he was engaged in shaking hands with well-wishers when Czolgosz approached him, a handkerchief covering his pistol. Czolgosz got off one shot that struck the president in the chest. McKinley, a Civil War veteran, remained standing until the police took Czolgosz into custody. He was taken to a local resident's house in Buffalo. McKinley died on September 14, 1901. Czolgosz was indicted and tried for murder within weeks of the president's death. Czolgosz had signed a confession admitting his guilt and claiming that McKinley deserved to die due to the vast inequality of wealth and power in the United States.[13]

Anarchists were to be denied entry to the United States based on political affiliation.[14] President Theodore Roosevelt addressed Congress calling for restrictions on freedom of speech by anarchists and characterizing anarchism as "high treason."[15] Congress established a special classification for dealing with anarchist immigrants that was neither criminal nor civil in nature. States adopted criminal syndicalism acts that were aimed at suppressing organized labor and by implication suppressing anarchists.[16]

William "Big Bill" Haywood, a Western Federation of Miners (WFM) labor organizer,[17] was one of the organizers of the 1899 Coeur d'Alene strike against the Bunker Hill Mine that featured a trainload of dynamite used to blow up the Bunker Hill Mine's concentrator.[18] Idaho governor Frank Steunenberg called for assistance from the U.S. Army to put down the strikers. Haywood issued a manifesto denouncing the use of soldiers to put down strikers.[19]

Someone planted a bomb at the front gate of former governor Steunenberg's home that blew off both his legs on December 30, 1905. Haywood, who had moved to Denver in 1900 to become the secretary of the WFM, was arrested and spirited away to Idaho for trial. WFM member Canadian Albert Horsley, who used the pseudonym Harry Orchard, confessed to planting the bomb at Steunenberg's front gate. Orchard described how he had been employed as a bomber by Haywood and the others from 1899 to 1905, committing grisly terror attacks on anti-union men. His confession implicated Haywood and two other WFM officers, President Charles Moyer and organizer George Pettibone.[20]

Haywood retained Clarence Darrow as his attorney, who persuaded the jury that even if Haywood and the others were complicit in Orchard's attack on Governor Steunenberg, their cause was just. The jury acquitted all three men.[21] Harry Orchard was given a life sentence. He died on April 13, 1954, in the Idaho State Penitentiary.[22]

In October 1910, twenty-one *Los Angeles Times* employees died as a result of a bomb set off at the rear of the building that ignited a flash fire. Two more unexploded dynamite bombs were found at the home of *Times* publisher Harrison Gray Otis and the home of Felix Zeehandelaar, president of the Los Angeles Merchants and Manufacturers Association. Private detective William J. Burns identified the bombers as John J. and Frank McNamara, members of the International Association of Bridge and Structural Iron Workers union. The McNamara brothers were arrested and brought back to Los Angeles to be tried for murder. Big Bill Haywood organized a crusade to free the McNamara brothers. Clarence Darrow volunteered his services to defend the McNamaras. The crusade fell apart when the McNamara brothers signed confessions that they were responsible for the *Times* bombing.[23]

In June 1919, the homes of prominent men in seven East Coast cities were bombed by unknown terrorists who left behind pink flyers stating that all men of power would be the next to die in a bombing. A night watchman for Judge Charles Nott was killed. Attorney General A. Mitchell Palmer's house was one of the seven targets.[24]

On September 16, 1920, a dump cart filled with dynamite exploded in front of J. P. Morgan & Company's Wall Street offices in New York City. Thirty-eight people were killed and 143 were injured. The Secret Service suspected Italian anarchists. William J. Burns, using an undercover operative, blamed the bombing on the Soviet Union.[25] No one was arrested or indicted for the bombing.

The resurgent Ku Klux Klan engaged in whippings, lynchings, and shootings directed against Jews, Catholics, and African Americans from 1915 through the mid-1920s. For a short while in 1921–1922, the Klan took over the state government in Oregon.[26] Klansmen were not prosecuted for these crimes, even after the Klan's influence declined.

In 1951, unknown terrorists in Florida committed a series of bombings and shootings, killing African Americans and destroying Jewish synagogues and Catholic churches.[27] The perpetrators of these attacks were never apprehended, and no one was charged with the deaths caused by bombs and shootings in central Florida.

Bombings and arson directed against on-campus ROTC buildings were part of the anti-war movement from 1965 through the early 1970s. Anti-war radicals used bombings to make a political statement in New York City in the period 1968–1970. The leading terrorists were Jane Alpert and Sam Melville, responsible for bombing the Marine Midland Bank, injuring twenty employees. Alpert and Melville were arrested. Alpert jumped bail and eluded capture for decades, finally surfacing in 1981 publishing her "tell-all" memoir admitting her complicity in a dozen bombings. Melville was tried and convicted and died during the 1971 Attica prison riot.[28]

Croatian terrorists hijacked a TWA airliner bound for Chicago from New York on September 10, 1976. The hijackers ordered the crew to fly the plane to Montreal, then to Gander, Newfoundland, after releasing some of the passengers. Meanwhile the New York Police Department followed a lead to Grand Central Station where the terrorists had planted a bomb in a locker. The bomb exploded while the police were defusing it, killing one police officer. The commandeered aircraft took off from Gander and landed in Paris. The terrorists demanded that a Croatian manifesto demanding independence from Yugoslavia be printed in English-language newspapers in Europe and in four United States dailies. The terrorists freed the remaining passengers and surrendered to French police. They were returned to New York and were tried and convicted in federal court for air piracy and murder.[29]

In 1984, the Rajneeshee movement, a Buddhist splinter sect, infected food at ten restaurants in The Dalles, Oregon, with salmonella bacteria. Seven hundred fifty-one people became ill, including county officers the movement hoped to replace with people sympathetic to their movement. No one was prosecuted for this attack, and federal investigators played down the incident due to fear about copycat episodes.[30]

On March 3, 1993, Ramzi Yousef drove a Ryder rental van filled with explosives into the World Trade Center garage. Yousef detonated the van, which destroyed a portion of the parking garage, killing six people and injuring more than one thousand. Yousef was acting on behalf of Sheikh Abdel-Rahman, a New Jersey Muslim imam who ordered the attack. The project was paid for with funds sent from abroad by Al Qaida member Khalid Sheikh Mohammed

. Yousef and his co-conspirators, including Sheikh Abdel-Rahman, were tried and convicted of murder and conspiracy.[31]

On April 19, 1995, Gulf War veteran Timothy McVeigh, member of a Michigan survivalist militia, parked a Ryder rental truck loaded with ammonium nitrate and diesel fuel in front of the Alfred P. Murrah Federal Building in Oklahoma City, Oklahoma, next to the day-care center. McVeigh lit two time fuses and walked away. The truck exploded at 9:02 a.m. The blast destroyed one-third of the Murrah building, killing 168 men, women, and children and injuring several hundred.

The FBI traced the Ryder truck to a rental agency in Junction City, Kansas. The employees gave the FBI a composite picture of the man who rented the truck. The composite was shown to the Oklahoma State Police, who identified the composite as McVeigh, who had been stopped by a trooper ninety minutes after the blast for speeding. McVeigh was arrested for carrying a concealed weapon. McVeigh was turned over to federal authorities.[32] The FBI discovered that Terry Nichols, another survivalist militia member, helped McVeigh build the bomb.[33] Michael Fortier was aware of the bomb plot but did not contact the police or the FBI prior to the blast.[34] All three were indicted and tried for murder and conspiracy in the U.S. District Court for the District of Colorado. McVeigh was sentenced to die under the Federal Death Penalty Act.[35] His accomplice Terry Nichols received a life sentence.

September 11, 2001

On September 11, 2001, at 8:47 a.m., an airliner loaded with fuel and passengers crashed into the south tower of the World Trade Center in New York.[36] Thirty minutes later, another airliner struck the north tower.[37] At the same time, a third airliner crashed into the west end of the Pentagon in Washington, D.C.,[38] and a fourth airliner crashed in a wooded section of western Pennsylvania.[39] The airliner attacks killed 2,997 people in the four airliners and on the ground, not counting the nineteen Al Qaida operatives aboard the four flights. All four airliners had been taken over by suicidal terrorists with instructions to destroy their targets and take the lives of U.S. nationals and anyone else who happened to be a passenger in the doomed aircraft or in the buildings struck on the ground. Al Qaida was originated by Osama Bin Laden, a Saudi heir to a multi-million-dollar fortune, and Ayman al-Zawahiri, an Egyptian physician. Both men were volunteer participants in the Afghanistani uprising against the Soviet-installed Communist government of Afghanistan in the 1980s. Both men followed the teachings of Egyptian Muslim thinker Sayyid Qutb, executed in 1966 by the Egyptian government. Qutb taught that the world was infected by barbarism, licentiousness, and unbelief, called *jahiliyya*. No one could remain neutral between *jahiliyya* and Islam. A struggle between Islam in and of God and *jahiliyya* was inevitable. All Muslims were called to take up arms in defense of Islam and against *jahiliyya*.[40] In 1992, Bin Laden and al-Zawahiri issued a statement interpreting the Koran ("fatwa") calling for a holy war ("jihad") against Western nations that occupied Islamic territory. A 1996 fatwa issued by Bin Laden singled out the United States for special vengeance.[41]

Al Qaida issued a fatwa in February 1998 asserting that the United States had declared war against Allah and his messengers, asserting that it was the duty of every Muslim throughout the word to murder U.S. citizens. In May 1998, ABC-TV interviewed Bin Laden. He elaborated on his fatwa, explaining that it was better to take U.S. lives than to kill other infidels. He said, "We believe that the worst thieves in the world today and the worst terrorists are Americans. Nothing could stop you except perhaps retaliation in kind. We do not have to differentiate between military or civilian. As far as we are concerned, they are all targets."[42]

Al Qaida attacks on U.S. installations included a December 1992 hotel bombing in Aden, shooting down two U.S. Blackhawk helicopters in Somalia in 1993; a car bomb explosion at a joint Saudi-U.S. training base in November 1995; and the truck bombing of Khobar Towers in Saudi Arabia in June 1996.[43] The 1993 World Trade Center bombing was directed by the blind Sheikh Abdel-Rahman, who was ordered to blow up the building by Al Qaida operative Khalid Sheikh Mohammed.[44] In 1998, the U.S. embassies in Nairobi, Kenya, and Tanzania were heavily damaged by car bombs that took hundreds of lives.[45] In 2000, the USS *Cole*, at anchor in a Yemeni harbor, was attacked by suicide bombers in a small boat, killing seventeen navy men and women.[46]

On September 11, President George W. Bush responded to the Al Qaida attacks by invoking the war power to declare a state of national emergency. The Bush administration sought congressional approval for a retaliatory attack on Afghanistan, the Taliban state where Al Qaida bases were located. Congress adopted a resolution authorizing the president "to use all necessary and appropriate force against those nations, organizations, or persons he determined planned, authorized, committed or aided the terrorist attacks that occurred on September 11, 2001."[47] This was an unlimited authorization to President Bush to use military forces against Al Qaida, the Taliban government of Afghanistan, and entities and individuals that provided funds to support Al Qaida.

THE PROTECTIONIST STATE

Congressional Angst over Presidential Assertions of Inherent Power to Conduct Combat Operations

Alan Dershowitz's provocative essay on United States objectives and strategies in the post-9/11 environment suggested that since September 11, 2001, the United States has shifted its paradigm from a reactive state (i.e., a state that captures criminals, tries, and punishes them after a crime has been committed) to a protective state that attempts to identify potentially hostile criminals engaged in terrorism before any overt terroristic act has been committed, detain the criminals, and treat them as a special class of offenders, distinct from common criminals. Dershowitz warned his readers that the shift to protectionism means jettisoning some very important rights of U.S. citizens and resident aliens (i.e., grand jury indictment, trial by jury, the presumption of innocence, and the principle that an alleged offender must be proven guilty of the offense charged beyond a reasonable doubt).[48]

Figure 7.1. President George W. Bush (White House).

The change began in the 1970s during the Nixon administration. Congressman Clement Zablocki's special House Foreign Affairs Subcommittee investigated the unilateral actions of Presidents Johnson and Nixon during the Vietnam War. The Tonkin Gulf Resolution concurring in President Johnson's use of force against North Vietnam had been passed on information furnished by Secretary of State Rusk and Secretary of Defense McNamara that later turned out to be false. Both houses of Congress passed the resolution with little examination of the underlying facts, accepting the administration's story as wholly true.[49] In April 1965, President Johnson ordered U.S. Marines and army paratroopers from the 82nd Airborne Division to land in the Dominican Republic, ostensibly to protect the lives and property of U.S. citizens, later exposed as a Johnson administration counter-coup to prevent a Socialist regime favorably inclined toward Fidel Castro's Cuba from seizing control of the government in the Dominican Republic. President Johnson acted without congressional assent or the authorization of the Organization of American States.[50] The Organization of American States belatedly acquiesced in the invasion of the Dominican Republic in late April, forming an OAS joint military command to relieve the U.S. Marines and cooperate with U.S. Army commander Lt. Gen. Bruce Palmer to control the city of Santo Domingo and broker a cease-fire and the installation of a coalition government.[51]

Senator William Fulbright initiated a Senate Foreign Affairs Committee investigation into the conduct of the White House relating to the Dominican crisis. The committee took up the Vietnam conflict in 1966, issuing a report that exposed some of the lies told to Congress in 1964 to obtain the Tonkin Gulf Resolution.[52] The Johnson administration's apologists asserted that the president had undisclosed, inherent power to commit U.S. armed forces to military action without a declaration of war or even a joint congressional resolution.[53] The doctrine of inherent power to wage armed conflict looked to Article II, § 2, clause 1, of the Constitution, which states, "The President shall be the Commander in Chief of the Army and Navy of the United States and the Militia of the several States, when called into the actual service of the United States." This argument surfaced over the next forty years to justify unilateral action by the executive branch of the government with respect to initiating military action in such places as Grenada and Somalia and in conducting espionage programs against U.S. and non-U.S. people and entities.

The Fulbright Committee's investigation led to proposals for a limiting resolution that defined the authority of the president to commit the United States to armed conflict. Senator Richard Russell's Resolution 151, later modified into Senate Resolution 85, was debated from 1967 to 1969. The Nixon administration claimed that the terms of the resolution were not binding on the executive branch.[54] The Senate action encouraged the House Foreign Affairs Committee chair, Rep. Clement Zablocki, to start an investigation into executive excesses in 1970. The Nixon administration had launched an invasion of Cambodia without seeking congressional approval. Mississippi senator John Stennis was briefed by the White House and sworn not to reveal the upcoming invasion.[55] President

Nixon carefully stated in his television address to the nation that the president had the inherent power to order the invasion of Cambodia.[56]

Congress reacted by repealing the Tonkin Gulf Resolution in 1970.[57] The House examined academicians' proposals for a standing resolution requiring the executive branch to report to Congress on its use of military force. The House Foreign Affairs Committee reviewed several proposed resolutions calling for some limits on executive power to commit U.S. forces to military operations during 1970–1973.[58]

Eventually the House and Senate agreed on a single joint resolution that was passed in October 1973.[59] President Nixon vetoed the resolution, claiming that it was an unconstitutional attempt to limit his Article II presidential power to conduct wars.[60] Congress overrode the veto, and the War Powers Resolution became law on November 7, 1973.[61] According to the joint report, the War Powers Resolution barred the unauthorized use of armed forces after sixty days elapsed from the employment of armed force, unless Congress passed a concurrent resolution authorizing the continued use or terminating the use of military force.[62]

The War Powers Resolution

The War Powers Resolution consists of six distinct parts: the first explains congressional concern with an overreaching White House. Section 1541 declares that the purpose of the resolution is "to fulfill the intent of the framers of the Constitution of the United States and ensure that the collective judgment of both the Congress and the President will apply to the introduction of United States Armed Forces into hostilities."[63] Section 1542 instructs the president that "the President in every possible instance shall consult with Congress" before employing U.S. armed forces in any form of hostilities.[64] Section 1543 obligates the president to file a report with Congress within forty-eight hours after employing U.S. armed forces in combat, or in preparation for hostilities if Congress has not passed a declaration of war.[65]

Section 1544 instructs the president that the president must terminate the use of U.S. armed forces within sixty days after filing the report required by section 1543 unless Congress either declares war, passes a resolution authorizing the use of armed forces, or grants a sixty-day extension for the hostilities.[66] Sections 1545, 1546, and 1546a provide for expedited review of any concurrent resolution relating to hostilities involving U.S. armed forces.[67] Section 1547 states that treaty obligations do not necessarily support the use of U.S. military forces. Specific legislative authority for the use of U.S. military forces must accompany the ratification of any treaty calling for the use of U.S. military forces.[68] Otherwise the employment of U.S. forces must follow sections 1541 through 1545. Section 1548 is a severability clause.

The War Powers Resolution is a challenge to the presidents who see their role of commander in chief under Article II, § 2, of the Constitution as a plenary grant of the inherent power of the sovereign to wage war.[69] Some presidents have argued that their power to wage war is not limited by the provisions of Article I that authorize Congress to declare war, call up the militia, and fund military operations.[70] The division of responsibility for inserting U.S. armed forces into foreign conflicts produced the wrangling between President George W. Bush and Congress over the manner in which President Bush conducted military operations in Afghanistan and Iraq.

Presidential compliance with the War Powers Resolution has been inconsistent. President Ford did not consult with Congress when U.S. military personnel were reinjected into Vietnam during the evacuation of Da Nang.[71] Congress was not consulted on the evacuation of U.S. personnel from Nom Phen, Cambodia.[72] He did consult with Congress over the evacuation of U.S. and Vietnamese personnel from the U.S. embassy in Saigon in May 1975.[73] President Ford also sent letters to the Speaker of the House and president pro tem of the Senate after the *Mayaguez* crisis in 1974. He also conducted briefings for key members of Congress.[74]

President Carter did not treat the Zaire rescue mission or the failed attempt to free the seventy-nine hostages held in Iran in 1979 as subject to the War Powers Resolution, characterizing both as non-combat operations.[75] President Reagan increased the number of military advisors in El Salvador early in his administration without first consulting Congress.[76] His deputy secretary of defense, Frank Carlucci, assured Congress that "every possible precaution has been taken, and will continue to be taken, to ensure that U.S. military personnel will not become engaged in, or be exposed to, the hostilities. . . . The possibility that U.S. military personnel would become engaged or endangered by the hostilities is remote."[77]

In 1983, Congress invoked the War Powers Resolution in the Multinational Force in Lebanon Resolution (P.L. 98-119), which authorized the marines to remain in Lebanon for eighteen months.[78] In 1990, President George H. W. Bush invoked the War Powers Resolution by reporting to Congress on the Iraqi seizure of Kuwait. Congress passed P.L. 102-1, authorizing the use of U.S. armed forces concerning the Iraqi aggression against Kuwait. The resolution stated that it authorized the president to use force against Iraq within the meaning of the War Powers Resolution.[79] The House invoked the War Powers Resolution during the Somalia crises on November 9, 1993. The House voted to order the withdrawal of U.S. forces from Somalia by March 31, 1994.[80] Congress passed P.L. 107-243 in October 2002 authorizing the use of military force against Iraq. The resolution has not been repealed.

The Foreign Intelligence Surveillance Act of 1978

In 1977, Senator Edward Kennedy introduced legislation that would allow the United States to detect terrorists and their accomplices proactively, before the terrorists had engaged in any overt criminal acts. The Foreign Intelligence Surveillance Act[81] was a response to the perceived excesses of J. Edgar Hoover's COINTEL surveillance programs exposed by the raid on the Media, Pennsylvania, FBI office. It was also a reaction to the Nixon administration's use of surveillance measures without judicial approval. Kennedy's co-sponsors included Senators Birch Bayh, James O. Eastland, Jake Garn, Walter Huddleston, Daniel Inouye, Charles Mathias, John L. McClellan, Gaylord Nelson, and Strom Thurmond. The bill passed both houses and was signed by President Carter in 1978.

The Foreign Intelligence Surveillance Act (FISA) was amended in 1996 and again by the PATRIOT Act in 2002. It is codified as 50 U.S.C., ch.36. In its current form, FISA contains four major subchapters relating to electronic surveillance programs,[82] search and seizure for intelligence purposes,[83] pen register and trap and trace surveillance,[84] followed by access to business records held by third parties.[85] The fourth subchapter relates to targeting and penalties.[86]

Subchapter 1 is devoted to substance and procedure for conducting electronic surveillance. Section 1801 contains key definitions that also contain substantive legal principles. The act permits electronic surveillance directed against "United States persons," defined as "a citizen, an alien lawfully admitted for permanent residence, an unincorporated association a substantial number of members of which are citizens of the United States . . . or a corporation which is incorporated in the United States."[87] Any human being, state, or entity that does not fit the definition of "United States person" is a "non–United States person" subject to different treatment under the act than United States persons.

"Foreign power" is defined to include any non-U.S. state. It also means "an entity that is openly acknowledged by a foreign government . . . directed and controlled by such foreign government," "a group engaged in international terrorism or activities in preparation therefor," and a foreign-based political organization or entity that engages in "international proliferation of weapons of mass destruction."[88] FISA allows government intelligence agency surveillance conducted against any of the "foreign powers." "Agent of a foreign power" is defined as "any person other than a United States person" who acts on behalf of a foreign power in the United States for a variety of operations, including terrorist activities or the "proliferation of weapons of mass destruction." The term "agent of a foreign power" also includes persons who engage in sabotage or spying. Anyone who aids or abets sabotage, spying, terrorist acts, or proliferation of weapons of mass destruction is also an "agent of a foreign power." This definition cleverly includes United States persons as well as non–United States persons.[89]

Subsection (c) defines "international terrorism" to include violent acts that would be a violation of the criminal laws of the United States that are intended to "intimidate or coerce a civilian population . . . influence the policy of a government by intimidation or coercion" and "affect the conduct of a government by assassination or kidnapping." The acts of international terrorism must occur outside the territorial boundaries of the United States or "transcend national boundaries" in terms of actions or the targets of terrorist acts.[90]

Subsection (e) defines "foreign intelligence information" as an "actual or potential attack or other grave hostile acts of a foreign power or an agent of a foreign power" as well as sabotage and "international terrorism" and proliferation of weapons of mass destruction. The definition also includes "any information concerning a United States person deemed necessary to . . . the national defense or the security of . . . or the conduct of the foreign affairs of the United States."[91]

"Electronic surveillance" is very broadly defined to include any form of electronic communication put out by a United States person operating within the boundaries of the United States "under circumstances in which a person has a reasonable expectation of privacy and a warrant would be required for law enforcement purposes." The definition covers the installation of listening devices as well as wiretaps and any other form of interception, including monitoring Internet service providers.[92]

Subsection (h) uses the definition of "minimization procedures" to describe the duty of the U.S. attorney general to adopt "specific procedures . . . to minimize the acquisition and retention, and prohibit the dissemination, of non-publicly available information" from people who do not consent to be subjected to electronic surveillance. "Minimization" does not exempt information disclosing that the person under surveillance has committed, is committing, or is about to commit a crime, a provision that directly involves an interpretation of the Fourth Amendment's prohibition on unreasonable searches and seizures.[93]

Section 1802 authorizes the attorney general to conduct electronic surveillance for a period of up to one year without court authorization for the purpose of collecting information from communications between or among foreign powers, acquiring technical intelligence, when there is no substantial likelihood that the surveillance program will acquire any communications involving a United States person.[94] The attorney general is authorized to direct that a "communications common carrier" assist the Department of Justice's surveillance activities and furnish technical support to the surveillance program.[95] The attorney general is required to certify that the attorney general has instituted appropriate minimization procedures and has complied with the minimization procedures in conducting the surveillance operation. The attorney general must report compliance to the House and Senate Select Committees on Intelligence.[96] Subsection (b) empowers the president and the attorney general to apply to the Federal Intelligence Surveillance Court for a court order to continue surveillance.[97]

Section 1803 establishes a special secret court for purposes of reviewing electronic surveillance programs carried out under section 1803 and other operative sections of the act. The eleven members of the court, U.S. District Court judges from seven of the eleven U.S. circuits, are appointed by the chief justice of the Supreme Court. The special court may hold hearings on applications for warrants authorizing surveillance on motion of the United States or sua sponte.[98] The chief justice also has the authority to designate a panel of three judges from any federal Article III court to act as a secret court of review when an application for a warrant is denied by the special court. The United States may file a petition for writ of certiorari to the U.S. Supreme Court if the reviewing panel rejects the application.[99] The special court may issue orders in aid of its jurisdiction, including stay orders, and adopt procedural rules.[100] Section 1804 sets out the specific requirements for an application for a warrant to conduct intelligence surveillance, requiring the Department of Justice to show that the target of the surveillance is a foreign power or an agent of a foreign power.[101] The special court is empowered to issue ex parte orders authorizing electronic surveillance. A proviso requires a showing that a United States person may not be considered a foreign power or agent of a foreign power solely on the basis of protected First Amendment speech or association.[102] Section 1805(e) provides for emergency employment of electronic devices without court order (in addition to the provisions of section 1802 authorizing surveillance without judicial supervision up to one year) by the attorney general.[103] Subsection (f) permits the attorney general to test surveillance equipment without prior court approval.[104] Subsection (h) bars a civil action against an electronic service provider, landlord, or custodian for violation of the rights of any person who was targeted for electronic surveillance.[105] An electronic surveillance order will contain authorization for use of pen registers and trap and trace devices in addition to authorizing surveillance.[106]

Section 1806 limits disclosure of intelligence recovered by electronic surveillance to intelligence agencies, the attorney general, and law enforcement officers.[107] If the government intends to use evidence disclosed by surveillance in a criminal prosecution or in a civil action, the government must notify the adverse party of intent to use information acquired by FISA electronic intelligence activities prior to trial. The same duty to disclose intent to use FISA electronic intelligence evidence devolves on state prosecutors. Subsection (e) authorizes an adverse party to file a motion to suppress electronic surveillance evidence on two disjunctive grounds: (1) the information was unlawfully acquired or (2) the information was collected not in conformity with any order from the FISA Court or from the attorney general.[108] Any attempt to discover FISA intelligence information or to suppress such evidence raised by motion in the U.S. District Court to which the attorney general has responded that disclosure of the information "would harm the national security of the United States."[109] It generates an ex parte in camera review of the FISA intelligence evidence by the court, which has limited discretion to disclose FISA intelligence evidence only so far as is "necessary to make an accurate determination of the legality of the surveillance."[110] Any emergency electronic intelligence information collected under 50 U.S.C. § 1805(e) that is not justified later by the FISA Court generates a limited privilege to disclose the fact of electronic surveillance being conducted against the party who was targeted.[111]

The attorney general must submit an annual report to the Administrative Office of the United States Court and to the House and Senate Select Committees on Intelligence showing the number of applications for surveillance orders and the total number granted. The congressional report should also show each criminal case in which FISA intelligence information is authorized for use at trial and the number of emergency electronic surveillance operations that the attorney general initiated during the year.[112] Any person who engages in unauthorized electronic surveillance, or discloses electronic surveillance information to anyone other than persons or entities authorized by section 1806, may be subject to a fine of up to $10,000 and imprisonment for not more than five years.[113] A civil right of action for actual damages not less than $1,000 or $100 per diem, punitive damages, and attorney's fees that does not waive U.S. sovereign immunity is established by section 1810 for any person, other than a foreign power or an agent of a foreign power, who has information collected by surveillance wrongfully disclosed by some individual.[114] Section 1811 is an additional emergency allowance of warrantless electronic surveillance for fifteen days' time following a congressional declaration of war.[115] The system established by sections 810 through 1811 are the exclusive means for conducting electronic surveillance.[116]

The second part of the FISA Act that authorizes searches for foreign intelligence purposes is structurally similar to the first: Section 1821 covers definitions, most of which are the same as those of section 1801. Section 1821 authorizes search by the attorney general of premises occupied by a foreign power if "there is no substantial likelihood" that the search involves searching space controlled by a United States person. The attorney general must certify that the search is directed at a foreign power and is compliant with minimization procedures. Each search conducted by the attorney general under section 1821 is reported to Congress and to the Foreign Intelligence Surveillance Court.[117] Section 1821(c) confers jurisdiction on the Foreign Intelligence Surveillance Court to consider the attorney general's application for an order authorizing a search anywhere in the United States.[118] The procedure for an order for physical search is similar to that required for a search warrant under Title 18 U.S.C.: a federal officer makes an ex parte application approved by the attorney general for a search order to a single judge of the Foreign Intelligence Surveillance Court demonstrating probable cause to believe that foreign intelligence information is located at the premises to be searched that cannot be "obtained by normal investigative techniques."[119] The attorney general also may be asked to review applications for search made by the FBI director, the secretary of defense, the director of national intelligence, or the director of the CIA, but the attorney general's review is not a mandatory condition for Foreign Intelligence Surveillance Court approval.[120] A search order may be issued by the single judge if the judge finds that "there is probable cause to believe that (A) the target of the search is a foreign power or an agent of a foreign power . . . (and) the premises or property to be searched is or is about to be owned, used, possessed by, or is in transit to or from an agent of a foreign power or a foreign power."[121] The search order has a ninety-day life, unless the order is issued against a foreign power for up to one year, and if issued against an agent of a foreign power, up to 120 days. The duration of a search may be extended by supplemental application to the single judge.[122] The attorney general may undertake a search in an emergency situation without prior approval by a single judge of the Foreign Intelligence Surveillance Court, provided that the attorney general files an application for search within seven days of authorizing the emergency search.[123]

Information obtained by an emergency search or search by court order is subject to the same limitations as information obtained by electronic surveillance.[124] If the search is carried out against a United States person and the information seized is no longer a matter of national security, the attorney general will notify the United States person of the search and the property seized by the officers making the search.[125] Use of property seized by the government as evidence in a criminal prosecution or civil suit is subject to ex parte review by the court before the property is disclosed to the opposition.[126] The attorney general is required to make a semi-annual report to Congress itemizing the number of applications and orders for search.[127] Civil and criminal penalties for unauthorized searches and unauthorized disclosure of property seized parallel those for unauthorized disclosure of electronic surveillance information.[128]

The third section of the act covers pen registers and trap and trace devices. A pen register is a device that records telephone numbers called from the telephone on which the device is installed. A trap and trace device records the telephone numbers of callers who place a call to the telephone that is under surveillance.[129] This section adopts the definitions portion of section 1801.[130] The attorney general or any attorney designated by the government may apply for an order to the Foreign Intelligence Surveillance Court to attach a pen register and trap and race device in any investigation that does not involve a United States person. A second sentence authorizes installation of these devices on telephones of United States persons if there is a belief that the attorney general needs to protect against "international terrorism or clandestine intelligence activities."[131] The application for a pen register and trap and trace device may be presented to a judge of the Foreign Intelligence Surveillance Court or to a magistrate judge designated by the chief justice. The attorney general's approval is required as part of the application.[132] Judicially ordered installation of pen register and trap and trace devices are for ninety days, with provisions for an additional ninety-day extension. If the federal officer requesting the installation of these devices certifies that "the information likely to be obtained is foreign intelligence information not concerning a United States person," the pen register and trap and trace order may be for a one-year period with possibility of a second year's surveillance by extension.[133] Section 1842 also immunizes communications service providers as well as landlords or custodians from suit for furnishing information to the federal officers conducting the pen register and trap and trace mission. Like the first subchapter, this subchapter contains an emergency provision allowing the attorney general to authorize installation of a pen register and trap and trace device and then apply for an order within seven days of initiating the devices.[134] A companion section authorizes installation for up to fifteen days without a court order when Congress declares war.[135] Disclosure of information obtained by pen register and trap and trace in criminal cases requires the attorney general's advance authorization and notice to the opposition of the existence of these devices.[136] This subchapter contains provisions for a motion to suppress evidence[137] and a requirement of semi-annual reporting to Congress relating to the use of pen registers and trap and trace devices[138] similar to those provisions in subchapter 1. Section 1861 allows the Foreign Intelligence Surveillance Court to permit the FBI to obtain business records from third parties relating to a targeted person or persons.[139] One section also reiterates the items of information to be collected and shared with Congress in the attorney general's semi-annual report.[140]

The final subchapter pertains to procedure before the Foreign Intelligence Surveillance Court for targeting of persons believed to be outside the boundaries of the United States who are not United States persons. This type of surveillance is supposed to be "conducted in a manner consistent with the fourth amendment."[141] Another section recites the chain of appeals from denial of a surveillance order through the Court of Review to the Supreme Court.[142] The procedure is similar to that applicable to domestic electronic surveillance applications and orders. Another section prescribes the procedure for targeting of a United States person located outside the United States for foreign intelligence surveillance. The procedure for targeting a United States person located outside the United

States is practically identical to that of targeting a non–United States person.[143] Joint surveillance activities inside and outside the United States for United States persons has similar procedural requirements.[144] The attorney general is also obligated to inform Congress of surveillance programs targeting non–United States persons and United States persons located outside the boundaries of the United States.[145]

To summarize: Congress delegated extraordinary power to the executive branch to conduct electronic surveillance and to conduct searches affecting United States citizens and resident aliens. Congress established a secret court that has sole jurisdiction to approve the attorney general's applications for an order authorizing surveillance, search and seizure, or installation of a pen register and trap and trace device on telephones. The responsible federal agencies that will conduct surveillance, search and seizure, and installation of pen registers and trap and trace devices include the FBI, the CIA, the NSA, and any other intelligence agency, so long as the stated purpose is to acquire intelligence pertaining to non-U.S. citizens or resident aliens. If a U.S. citizen or a resident alien is deemed "an agent of a foreign power," FISA authorizes acquisition of information from the citizen or alien to be used to protect the people of the United States from terrorism. The effect is to blacklist citizens and resident aliens, as will be shown during the discussion of "no-fly lists" and legal representation of accused terrorists.

FISA permits the attorney general to conduct surveillance without court order in cases of national emergency. It also authorizes the attorney general to collect surveillance information for up to one year so long as the surveillance operation is not likely to involve a U.S. citizen or resident alien. Again, the emergency surveillance operation may involve seizing information from a U.S. citizen or resident alien as an "agent of a foreign power."

National Security Letters

The national security letter permits a federal agency to order the turnover of records involving a targeted individual from that individual's bank, credit card issuers, and library. The business or entity that receives a national security letter cannot notify the individual whose records have been seized. It cannot disclose that it received a national security letter to anyone, including outside counsel retained to protect the entity's rights. No court has sustained a challenge to an NSL as of the date of this chapter.

Although electronic information, searches and seizures, and national security letters to third parties to obtain business records are stated to be used for intelligence purposes, the attorney general has the authority to turn over surveillance to any federal prosecutor to conduct a criminal investigation if the surveillance operation detects criminal activity.

Since the attorney general, relevant federal agencies, and the Federal Intelligence Surveillance Court operate in closed session, U.S. citizens and resident aliens have no practical way to challenge collection of information by the executive branch of government, since the identity of persons targeted for surveillance is classified. Two federal courts have dismissed civil actions filed by parties who alleged that the attorney general had authorized surveillance.[146] Neither plaintiff could prove that they were under FISA surveillance, because the United States asserted the state secret privilege to protect the operations of the surveillance agencies.

SUSPECTED TERRORISTS AND OUTLAWS

FISA and other similar laws established a special class of persons who are not entitled to most of the constitutional safeguards under the Fourth, Fifth, and Sixth Amendments and to protected political speech under the First Amendment. Class members are to be treated as especially dangerous to life and property, warranting suppression of their civil liberties to ward off terrorist attacks on the United States. The common-law antecedent for this process was "outlawing." At common law, a man over the age of fourteen could be put beyond the protection of the law for engaging in heinous crimes. In the 1970s, Congress and the executive branch established FISA, a scheme to invade the privacy of persons classified as potential terrorists (i.e., "outlaws"). The executive branch could conduct electronic surveillance without probable cause under the loose supervision of a secret U.S. court charged with approving and judicially supervising surveillance.

At the same time, Congress revised portions of the immigrant and naturalization laws to classify terrorists as persons who would not be admitted to the United States for any purpose. Congress also reached out to squash organizations that supported terrorist activity. Congress made it a felony for charitable corporations or individuals to provide support for a terrorist organization. Any person who lent material support or advice to an organization that supported terrorism was also committing a felony.

After September 11, 2001, Congress added additional structure to immigration and naturalization laws designed to curb terrorism.[147] Scholars such as Alan Dershowitz lament the change in federal criminal law and procedure from a system that punishes wrongdoers after the fact to one that invades wrongdoers' constitutional rights to stop wrongdoing before it occurs. The proactive approach to curbing terrorism had wide public support post-9/11, so long as the targeted individuals are Muslims.[148]

Vice President Cheney was the lead planner for the anti-terrorism program during the Bush administration. It is not clear if anyone has filled Cheney's shoes since 2009. One of the known components of the plan consists of identifying U.S.-based charitable corporations that may contribute funds to terrorist organizations, known as "material support of terrorism." The second component is the "no-fly list" blocking air travel for anyone identified as an agent of a foreign power. The third component is electronic surveillance of U.S. corporations, citizens, and resident aliens believed to be aiding and abetting terrorist groups, directly or indirectly, using FISA and the "inherent authority of the president" to justify surveillance measures. The fourth prong deals with men captured on the battlefield in Afghanistan and Iraq, as well as men detained as material witnesses within the borders of the United States, including U.S. citizens. The captives were not to be treated as prisoners of war. Rather, the prisoners were to be treated as a special class of individuals who were to be detained in a U.S.-manned facility at Guantanamo Bay, Cuba, or in military prisons in the United States. Members of this special class may also be subject to intensive interrogation by U.S. intelligence agents or be sent to prison facilities in other nations where extraordinary means of interrogation would be employed. Information derived by this prong would be used by intelligence agencies in tracking down Al Qaida terrorist plots and leadership cells. It would also be used as evidence against the captives who were to be tried by a military commission. The executive branch initiated the program without express congressional authorization in 2001. Later, the U.S. Supreme Court and Congress intervened.

Material Support of Terrorism Acts

Title 18 U.S.C. § 2339A provides that "whoever provides material support or resources or conceals or disguises the nature, location, source, or ownership of material support or resources, knowing or intending that they are to be used in preparation for, or in carrying out" terrorist attacks "or in preparation for, or in carrying out, the concealment of an escape from the commission of any such violation, or attempts or conspires to do such an act" commits a crime punishable by imprisonment for up to fifteen years and an unlimited fine.[149] The statute also defined "material support or resources" as "any property, tangible or intangible, or service, including currency or monetary instruments or financial securities, financial services, lodging, training, expert advice or assistance, safe houses, false documentation or identification, communications equipment, facilities, weapons, lethal substances, explosives, personnel (1 or more individuals who may be or include oneself), and transportation, except medicine or religious materials," a definition broad enough to include an attorney who gives legal advice to an individual charged with violating this section.[150] The Department of Justice has conducted a number of prosecutions under this statute since 2001.[151]

Sami Omar al-Hussayen

Since the purpose of the statute was proactive, the Justice Department's zealous prosecutions often resulted in indictments, arrests, and lengthy trials involving innocent people. For instance, University of Idaho graduate student Sami Omar al-Hussayen was indicted for providing material support for terrorists because he volunteered to be a webmaster for the Islamic Assembly of North America.[152] Al-Hussayen was arrested in February 2003 on immigration fraud charges and detained in the Ada County jail under contract with the Bureau of Citizenship and Immigration. FBI agents conducted interrogation of hundreds of University of Idaho students in an effort to identify a terrorist "sleeper cell" at the university without success.[153] After being detained for almost a year, al-Hussayen was indicted for giving material support to a terrorist organization by means of acting as a webmaster for the Islamic Assembly. The government theory was that al-Hussayen was responsible for postings of anti-American, anti-Semitic, and jihadist statements on the website.[154] The government introduced evidence that al-Hussayen's computer was used to broadcast a January 2003 speech by Sheikh Safar al-Hawali full of anti-Semitism and anti-Israeli assertions. The Sheikh did not advocate any immediate terrorist acts against Israel or against Jews.[155] The government's strategy in using this speech was unclear, but it showed that al-Hussayen associated or sympathized with anti-Semitic fanatics.

The government had identified four fatwas posted on the website by Muslim clerics dealing with the issue of suicide as the key pieces of evidence against al-Hussayen.[156] The contents of the fatwas were inadmissible, the trial judge ruled, until the government first established that the documents were connected to al-Hussayen. Al-Hussayen's defense counsel challenged government testimony of this type on the ground that the First Amendment protected utterers of political speech from prosecution for statements that were not intended to incite unlawful acts.[157] The government displayed the fatwas in Arabic, on the theory that none of the jurors understood Arabic. The government also won an important evidentiary fight: introduction of statements by fanatics who were allegedly co-conspirators with al-Hussayen to give material aid and support to terrorist groups.[158] Government expert witness Curtis W. Rose testified that al-Hussayen was involved in numerous online financial transactions. A great proportion of the transactions were charitable donations to Islamic charities.[159] Government expert on terrorism Rita Katz, testifying as a lay witness who was fluent in Arabic, was permitted to translate three of the fatwas into English for the jury.[160] The government's star witness, Khwaja Hasan, told the jury that he left the United States to go to a terrorist training camp because of what he saw on websites. Defense counsel discredited his testimony on cross-examination, getting Hasan to admit that it was the 9/11 attack that prompted him to go to Afghanistan on the advice of a Muslim cleric, Sheikh Ali al-Timimi, who urged Hasan to fight against the United States. Hasan admitted that he would be repaid for his testimony with time off from his eleven-year, three-month conspiracy sentence.[161]

The defendant called one witness, Frank Anderson, a former CIA agent and security consultant, who told the jury that two of the websites linked to al-Hussayen, www.islamway.com, a religious outreach website, and www.alasr.ws, an online magazine, were not terrorist organs. Anderson also testified that the four fatwas that were the basis of the government's case were published "to advance analysis," not to advocate suicide bombing attacks.[162]

The jury found Al-Hussayen "not guilty" on the three terrorism charges and was unable to agree on a verdict on the immigration law violations. Al-Hussayen was under a deportation order and was detained post-trial, and the U.S. Attorney's Office threatened to retry him on the immigration law violations. Al-Hussayen agreed to leave the United States to avoid retrial. He forsook an appeal from the deportation order and rejoined his family in Saudi Arabia.[163]

Al-Hussayen spent sixteen months in detention even though the material support of terrorism case against him was conceptually and factually weak. The University of Idaho campus was disrupted by an FBI strike force invasion of the campus that uncovered no evidence of any secret terrorist cell on campus. The FBI searched al-Hussayen's apartment, seized his computer, and threatened his wife and family with deportation. The FBI's conduct and that of the U.S. Attorney's Office in Boise cannot be explained unless one looks to the policy measures taken by the White House after September 11, 2001. Al-Hussayen was a Saudi national in the United States on a student visa. Foreign nationals lawfully in the United States are entitled to basic constitutional due process, just as if the foreign national were a U.S. citizen.

Abdullah al-Kidd

Abdullah al-Kidd, a native-born African American U.S. citizen and convert to Islam was a running back at the University of Idaho in the 1990s. He received a scholarship from a Saudi Arabian university to study Arabic in 2003. The FBI arrested al-Kidd at Dulles Airport as a material witness in the al-Hussayen prosecution and detained him for sixteen days, transporting Kidd to a series of federal detention centers in Oklahoma, Wyoming, and Idaho.[164] He was released on condition that he surrender his passport, confine his travel to four states, live with his in-laws in Nevada, and report to a federal probation officer on a regular basis. A federal judge returned his passport in June 2004.[165]

No-Fly Lists

The United States established the no-fly list as a control measure to prevent any reoccurrence of a hijacking of an airliner by terrorists. The Bush administration established the FBI-operated Terrorist Screening Center (TSC) shortly after 9/11. That agency maintains records of all persons having any ties to known terrorist groups. This operational unit maintains a consolidated Terrorist Screening Database (TSDB), otherwise known as the Terrorist Watchlist. This list has about one hundred thousand names. The smaller no-fly list contains about twenty thousand listed individuals. The criteria for posting anyone on the no-fly list and the TSA's watchlisting guidance materials are classified documents unavailable to the public. TSC accepts nominations for the no-fly list if there is a "reasonable suspicion that a nominee is a known or suspected terrorist." TSC's standard for finding that reasonable suspicion exists is a finding that "articulable facts which, taken together with rational inferences, reasonably warrant the determination that an individual is known or suspected to be, or has been engaged in conduct constituting, in preparation for, in aid of or related to, terrorism or terrorist activities."[166] TSC supplies the no-fly list to the Department of Homeland Security's Transportation Security Administration (TSA). All TSA stations in all U.S. airports have a copy of this list which it shared with commercial airlines. Ticketing information is checked electronically, and any person who appears on the no-fly list will be denied ticketing and boarding. The theory is that suspected terrorists will be excluded from hijacking a commercial airliner. In 2011, more than twenty thousand individuals were on the list. The government has its own classified "Watchlisting Guidance" for internal law enforcement and intelligence use, and the no-fly list has its own classified minimum substantive derogatory criteria. The United States considers these documents "sensitive" national security matters and will not release them.

The list is not based on a standard of probable cause; it is based on hearsay reports and other information that would probably not be admissible in court. The list has the usual failing of such comprehensive control devices: "false positives," including the faux pas listing of Massachusetts senator Edward F. Kennedy as a person excluded from flying.[167]

The American Civil Liberties Union brought a Freedom of Information Act suit in the Northern District of California in 2004.[168] The two individual plaintiffs and the ACLU argued that the U.S. Department of Justice erroneously denied their FOIA request for information relating to the no-fly list by asserting that the information was exempt from the Freedom of Information Act.[169] The United States asserted that the information sought was protected from disclosure by 49 U.S.C. §§ 114(s) and 40119(b). Section 114(s) commands that the secretary of homeland security develop a plan for transportation security.[170] Section 40119(b) authorized the secretary of transportation to make regulations prohibiting disclosure of information that invaded personal privacy, constituted a trade secret, or was "detrimental to transportation safety."[171] The United States also tried to apply exemptions (6)[172] and (7)[173] to the Freedom of Information Act to exclude no-fly list data (without names) as invasions of privacy rights, but the district court dismissed these contentions because the United States failed to carry the burden of persuasion that disclosure would invade individual privacy rights.[174]

The court concluded that the United States failed to carry the burden of proof that the data sought by the plaintiffs was exempt from disclosure. The court's preliminary review of the voluminous material demonstrates that the government did not come close to meeting its burden and made frivolous claims of exemption. The appropriate remedy is to have defendants review all of the withheld material to determine whether they believe in good faith that the material is in fact exempt and, if defendants contend it is exempt, to provide a detailed affidavit that explains why the particular material is exempt. General statements that the information is sensitive security information are inadequate to satisfy the government's burden. Material that is not exempt shall be promptly disclosed to plaintiffs in response to their FOIA requests.[175]

The court then continued the case to permit the United States to review the material claimed to be exempt from disclosure. In 2006, the parties settled this lawsuit. The United States agreed to pay attorneys' fees of $200,000 to the ACLU of Northern California and to release records relating to the no-fly list.[176]

The ACLU filed a complaint in 2014 for fourteen plaintiffs who claimed that they were placed on the no-fly list and were forbidden to travel via airline within or without the United States. The plaintiffs, who were U.S. citizens of western Asian ancestry, claimed that the no-fly list was an unconstitutional impairment of their right to travel.[177] The plaintiffs and the defendant, Attorney General Eric Holder, cross-moved for summary judgment. The court issued an order granting plaintiffs' summary judgment motion and denying the government's motion. The court noted that an internal administrative review process was available to any prospective passenger who was denied boarding, and judicial review of that administrative decision by a U.S. court of appeals was available to an aggrieved party.[178]

Other challenges have been less successful. In 2005, the Ninth Circuit Court of Appeals ruled in *Gilmore v. Gonzales*[179] that a person listed by the United States' civilian airline passenger identification policy may challenge the constitutionality of the policy but may not challenge listing on the no-fly list. Gilmore argued that the passenger identification policy impinged on his right to travel, claiming that the right to travel by airline is an essential right, but the court held that Gilmore's right to travel was not unconstitutionally curtailed because Gilmore had other means to travel to his destination.[180]

Despite limited success under the Freedom of Information Act, the general public does not know who is listed on the Terrorist Watchlist or on the no-fly list. Anyone who is denied boarding privileges at any airport can file for administrative review of his or her designation on the no-fly list, but that won't permit the traveler to take a seat on his or her flight. This system is the best-known example of the protectionist state at work. Evidently, the attorney general and the Department of Homeland Security believe that the interest of the people of the United States is best served by making lists based on hearsay reports that bar people from flying in any aircraft departing from the United States or from entering the United States from another departure point. The majority of U.S. citizens and resident aliens will be protected from another terrorist airline hijacking, even though a number of innocent people are included in the lists of those who cannot fly in airliners.

Electronic Surveillance without Court Order

As of the writing of this chapter, no one knows if the FBI, CIA, DIA, or NSA is conducting warrantless electronic surveillance of anyone's telephone, cell phone, tablet, or computer transmissions or activities. The reason for conducting warrantless surveillance evoked by all these agencies is protection from another terrorist attack. President Clinton authorized the attorney general to conduct warrantless foreign intelligence surveillance for up to one year if the attorney general issued certification of need as required by FISA.[181] The FBI has employed drones since 2006 to collect electronic data without warrant on suspected foreign terrorists and domestic criminals.[182] In 2013, the Justice Department sought and received an indictment against Jamshid Muhtorov, believed to be involved in plotting a terrorist attack. The court granted the government's motion to refuse to produce classified information with respect to the FBI drone surveillance program and allowed the United States to substitute unclassified summaries of certain documents under Fed. R. Crim. Pro. 16.[183] Because the case has not gone to trial, the outcome of a case based on warrantless drone search information will not be determined for some time. A parallel Illinois case, *United States v. Daoud,* allowed defense counsel to review classified information pertaining to electronic surveillance of Adel Daoud who was accused of plotting to blow up a Chicago bar. Since Daoud's attorney had a security clearance, the trial judge allowed him to review classified material. He did not order public disclosure of the contents of the documents.[184] The rationale of the protectionist state for employing domestic drone surveillance remains "national security." The Seventh Circuit Court of Appeals reversed the trial judge and ordered the trial court not to allow defense counsel to review classified materials relating to warrantless surveillance.[185] Judge Posner said that FISA was an attempt to strike a balance between national security and an open judicial proceeding. He concluded that the government had an interest in preventing Daoud from using drones to commit terrorist acts that trumped any need for public disclosure.[186] Judge Posner acknowledged by this statement that the regime of the protectionist state permits the United States to disregard ordinary search and seizure laws in order to protect the public from terrorist attacks.

Edward Snowden's disclosure of NSA's widespread data-capturing program related only to one federal agency's domestic electronic surveillance. NSA's use of warrantless surveillance was known prior to Snowden's publication of classified NSA information. NSA's avoidance of the Foreign Intelligence Surveillance Act's warrant requirement is the best-known system thanks to a 2006 exposé published by the *New York Times* and carried by many other newspapers including the *Baltimore Sun*.[187] In 2002, President Bush had secretly authorized the NSA to intercept phone calls and e-mails to and from persons believed to be Al Qaida sympathizers and supporters. NSA could bypass the FISA provisions that required a warrant to conduct such searches. NSA code named the collection of raw data on phone calls and e-mails on a number of suspicious persons "Stellar Wind."[188] The *New York Times* published an article exposing the program on December 16, 2005. Attorney General Gonzales admitted that the Stellar Wind program existed shortly after the disclosure was published. In a December 2005 news conference, Gonzales defended the president's initiation of Stellar Wind, saying to the media that "the authorization by the President is only to engage in surveillance of communications where one party is outside the United States, and where we have a reasonable basis to conclude that one of the parties of the communication is either a member of al Qaeda or affiliated with al Qaeda."[189] The attorney general stated in a March 2006 news conference that "it has been the position of this administration, the Department of Justice, from the outset that the president does have the authority as commander of chief during a time of war supplemented under the Constitution, supplemented by the Authorization for the Use of Military Force passed by Congress shortly after the attacks of September 11th."[190]

President Bush invoked his power as commander in chief to defend the warrantless intercept program, asserting that "we are at war with an enemy who wants to hurt us again. . . . If somebody from Al Qaeda is calling you, we'd like to know why. We're at war with a bunch of cold-blooded killers."[191] Bush also relied on the congressional delegation of authority lodged in the AUMF act to justify this program.[192]

NSA chief Gen. Michael Hayden stepped down because of the disclosure of the Stellar Wind program. Lieutenant Gen. Keith B. Alexander replaced Hayden and immediately transferred Deputy Director William

B. Black Jr., who was responsible for the warrantless search program, to a foreign post.[193]

Thomas Tamm, a former Department of Justice employee, admitted to Michael Isakoff of *Newsweek* in 2008 that he "blew the whistle" on Stellar Wind to the *New York Times* in 2005. Tamm told the reporter that he was motivated by the knowledge that the Justice Department was involved in an illegal program run by the NSA. He tried to share his concerns with a friend who served on the staff of the Senate Justice Committee. She later told Tamm not to reveal what he knew.[194]

President Bush's position relied on the expansive construction of his Article II power as commander in chief advocated by Prof. John Yoo in his 1996 law review article. He accepted the rationale that would have been approved by Abraham Lincoln—the president sometimes has to disregard the law in order to save the nation. The attorney general advised Senate leaders on January 17, 2007, that the president would not reauthorize Stellar Wind. Attorney General Gonzales stated that "any electronic surveillance that was occurring as part of the Terrorist Surveillance Program will now be conducted subject to the approval of the Foreign Intelligence Surveillance Court."[195]

Stellar Wind was also challenged in 2008 by the Electronic Frontier Foundation, which sued the NSA, President Bush, Vice President Cheney, and former attorney general Gonzales, among others. This was a class action brought on behalf of AT&T customers claiming that the customers' right to privacy was violated by the Stellar Wind program. It was consolidated with other similar cases and resulted in summary judgment for telephone service providers in 2009.[196]

Attorney General Eric Holder filed a post-trial motion in January 2009 to set aside the court's judgment, agreeing with his predecessor's argument that Congress had authorized this type of surveillance and had specifically insulated AT&T and other telephone companies from liability for cooperating with the NSA. The court nonetheless sustained its original decision in 2010.[197] The Ninth Circuit reversed the trial court, vacating the judgment against the United States and affirming the district court's dismissal of the claim against Mueller, trailblazer and whistleblowing prosecution.[198]

The final chapter in the continuing saga of electronic surveillance within the United States has not been written. Edward Snowden released classified documents in 2013 showing that the NSA was capturing all cell phone numbers to and from individuals suspected of having some connection to Al Qaida and monitoring e-mails with the cooperation of Internet service providers. The NSA continued to assert that it did not intercept actual telecommunications without a warrant. Internet service providers and telephone service providers gave the NSA unsupervised access to all fiber-optic communications going between some of the nation's largest telecommunication companies' major interconnected locations, including phone conversations, e-mail, web browsing, and corporate private network traffic.[199]

Immigration and Naturalization

The proactive approach to preventing future terrorist attacks also affected immigration and naturalization practices after September 11, 2001. The terrorists who perpetrated the airliner hijackings were traveling on student visa cards, even though at least one of the terrorists was known to be a potential security risk. Congress passed the Homeland Security Act in 2002 that brought the Immigration and Naturalization Service into the Department of Homeland Security. Congress liberally funded the new central agency. This permitted the INS to spend more time and money watching the border between Mexico and the United States. It also accelerated deportations of illegal immigrants. About two hundred thousand illegal immigrants were deported in 2001, and by 2011, more than four hundred thousand illegal immigrants were deported.[200] About 188,000 deportations were "criminal" deportations. If an alien is accused of a crime, the alien may be deported without any findings of guilt.[201] They appeared before an administrative law judge who would decide the issue of deportation on the evidence submitted by the Immigration and Naturalization Service. The immigrant could have the benefit of legal counsel if the immigrant could afford a lawyer.[202] The vast bulk of those deported were Hispanic illegal immigrants, not Arab terrorists.[203] Since September 11, 2001, the government has used deportation proceedings to rid the United States of Hispanic illegal immigrants. The increase in funding and in deportations had little to do with stopping Arab terrorists.

THE USA PATRIOT ACT

In October 2001, Congress quickly passed a comprehensive act called the Uniting and Strengthening America by Providing Appropriate Tools Required to Intercept and Obstruct Terrorism Act of 2001, better known by its acronym, the USA PATRIOT Act. The act amended many existing statutes such as the FISA Act as already noted. The act also permitted the executive branch of government to make incursions into areas of personal conduct without a showing of probable cause.

Some of the more objectionable portions of the act have been held unconstitutional. Congress established three provisions that intruded upon personal freedom. The "sneak and peek" warrant provision allowed law enforcement agencies to obtain a warrant for surveillance, carry out surveillance, and delay the return on the warrant indefinitely. The "sneak and peak" warrant was held to be an unreasonable search and seizure in *Mayfield v. United States*.[204] Brandon Mayfield, an Oregon attorney who converted to Islam, was arrested on May 6, 2004, and charged with being an accessory to the March 11, 2004, bombing of a commuter train in Madrid that killed 191 people. The arrest was based on the identification of a partial fingerprint by U.S. fingerprint analysts that was recovered from a bag containing detonating devices found in the wreckage of the train. Computer comparison of the partial print known as LFP #17 by the FBI came up with twenty individuals whose fingerprints had some common elements with that of the unidentified terrorist. Mayfield, a middle-aged Portland, Oregon, attorney and former army veteran, was one of the twenty persons of interest. The FBI concluded on St. Patrick's Day 2004 that Mayfield made the partial print LFP #17. The FBI put Mayfield and his family under surveillance on March 21, 2004. The FBI applied to the FISA Court for a warrant authorizing the placement of a listening device in Mayfield's home and at the same time searched Mayfield's home when no one was there. The FBI also acquired private and protected information about the Mayfields from third parties, searched his law office, and tapped his office and home telephones.[205]

The FBI sent Mayfield's fingerprints to the Spanish government early in April 2004. The Spanish National Police reviewed the fingerprint and the FBI report and concluded that there were too many unexplained dissimilarities between Mayfield's prints and LFP #17 to verify the match. FBI agents then met with their Spanish counterparts in Madrid, who refuted the FBI's conclusion that there was a match.[206]

Despite the Spanish National Police determination that Mayfield's print was not a match, the FBI filed an affidavit with the U.S. District Court, claiming that that experts considered LFP #17 a "100 percent positive identification" of Mayfield. The FBI included irrelevant information about Mayfield's religious practice and association with other Muslims. The FBI declared that Mayfield was a material witness on May 4, 2004, and filed an application for a material witness order.[207] With the approval of Mayfield and his attorney, Kenneth Moses, an independent fingerprint expert, analyzed the print found at the scene of the Spanish train bombing and Mayfield's fingerprints. Moses concluded that LFP #17 was from Mayfield's left index finger.[208]

Mayfield's home and his law office were searched by FBI agents executing search warrants. The agents recovered his computers, his paper files, and his children's homework. On May 6, 2004, the FBI arrested Mayfield as a material witness.[209] He was held for two weeks. On May 17, the Spanish police told the FBI that it had matched up the print from the train bombing to an Algerian named Ouhane Daoud. Mayfield was released from confinement on May 18, 2004.[210]

The FBI issued a report on July 16, 2004, stating that the fingerprint taken from the train bombing was that of Daoud. On October 4, 2004, Mayfield, his wife, and his children filed suit against the government in the U.S. District Court for the District of Oregon.[211] Mayfield alleged that the FBI agents who searched his house and office and arrested him committed an actionable wrong against him and his family, relying on *Bivens v. Six Unknown Named Agents*,[212] the 1971 U.S. Supreme Court decision holding that individual law enforcement officers who committed intentional torts that violated the plaintiff's constitutional rights during duty status were individually liable to the victim of their tortious conduct. Mayfield also pled a claim under the Privacy Act[213] against the FBI for leaking information to the press relating to his detention as a material witness. Mayfield also challenged FISA and the PATRIOT Act as authorizing unreasonable searches and seizures.[214]

Mayfield and the United States settled his claim, which was approved on November 29, 2006. The government agreed to pay $2 million to Mayfield and his family in compensatory damages and to destroy documents relating to the FBI electronic surveillance intercepts. The government also agreed to return every document and item of personal property seized by the FBI in execution of its FISA search warrants. Both sides agreed that Mayfield was limited to a declaratory judgment action in U.S. District Court. The parties executed a Recitation of Stipulated Facts that would govern all further proceedings.[215] Mayfield won a declaratory judgment of unconstitutionality against the United States in the district court, but the Ninth Circuit reversed and remanded Mayfield's case. The issues included the constitutionality of three PATRIOT Act provisions: the "sneak and peek" warrants, roving wiretaps, and the ability of the FBI to gain access to documents that reveal the patterns of U.S. citizens. The "sneak and peek" law permitted the FBI to delay notification of the execution of search warrants without stating how long the delay period would last. It allowed for delayed notification of the execution of search warrants. The period before which the FBI must notify the recipients of the order was unspecified in the act. The FBI field manual says that it is a "flexible standard" and it may be extended at the court's discretion.[216] The Ninth Circuit validated this type of warrant in 1988.[217]

Roving wiretaps are wiretap orders that do not need to specify all common carriers and third parties in a surveillance court order. The Department of Justice prefers a roving wiretap order because a terrorist can change location and communication devices rapidly. The roving wiretap order allows the FBI to execute a wiretap every time the suspected terrorist changes communications systems and carriers without reapplying for a new warrant.[218] The Second Circuit held that the roving wiretap was a reasonable search and seizure.[219] The PATRIOT Act also authorized the FBI to make an order "requiring the production of any tangible things (including books, records, papers, documents, and other items) for an investigation to protect against international terrorism or clandestine intelligence activities, provided that such investigation of a United States person is not conducted solely upon the basis of activities protected by the first amendment to the Constitution." Arguably, the production order could be enforced against any library that a suspected terrorist or aider and abettor used. The FBI may need to see the suspect's checkouts to see if the suspect was reading up on bomb making or other terroristic devices. The American Library Association (ALA) protested the search orders in a June 29, 2005, resolution. The Manhattan Institute's Heather MacDonald said in her article for the *New York City Journal* that "the furor over Section 215 is a case study in Patriot Act fear-mongering." The 2006 amendments to the PATRIOT Act exempted ordinary lending libraries from production orders.[220]

THE DETAINEES

The Invasion of Afghanistan

When U.S. forces landed in Afghanistan in 2001, that state was controlled by a religiously oriented Islamic political party known as the Taliban. That party had been one of the coalition of Afghans that had resisted Soviet seizure of Afghanistan in the 1980s. Then known as the Mujahadin, they were trained by Pakistani military men on the order of Muhammad Zia-ul-Haq, then Pakistan's president. After the Soviets were driven out of Afghanistan, the Mujahadin were included in the coalition government set up in 1992. A former Mujahadin imam named Mullah Omar, who had been trained by the Pakistani military, organized a paramilitary group to support his interpretation of Islamic law in Afghanistan. In 1994, Mullah Omar's forces marched on Kandahar. They captured the city, and it became the capital of Mullah Omar's Islamic state. Within a year, his fighters controlled twelve Afghan provinces and were in position to oppose the central government in Kabul. Amad Shah Massoud was the principal leader of the Kabul government. He was able to form an alliance between the two principal tribes that inhabited Afghanistan, the Pashtuns and Tajiks. Massoud's coalition was able to defeat the Taliban on its first attempt to seize Kabul. Massoud was assassinated in September 2001, shortly before the attacks on the United States. The Taliban won the civil war and set up a government in Kabul based on sharia law as interpreted by Mullah Omar. Mullah Omar taught that Western dress and Western ways were antithetical to a good Islamic life.[221] Mullah Omar forbade women from attending school and required that no woman could leave her home without a male escort. All women were required to wear the burka, a robe with head piece that covered most of the wearer's face, when in public.[222] Some Taliban commanders kidnapped women to be sold into slavery in Pakistan.[223]

In 1994, Osama Bin Laden and his followers turned up in Afghanistan. His Al Qaida fighters were determined to restore Palestine to Arab control, drive the Israelis and the United States out of the Mideast, and restore Islam to its seventh-century roots. Within two years' time, Bin Laden had forged an alliance with Mullah Omar.[224] Al Qaida had base camps in Afghanistan with permission from Omar. The terrorists who entered the United States in 2000 who committed the 9/11 attacks were trained in Afghanistan.[225]

Following the 9/11 attacks on the United States, the United States, allied with the Afghan anti-Taliban Northern Alliance and eventually assisted by NATO units, invaded Afghanistan and drove the Taliban regime out of Kabul, setting up a pro–United States regime headed by Hamid Karzai. The United States captured Taliban and Al Qaida fighters in the course of its military operations from 2001 through 2014. Since these fighters were not regularly enlisted members of some state's armed services, the Bush administration refused to grant these captives prisoner-of-war status under the Geneva Convention.

The Invasion of Iraq

In 2003, the Bush administration launched an invasion of Iraq to prevent Iraqi dictator Saddam Hussein from using weapons of mass destruction on civilians inside and outside of Iraq. Hussein's regime collapsed, and Saddam Hussein was captured in a spider hole hiding from U.S. troops later that year. U.S. forces captured irregular fighters who were not part of Iraq's army and lodged the captives in several locations inside and outside Iraq. According to several sources, these captives and some of the fighters captured in Afghanistan were victims of "extraordinary rendition," a policy that sent alleged terrorists to states that used torture to extract information from these captives relevant to future attacks on the United States and other states. Despite an official policy that did not condone torture by U.S. forces, CIA interrogation of captives often included sleep deprivation, nudity before people of the opposite sex, and in some instances waterboarding.[226] The Bush administration relied on a memorandum prepared by John Yoo that asserted that waterboarding, nudity, unusual positions, and other interrogation techniques were not torture as defined by the Geneva Convention.[227] Military police corrections NCOs and officers at Abu Ghraib prison in Iraq engaged in similar practices that were made public in the fall of 2003, resulting in the court-martial of several enlisted corrections personnel and the removal of the brigadier general commanding the prison.[228] The Abu Ghraib staff was accused of beating prisoners; of forcing them to lie in the sun, be nude for hours, crawl around the compound, and be ridden by the guards like animals; and of raping and sodomizing some prisoners with a baton and similar attempts to break down the captives' resistance to interrogation. Some of the military police staff at Abu Ghraib took photos of these abuses and sent them to friends in the United States.[229] The Bush administration ordered an investigation into the torture allegations, and Secretary of Defense Rumsfeld testified before Congress specifically on authorization of interrogation techniques. Rumsfeld insisted that the United States did not condone torture of its captives.[230]

The Problem: What to Do with Stateless Terrorists Taken Prisoner

The United States also opened its own concentration camp for captives in Guantanamo Bay, Cuba, in 2002. Relying on another Justice Department memo, the Bush administration decided that captives held at Guantanamo were not subject to the constitutional protections afforded anyone charged with a crime in the United States. Some 779 captives were detained at Guantanamo since 2002. According to the Seton Hall Law School Center for Policy and Research, which periodically reviews official government documents concerning Guantanamo's captives,

1. Fifty-five percent (55%) of the detainees are not determined to have committed any hostile acts against the United States or its coalition allies.
2. Only 8% of the detainees were characterized as al Qaeda fighters. Of the remaining detainees, 40% have no definitive connection with al Qaeda at all and 18% have no definitive affiliation with either al Qaeda or the Taliban.
3. The Government has detained numerous persons based on mere affiliations with a large number of groups that in fact, are not on the Department of Homeland Security terrorist watchlist. Moreover, the nexus between such a detainee and such organizations varies considerably. Eight percent are detained because they are deemed "fighters for;" 30% considered "members of;" a large majority 60%—are detained merely because they are "associated with" a group or groups the Government asserts are terrorist organizations. For 2% of the prisoners, their nexus to any terrorist group is unidentified.
4. Only 5% of the detainees were captured by United States forces. 86% of the detainees were arrested by either Pakistan or the Northern Alliance and turned over to United States custody.[231]

The Seton Hall Center also discovered that many of the Guantanamo captives were interrogated using methods that could be described as torture.[232] Relying on the Yoo memo, President Bush determined that after the CIA and other intelligence operatives had finished extracting information from the captives, using waterboarding, prolonged interrogation without sleep, and other means validated by Yoo, the captives should be tried by military commission.

Intelligence Gathering: Extraordinary Rendition

The CIA and other intelligence agencies felt hampered by anti-torture guidelines. In order to produce more information from some of the captives, the Bush administration permitted 156 captives to be transferred to such states as Syria, Jordan, and Macedonia for further interrogation between 2002 and 2013[233] because these states were not bound by any anti-torture guidelines.[234] The treatment of these captives did not meet the standards of the Geneva Convention and the anti-torture guidelines. The CIA operated "dark prisons" for captives in Afghanistan, Lithuania, Morocco, Poland, Romania, and Thailand. A few examples from "Twenty Extraordinary Facts about Extraordinary Rendition" suffice to show how the extraordinary rendition program operated.

Wesam Abdulrahman Ahmed al-Deemawi was captured in Iran and taken to a "dark prison" in Afghanistan, then transferred to the Bagram Air Base prison. Al-Deemawi was hung from the ceiling in the strappado position. His interrogators threatened him with dogs and forced him to watch torture videos. The interrogators devised a subtle form of audio torture: playing the sound of electric sawing and having someone cry out in pain.[235]

A pregnant woman named Fatima Bouchar was taken into custody at the Bangkok airport and chained up to a wall for five days without food. She and Abdel Hakim Belhaj, her husband, were taken to Libya for further interrogation. Eventually after Belhaj was tortured for several months, the couple was released. They filed suit for damages against the British intelligence Agency MI6. Their case is still pending at this time.[236]

Muslim cleric Abu Omar lived in Milan. He was apprehended by CIA agents and taken to Egypt for interrogation using electric shock. One of his plural wives visited him in Egypt bringing food, clothes, and money. She told the media about her husband's treatment in 2005.[237] This treatment resulted in criminal charges being filed in a criminal court in Milan against twenty-two CIA agents and an air force officer who were convicted by an Italian court in absentia for various crimes against humanity.[238]

Abd al-Rahim al-Nashiri, suspected of being the mastermind behind the attack on the USS *Cole,* was held in a Polish secret prison before being transferred to Guantanamo in 2006. While secretly detained in Poland, U.S. interrogators subjected al-Nashiri to a mock execution with a power drill as he stood naked and hooded, racked a semi-automatic handgun close to his head as he sat shackled before them, held him in "standing stress positions," and threatened to bring in his mother and sexually abuse her in front of him.[239]

The Guantanamo Detainees

The U.S. camp in Guantanamo held more than 770 individuals considered to be suspects. The camp included a special interrogation compound where CIA interrogators used "enhanced interrogation techniques" to extract information on Al Qaida and related organizations, and regular compounds for captives who had been interrogated and were awaiting some resolution to their confinement.[240] All the captives were classified by the Bush administration as "enemy combatants,"[241] exempt from the minimal protection for prisoners of war under the Geneva Convention.[242] Captives were flown to Guantanamo wearing goggles, a mask, and headphones to prevent them from knowing where they had been and where they were upon arrival.[243] According to *The Report on Torture and Cruel, Inhuman and Degrading Treatment of Prisoners at Guantanamo Bay, Cuba,*[244] prisoners who were treated with the enhanced interrogation techniques employed by the CIA at Guantanamo were

- held in solitary confinement for periods exceeding a year;
- deprived of sleep for days and weeks and, in at least one case, months;
- exposed to prolonged temperature extremes;
- beaten;
- threatened with transfer to a foreign country, for torture;
- tortured in foreign countries or at U.S. military bases abroad before transfer to Guantánamo;
- sexually harassed and raped or threatened with rape;
- deprived of medical treatment for serious conditions; or allowed treatment only on the condition that they "cooperate" with interrogators; and
- routinely "short-shackled" (wrists and ankles bound together and to the floor) for hours and even days during interrogations.[245]

The report asserted, based on lawyers' conversations with Guantanamo captives while incarcerated, that "most prisoners live in conditions that are debilitating. Many have serious, untreated medical problems, often caused by living conditions or physical punishment. Some have lost their sanity. Numerous prisoners have tried to commit suicide, some multiple times, one in October 2005 during a visit by his lawyer."[246]

Guantanamo captives staged hunger strikes to protest living conditions at the camps, the most memorable being the August 2005 hunger strike. The guards resorted to force-feeding some prisoners to keep them alive. In 2013, during another hunger strike, the captives were force-fed again. The American Civil Liberties Union considered force-feeding to be torture on par with waterboarding.[247]

President Obama issued an executive order in 2009 directing CIA and other intelligence agencies not to use torture to aid in interrogation of suspected terrorists. This order is remarkable for its ambiguity. It directs all agencies to follow interrogation practices and procedures outlined in Army Field Manual 2.22.3, but qualifies that order by stating, "Nothing in this section shall preclude the Federal Bureau of Investigation, or other federal law enforcement agencies, from continuing to use authorized, non-coercive techniques of interrogation that are designed to elicit voluntary statements and do not involve the use of force, threats, or promises."[248] The order also directs interrogators not to rely on any interpretations of FM 2.22.3 or its predecessor issued between September 11, 2001, and January 20, 2009. This clause was intended to override the Yoo memo. The CIA was ordered to close any detention facilities at once, referring to the secret CIA detention centers in Poland, Syria, and other non-U.S. states. That 2009 order also established a special task force to review interrogation techniques and FM 2.22.3 when used by other than armed forces interrogators to determine if FM 2.22.3 does "provide an appropriate means of acquiring the intelligence necessary to protect the Nation, and, if warranted, to recommend any additional or different guidance for other departments or agencies."[249]

The Guantanamo captives are not U.S. citizens, nor are they resident aliens. A few of the more than six hundred men held captive are members of Al Qaida or some other stateless terrorist group or are "fellow travelers." Most of the captives, as stated above, were taken by local armed forces in Afghanistan and elsewhere and turned over to the United States for a reward. The Bush administration released more than five hundred captives.[250] The Obama administration began screening the captives, eventually releasing more than two hundred of them because there was no reason to believe that they were Al Qaida members or fellow travelers. The government has retained 169 captives, some or all of whom may be subject to trial by military commission for various crimes.[251]

TRIAL BY MILITARY COMMISSION

President Bush's Executive Order on Military Trials

The United States had not tried anyone by military commission since the conclusion of the Japanese war crime trials in 1947. Following the U.S. invasion of Afghanistan in 2001, the Bush administration collected hundreds of captives, some of whom could have been Al Qaida operatives or Taliban leaders. Many of these individuals were brought to the detention center at Guantanamo Bay. Since the Bush administration had classified these individuals as enemy combatants not protected by the Geneva Convention or any other international accord relating to treatment of prisoners of war, the last thing the administration intended to allow would be indictment and trial by jury in the United States for crimes against the United States or international law.

The only alternative was to establish military commissions that would try the captives and mete out punishment for violations of the law of war, following the same path as Presidents Lincoln and Roosevelt had followed in the past. President Bush then issued a state document on November 16, 2001. This document stated that "individuals subject to this order" could not be tried by the civil courts in the United States. The president authorized detention of "individuals subject to this order" defined as:

> 1. (a) The term "individual subject to this order" shall mean any individual who is not a United States citizen with respect to whom I determine from time to time in writing that:
> (1) there is reason to believe that such individual, at the relevant times,
> (i) is or was a member of the organization known as al Qaida;
> (ii) has engaged in, aided or abetted, or conspired to commit, acts of international terrorism, or acts in preparation therefor, that have caused, threaten to cause, or have as their aim to cause, injury to or adverse effects on the United States, its citizens, national security, foreign policy, or economy; or
> (iii) has knowingly harbored one or more individuals described in subparagraphs (i) or (ii) of subsection 2(a)(1) of this order.[252]

Section 4 of the president's document authorized the secretary of defense to try an "individual subject to this order" by military commission. The secretary of defense was authorized to prescribe rules of conduct for military commissions including pre-trial, trial, and post-trial procedures.[253] The same document barred any "person subject to this order" from seeking any relief in U.S. courts.[254] The president authorized conviction and sentencing by two-thirds majority vote of the commission.

The Department of Defense prescribed rules for the conduct of military commissions, and the legal machinery of the Judge Advocate General's Office was invoked to start proceedings under this presidential document. Commission Order 1 stated that Guantanamo captives would be tried according to the law of war. The captive would be given the right to counsel, the right to make an opening statement and closing argument at trial, the right to compulsory process, and the right to present evidence to the commission during the guilt and the sentencing phase. The captive could be convicted by two-thirds majority vote. A death sentence could be imposed by the same majority. The order also provided for a trial that included closed sessions for evidence deemed important to national security and open sessions for other evidence of guilt.[255] The model for the order dictated that a captive and his counsel may be excluded from any closed sessions of the military commission assigned to try his case. However, the captives had allies outside the Guantanamo compound, and these allies began to attack President Bush's order, starting with the order barring resort to U.S. courts for habeas corpus proceedings and other challenges to the detention of the captives. Congress meanwhile passed the Detainee Treatment Act (DTA) of 2005, which provided that "no court . . . shall have jurisdiction to hear or consider . . . an application for . . . habeas corpus filed by . . . an alien detained . . . at Guantanamo Bay."[256]

If Congress had the authority under the Constitution to bar access to courts for non-U.S. citizens, then the Detainee Treatment Act foreclosed the habeas corpus petition filed by lawyers for Salim Ahmed Hamdan in the U.S. District Court for the District of Columbia. That court held that the Third Geneva Convention applied to Hamdan and that his habeas corpus petition should be granted.[257] The D.C. Circuit reversed, citing congressional withdrawal of the availability of U.S. courts to Hamdan via the Detainee Treatment Act.[258] Hamdan filed a petition for writ of certiorari, which was granted after the passage of the Detainee Treatment Act. The government argued that the Detainee Treatment Act should apply to Hamdan's habeas corpus petition, but the Supreme Court held that the act was not intended to apply to a petition by a Guantanamo captive that had been filed before the passage of the act.[259] The Court also noted that *Ex parte Quirin* was authority for the Supreme Court to take jurisdiction over a pending habeas corpus petition.[260]

The Court noted that

> Hamdan and the Government both have a compelling interest in knowing in advance whether Hamdan may be tried by a military commission that arguably is without any basis in law and operates free from many of the procedural rules prescribed by Congress for courts-martial—rules intended to safeguard the accused and ensure the reliability of any conviction.[261]

The Court then engaged in a historical analysis of Article 15 of the Articles of War and its UCMJ successor, Article 21. It reached the conclusion that neither statute authorized the trial of a Guantanamo Bay captive by military commission. The Court held that the UCMJ, the AUMNF, and the DTA did not authorize the president to convene military commissions. It then inquired whether the president could order detainees tried by military commission.[262] The Court found that military commissions could be convened to try civilians when martial law has been declared, when a temporary military government has been instituted over an occupied territory, and, a third instance, "when there is a need to seize and subject to disciplinary measures those enemies who in their attempt to thwart or impede our military effort have violated the law of war."[263]

The Court noted that the government correctly invoked *Quirin* to support trying the Guantanamo captives because *Quirin* represented the third type of circumstances warranting trial of civilians by military commission. Citing Winthrop's Military Precedents, the Court held that the

Quirin type of trial by military commission was justified (a) if an offense was committed within the field of a command, (b) if the offense committed was within the period of war, (c) only for "individuals of the enemy army who have been guilty of illegitimate warfare" or members of the host nation's army who are not triable by a regular court-martial or civilian criminal court, and that (d) the only offenses that can be tried by military commission are "violations of the laws and usages of war cognizable by military tribunals only" and "breaches of military orders or regulations for which offenders are not legally triable by court-martial under the Articles of war."[264] The Court held that Hamdan was charged with conspiracy beginning in 1996 and ending in November 2001, only a short portion of which fell into Winthrop's criteria for invoking a military commission. None of the alleged overt acts committed by Hamdan and other conspirators occurred on or after September 11, 2001. The offense with which Hamdan was charged was not a violation of the law of war.[265] Congress had not defined "conspiracy" as a war crime. The offense charged, conspiracy, was not defined by statute or treaty, and its status as a war crime must be plain and unambiguous. The government failed to meet that requirement in Hamdan's case.[266]

The Court decided that President Bush lacked the authority to convene a military commission because neither the Uniform Code of Military Justice nor the Authorization for Use of Military Force passed in 2001 expressly or impliedly authorized him to set up military commissions for captives.[267] The Court ruled that Commission Order 1's procedures violated the Geneva Convention.[268] Brushing aside the government's contention that Hamdan was not protected by the Geneva Convention because he was not a member of a regularly constituted military force, the Court determined that the Geneva Convention of 1949 was a part of the law of war and bound the United States to comply with the convention. The Court noted that Common Article 3 applied to Al Qaida fighters in Afghanistan, which was one of the high contracting parties to the Geneva Convention, and Common Article 3 stated that in a "conflict not of an international character occurring in the territory of one of the High Contracting Parties, each Party to the conflict shall be bound to apply, as a minimum, 'certain provisions protecting . . . persons taking no active part in the hostilities, including members of armed forces who have laid down their arms and those placed *hors de combat* by . . . detention.'"[269] Article 3(d), as the Court noted, bars "the passing of sentences and the carrying out of executions without previous judgment pronounced by a regularly constituted . . . court affording all the judicial guarantees which are recognized as indispensable by civilized peoples."[270]

Justice Scalia wrote the dissenting opinion for the three justices who disagreed with the majority. He argued that the Detainee Treatment Act of 2005 barred any Guantanamo captive from filing a habeas corpus petition in a U.S. federal court, giving the statute retrospectant effect to habeas corpus petitions already filed prior to its passage.[271] He argued that the post-decision review provided for by section 1005(e)(3) was the exclusive remedy for any errors of law relating to Hamdan's confinement and trial.[272] Even if the Detainee Act did not take away federal jurisdiction, Justice Scalia argued, the Court should abstain from issuing any injunction on grounds of comity.[273] Justice Thomas's separate dissent argued that Hamdan's case fit the four requirements for an extraordinary military commission cited by the majority relying on Winthrop's Precedents.[274]

The Court's majority opinion made it clear that the president needed specific congressional authorization to try any captive by military commission. Congress needed to adopt procedures for military commissions that mirrored the provisions of the UCMJ. That is precisely what Congress did in 2006. The Military Commissions Act of 2006 authorized trial of those individuals held captive by the United States deemed to be "unprivileged enemy belligerents."[275] The same act defined thirty-two separate crimes that would be triable by military commission, stating that these crimes were part of the common law of war and were merely codified by the act.[276] Congress intended that the act would apply to captives who were already in custody and awaiting trial. Congress also set up a procedural system that paralleled the UCMJ, granting compulsory process to the accused,[277] pre-trial discovery for classified information,[278] protection for disclosure of classified information,[279] and trial and post-trial practice.[280] Congress established a special court called the Court of Military Commission Review to review convictions by military commission.[281] The act also provided for an appeal from the Court of Military Commission Appeals to the D.C. Circuit and, ultimately, certiorari to the Supreme Court.[282]

The Department of Defense was also authorized to make rules consistent with the act, including rules of evidence. If no new rules were adopted, then the procedures and rules of evidence for general courts-martial would apply to military commission trials.[283]

The *Hamdan* decision required that Congress expressly authorize trial by military commission stands, applying the rule from *Ex parte Milligan*. The decision also validated *Ex parte Quirin* by requiring that Congress expressly authorize trial by military commission for certain classes of combatants. It did not hold that the Guantanamo captives, who are not U.S. citizens, could never be tried by military commission when U.S. courts are open and there is no threat of enemy invasion. Despite the Obama administration's protests against trying the captives by military commission and Attorney General Holder's abortive attempt to bring Khalid Sheikh Mohammad to New York City for a civilian court trial, five captives have been formally charged with crimes and are awaiting trial by military commission.[284]

Yaser Hamdi

Yaser Hamdi, a U.S. citizen, was captured in Afghanistan. He was alleged to be a Taliban fighter. Hamdi was taken to the U.S. mainland and confined in the navy brig at Norfolk, Virginia. His father hired an attorney to file a habeas corpus petition alleging that Hamdi was unlawfully confined. The U.S. District Court for the District of Virginia granted the petition, but the Fourth Circuit reversed the district court. On remand, the United States submitted a declaration by Michael Mobbs, a special advisor to the undersecretary of defense for policy, that summarized the circumstances of Hamdi's capture in Afghanistan. Hamdi was captured by Northern Alliance troops, and according to Mobbs, Hamdi was carrying an assault rifle and was affiliated with a Taliban unit when taken prisoner. The district judge ruled that the Mobbs declaration alone was insufficient to justify holding Hamdi prisoner without charges and a hearing. The district judge certified that issue to the Fourth Circuit.[285] The circuit court held that the declaration was sufficient to hold Hamdi as an enemy belligerent for eventual trial by military commission, despite his U.S. citizenship.[286] The circuit court also noted that the Authorization for Use of Military Force resolution empowered President Bush to detain fighters captured in Afghanistan, whether they were U.S. citizens or not.[287]

Hamdi filed a petition for writ of certiorari which was granted. The Supreme Court reversed the Fourth Circuit and vacated its decision to hold Hamdi in custody without charges.[288] The majority opinion written by Justice O'Connor stated that the only issue before the Court was "whether the Executive has the authority to detain citizens who qualify as 'enemy combatants.' . . . We therefore answer only the narrow question before us: whether the detention of citizens falling within that definition is authorized."[289] The majority held that the Authorization for Use of Military Force resolution granted President Bush power to detain Hamdi, despite his U.S. citizenship and entitlement to due process of law under the Fifth Amendment.[290] The majority also held that Hamdi was entitled to some of the basic Fifth Amendment rights accorded U.S. citizens accused of crimes. First, Hamdi has the privilege of filing a writ of habeas corpus to test the legitimacy of his confinement.[291] The plurality opinion stated, "We therefore hold that a citizen detainee seeking to challenge his classification as an enemy combatant must receive notice of the factual basis for his classification, and a fair opportunity to rebut the Government's factual assertions before a neutral decisionmaker."[292]

Following the Supreme Court ruling, Hamdi renounced his U.S. citizenship. He was released from custody and deported to Saudi Arabia. The terms of his release prohibit him from returning to the United States or traveling to Afghanistan or other western Asian states.[293]

Hamdi, decided the same day as *Rasul v. Bush*,[294] which held that Guantanamo captives could challenge their custody in an appropriate U.S. District Court because Guantanamo was arguably under U.S. control, even though Cuba was the recognized sovereign over the military base, was consistent with *Rasul* and *Hamdan* and also fit well with *Ex parte Quirin* and *Ex parte Milligan*. Any individual who was detained by the U.S. military could not be held without charges indefinitely. Congress could provide that individuals detained as suspected terrorists were to be tried by a military commission, but the president lacked the authority to order individuals to be tried by military commission under the war power without congressional authorization. Those men who were captives were not barred from seeking habeas corpus relief in the absence of legislation that expressly deprived the federal courts of jurisdiction over the captives' detention. The Military Commissions Act of 2006 supplied the authority for President Bush and President Obama to continue to hold suspected terrorists in Guantanamo for trial by military commission without recourse to habeas corpus or other ways to challenge their captivity in federal courts.

José Padilla

José Padilla, a member of the Latin Kings street gang, was tried and convicted of aggravated assault and manslaughter. After serving his sentence, he became a Muslim and made a trip to Saudi Arabia in 2002. When he returned to Chicago, he was arrested as a material witness and held without charges being preferred. The president then directed that Padilla's custody be changed from that of "material witness" to "enemy combatant."[295] Padilla filed a petition for writ of habeas corpus in the Southern District of New York, testing the lawfulness of his confinement without charges. The government moved to dismiss the petition because Padilla was confined in Charleston, depriving the Southern District of New York of any jurisdiction over Padilla.[296] The district court held that it had jurisdiction to issue the writ but that the president was authorized by statute and the Constitution to detain Padilla without charges. The court granted Padilla's lawyer, Donna Newman, access to her client in the Charleston brig, which the government opposed on grounds of breach of national security (inferring that Padilla would be transmitting messages to Al Qaida through his attorney). Judge Michael Mukasey certified that issue to the Second Circuit after initially rejecting the government's motion.[297] Judge Mukasey formulated six issues for the Second Circuit:

1. Is the Secretary of Defense, Donald Rumsfeld, a proper respondent in this case?

2. Does this court have personal jurisdiction over Secretary Rumsfeld?
3. Does the President have the authority to designate as an enemy combatant an American citizen captured within the United States, and, through the Secretary of Defense, to detain him for the duration of armed conflict with al Qaeda?
4. What burden must the government meet to detain petitioner as an enemy combatant?
5. Does petitioner have the right to present facts in support of his habeas corpus petition?
6. Was it a proper exercise of this court's discretion and its authority under the *All Writs Act* to direct that petitioner be afforded access to counsel for the purpose of presenting facts in support of his petition?[298]

The Second Circuit ruled that the district court had jurisdiction insofar as Padilla's petition was concerned because the secretary of defense made an extraordinary order transferring Padilla out of the physical jurisdiction of the Southern District of New York and changing his status from "material witness" to "enemy combatant." The district court had the aid of the New York long-arm statute to assist it in taking jurisdiction.[299] The Second Circuit then held that President Bush and Secretary of Defense Rumsfeld acting as his delegate lacked the inherent authority to hold Padilla without charges as an "enemy combatant," citing *Ex parte Milligan* and *Ex parte Quirin*.[300] The court also decided that Congress had not indirectly authorized the detention of U.S. citizens, citing the Non-Detention Act of 1971.[301] The government argued that the Non-Detention Act did not apply to military detentions, but the court rejected that argument.[302] The court also held that the Authorization for Use of Military Force resolution of 2001 did not grant authority to the executive branch to detain Padilla without charges.[303] The court then remanded Padilla's case to the district court, directing it to issue the writ and discharge Padilla. The government moved for a stay and filed a petition for writ of certiorari with the Supreme Court.[304] The Supreme Court upset the Second Circuit decision without deciding the certified question. It held that Padilla's writ petition should have been filed in South Carolina where he was held, and the proper party defendant was the officer in charge of the navy brig where he was confined.[305] Eventually, Padilla's lawyer filed a habeas corpus petition in the U.S. District Court for South Carolina. The district court granted the writ, finding that Padilla was unlawfully detained as an enemy combatant.[306] The government appealed, and the Fourth Circuit reversed the trial court, holding that the Authorization for Use of Military Force resolution passed in 2001 empowered the president to hold Padilla as an enemy combatant without charges, without submitting his case to a grand jury.[307] The Supreme Court denied certiorari.[308]

In 2006, Padilla was indicted for conspiracy to commit murder and for conspiracy to give material aid for terrorists. He was convicted in 2007 and sentenced to seventeen years.[309] In 2014, after the Fourth Circuit disposed of the government's appeal by ordering the district judge to resentence Padilla, the district judge sentenced him to twenty-one years in prison. Meanwhile, Padilla sued Prof. John Yoo for injuries he suffered while being tortured by U.S. intelligence operatives, because Yoo advised the intelligence apparatus of the United States that torturing captives allegedly belonging to Al Qaida was lawful.[310] Padilla's theory was that Yoo personally involved himself in the torture regime. The district court denied Yoo's motion to dismiss based on Yoo's claim of qualified immunity as a governmental employee and granted the motion to dismiss a Fifth Amendment claim against the United States. The government appealed, and the Ninth Circuit reversed the lower court, holding that Prof. Yoo enjoyed qualified immunity from tort liability while working for the United States.[311] Padilla did not seek certiorari, and his claim was ultimately dismissed with prejudice.

Lakhdar Boumedienne

The tangled threads of Supreme Court jurisprudence following 9/11 did not deal with congressional termination of the writ of habeas corpus for Guantanamo detainees. The 2005 Detainee Treatment Act suspended the right of Guantanamo captives to file writs of habeas corpus in U.S. courts.[312] The 2006 Military Commission Act set up a review process allowing Guantanamo captives to take interlocutory appeals before trial by military commission to a special Article I court set up to act as an intermediate appellate court to redress any errors made during trial, with a potential appeal to the D.C. Circuit.[313] Lakhdar Boumedienne and several other Guantanamo captives filed habeas corpus writs in the D.C. District Court before either act became law. The district court held that the acts barred their writ applications. Boumedienne and the other applicants appealed, asserting that Congress failed to provide a meaningful alternative to writ practice in the Military Commissions Act. Therefore, the applicants argued, the provisions of the Detainee Treatment Act were unconstitutional. The government pointed to the Supreme Court's decision in *Johnson v. Eisentrager*,[314] refusing to allow a German national detained in a U.S. facility in Germany after World War II to file a writ of habeas corpus in a U.S. court to test the lawfulness of his confinement. The D.C. Circuit held that it had no jurisdiction over the Guantanamo captives' habeas corpus petitions because 28 U.S.C. § 2241(e) deprived the court of all jurisdiction.[315]

The captives petitioned for certiorari, which was granted. The Supreme Court reversed the D.C. Circuit on constitutional grounds, holding that Congress had to comply with Article II, section 9, of the Constitution that granted Congress power to suspend the writ of habeas corpus "when in cases of rebellion or invasion the public safety requires it."[316]

The Supreme Court noted that Cuba retained sovereignty over Guantanamo, which was leased to the United States. It then held that the United States had "de facto" sovereignty over the naval base because it had exclusive control over the base premises.[317] In the early twentieth century, the Supreme Court issued decisions involving jurisdiction over Guam, the Philippines, and Puerto Rico that extended the Constitution in part to these territories that were not to be incorporated as states of the union.[318] The Court held that the United States' interest in Guantanamo was like that of the United States after the Spanish–American War with respect to Puerto Rico and the Philippines. The Court cited *Reid v. Covert*[319] as authority for the proposition that extraterritorial extension of the Constitution depended upon the circumstances associated with practical necessities. In *Reid*, the Court held that the Fifth and Sixth Amendments applied to a United States citizen tried outside the territorial jurisdiction of the United States.[320] The Court viewed the controversy from the perspective that Congress alone could pass legislation suspending the writ of habeas corpus under Article I, § 9. Congress did pass a statute excluding the Guantanamo captives from federal courts, but not specifically suspending the writ of habeas corpus. The Court questioned whether Article I, section 9, protected the Guantanamo captives or not. It concluded that it did.[321] The Court also concluded, applying the *Johnson v. Eisentrager* factors, that the Guantanamo captives were not barred from filing habeas corpus petitions because Congress did not expressly suspend the writ. The captives' enemy combatant status had been challenged, and they were held captive in a facility exclusively under U.S. control on land leased by the United States.

CONCLUSION

The United States is passing through a transformation from a state that punishes criminal activities after the fact to a state that seeks to prevent criminal activities before an offense is committed. In order to effectuate this transformation, the executive branch of government has instituted a comprehensive program of surveillance and invasion of what was once thought to be privacy. The process of transformation began during the presidency of Jimmy Carter in response to terrorist attacks on U.S. citizens and U.S. installations. The FISA was the first congressional charter for preemptive surveillance without the traditional requirement of a criminal act precipitating the need for a warrant authorizing surveillance. Since 1978, Congress has accelerated the delegation of authority to invade privacy via the PATRIOT Act. The message is clear: some constitutionally protected rights must be suspended in order to apprehend terrorists, drug traffickers, and other evil persons before their criminal plots crystallize into an overt criminal act.

The Al Qaida attack on the World Trade Center and Pentagon in 2001 intensified the public need for further intrusions into constitutionally protected privacy rights. The National Security Agency, formerly limited to conducting electronic surveillance in non-U.S. venues, has extended its electronic information gathering to include outgoing electronic transmissions to non-U.S. venues. The true range of surveillance activity conducted by the FBI, the CIA, and the NSA is unknown. Two former surveillance technicians have leaked thousands of documents and classified surveillance techniques, exposing a portion of these surveillance operations.

The Bush administration's program to suppress Islamic support for western Asian militancy was well organized and was carried out with signal success. The Bush administration knew that Arab terrorists were funded in part by charitable donations made by U.S. Muslims to charitable foundations that were "fronts" for terrorist groups, authorizing the executive branch to investigate Muslim foundation giving practices.

The executive and legislative branches' justification for imposing a long-term partial suspension of civil liberties on U.S. citizens and resident aliens was strikingly similar to President Lincoln's justification for imposing similar restrictions during the Civil War. Relying on the presidential authority to act as commander in chief during time of war, Congress furnished Presidents Bush and Obama with a broad range of extraordinary power to anticipate terrorist wrongdoing by surveillance and by search and seizure before any crime has been committed. The Bush administration claimed that it had the authority under the presidential war power to detain non-U.S. citizens and non-resident aliens captured in Afghanistan and Iraq in order to interrogate the captives using means that amounted to forms of torture in order to extract intelligence information relating to Al Qaida operations. It claimed to have the authority to turn over these captives to other states that had no scruple about extracting information by torture. It claimed to have the authority to house some captives in CIA secret prisons in Europe and Africa where restrictions on torture may not apply and to hold the non-U.S. nationals in Guantanamo indefinitely without preferring charges. President Obama promised during his 2008 campaign to close the Guantanamo center and to cease using extraordinary means to obtain intelligence from captives. As of August 2016, some seventy-six captives are still held against their will in Guantanamo.

The justification for bypassing the Bill of Rights in 2016 is similar to the justifications used by the Lincoln, Wilson, and Roosevelt administrations: the crisis provoked by 9/11 justifies extraordinary means to protect the people of the United States that would ordinarily be impermissible under the Bill of Rights.

NOTES

1. "Terrorism," *Merriam-Webster Online Dictionary*, last accessed Feb. 19, 2017, http://www.merriam-webster.com/dictionary/terrorism.

2. John Philip Jenkins, "Terrorism," *Encyclopaedia Britannica Online*, last accessed Feb. 19, 2017, http://www.britannica.com/EBchecked/topic/588371/terrorism.

3. 17 Stat. 13, ch. 22, 42nd Cong., 1st Sess. (1871). The criminal portion of the act is contained in 18 U.S.C. § 242, and the civil portion of the Anti-Klan Act is included in 42 U.S.C. § 1983 as the grounds for a civil action against hooded night riders.

4. See Herbert Shapiro, "The Ku Klux Klan during Reconstruction: The South Carolina Episode," *Journal of Negro History* 46 (1964): 45–46.

5. Presidential Proclamation 201, 17 Stat. 951 (1871). The South Carolina counties affected were Spartansburg, York, Marion, Chester, Laurens, Newberry, Fairfield, Lancaster, and Chesterfield.

6. Caneisha Mills, "The Law That Put the Klan on the Run: Lessons from the Civil Rights Act of 1871," last accessed Feb. 19, 2017, http://www.pslweb.org/liberationnews/news/140-years-since-civil-rights-act-1871.html.

7. Beverly Gage, *The Day Wall Street Exploded: A Story of America in Its First Age of Terror* (New York: Oxford University Press, 2009), 41–42.

8. Gage, *The Day Wall Street Exploded*, 50–51.

9. Gage, *The Day Wall Street Exploded*, 58–60.

10. Gage, *The Day Wall Street Exploded*, 60–61.

11. Gage, *The Day Wall Street Exploded*, 63.

12. Gage, *The Day Wall Street Exploded*, 111–112, 119–121. Goldman and Berkman were sentenced to two years' confinement followed by deportation.

13. Jennifer Rosenberg, "1901 U.S. President William McKinley Assassinated," last accessed Feb. 19, 2017, http://history1900s.about.com/od/1900s/qt/mckinleykilled.htm. Czolgosz said, "I killed President McKinley because I done my duty. I didn't believe one man should have so much service and another man should have none." See also Gage, *The Day Wall Street Exploded*, 64–66.

14. The anti-anarchist clause in the immigration act was finally removed by amendment in 1990. See P.L. 101-46, 104 Stat. 15, § 131, 101st Cong., 2nd Sess., Feb. 16, 1990. See 18 U.S.C. § 1812.

15. Gage, *The Day Wall Street Exploded*, 66.

16. See, for example, the New York Criminal Anarchism Act, Laws 1902, ch. 371 (1902).

17. Gage, *The Day Wall Street Exploded*, 70–72.

18. Gage, *The Day Wall Street Exploded*, 73.

19. Gage, *The Day Wall Street Exploded*, 73–74.

20. Gage, *The Day Wall Street Exploded*, 81.

21. Gage, *The Day Wall Street Exploded*, 76–82. See also John A. Farrell, *Clarence Darrow: Attorney for the Damned* (New York: Knopf Doubleday, 2011), 163–184.

22. *Lewiston Morning Tribune*, Apr. 14, 1954, 1.

23. Gage, *The Day Wall Street Exploded*, 89–91.

24. Gage, *The Day Wall Street Exploded*, 27.

25. Gage, *The Day Wall Street Exploded*, 31–37, 121–151, 283–285. See also *New York Times*, Sept. 17, 1920, 1; Sept. 19, 1920, 1; Dec. 20, 1921, 7.

26. See Southern Poverty Law Center, *Ku Klux Klan: A History of Racism and Violence*, 6th ed. (Montgomery, AL: Southern Poverty Law Center, 2011), 15–17, 20.

27. *St. Petersburg Times*, Dec. 30, 1951, 1 (AP story). A Christmas night bombing killed Harry Moore, the Florida state coordinator for the NAACP.

28. Eden Ross Lipson, *New York Times*, book review, Oct. 25, 1981.

29. Angelo Patrizio and Mike Mudge, "TW355 Hijacked!," last accessed Feb. 19, 2017, http://www.twaseniorsclub.org/memories/contrails/tw355hijacked.html.

30. Philip Elmer DeWitt, "America's First Bioterrorism Attack," *Time*, Sept. 30, 2001.

31. See *United States v. Salameh*, 152 F.3d 88, 1998 (2d Cir. 1998), cert. denied 1999 U.S. LEXIS 700 (1999).

32. See Christopher Sullivan and Dan Sewell, "Caught JOHN DOE NO. 1: Nabbed 60 Miles outside Oklahoma City, He's Identified as Timothy McVeigh, 27 PARAMILITARY LINK: FBI Reportedly Seeking More Suspects Associated with a Far-Right Militia in Michigan Farmhouse FAST ARREST: Suspect Stopped for Speeding 90 Minutes after Bombing TERROR IN THE HEART OF AMERICA," *San Francisco Examiner*, Apr. 21, 1995, A1.

33. See Ford Fessenden, "Neighbors Recall Men, Explosives on Michigan Farm," *Newsday Buffalo News*, Apr. 22, 1995, A6.

34. FBI Staff, "Terror Hits Home: The Oklahoma City Bombing," last accessed Feb. 19, 2017, http://www.fbi.gov/history/famous-cases/oklahoma-city-bombing.

35. *New York Times*, June 12, 2001, A1. See also 18 U.S.C. §§ 3591–3596.

36. American Airlines flight 11 from Boston to Los Angeles was hijacked by five men who were Al Qaida operatives. Mohamed Atta, who had been trained to pilot commercial jet aircraft in a U.S. flying school; Abdul Azzis el Omari; Satam el Suqami; Wail el Shehri; and Waleed al-Sherhri captured the plane, stabbed two flight attendants and a first-class passenger, broke into the cockpit, and dispatched the air crew shortly after 8:00 a.m. Atta presumably flew the plane into the south tower of the World Trade Center. *Final Report of the National Commission on Terrorist Attacks upon the United States* (Washington, D.C.: Government Printing Office, 2004), 1, 4–7.

37. United Airlines flight 175 from Boston to Los Angeles departed Logan Airport carrying Al Qaida operatives Marwan al-Shehhi, Fayez Banihammed, Mohand al-Shehri, Ahmad al-Ghamdi, and Hamza al-Ghamdi. The operatives took over the aircraft, stabbed the flight crew, and flew the aircraft into New York City, striking the north tower of the World Trade Center at 9:03 a.m. *Final Report of the National Commission on Terrorist Attacks*, 1–2, 7–8.

38. American Airlines flight 77 from Washington, D.C., Dulles Airport to Los Angeles was boarded by Khalid al-Mihdhar, Majed Moqed, Hami Hanjour, Nawaf al-Hazmi, and his brother Salem al-Hazmi. The operatives took over the plane at 9:12 a.m. and turned the flight around toward the Pentagon. The aircraft struck the Pentagon at 9:37 a.m. *Final Report of the National Commission on Terrorist Attacks*, 2–3, 8–10.

39. United Airlines flight 93 from Newark to San Francisco was boarded by Al Qaida operatives Saed al-Ghamdi, Ahmad al-Nami, Ahmad al-Haznawai, and Ziad Jarrah. The aircraft was taken over at 9:28 a.m. and turned to the southeast, heading toward Washington, D.C. As the plane headed southeast, several passengers organized an assault to retake the plane from the Al Qaida operatives. The operative flying the plane yawed and pitched the aircraft, trying to stop the passengers' rush on the cockpit. When that failed, he flew the plane into the ground near Shanksville, Pennsylvania, more than one hundred air miles from the intended targets in Washington. *Final Report of the National Commission on Terrorist Attacks*, 4, 10–14.

40. The similarity between the struggle between *jahiliyya* and Islam and the biblical description of Armageddon is apparent. See Revelations 6:16. It is also mentioned in the Hadith, the Islamic recording of Muhammad's prophecies. See Sunan Abi Dawud 4311, in-book reference: Book 39, Hadith 21, English translation: Book 38, Hadith 4297; Sunan Abi Dawud 4321, in-book reference: Book 39, Hadith 31, English translation: Book 38, Hadith 4307; Sunan Abi Dawud 4324, in-book reference: Book 39, Hadith 34, English translation: Book 38, Hadith 4310.

41. *Final Report of the National Commission on Terrorist Attacks*, 59.

42. *Final Report of the National Commission on Terrorist Attacks*, 47.

43. *Final Report of the National Commission on Terrorist Attacks*, 60.

44. *Final Report of the National Commission on Terrorist Attacks*, 71–73. Khalid Sheikh Mohammed's career as an Al Qaida operative is detailed in *Final Report of the National Commission on Terrorist Attacks*, 145–150.

45. *Final Report of the National Commission on Terrorist Attacks*, 68–70.

46. *Final Report of the National Commission on Terrorist Attacks,* 190–193. The 9/11 Report states that the attack on the *Cole* was personally supervised by Osama Bin Laden, who paid for the explosives used to attack the ship.

47. S. J. Res. 23, Joint Resolution on Authorization for Use of Military Forces, 115 Stat. 224 (2000).

48. See Alan M. Dershowitz, "The Preventive State: Uncharted Waters after 9/11," in *The Impact of 9/11 and the New Legal Landscape,* ed. Matthew J. Morgan (New York: Palgrave Macmillan, 2009), 7–26.

49. See House Committee on Foreign Affairs, *The War Powers Resolution: A Special Study of the Committee on Foreign Affairs* (Washington, D.C.: Government Printing Office, 1982), 5–6.

50. House Committee on Foreign Affairs, *The War Powers Resolution,* 7–8.

51. See Lyndon B. Johnson Presidential Library and Museum, Telegram from White House Situation Room to President Johnson, dated Apr. 25, 1965; transcript of telephone conversation between Pres. Johnson and Undersecretary of State Mann, dated Apr. 26, 1965; Jack Valenti notes Apr. 30, 1965; Instructions from Gen. Earl Wheeler to commanders Dominican Republic, dated May 1, 1965, last accessed, http://www.utexas.edu/hemispheres/_filespdf/newsletters/cold_war_docs/DominicanCrisis.pdf.

52. See House Committee on Foreign Affairs, *The War Powers Resolution,* 9–11.

53. House Committee on Foreign Affairs, *The War Powers Resolution,* 13.

54. House Committee on Foreign Affairs, *The War Powers Resolution,* 18–19, 20.

55. House Committee on Foreign Affairs, *The War Powers Resolution,* 27.

56. House Committee on Foreign Affairs, *The War Powers Resolution,* 29; see also the history of the Cooper–Church Amendment to freeze appropriations for the Cambodian invasion at pp. 31–34.

57. House Committee on Foreign Affairs, *The War Powers Resolution,* 38–39.

58. House Committee on Foreign Affairs, *The War Powers Resolution,* 44–50, hearings at 55–59. A similar resolution sponsored by Sen. Javitts was pending during the same period (pp. 52–54).

59. House Committee on Foreign Affairs, *The War Powers Resolution,* 99–100, 110–113, 138–148 (conference committee), 152–155 (passage of joint resolution by both houses).

60. House Committee on Foreign Affairs, *The War Powers Resolution,* 156–157.

61. House Committee on Foreign Affairs, *The War Powers Resolution,* 158–166.

62. House Committee on Foreign Affairs, *The War Powers Resolution,* 148.

63. 50 U.S.C. § 1541(a). Subsection (b) invokes the "necessary and proper" clause of Art. I, § 8, of the U.S. Constitution as justification for the resolution. Subsection (c) states a limitation on the president's power as commander in chief, requiring that the president may employ U.S. forces only when Congress declares war or a national emergency is "created by attack upon the United States, its territories or possessions, or its armed forces."

64. 50 U.S.C. § 1542.

65. 50 U.S.C. § 1543.

66. 50 U.S.C. § 1544.

67. 50 U.S.C. §§ 1545–1546.

68. 83. 50 U.S.C. § 1547. President Johnson occasionally relied on the SEATO treaty to justify U.S. military involvement in Vietnam.

69. Clause 1 of Art. II, § 2, reads as follows: "The President shall be Commander in Chief of the Army and Navy of the United States, and of the Militia of the several states when called into the actual service of the United States."

70. U.S. Const., Art. I, § 8, clause 11, grants Congress authority "to declare War, grant letters of Marque and Reprisal and make rules concerning Captures on Land and Water." Clause 12 authorizes Congress to "Raise and Support Armies." Clause 13 authorizes the establishment of the U.S. Navy, and clause 14 grants Congress the power to pass statutes relating to "Government and regulation of land and naval

forces." Clause 15 grants Congress power to call up the militia. Clause 17 authorizes Congress to "provide for the organizing, arming and disciplining the militia."

71. House Committee on Foreign Affairs, *The War Powers Resolution*, 181–185. The Ford administration did try to reach some members of Congress, which was in recess at the time Da Nang was evacuated. No formal consultation or reporting took place.

72. House Committee on Foreign Affairs, *The War Powers Resolution*, 186–189.

73. House Committee on Foreign Affairs, *The War Powers Resolution*, 198–199 (Saigon).

74. House Committee on Foreign Affairs, *The War Powers Resolution*, 208–219 (Mayaguez rescue mission).

75. House Committee on Foreign Affairs, *The War Powers Resolution*, 232–237 (Zaire), 238–246 (Iran rescue operation). President Carter filed a report with Congress on the Iran rescue operation within the War Powers Resolution time limit but denied that he was required to do so.

76. House Committee on Foreign Affairs, *The War Powers Resolution*, 247–252. President Reagan sent assurances to Congress that U.S. involvement in El Salvador would not escalate to a U.S. military expedition in support of the El Salvadorean government's attempts to put down the Marxist rebellion.

77. House Committee on Foreign Affairs, *The War Powers Resolution*, 251.

78. Library of Congress, ed., "War Powers," 2013, last accessed Feb. 15, 2017, http://www.loc.gov/law/help/war-powers.php.

79. 105 Stat. 3 (1991).

80. See General Accounting Office, *Report to Congressional Requesters: Withdrawal from Somalia* (Washington, D.C.: Government Printing Office, 1994). Congress passed P.L. 103-139, the Defense Appropriation Bill, 107 Stat. 1418 (1993), which specified in Section 8151 that military operations in Somalia would not be funded after Mar. 31, 1994.

81. P.L. 95-511, 92 Stat. 1783, codified as 50 U.S.C., ch. 36.

82. 50 U.S.C. §§ 1801–1812.

83. 50 U.S.C. §§ 1821–1829.

84. 50 U.S.C. §§ 1841–1846.

85. 50 U.S.C. §§ 1861–1871.

86. 50 U.S.C. §§ 1881–1885b.

87. 50 U.S.C. § 1801(i).

88. 50 U.S.C. § 1801(a).

89. 50 U.S.C. § 1801(b).

90. 50 U.S.C. § 1801(c).

91. 50 U.S.C. § 1801(e).

92. 50 U.S.C. § 1801(f).

93. 50 U.S.C. § 1801(h). The Fourth Amendment reads as follows: "The right of the people to be secure in their persons, houses, papers, and effects, against unreasonable searches and seizures, shall not be violated, and no Warrants shall issue, but upon probable cause, supported by Oath or affirmation, and particularly describing the place to be searched, and the persons or things to be seized."

94. 50 U.S.C. § 1802(a).

95. 50 U.S.C. § 8102(a)(4).

96. 50 U.S.C. § 1802(a)(2) and (3).

97. 50 U.S.C. § 1802(b).

98. 50 U.S.C. § 1803(a).

99. 50 U.S.C. § 1803(b).

100. 50 U.S.C. § 1803(g).

101. 50 U.S.C. § 1804.

102. 50 U.S.C. § 1805.

103. 50 U.S.C. § 1805(e).

104. 50 U.S.C. § 1805(f).

105. 50 U.S.C. § 1805(h).

106. 50 U.S.C. § 1805(i).
107. 50 U.S.C. § 1806 (a) and (b). Subsection (b) states: "No information acquired pursuant to this title [50 USCS §§ 1801 et seq.] shall be disclosed for law enforcement purposes unless such disclosure is accompanied by a statement that such information, or any information derived therefrom, may only be used in a criminal proceeding with the advance authorization of the Attorney General."
108. 50 U.S.C. § 1806(e)(1) and (2).
109. 50 U.S.C. § 1806(f).
110. 50 U.S.C. § 1806(f). Any court order issued after ex parte inspection by the court will be deemed final orders generating the right to appeal to the court of appeals.
111. 50 U.S.C. § 1806(j).
112. 50 U.S.C. § 1807 and 1808.
113. 50 U.S.C. § 1809.
114. 50 U.S.C. § 1810.
115. 50 U.S.C. § 1811.
116. 50 U.S.C. § 1812.
117. 50 U.S.C. § 1821(a)(1) and (2). Subsection (3) requires that the attorney general also transmit the certification for any search to the Foreign Intelligence Surveillance Court.
118. 50 U.S.C. § 1821(c).
119. 50 U.S.C. § 1823.
120. 50 U.S.C. § 1823(d)(1) and (2) (attorney general's obligation to suggest modifications of application).
121. 50 U.S.C. § 1824(a)(1).
122. 50 U.S.C. § 1824(d).
123. 50 U.S.C. § 1824(e).
124. 50 U.S.C. § 1825.
125. 50 U.S.C. § 1825(b).
126. 50 U.S.C. § 1825(h).
127. 50 U.S.C. § 1826.
128. 50 U.S.C. §§ 1827–1828.
129. See the definition and description of pen registers and trap and trace devices at Cornell University Law School Legal Information Institute, last accessed Feb. 15, 2017, https://www.law.cornel.edu/wex/pen_register.
130. 50 U.S.C. § 1841.
131. 50 U.S.C. § 1842.
132. 50 U.S.C. § 1842(b) and (c).
133. 50 U.S.C. § 1842(e).
134. 50 U.S.C. § 1843(a).
135. 50 U.S.C. § 1844.
136. 50 U.S.C. § 1845(b).
137. 50 U.S.C. § 1845(e), (f), and (g).
138. 50 U.S.C. § 1846(a).
139. 50 U.S.C. § 1561.
140. 50 U.S.C. § 1571.
141. 50 U.S.C. § 1881a(b) and (c).
142. 50 U.S.C. § 1881a(i).
143. 50 U.S.C. § 1881b.
144. 50 U.S.C. § 1881d.
145. 50 U.S.C. § 1881(e).
146. *Al-Haramain Islamic Found., Inc. v. Obama*, 690 F.3d 1089 (9th Cir. 2012), held: 50 U.S.C. § 1810 is not a waiver of sovereign immunity; hence plaintiffs have no right to sue the United States. *ACLU v. NSA*, 493 F.3d 644 (6th Cir. 2007), held: ACLU suit dismissed for lack of federal jurisdiction.

147. David Martin, "Refining Immigration's Role in Counterterrorism," in *Legislating the War on Terror: An Agenda for Reform*, ed. Benjamin Wittes (Washington, D.C.: Brookings Institution Press, 2009), 180–211.

148. See Quinnipiac College Public Opinion Poll, January 2010 and July 2013, last accessed Feb. 15, 2017, http://www.poll.qu.edu/release-detail?ReleaseID=1919.

149. 18 U.S.C. § 2339A.

150. 18 U.S.C. § 2339A(3), "advice or assistance," means advice or assistance derived from scientific, technical, or other specialized knowledge.

151. See, e.g., *United States v. Farhane*, 634 F.3d 127 (2d Cir. 2011) (defendant a martial arts instructor charged with giving material aid to Al Qaida operatives by giving them martial arts instruction); *United States v. Chandia*, 514 F.3d 365 (4th Cir. 2008); *United States v. Hassoun*, 476 F.3d 1181 (11th Cir. 2007) (defendants charged with belonging to a cell in the United States that conspired to carry out murders in support of Al Qaida); *United States v. Khan*, 461 F.3d 477 (4th Cir. 2006) amended by *United States v. Khan*, 2006 U.S. App. LEXIS 22748 (4th Cir. Va., Sept. 1, 2006), cert. denied 550 U.S. 956 (2007). Post-conviction relief denied *United States v. Chapman*, 2010 U.S. App. LEXIS 20569 (4th Cir. Va., Oct. 4, 2010) (defendants members of Dar al Arqam Islamic Center Falls Church, Virginia, trained other members with paintball simulations aiding LET terrorists in Pakistan; one defendant also went to LET camp and helped agent of terrorist group purchase weapons); *United States v. Warsame*, 537 F. Supp. 2d 1005 (D. Minn. 2008) (defendant charged with traveling to Afghanistan to receive Al Qaida training); *United States v. Shah*, 474 F. Supp. 2d 492 (S.D. N.Y. 2007) (doctor charged with providing medical aid to Al Qaida members); *United States v. Awan*, 459 F. Supp. 2d 167 (E.D. N.Y. 2006) (defendant charged with transferring own money and assisting others to transfer money to the Khalistan Commando Force, a Sikh separatist organization based in Pakistan); *United States v. Sattar*, 314 F. Supp. 2d 279 (S.D. N.Y. 2004) (defendants including lawyer for accused terrorist charged with conspiracy to aid foreign terrorists).

152. See *United States v. Al-Hussayen*, No. CR03-048-C-EJL, 2004 U.S. Dist. LEXIS 29793 (D. Idaho Apr. 7, 2004), discussed in David Cole, "Out of the Shadows: Preventive Detention, Suspected Terrorists, and War," 97 *California Law Review* 693 (2009) 703, and in Susan N. Herman, *Taking Liberties: The War on Terror and the Erosion of American Democracy* (New York: Oxford University Press, 2011), 23–32.

153. Herman, *Taking Liberties*, 26.

154. See *Spokane Spokesman Review*, Apr. 5, 2003, B1.

155. *Spokane Spokesman Review*, May 6, 2004, A1.

156. *Spokane Spokesman Review*, May 12, 2004, B1.

157. Herman, *Taking Liberties*, 26.

158. *Spokane Spokesman Review*, May 19, 2004, B1.

159. *Spokane Spokesman Review*, May 12, 2004, B1.

160. *Spokane Spokesman Review*, May 16, 2004, B1.

161. *Spokane Spokesman Review*, May 25, 2004, B3.

162. *Spokane Spokesman Review*, May 27, 2004, B1.

163. *Spokane Spokesman Review*, July 22, 2004, B1.

164. See 18 U.S.C. § 3144 (material witness statute).

165. Herman, *Taking Liberties*, 33; *Spokane Spokesman Review*, June 22, 2004, B3. Kidd was held as a material witness in the al-Hussayen prosecution.

166. *Latif v. Holder*, 2014 U.S. Dist. LEXIS 85450 (D. Or. 3:10-cv-00750-BR June 24, 2014), at 6–8 (Joint Statement of Stipulated Facts [#84] at 4).

167. See Ted Barrett, "Kennedy Has Company on Airline Watch List," CNN, Aug. 20, 2004, last accessed Feb. 15, 2017, http://www.cnn.com/2004/ALLPOLITICS/08/20/lewis.watchlist/index.html. U.S. congressman John Lewis was also inadvertently put on the list.

168. *Gordon v. FBI*, 390 F. Supp. 2d 897 (N.D. Cal. 2004).

169. *Gordon*, 390 F. Supp. 2d 900. See also 5 U.S.C. § 552(b)(3).

170. 49 U.S.C. § 114(s).

171. 49 U.S.C. § 40119(b).

172. Exemption (6) excludes from disclosure "personnel and medical files and similar files the disclosure of which would constitute a clearly unwarranted invasion of privacy." 5 U.S.C. § 552(b)(6).

173. Exemption (7) applies to "records compiled for law enforcement purposes but only to the extent that providing these records" fulfills certain conditions.

174. *Gordon*, 390 F. Supp. 2d 899–902.

175. *Gordon*, 390 F. Supp. 2d 902.

176. "TSA and FBI Ordered to Pay $200,000 to Settle 'No Fly' Lawsuit" (press release), American Civil Liberties Union, Jan. 24, 2006; "Justice Department Report Tells of Flaws in Terrorist Watch List," CNN, Sept. 6, 2007, last accessed Feb. 20, 2017, http://www.cnn.com/2007/US/09/06/terror.watchlist.

177. *Latif v. Holder*, 2014 U.S. Dist. LEXIS 85450 (D. Or. 3:10-cv-00750-BR June 24, 2014).

178. *Latif v. Holder*, 2014 U.S. Dist. LEXIS 85450, 10–12.

179. *Gilmore v. Gonzales*, 435 F.3d 1125 (9th Cir. 2006).

180. *Gilmore v. Gonzales*, 1136–1137.

181. Executive Order 12949, Feb. 9, 1995.

182. See *The Guardian*, "Warrantless Surveillance Evidence Faces Court Test in Terrorist Case," last accessed Feb. 15, 2017, http://www.theguardian.com/world/2013/oct/26/warrantless-surveillance-jamshid-muhtorov-court; "Declassified FBI Docs Detail Warrantless Drone Surveillance," Dec. 13, 2013, last accessed Feb. 20, 2017, http://rt.com/usa/fbi-internal-drone-guidelines-revealed-169.

183. *United States v. Muhtorov*, 2013 U.S. Dist. LEXIS 61756 (D. Colo. No. 1:12-cr-00033-JLK Apr. 30, 2013).

184. See *United States v. Daoud*, 755 F.3d 479, 480–482 (7th Cir. 2014). See also Charles Savage, "Warrantless Surveillance Challenged by Defendant," *New York Times*, Jan. 29, 2014.

185. *United States v. Daoud*, 755 F.3d 479 (7th Cir. 2014); "Court Denies Access to FISA Surveillance Documents in Adel Daoud Terror Case," *The Guardian*, June 16, 2014, last accessed Feb. 17, 2017, http://www.theguardian.com/law/2014/jun/16/fisa-surveillance-documents-daoud-court-overturn-chicago.

186. Daoud, 755 F.3d 483.

187. See, e.g., Siobhan Gorman, "NSA Rejected System That Sifted Phone Data Legally," *Baltimore Sun* (Washington), May 18, 2006.

188. The special project was known as "Trail-Blazer," a $1.2 billion intercept program that ultimately turned out to be a dismal failure. The NSA rejected a competing program—Thin Thread—that would have complied with FISA and would not have invaded the privacy of callers or messages. It was an encrypted program. See also Deb Reichmann, "Bush Defends Spying Program; Calls Effort Legal, Vital; Leak Seen Hurting Nation," *Buffalo News*, Jan. 2, 2006.

189. Morton Halperin, "A Legal Analysis of the NSA Warrantless Surveillance Program," last accessed Feb. 15, 2017, https://opensocietypolicycenter.org/wp-content/uploads/mhh-fisa-6-Jan.pdf.

190. Halperin, "A Legal Analysis of the NSA Warrantless Surveillance Program."

191. Walter F. Roche Jr. and Edwin Chen, "Bush Defends Decision on U.S. Wiretaps," *Chicago Tribune*, Jan. 2, 2006.

192. Roche and Chen, "Bush Defends Decision on U.S. Wiretaps."

193. See Sibohan Gorman, "Second-Ranking NSA Official Forced out of Job by Director," *Baltimore Sun*, May 31, 2006.

194. Michael Isikoff, "The Whistleblower Who Exposed Warrantless Wiretaps," *Newsweek*, Dec. 12, 2008, last accessed Feb. 15, 2017, http://www.newsweek.com/whistleblower-who-exposed-warrantless-wiretaps-82805.

195. Congressional Record (Senate) S646–S647, Jan. 17, 2007.

196. See *In re NSA Telecomms*. Records Litig., 700 F. Supp. 2d 1182 (N.D. Cal. 2010).

197. Charles Savage and James Risen, "Federal Judge Finds N.S.A. Wiretaps Were Illegal," *New York Times*, Mar. 31, 2010.
198. *Al-Haramain Islamic Found., Inc. v. Obama*, 690 F.3d 1089 (9th Cir. 2012).
199. Barton Gellman and Ashkan Soltani, "NSA Tracking Cellphone Locations Worldwide, Snowden Documents Show," *Washington Post*, Dec. 4, 2013.
200. Ted Hesson, "Five Ways Immigration System Changed after 9/11," 2012, last accessed Feb. 15, 2017, http://abcnews.go.com/ABC_Univision/News/ways-immigration-system-changed-911/story?id=17231590.
201. Hesson, "Five Ways Immigration System Changed."
202. 8 U.S.C. § 1229a describes the scope of deportation proceedings and the limited civil rights of alleged illegal aliens before the immigration judge.
203. Hesson, "Five Ways Immigration System Changed." Hesson noted that private detention centers for illegal immigrants run by profit-making corporations brought in substantial revenue to their corporate owners.
204. *Mayfield v. United States*, 504 F. Supp. 2d 1023 (D. Or. 2007).
205. *Mayfield v. United States*, 588 F.3d 1252, 1255 (9th Cir. 2009). See also U.S. Dept. of Justice, Office of Inspector General, *A Review of the FBI's Handling of the Brandon Mayfield Case* (Washington, D.C.: Government Printing Office, 2006), 1.
206. Dept. of Justice, *A Review of the FBI's Handling*, 2.
207. Dept. of Justice, *A Review of the FBI's Handling*, 3–4.
208. Dept. of Justice, *A Review of the FBI's Handling*, 3.
209. Dept. of Justice, *A Review of the FBI's Handling*, 3.
210. Dept. of Justice, *A Review of the FBI's Handling*, 3.
211. Dept. of Justice, *A Review of the FBI's Handling*, 4.
212. *Bivens v. Six Unknown Named Agents*, 403 U.S. 388 (1971). The *Bivens* decision allowed the plaintiff to bring suit against the narcotics agents for violating his Fourth Amendment protection from unreasonable search and seizure.
213. 5 U.S.C. § 552a.
214. Mayfield, 599 F.3d 966–970.
215. Mayfield, 599 F.3d 966–970.
216. Mark Jaycox, "Peekaboo, I See You: Government Authority Intended for Terrorism Is Used for Other Purposes," *Electronic Frontier Foundation*, Oct. 26, 2014, last accessed Feb. 15, 2017, https://www.eff.org/deeplinks/2014/10/peekaboo-i-see-you-government-uses-authority-meant-terrorism-other-uses.
217. *United States v. Freitas*, 800 F.2d 1451, 1456 (9th Cir. 1986). The court warned readers that the warrant was defective because it lacked a definite time to make notice, but affirmed the seizure under the good faith exception to the suppression rule.
218. Fred E. Foldvary, "Roving Wiretaps Deplored by Fred Foldvary," *Progress Report*, Sept. 23, 2004, last accessed Feb. 15, 2017, http://www.progress.org/fold79.htm.
219. *United States v. Abu-Jihadd*, 630 F.3d 102 (2nd Cir. 2010), cert. denied 2011 U.S. LEXIS 4819 (No.10-9651, June 27, 2011).
220. Laura Donohue, "Criminal Law: Anglo-American Privacy and Surveillance," *Journal of Criminal Law & Criminology* 96 (2006): 1059.
221. See Emran Qureshi, "Taliban," Oxford Islamic Studies Online, Sept. 13, 2014, last accessed Feb. 15, 2017, http://www.oxfordislamicstudies.com/article/opr/t236/e0895.
222. Qureshi, "Taliban."
223. Tim McGirk and Shomali Plain, "Lifting the Veil on Taliban Sex Slavery," *Time*, Feb. 10, 2002.
224. Pierre Tristam, "History of the Taliban: Who They Are, What They Want," last accessed Feb. 15, 2017, http://middleeast.about.com/od/afghanistan/ss/me080914a.htm.
225. Tristam, "History of the Taliban."
226. Alex Cane, "5 Stunning Revelations from Senate Report Exposing CIA Torture," *Salon*, last accessed Feb. 15, 2017, http://www.salon.com/2014/04/17/5_stunning_revelations_from_senate_report_exposing_cia_torture_partner. See also "Dianne Fein-

stein: Administration Is Hiding Key Facts in Senate's CIA Torture Report," *Huffington Post*, Aug. 6, 2014. The writer states that leaks from the government indicate that the CIA used a variety of torture techniques to extract intelligence information from captives.

227. Jay Bybee and John Yoo, "Letter to Hon. Alberto Gonzales Dated Aug. 1, 2002," last accessed Feb. 15, 2017, http://nsarchiv.gwu.edu/NSAEBB/NSAEBB127/020801.pdf. Bybee and Yoo argue that the interrogation methods used on Al Qaida captives were not torture as defined by 18 U.S.C. § 234-2340a, which defined the use of torture as a felony, nor did the United States violate any provision of the Geneva Conventions.

228. See Charles J. Hanley, "Former Iraqi Detainees Tell of Riots, Punishment in the Sun, Good Americans and Pitiless Ones," *Associated Press*, Nov. 1, 2003, last accessed Feb. 20, 2017, http://legacysandiegotribune.com/news/wprld/iraq/w20031101-0936-iraq-thecamps.html.

229. These abuses were detailed in an official investigative report conducted by Brig. Gen. Antonio Taguba released in May 2004. See "Executive Summary of Article 15-6 Investigation of the 800th Military Police Brigade by Maj. Gen. Antonio M. Taguba," last accessed Feb. 20, 2017, http://www.NPR.org/Iraq/2004/prison-abuse-report.pdf.

230. Taguba, "Executive Summary of Article 15-6 Investigation."

231. Mark Denbeaux, Joshua Denbeaux, David Gratz, John Gregorek, Matthew Darby, Shana Edwards, Shane Hartman, Daniel Mann, and Helen Skinner, *Report on Guantanamo Detainees: A Profile of 517 Detainees through Analysis of Department of Defense Data* (Seton Hall Law School Center for Policy and Research, 2006), last accessed Feb. 15, 2017, http://law.shu.edu/publications/guantanamoReports/guantanamo_report_final_2_08_06.pdf.

232. Mark Denbeaux, Joshua Denbeaux, R. David Getz, Megan Sassaman, Daniel Mann, Matthew Darby, and Michael Ricciardelli (2008); Jennifer Ellick, Grace Brown, Jillian Camarote, Douglas Eadie, Daniel Lorenzo, Mark Muoio, and Courtney Ray (2009); Adam Deutsch, Deborah Fish, Gabrielle Hughes, Michael Patterson, and Paul Taylor (2010), *Torture: Who Knew; An Analysis of the FBI and Department of Defense Reactions to Harsh Interrogation Methods at Guantanamo* (Seton Hall Law School Center for Policy and Research, 2008–2010), last accessed Feb. 20, 2017, http://law.shu.edu/policy-research/guantanamo-reports.cfm.

233. Jonathan Horowitz and Stacy Cammarano, "20 Extraordinary Facts about CIA Extraordinary Rendition and Secret Detention," Open Society Justice Initiative, 2013, last accessed Feb. 15, 2017, http://www.opensocietyfoundations.org/voices/20-extraordinary-facts-about-cia-extraordinary-rendition-and-secret-detention-comments.

234. Horowitz and Cammarano, "20 Extraordinary Facts."

235. Horowitz and Cammarano, "20 Extraordinary Facts."

236. See Ian Cobain, "Rendered to Libya," *The Guardian*, Mar. 4, 2013. Horowitz and Cammarano, "20 Extraordinary Facts."

237. John Crewdson, "Wife of Abu Omar Recounts Visits with Husband," *Chicago Tribune*, Dec. 28, 2005; Horowitz and Cammarano, "20 Extraordinary Facts."

238. See "Italian Court Convicts Egypt Cleric Abu Omar to 6 Years for Terrorism," *Xinhua News Agency—CEI* (Woodside), Dec. 6, 2013; John Crewdson and Alessandra Maggiorani, "CIA Chiefs Reportedly Split over Cleric Plot; Agency Schisms Come to Light in Italy Probe," *Chicago Tribune*, Jan. 8, 2007.

239. See Peter Foster, "CIA Took Suspects 'to Point of Death,'" *Calgary Herald*, Sept. 8, 2014; "Why Did CIA Shut Down Black Site in Poland?," *Polish News Bulletin* (Weekend Supplement) (Warsaw), Aug. 7, 2014; Horowitz and Cammarano, "20 Extraordinary Facts."

240. This account is based on Center for Constitutional Rights, *Report: Torture and Cruel, Inhuman, and Degrading Treatment of Prisoners at Guantanamo*, 2006, last accessed Feb. 15, 2017, http://ccrjustice.org/learn-more/reports/report:-torture-and-cruel,-inhuman,-and-degrading-treatment-prisoners-guantanamo-.

241. Initially, this term was undefined. After *Rasul v. Bush*, 542 U.S. 406 (2004), the Supreme Court decision that authorized individuals held at Guantanamo to file writs of habeas corpus to test the legality of their confinement, Undersecretary of Defense Wolfowitz issued an order defining *enemy combatant* as "an individual who was part of or supporting Taliban or al Qaeda forces, or associated forces that are engaged in hostilities against the U.S. or its coalition partners. This includes any person who has committed a belligerent act or has directly supported hostilities in aid of enemy armed forces." *Rasul* has been overruled by statute. See 28 U.S.C. § 2241(e) removing jurisdiction over any individual detained as an enemy combatant from all federal courts.
242. Center for Constitutional Rights, *Report*, 7.
243. Center for Constitutional Rights, *Report*, 4–5.
244. Center for Constitutional Rights, *Report*.
245. Center for Constitutional Rights, *Report*.
246. Center for Constitutional Rights, *Report*.
247. See "ACLU Calls for End to Inhumane Force Feeding of Guantanamo Prisoners," last accessed Feb. 15, 2017, https://www.aclu.org/news/aclu-calls-end-inhumane-force-feeding-guantanamo-prisoners.
248. Executive Order 13491 (2009). Executive Order 13491.
249. Executive Order 13491.
250. Human Rights First, "Guantanamo by the Numbers," last accessed Feb. 15, 2017, http://www.humanrightsfirst.org/wp-content/uploads/pdf/USLS-Fact-Sheet-Gitmo-Numbers.pdf. This source lists the total number of detainees at 779 between 2001 and 2014.
251. Human Rights First, "Guantanamo by the Numbers."
252. Detention, Treatment, and Trial of Certain Non-Citizens in the War against Terrorism, 66 Fed. Reg. 57833 (Nov. 16, 2001).
253. Detention, Treatment, and Trial of Certain Non-Citizens.
254. Detention, Treatment, and Trial of Certain Non-Citizens.
255. Dept. of Defense Military Commission Order No. 1, Mar. 21, 2002.
256. P.L. 109-148, 109th Cong., 119 Stat. 2739 (2005).
257. *Hamdan v. Rumsfeld*, 344 F. Supp. 2d 152 (D. D.C. 2004).
258. *Hamdan v. Rumsfeld*, 415 F.3d 33 (2005). The D.C. Circuit concluded that Hamdan was not entitled to a writ of habeas corpus because the Geneva Convention may not be enforced by judicial decree. The same court held that *Ex parte Quirin*, 317 U.S. 1 (1943), authorized the president to try Hamdan by military commission.
259. *Hamdan v. Rumsfeld*, 548 U.S. 557 (2006).
260. *Hamdan v. Rumsfeld*, 548 U.S. 588–589.
261. *Hamdan v. Rumsfeld*, 548 U.S. 589–590.
262. *Hamdan v. Rumsfeld*, 548 U.S. 594–595.
263. *Hamdan v. Rumsfeld*, 548 U.S. 596.
264. *Hamdan v. Rumsfeld*, 548 U.S. 598.
265. *Hamdan v. Rumsfeld*, 548 U.S. 600.
266. *Hamdan v. Rumsfeld*, 548 U.S. 602–603, 604–606.
267. *Hamdan v. Rumsfeld*, 548 U.S. 614–616, 619–621. The court was particularly disturbed by the provisions of Commission Order 1, which allowed the commission to eject the accused and counsel during secret sessions involving classified matter and its many deviations from the UCMJ's provisions for courts-martial.
268. *Hamdan v. Rumsfeld*, 548 U.S. 631.
269. Geneva Convention 1949 U.S.T. LEXIS 483–484.
270. Geneva Convention 1949.
271. *Hamdan v. Rumsfeld*, 548 U.S. 656–657.
272. *Hamdan v. Rumsfeld*, 548 U.S. 670–671.
273. *Hamdan v. Rumsfeld*, 548 U.S. 672–673.
274. *Hamdan v. Rumsfeld*, 548 U.S. 683–684.
275. 10 U.S.C. § 948b.
276. 10 U.S.C. § 950t.

277. 10 U.S.C. § 949j (also containing provisions for prosecution disclosure of exculpatory evidence).
278. 10 U.S.C. § 949, p. 4 (discovery of classified information).
279. 10 U.S.C. § 949, pp. 1–7.
280. See 10 U.S.C. § 950a–o.
281. See 10 U.S.C. § 950c, 950f.
282. See 10 U.S.C. § 950g.
283. 10 U.S.C. § 949a.
284. Human Rights Watch, "The Guantanamo Trials," last accessed Feb. 15, 2017, http://www.hrw.org/features/guantanamo.
285. *Hamdi v. Rumsfeld*, 316 F.3d 450 (4th Cir. 2002).
286. *Hamdi v. Rumsfeld*, 316 F.3d 465–467. See also *Hamdi v. Rumsfeld*, 542 U.S. 507, 513–514 (2004).
287. *Hamdi v. Rumsfeld*, 316 F.3d 467–469. The court expressed a duty of deference to the president's authority as commander in chief under Article II required the result.
288. *Hamdi v. Rumsfeld*, 542 U.S. 507, 509 (2004).
289. *Hamdi v. Rumsfeld*, 542 U.S. 516.
290. *Hamdi v. Rumsfeld*, 542 U.S. 516–517.
291. *Hamdi v. Rumsfeld*, 542 U.S. 525. The court qualified this holding, stating that the right to habeas corpus could be suspended by Congress.
292. *Hamdi v. Rumsfeld*, 542 U.S. 533. Later in the opinion the plurality stated, "In sum, while the full protections that accompany challenges to detentions in other settings may prove unworkable and inappropriate in the enemy-combatant setting, the threats to military operations posed by a basic system of independent review are not so weighty as to trump a citizen's core rights to challenge meaningfully the Government's case and to be heard by an impartial adjudicator." *Hamdi v. Rumsfeld*, 542 U.S. 535.The Court also noted that the president's war power "does not remove constitutional limitations safeguarding essential liberties." *Hamdi v. Rumsfeld*, 542 U.S. 536.
293. "U.S.-Freed Combatant Is Returned to Saudi Arabia; Yaser Esam Hamdi's Case Was a Factor in a High Court Ruling That Said Such Prisoners Must Be Charged. 'He Is Not a Taliban,' His Father Says," *Los Angeles Times*, Oct. 12, 2004, A8.
294. *Rasul v. Bush*, 542 U.S. 466 (2004).
295. *Padilla v. Rumsfeld*, 542 U.S. 426 (2004).
296. *Padilla v. Bush*, 233 F. Supp. 2d 564 (S.D. N.Y., 2002).
297. *Padilla v. Bush*, 233 F. Supp. 2d 569–570. The district court ordered the secretary of defense to permit Padilla to consult with his attorney, Ms. Newman. The government then moved for reconsideration of the district court's order that allowed Ms. Newman to talk with her client, because no conditions could be set that would protect the national security. See *Padilla ex rel. Newman v. Rumsfeld*, 256 F. Supp. 2d 218 (S.D. N.Y. 2003).
298. *Padilla v. Bush*, 243 F. Supp. 2d 223.
299. *Padilla v. Rumsfeld*, 352 F.3d 695, 710 (2d Cir. 2003).
300. *Padilla v. Rumsfeld*, 352 F.3d 718.
301. 18 U.S.C. § 4001(a).
302. *Padilla v. Rumsfeld*, 352 F.3d 721.
303. *Padilla v. Rumsfeld*, 352 F.3d 723–724.
304. *Padilla v. Rumsfeld*, 542 U.S. 426, 434 (2004).
305. *Padilla v. Rumsfeld*, 542 U.S. 435.
306. *Padilla v. Hanft*, 389 F. Supp. 2d 678 (D. S.C. 2005).
307. *Padilla v. Hanft*, 423 F.3d 386 (4th Cir. 2005).
308. 2006 U.S. LEXIS 2705 (U.S. 3 Apr. 2006).
309. Jenny Martinez, "The Real Verdict on Jose Padilla," *Washington Post*, Aug. 17, 2007.
310. Anonymous, "Tale of Abuse; Was Jose Padilla, an American Arrested in the United States, Subjected to Illegal Torture? Congress Should Find Out," *Washington Post*, Jan. 17, 2008. Padilla's theory of the case relied on *Bivens v. Six Unknown Named*

Agents of Fed. Bureau of Narcotics, 403 U.S. 388 (1971). The Supreme Court ruled that the plaintiff could sue the narcotics agents that allegedly used excessive force on him while in custody because they violated his due process rights under the Fifth Amendment.

311. *Padilla v. Yoo*, 678 F.3d 748 (9th Cir. 2012).

312. 28 U.S.C. § 2241 was amended to state that "no court, justice, or judge shall have jurisdiction to . . . consider . . . an application for . . . habeas corpus filed by or on behalf of an alien detained . . . at Guantanamo."

313. See 10 U.S.C. §§ 950c, 950f, 950g.

314. *Johnson v. Eisentrager*, 339 U.S. 763, 775 (1950). The court said in barring Eisentrager's access to federal courts, "The nonresident enemy alien, especially one who has remained in the service of the enemy, does not have even this qualified access to our courts, for he neither has comparable claims upon our institutions nor could his use of them fail to be helpful to the enemy."

315. That section read:

1. No court, justice, or judge shall have jurisdiction to hear or consider an application for a writ of habeas corpus filed by or on behalf of an alien detained by the United States who has been determined by the United States to have been properly detained as an enemy combatant or is awaiting such determination.
2. Except as provided in paragraphs (2) and (3) of Section 1005(e) of the Detainee Treatment Act of 2005 (10 U.S.C. 801 note), no court, justice, or judge shall have jurisdiction to hear or consider any other action against the United States or its agents relating to any aspect of the detention, transfer, treatment, trial, or conditions of confinement of an alien who is or was detained by the United States and has been determined by the United States to have been properly detained as an enemy combatant or is awaiting such determination.

316. U.S. Const., Art. I, § 9.

317. *Boumedienne v. Bush*, 553 U.S. 723, 754 (2008). The Court concluded that sovereignty was not absolutely necessary to jurisdiction. It found that the United States had complete jurisdiction over the Guantanamo naval base.

318. See *Balzac v. Porto Rico*, 258 U.S. 298 (1922). See also *Dorr v. United States*, 195 U.S. 138, 145 (1905); *Hawaii v. Mankichi*, 190 U.S. 197 (1903); *Downes v. Bidwell*, 182 U.S. 244 (1901) (all holding that Congress had the power to make laws and rules for territories under Art. I, § 8, clause 17). The same cases extended the constitutional protection of the right to due process to territories not intended to become states.

319. *Reid v. Covert*, 351 U.S. 487 (1956). The petitioner was a civilian whose husband was stationed at a USAF–RAF joint base in England. She was accused of murdering her husband and was tried and convicted by a general court-martial. Her conviction was set aside, and she was scheduled for a retrial. Meanwhile she was transferred to the continental United States. She filed a habeas corpus petition in the District Court for the District of Columbia. The court held that the District of Columbia courts had jurisdiction to review her petition but ruled against her on the merits.

320. *Reid v. Covert*, 351 U.S. 487. See reservations of Frankfurter, J.

321. *Boumedienne v. Bush*, 553 U.S. 767, quoting *Johnson v. Eisentrager*, 339 U.S. 777.

EIGHT

Summary and Conclusions

This book has been an examination of the means used by the federal and state governments to achieve a series of morally permissible ends, starting with freedom from British rule and including the preservation of the United States from internal dissolution or external attack by hostile states or stateless terrorists. In each of the situations reviewed, the politicians responsible for achieving the common ends of the United States as a social and political entity have selected highly questionable means to preserve and protect the United States in time of crisis.

Politics is the art and science of the choice of means to achieve an end defined by the history, culture, and legal structure of the political society that is to be governed. There are two, possibly three, schools of thought on the relationship between ends and means in politics. One school, that of Thomas Aquinas and his intellectual heirs, adopts the principle that the means selected to attain an end must be proportionate to the end. A politician may not employ a particular means that is intrinsically disordered (i.e., morally and legally wrong) to achieve the just end.[1] This insight is often shorthanded to "the end does not justify the means."

A second school, represented by philosophers such as Thomas Scanlon, called "contractualism," states the problem in a different conceptual form: one must not behave with respect to others or to political society in such a way that the other would not choose to act.[2] This form of conceiving political action depends upon some intellectual common ground among the government and the governed that permits analysis of a political act from the standpoint of a supposed social contract or original position, such as that described by John Rawls in his *Theory of Justice*. This view may be shorthanded as the end and the means must be reciprocally acceptable to the government and the governed. In this conceptual framework, the ends may or may not justify the means used to attain the end based on a presupposed general agreement not to harm others.

The third school, that of Machiavelli, Jeremy Bentham, John Stuart Mill, and their modern disciples, may be labeled for convenience's sake as "consequentialism," the principal that the end sought may be attained by any means that will produce the end without regard to the character of the means chosen.[3] In short, politicians may employ means to attain a desirable end by using lies, fraud, and any manner of unjust treatment of the people, so long as the end is accomplished. Maritan referred to this view as a "technical or artistic rationalisation of political life."[4] The choice of moral political position makes all the difference in the world.

If one adheres to the consequentialist viewpoint, such actions as Lincoln's arbitrary arrests of civilians and Wilson's use of vigilantes to root out draft dodgers are justified because each course of conduct promoted winning the war. The just end was achieved by these means, among others. By the same criteria, Johnson's inability to crack down on the student anti-war movement was a major political failure because Johnson's failure to root out dissent crippled the war effort in Vietnam, causing the United States to make a shamefaced withdrawal from Vietnam in 1973.

If one adopts the contractarian viewpoint, one looks to the basic contractual position that supports moral choice to determine which means were appropriate. In such an evaluation, Lincoln's arbitrary arrests could be considered an immoral means to winning the Civil War because no one would wish to be imprisoned without knowledge of the charges against him or her, but Wilson's vigilantes policing the draft would probably be considered moral because all would agree that the draft had to function effectively if the war was to be won, even at the cost of some civil liberties. President Johnson's failure to arrest and prosecute student anti-war activists was not moral because the student protestors impeded the draft and the war effort in Vietnam and gave comfort to the Vietnamese People's Republic that it could withstand U.S. bombings because the United States lacked the will to win the war. The basic agreement among the government and the people originally favored U.S. intervention in Vietnam and a quick victory over the pro-Communist Viet Cong and the Vietnamese People's Republic.

If one follows the Thomist view, one must first decide if the means chosen by the government are intrinsically wrong or not. Political society exists to attain the common good for the people who are governed (i.e., security, justice, education, and prosperity), the good of all the people that can be shared by all the people.[5] The primary analysis under this theory is the determination whether the means are just or unjust. Justice is one of Aquinas's primary virtues, one directed toward society rather than to the individual actor. Justice is the virtue or habit of giving to each his or her due and observing a duty that each member of society contributes to the common good.[6] Just laws are those that promote the common good; unjust laws do not.[7] Imprisoning people without charges for the duration of the war on the rumor that they were disloyal is intrinsically unjust because these individuals did not deserve to be detained without notice and an opportunity to be heard in their own defense. Lincoln's use of intrinsically evil means to win the war was wrong. Wilson's use of vigilantes to enforce the draft, allowing vigilantes to identify alleged pro-German or anti-draft people based on rumor, was also intrinsically evil because the employment of private citizens to investigate and to invade others' private lives and thoughts was unjust. President Johnson's refusal to engage in mass arrests and prosecutions is an indication of his refusal to use morally dysfunctional means to produce victory in Vietnam. Therefore, withholding police crackdown on student protesters was morally correct because it was an act of fundamental justice not to take retribution on students who disagreed with the government's policies regarding Vietnam.

The following historical review shows that an oversimplified version of consequentialism was the prevailing governmental moral view from the Revolution through the Global War on Terrorism. It also reflects the prevailing moral opinion of the people of the United States. Opposition to the Vietnam War showed how this unsophisticated utilitarianism worked to the disadvantage of the Johnson and Nixon administrations' war effort. Excluding the traditional peace church members' opposition to all wars and the views of the Nation of Islam, anti-war opposition was rooted in part in the apprehension that young male students would be drafted and sent into combat in a war zone that did not immediately threaten the internal security of the United States. Later, when the majority of U.S. citizens polled became opposed to the war, the failure of the executive branch of the government to bring the war to a swift final favorable victory over the Viet Cong and the People's Republic of Vietnam in 1966–1967 produced war weariness and disgust among the public without regard to the justice of intervention in Vietnam.

THE HISTORICAL PATTERN

The preceding seven chapters demonstrate a recurrent political and legal behavior pattern in time of national crisis. First, political leaders adopt a series of goals designed to protect the body politic from the worst effects of the crisis. Second, a substantial minority of citizens oppose those goals and work to frustrate the politicians' goals. Third, the politicians retaliate by repressing the dissenters using vigilante tactics, military actions, and various legal devices designed to deter dissent. Fourth, the judiciary cooperates with the politicians of the executive and legislative branches to bend or twist constitutional law to support the crisis-ending goals.

Fifth, when the crisis subsides, the same politicians who set the original controversial goals may continue the repressive measures long after the end of the perceived danger, but the judiciary no longer supports the political program to curb dissenters.

Perceived Crises and Repressive Measures

During the Revolution, the Whigs who controlled the Continental Congress and the legislatures of the thirteen states sought to throw off British rule and establish an independent republic. The perceived danger was the Tory fifth column that supplied soldiers, provisions, and munitions to the Royal Army to suppress the Whig revolution. Political leaders reacted by using a variety of vigilante and extra-legal means to frustrate the Tories. That included tarring and feathering Tories, destroying Tory-owned newspapers, boycotting Tory-owned businesses, confiscating Tory livestock and real estate, barring Tories from holding public office or voting in elections, ejecting Tories from the state, and trying suspected Tories for aiding and abetting the British Crown.[8] The formal legal suppression of Tories by the thirteen states was initiated by Continental Congress resolutions calling for each state to pass repressive laws respecting Tories and their property. Since there was no federal judiciary during this period, the courts of the thirteen states refused to intervene to protect Tory civil and property rights. The Treaty of Paris partially restored civil rights to the Tories, but the thirteen states did not rush to undo the harm that had been generated by the anti-Tory campaign. The British Crown provided some relief to Tories who fled the thirteen United States. The records of the Crown's Claim Commission document legal and vigilante destruction and confiscation in painful detail. Most Tories either remained in their states during the war or returned from exile shortly after the Treaty of Paris. Despite the Treaty of Paris's requirement that the United States return Tory property, the new order of prosperous Whig merchants and farmers never fully complied with the treaty.

The Civil War

The Civil War crisis was the attempt made by eleven states to leave the Union and set up a new nation-state on the North American continent. Lincoln made war on the seceding states, intending to force them back into union. A substantial minority of citizens, principally members of the Democratic Party, sought peace at any price. The Lincoln administration's response included arbitrary arrests of suspected disloyal persons, denial of notice and hearing on any charges of treason or other crimes, denial of trial by jury, and suspension of the writ of habeas corpus. Anywhere between thirteen thousand and thirty thousand U.S. citizens were arbitrarily arrested and held without charges in military prisons during the war. At least two thousand individuals were tried for various crimes by military commissions in Missouri, Kentucky, and the Union-occupied portions of Tennessee during the war. Many of these individuals were accused of guerilla depredations such as burning railroad bridges, shooting up towns, and gunning down Union soldiers from ambush. Cotton speculators who traded in Confederate cotton under forged passes from the United States suffered similar fates. Civilian courts were open for business in the border states, and despite guerilla warfare and occasional Confederate forays into the border states, the courts remained open and civilian prosecutors continued to indict and try offenders throughout the war. A handful of individuals living in Northern states were also tried by military commission from mid-1863 onward for interfering with the draft, committing treason, and aiding the Confederacy. Legal challenges to arbitrary arrest and incarceration during the war were rejected by the Supreme Court and lower federal courts, sometimes on specious grounds, as in *Ex parte Vallandigham*. Post-war, the Supreme Court had a change of heart, exhibited by its decision in *Ex parte Milligan* that sought to curb the executive branch's use of military commissions to dispose of dissenters who were accused of committing treason.

The vast majority of the men and women imprisoned by the Lincoln administration were let go after a substantial detention period without indictment, trial, or conviction, despite Congress's mandate in the Habeas Corpus Act of 1863 that persons arrested by the military be turned over to civilian authorities for indictment and prosecution.[9]

World War I

The perceived domestic crisis generated by the United States' declaration of war on the German Empire, Austria-Hungary, and Turkey in April 1917 was more complex than the 1861 secession crisis. The Wilson administration sought to support England and France against the German and Austro-Hungarian Empires because of fear that Germany would win the war, dictate a hostile peace to the losing side, and become the world's greatest national power. Woodrow Wilson also believed that the war aims of Germany and Austria-Hungary were contrary to the United States' economic and political policies. The precipitating cause was said to be the kaiser's proclamation of unrestricted submarine warfare on all shipping, including neutral shipping destined for English and French ports. Prior to April 1917, millions of U.S. citizens were either born in Germany or descended from German immigrants. They were pro-German and favored a victory by the kaiser and his allies over England and France. Prior to 1917, thousands of U.S. citizens and resident aliens opposed all wars as part of the Socialist program to impose a legal system that would transfer ownership of the means of production, if the war involved two capitalist regimes fighting over economic and social power. Prior to April 1917, thousands of workers belonged to the Industrial Workers of the World, a trade union that crossed craft lines to represent entire industries. The IWW was not part of the domestic Socialist Party led by Eugene Debs, but its leadership supported Socialist policies and threatened general multi-industrial strikes to stop the war effort.

Wilson and his cabinet, with the willing help of Congress, initiated a well-organized program of repressive measures against pro-Germans, Socialists, and IWW members. Wilson appointed George Creel chairman of the Committee on Public Information that generated distorted propaganda supporting the war effort and controlled news from the Western Front. This was the first attempt by the executive branch to control public opinion by selective repression of unfavorable war news and promotion of an emotional, jingoistic form of patriotism at home. The 1917 espionage act and 1918 sedition act granted the Wilson administration authority to arrest and try pro-German sympathizers for the crime of supporting the kaiser. Postmaster General Burleson was authorized to censor the mails and to refuse bulk mailing privileges to Socialist and union newspapers and magazines that were perceived to be anti-war. Wilson's attorney general staged high-profile prosecutions of Socialist leaders such as Eugene V. Debs and Rose Pastor Stokes for advocating resistance to the draft. The attorney general also prosecuted IWW members in a mass trial in Chicago that resulted in long prison terms for the union leaders. A handful of U.S.-based anarchists such as Emma Goldman and her lover Alexander Berkman were tried for violating the espionage act and then deported after serving their prison time. Espionage act convictions were regularly affirmed by the circuit courts, and in a series of three major decisions, the Supreme Court supported and affirmed the espionage act convictions of Socialist Party members Eugene Debs and Charles Schenck. The defendants were charged with making anti-war speeches that could convince a listener not to report for induction. The rationale for supporting these convictions was unconvincing because the First Amendment traditionally protected dissenters' right to speak against an act of Congress, and Justices Holmes and Brandeis retreated from their extreme support for the executive branch's suppression of Socialists in the post-war *Abrams* case.

President Wilson did almost nothing to discourage vigilante attacks on Socialists and IWW organizers, and his attorney general made use of a civilian corps of vigilantes called the American Protective League who were commissioned to spy on their fellow Americans by the attorney general. The league often assisted law enforcement officials in making arrests of allegedly disloyal people and staged its own anti-slacker program in New York City, rounding up thousands of men who were accused of failing to register for the draft.

When the war ended with Allied victory and German surrender in 1918, capped by the Treaty of Versailles, the Republican administration allowed many Wilson-era political prisoners to be freed, including Eugene V. Debs and Rose Pastor Stokes.[10]

World War II

President Franklin Roosevelt tried his best to drag the United States into World War II on the Allied side as early as late 1939. His advisors told him that an Axis victory would destroy maritime commerce and pose a direct threat of Nazi invasion of the United States. Thousands of U.S. citizens were opposed to the war. They organized action groups to keep the United States out of war. One such group, the German American Bund, was openly pro-Nazi; Father Coughlin's Social Justice movement opposed the war on political and religious grounds, and Charles Lindberg's American First organization advocated a pre-1912 version of isolationism. The Bund and Father Coughlin were suppressed by non-governmental initiatives, and America First collapsed when the Japanese bombed Pearl Harbor.

Unlike Woodrow Wilson, Franklin Roosevelt had no organized program to suppress anti-war dissenters. The West Coast suffered a wave of anti-Japanese hysteria after Pearl Harbor, fearing Japanese invasion of the mainland. Hundreds of thousands of U.S. native-born citizens of Japanese descent and their resident alien parents lived on the West Coast. Japanese Americans had become a well-educated successful middle-class constituency by wartime. Despite no hard evidence showing that any of these people were actively supporting Imperial Japanese war efforts, Lt. Gen. John DeWitt, the commanding general of the Pacific Frontier, proposed to intern all Japanese Americans and resident aliens "for the duration." Roosevelt and his attorney general obligingly drafted an executive order permitting DeWitt to round up the Japanese Americans and truck them off to concentration camps in Utah and New Mexico. Two Japanese Americans refused to comply with the removal order, resulting in separate criminal prosecutions that were reviewed by the Supreme Court. That court affirmed both convictions, showing remarkable deference to the executive branch and to military necessity, permitting no Brandeis brief showing that almost none of the interns, including Hirabayshi and Korematsu, the two men whose convictions were reviewed by the Supreme Court, had any ties to Imperial Japan. The Court founded President Roosevelt's action on the war power and refused to second-guess the presidential decision to order the Japanese American internment. The Court would have second thoughts toward the end of the war. It invalidated convictions by a military commission sitting in Hawaii when Hawaii was under martial law after the attack on Pearl Harbor. Adopting the rationale of *Ex parte Milligan*, the Court held that the imminent threat of Japanese invasion ended in 1942, making the trials of two men guilty of ordinary civilian criminal acts unconstitutional. In the same year, it found that Mitsuyi Endo was wrongfully detained in a concentration camp when she was proven to be a loyal citizen with a job opportunity in Chicago, away from the Pacific coast.

During World War II, the Roosevelt administration also interned thousands of German and Italian resident aliens under the Alien Enemy Act. These individuals had a right to an administrative hearing to determine cause for internment, a right not accorded to Japanese American citizens. If the alien lost at the administrative hearing, the alien could not appeal but could pursue habeas corpus as an alternative to an appeal.

The Roosevelt administration also sent Nazi saboteurs and spies to their deaths or to long prison terms via military commission trials. The hook on which military jurisdiction over these individuals was extended was a provision in the Articles of War that allowed for trial by military commission for certain classes of offenders, including those who violated the law of war. The civilian courts were open throughout the United States, and the United States was under no imminent threat of invasion. Nonetheless, the Supreme Court upheld trial by military commission for Nazi saboteurs, including one native-born U.S. citizen who had joined Nazi Germany's intelligence network.

The 1940 Smith Act, intended to apply to publication of Communist literature advocating violent overthrow of the government, was employed as the basis for trying longshoreman's union boss Harry Bridges on the ground that he was advocating violent overthrow of the government. It was also used on the Crusader White Shirts, a Nazi-oriented right-wing fringe group. The Justice Department obtained indictments against thirty men and women for advocating overthrow of the government. The Justice Department dismissed its indictments against all defendants in 1946 because it was apparent it could not prove a prima facie case.

Post-war, the courts and the Congress attempted to make reparations to the Japanese Americans interned in 1942. Congress authorized compensation payments to the victims, and the Ninth Circuit found a way to set aside Yamashita's 1943 conviction because it was based on false evidence.[11]

The Cold War

From 1946 to 1989, the United States and the Soviet Union confronted one another in an international struggle for political control of most of the known world. While neither side commenced a shooting war, both sides used surreptitious means to undermine the other's position in the world. This period was commonly known as the "Cold War." Both sides possessed enough nuclear devices to wipe out all the people on earth, and both sides threatened to wage nuclear war periodically. Since the Soviet Union was organized under the aegis of the Communist Party, people in the United States were terrified that a Communist coup would overthrow the government and impose a dictatorship on the United States. This fear egged on President Truman's loyalty oath program, adopted by President Eisenhower with minor changes in the early 1950s. Federal employees who refused to take the loyalty oath were fired. State government also imposed loyalty oath requirements on state employees, including teachers at state-run colleges and universities. The loyalty oath program was assisted by self-appointed censors who established blacklists for performers and teachers that wrecked the careers of a number of left-leaning movie and television stars in the 1950s. The people that were most damaged by these measures were liberal-left-leaning politicians, actors, and teachers who may have once belonged to the Communist Party in the 1930s or attended events sponsored by the party, who still held left-Socialist views about the economy and appropriation of private property.

A new dimension to the attack on dissenters emerged during the Cold War, the congressional investigative committee. The House Un-American Activities Committee called government officials as witnesses under oath to explain why they were "soft on Communism." Alger Hiss, a State Department official, went before the committee and swore that he was not a Communist and never passed secret documents to Communist agents. Whittaker Chambers, a *Time* magazine editor and avowed former Communist, testified after Hiss and told the committee that Hiss had passed microfilms of classified State Department documents to him in the late 1930s to be turned over to the Soviet Union. Chambers's disclosure resulted in Hiss's indictment and conviction for perjury. Hiss spent the remaining thirty years of his life trying to clear his name without success, although Massachusetts restored his license to practice law.

The most successful manipulator of the congressional committee process was Wisconsin's junior senator, Joseph R. McCarthy. In 1950, he made a speech before a Republican women's group in Wheeling, West Virginia, in which he waved a paper stating that he had a list of 205 card-carrying Communists who had infiltrated the State Department. McCarthy changed the number of party members in subsequent accusations, settling on "fifty-seven" as the best number. He turned an obscure Senate Committee on Government Expenditures into an anti-Communist kangaroo court, hauling government officials before it for third-degree cross-examination by Sen. McCarthy or Roy Cohn, his chief of staff. McCarthy had a large following among more conservative citizens, but he self-destructed when he accused the army of allowing its top-secret projects to be infiltrated by Communists. The army fought back during the extended 1954 Army-McCarthy hearings, showing that McCarthy's accusations were baseless. The Senate censured McCarthy who died in office two years later.

The Justice Department indicted a number of left-wing citizens under the Smith Act during the Cold War, including most of the leadership of the tiny U.S. Communist Party. Eugene Dennis, the Communist Party's chair, and ten other party officials were convicted of advocating the violent overthrow of the government. None of the mounds of evidence produced during their trial in Chicago showed that the Communists took any affirmative steps to overthrow the government. The government proved that Dennis and his leadership talked about an overthrow and told people that someday the workers would overthrow the government. The convictions of the eleven party officials were affirmed by the Seventh Circuit and the Supreme Court. During the early Cold War period, the Supreme Court validated punishment for the publication of ideas rather than direct action. The Court would later back away from this position during the Vietnam era.[12]

The Cold War attack on dissenters added the exploitation of the congressional committee system with access to television to the uncoordinated attempts to suppress Communists and fellow travelers. Exposure of a government employee's ties to alleged Communist front groups, or innuendo that a government employee passed secret information to Communist operatives, caused government workers to lose their jobs for disloyalty. The Cold War also added a new form of vigilante activity to the arsenal of weapons against dissenters: the establishment of blacklists for entertainers and other occupations. Anyone listed on a blacklist could clear himself of alleged pro-Communist leanings by subjecting himself or herself to screening by an approved anti-Communist screener. The screener often required the alleged pro-Communist to do penance by writing articles or giving speeches that were anti-Communist.

The executive branch did not ask Congress to suspend the writ of habeas corpus or pass a new sedition act to control domestic Communists. The executive branch did not use military commissions to try alleged Communists for violating the international laws of war. Instead, it relied on the Smith Act and loyalty oath programs to curb Communists in government.

The Vietnam War

Although the Vietnam War was within the Cold War period, it generated its own crises independent of the general fear of a Communist takeover of the United States. The public generally supported the 1964 Tonkin Gulf Resolution supporting President Johnson's retaliation against an alleged torpedo boat attack by the North Vietnamese navy against U.S. destroyers in neutral waters off North Vietnam. Anti-war opposition grew from the inception of the landing of U.S. Marines at Da Nang in February 1965 because the government used the draft to compel men to fight in Vietnam.

Initially, the United States was able to prosecute draft evaders and draft resisters. The Supreme Court confirmed the constitutionality of the draft and of prosecuting anti-war activists who refused to participate in the draft. The Court held in *United States v. Seeger* that a man who professed a belief in a power greater than himself, not necessarily the traditional God, which had ordained that all wars were evil and immoral could be classified as a conscientious objector and excused from military service. Two years later, boxer Muhammad Ali was indicted for failure to report for induction. Ali, a member of the Nation of Islam which granted minister status to all male members of the Nation, claimed he was exempt from the draft because he was a minister. The trial court and the Fifth Circuit held that Ali was not a sincere conscientious objector, and he was incarcerated for a short period before the Supreme Court overturned his conviction.

The anti-war protest movement was first supported only by traditional peace groups and by the Society of Friends, Mennonites, and other "peace churches," but the cause was taken up by left-wing radical organizations and a loose coalition of college student groups (e.g., Students for a Democratic Society). In 1965–1966, public opinion supported the Vietnam War, but support eroded from 1966 to the end of U.S. participation in 1973. During the 1968 Democratic Convention in Chicago, peace activists led by David Dellinger, Abbie Hoffman, Black Panther Party chief Bobby Seale, Rennie Davis, Students for a Democratic Society leader Tom Hayden, and other leftists were involved in a series of altercations with the Chicago police. Dellinger, Hoffman, and their associates were indicted for violating the federal riot act, resulting in a three-ring-circus trial before federal judge Julius Hoffman. Although the jury returned judgments of conviction, the convictions for crossing state lines to instigate a riot were thrown out on appeal.

The worst retaliatory act against the anti-war movement occurred on the campus of Kent State University in Ohio on May 4, 1970. Ohio National Guard troops opened fire on unarmed student demonstrators, killing four students and wounding nine. When President Nixon called off the draft, the number and intensity of anti-war demonstrations by college students declined.[13]

The executive branch did not ask Congress to suspend habeas corpus for anti-war protestors. It did not arrest anti-war activists without probable cause, nor were any anti-war activists tried by military commission for violating the laws of war. Government by opinion poll vitiated any concerted attempt to suppress anti-war dissenters during the Vietnam War. Citizens did not engage in vigilante action against the anti-war movement, with one notable exception, the hard-hat attack on anti-war protesters in New York City. Neither Presidents Johnson nor Nixon was willing to go against mounting popular disapproval of the war in Vietnam. With the exception of the prosecution of draft dodgers, the Justice Department did nothing to interfere with anti-war marches and rallies.

The Global War against Terrorism

The Al Qaida suicide attack on the World Trade Center and Pentagon on September 11, 2001, precipitated a retaliatory United States attack on Afghanistan, the country from which Al Qaida launched its terrorist attack on the United States. Two years later, the Bush administration attacked Iraq and brought down the regime of Saddam Hussein. Popular opinion supported both military expeditions in retaliation for the 9/11 attack. Congress and the Bush administration cooperated in a program to identify and stop potential terrorists operating in the United States. The PATRIOT Act, passed in 2001, substantially modified many statutes, including the obscure Foreign Intelligence Surveillance Act, expanding the investigatory power of the FBI and other federal law enforcement agencies to identify and arrest men and women who showed signs of potential terrorist activities or affiliations. The Bush administration instituted the "no-fly" list barring persons with suspected ties to Arab terrorist groups from boarding commercial airliners. It developed national security letters that worked as a species of warrant for forcing a targeted individual or corporation to turn over records relating to suspected terrorists and their accomplices in the United States. Failure to comply with a national security letter's demands was a crime. The Bush administration also made thousands of searches and seizures using the sneak-and-peak provision of FISA search warrants. The FBI also conducted wiretaps and electronic intercepts without first obtaining warrants from FISA. The NSA collected data on telephone and Internet transmissions to and from persons inside and outside the United States suspected of having pro-terrorist sympathy, resulting in a media uproar in 2005 and again in 2013 when NSA's data collection activities were exposed by former NSA employees and by Edward Snowden.

The Bush administration's anti-terrorist programs accelerated a sea change in U.S. criminal law that had begun during the administration of Jimmy Carter, a shift from after-the-fact apprehension and punishment of offenders to actions taken to prevent potential offenders from committing crimes. The federal government became proactive, adopting investigative tactics designed to identify potential offenders and to apprehend them before commission of any overt act. This was thought to be necessary in the case of Al Qaida terrorists who would carry out suicide attacks unless apprehended before any overt act against the United States resulted in death or injury to any U.S. citizen.

The tiny Arab American ethnic community was not subjected to significant vigilante attacks after 9/11. Popular opinion supported proactive measures designed to stop future terrorists from making suicide attacks on U.S. soil. The anti-war movement against U.S. involvement in Iraq and Afghanistan did not become a serious deterrent to the war effort. Congress did not reinstitute the draft, thus not provoking anti-war, anti-draft opposition to the military operations in Iraq and Afghanistan.

The Supreme Court did deal with the Bush administration's program to debrief captured suspected terrorists using tactics considered by some sober thinkers to be torture. This included waterboarding, sleep deprivation, and subjection to humiliating sexual events (e.g., standing naked before women). Some of the suspected terrorists were sent to secret prisons in Poland, Syria, and Macedonia to be interrogated by investigators from those nations who were not bound to observe the UN and Geneva guidelines outlawing torture. This program was labeled "extraordinary rendition." Meanwhile, other captives were taken to a maximum-security compound at the Guantanamo naval base for interrogation. The Bush administration, without express congressional approval, set up military commissions to try the Guantanamo captives for crimes against the law of war. The Bush administration reverted to President Lincoln's justification for arbitrary arrests and trials by military commission. The United States captured men in Afghanistan and Iraq who were thought to be Al Qaida members or Taliban members. President Bush asserted the authority to interrogate these captives and to try them for violations of the international law of war without congressional enabling legislation.

The Supreme Court, reverting to the *Ex parte Milligan* standard for trying people by military commission, told President Bush that he did not have the authority under the war power to do as Lincoln had done. Congress then authorized the executive branch to try captives by military commission.

An act of Congress attempted to bar access to U.S. courts by the Guantanamo captives to prevent them from testing the lawfulness of their confinement by seeking a writ of habeas corpus. Ultimately, the Supreme Court resurrected *Ex parte Milligan* to prevent Yaser Hamdi, a U.S. citizen captured on the battlefield in Afghanistan, from being held without charges being preferred for an indefinite period. In *Rasul v. Bush*, a companion case, the court held that Guantanamo captives could have access to U.S. courts for the purpose of filing habeas corpus petitions. That same court held that the president lacked authority to convene military commissions without express congressional authorization. The *Hamdan* case established that the 2001 congressional Authorization for Use of Military Force did not invoke the basis for trial by military commission, despite the series of memos prepared by Prof. John Yoo supporting a very broad reading of that resolution. Congress then passed specific enabling legislation empowering the president to set up military commissions to try Guantanamo captives.[14] The Obama administration has quietly adopted the policy of the Bush administration with regard to the Guantanamo captives. After screening, those captives deemed harmless were repatriated, and the handful of alleged terrorists are being held for trial by military commission.

The Bush administration developed a program for apprehending and interrogating potential terrorists that included NSA spying on domestic telephone calls and conducting warrantless searches and seizures of suspected potential terrorists and supporters, resulting in several prosecutions.

Vigilante action against Muslim American citizens and resident Arab aliens was practically non-existent. Muslim Americans were such a tiny minority that the public did not fear internal terrorist threats from the Arab settlements in Detroit or on the West Coast, nor did the public concern itself with Pakistani and Indonesian Muslim immigrants.

The latest anti-American, anti-Israeli threat to U.S. internal security may change the public's attitude toward domestic Muslim settlements. A political party known by the acronym "ISIS" that was born out of the insurrection in Syria uses social medial to urge Muslims living in the United States to attack U.S. targets to avenge the death of ISIS fighters killed by U.S. air strikes in support of the Kurdish and Iraqi resistance to an ISIS takeover.

WHY THERE ARE TWO CONSTITUTIONS

The political behavioral patterns in all the crises described in this book are remarkably similar. The United States is in a real or perceived crisis threatening its vital interests. The people demand action to head off the impending crisis. The executive and legislative branches respond with repressive measures against those individuals and groups deemed hostile to the United States. The executive branch responds by a program that erodes or temporarily extinguishes the constitutional guaranties of freedom of expression and association. The executive branch reinterprets the Fourth Amendment restriction on unreasonable searches and seizures to permit widespread invasion of personal privacy. The executive branch also limits or disregards the Fifth and Sixth Amendment guaranties of due process and fair procedure. Suspected dissenters are incarcerated for the duration. With the notable exceptions of the Vietnam era and the current war on terror, the executive branch condones or even encourages vigilante action against dissenters. The legislative branch cooperates by authorizing repressive measures, such as the 1917 and 1918 sedition acts and the Smith Act.

The Constitution is altered during these crisis situations. The federal courts condone the alteration reducing civil liberties. By construing the presidential war power to permit major invasions of constitutional civil liberties, the courts support the alteration. So far, the invocation of the war power to trump civil liberties has not persisted after the crisis has been resolved. Clinton Rossiter and the late Chief Justice Rehnquist correctly identified this process as a de facto adoption of a second constitution, a war-making constitution. There is no constitutional safeguard against executive expansion of the war power in the context of perpetual warfare, the context of the early twenty-first-century military expeditions in Afghanistan and Iraq. No commentator has suggested that the United States formally amend its 1787 Constitution by way of adding provisions for the exercise of emergency powers, a feature of several French constitutions and the constitutions of Italy, Austria, and Germany. European commentators have given a great deal of thought to the emergency clauses in European constitutions.[15] Some commentators in the United States have written about emergency constitutional powers as well.[16] The commentators have no unified position on the effectiveness of the protection of civil liberties in state of emergency clauses.

In a typically American way, a non-doctrinal "second constitution" has been generated by a succession of presidential decisions backed by Congress and the courts. The non-doctrinal second constitution's premises may be summarized as follows:

> The president in exercise of the war power may take extraordinary measures during a crisis that is perceived by the executive and legislative branches supported by popular opinion, to threaten the existence of the United States;
>
> Congress may enable the president to take action in a crisis that exceeds the war power if Congress deems that the United States is threatened;
>
> The judiciary will support the combined executive and congressional adoption of emergency measures that override the provisions of the Bill of Rights for the duration of the crisis; and when the crisis is perceived to have ended, full civil rights and limitations on presidential power will return.

So far, our constitutional history shows that these brief aberrations from the civil liberties guaranteed by the Bill of Rights will not lead to a permanent reduction of civil liberties, although there are no legal impediments to ensure that the executive and legislative branches will return to the pre-crisis state of civil liberties. Many innocent men and women have been physically and psychically injured during the crises periods by repressive measures such as imprisonment, vigilante action, and deportation, and in the current crisis, torture and related prolonged interrogation by intelligence operatives without Fifth Amendment protection. One cannot condone repressive measures unless one is willing to concede that the suspension of civil liberties arising from an extraordinary joint power to wage war due to "exigent circumstances" is the price this nation pays for its continued existence as a free republic. Rossiter and Rehnquist support this trade-off.

A formal emergency powers amendment to the Constitution would not guarantee that the executive and legislative branches would act within the limits imposed by an emergency clause. Congress's attempts post–Vietnam to rein in the executive's unilateral use of the war power have been marginally successful. At any rate, Congress has condoned warrantless surveillance and trial by military commission for violations of the law of war more than once since the Civil War.

Public opinion in time of crisis favors repressive measures directed against dissenters who are deemed to threaten the continued existence and stability of the United States. Prior to World War II, no accurate system for measurement of public opinion was available to the executive and legislative branches. Typically, these branches of government were unduly influenced by newspaper rants and by self-appointed spokespersons. The advent of fairly reliable opinion polls allowed the Truman and Eisenhower administrations and Congress to determine how much repression the public demanded or would tolerate.[17] During the Vietnam War, public opinion swung from support for the war to opposition, a warning that repression of student-led anti-war demonstrations would not be received favorably by the public.[18] In the present crisis, public opinion supported the Bush administration's intrusion into privacy at first.[19] When the public grew tired of the long wars in Iraq and Afghanistan, opinion shifted, not because the public was particularly aware of the significant invasion of civil liberties perpetrated by the Bush administration, but because the public lacked the patience to see these two wars through to a successful conclusion.[20]

In closing, unless the public is animated by a strongly held opinion that constitutional civil liberties should be preserved during a crisis and the normal processes of the criminal law produce satisfactory resolution of criminal conduct during the crisis, the "exigent circumstances" argument will prevail, and the executive and legislative branches will engage in repressive measures against dissenters who appear to threaten the existence of the United States.

NOTES

1. See Jacques Maritan, *Man and the State* (Chicago: University of Chicago Press, 1951), 58–64. See also *Catechism of the Catholic Church, Part Three, Life in Christ*, ch. 1, Art. IV, "The Morality of Human Acts & 1753." That statement asserts that "a good intention (for example, the helping of one's neighbor) does not make behavior that is intrinsically disordered, such as lying and calumny, good or just. The end does not justify the means."

2. See, for example, Thomas Scanlon, *What We Owe to Others* (Cambridge, MA: Harvard University Press, 2000), 153. An act is wrong if its performance under the circumstances would be disallowed by any set of principles for the general regulation of behavior that no one could reasonably reject as a basis for informed, unforced, general agreement.

3. See, for example, John Stuart Mill, *Utilitarianism* (London, 1863; Oxford: Oxford University Press, 1998), chs. 2, 4 (on justice as a principle of social utility); Niccolo Machiavelli, *The Prince*, trans. W. K. Marriott (State College: Pennsylvania State University Electronic Classics Series, 2001–2012), ch. 15, "Concerning Things for Which Men and Especially Princes Are Praised or Blamed". According to the Internet Encyclopedia of Philosophy, consequentialism is the view that morality is all about producing the right kinds of overall consequences. Here the phrase "overall consequences" of an action means everything the action brings about, including the action itself. For example, if you think that the whole point of morality is (a) to spread happiness and relieve suffering, or (b) to create as much freedom as possible in the world, or (c) to promote the survival of our species, then you accept consequentialism. Although those three views disagree about which kinds of consequences matter, they agree that consequences are all that matter. So they agree that consequentialism is true. The utilitarianism of John Stuart Mill and Jeremy Bentham is a well-known example of consequentialism. By contrast, the deontological theories of John Locke and Immanuel Kant are non-consequentialist. (Internet Encyclopedia of Philosophy, last accessed Feb. 9, 2017, http://www.iep.utm.edu/conseque.) The political theory of Chinese scholar Mo Di, or "Mozi," who lived ca. 430 BCE, describes the concept of *fa*, meaning a "model" for human behavior that is directed at achieving collective well-being. *Fa* is not necessarily a logical principle, since the behavior of a parent may also be *fa*. *Fa* requires that any statement must have a historical root, a source or empirical basis and use or utility; that is, it must produce a *li* (benefit) for the state. "Actions, practices and policies that promote the overall welfare of society are considered morally right. . . . For the Mohists, then, the purpose of government is to achieve a stable social order by promulgating a unified conception of morality." This is a form of consequentialism that justifies the means to produce a well-ordered society. (Stanford Encyclopedia of Philosophy, last accessed Feb. 9, 2017, http://plato.stanford.edu/entries/mohism.)

4. Maritan, *Man and the State*, 56.

5. *Encyclopaedia Britannica Online*, last accessed Feb. 9, 2017, http://www.britannica.com/EBchecked/topic/128312/common-good.

6. Thomas Aquinas, *Summa Theologica*, II, I, Art. I, Q. 90 (the law) and II, II, Art. 1 (justice defined) (Chicago: Bensiger, 1947).

7. Thomas Aquinas, *Summa Theologica*, II, I, Art. 1, Q.90.

8. See ch. 1 for details.

9. See ch. 2 for details.

10. See ch. 3 for details.

11. See ch. 4 for details.

12. See ch. 5 for details.

13. See ch. 6 for details.

14. See ch. 7 for details.

15. See, for example, "Emergency Powers and Constitutionalism," *Oxford Journal of International Constitutional Law* 2 (2004): 207, last accessed Feb. 9, 2017, http://icon.oxfordjournals.org/content/2/2/207.extract, for a thorough discussion of emergency powers clause advantages and disadvantages.

16. See, e.g., Linda Camp Keith and Steven C. Poe, "Are Constitutional State of Emergency Clauses Effective? An Empirical Exploration," *Human Rights Quarterly* 26 (2004): 1071. These authors engaged in an empirical analysis of the paper constitutions of many modern states. They concluded that individual civil liberties were best protected when the legislature invoked the state of emergency and preserved certain basic civil rights during the perceived crisis. Those states that allowed the executive to declare an emergency of unlimited duration gave much less protection to civil liberties.

17. See John Kenneth White, "Seeing Red: The Cold War and American Public Opinion" (Conference on the Power of Free Inquiry and Cold War International History Session, Sept. 1998), last accessed Feb. 9, 2017, http://www.archives.gov/research/foreign-policy/cold-war/conference/white.html.

18. White, "Seeing Red." See also Adam J. Berinsky, "Public Opinion during the Vietnam War: A Revised Measure of the Public Will," Princeton University, 2001, last accessed Feb. 9, 2017, http://polmeth.wustl.edu/media/Paper/berin01.pdf.

19. Pew Institute, "Public Attitudes toward the War in Iraq: 2003–2008," last accessed Feb. 9, 2017, http://www.pewresearch.org/2008/03/19/public-attitudes-toward-the-war-in-iraq-20032008.

20. See Frank Newport, "More Americans Now View Afghan War as a Mistake," Gallup Services, 2014, last accessed Feb. 9, 2017, http://www.gallup.com/poll/167471/americans-view-afghanistan-war-mistake.aspx.

Glossary of Legal Terms

attainder, bill of: Legal device employed in England to punish an individual who was thought to be guilty of a criminal act without the right to trial by means of an act of Parliament.

conspiracy: A criminal offence committed when two or more individuals agree to commit a crime. Under prevailing federal law, all conspiracy members are equally guilty of any substantive crime committed by a conspirator in furtherance of the conspiracy.

demurrer: A pleading in civil and criminal cases in the nineteenth and early twentieth centuries that admitted the trust of all the allegations in a civil complaint or criminal indictment and asserted that those allegations did not constitute a civil cause of action or a crime. The demurrer has been replaced by the more modern motion to dismiss.

error, writ of: A writ issued by an appellate court to a lower court, ordering the lower court to transmit the record of a case to the appellate court so that the record may be reviewed for alleged errors of law.

escheat: The appropriation of real or personal property by the state when the owner of the property is unknown or has abandoned the property.

ex parte: Unilateral action by one of the parties to a dispute without the presence of any opponent. It also refers to a judge making a decision for one party without the presence of any other party.

ex post facto law: A statute that made a past act which was not criminal a criminal offense when committed in the past.

fee simple: The equivalent of absolute ownership of real estate under English and American property law.

habeas corpus, writ of: A writ issued by a court directing the person detaining another person in custody to appear and to show cause why the detainee was lawfully held.

hue and cry: An English common-law measure that required any citizen who witnessed the commission of a felony to call out his neighbors to pursue the felon. It was recognized in most U.S. jurisdictions in the early nineteenth century.

jurisdiction: The power granted to a court by legislation to hear certain kinds of cases.

jury nullification: The legal doctrine that permits a jury to decide a case contrary to the law as instructed by the trial judge.

libel: A term used in admiralty proceedings in U.S. courts prior to the 1960s for the complaint initiated by an injured party against a ship or to condemn the ship and cargo as contraband.

per curiam: A Latin phrase literally translated as "by the court" used in U.S. appellate practice when an appellate opinion is not to be attributed to any judge.

posse comitatus: An English common law measure that permitted the county Sheriff to organize citizens into a temporary band to apprehend felons. The U.S. posse comitatus law forbids the use of military forces to apprehend felons as part of a posse comitatus.

postliminium: An international law principle that states that when persons or things taken by an enemy in war are again under the control of their own state they as a general rule regain the rights belonging or relating to them before capture.

sua sponte: Literally "on the own" refers to a judge making a ruling or order that was not initiated by any party to a lawsuit or criminal prosecution.

voir dire: A medieval French term still used today with reference to questioning prospective jurors in civil and criminal cases to determine the eligibility of prospective jurors to sit as jurors.

Bibliography

Allen, Thomas B. *Tories: Fighting for the King in America's First Civil War*. New York: Harper Collins, 2010.

Amar, Akill Reed. "Fourth Amendment First Principles." *Harvard Law Review* 107 (1994): 757, 802–804.

American Civil Liberties Union. "TSA and FBI Ordered to Pay $200,000 to Settle 'No Fly' Lawsuit." Press release, American Civil Liberties Union, January 24, 2006.

Anders, Roger M. "The Rosenberg Case Revisited: The Greenglass Testimony and the Protection of Atomic Secrets." *American Historical Review* 83 (1978): 388.

Anonymous. *A Fair Account of the Unhappy Disturbance at Boston in New England Extracted from the Depositions That Have Been Made by All Parties with an Appendix Containing Some Affidavits and Other Evidences Not Mentioned in the Narrative of It That Has Been Published in Boston*. London: B. White Fleet St., 1770.

———. *A List of Those Tories Who Took Part with Great-Britain in the Revolutionary War, and Who Were Attainted with Treason Commonly Called the Black List, to Which Is Prefixed the Opinions of Attorneys McKean and Dallas Philadelphia, 1802*. New York, 1865.

———. *A Short Narrative of the Horrid Massacre in Boston Perpetrated in the Evening of the 5th Day of March by Soldiers of the XXIXth Regiment with Which the XIVth Regiment Was Quartered There: With Some Observations on the State of Things Prior to the Catastrophe, to Which Is Added an Appendix, Containing the Several Depositions Referred to in the Preceding Narrative; and Also Other Depositions Relative to the Subject of It*. Boston: Edes & Gill, 1770.

———. "Tale of Abuse; Was Jose Padilla, an American Arrested in the United States, Subjected to Illegal Torture? Congress Should Find Out." *Washington Post*, January 17, 2008.

Aquinas, Thomas. *Summa Theologica*. Chicago: Bensiger, 1947.

Austin, Allen W. "Eastward Pioneers: Japanese American Resettlement during World War II and the Contested Meaning of Exile and Incarceration." *Journal of American Ethnic History* 26 (2007): 59–60.

Bailey, Percival R. "The Case of the National Lawyers Guild, 1939 to 1958." In *Beyond the Hiss Case: The FBI, Congress and the Cold War*, edited by Athan G. Theoharis. Philadelphia: Temple University Press, 1982.

Bailey, Thomas A. "The Sinking of the Lusitania." *American Historical Review* 41 (1935): 54.

Bancroft, Frederick A. *The Life of William A. Seward*. New York: Harper, 1899.

Basler, Roy E., ed. *Collected Works of Abraham Lincoln*. New Brunswick, NJ: Rutgers University Press, 1953.

Bassett, John Spencer. *The Regulators of North Carolina*. Washington, DC: Government Printing Office, 1895.

Belknap, Michael R. *Cold War Political Justice*. Westport, CT: Greenwood, 1977.

Blum, John Morton. *Joe Tumulty and the Wilson Era*. New York: Houghton Mifflin, 1951.

Bodenhamer, David. *Fair Trial: Rights of the Accused in American History*. New York: Oxford University Press, 1992.

Boucher, Jonathan, ed. *Reminiscences of an American Loyalist 1738–1789, Being the Autobiography of the Rev'd Jonathan Boucher, Rector of Annapolis in Maryland and afterwards Vicar of Epson, Surrey, England*. Cambridge and New York: Houghton Mifflin and Riverside Press, 1925.

Broadwater, Jeff. *Eisenhower and the Anti-Communist Crusade*. Chapel Hill: University of North Carolina Press, 2010.

Brown, Richard D. "The Confiscation and Disposition of Loyalists' Estates in Suffolk County." *William and Mary Quarterly (Third Series)* 21 (1964): 534.

Brown, Wallace. "The American Farmer during the Revolution: Rebel or Loyalist?" *Agricultural History* 42 (1968): 327–330.

Budenz, Louis. *This Is My Story*. New York: McGraw-Hill, 1947.

Bulla, David W., and Gregory A. Borchard. *Journalism during the Civil War*. New York: Peter Lang, 2010.

Bulla, David W., and Justyna Sempruch. *Lincoln's Censor Milo Hascall and Freedom of the Press in Civil War Indiana*. West Lafayette, IN: Purdue University Press, 2008.

Byington, Lewis Francos. *History of San Francisco*. 2 vols. Chicago: S. J. Clarke, 1931.

Calhoon, Robert McCluer. *The Loyalists in Revolutionary America, 1760–1781*. New York: Harcourt Brace Jovanovich, 1963.

Callahan, North. *Royal Raiders: The Tories of the American Revolution*. Indianapolis: Bobbs-Merrill, 1963.

Capozzola, Christopher. "The Only Badge You Need Is Your Patriotic Fervor: Vigilance, Coercion and the Law in World War I America." *Journal of American History* 88 (2002): 1354, 1360–1361.

———. *Uncle Sam Wants You: World War I and the Making of the Modern American Citizen*. New York: Oxford University Press, 2008.

Catechism of the Catholic Church, Part Three, Life in Christ. Chapter 1, Article 4, "The Morality of Human Acts." 1753.

Ceplair, Larry. *Anti-Communism in Twentieth-Century America: A Critical History*. Santa Barbara, CA: ABC-CLIO, 2011.

Chambers, Whittaker. *Witness*. New York: Random House, 1952; Washington, DC: Regnery, 1987.

Chorley, Robert Samuel Theodore. "Inquest on the Rosenberg–Sobell Case." *Modern Law Review* 33, no. 2 (1970): 121.

Cobain, Ian. "Rendered to Libya." *The Guardian*, March 4, 2013.

Cohen, William. "Justice Douglas and the Rosenberg Case: Setting the Record Straight." *Cornell Law Review* 70 (1985): 211.

Cohn, Roy. *McCarthy*. New York: New American Library, 1968.

Cole, David. "Out of the Shadows: Preventive Detention, Suspected Terrorists, and War." *California Law Review* 97 (2009): 693.

Creel, George. *How We Advertised America: The First Telling of the Amazing Story of the Committee on Public Information That Carried the Gospel of Americanism to Every Corner of the Globe*. New York: Harper, 1920.

Crewdson, John. "Wife of Abu Omar Recounts Visits with Husband." *Chicago Tribune*, December 28, 2005.

Crewdson, John, and Alessandra Maggiorani. "CIA Chiefs Reportedly Split over Cleric Plot; Agency Schisms Come to Light in Italy Probe." *Chicago Tribune*, January 8, 2007.

Crow, Jeffrey J., and Larry E. Tise, eds. *The Southern Experience in the American Revolution*. Chapel Hill: University of North Carolina Press, 1978.

Davis, William C. *The Images of War*, vol. 6 (New York: Doubleday, 1984.

———, ed. *National Historical Society, The Images of War*. 6 vols. New York: Doubleday, 1984.

Dawson, Henry B. *Rutgers v. Waddington*. New York: Samuel Loudon, 1784; repr., Morisiania, NY, 1866.

De Benedetti, Charles, and Charles Chatfield. *An American Ordeal: The Antiwar Movement of the Viet Nam Era*. Syracuse, NY: Syracuse University Press, 1990.

Dershowitz, Alan M. "The Preventive State: Uncharted Waters after 9/11." In *The Impact of 9/11 and the New Legal Landscape*, edited by Matthew J. Morgan. New York: Palgrave Macmillan, 2009.

Dewitt, Philip Elmer. "America's First Bioterrorism Attack." *Time*, September 30, 2001.

"Dianne Feinstein: Administration Is Hiding Key Facts in Senate's CIA Torture Report." *Huffington Post*, August 6, 2014.

Doenecke, Justus. *Nothing Less than War: A New History of America's Entry into World War I*. Lexington: University Press of Kentucky, 2011.

Donohue, Laura. "Criminal Law: Anglo-American Privacy and Surveillance." *Journal of Criminal Law and Criminology* 96, no. 3 (2006): 1059.

Doyle, John. *English Colonies in America: The Middle Colonies*. 3 vols. New York: Henry Holt, 1907.

Earley-Wilmot, John. *Historical View of the Commission for Enquiring into the Losses, Services, and Claims of American Loyalists, at the Close of the War between Great Britain and Her Colonies in 1783*. London: J. Nichols, Son & Bentley, 1815; Boston: Gregg Press, 1972.

Eastern Sea Frontier War Diary. College Park, MD: Modern Military Branch, National Archives and Records Administration, 1944.

Ellis, Edward Robb. *Echoes of Distant Thunder: Life in the United States, 1914–1918*. New York: Coward, McCann & Geoghegan, 1975.

Eugene, Oregon, Register-Guard, August 30, 1973.

Farber, Daniel, ed. *Security v. Liberty: Conflicts between Civil Liberties and National Security in American History*. New York: Russell Sage Foundation, 2008.

Farber, David. "The Counterculture and the Peace Movement." In *Give Peace a Chance: Exploring the Viet Nam Anti-War Movement*, edited by Melvin Small and William D. Hoover. Syracuse, NY: Syracuse University Press, 1992.

Farrell, Brian. "Habeas Corpus in Time of Emergency: A Historical and Comparative View." *Pace International Law Review* (Online Companion), April 2010.

Farrell, John A. *Clarence Darrow: Attorney for the Damned*. New York: Knopf, 2011.

Federal Bureau of Investigation. *German Espionage and Sabotage against the U.S. in World War II: George John Dasch and the Nazi Saboteurs*. FBI Handout. Washington, DC: U.S. Department of the Navy.

Feklisov, Alexander, and Sergei Kostin. *The Man behind the Rosenbergs*. New York: Enigma, 2001.

Ferling, John E. *The Loyalist Mind: Joseph Galloway and the American Revolution*. State College: Pennsylvania State University Press, 1977.

Fessenden, Ford. "Neighbors Recall Men, Explosives on Michigan Farm." *Newsday Buffalo News*, April 22, 1995.

Final Report: Japanese Evacuation from the West Coast, 1942. Headquarters Western Defense Command and Fourth Army Office of the Commanding General Presidio of San Francisco, California, 1943.

Final Report of the National Commission on Terrorist Attacks upon the United States. Washington, DC: Government Printing Office, 2004.

Fisher, Louis. *The Constitution and 9/11: Recurring Threats to America's Freedom*. Lawrence: University Press of Kansas, 2008.

———. "Military Commissions: Problems of Authority and Practice." *Boston University International Law Journal* 24, no. 1 (2006): 15–53.

———. *Military Tribunals & Presidential Power American Revolution to the War on Terrorism*. Lawrence: University Press of Kansas, 2005.

Ford, Guy Stanton. "The Committee on Public Information." *Historic Outlook* 11 (1919): 97.

Ford, Worthington Chauncy, ed. *Journal of the Continental Congress, 1774–1789*. Edited from the original records in the Library of Congress by Worthington Chauncy Ford, chief of the Division of Manuscripts. Vol. 1. Washington, DC: Government Printing Office, 1904.

Foster, Peter Foster. "CIA Took Suspects 'to Point of Death.'" *Calgary Herald*, September 8, 2014.

Franklin, F. G. "Preserving the Honor of the Flag: Anti-Syndicalist Legislation in Several States: Penalties Provided for Desecration of the Flag, League of American Municipalities." *Modern City* 5 (July 1920): 20.

Freeberg, Ernest. *Democracy's Prisoner: Eugene V. Debs, the Great War and the Right to Dissent*. Cambridge: Harvard University Press, 2008.

Gage, Beverly. *The Day Wall Street Exploded: A Story of America in Its First Age of Terror*. New York: Oxford University Press, 2009.

Gannon, Michael. *Operation Drumbeat: The Dramatic True Story of Germany's First U-boat Attacks along the American Coast in World War II*. New York: Harper & Row, 1990.

Garrison, Lloyd. "Some Observations on the Loyalty-Security Program." *University of Chicago Law Review* 23, no. 1 (1955): 1–11.

Gayarré, Charles E., William Beer, and Grace Elizabeth King. *History of Louisiana*. New York: W. J. Widdleton, 1867; New Orleans: Pelican, 1965.

Gellhorn, Walter. *The States and Subversion*. Ithaca, NY: Cornell University Press, 1952.

Gellman, Barton, and Ashkan Soltani. "NSA Tracking Cellphone Locations Worldwide, Snowden Documents Show." *Washington Post*, December 4, 2013.

Genders, William L. "Woodrow Wilson and the Preparedness Tour of the Midwest January–February 1916." *Australasian Journal of American Studies* 9 (1990): 75.

General Accounting Office. *Report to Congressional Requesters: Withdrawal from Somalia*. Washington, DC: Government Printing Office, 1994.

Gentry, Curt. *J. Edgar Hoover: The Man and the Secrets*. New York: Norton, 1991.

Gilbert, Martin. *The First World War: A Complete History*. New York: Henry Holt, 1994.

Goodman, Walter Goodman. *The Committee: The Extraordinary Career of the House Committee on Un-American Activities*. New York: Farrar, Straus & Giroux, 1968.

Gorman, Siobhan. "NSA Rejected System That Sifted Phone Data Legally." *Baltimore Sun*, May 18, 2006.

Gould, Christopher. "The South Carolina and Continental Associations: Prelude to Revolution." *South Carolina Historical Magazine* 87 (1986): 36.

Griffith, Robert. *The Politics of Fear*. Amherst: University Massachusetts Press, 1970; rev. ed., 1987.

Hadith. Sunan Abi Dawud 4311, in-book reference: Book 39, Hadith 21; English translation: Book 38, Hadith 4297. Sunan Abi Dawud 4321, in-book reference: Book 39, Hadith 31; English translation: Book 38, Hadith 4307. Sunan Abi Dawud 4324, in-book reference: Book 39, Hadith 34; English translation: Book 38, Hadith 4310.

Hahn, Harlan. "Correlates of Public Sentiments about War: Local Referenda on the Vietnam Issue." *American Political Science Review* 64 (1970): 1186.

Hancock, Harold. *The Loyalists of Revolutionary Delaware*. Newark: University of Delaware Press, 1976.

Handy, Isaac W. P. *U.S. Bonds or Duress by Federal Authorities*. Baltimore, MD: Turnbull, 1874.

Heale, M. J. *American Anti-Communism: Purging the Enemy Within*. Baltimore, MD: Johns Hopkins Press, 1990.

Heisler, Francis Heisler. "The Law versus the Conscientious Objector." *University of Chicago Law Review* 20 (1953): 441.

Herman, Susan N. *Taking Liberties: The War on Terror and the Erosion of American Democracy*. New York: Oxford University Press, 2011.

Herring, George C. "The Cold War and Vietnam." *OAH Magazine of History* 18 (2004).

Higham, Charles. *Howard Hughes: The Secret Life*. New York: St. Martin's, 1993.

Hough, Emerson. *The Web: The Authorized History of the American Protective League*. Chicago: Reilly & Lee, 1919.

House Committee on Foreign Affairs. *The War Powers Resolution: A Special Study of the Committee on Foreign Affairs*. Washington, DC: Government Printing Office, 1982.

Hulsebosch, Daniel J. "Discrete and Cosmopolitan Minority: The Loyalists, the Atlantic World, and the Origins of Judicial Review." *Chicago-Kent Law Review* 81 (2006): 825.

———. *A Symposium on the People Themselves: Popular Constitutionalism and Judicial Review*. Chicago: Chicago-Kent College of Law, Illinois Institute of Technology, 2006.

"Italian Court Convicts Egypt Cleric Abu Omar to 6 Years for Terrorism." *Xinhua News Agency—CEI* (Woodside), December 6, 2013.

Jameson, John Franklin. *The American Revolution as a Social Movement*. Princeton, NJ: Princeton University Press, 1967.

Johnson, Bradley T. "Confederate Military History: Maryland." In *Confederate Military History: A Library of Confederate States History, in Twelve Volumes, Written by Distinguished Men of the South, and Edited by Gen. Clement. A. Evans of Georgia*, edited by Clement A. Evans, 12 vols. Atlanta: Confederate Publishing, 1899; Secaucus, NJ: Blue & Grey Press, 1981.

Journal of the First Congress of the American Colonies, in Opposition to the Tyrannical Acts of the British Parliament Held at New York, October 7, 1765. New York, 1845.

Keegan, John. *The First World War*. New York: Hutchinson Books, 1998; New York: Knopf, 1999.

Keith, Linda Camp, and Steven C. Poe. "Are Constitutional State of Emergency Clauses Effective? An Empirical Exploration." *Human Rights Quarterly* 26 (2004): 1071.

Kennedy, David M. *Over Here: The First World War and American Society*. New York: Oxford University Press, 1980.

Klein, Rachel N. "Ordering the Back Country: The South Carolina Regulation." *William and Mary Quarterly (Third Series)* 38 (1981): 661.

Klement, Frank L. *The Limits of Dissent: Clement L. Vallandigham and the Civil War*. New York: Fordham University Press, 1998.

Knight, Amy. *How the Cold War Began: The Igor Gouzenko Affair and the Hunt for Soviet Spies*. New York: Carroll, 2005.

Kostianen, Auvo. "Policies of the Left and Right." In *Finns in the United States: A History of Settlement, Dissent and Integration*, edited by Auvo Kostianen. Lansing: Michigan State University Press, 2014.

Kuhnhardt, Dorothy Meserve, and Philip B. Kuhnhardt. *Twenty Days: A Narrative in Text and Pictures of the Assassination of Abraham Lincoln*. New York: Harper & Row, 1965; Wayne, NJ: Career Press, 1985.

Lambert, Robert S. "The Confiscation of Loyalist Property in Georgia, 1782–1786." *William and Mary Quarterly (Third Series)* 20 (1963): 91.

Lambert, Robert Stansbury. *South Carolina Loyalist in the American Revolution*. Columbia: University of South Carolina Press, 1987.

Lawson, John D., ed. *American State Trials*. 36 vols. St. Louis, MO: F. H. Thomas Law Books, 1914–1936.

Leech, Margaret. *Reveille in Washington, 1860–65*. New York: Harper, 1941; New York: Time-Life, 1962.

Lewis, Jerry M., and Thomas R. Hensley. "The May 4 Shootings at Kent State: The Search for Historical Accuracy" (unpaginated). Last accessed February 10, 2017.http://www.kent.edu/may-4-historical-accuracy.

Lewiston Morning Tribune, April 14, 1954.

Lipson, Eden Ross. *New York Times*, book review, October 25, 1981.

Lodge, Henry Cabot. *A Short History of the English Colonies in America*. New York: Harper, 1881.

Machiavelli, Niccolo. *The Prince*. Translated by W. K. Marriott. State College: Pennsylvania State University Electronic Classics Series, 2001–2012.

Main, Jackson Turner. *The Sovereign States, 1775–1783*. New York: New Viewpoints, 1973.

March, Francis A., and Richard J. Beamish. *History of the First World War*. Philadelphia, Chicago, and Toronto: United Publishers of the United States and Canada, 1919.

Maritan, Jacques. *Man and the State*. Chicago: University of Chicago Press, 1951.

Marshall, Simon Lyman Atwood. *World War I*. New York: American Heritage Series, 1964; American Heritage Library edition, New York: Houghton Mifflin, 1987.

Martin, David. "Refining Immigration's Role in Counterterrorism." In *Legislating the War on Terror: An Agenda for Reform*, edited by Benjamin Wittes. Washington, DC: Brookings Institution Press, 2009.

Martinez, Jenny Martinez. "The Real Verdict on Jose Padilla." *Washington Post*, August 17, 2007.

McGirk, Tim, and Plain Shomali. "Lifting the Veil on Taliban Sex Slavery." *Time*, February 10, 2002.

Meeropol, Robert. *An Execution in the Family*. New York: St. Martin's, 2003.

Meeropol, Robert, and Michael Meeropol. *We Are Your Sons*. Urbana: University of Illinois Press, 1986.

Meyers, Jeffrey. *John Huston: Courage and Art*. New York: Crown, 2011.

Mill, John Stuart. *Utilitarianism*. London, 1863; Oxford University Press, 1998.

Miller, Edward A., Jr. *Lincoln's Abolitionist General*. Columbia: University of South Carolina Press, 1997.

Miller, I. "The Second Virginia Committee of Correspondence." *William and Mary Quarterly (Second Series)* 22 (1913): 99.

Miller, John C. *Origins of the American Revolution*. Palo Alto, CA: Stanford University Press, 1943.

Millett, Allan R. *Semper Fidelis: The History of the United States Marine Corps*. New York: Macmillan, 1980.

Mitchell, Broadus. *The Price of Independence*. New York: Oxford University Press, 1974.

Mitford, Jessica Mitford. *The Trial of Dr. Spock, the Rev. William Sloane Coffin, Jr., Michael Ferber, Mitchell Goodman, and Marcus Raskin*. New York: Knopf, 1969.

Moody, John Sheldon, Calvin Duval Meeropol, Frederick Caryton Ainsworth, Robert N. Scott, Henry Martyn Lazelle, George Breckenridge Davis, Leslie J. Perry, and Joseph Kirkley, eds. *The Official Record of the War of the Rebellion*. Series 1 and 2. Washington, DC: Government Printing Office, 1888–1901.

Morais, Herbert M. "Artisan Democracy and the American Revolution." *Science & Society* 6, no. 3 (1942): 227–241.

Morgan, Matthew J., ed. *The Impact of 9/11 and the New Legal Landscape*. New York: Palgrave Macmillan, 2009.

Neely, Mark E., Jr. *The Fate of Liberty; Abraham Lincoln and Civil Liberties*. New York: Oxford University Press, 1991.

New, M. Christopher. *Maryland Loyalists in the American Revolution*. Centreville, MD: Tidewater, 1996.

New Jersey, State of. *Minutes of the Provincial Congress and the Council of Safety of the State of New Jersey*. Trenton, NJ: Naar, Day & Narr, 1879.

Nizer, Louis. *The Implosion Conspiracy*. New York: Doubleday, 1973.

———. *The Jury Returns*. New York: Doubleday, 1966.

Olmstead, Kathryn S. *The Red Spy Queen: A Biography of Elizabeth Bentley*. Chapel Hill: University of North Carolina Press, 2002.

O'Neill, William. *Coming Apart: An Informal History of America in the 1960's*. New York: Times Books, 1971.

Perret, Geoffrey. *Lincoln's War: The Untold Story of America's Greatest President as Commander in Chief*. New York: Random House, 2004.

Poore, Ben Perley, ed. *The Conspiracy Trial for the Murder of the President, and the Attempt to Overthrow the Government by the Assassination of its Principal Officers*. Edited with an introduction by Ben Perley Poore. Boston: J. Tilton, 1865.

Prange, Gordon W. *At Dawn We Slept: The Untold Story of Pearl Harbor*. New York: McGraw-Hill, 1981.

Radcliffe, George L. P. *Governor Thomas H. Hicks of Maryland and the Civil War*. Baltimore, MD: Johns Hopkins University Studies in Historical and Political Science, 1901.

Radosh, Ronald, and Joyce Milton. *The Rosenberg File: A Search for the Truth*. New York: Vintage, 1984.

Ramsby, Thomas W. "The Sons of Liberty: The Early Inter-Colonial Organization." *International Review of Modern Sociology* 17 (1987): 313–334.

Randall, James G. *Constitutional Problems under Lincoln*. Urbana: University of Illinois Press, 1926; 2nd ed., 1956.

———. "The Newspaper Problem in Its Bearing upon Military Secrecy during the Civil War." *American Historical Review* 23 (1918): 303.

Rehnquist, William H. *All the Laws but One: Civil Liberties in Wartime*. New York: Knopf, 1998.

Reichmann, Deb. "Bush Defends Spying Program; Calls Effort Legal, Vital; Leak Seen Hurting Nation." *Buffalo News*, January 2, 2006.

Ridpath, John Clark. *James Otis the Pre-Revolutionist*. Project Gutenberg, 1996.

Ringle, Denis J. *Mr. Lincoln's Navy*. Annapolis, MD: U.S. Naval Institute Press, 1998.

Robinson, Greg. *By Order of the President: FDR and the Internment of Japanese Americans*. Cambridge, MA: Harvard University Press, 2001.

Roche, Walter F., Jr., and Edwin Chen. "Bush Defends Decision on U.S. Wiretaps." *Chicago Tribune*, January 2, 2006.

Rogow, Arnold A. "Loyalty Oath Issue in Iowa, 1951." *American Political Science Review* 55 (1961): 861.

Rossman, David. "Criminal Law: 'Were There No Appeal'; The History of Review in American Criminal Courts." *Journal of Criminal Law & Criminology* 81 (1990): 518.

Ryerson, Egerton. *The Loyalists of American and Their Times*. Toronto, 1880; New York: Haskell House, 1970.

Savage, Charles. "Warrantless Surveillance Challenged by Defendant." *New York Times*, January 29, 2014.

Savage, Charles, and James Risen. "Federal Judge Finds N.S.A. Wiretaps Were Illegal." *New York Times*, March 31, 2010.

Sayers, Michael, and Albert E. Kahn. *Sabotage! The Secret War against America*. New York: Harper, 1942.

Schneir, Walter, and Miram Schneir. *Invitation to an Inquest: Reopening the Rosenberg "Atom Spy" Case*. 3rd ed. Baltimore: Penguin, 1973.

Schrecker, Ellen. *The Age of McCarthyism: A Brief History with Documents*. New York: Bedford St. Martin's, 2002.

Schultz, John. *The Chicago Conspiracy Trial*. Chicago: University of Chicago Press, 1970; 3rd ed., 1992.

Schwartz, Edward A. "The Lynching of Robert Prager, the United Mine Workers and the Problems of Patriotism in 1918." *Illinois Historical Society Journal* 95 (2002): 414–415.

Shankman, Arnold. "Draft Resistance in Civil War Pennsylvania." *Pennsylvania Magazine of History and Biography* 101 (1977): 190.

Shapiro, Herbert. "The Ku Klux Klan during Reconstruction: The South Carolina Episode." *Journal of Negro History* 46 (1964): 45.

Shaw, Albert, ed. *Messages and Papers of Woodrow Wilson*. 3 vols. New York: Review of Reviews, 1924.

Smith, Jeffrey A. *Franklin and Bache: Envisioning the Enlightened Republic*. New York: Oxford University Press, 1990.

Smith, Zachary F. *The Battle of New Orleans, Including the Previous Engagements between the Americans and the British, the Indians, and the Spanish Which Led to the Final Conflict on the 8th of January, 1815*. Filson Club Publication 19. Louisville, KY: John P. Morton, 1904.

Southern Poverty Law Center. *Ku Klux Klan: A History of Racism and Violence*. 6th ed. Montgomery, AL: Southern Poverty Law Center, 2011.

Sterling, Robert E. *Civil War Draft Resistance in the Midwest*. De Kalb: Northern Illinois University Press, 1977.

Story, Joseph. *Commentary on the Constitution of the United States with a Preliminary Review of the Constitutional History of the Colonies and States before the Adoption of the Constitution*. 3 vols. 5th ed. Boston: Little, Brown, 1891 [1833].

Suber, Howard. "Dalton Trumbo's Real Role in 'Roman Holiday.'" *Los Angeles Times*, August 19, 1991.

Sullivan, Christopher, and Dan Sewel. "Caught John Doe No. 1: Nabbed 60 Miles outside Oklahoma City, He's Identified as Timothy McVeigh, 27 Paramilitary Link: FBI Reportedly Seeking More Suspects Associated with a Far-Right Militia in Michigan Farmhouse Fast Arrest: Suspect Stopped for Speeding 90 Minutes after Bombing Terror in the Heart of America." *San Francisco Examiner*, April 21, 1995.

Summers, Anthony. *Official and Confidential: The Secret Life of J. Edgar Hoover*. New York: Putnam, 1993.

Thayer, James B. *Cases on Constitutional Law*. 2 vols. Cambridge, MA: Charles W. Sever, 1895.

Thomas, William H., Jr. *Unsafe for Democracy: World War I and the U.S. Justice Department's Covert Campaign to Suppress Dissent*. Madison: University of Wisconsin Press, 2008.

Tredway, Gilbert. *Democratic Opposition to the Lincoln Administration in Indiana*. Indianapolis: Indiana Historical Bureau, 1973.

Tucker, St. George, ed. *William Blackstone, Commentaries on the Common Law of England*. Philadelphia: Birch & Small, 1803.

Tyler, Moses Coit. "The Party of the Loyalists in the American Revolution." *American Historical Review* 1 (1895): 24–45.

U.S. Chamber of Commerce. *A Program for Community Anti-Communist Action*. Washington, DC: U.S. Chamber of Commerce, 1948.

U.S. Department of Justice. *Report to the Congress of the United States: A Review of the Restrictions on Persons of Italian Ancestry during World War II*. Appendix B: "Chronology of Events Surrounding the Evacuation, Relocation, and Internment of Persons of Italian Ancestry during World War II." November 2001.

U.S. Department of Justice, Office of Inspector General. *A Review of the FBI's Handling of the Brandon Mayfield Case*. Washington, DC: Government Printing Office, 2006.

"U.S.-Freed Combatant Is Returned to Saudi Arabia; Yaser Esam Hamdi's Case Was a factor in a High Court Ruling That Said Such Prisoners Must Be Charged. 'He Is Not a Taliban,' His Father Says." *Los Angeles Times*, October 12, 2004.

Vallandigham, James L. *The Life of Clement L. Vallandigham*. Baltimore, MD: Turnbull, 1872.

Van Tyne, Claude H. *The Loyalists in the American Revolution*. New York: Macmillan, 1902; repr., 1959.

Vattel, Emmerich de. *The Law of Nations or the Principles of Natural Law in Four Books*. Zurich, 1758. Translated by Joseph Chitty, 1833. Lonang Institute electronic edition, 2003, 2005.

Warner, Ezra. *Generals in Blue*. Baton Rouge: Louisiana State University Press, 1964.

Weinberg, Gerhardt L. *A World at Arms*. New York: Cambridge University Press, 1994.

Weinstein, Allen. *Perjury: The Hiss–Chambers Case*. New York: Knopf, 1978.

West, Ellis M. "The Right to Religion-Based Exemptions in Early America: The Case of Conscientious Objectors to Conscription." *Journal of Law and Religion* 10, no. 2 (1993): 367–401.

"Why Did CIA Shut Down Black Site in Poland?" *Polish News Bulletin*, Weekend Supplement (Warsaw), August 7, 2014.

Wickware, Frances. *The American Year Book*. Vol. 8. New York: D. Appleton, 1918.

Wiecek, William W. "The Legal Foundations of Domestic Anticommunism: The Background of Dennis v. United States." *Supreme Court Review* 417 (2001).

Will, Allen Sinclair. *Life of Cardinal Gibbons, Archbishop of Baltimore*. New York: E. P. Dutton, 1922.

Williams, Mary Floyd. *History of the San Francisco Vigilance Committee of 1851: A Study of Social Control on the California Frontier in the Day of the Gold Rush*. Vol. 12. Edited by Bolton E. Herbert. Publications in History. Berkeley: University of California, 1921.

Woodward, Bob, and Scott Armstrong. *The Brethren: Inside the Supreme Court*. New York: Simon & Schuster, 1979.

Work Projects Administration. *List of Presidential Executive Orders Compiled by W.P.A. Historical Records Survey*. New York: Archives, a Division of Hastings House, 1944.

Yoshpe, Harry B. *The Disposition of Loyalist Estates in the Southern District of the State of New York*. New York: Columbia University Press, 1939.

Zinn, Howard. *A People's History of the United States*. New York: Harper & Row, 1980.

Index

About the Author

Thomas J. Reed is professor emeritus of law, Widener University School of Law, Wilmington, Delaware. He received his undergraduate B.A. from Marquette University in 1962 and his J.D. from Notre Dame Law School in 1969. He served in the U.S. Marine Corps from 1962 to 1966, winning an Air Medal for combat action in the Dominican Republic in 1965. His teaching career began at Western New England College School of Law, Springfield, Massachusetts, in 1976. In 1981, he accepted a position at Widener University School of Law and served as associate dean of the law school from 1984 to 1992 in addition to teaching a broad spectrum of law courses. He was the director of the Veterans Law Clinic from 1997 to 2010. He has continued to work in the Veterans Law Clinic as a volunteer staff attorney since 2010. He is the author of two Civil War books, *Tibbits' Boys: A History of the 21st New York Cavalry Regiment* (1997) and *The Original Iron Brigade* (2011), and co-author with Andrew McKay and Rev. Anthony Wade of *Untying the Political Knot: Delaware during the War between the States* (2001). Professor Reed edited the diaries and letters of Orderly Sergeant John F. C. Hartwell with Prof. Ann. H. Britton, published as *To My Beloved Wife and Boy at Home* (1997).

Professor Reed has written more than twenty articles for law journals and is the co-author with Eunice L. Ross of *Will Contests*. He lives with his wife and two cats in New Castle, Delaware, in a house built in 1872 by a Civil War veteran.